A *Backwoods Home* Anthology:

The Nineteenth Year

Published by
Backwoods Home Magazine
P.O. Box 712
Gold Beach, OR 97444

Copyright 2008, 2012 by *Backwoods Home Magazine*

ISBN: 978-0-9846222-4-5

Editor: Dave Duffy

Senior Editor: John Silveira

Art Director: Don Childers

Contributors: *Jerry Allen Hourigan, Jackie Clay, Claire Wolfe, Jeffrey R. Yago, Massad Ayoob, Gail Butler, Lee Greiman, Len McDougall, John Silveira, Dave Duffy, Ilene Duffy, Dorothy Ainsworth, Linda Gabris, Allen Easterly, Rev. J.D. Hooker, Corey Gage, Brewster Gillett, Richard Blunt, Paul Miller, Charles Sanders, Randy Erskine, Sylvia Gist, Annie Tuttle, Vicky Rose, Joe Knight, Sandy Coates, Selina Rifkin*

Cover Art: Don Childers

Layout Design and Proofreading: Lisa Nourse, Rhoda Denning, Annie Tuttle, Ilene Duffy

For Katherine Myers,
who persevered in her mid-80s to make "3 day pies,"
one day for the crust, one day for the filling,
and one more day to bake it. Her patience, tenacity,
and delicious pies will be remembered.

Contents —

Issue Number 109

Issue Number 110

Issue Number 113

Issue Number 114

Jan/Feb 2008
Issue #109
$5.95 US
$7.50 CAN

Backwoods

Home magazine

practical ideas for self-reliant living

A cabin for one

The joys of idleness
All about rhubarb
The .22 handgun
Wildlife tracking 101
Affordable beach home

Chickens
the most valuable animals
on the homestead

$5.95US $7.50CAN

0 2>

0 74470 99712 2

www.backwoodshome.com

My view

Starting the hurricane

My predictions for 2008:

(1) A Democrat or Republican will be elected President.

(2) Overwhelmingly, Democrats and Republicans will be elected to Congress, state legislatures, and city halls.

(3) Government at all levels, staffed by loyal Democrats and Republicans, will grow bigger while our individual freedoms will grow smaller.

(4) Other serious American problems, such as a loss of good paying jobs, porous borders, growing debt, a declining dollar, dependence on foreign oil, and unaffordable housing will get worse.

Are you laughing or crying? They're easy predictions to make. Most Americans who think about such things would make them. You could make the same predictions for 2009 and 2010. It's like predicting the sun will set at sundown.

But I'm not going to be among the people who help these predictions come true. I'm swearing off the stuff that's been making America sick. I'm going to take that first step in recovery by not voting for Democrats or Republicans.

I'll still vote; I think that's my duty as an American citizen. But I'm not sure for whom. Most likely the Libertarian candidate, even though he or she doesn't have a chance of winning. Maybe another third party candidate who can't win. Even Green Party candidate Ralph Nader, who I don't agree with on most things, is a possibility because a vote for someone other than a Democrat or Republican is a step away from the disastrous lock on power the Demopublicans have had in my lifetime.

Even if it means spitting into the wind, it's a start. If the slightest breeze can have an impact on a major storm sometime in the distant future, perhaps my vote for change in the face of overwhelming odds will have an effect on politics some day.

All the pundits, you know, those Democrats who give their opinions as TV newscasters, and those Republicans who give their opinions as talk radio hosts, say I'm wrong. They claim that people who vote for third party candidates throw away their vote because it takes away support from the Democrat or Republican candidate who comes closest to their views. But most TV newscasters and talk show hosts are shills for the Democrat and Republican Parties. They mislead us for the sake of their political parties.

Many of us, even I, had been suckered in by the apparent logic that third party voting was a mistake. I voted for the current President because I feared that if I didn't, the big spending, big government Democratic candidate, John Kerry, might get elected and spend the country into oblivion and trample my freedoms. Gee, guess what happened?

Dave Duffy

Bush spent the country's treasury like a drunken politician and passed all sorts of laws that trampled my freedoms. He did the same thing that every Democrat and Republican President in my lifetime has done: He grew government and shrunk my freedoms.

Almost half of eligible voters no longer vote in most elections, and surveys show that seven or more out of every ten Americans disapprove of the way both the President and Congress run the country. Yet most people who *do* vote continue to vote Democrat or Republican.

It's time to stop! Bush's performance should have demonstrated that clearly to conservative/Libertarian types like me. From my perspective, voting for a Democrat means a quick growth of government and a quick abdication of individual freedoms, while voting for a Republican means a slightly slower process, sort of a frog-in-the-slowly-heated-pot method. But the result is the same.

I am a limited government man, I admit. I feel government has only a few legitimate functions, mainly providing protection against criminals and foreign enemies, and keeping the roads repaired so citizens can move about. Otherwise, I think citizens can handle things pretty well themselves. History demonstrates rather conclusively that when governments get too big, its citizens suffer abuses. The number one abuse is the growth in the prison population. Right now, America's prison population is the highest in the world, and the highest in our history. That should tell you something.

America needs some sort of reform. The Democrat and Republican Parties have been marching us down the road to bankruptcy and tyranny for decades. It's time to stop our part of the parade. We may get trampled on for now, and the pundits on TV and radio will no doubt continue to laugh at us, telling us we're wasting our vote. But maybe our refusal to participate will have a ripple effect, causing a slight disruption that will get magnified later. I think that's a start. Later we can take credit for starting the hurricane.

— **Dave Duffy**

Get to know your spiders

By Jerry Hourigan

Every landowner and home-owner creates the perfect environment for spiders. Not intentionally, of course, but spiders seem to like all the little nooks and crannies created from how we store our equipment, tools, hay, feed, supplies, and other items. Spiders are especially fond of our wood-piles, storage bins, clos-ets, and tack rooms. They love our homes, gardens, orchards, flow-er beds, and landscap-ing. They live everywhere we do except Antarctica.

For the most part spiders are a good thing. These creepy crawlies are a normal everyday part of life and eat tons of other insects. Without them we would be up to our ears in other insects who would eat us out of

The Black Widow is easily identified by the red hourglass shape on its abdomen.

house and home. We humans think we own the world, but in reality it would really belong to the insects if it weren't for the birds, bees, bats, and yes, spiders.

Even though we cringe at the thought of spi-ders, they have been immortal-ized through movies, songs, and sto-ries. Who hasn't taught their children the Itsy Bitsy Spider nursery rhyme or read them the story of *Charlotte's Web*. This story did wonders to help erase centuries of myths and legends and people's innate fear of this crea-ture. Everyone at one time or another has marveled at the wonder of a beautiful cobweb covered in dew and catching the rays of the sun.

There are more than 38,000 differ-ent types of spiders around the world but only a few of these are potentially harmful to people. Here in the conti-nental United States there are only a few types of poisonous spiders we need to be able to identify and to teach our children to be able to iden-tify and avoid. To simplify things, group all spiders into two categories. You have 38,000+ types in the good category and only a few in the bad category. The good category is too overwhelming and unless you are a spider enthusiast or arachnologist, just accept them for what they are

and forget about it. Now we are down to just a few spiders in the bad cate-gory. That's manageable and some-thing we can take the time to learn and be able to identify.

Here in the Southeast our family is concerned about teaching ourselves and our grandson to identify two spiders in the "bad" category. They are the most likely to be found in our house and outbuild-ings. Those two are the Black Widow and the Brown Recluse.

Once you have edu-cated yourself, it is important that you not go on a rampage and start destroying all spiders. No matter how you feel about them, believe that our lives benefit from having them around and learning to co-exist with them. Accept them for what they are and give them a wide berth when you can. When you can't, simply destroy their webs to encourage them to move elsewhere. Removing their food source will also discourage spi-ders from setting up housekeeping in your barns and outbuildings. You can place pheromone flytraps to control flies, which are a favorite food source of the spider. Another way to help control spider populations is not to destroy mud dauber wasps' nests. These predator wasps prey on the spi-der's eggsacks and are people friend-ly. Regular maintenance of your feed and storage areas will also help dis-courage spiders from moving in. Leaf blowers are great tools to clean out dusty areas where spiders like to hide. They like quiet, undisturbed areas with little or no traffic. Once they are disturbed they will usually get insulted and vacate the premises.

Normally I don't pay much attention to spiders. As long as they are not in my face I'm fine with them, but I don't hesitate to destroy them when they become unwanted squatters. Recently, I went to use one of my plastic watering tubs in the barnyard. When not in use, I overturn them to prevent stagnant water which attracts mosquitoes and the chance of West Nile Virus. When I overturned the tub I discovered a spider had set up housekeeping there. I immediately knew this was an unusual spider and upon closer inspection, I found that it was the Black Widow. I had never seen this spider before but I have seen pictures. Trying to avoid one bad thing, I created the perfect environment for this harmful spider. Sometimes you just can't win for losing! I didn't find any egg sacks so hopefully I discovered her before she got her house in order and started her family.

The Black Widow

The Black Widow is a very glossy black with a smooth round body about the size of a pea. The most distinguishing feature is the bright red hourglass shape on its abdomen. Typically she builds her web close to the ground and in a closed, protected, undisturbed area. She never leaves her web and is usually found upside down near the center. She will make her egg sacks and place them near the edges of the web where she can protect them. She may be accompanied by the smaller male, but in most cases once she has mated she will usually kill and eat the male. One mating will last her a lifetime so she no longer needs her mate. Hence the name Black Widow. If the male is allowed to live after mating he is rendered harmless and has to depend on the female for food. He is no longer able to produce venom and kill his own food. The venom of the Black Widow

is a neurotoxin and affects the central nervous system. Per volume it is more toxic than that of the cobra, corral, and rattlesnake. Bites are seldom fatal but will require a trip to the hospital for treatment to prevent breathing difficulty and muscle spasms. In all the reported cases about 5% have been fatal. Once you are able to identify this spider, mentally associate it with the skull and crossbones.

Your chances of being bitten by a Black Widow are small but it is possible, especially if you have them on your property. In most cases you will first see the web which will alert you to the fact there may be a spider as well. Once you discover a Widow, destroy her and then search for her egg sacks and destroy them as well. There may be more than one. Unlike most spiders who die after completing their egg sacks, the Widow can live as many as three years. There is a very similar spider called the Redback which is almost identical to the Black Widow except that it has a red slash or bar down the back. At first glance you would naturally assume that it is a Black Widow. While you may not want this spider around your barn or buildings, there is no need to be concerned.

Like many of us, I have little ones running around the property. They could just as easily have turned over this watering tub and crawled in to play, as all kids will do. Since I was able to identify this spider, I now know that a little spider patrol may be in order. There is never just one of anything. My six year old grandson got his first lesson in spider identification right after this discovery. We don't want our children to be terrified and run screaming when they see a spider, but they do need to gain a healthy respect and learn how to react when they do see one. The Black Widow is

well worth the time to get to know and be able to identify.

The Brown Recluse

The second in the bad category is the Brown Recluse spider. It is highly unlikely that you will ever see this one or it will be too late. It does not build a web but prefers to hunt at night. It searches for dead insects but will attack live ones as well. I call it the buzzard of the spider world. It likes to live in our heated homes and garages. It hides in our closets, clothes, shoes, and behind our pictures. Most people are bitten in their beds at night or when they put on their clothes. The venom from this spider is necrotic. It destroys the flesh at the site of the bite and is very difficult to heal. Doctors can help to prevent infection but there is nothing that will restore the rotting flesh. What this spider bite can do is *ugly*.

Adult Brown Recluse spiders are yellowish-tan to dark brown. The most distinguishing feature is the dark brown or black fiddle or violin shape along its head with the neck of the fiddle pointed towards the rear of

The Brown Recluse is identified by a fiddle or violin shape that points toward the rear of its body.

of our existence and have been for millions of years. All spiders have venom and will bite if you come into close contact with them. However, their fangs are weak and are not intended to pierce thick skin but rather the soft body parts of insects. If they do bite, the amount of venom will usually be so small that a mild reaction or none at all will be noticed. Spiders are formidable predators in their insect world. Once threatened by humans they are more likely to scurry off than to attack. Most are trappers, hence the cobwebs. They wait patiently for their prey to become entangled in their web. After the prey weakens, the spider will advance and begin to wrap it in a cocoon and then inject its poison. It is usually a very slow process.

But, like everything else, there are two sides to every issue. There have been reported cases where a bite had been delivered well enough to cause a serious reaction and severe complications. The point of all this is that we can arm ourselves with a little knowledge and not have to fear spiders as a whole. That is why it is important to get to know these two spiders in the Southeast states. For those living in other parts of the world, let's just say you have more than *two* varieties to get to know. Δ

its body. They have long, thin gray to dark brown legs covered with short dark hairs. They are about the size of a quarter.

The best way to prevent this spider from setting up housekeeping in your home is first to find out if you have them. Set spider glue traps in several areas of your house and periodically check to see what you catch. Most of your major home improvement stores carry these traps. Once you have identified the spider you can make better decisions about what to do. Don't overreact and have the house fumigated with pesticides. This spider loves dead insects and will appreciate you taking the time to provide a good supply. Vacuum your closets, under beds, window sills, and storage areas periodically and store extra clothing and shoes in spider-proof bags and cartons. Learn to identify this spider and react accordingly. Forget the

other 38,000 but get to know this spider on a first name basis and mentally associate it with the skull and crossbones.

This article is intended only to inform the reader. Spiders are a part

Harvesting the Wild

- *Clover*
- *Greens*
- *Asparagus*
- *Flower buds*
- *Raspberries*
- *Blueberries*
- *Wild garlic*

- *Plantain*
- *Cactus*
- *Birch syrup*
- *Acorns*
- *Hazelnuts*
- *Mushrooms*
- *Wilderness wine*

Chickens
the *most* valuable animals on the homestead

By Jackie Clay

When I was a child, I used to read and re-read the chick section in our Sears and Roebuck catalog. Imagine! For only two cents you could buy a perfectly good baby chick. Of course back then I didn't understand that one had to buy a minimum of 25 chicks to get this price...or to buy them at all. I had my six pennies saved up special and for the life of me I couldn't understand why my parents, who lived in Detroit at the time, wouldn't send for them.

Even back then, somehow I *knew* I had to have my own piece of ground, a garden, and a few chickens on it. And yep, as soon as I had my very own first homestead, shortly after graduating from high school, there were chickens on it. For 43 years, there have always been chickens on our various homesteads.

But there is a reason. Those oh-so-cute chicks grow up into *the* most valuable animal on the homestead. Sure they're cute when they're little and pretty when they're big. However, they are also an integral part of the homestead. When they are grown, hens provide a bounty of eggs, given happily and freely, to pay

for their tender care. Extra roosters, of course, can be butchered and you will enjoy meat that cannot be bought in the store. It is tender, juicy, and so tasty you won't believe what you've been missing. Or you can raise a batch of chicks, just for the meat. And that luscious meat is also free of hormones, dubious feed additives, chemicals, or antibiotics.

Those are the most often thought of benefits from keeping chickens, but what of the feathers? A breast feather comforter is nearly as warm as a goose

Buff Orpington

down comforter.

And all that free fertilizer? Perhaps the least appreciated benefit of having a flock of chickens is the manure. Not only is it of extremely high quali-ty, but chickens totally digest all weed seeds. You'll never "plant" weeds or grasses by spreading not-quite-composted chicken manure on your garden, as with horse or cow manure.

In fact, a good way to house your flock of chickens is to make the coop in the center, with a large fenced run on either side. You can then rotate the chickens from one side to the other, using the unused run for a garden plot. Not only is it richly fertilized, but your helpful hens have dug up and eaten all of the weeds and grass, including the seeds, in your garden-to-be. Because they love to dig and scratch, they have also eaten up most of the destructive insects present, from cut-worms to ticks.

I say "destructive insects" because they won't bother earth-worms as earthworms live deeper than hens scratch and only come out at night to deposit their castings. By that time your happy hens are roosting and dreaming of scratch feed and dust baths.

Chickens are also very easy to han-dle. I've never had a "mean" hen. Roosters, yes, but very seldom and you don't need a rooster for your girls to lay lots of eggs. You only need a rooster if you want fertile eggs for hatching your own chicks or just because you want one strutting and crowing about the place.

My son, David, used to carry our hens around when he was two years old. Children and the elderly can easily handle a small flock of chickens; the chores are fun and not burdensome. In addition, a few hens can be housed in a very small coop and run, so you can keep them in any legal place, including towns and some cities (be sure to check regulations).

There is no smell to a chicken or coop that has the bedding changed regularly. It's only when it is not changed that visitors wrinkle their noses when they enter to see your hens. It's amazing how nice a clean chicken coop can really smell. Of course, the more chickens you have, the harder it is to keep that coop pristine. A dozen hens make little odor from the ammonia in their waste. Housing for 500 hens always has that "breathtaking" odor, no matter how often it is cleaned. But we homesteaders seldom need more than a couple dozen birds unless we are raising them for meat, so we don't have to deal with odor problems.

Choosing a breed that suits your purpose

Fortunately, there are dozens and dozens of common breeds of chickens, from the huge Jersey Giants down to petite bantams the size of a quail. Some are extremely beautiful while others are less gorgeous but extremely good at what they do (producing eggs or meat). Many chickens are good at foraging for a good portion of their food and are colored to avoid detection by predators. Others are brightly colored and more "domestic" in attitude.

EGG PRODUCTION

If you really don't plan on eating many of your birds and only want eggs, and lots of them, consider one of the egg laying breeds. The most popular is the White Leghorn.

David when he was young with one of his pet chicks.
Chickens are easily handled by anyone.

Leghorn hens are lightweight and active, with a tendency to being a bit flighty. But boy do they lay eggs! Getting over 300 eggs a year from a good hen is not uncommon.

Want a prettier color than plain old white? Just look in a poultry catalog and find a prettier breed that still lays plenty of good eggs. Most of the highest producing egg layers lay white eggs and are lighter weight hens.

MEAT PRODUCTION

I've raised lots and lots of chickens, but for the sheer feed conversion factor, the white Cornish Rock crosses far surpass anything else you can buy.

In less than two months, you can go from tiny chicks to large, butchering-sized birds. We raise these and at three months, these birds dress out looking like young turkeys.

DUAL PURPOSE BREEDS

Okay, you want it *all*, both eggs and meat? There are many so-called dual purpose breeds. These are heavier than the lightweight layers but still lay lots of soft brown eggs. You won't get the super fast turnover in a butchering bird like you do with the Cornish Rock hybrids, but then you can let your hens hatch their own eggs and raise the chicks. I've tried to save a few Cornish Rock hens for breeders, hoping to introduce a large size into my flock. Doesn't work. Their legs are their weak spot. Sooner or later, usually sooner, they develop sore feet or torn muscles. Then they go down and cannot even walk.

Fortunately, you can raise White Rocks, which are a parent of the Cornish Rocks, Buff Orpingtons, Rhode Island Reds, Barred Rocks, or one of the other many heavy breeds that are used for cross-purposes. These heavy hens are also much more sedate and easily handled, especially when you have small children or a yapping puppy around.

The heavies don't produce as many eggs in a year, usually averaging around 200 per hen. But it's enough for most families.

Still want something more unique around? How about the Aracauna? It not only looks different, often having olive green legs and "ear muffs," but it lays blue or green eggs. How cool is that? We think it's neat and always have at least a few Aracauna hens around. They also produce quite a few eggs, and are excellent at rustling around the yard for insects and wild food.

There are many different rare and unusual breeds available, and I've raised many of them. Not only do you get your eggs, but you can sell either the excess young birds or breeders to other hobbyists for a decent price. My kids always had some different chickens as 4-H projects while they were growing up. And through the 4-H and your county fair, a homesteader can pick up many potential buyers for their purebred chickens.

With these "fancy" breeds, you can choose, again, from larger "standard" breeds, such as the different colors of feather-footed Cochins and mopheaded Polish to tiny Mille Fleur banties that fit in your hand. Just pick up a poultry catalog and browse the selection.

Besides browsing (and drooling over) poultry catalogs, you can visit poultry breeders in your area and attend poultry swaps and fairs to learn about different breeds and see them in "person."

How many chickens?

When buying chicks or chickens, we always tend to overdo. This isn't a good idea, especially for beginners in poultry.

A family of five can do quite well with a dozen hens for eggs. If, after awhile, you feel that you need more eggs, you can always add a few more hens. This allows for minimal housing, chores, feed, and space.

Okay, you really do want to raise some chickens both for eggs and to butcher later on.

Cochin

Why not start with 25 chicks, plus a few fancy ones for fun? Those tiny chicks don't take much space, feed, or work. But when they reach full size, suddenly, they crowd a smaller coop and gobble down a 50-pound sack of feed every week.

How much room do you really have for chickens? It's easy to house hens during the summer. They require only a safe place to roost at night and an area to run outside during the daytime. But if you live in an area of the country with cold winters, they will need more windproof, warmer, indoor living quarters. Twenty-five or thirty hens need as much space as half our goat barn, or an area roughly 8'x20', and that's not including an outside run. Even in the coldest parts of the winter, we let our hens out on nice sunny days.

Housing your flock

There *is* no one way to house your chickens. Fortunately, chickens are the easiest of all homestead livestock to house. I've seen them successfully housed in old school buses, vans, travel trailers, adobe huts, traditional chicken coops, log cabins, and even a tent, in the summer, of course. And

A basket of fresh eggs is always welcome.

I've housed my various flocks in a variety of these, myself. Yep, my half-grown chicks resided in a tent I rescued from the dump once, while we hurriedly finished their log coop. These were also the chickens that rode up the mountain on a snowmobile from the post office, and resided in a kerosene brooder in our kitchen until they were feathered out (and the kitchen was chicken dust, from top to bottom, might I add).

Nope, chickens *are* versatile in housing requirements, for sure. All they need is a dry, airy, yet warm in the winter home that is secure from predators, a place to happily roost off the floor, and spots in which to cuddle down and lay all those eggs. They don't care if their nest boxes are plain wooden nests, recycled old store bins, or even cardboard boxes, and they don't give a rip if their roosts are made from an old ladder or poles from your woods. High society, your girls are not!

How big should the coop be? A dozen hens fit nicely in a coop that is 8'x10'. This gives them space to roost, nest, and have their feed and water,

White Leghorns are good egg layers.

yet still be able to move about and dig and scratch as chickens love to do. Do you know that those nice sterile-looking eggs in the stores come from disheveled hens that are crammed five to a cage, in which they cannot walk about, only sit and lay their egg-a-day? I've "rescued" a few of them when I helped catch them to ship them to Campbell's Soup Company, as part payment for my all-night work. Those poor hens didn't know how to walk, eat, or roost and were afraid of the sun. Luckily in a few days they followed their instinct and became true chickens.

And, like I said before, 25-30 hens need a coop that is at least 8'x 20', for year-round housing.

Very popular right now is the "chicken tractor." This is basically a small enclosed coop on wheels with a portable enclosed yard attached. I've used this for my purebred chickens and could move the individual coops around the yard every few days. This gives the chickens fresh ground to peck and walk around on. They eat quite a bit of foraged food this way, from grass to weeds and insects. They also fertilize the area as they occupy it.

The coop part includes a roost and nest boxes. You generally feed and water the birds in their outdoor run. In hot weather it's a good idea to tie a tarp down over one end of the run for shade. Chickens overheat quite easily and a breezy shaded area is always appreciated.

I would put a rooster and two or three hens in a chicken tractor that had a coop 4 feet wide, 2 feet deep and 18 inches high, the coop having a sloping roof that was hinged where it

Cornish Rocks are great for meat production.

met the run. The runs were 8 feet long and 4 feet wide and 2 feet high, made of 1"x4" lumber and 1-inch chicken wire. This made it very lightweight and easily movable by one person (me). I had two handles on the back of the coop and I just pulled the whole sheebang backwards until I reached fresh ground. When you have a "chicken tractor" that is larger or transported further distances, it should have wheels.

The only problems I had with my chicken tractors were predators, especially larger ones such as stray dogs and raccoons. (If you don't think a "cute" raccoon is a chicken predator, think again.) The chicken wire is easily breached by a larger animal and the predator can flip the edges of the pen up and get at the birds.

The chicken tractor is not a winter home for your hens in any cold winter climate. To make the coop warm enough, it is too heavy to transport. And that short run soon fills up with snow, blocking all access to needed exercising room.

Many folks who only have a few hens house them in doll-house type coops. These are as artsy as you care to make them, from simple but effective plain dog-house style coops to gnome homes for your pets. The basics are few: draft-free and dry, light and airy, yet warm in the winter. The chickens can run loose, known as free ranging, or can be in a protected

*Our chicken coop/goat shed in Wolf Creek,
Montana was built using salvaged materials.*

run. Remember though, that chickens *will* dig in your flower beds, pull up your prize begonias as well as weeds, and sample that just-ripe tomato that you have been watching for weeks. They'll poop on your porch and eat the dog's food.

So think twice about letting your girls run wild. We *do* let our poultry range at will. But then we *have* no neighbors, fence our garden and yard, feed our dogs away from the house, and train our birds that the porch is off-limits. It's amazing what screaming and waving a broom will do.

Winter accommodations for chickens in colder climates include windows on the south for solar gain in the daytime—much appreciated by your hens. In very cold areas, it's a good idea to add insulation to the walls and ceiling. But be sure to cover it with OSB, boards, or plywood. Chickens will eat insulation like dessert. If you are on grid, a light hung in the coop will provide some heat and will also ensure a whole lot more egg laying going on during those long dark months. No light equals no eggs. For us off-grid homesteaders, I *used* to hang a kerosene lamp in the feed bin area that was wired off from the

regular part of the coop with chicken wire. It gave light and also a little heat, so we got eggs all during the winter. When they raised the price of kerosene to gold I stopped doing that.

This winter, our girls will get a new compact fluorescent light hung from the ceiling, powered by its own deep cycle battery and small charger. When we run the generator, not only will it charge the house's system, but also our chickens'. Imagine, hens having their own power system. How classy.

Be sure to add extra bedding in the winter, whether it is shavings or straw. Not only will it keep them warmer, but it will encourage them to move about more, scratching and digging. This will also keep the hens warmer.

If you can't keep water from freezing in the coop, at least dump the ice out or change the containers twice a day. If they don't get enough water they won't produce as many eggs or stay healthy. Yes, you *can* dump snow in their coop for them to eat. But if this is all the "water" they get, they will eat more feed because it takes more calories to melt that snow. When you save steps by watering

with snow, you spend more money at the feed store.

Whatever housing you decide on for your new flock of chickens, be sure that it is built *before* you get those chicks. (Remember my tent chickens? I speak from first hand experience, here.) At least our tent had a zip-tight door, a waterproof roof, and a sewn-in floor. If you just turn your grown chickens loose without adequate housing, a predator will get them for sure.

Raising day-old chicks

Sometimes you'll just go to the feed store and order or buy your baby chicks. But when you order them from a catalog, you will pick them up at the post office. Mail-order chicks come in short, sturdy cardboard boxes with holes in them for ventilation. There is no need for feed or water as day old chicks are still living off the nutrients absorbed from the egg. But they are thirsty and hungry when they get home.

These tender babies need four things: a safe, dry, draft-free brooding area, warmth provided by a heat source so they can stay warm enough (hot room temperature is not enough; they need to have a temperature of 92-95° F available to them at first), feed, and water.

BROODING AREA

Bedding for new chicks should be newspaper at first. If you put down shavings, they may eat more shavings than feed. I told you they weren't too smart at first. After they are eating well, replace the newspaper with wood shavings or ground corn cobs. Don't use sawdust or they will eat it. It is very dusty and may cause respiratory problems. With meat breeds, it's a good idea to only leave the newspapers down for one day. These chicks are heavier, and their bones and muscles are still weak. They can develop leg troubles as their feet slip

*Mille Fleur; a banty that
will fit in your hand*

and their legs spraddle on the slippery surface of the papers.

After four weeks, and when the chicks are feathered out, you can move them to their new adult home, complete with roosts. Roosts for these young birds should be stepped up so they can hop up on the lower rungs, then on up to the higher ones they prefer. It won't be long before they just fly up to the top. Chickens prefer rounded roosts to square material and it is easier on their feet.

You'll want to allow at least six inches shoulder room for each bird and have the roost poles eight inches apart to avoid having the birds "splatter" their roost-mates with you-know-what. I wouldn't provide nest boxes until the chicks are at least four months old. If they are given access to them sooner, they'll start to roost in the nests. This is a bad habit because the birds will foul the nests.

You can buy metal nest boxes or make your own. I've had real good luck using plywood for the back, bottom, and top and 1" x 12" lumber for the dividers. I like my boxes about a foot wide and high, and about 18 inches deep. This is large for a small hen, but a big hen finds it comfy, so your boxes will be versatile.

The top of your nest box tier should be steeply sloped toward the front to prevent chickens from roosting on the nest boxes.

Along the front, run a 1-inch pole a few inches out from the front of the boxes so that a hen can fly up, land on it, and choose the box she wants.

It results in less "arguments" over nests and less broken eggs as a result.

HEAT REQUIREMENTS

When you first bring your chicks home, make sure their brooding area maintains 92-95° F. This should be kept up for the first week. Then you can reduce the temperature 5° each week until you get to 70° F and the chicks are quite well-feathered. It's better to use a red heat lamp than a clear one. It often will keep picking down. Picking is when one or more chicks are being pecked by the other birds. They will start pulling feathers, then get aggressively worse until the poor chick is a bloody mess or is actually killed and eaten by its pen mates. If this begins to happen, and watch carefully for it, scatter some grass or fruit pieces in the pen, put a little pine tar on the pecked bird, and dim the lights. This can often be best done by hanging a sack over one or more windows. If they continue to pick on the one chick, you'll have to remove it or they'll kill it. After the feathers regrow, you can put it back and they will usually leave it alone.

Picking is also a sign of chicks that are too hot or too crowded, so avoid these situations. It's easier to prevent picking than cure it!

If you will be brooding your chicks in a small building, you can hang a heat lamp from the ceiling, near one corner. It's a good idea to make a cardboard

circle a foot high and 6 feet in diameter. This keeps the new (not so smart!) chicks corralled near the heat, yet able to get away from it if they wish, as well as near the food and water.

If you are using another source, rather than a heat lamp, such as a commercial or farm brooder, it's a good idea to also provide a small light at night. This keeps the chicks from piling in a corner and smothering each other. I had this trouble with our homebuilt kerosene brooder on our remote Montana mountain homestead so we set a kerosene lamp on the table at the end of the brooder pen and the piling instantly stopped.

I've also used an empty stock tank and it works quite well. You can hang a heat lamp at each end of an 8 foot tank, leaving the center for a cooler area with the food and water.

FEED

Probably the easiest feed to use is commercial chick starter. This is crumbled grain, not too fine, nor too coarse, which includes vitamins and minerals to keep them growing quickly. "But what did Grandma do?" I can hear you ask. Grandma raised her chicks on a mix of coarse ground cornmeal, oatmeal, milk, and hard-

Rhode Island Red

19

boiled eggs. She probably mixed it up so it made a crumbly dough-like feed and fed them several times a day, leaving just enough in their pan so they didn't have any left at the next feeding (to prevent it from molding), but weren't too hungry waiting for the next feeding.

Also, remember that Grandma did *not* have those super duper Cornish Rock hybrid chicks to raise, either. They grow so fast they have special feed needs. They cannot have feed left in front of them 24/7 or they will develop leg problems, and become unable to walk and will die. With these broiler chicks, you should provide all the feed they can eat in a day, then let it run out at evening time, and fill the feeders again in the morning.

WATER REQUIREMENTS

For each 25 chicks, you'll need a 2-foot long chick feeder and a 2-quart watering jar. Chicks are very prone to drowning, so use a waterer while they are young. If you just put a pan of water in the brooding area, you are sure to lose a few babies. Just as soon as you get your box of chicks home, take the time to dip the beak of each chick in the water so they learn how to drink and where the water is. It's also a good idea for the first three days to put 3 Tbsp. of sugar in the waterer to give the new chicks energy so they will eat, drink, and be active. It helps get them off to a good start. There are packages of special chick vitamins, minerals, and electrolytes available to help get the babies going. We usually use this, as well.

Keep those feeders (except at night for the broiler chicks) and waterers full. It's amazing how fast baby chicks can dehydrate or can actually starve to death.

In addition to feed and water, chicks need grit to digest their food. Sprinkle a little grit on the feed every day. Don't use a lot or they'll eat the grit, not the feed.

Predator protection

Everyone has a "fox that got my chickens" story. Yet in all the years we've lived in wild and remote country, we've only lost one setting hen to a predator. And it's not because we didn't have any around. Our homestead was also home to coyotes, wolves, mountain lions, bears, lynx, bobcats, foxes, raccoons, weasels, fishers, mink, pine martens, hawks, eagles, and owls—all of which would truly love a free meal of tender chicken. The hen we lost hid her nest out in the brush and absolutely refused to be lured into the coop.

I believe the biggest reason we have had such good luck is that we always, without fail, shut our livestock and chickens in at night. And once *in* it is hard for predators to gain access. Of course, having several big dogs around the place does help.

Weasels are bloodthirsty little buggers. They really *are* cute, with black, shoe-button eyes, alert stand-up ears, and round little cat-like paws. In the summer they are brown with a white belly and in the winter, they turn ermine white with a black tip on their tail. One weasel can squeeze through a knothole the size of your thumb and kill all your chickens in one night. I had it happen long ago, back on the farm.

I didn't know a weasel could squeeze through a hole that small, nor did I know that they could climb like a squirrel. I do now. That big crack over the door? Or under it? That place where the board is rotted off? Yep, a weasel can pop right through. We even had a friend who had a weasel pry up the hardware cloth covering the stock tank serving as a chick brooder in the barn. No more chicks. The moral to this story is to make your coop weasel-tight.

If larger predators are a possibility in your area, it is a good idea to make your doors stronger and to bury heavy gauge wire below the door and along your outside pen. I plan on using 6-foot chicken wire for my large chicken yard/orchard. But this wouldn't keep out a determined coyote or stray dog. So on the outside I'm using 16-foot welded wire stock panels for added security. It's also a good idea to bury your fence in the ground to dissuade aggressive diggers too.

In many areas, your most dangerous chicken predator is a dog or several loose dogs. They can be nice dogs, but seeing those noisy, fluttering chickens makes them lose their cool and turn predator. If you live where stray dogs, or even your neighbors' dogs roam, it's a good idea to reinforce your run with stock panels and electric wire. Just in case.

If raccoons are plentiful in your area, I would strongly suggest adding an electric wire six inches up from the bottom of your fence and an additional strand on top of the fence to keep those adorable, fluffy, bloodthirsty buggers out of your chicken run. I once (again on the old farm) had 33 turkeys killed and dragged off by raccoons who dug under the door, broke a window, and chewed through the chicken wire fence. I trapped five of them just outside the fence and shot one in the act of grabbing a hen off the roost. No circumstantial evidence here.

If hawks and owls are a problem, it's easiest to put a netting over your outside run and *don't* let the birds free range. If you do, there is not much chance of protecting them. You cannot legally shoot a hawk or owl, nor should you. They are just doing what nature built them to do.

Feeding the homestead flock

There are varied opinions as to what you should feed your chickens. Some people, especially commercial producers and feed store salesmen, staunchly recommend that you only feed your chickens commercial feed appropriate to their age and use: chick starter, chick grower, broiler maker, egg mash, etc.

Personally, I do not like all the additives that are in commercial feed. Yes, I *do* start my chicks on commercial chick starter; I can't spend the time making "baby formula" like Grandma did. But as soon as they start to feather out, I gradually switch to a mixture of a good scratch feed (cracked corn, milo, and wheat, primarily), in addition to all the fresh milk they can drink, and all the kitchen scraps and garden produce I have available for them.

My chicks grow like weeds on this and mature to fill my canning jars and lay all the eggs our family could ever use.

I always plant a little "extra" in the garden for the goats and chickens: corn, greens, squash, and root crops. It's amazing how a regular handful of garden produce year-round can cut your feed bill and raise the quality of your eggs. When I crack open one of our eggs, it has an orange yolk that stands up firmly on the white. The store eggs are so pale by comparison that when my son, David, saw a neighbor break one into a pan he whispered to me, "Mom! What's wrong with their eggs?"

You know the old saying "You are what you eat?" Well, it holds true for your chickens, too. And I have hens that are seven years old and still lay their egg a day unless they are molting. Commercial hens are burned up by the age of one year and are made into soup. Ever wonder why? It's a combination of breeding a hen that just about lays herself to death and the feed she must eat all her life.

I want to know what my birds are eating. Try to find that out from the tag on your commercial chicken feed. There's things in it that I can't even pronounce, let alone know what they are. Then there are the "products" and "digests," etc. I feel better giving my chickens *real food*.

In the winter, when they can't forage outside, I always bring them some vegetables or vegetable scraps from the basement, along with the pail of food scraps they also get daily. In real cold weather, they appreciate a treat of alfalfa leaves or pellets soaked in boiling water until they are nicely warm, but cooled down enough to eat.

Health concerns

First let me say that I have had very few sick chickens. Ever. Once in awhile, one will just die. People do, too. But by feeding your flock well and providing them with relatively warm, airy, dry housing, you will seldom see sick birds. Most poultry diseases only occur in large commercial flocks.

When our kids showed chickens at the fair and 4-H shows, we always quarantined them for three weeks after they came home. You never know what your birds may pick up from neighboring birds caged next door. By taking this precaution, we never had a problem.

What does a healthy bird look like? It is alert and active. Its feathers are smooth and it holds them close to its body. (Except when it's a hen running with roosters, who will quickly denude her back and the back of her head during repeated breedings, or when she's in molt twice a year.) The eyes and nostrils are clear of running or crusty discharge. When you pick the chicken up, she should feel plump and heavy. A very light chicken is usually thin because of a health problem.

PARASITES

Even flocks that are well cared for will occasionally pick up external parasites, usually chicken lice or mites. Chickens will try to keep themselves free of these by taking frequent dust baths and by preening. But sometimes they need a little help. It's a good idea once in a while to catch a

bird and closely examine its skin, beneath its feathers. Use a magnifying glass, if necessary. Chicken mites are about the size of the dot a pencil makes on a paper. Lice are larger and are pinkish clear. Both will get on humans for a short time, but will not stay.

In the old days, they dusted the nests with DDT and nicotine dust. Obviously, you wouldn't even consider the DDT, and nicotine dust is very poisonous. Nicotine, as in tobacco, as in cigarettes…point made. Instead, I dust my chickens with a 1% rotenone compound that is often sold in gardening sections at hardware and feed stores. This is mild and does the trick. It's a good idea to clean and dust the coop first, then dust the chickens. Be sure you totally remove the bedding and clean out the nest boxes too or you'll risk reinfestation.

SCALY LEG

This is a quite common problem, also caused by external parasites, the leg mite. You cannot see these mites, so there's no sense in looking for them. They cause the legs to become rough and scaly. In severe cases they cause bleeding and the bird will lose weight and die. Fortunately, they are quite easily treated. Simply dip both legs, one at a time, in a tall can of vegetable oil. Repeat this once a week until the legs show signs of improvement. The oil not only smothers the mites but helps soften and remove the scales.

COCCIDIOSIS

Coccidiosis is most often seen in chicks confined to a brooding area. It is caused by an internal protozoa. The symptoms include diarrhea, weakness, sitting around with feathers puffed up, and lack of growth. Death often results without treatment. Fortunately, coccidiosis can usually be prevented by keeping dry, clean bedding under your chicks at all times. It can be diagnosed by taking a small sample to your veterinarian for a fecal examination.

Most cases of coccidiosis can be effectively treated by putting medication in the drinking water. Many veterinarians use Sulfadimethoxine at a dosage of 2 tsp. per gallon of drinking water.

UPPER RESPIRATORY PROBLEMS

There are several chicken diseases that can show up with upper respiratory symptoms. To complicate matters, some of these are viruses which have no effective treatment but good care, while others are bacterial and often respond to antibiotics.

Upper respiratory symptoms include mattered eyes and nostrils, discharge from the nostrils, sneezing, and wheezing.

In the home flock, most cases of upper respiratory diseases can be traced to two things: a coop that is continually damp and closed in, and a dry coop, often bedded with sawdust. In both cases, getting some good ventilation really helps. We're not talking about windy, but some steady cross-ventilation to keep fresh air in the coop. The damp closed-in coop is often seen in the winter when some chickens are not allowed to go outdoors. A combination of built-up litter and the ammonia generated by the manure sets the chickens up for a serious problem with upper respiratory diseases.

If your chickens are not allowed out in the winter, be sure to change the bedding frequently, and crack open a south facing window a bit to let in fresh air, at least during the daytime when it is milder out.

Should these care tips not provide prompt relief, it would be a good idea to treat the flock with an antibiotic, such as Terramycin, for ten days. While this will not "cure" a viral infection, it will usually take care of bacterial diseases and will prevent a secondary infection from occurring,

following, or in conjunction with the viral illness.

IMPACTED CROP

Because chickens are instinctively "peckers," they will often eat anything they can swallow. Their crop can become impacted with a great variety of foreign objects as well as too much straw, dry grass, or bedding. David once lost a pet chick because it picked up many little pieces of paper that David had punched with a hole punch. By the time we knew what had happened it was too late. This was a sad lesson.

The chicken with an impacted crop will have a large crop that stays large for over two hours. The bird acts distressed and repeatedly works its neck, trying to move the impaction down into the digestive tract. Finally it becomes weak and lethargic. And, as David experienced, it can die.

Usually you can effectively treat an impacted crop, *if* you notice the bird in time and treat it. The treatment consists of 2 Tbsp. of vegetable oil sucked into a bulb syringe and squeezed slowly into the chicken's mouth. Don't rush this or the bird may choke. When the oil is all in, gently massage the oil into the mass in the crop, trying to work it apart and either up into the mouth, where she will violently shake her head and fling the offending pieces away, or down into the digestive tract. When the crop is less distended, keep the chicken quiet and warm, withholding feed for 24 hours, yet providing plenty of water.

EGG BOUND

On the other end of the chicken, the working end, is another fairly common problem. For some reason or another, the hen can't push out the egg. It's sort of like constipation only with an egg. Often it is a very large egg or else one that is dry. Again, get out your trusty bulb syringe and vegetable oil and gently inject 2 Tbsp. of

vegetable oil into the vent around the egg. This usually works rapidly and quite well. In extreme cases, when the egg cannot be passed, you may be able to save her life by poking the egg with needle-nosed pliers to break it and very gently pull pieces out so the egg shell will collapse, then be able to be passed.

WHAT ABOUT BIRD FLU?

Yeah, okay. Yes, it is possible for a flock of chickens to catch bird flu from wild birds. It's also possible that they may be hit with a meteor. Bird flu is caused by a virus, H5N1. Although it has been found in Asia, it never has been seen in the United States. Never. So unless it does cross the ocean, I wouldn't worry about that problem. Yet.

If it should, I would recommend completely isolating your flock from wild birds. This means having them in an enclosed, bird-proof coop and an enclosed bird-proof outdoor run. Then your birds will probably be safer than you will be. They don't go shopping, traveling, to school, to work or play, or to mix with other vectors.

Setting your own hens

You can certainly buy new chicks every time you want a new flock or a few new birds. But there are certain advantages to breeding your own replacement chicks. First of all, it's fun and entertaining to let a hen go broody and hatch out a bunch of fuzzy little peepers. Then, when you hatch your own chicks, there is no chance of introducing some health problem into your flock from outside sources. Reputable hatcheries have exceedingly healthy chicks, but there is always a chance for the baby chicks to pick up something along the way. You see this most often with "feed store" chicks, where they come in from a hatchery, then are available to the public for several days, often in open stock tank-type brooders.

Then, too, you never know when some sort of country-wide disaster may hit, severely limiting the *ability* to buy chicks...or much else. If you have hens that can raise chicks, you are never at the whims of fortune...or lack of it.

Heavy breed hens and banties are exceedingly good at sitting on a nestful of eggs, come hell or high water. My kids used to be scared to reach under a setting hen to check her eggs. My oldest son, Bill, told me of his experience one day, checking under a setting hen. "How many eggs does she have?" I asked. He shrugged. "She went like this," he squinted his eyes viciously and stuck out his elbows, "and she yelled at me!" They will peck, too, protecting their flock of eggs.

It's usually a hen over two years old that will go broody and want to sit on eggs. When this happens and you want to let her hatch eggs, make sure she receives a clutch of fresh eggs of a breed you want to hatch. The hen does not have to sit on eggs of her own breed. While I love banties, I always put heavy breed eggs under her to sit on. I don't need scads of teeny, tiny chickens.

Keep her in a comfortable, private location. If she is in a nest box and refuses to be moved to another "sitting nest," hang a piece of feed sack down over the door to keep other hens out. If you don't you'll have hens laying eggs in the nest with the sitting hen and they won't hatch with the first batch and will only go bad.

If left alone and only daily offered food and water, she will handle hatching the eggs just fine, turning them several times daily to ensure that they hatch well. One day you'll hear little peeps coming from under her, and lo and behold, there are several fuzzy heads peeping out from under her wings. Keep the chicks in the nest until all have hatched. There are often a few eggs that are bad and won't hatch. They do not need feed and

water for 24 hours, but should be offered some the next day if the hen is still on the eggs. I offer water in a shallow dish three times a day and leave food in the front of the nest for them.

When they are out of the nest, they will follow Mom around the yard, scratching and eating happily. Again, chicks drown easily so be sure there are no deep water containers available. Chicks flying up to get a drink out of my goat water tank and falling in have caused my biggest losses through the years.

When you raise your own chicks, you often have a ready market for the young, grown birds—provided that they are a pure breed of a popular type or a rare breed that is in demand. This helps pay for the flock's feed and other costs. Sometimes a person only wants a rooster to cross with their hens, but selling a trio consisting of a cockerel (young rooster) and two pullets (young hens) is a common practice.

In addition to selling surplus young stock, selling your surplus eggs also provides income for the homestead. Today many health-conscious people eagerly seek out home-raised free-range eggs, as opposed to "chicken concentration camp" eggs from the

local store. And they will happily pay a premium price for them too. I would not want to have enough hens to make a substantial income from the eggs, but you never have a problem selling any excess eggs from time to time. A simple roadside sign or a note on the bulletin board at the feed store usually directs more customers to you than you can believe. Farm fresh eggs are a very marketable commodity at local farmers' markets, as well. And not only will you develop regular customers, but new friends to boot! Δ

City girl ❦ Country life

The joys of idleness

By Claire Wolfe

"If work were so pleasant, the rich would keep it for themselves." — Mark Twain

Chances are, your granny used to tell you something like this: *"Fac et aliquid operis, ut semper te diabolus inveniat occupatum."* Okay, she probably didn't put it in exactly those words. But very likely Granny or a Sunday School teacher or your least-favorite uncle liked to remind you, "Idle hands are the devil's playground." Or maybe, "An idle brain is the devil's workshop."

They were echoing St. Jerome, who wrote the Latin tongue-twister above in the 4th Century. (A rough translation is, "Do good deeds and the devil will always find you occupied.") No doubt Jerome was echoing some earlier moralist. Who was echoing some earlier moralist. Who… well, you get the point.

Fact is that, ever since human beings settled down into societies where one man works for another, earnest sorts have warned of the perils of idleness and promoted the alleged virtue of work, work, work, and more darned work until you drop.

"You" is the operative word. As often as not, the biggest promoters of work have been landed gents, philosophers, wealthy factory owners, preachers, and other fine folk not noted for getting their own lily-whites dirty.

Now, don't get me wrong. I'm not opposed to work. In the backwoods, work never ends, so who has time to sit around opposing it? And although I may snort and sneer at the folks who sit in their cozy libraries and assure us work is a great idea for other people, they have a point.

History tells us what happens when we mere mortal weaklings fall into the abyss of idleness. Let us count the ways:

• **We get violent.** We hang out on street corners, plot mayhem, and beat up little old ladies. Sometimes we become pool sharks or Mafia hit men. Or get shanghaied and meet an early and watery grave. (Well, not you fine *BHM* readers, of course, but those other idle people, especially aimless young men with too much time on their hands.)

• **We go broke.** Like grasshopper (the one in the Aesop fable, not the one on the old Kung-Fu TV series), we "idle" ourselves right into poverty and starvation, dragging our helpless loved ones into the gutter with us.

• **We indulge.** Idleness is a moral weakness that leads to even more moral weakness. The idle get hooked on Demon Weed. They're seduced by jazz music. They fall into

> **…ever since human beings settled down into societies where one man works for another, earnest sorts have warned of the perils of idleness…**

debauchery. (Or whatever the chemical, musical, and sexual tabloid material of the age might be.)

It's all dreadful to contemplate. Worse, even in this non-religious age, we moderns have managed to add a couple more pitfalls to the horrible historic toll of idleness:

• **Idleness is unproductive.** Idle time is inefficient. It doesn't increase our stock portfolios, pay our second mortgage, or add a third vehicle to our driveway.

• **We get bored.** We might, God forbid, go right screaming out of our hairy wits with dullness and lassitude, not to mention the much more fashionable ennui and enervation, if we don't have a full schedule of work, Pilates workouts, soccer carpools, and community-college classes.

All this is true. (Well, perhaps not the part about Demon Weed.) Idleness is a troublemaker. So *fac et aliquid operis* and *sic transit gloria mundi* and *excelsior!* and all that. Three cheers for keeping ourselves so busy we can't stop to think about how draggle-tailed miserable and settling-for-nothing we are.

Nevertheless, let me take the contrary view.

I'm vigorously, 100%, in favor of idleness. We need more idleness. I'm working hard to put the cause of idleness on the map. I don't want Congress to go forcing it upon us, mind you. But I want each of us, voluntarily, in our heart of hearts, including me, to become more attuned to personal idleness, in fact and in philosophy.

And one reason I'm in favor of it is that, yep indeed, it IS a troublemaker. But more about that in a minute. First, a bit on the human history, not to mention the current events, of work and idleness.

Death by overwork

In hunter-gatherer societies—the way humans lived before they settled down to civilization and formal agriculture—nobody had the slightest need to exhort other people with more callused hands to work, work, work. It was very simple: you worked to eat. No work, no chow. Choose not to work and you either didn't get your share of the mastodon meat or in extreme cases, you got kicked out of the tribe altogether, which very likely meant death. These societies fed their non-working old and small children to the best of their ability, but if you were capable of labor, you labored. No moralists needed.

So given the imperative for survival, how much of their day did hunter-gatherers devote to work, work, work? About three hours, say anthropologists. Yes, you read that right. Our deep, dark, primitive, unfortunate, benighted ancestors worked about three hours a day. Maybe four when things got rough.

Wow. Think about that next time you're hunting the canyons of modern urban office blocks, watching wan and pallid office workers stuff sugar and grease down their gullets on their guiltily-grabbed lunch breaks.

Daniel Pink, in his book *Free Agent Nation*, points out this painful fact: "Americans work 350 hours more per year than Europeans, and 70 hours more per year than even the Japanese, whose language contains a word, *karoshi*, that means 'death from overwork'."

Three hours a day versus death from overwork. Hm. Which to choose…which to choose?

But then, it's not a fair comparison. Hunter-gatherers may have had a light schedule. But they didn't have iPods, SUVs, Xtreme ski vacations, $1,500 per month health-insurance premiums, or Viagra. And they did have a myriad of nasty diseases, not to mention the occasional spot of cannibalism. They were at the mercy of drought, disease, and habitat change to a degree we can't even imagine unless we've just watched a documentary about it on our satellite-dish or cable TV.

So if neither three hours a day nor death by cubicle is the way to go, what is the "right" amount of work?

Well, the "right" amount of work, of course, is the amount that *you* decide suits your life circumstances, your goals, and your temperament.

But to figure *that* out, you need…idleness.

And you know, when it comes to putting a little *carpe diem* into the subject of active idleness, there are powerful forces in this world massed against the possibility of you ever getting any. They've been at it for a long time.

Creating the virtue (ack!) of work

As the Industrial Revolution began to boom and machinery began to make more production possible, entrepreneurs and their moral supporters sought ways to make workers more productive. Although our image of the Industrial Revolution features dark, Dickensian factories, those actually came a bit later. The first machinery of the revolution—textile-producing looms—was often located in homes and little privately owned workshops.

Families would make cloth. Or caps. Or capes. Or whatever. And they'd sell their wares wholesale to distributor-clients.

An early problem the "proto-capitalists" faced: How to get these independent family units to produce more? Aha, let's do the humane thing and offer them more pay!

> With sufficient true idleness, we might just start asking questions about why we've been spending so much of our lives busily serving the interests of those who really don't have *our* interests at heart.

But, unfortunately that little burst of good intentions didn't pan out.

What did independent people do when the offered higher pay per item delivered? Well, like any sensible people, they produced fewer items, pocketed the same amount of money, and took more time off to enjoy themselves.

Those Dickensian factories were the entrepreneurs' answer. Drive the independent sorts out of business and bring the men, women, and kiddies into the mill or garment factory under the gaze of the overseer—and tell them hard work is a virtue. It was more efficient, anyhow—even if the system did stamp out independence and individuality.

It was about that time that phrases like "idle hands are the devil's playground," which had been around for a long time, suddenly proliferated like kudzu in books and sermons.

Then comes the 20th century and the beginning of the modern assembly line. Mass production had already been going on for decades, and in that system workers were just replaceable cogs in replaceable wheels—those Dickensian factories, you know. But some workers—like those who built machinery, proudly saw themselves as craftsmen. A man who could build a reaper or a bicycle or assemble an automobile didn't like to see himself as nothing but a sort of human machine, welding a stream of identical welds all day, or repetitively lifting one part into place, never taking pride in the whole. These men expected their chosen work to bring personal satisfaction. They wanted to put their own integrity into the work, then watch that integrity come back out as fine product.

Even when Henry Ford offered the then-fabulous inducement of paying his workers $5 a day, he initially had a hard time hiring and keeping employees. All budding assembly line businesses did. Skilled people simply saw it as beneath their dignity, and as dehumanizing, to work that way—no matter how good the pay.

So entrepreneurs and their moral supporters came up with another bright idea. And, you have to admit, this one served brilliantly. For the first time in history, they promoted *debt* as a virtue. Before that, for the average person, being in debt was a shameful thing. A moral failing. But now…well, with credit you could own your own home (even if you owed most of it to the bank). You could actually drive one of those new cars you were building. You could have more than you ever imagined. And all you had to do to get it was accept a "secure" job that would enable you reliably to borrow and pay. Never mind how dreary it was, never mind what grim hours you had to work, and under what grim conditions.

So the craftsmen fell. And the money, the money alone, became the thing. (Later "benefits" were added to the mix of musts.) The expectation of work satisfaction…the desire for independence…the belief in determining one's own proper mix of work and leisure…pride of craftsmanship… any commitment for working closely with one's family… all went out the window.

Nowadays, our culture heroes are pale, stooped men and women with coke-bottle glasses and incipient autism who work 20-hour days—entrepreneurs and high-tech geniuses who work harder than Victorian factory serfs. Wow. Progress, eh?

And never mind what they produce. Don't ask, "Does it benefit us? Do we really need it? Does it improve life?" Just ask, "Can I get some of that?" We know the consumer price index better than we know our neighbor down the street. The Dow-Jones industrial average gets more attention than the local fishing pond. We don't &^%$#@!ing care that our new vehicle is going to cost us $60,000 once we've finished paying the interest on it; we just gotta have it. We know what's happening on Slashdot or MySpace more than we know what's happening in our own neighborhoods. And we work, work, work, work, work to support all this vast, glorious, glittering just-gotta-have-it prosperity.

Since the beginning of automation, a few contrarian writers have claimed to promote the value of idleness. The philosopher Bertrand Russell wrote a 1932 essay "In Praise of Idleness." The anarchist Bob Black produced a 1985 essay, "The Abolition of Work," that boldly states, "No one should ever work. Work is the source of nearly all the misery in the world. Almost any evil you'd care to name comes from working or from living in a world designed for work. In order to stop suffering, we have to stop working."

But oddly enough, essays like these don't actually spend much time on the virtues of idleness. They're mostly political rants—against capitalists or communists or the rich or the system or all of the above.

From my own little industrial rant just above, you can see how easy it is to fall into that trap. The alleged "pro-idleness" thinkers say, "How awful all that enforced labor is!" They don't say enough about how joyful idleness might be.

Russell, Black, and their rare little ilk are sort of like theologians who can paint a whiz-bang picture of hell but who can't even attempt to conjure up an image of a heaven that's worth aiming for. Seems it's always more interesting to relate what you oppose than what you favor. Have you ever noticed that? Descriptions of hell, from Dante onward, are as spine-chillingly vivid as *Freddie Meets Jason at the Bates Motel*, but even the most authentically saintly visions of heaven sound as dull as an afternoon spent paying a courtesy call on your rich great aunt. Thus it is with writing about work and leisure. Nobody ever seems to have a good idea about what makes leisure so desirable.

I mean, once you've played a few rounds of golf or gotten sunburned in a hammock, what's left? It's like sitting around heaven twanging a harp and trying not to yawn, right?

Well, I'm here to tell you…there's a whole lot left to leisure—that is, to true idleness. A whole, vast, unexplored universe is left. And unfortunately, it's being left unexplored.

The virtues of idleness (including the virtue of troublemaking)

Idleness—even when it's bad—is good.

Sometimes idleness is good *precisely because it's bad*.

But before I get down to praising idleness, let me distinguish: Idleness that says, "I don't have to lift a finger; the rest of the world should serve me" is contemptible. (Thank you, Modern Welfare State; our caveman ancestors look sophisticated by comparison.)

Enforced idleness is also not good. Sticking an otherwise productive person into a prison cell and letting him rot… well, there just aren't words for the waste. Telling somebody he can't work because he can't get government permission…very bad.

Nor is idleness good when it's unbalanced. Productive work and idleness complement each other. Some of the best idleness comes in those moments when the wood is newly chopped and you lean against the fresh woodpile and watch the snow fall in silence.

What an old-fashioned image that is! But then, the last time our culture had space for much idleness was when it was the common way of life, just as it is now for a few of us. And there's something in those moments and those substances—wood, water, rock, greenery—that heal the heart far better than a dose of Prozac, the happy results of Viagra, or watching your team win the StuporBowl. In fact, isn't it funny how our culture pitches "pleasure" and relief of pain at us 24 hours a day—*Take that pill, buy that car, root for that team, enjoy that TV show, relax with that drink, buy that brand, ease that ache.* Yet so many of the supposed "pleasures" merely pretend to temporarily relieve *the chronic misery or what we're presumed to be suffering.* How come nobody ever asks: Why are we suffering so many vague, chronic ills and discontents in the first place?

But I digress. Anyway…idleness as a choice, balanced against meaningful and gratifying work…now that is a virtue we deprive ourselves of at our own peril.

Let's go back and look at those five dire consequences of the satanic (or merely inefficient, in modern terms) "vice" of idleness covered above and turn them into their corresponding virtues. Take the last first:

Boredom. Yep, idleness—true idleness, not soccer games or cocktails by the pool, but absolute, true Just Doing Nothing—can be so boring you can almost hear your fingernails grow. This is exactly— precisely!—when idleness begins to get good. Just stay right at that spot. Don't go turn on the TV set. Don't call up a girlfriend. Don't busy yourself in the woodshop (although later, much later, the woodshop may, for other reasons, become a place of joyful idleness). Just be bored for now. It isn't fatal.

Eventually something, you can be sure of it, will bubble out of this deadening of mind and body. You'll recall some old dream you never followed through on. You'll start wondering how a prism works. You'll invent a fictional alterego. You'll remember a neglected knitting project from five years ago. You'll design your dream house. Who knows?

Possibly, the thing that bubbles up out of boredom may seem negative at first: With time to think, you gradually realize your marriage has been shot for a long time but nobody wants to talk about it. You realize you've lost your faith in God. Or you realize that the atheism and logic you've always touted no longer fill a void in you. You discover you hate your job. You realize your oldest kid has a

drug problem you were previously too busy to be fully aware of.

Nevertheless, wherever your mind goes, this is where boredom leads you and it's where you need to go. You may discover unexpected talents or joys. You may just as easily discover old woes and pains you thought you'd forgotten decades ago. But you will find *you*. You'll find your life and live it wherever it takes you. And even suffering may be a form of healing, as you go through a dark night of the soul to emerge into a rosy-fingered dawn (thank you, St. John of the Cross and Homer (the old one, not Simpson) for the rather florid imagery).

Please don't be put off by this talk of spiritual or familial crises, though. Chances are good that when you just let yourself relax long enough to get through the pressures of "Oh, I really should be *doing something*" you'll have a lovely, positive experience. You'll discover how fun it is to help the kids build a fort. You'll notice how those light hairs on the dog's coat sparkle in the sun. You'll breathe deep. You'll enjoy.

Now on to the modern claims that **idleness is inefficient and unprofitable.** What can I say? Stuff and nonsense! Nothing, nothing, nothing in the world is more profitable than idleness in the long run.

> …Idleness…gives birth to the most creative ideas, the greatest works of art, the coolest entrepreneurial ventures, the wildest video-game concepts, the greatest movies in the world…

Idleness—and again, we're talking true just *being* sort of idleness (though there are times it gets mixed with more active talents)—gives birth to the most creative ideas, the greatest works of art, the coolest entrepreneurial ventures, the wildest video-game concepts, the greatest movies in the world. It gives birth to philosophy (though, sorry, so much of that has been crap). It advances mathematics. It produces the greatest "Eureka!" moments of all time. (Remember, the original "Eureka" moment came when Archimedes had given up working on his gold crown problem and was slipping into a nice, relaxing bath.) In fact, history is bursting at the seams with artists, scientists, or mathematicians relaxing after beating their brains on a problem, only to have the solution fly into their heads as if delivered by FedExing angels.

And even for us non-genius types, how many ideas for little business ventures, how many great cabin designs, how many stories, how many drawings, how many improvements to life have come out of those moments? If we only let ourselves have those moments.

And finally, on the subject of efficiency, you know darned well that when we're beat we all work more efficiently after a long mental and physical rest. Not a hectic vacation, but a real rest.

Ah, but here is where those old moralists thunder into our brains once again. Because you see, this is also where the true troublemaking terror of idleness comes in.

The ideas you get when you're coming out the other side of boredom into idea-nirvana just might be dangerous. Oh, not dangerous in the sense of "Let's hang out on a street corner and mug a little old lady."

No, strange as it sounds, the moralist powers-that-be actually thrive on those unthinking or rare products of idleness. Dealing with the bad guys *justifies the moralists' existence*. Keeping us scared of the bad guys is one of the ways they keep us from asking questions—questions not about the bad guys, but about the moralists themselves and the huge institutional structures they construct to cage us.

With sufficient true idleness, we might just start asking questions about why we've been spending so much of our lives busily serving the interests of those who really don't have *our* interests at heart. Why we consider perpetual debt to be happiness. Why we're more interested in *stuff* than in people—including our own selves.

Church and state and mega-corporation and media—whatever you call them, all those forces, institutions, and agencies that want to manipulate your life for their benefit (while tossing you some tasty crumbs)—have always feared, above all, one fundamental threat to their power: that the common man might start asking some "interesting" questions and not take propaganda for an answer.

Ah. So there, you see, is why the "anti-idleacs" have been with us since civilization began, and especially since we began to serve as human cogs in a system not of our own design. Because "they" (a "they" which changes over the centuries, but can always be classed as "the establishment" or "the system") gotta keep us moving their way or we might move in the wrong (that is our own) direction.

Knowing all that, we can go on to quickly demolish the moralists' original three anti-idleness points: that idleness is moral vice, that idleness leads to poverty, that idleness prompts us to bop old ladies over the head for the sake of $1.57 and a tattered picture of some granny's cat.

Sure, idleness can *sometimes* give a body the opportunity for moral depravity. As a writer, I indulged in a bit of that in my wicked youth, and I must say I don't regret a bit of it. I regard it as part of the writer's apprenticeship. Gotta live to learn. We mustn't forget that experience teaches us far more about life than any sermon, class, or how-to book ever will.

Do some people fall into what Victorian tabloids breathlessly (and vaguely) called "debauchery" and find themselves unable or unwilling to crawl out? Well, yeah. Just as some drop dead from overwork or die of black-lung disease. Life has its casualties. But when we take responsibility for our own actions—both our idleness and activity, our sins of omission and commission—idleness is far less likely to go in the direction of depravity and irresponsibility. When idleness is a natural and healthy part of life, rather than a pleasure guiltily wrested from the clutches of dehumanizing work, it's no longer forbidden fruit, no longer a snare to capture the weak and vulnerable.

And do some idle folk bop old ladies, and pop each other with .357s in disputes over a gram of some substance or another? Alas, yes. And people are more likely to do that in alienated, fragmented societies where work has no connection to family or neighborhood and a governmental system spawns and nurtures generations of entitled idle. In a world of healthy mixed work and idleness, you have a chance to get to know all kinds of people around you and to interact with them in all kinds of creative ways. So are you more, or less, likely to end up on the bromidic street corner, glassy-eyed from meth and ready to kick butt?

Finally, the very last moralist argument to topple: When you're idle you may fall into the pit of poverty and drag your progeny and posterity along with you.

Yeah, well that, too, can happen. And it's perhaps the one anti-idleness point to take seriously. The day of the loom in the living room is long gone. Say you're sold on this idleness thing and you want only to work four hours a day, and maybe not have to work at all on the days of your choice. Uh huh. Good luck there.

For good or ill, modern society just ain't set up to accommodate dreamers and poets and pure back-to-the-landers and parents who want to take their kids to work (and *not* just to insert the little darlings into the company day-care center.) So it's a little hard to create what you want. *Genuine change* is always hard on the pioneers.

You can work for yourself, of course. But in this go-go-go age, it's very hard not to end up pushing yourself so hard you have even less rest than before. (As the old entrepreneurs' joke goes, "I'm in business for myself, so I only have to work half a day. And I even get to choose which 12 hours!")

So unless you're among the fortunate who've already found it, or already have a gift for it, idleness must be cherished and cultivated like a fragile rose. It must be carved out of hectic schedules, crafted from otherwise-filled space, and even sneaked away to as a guilty pleasure. In other words, you might have to work hard to earn the idleness that is one of your ancestors' most natural gifts.

But don't give up hope. It can be done with some creativity and sometimes a little help from our friends and families. And once achieved…how glorious! There it is—your own real life, your own real work, your own real pleasure all lie ahead of you. All the gift of your hard-won idleness. Δ

Read more by Claire Wolfe in her book, *Hardyville Tales*

Feathered to finished in 15 minutes

clean a chicken quickly and easily with these simple steps

By Jackie Clay

The first time I cleaned a chicken, I had no idea of what to do. I was handed a beheaded chicken and had to figure it out for myself. I managed. After all, the basics are to take the feathers off or skin the bird and take the insides out without dumping nasty stuff into the body cavity. But there is definitely an easy way and a hard way. Here are a couple of methods we use that make the process much easier and faster.

Before the birds are killed, I either heat a big canning kettle of water to boiling if I'm going to pluck them, which I usually do, or just have a hose handy for washing the birds and my table, plus a washtub of ice water to put the birds into after they have been cleaned.

I bring out the canning kettle of boiling water and set it next to the washtub of ice water. We use my

Jackie and Jeri pluck chickens. The plastic table is easy to keep clean during the entire process.

handy dandy old plastic round table for a work surface—the same one I use for garden produce trimming, corn husking and desilking, etc. It's easy to clean during the process.

Plucking

One at a time, I dip the chickens fully into the water by the feet, holding them immersed for about 20 seconds. Then we set about plucking the birds. An old plastic garbage can sits between us to receive the handfuls of feathers and a small plastic bucket stands on the ground for the feet and entrails. You can dry pluck the birds, but I prefer to scald them because the heavy wing and tail feathers come out *much* better after scalding.

Most of the feathers come out very easily. You just grab handfuls and toss them in the garbage can. But there always are a few stubborn ones. I use a paring knife against the base of the feather, push the feather against it with my thumb, and pull. This gets them all. If the feathers are mostly reluctant to come out, the bird was not scalded long enough or the water is becoming cool. It helps to scald all the birds at once, while the water is very hot or else use two kettles of boiling water, alternating them to make sure you have fresh boiling water in which to dip the birds.

Skinning

Sometimes we skin the birds instead of plucking them, especially when we do a bunch of small birds, such as fryers or banties that we are going to can up. There are several methods of doing this, but a common way is to pull a pinch of skin up

above the point of the breast, cut that piece off with a sharp knife, then slit down the breast, holding the knife with the sharp edge up. Then the skin (feathers and all) can be pulled away from the body. With young chickens, this is very easy, but with older birds, the skin comes off harder.

Keep pulling and working the skin off; it often comes off in large pieces. At the wings, help it with your knife. I often just cut the wing tips off; there's hardly any meat on them and you really don't need to have a "pretty" carcass with a skinned bird. As you pull the skin down the legs, toward the feet, cut the feet off neatly at the "elbow" joints. Then pull the rest down and simply cut off the tail.

Hose off the bird and pick any stray feathers. It is now ready for evisceration.

Cleaning

Gently remove the crop. If you withheld feed overnight, the crop will be empty and will not spill the contents all over the table.

With a very sharp small knife, open the carcass carefully from the point of the breastbone, around the vent. Repeat on the other side, carefully loosening the rectum area. Then, carefully, insert your hand up high, next to the point of the breast and scoop/pull the entrails out. Once the big batch is out, reach up and loosen the windpipe and pull it out. The lungs are sort of attached to the ribs, so they need to be scraped, and pulled out. Really, this is not a terribly messy job and it is certainly not bloody. It's funny I can do this but can't whack off the heads.

Skinning a bird

1. Pull up the skin just below the breast and cut a hole, then with the blade of the knife away from the meat, hold skin up and cut down toward tail. Be careful not to cut into the abdominal cavity.
2. Hold down carcass and rip skin loose.
3. Work skin down legs to joint, then bend joint and cut there to remove feet and skin. Repeat with wings, remove tips.

Once they are cleaned, turn on the hose and rinse the outside of the birds, then the insides very well. (I have the generator going, then turn the switch for the pump when it's time. Between the birds, I just let the hose run on the ground, down hill, away from our feet.)

The cleaned birds are then put in the tub of ice water to begin cooling down. To cook or can chickens, you need to cool them, preferable overnight, to ensure every bit of body heat has left the bird. If you don't you will have very tough chicken dinners. I've

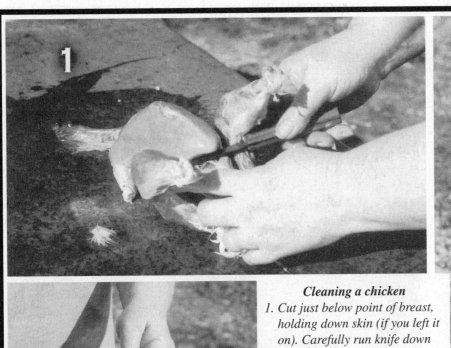

Cleaning a chicken

1. Cut just below point of breast, holding down skin (if you left it on). Carefully run knife down on each side of rectum and under—do not cut into it!
2. Remove crop by pulling up and slicing it off. This frees the esophagus.
3. Reach in and pull out the guts.
4. When guts are out scrape lungs, attached to back ribs, loose. Cut tail off or remove oil sac.
5. Rinse carcass inside and out. Place in a bucket of fresh cold water.

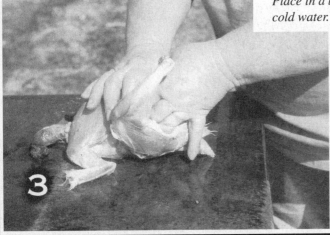

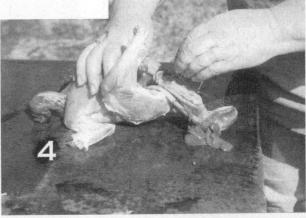

had this happen myself and the chicken was like rubber. Since then, I've talked to numerous others who had the same experience. Young, home-raised chicken is supposed to be ten-der, and it is, but you have to cool it well before you cook it.

All totaled, you should be able to pluck and clean a chicken in about 15 minutes if you're new at it. As you become more experienced you will be quicker. The time is about the same for when you skin and clean a bird. It's amazing to see the transformation of a feathered chicken to gorgeous chicken meat before your eyes. Δ

Solar power trailer: Part 2

By Jeffrey R. Yago, P.E., CEM

In Part I of this article in the 18th year anthology, I described the many uses for a solar power system that could be made totally portable. If you took up the challenge to build your own version of this solar project, your assignment was to find an enclosed utility trailer to serve as the basis for your own portable power system.

In this issue, I am going to describe in more detail the electrical components you will need, and how to wire everything together.

Batteries

The force behind any off-grid or portable solar-power system is the battery bank. Since this system is portable, the number of batteries your system can use will be limited by battery weight and proper weight distribution on the tires of the trailer. Due to the daily charge and discharge cycling any solar battery will experience, you cannot use lightweight automotive-type batteries which will fail in a matter of weeks.

For small residential-size photovoltaic systems, there are several reasonably-priced battery types that have the heavy construction required for this daily deep-discharge cycling. The T-105 (6 volt golf-cart battery) is an excellent choice since it is usually available locally. Its 62 pound weight and 7" x 11" base x 12" height should allow 8-16 batteries this size to fit into the trailer we are using.

For system sizing purposes, this battery will store about 1 kWh of useful electrical power during a normal charge/discharge cycle. For example, if your system will have eight of these batteries, you could power a 1,000

watt load for eight hours, or a 2,000 watt load for four hours, assuming the inverter and other electrical components are properly sized.

This smaller T-105 golf-cart battery is also available as a sealed gel battery that is spill-proof and does not require any periodic maintenance. Since there is no liquid form of acid

being used, this is a real advantage for portable applications, but will add 40-50% to the battery cost without gaining any additional charge capacity or life.

The L-16 size battery I used for the solar power trailer shown in these photos has a 7" x 12" base x 17" height, and weighs 128 pounds.

Solar trailer battery bank consisting of eight (8) L-16 size 6 volt batteries.

Unless your trailer has dual axles, it is doubtful you will be able to use more than eight of these L-16 size batteries without serious weight distribution problems. The L-16 size solar battery will store about 2 kWh of useful electrical power, and its heavier construction provides a useful life in the 6-8-year range. This is three times the life expectancy of the smaller T-105 golf-cart battery.

Unfortunately, the L-16 battery also costs three times the price of the T-105 golf-cart battery, and is only available from industrial battery-distribution centers. This means you may have a problem finding a local battery distributor that stocks this larger battery, which was originally designed for battery-powered floor scrubbers.

You will need to decide early on which size battery you will be using and how many will be installed before the other power-system components can be determined. You will want to use an even number of 6 volt batteries since all residential-size power inverters have a 12, 24, or 48 volt DC input. This means a 48 volt inverter will be connected to a single "string" of eight batteries in series (8×6=48). A 24 volt inverter could be connected to a single-string of four batteries (4×6=24), or two parallel strings of four batteries each for double this capacity.

Inverter

Unless your system will be very small, it is doubtful you will find a 12 volt DC inverter with the capacity to power more than 1,000 watts of electrical load, regardless of battery size. You should have an inverter with a 2 kW or higher load capacity, so your solar power trailer will be using either a 24 or 48 volt DC inverter. Most 24 volt inverters will have a 120 volt AC output capacity in the 2-3 kW range, which will easily power a well pump, microwave oven, small power tools, and most lights and kitchen appliances. I selected a 24 volt DC OutBack inverter since the DC refrigerator I installed in the trailer was not available in a 48 volt model, and both are connected to the same 24 volt DC battery bank.

Inverters for 48 volt battery systems will have output capacities in the higher 3.5-5.5 kW range. In addition, regardless of the electrical loads being supplied, a 48 volt inverter will draw exactly half the current from the batteries that a 24 volt inverter draws. This means you will be able to utilize smaller battery-to-inverter cables when using a higher voltage 48 volt DC battery bank.

Inverters are available in "modified sinewave" and "pure sinewave" versions. A modified sinewave inverter produces 120-volt AC power using a voltage waveform that increases and decreases in several small steps to simulate the utility grid's smoother sinewave-shaped voltage profile. If the waveform output of the inverter is not exactly 60 cycles-per-second, clocks will speed up or slow down, and sensitive electronic appliances can be damaged. However, power tools, lights, and most computers will usually operate without any problems on a modified sinewave inverter. Photocopiers, fax machines, and light dimmers usually have serious problems when connected to a modified sinewave inverter, so be careful what loads you supply.

A pure sinewave inverter costs significantly more than a modified sinewave inverter with the same capacity, but you will be able to operate almost any 120 VAC device on this inverter. The power output from a pure sinewave inverter is actually cleaner and more stable than the power supplied by most utility grids.

I recommend using the Xantrex DR series inverter if you want a quality modified sinewave inverter, and either the Xantrex SW or Outback FX sinewave inverter for more demanding applications requiring grid-quality power. All are available in several kW sizes.

OutBack sinewave inverter with 120 VAC circuit breaker panel (left) and 24 volt DC disconnect panel on right. Solar charge controller is located at extreme right.

Solar array

Solar modules can be wired in series, parallel, or series-parallel

*Raised solar array showing side-mounted
array combiner box and GFI duplex 120 VAC outlet box.*

arrangements to match the battery voltage you are using. Solar modules under 100 watts in size usually have a 17 volt DC output under load, but are still referred to as "12 volt" modules. This is because the voltage output of any solar module must be higher than the voltage of the battery it is trying to charge or no charging current will flow. This was found to be the ideal charging voltage for the early solar charging systems first used with 12 volt batteries.

Solar modules over 100 watts in size have a 34 volt DC output under load, but are referred to as a "24 volt" module for the same reason. My trailer's solar array uses two pairs of 24 volt modules wired in series to produce a 48 volts output.

The actual number and size of solar modules you will be using will be determined by the size and shape of the trailer you have and by your project budget. Solar array selection and mounting was discussed in more detail in Part I of this article.

Array combiner box

I recommend using an exterior-mounted array combiner box between the solar array and the solar charge-controller. The combiner box is a wiring junction box with multiple DC circuit breakers or fuses and terminal blocks. This makes it easy to connect and disconnect multiple individual strings of solar modules for testing and servicing while requiring only one pair of wires connected to the charge controller located inside. You

can also make your own array combiner using a rainproof junction box, but be sure to use only DC rated fuses or circuit breakers. The Square D "QO" line of 120 VAC circuit breakers are also UL listed for 12 and 24 volt DC service, but this is the only residential AC product line I am aware of that has this dual AC and DC rating.

Solar charge controller

Regardless of your solar array and battery bank size, you will need a solar charge controller. The charge controller's job is to control the battery charging process, and protect the battery from damage due to over-charging.

This device has input terminals for the solar array and output terminals for the battery bank. More expensive charge controllers adjust the charging rate based on battery temperature, and can be programmed for a battery voltage that is different from the solar array voltage, but most solar modules are wired to match the battery voltage.

A maximum power-point tracking (MPPT) charge-controller can be used with a solar array that is at a higher voltage than the batteries. These more expensive charge-controllers constantly adjust the charging voltage and current to maximize battery charging. This puts more solar charge into the batteries than a lower-cost non-MPPT solar charge-controller.

Since I had to stay with a 24 volt battery bank to power the DC refrigerator, I programmed this charge controller to charge a 24 volt battery from the 48 volt solar array.

System wiring

As shown in the wiring diagram, the solar modules are wired to the solar charge controller, which in turn is wired to the battery bank. Notice the DC circuit-breaker safely disconnects

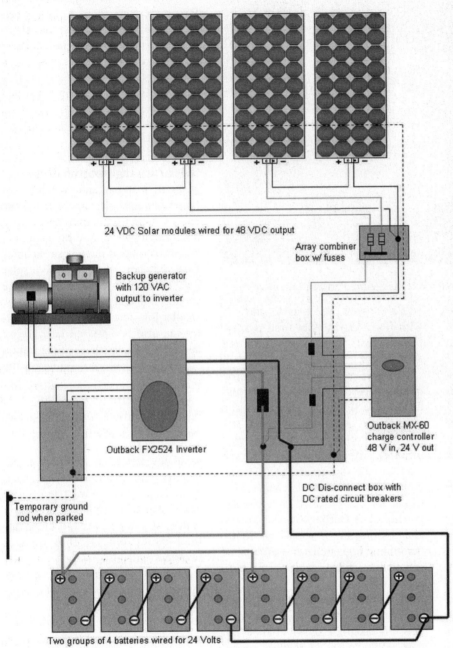

24 VDC Solar modules wired for 48 VDC output

Array combiner box w/ fuses

Backup generator with 120 VAC output to inverter

Outback FX2524 Inverter

Temporary ground rod when parked

Outback MX-60 charge controller 48 V in, 24 V out

DC Dis-connect box with DC rated circuit breakers

Two groups of 4 batteries wired for 24 Volts

a very high current during the first few seconds of start-up. This can easily produce a 200 amp battery load which is why the inverter-to-battery cables must be very large and as short as possible.

The inverter battery cables are pre-made in five and ten foot lengths, so your inverter will need to be mounted close to the battery bank. Note the large DC circuit breaker between the battery positive (+) terminal and the inverter positive (+) terminal. Do not use standard AC circuit breakers in DC circuits as they can arc and "weld" shut when trying to switch off these larger current flows. All circuit breakers, fuses, and switches must be rated for DC type service or you will have a very unsafe wiring system.

Since the quality and size of the inverter, batteries, and solar modules will be different for each solar power trailer builder, I am providing only general wiring instructions. You will need to modify this wiring layout if you are using a different battery or array voltage.

Backup generator

I recommend including a small 4,500 watt generator to complete your solar trailer and to have a truly reliable all-weather backup power system for all applications. Unlike your typical emergency generator which must operate continuously, this generator only needs to operate when the batteries are low. When the generator is started, the inverter will automatically switch from inverting mode to battery charging mode, and will charge the batteries as fast as possible. During generator operation, all system loads will be supplied directly from the generator and not the battery bank while it is being re-charged.

The battery charger built into these inverters is much more robust than a typical stand-alone battery charger, as

on both the solar array side and the battery side of the charge controller.

The inverter has its own separate circuit breaker and wiring connection to the battery bank, which requires size #2/0 or larger cables. This is a very large cable size with special copper lugs crimped on each end. These battery cables should be purchased with the inverter to make sure you have the correct size.

An inverter rated for 48 volt DC will have a battery cable current flow 2.5 times the current load on the 120 VAC side (120/48 = 2.5). This current will be five times the load on the 120 VAC side of a 24 volt DC inverter (120/24 = 5). This means a 15 amp AC load on a 24 volt DC inverter will draw over 75 amps from the battery (15x5=75). Larger motor loads like well pumps and compressors require

Completed solar power trailer powering a campsite on a remote mountain top.

the inverter designers realize you want to minimize generator run time to reduce fuel use and noise. Most retail battery chargers will not charge properly when powered from an emergency generator, while the charger built into most inverters is designed to utilize generator power, which typically have lower-quality voltage regulation. The OutBack inverter I used for this project can recharge this large battery in less than three hours. This allows a quick system re-charge during days of cloudy weather.

System costs and material sources

I am always asked what a solar power system will cost, and I usually answer that this is like asking a NAPA auto-parts dealer what it will cost to build a car. Each system will be different, and some of you may already own the trailer and some of the needed electrical components. You will find that individual solar modules in the 40 to 100 watt size range will cost in the $10 per watt range, while larger solar modules will be priced in the $8 per watt range. The solar array for my trailer has six modules totaling 990 watts and cost

$6,500, so you may want to start out with fewer modules at first to keep project costs low and expand your system later.

Expect to pay around $1,100 for a quality modified sinewave inverter, and double this for a pure sinewave inverter. A Xantrex Model C-40 charge-controller will cost $160 and is an excellent controller for this smaller size solar array. Internal jumpers allow using this charge controller for 12, 24, or 48 volt battery systems. The OutBack Model MX60 charge-controller I used cost $650, but it has a higher charging efficiency and many useful charging control features I wanted.

The OutBack combiner box shown in Photo #3 cost $150, and the DC circuit breaker box shown in Photo #2 cost $329. You will probably spend another $150 for the inverter battery cables and special cable adapters that will need to be ordered. However, the 120 VAC wiring devices and the 120 VAC circuit breaker panel are very low-cost and can be found at any building supply outlet. The eight L-16 batteries I used cost $2,500 total, but you can spend less than $900 if you substitute the smaller T-105 golf-cart batteries.

Your actual costs can be much less than these costs by using fewer batteries and solar modules, and shopping around for a used trailer. There are solar parts distributors who advertise in this magazine that can provide any of these solar components if you cannot find them locally.

Conclusions

If you are working with a limited budget, you can start with the smaller golf-cart batteries and switch to the larger batteries after these reach the end of their useful life. You should also design your solar-array mounting system to support more solar modules than you start out with, since a solar array is easy to expand later if the support frame is properly designed. A smaller low-cost solar charge controller can also be up-sized later if you add more solar modules in the future. However, I would not skimp on the inverter.

Decide what you want the total system capacity to be and purchase the right inverter to begin with, as it will be very costly to replace an undersized inverter later. Remember, the inverter is the heart and brains of the system, and you will want an inverter model and brand that will provide a stable AC output voltage under all load conditions. Higher quality inverters will also include a digital display that can show system performance, error messages, and other useful system information.

Good luck with your own solar power trailer construction, and let us know how your trailer turned out.

Jeff Yago is a licensed professional engineer and certified energy manager with more than 25 years experience in the energy conservation field. He has extensive solar thermal and solar photovoltaic system design experience and has authored numerous articles and texts. His web site: www. pvforyou.com Δ

Ayoob on Firearms

The .22 handgun: A backwoods home staple

By Massad Ayoob

Thanksgiving. I was in the sunny South, thanking the fates that I was not freezing my butt off in the frozen wasteland where I had spent most of my Novembers, and after the turkey had been rendered hors de combat, the folks I had feasted with decided to take the kids out back of the house to do a bit of shooting.

Ruger's neat new kid-size 10/22 autoloading rifle did just fine. Never a malfunction, and the kids shot this properly sized .22 very well. Then one of them said, "Hey, can we shoot pistols?"

Grandpa had a spare box of ammo in the van for his Glock 19, but only the oldest—the only genuine adolescent in the bunch—was up for shooting a 9mm automatic. He did well with it, too. The younger kids started asking if we had something they could shoot that wasn't as loud and didn't kick as much.

Well, Uncle John's Glock .40 was a step up in power from his dad's 9mm, and the snub-nose .357 Magnum revolver on my hip wasn't a kid's gun at all. Our hosts were about to go into the house and dig out a Ruger .22 pistol from the gun safe when I said, "Wait a minute, I've got something in the car."

The "something" was a SIG-Sauer Mosquito that I had picked up from my local gun dealer the day before. SIGARMS had sent it to me to test for one of the gun magazines. A scaled-down version of SIG-Sauer's famous military and law enforcement service pistols, the Mosquito has a manual safety, a magazine-disconnec-tor device that keeps the chambered round from firing if the magazine is removed, and is a double-action semi-automatic pistol that cocks itself to single action for an easier trigger pull after the first shot is fired. Its small size and light weight are just right for junior-age shooters.

All the kids, including the youngest, shot it with delight under adult super-vision until the .22 ammo ran out. It's safe to say that this après-turkey delight was repeated throughout rural America on that Thanksgiving, as on so many before.

A bit of rural history

The .22 caliber handgun is a staple of the backwoods home armory and has been so for a very long time. Its light recoil and mild bark makes it easy and forgiving for new shooters to learn with. As the traditional turkey is a microcosm of the feast of the original Pilgrims, the .22 pistol is a tiny version of the ancient blunder-buss that the Pilgrims used to harvest said turkeys. Indeed, when people Dave Duffy's age and mine were kids, that Pilgrim with the flared-muzzle musket was as iconic of the Day of Thanks as the turkey itself.

The firearm remains a traditional tool of the rural American. The small-caliber handgun is a particularly use-ful subset of that technology. It's the right size for shooting a marauding woodchuck in the garden, or the pro-verbial fox in the henhouse. The very low cost of its ammunition makes it affordable as a tool with which to learn marksmanship. It is, particularly when loaded with "snakeshot" ammu-nition, a handy thing to have if you

Massad Ayoob

live in serpent country. If you've put your time in to learn to shoot it well, it can pot squirrels and rabbits for the table. And, if raccoons have been driving you nuts, it's the gun of choice for 'coon huntin'.

In the late 19th century, single-shot .22 pistols proved themselves to be useful for these purposes. However, not everyone was a dead shot, and sometimes the animals were too tough to drop with a single bullet through the vitals, so a market mani-fested itself for .22 handguns that had more cartridges than a single shot, but still had precise accuracy.

In the early 20th century, Smith & Wesson produced match-grade six-shot revolvers chambered for the .22 Long Rifle cartridge, and Colt intro-duced before World War I their clas-sic Woodsman semiautomatic pistol. By the mid-20th century, these guns—and the Woodsman-like High Standard .22 auto pistol—had beaten the .22 single shots into submission and were winning national pistol championships. The 1950s saw the development of newer, heavier .22

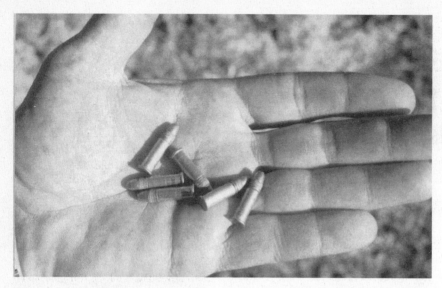

The low recoil, blast, and cost of these tiny .22 Long Rifle cartridges make the caliber ideal for many rural needs.

autoloaders that were even more accurate and more "shootable" in terms of winning matches, but had evolved into guns too big to be comfortable for all-day hiking or to wear on the hip on a farm.

The year 1949 saw Bill Ruger's introduction of the pistol that created the dominant firearms manufacturing company in America today. A bit heavier than the Colt Woodsman, but every bit as accurate and much cheaper, the Ruger Standard Model .22 semiautomatic soon became the single most popular "farmer's pistol" in its caliber. Ruger today manufactures several updated versions of this classic handgun, including very handy lightweight models with polymer frames.

Revolver or semiautomatic?

The semiautomatic .22 pistol will hold up to 11 cartridges, 10 in the magazine and one more in the firing chamber. The old Colt Woodsman actually wasn't safe to carry fully loaded by today's standards because its design did not include an internal firing-pin lock, and if it was dropped or struck at a certain angle, the unsecured firing pin could snap forward and "inertia-fire" the gun, sometimes

with catastrophic results. Modern designs—the Rugers, the lightweight Smith & Wesson .22 autoloaders, Walther's splendid little compact P22 with polymer frame, and the SIG Mosquito—are "drop safe," and I feel perfectly comfortable carrying them with a live round in the firing chamber. The self-cocking nature of most .22 autoloaders means that you have a light, easy, crisply breaking pull of the trigger for every shot including the first, and this helps guarantee that

the first shot hits the target, which after all is the object of the exercise.

The .22 caliber revolvers carry fewer rounds, generally 6 to a rarely seen 10 depending on the make, model, and size. For the light-trigger pull, you have to cock the hammer with your thumb. However, a double-action model allows you to instantly fire just by pulling the trigger; the "double action" of its nomenclature refers to a mechanism that first raises and then drops the hammer to fire the shot via one trigger stroke that will be long and heavy. The long, heavy pull is considered a safety feature that guards against inadvertent discharge, but it takes some practice to be able to do it smoothly enough to hit a close-range snake in a moment of stress or a distant rabbit in a moment of opportunity.

The revolver is easier to handle in terms of loading, unloading, checking, and cleaning. The semiautomatic pistol is more complex to handle in these regards, but rewards the shooter with an easier trigger pull once the shooting starts, since its autoloading mechanism self-cocks it between shots.

Because the autoloading pistol is dependent on the power of each pre-

High tech .22: SIG's modern Mosquito accepts InSight flashlight attachment for night shooting of raccoons and other varmints.

*The .22 caliber SIG Mosquito is a scaled-down version of
their popular service pistols in larger calibers.*

viously fired shot to cycle the mechanism that chambers the next cartridge, it is not as versatile as the revolver in terms of ammunition. A pistol chambered for the .22 Long Rifle cartridge will only work reliably with that particular cartridge. Moreover, some models may jam when fired with low-velocity target ammunition, or with snake-shot or rat-shot cartridges.

On the other hand, the revolver is operated mechanically by the hand of the shooter and can fire super-mild .22 CB ammunition, .22 Short, .22 Long, or the much more popular .22 Long Rifle. It will function perfectly with the shot-spraying cartridges designed for close-range use on rats or snakes.

Revolvers, unlike auto pistols, can also be had in .22 Magnum caliber. This is a much hotter loading than the .22 Long Rifle, though still not on a par with a true self-defense cartridge like the 9mm Luger, the .38 Special, or other more potent rounds designed for self defense and the hunting of animals larger than small-game size.

Picking a .22 auto pistol

The classic Colt Woodsman has long been discontinued, and you'll have to haunt the gun shops, the gun shows, and the Internet to find them.

They're worth looking for. Slim and compact, particularly the pre-WWII models with small grip frames, they are utterly reliable and offer the accuracy of target pistols. High Standard made some fine field-grade .22s with good handling and great accuracy, such as the Sport King and Field King, but those, too, are "out of print," though the big target versions of the excellent High Standard have been resurrected by new companies.

Perhaps the classic rural .22 auto of today is the one that sealed the doom of the Woodsman—the Ruger

Standard Model and its descendants. Delivering the accuracy of the Woodsman with only a little more bulk and weight, and at a much lower price, it drove the classic old gun off the market and became a modern classic itself. These guns are very reliable, and the price is right. The polymer-framed 45/22 variation is particularly light and handy for all-day carry, and the lighter guns are easier for youngsters to learn with.

Other medium-size polymer frame guns have come along. These include the SIG Trailside produced by Hammerli—flat, light, very accurate and shootable, and all things considered, "the Colt Woodsman of today." S&W has found a winner by importing the handy little Walther P22, barely bigger than a pocket pistol yet accurate, reliable, and very affordable. Many gun shops tell me it's their fastest-selling handgun. Being a scaled-down variation of Walther's full-size service pistols in 9mm and .40, it is a popular "understudy gun" for those who carry that style in a more powerful pistol. The new SIG Mosquito mentioned above is in the same vein. Slightly larger is the Smith & Wesson series, typified by the Model 22A, which like most of the above, except the SIG, is produced with polymer frame. Beretta's "plas-

*One of author's favorite "around the country place" guns is this
snub-nose, pocket-size Smith & Wesson .22 Kit Gun.*

Ruger autos may be the most commonly used .22 "farm pistols" today. This one is an older model Mark I Target variation with five-inch heavy barrel.

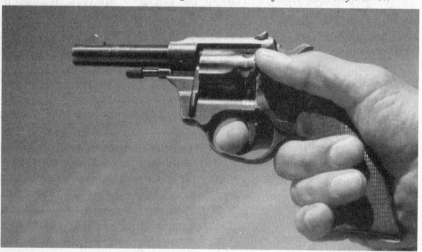

The old High Standard Sentinel 9-shot .22 was author's favorite woods-walking gun as a kid, and he still considers it a best buy on the used gun market.

For those who want to amp up their .22 rimfire power level, Taurus makes this Ultra-Lite .22 Magnum with 2" barrel. Note the eight-chambered cylinder.

tic frame" Neos has won a lot of fans, though I find it a bit large and don't care for its ergonomics.

Finally, consider a small pocket pistol in caliber .22 Long Rifle. In the pocket, or riding with maximum comfort inside or on the belt, the Walther PPK and TP22 in .22 LR deliver good reliability and accuracy. Always carry them on-safe; except for the very latest PPK's imported by S&W and built to their specs, these particular Walthers are not drop-safe when a round is in the chamber unless the thumb safety is engaged. Another neat little .22 pocket auto is Beretta's Model 21. Its tip-up barrel is a blessing to those with arthritis or limited upper-body strength, since they don't have to "jack" the pistol's slide to chamber or unload the first round. Accuracy potential with these small guns is limited beyond short range, but for many mission profiles, short range is all the owner has in mind.

Picking a .22 revolver

Revolvers tend to be more reliable than autos so long as the chambers are kept clean. Smith & Wesson's target-grade revolvers go back a long way, and range from small-frame "Kit Guns" to medium-frame target guns. The big K-22 was a favorite of such great outdoorsmen as Jack O'Connor and Elmer Keith, who disagreed on most everything else. The K-22 has been produced in a 10-shot variation, though most are six-shooters. When I was a kid, my favorite squirrel gun was a K-22 with 6" barrel.

Particularly desirable are the small-frame Kit Guns. Most were produced with 4" barrels, but there was a 6" target model, some 3½" variations, and a somewhat popular 2" barrel. The latter was and is great for pocket carry. Its descendant in today's S&W catalog is the Model 317 series. Weighing as little as 10½ ounces with Titanium frame, it holds eight shots and delivers reasonable accuracy. Taurus has similar designs at lower price, and

.22s are great for teaching handgun marksmanship to young people. Here, Brandon Taylor shoots well with the SIG Mosquito...

with 9-shot .22 Long Rifle cylinders. I've found the less expensive Taurus to compare remarkably well with the pricier Kit Gun, and often, to outshoot it in terms of accuracy.

You run across a lot of Iver Johnson and Harrington & Richardson .22 revolvers when you visit rural homes. Neither are still in production. They were fairly rugged for their cost, which was low, but tended to be characterized by rough, heavy actions that didn't lend themselves well to precision shooting. The best of the old, discontinued guns are the High Standard Sentinel and Double Nine revolvers produced during the third quarter of the 20th century. I cut my teeth on one of these as a youngster, and still own and cherish that lightweight, 4" barrel 9-shot .22. Often selling for as little as $100, a High Standard Sentinel is one of the best buys available on the used handgun market.

Revolvers chambered for the .22 Long Rifle cartridge, unlike autoloaders in the same caliber, will work with rat-shot and snake-shot cartridges. They will feed quieter .22 Shorts, and even .22 CB caps, which can be useful for rats in the barn that are out of reach of the short-range shot cartridges. With a much lighter recoil impulse, these mild loads won't oper-

ate the slide of a .22 LR semiautomatic pistol.

So far, we've been talking about double-action revolvers, which can be thumb-cocked for an easier trigger pull, or fired with a single long, heavy pull of the trigger. They usually have swing-out cylinders for simultaneous ejection and fast reloading. Many traditionalists prefer single action revolvers in the style of the 19th century Peacemaker of the frontier, which must be thumb-cocked for every shot. Cartridges must be

removed or inserted one at a time through a loading gate on the right side behind the cylinder. Ruger's Single Six is probably the most popular of this type, and those who like this style might consider its tiny but well-made sibling, the Bearcat.

For those who want a little more power when dealing with foxes and coyotes, revolvers can be had chambered for the .22 Winchester Magnum Rimfire cartridge. Some even have alternate cylinders for the less expensive .22 Long Rifle. However, those "convertible" guns have the same barrel, and the .22 Long Rifle has a subtly different bore diameter than the .22 Magnum. This means that, while either is safe to fire if the correct cylinder is in place, one caliber will always be less accurate than the other. In a .22 Magnum, I think you're better off with a revolver dedicated to the caliber: My favorite is a little Taurus Ultra-Lite with Titanium frame, which holds eight of the .22 Magnum cartridges.

There are many other fine .22 handguns out there, more than there is room here to name and describe, but you get the drift. It's a buyer's market

...as does his sister Libby, 11. Note presence of supervising adult, and vigilant use of ear and eye protection.

in terms of desired features and quality for the dollar.

A question of purpose

Ammunition for a .22 Long Rifle is so inexpensive today that a handgun in that caliber is ideal for learning good marksmanship. This cartridge, despite its lower velocity out of a short-barreled handgun compared to a long-barreled rifle in the same caliber, is considered adequate for small game such as squirrels and rabbits. It is the standard raccoon hunter's caliber, because they go for brain shots on these tough little critters. For shooting a rabid specimen, however, it is a different matter. The docs will need the animal's whole brain to determine if it is indeed rabid. This is important, because if you find out five minutes after you blew its brains out that it bit a kid an hour ago, the medicos will have to err on the side of caution and give the child the full prophylactic injection series for rabies. This is not only painful, but potentially dangerous; keeping the brain intact can save the bite victim from something serious. Raccoons can take a lot of lead when you can't aim for the brain; it once took me five rounds of 185-grain hollow point out of a .45 automatic to nail down a rabid 'coon. The first four went through its chest, while the fifth broke the cervical spine and finished the job.

Many hunters feel that something the size of a coyote or even a fox demands .22 Magnum for an instant kill, though some have used the .22 Long Rifle with good results. Placement is the key. The Inuits have been known to kill huge brown bear with .22 rifles. There is one African elephant on record killed with a .22 rifle. However, taking on something so large and dangerous with something so small and low-powered is akin to trying to stab a 400-pound rapist to death with a hat-pin. Yes, you can do it in theory, and someone somewhere may actually have done it

for real, but it's not something you want to bet your or your children's lives on.

The .22 caliber handgun has been used successfully for self defense, but no genuine authority in the field would ever recommend it except for someone so severely handicapped that they could handle nothing larger. Yeah, yeah, I know: The Mafia is famous for using .22 pistols to carry out gangland hits. That's apples and oranges. They carry out those hits by lulling unsuspecting "friends" into a relaxed posture, then shooting them several times in the back of the head. It is most unlikely that you can convince an enraged human criminal to turn his back to you and hold still.

I remember as a police officer responding to a situation where a healthy young man had been shot through the "K5 vital zone" of his torso with a .22 rifle. He was not in any great discomfort when I got there, and was walking and talking normally. He was treated and recovered without complication. Had he been an enraged criminal, the .22 hit might only have enraged him more.

One of my students stopped a rapist with a .22 Kit Gun, but needed all six shots to do it. He broke off his attack and ran out of her apartment. He made it to the hallway where he screamed, "The b---- shot me for nuthin'," and then collapsed and died. I was an expert witness hired for the defense of a physician who was charged with manslaughter after he shot a charging burglar twice with his S&W .22 Kit Gun. The suspect turned, and not only ran, but got about a mile before he bled out and died from the effects of a hyper-velocity CCI Stinger hollow point through his liver. In a third case, I spoke for a battered woman who killed her abuser with three shots from a cheap little RG .22, thankfully one of the few that company made that worked properly. He turned and ran also, and made it to the front yard

of her trailer home before he collapsed and died from the one of those bullets that had pierced his heart. All three of those shooters were ultimately exonerated.

Note that after lethal wounds from multiple little .22 slugs, all three criminals were able to carry on some degree of strenuous, purposeful activity for varying lengths of time. All three were cowardly predators, fortunately, and fled instead of attacking the righteous citizens who had shot them in self-defense. It could have turned out differently. That's why most of us recommend nothing less than a .38 Special revolver or a 9mm semiautomatic for personal defense.

If you must use a .22 against a human attacker, aim for the brain. It's a tough shot to make, but the low cost of .22 Long Rifle ammunition and the ease of its almost non-existent recoil encourages skill-building practice.

For the most part, the .22 caliber handgun is a pest eradicator, small game harvester, and tool of recreation and marksmanship training. Use it for its intended purpose, and you'll understand why it has so long been welcomed as standard equipment in so many backwoods homes. Δ

More good reading on gun ownership and responsibility:

In the Gravest Extreme

by Massad Ayoob

Ask Jackie

If you have a question about rural living, send it in to Jackie Clay and she'll try to answer it. Address your letter to Ask Jackie, PO Box 712, Gold Beach, OR 97444. Questions will only be answered in this column.

— Editor

Preserving chestnuts

My chestnut trees are loaded with chestnuts this year and I would like to know how I could preserve some of them for winter use. Can you can chestnuts? I thought I read something somewhere about canning chestnuts but I can't remember where or how.

Marion Calhoun
Everett, Pennsylvania

Yes, you can can chestnuts and other nut meats. And it's quick and easy, too. Just peel your chestnuts and lay them in a single layer on a cookie sheet in your oven. Slowly roast them at 250° F, turning them to prevent scorching. Use two or more pans to make a good big batch for canning at one time. You want all the nut meats hot for packing. Pack hot into hot jars, leaving ½ inch of head room at the top of the jar. Use either pint or half-pint jars only. Process the jars at 5 pounds pressure for 10 minutes (unless you live at an altitude above 1,000 feet and must adjust your pressure to suit your altitude, if necessary; check your canning manual). You'll note that this pressure is different from the usual 10 pounds that most other foods are processed at.

You can also process nut meats in a water bath canner, but do not fill the canner with water higher than the shoulders of the jars. This is one of the only foods that this applies to; most foods have the water level at least 2 inches above the jar tops. But you want absolutely no moisture to enter the jars or the nut meats might mold. — *Jackie*

Making lye for soap

I just celebrated my eighth summer living in the country. This past May I added cows to my farm, and I plan to slaughter one this coming spring. I would like to make homemade soap from the steer fat as mentioned in (a previous) "Ask Jackie" section. The recipes I have require lye, which is no longer available in most stores. Do you have some recipes that don't need this ingredient?

Barbara Berghoff
Bunker Hill, Illinois

I know it's hard to find lye at local stores, although some still carry it. Lehman's Hardware still carries it. You can also go the whole route and leach your own lye by taking a wood barrel and drilling a hole near the bottom, then adding a layer of fist-sized rocks with a wide layer of hay over that (it filters out the ashes), then adding wood ash nearly to the top of the barrel. You pour fresh water carefully into the top and it runs down through the ashes, through the hay and rocks which keep the hay off the bottom of the barrel. The resultant lye runs out a non-metal spigot put into the hole you drilled and into a non-metal holding container.

When lye is strong enough, a fresh egg will float with a bit above the water. If the egg sinks, the lye is too weak; pour it back through the ashes again. If it floats very high, it's too strong; add just a bit of fresh water and try again.

I've never made soap without lye, either store-bought which is more convenient or with homemade, which is more self-reliant. — *Jackie*

Jackie Clay

Making lye soap

You mentioned homemade lye soap in the September/October 2007 issue (#107). Please share how to make it.

Rosilyn Couturier
Phoenix, Arizona

Soap is very easy to make, but like most things you do have to be careful and watch what you're doing. The great thing about making soap is that a big batch, which you usually make anyway, will last a long time, even when you grate it and use it for your laundry. To make soap, first render your fat. Grind it, then heat it gently until it becomes liquid, straining off any bits of meat or debris. You can make soap from any amount of fat, but like any recipe, there are certain amounts of lye, fat, and water that must be used to get a good, useable product.

Keep in mind that lye burns and the fumes are strong enough to make your eyes water and your lungs burn. So be careful not to splash the lye about, have all young children and pets out of the area, and make your soap in a well-ventilated area.

There are many different "recipes" for soapmaking, and here is one that is very basic. The soap won't be "gourmet" quality, but it's easy and quick to do.

Have your soap forms ready. I use shallow boxes, like the kind that canned pop comes in. Or cut down your own boxes. Line them with heavy plastic sheeting. You can also use any non-metal bowl, disposable plastic carton, etc. Grease your molds with petroleum jelly to get the soap to release easier when it hardens.

Slowly stir 1 can of lye into 5 cups of cold water in a large enameled pan with no chips. Never use lye with a metal pan of any kind; it about eats it up. There are real strong fumes at this point, so don't hang over the pan. I use a wooden spoon to gently stir them together. It will heat up as the crystals dissolve. When they are all dissolved, cool the lye water to 70-75° F — lukewarm, but use a thermometer to make sure.

If your fat is tallow, instead of pig fat, only cool the temperature to 90-95° because tallow (venison, beef, and sheep fat) melts at a higher temperature than pig fat (lard).

Heat 10 cups melted fat to 120° (pig) or 130° for tallow. You want the lye water and the melted fat at close to the ideal temperatures when you mix them.

Pour the melted fat slowly into the lye water and stir round and round (don't go back and forth or you'll splash) till the mixture gets about like honey. Expect it to take about 15 minutes. The soap is ready to pour into your molds when your mixing spoon will stand upright in it without tipping over.

When it's ready, quickly pour the mixture out into your molds and work it until it's pretty flat. Don't worry if it's a little dark; it bleaches itself out in a few days. The longer soap cures, the harder it becomes. In about 2 weeks it should be just about right to take out of the molds. At this point, you can easily cut it into bars with a stout wire or an old knife.

I grate a bar of older homemade soap with an old cheese grater for laundry soap. If you want to use it for dish soap, I've had better luck by making soft soap out of the grated pieces by adding boiling water enough to melt the soap into a thick jell. This really works well for dish washing. The dishes come sparkling clean. But don't expect it to bubble and be like dish detergent; it's not. But when you wash your dishes with hot water and rinse them well with hot clear water, you'll be amazed at how nice it washes. — *Jackie*

Habañero jelly

My habañero peppers went crazy wild this year. I've been dehydrating them, then grinding to a powder. I have well over a quart and a half of the powder. Probably enough for the next 10 years. They are still coming on strong so I wondered about trying hot pepper jelly. Can't find it in my Ball book or any other. Do you know of a recipe for habañero jelly? Or perhaps any use for them? (Besides regular cooking.)

Dani Payne
Rose, Oklahoma

Sure Dani, here's one habañero jelly recipe you might like. You already know to use gloves when handling these fire-breathing peppers!

10 ripe habañeros
3 large orange bell peppers
9 oz. liquid pectin
1½ cups white vinegar
7 cups sugar

Remove stems, seeds and membranes from all peppers. Use gloves. Put peppers and vinegar in a blender and whiz till smooth. Combine pepper puree and sugar in an enameled pan and bring to a boil. Reduce heat and simmer for 20 minutes, stirring frequently to keep from scorching. Remove from heat and strain through cheesecloth into another pan. Add pectin and bring to a full rolling boil while stirring. Boil one minute and ladle into hot sterile jars. Process in a boiling water bath canner for 10 minutes to ensure a seal.

If you like your peppers hot, you might try making cherry jelly with pie cherries or wild cherries and simmering a couple seeded, de-membraned habañeros with the juice and sugar as it's boiling. This makes a real spicy, fruity jelly dip for chicken or fish, and also a good fruity glaze as well. I make this with jalapeños because my crew doesn't like their "hot" that hot!
— *Jackie*

Chickens in the city

I live on the outer edge of the city; backyard is fenced in by 6-foot high privacy fence, neighbors on two sides, none in back or ever will be. I have a space in rear corner of yard about 12' x 12' that I would like to put chickens in. We use approximately 2 dozen eggs a week.

Which chickens are the quietest, best layers, and how many do I need? I was thinking 4. No rooster allowed, too noisy.

I really don't want to use laying mash because of hormones and other additives. Will the hens lay sufficiently without it?

Richard L. Anderson
Savannah, Georgia

Any of the heavy breeds are quite docile and calm, especially cochins (but they aren't as good an egg layer as, say Buff Orphingtons or Rhode Island Reds). Hens are pretty quiet, as a rule, singing and clucking as they go about their business. The only time there's noise is when they lay an egg or something is chasing them; then they'll loudly cackle and squawk. Most heavy hens will lay an egg a day during the spring and summer, then taper off to maybe an egg every other day during the fall and winter (if you keep a light on for them for a few extra hours during the short-day period). But realistically, there are just days they don't lay, especially during the two molting periods they go through every year. So you have to take this into consideration.

You don't need a rooster unless you want to hatch eggs and need fertile ones.

Yes, hens will lay without laying mash. I don't feed it to my hens and they do fine. But I *do* give them plenty of greens, year-around, house scraps, and goat milk when I have it. Hens will lay *more* on laying mash, but will have a longer useful life without it.

Be sure your neighbors will not be against your new project. Perhaps a promise of fresh eggs every once in awhile (your extras) would make them more agreeable to having chicken neighbors. It often works that way. — *Jackie*

Brined dill pickles

I have been successfully fermenting sauerkraut just using canning salt and cabbage without a recipe. I tried fermenting cucumbers, but ended up with a slimy mess. I know there are many recipes using vinegar and cooking. But, I remember my parents buying a pickle at a grocery store where they fished one out of just a wooden barrel full of brine. I remember they were crisp and tasty, with no vinegar taste. I would appreciate it if you could provide a recipe. By the way, I have found that one head of red cabbage in a bucket of green cabbage will turn the entire batch red (chopped up and fermenting of course).

Bernard Falkowski
Merlin, Oregon

What you are referring to is brined dill pickles. But even these have vinegar; just not as much. To make brined dill pickles, you'll need (roughly):

10 pounds 4 to 6-inch cucumbers
6-8 bunches fresh dill
1½ cups canning salt
2 cups vinegar
2 gallons water
6 cloves garlic (optional)

Wash and drain cucumbers. Remove blossom end; leave ¼ inch of stem. Place a layer of dill in a clean crock. Add cucumbers to within 4 inches of the top. Combine salt, vinegar, and water; use pickling salt. Ladle over cucumbers. Place another layer of dill over the top and garlic, if desired. Weight cucumbers under the brine with a plate and a clean weight.

Store container in a cool place. Let cucumbers ferment until well-flavored and clear throughout. Check periodically for scum. If it forms, skim as necessary. Keep the pickles under the brine. You can can the pickles in about 3 weeks. These pickles will usually keep in the crock until they are eaten. But if they are allowed exposure to the air, they will rot. So most folks go ahead and can them up. To do this, remove the pickles from the brine. Strain the brine and bring it to a boil in a large kettle. Pack the pickles into hot jars, leaving ½ inch of headroom. Ladle hot liquid over pickles, leaving ½ inch of headroom. Process in a boiling water bath for 15 minutes. — *Jackie*

Small ears of corn

I had a nice little patch of corn this past year. The corn was tasty, but my ears were really puny and small. How do I get bigger and better corn for my work? Maybe I didn't water them enough? And at what point should I stop watering the plants from above and just water the rows and furrows without getting the plants themselves wet...or doesn't it matter?

Ilene Duffy
Gold Beach, Oregon

Corn is a hog. It is a lush plant and it likes plenty of water and also plenty of fertilizer. In our new garden area, next to the old one, there was an area about 20 feet by 10 feet that was new and I didn't get any rotted manure on before I tilled and planted the corn. My whole corn plot was about 20 feet by 50 feet. The manured part of that

plot grew tall plants with large cobs. The unmanured end grew short corn with runty cobs. That was my problem. Corn likes nitrogen, which will burn many other garden plants. Sometimes I've hauled relatively fresh manure and side-dressed the corn rows and had excellent corn. (It also kind of mulches the roots, as well, holding in the water.)

I really don't think it matters which way you water corn. I've done it several ways and it didn't seem to matter. The leaves are built like funnels to run water down the stalks to the roots. Pretty smart of the corn plants, huh? Sort of self-watering. The thing to do is to make sure that the roots are getting at least an inch of water every other day when the plants are growing quickly and setting ears (providing the weather is hot and it's not raining).

Did you plant a variety of sweet corn that you've had luck with before? I've known folks that bought Golden Bantam sweet corn and were disappointed when the plants were really short and the ears small, compared to most modern varieties of corn. I always read the plant descriptions in the catalogs as to plant height and cob length/number of rows per cob. I figure that big cobs on big plants, with plenty of rows per cob, equals more corn for my work.

Another tip is to plant at least four rows, even if they are kind of short rows; make a block rather than a row or two that are longer. Corn is wind-pollinated and you want that pollen to land on the corn silks, not on a patch of beans next door to the corn row. Poorly pollinated corn ends up in misshapen cobs (kind of "C" shaped), with missing kernels at the tip or even down the row.

I hope this helps; corn is so much a part of the garden and everyone needs a successful crop! — *Jackie*

There's more Ask Jackie in all 18 anthologies.

Starting Over
PART 14

By Jackie Clay

When I look back over the last year, I can scarcely believe so *much* has happened here on our homestead. It's amazing at what can be crunched together into a few months. And now it's late fall and again we're getting ready for winter. But let me tell you what we've been doing (along with why we didn't get *more* done).

Bill and the crawler

When the temperatures warmed up in May, I was dying to get the garden planted. But my oldest son, Bill, said he'd come up again with his crawler and do some enlarging and grading for me. I didn't want to plant, then have things in his way, so I waited. Bill's a busy guy with work, helping neighbors, and building on his own homestead. But one day he came up the trail with his Case crawler chained down to his flatbed trailer. I was really tickled because we have kind of rough land, having been partially logged about fifteen years ago. I needed the orchard cleaned of brush, log piles, ruts, and rocks, the garden enlarged, and the trail down to the horse pasture widened. Our little 9N Ford tractor just wasn't up to that much pushing.

Bill set right to work in the garden. He shoved old dozer piles down the hill, flattening them out so they wouldn't be such an eye-sore, pushed little popple trees over, leveled and graded the garden area, and dug up a few big old stumps that were a real problem. When he got done, all but a 10-foot area next to the fence was clean, level, and smooth. My garden had suddenly doubled in size, and we sure needed it. Now it's about 60 feet by 100 feet. When we started here, I had a spot only 25 feet by 10 feet after clearing it all by hand.

Next Bill started in on the orchard, which was basically some young fruit trees planted amongst wild raspberries, rocks, logs, and piles a dozer had left years ago. Ugly? Oh yeah! Bill carefully shoved debris around my little fruit trees, taking great care not to get too close to them. I had marked some good wild cherry and choke-cherry trees (and my orchard trees!) with flagging tape, as well as a few pretty birch trees I wanted to save along the edges. When Bill got done, the orchard was quite flat and clean.

I want to fence it with 6-foot-tall 2 by 4-inch welded wire to keep the deer out. Right now most of the trees are individually fenced and have their trunks protected with screen to keep voles, rabbits, and field mice from girdling them. But the deer can still reach over and nibble a bit. I also want to have the chickens in the orchard, running free inside the fence to keep down the grass and weeds, and also to keep them out of my flower beds!

Right now, our little orchard is about 60 feet wide by about 150 feet long. We have Haralson, Haralred, Honeygold, Honeycrisp, Fireside, and Yellow Transparent apples growing in there. We'll add other fruits next year. Down in the garden, we have planted a Pipestone plum, some Manchurian apricots, and smaller bush and bramble fruits so far.

While Bill was here, he also rooted up a lot of stumps in our horse pasture, widened the trail down there, and opened up a four wheeler trail around the hill.

Bill clears the orchard. The apple tree in the foreground is wrapped with screen to protect it from voles and rabbits, and flagged with tape to protect it from Bill!

Bill also dug a small test hole at a spring site below the house. We wanted to see how long it stayed full. It was full except for three weeks during the drought that lasted all summer. Now if it was deeper and developed...

The garden

As soon as Bill left, David and I quickly set about pounding the steel T posts on the garden fence line and stretching the 6-foot welded wire back up tight. I was *not* going to have deer in my garden again this year—and I didn't.

I tilled up most of the garden and got it planted. It was getting late and you *don't* plant late in northern Minnesota if you can help it. Even my tomatoes and peppers, in their Wall'o'Waters, went in a month later than they should have. Even so, it was worth it to get the garden made so much bigger. Since we were late, we planted and planted and planted. I don't think I've ever worked so frantically to get a garden in.

Because we were also starting on the new greenhouse/porch, I hadn't been able to start my squash and melons inside as I usually do. I just hoped we'd get lucky. (We did.)

After we got the main part of the garden planted, I started hand clearing the last ten feet of garden that Bill couldn't get to because of the fence. David brought the tractor down and we pulled about a dozen 10-foot-tall popple trees out by the roots. (By the way, for you non-Minnesotans, "popple" is the northern nickname for poplar trees, or in the west, aspen.) I've found that it's better to pull smaller trees, rather than cut them off. Not only do you eliminate stumps and root masses, but also the many sprouts that tend to come up from the roots.

I took a large pair of hand clippers and cut off all the brush I could, as low as I could. Then I tossed all the rocks, logs, and branches over the

Jim Bonnette shows some of our "leftover" green beans.

fence as I came to them. After the area was relatively clear, I tilled it a few times. It was kind of rough, but it did get worked up. Then I would do another strip about 2 feet wide or so until I got to the fence. When it was all worked up nicely, I looked back on it and thought about it. Here was this nicely worked 10-foot strip, 100 feet long. Would anything grow on it, or would it just grow up to brush again?

I couldn't stand it. I'd already planted plenty of beans, potatoes, melons, and squash, but I got out the seed again and went to town. I also planted rutabagas and parsnips.

The only problem was that when harvest came, I canned green beans every other day until I had a whole two-foot deep shelf full. So I called

my friends Jim and Jeri (whose goats had broken into their green beans) and invited them to come pick green beans. As it ended up, we both had way plenty!

A new chipper

Our *big* spring purchase this year was a chipper. We'd been talking about one for years. Here we have all these trees to get rid of, brush, branches, debris, and we need lots of mulch. It only made sense. So when one went on sale, I took our saved money to town and came home with "Big Red." David couldn't wait to fire it up. I was a little disappointed because I thought once you shoved a branch in that it would grab it and pull it on through. It doesn't. I guess they changed them for safety reasons. On the plus side, all we had left after we chipped those trees was a pile of nice wood chips that served to mulch the asparagus and raspberries nicely.

We are enjoying it. I would have liked to get a big DR model chipper, but our little savings just wasn't big

Tom and David notch in the support beam on the new porch this spring.

enough. Big Red is working fine, albeit a little slow. David ran the spent corn stalks and tomato vines through it and it made very fine material that worked in on the first pass. Of course, being a *boy*, he just had to toss in a few squash, frozen tomatoes, and broccoli plants! "Wow Mom! Look at *that!*"

David vs flesh eating bacteria

The garden was growing nicely, the new greenhouse/porch was under way and David was haying for our neighbor again this year. Bill had invited David down to go camping with him and his wife, Kelly, for the Fourth of July. But the morning of the 3rd, when he was getting up to leave, he said he must have snored because he had a little sore throat. And his first knuckle on his left hand was kind of sore. He must have thrashed around in his sleep and banged it.

By 10 o'clock that night, Bill called to say David was sick. He was cold, droopy, and his hand was swelling. I agreed that David better head for the emergency room. So they put out the campfire and drove to Cloquet, to the hospital.

At the hospital, the doctor thought David had poked something into his knuckle, starting an infection in his hand, so they kept him and started I.V. antibiotics. When I drove down the next morning, I expected him to be better. Instead the swelling was getting worse and he was in intense

Tom lowering first floor joist into the steel bracket he made

pain. The following morning the swelling was going up his arm, along with a red streak. Was I panicked? Oh yeah! I got a healthy flashback to when Bob had died, and I started to shake.

Luckily, David's doctor had called the infectious disease specialist in Duluth and she told them to get a CT scan of his hand and arm and get him up to St. Luke's Hospital for immediate surgery. She believed it was flesh eating bacteria and that even with immediate surgery, she wasn't sure they'd be able to save his arm.

To make a long story shorter, David had the surgery, then another one a couple days later. Both were very successful. He came home a week later with a main line I.V. hooked to a little computerized pump that he wore around his waist in a belly pack. This was a part of his life for another three weeks to maintain heavy duty antibiotics to prevent any possible recurrence.

Of course David didn't wimp around; two weeks after his surgery, he was back on the tractor, haying... I.V. and all. Later, the doctors all said they'd never seen anyone heal up so well, so quickly.

I learned a lot about flesh eating bacteria. It didn't come from a cut, nick, poke, or sliver. It came from the mild strep infection in his throat. The doctor said that one in a million type A strep infections breaks loose and goes through the bloodstream to lodge in an extremity; a foot, hand, or even head/brain, where it causes intense pain. The bacteria produces a toxin which eats the muscle covering, causing necrosis. And it moves very quickly. The doctor said that in another day, David would have lost his arm and in one more, he could have lost his life. I tell everyone I talk to about his experience in the hopes that should this ever happen to someone in their family that they would be better informed than I was. We were very lucky—blessed!

Football season started about three weeks after David had his 37 staples and 12 stitches removed, and had the I.V. line pulled out of his chest. He badly wanted to play this year, but figured he wasn't recovered enough to play. Within three weeks he was back at karate and had the doctor's go-ahead to play. He had an awesome season as both kicker and on defense. Needless to say, I'm a very proud mom!

The house

Our little log house is growing. After we got those huge used power poles in the ground early this spring, we set about getting the greenhouse/porch put together. Tom, our carpenter friend, is a very handy guy. Special pole floor joist supports cost $200 each and we were going to need several. So instead he took measurements, went to a steel salvage yard in Hibbing, and welded his own version. Basically, they're cup-shaped brackets that fit under the house end of the log and lag screw to the sill plate.

Each pole floor joist was lowered into the bracket and spiked to the sill plate. The other end was notched to fit over the long log ledger plate, which in turn was notched into each upright post and bolted securely into place. It was a lot of scribing, cutting,

The box rafter waiting to go up

and work, but Tom made steady progress fitting the whole floor support system together. It was especially tricky working over the basement walk-out area. You can't stand there, let alone hoist a heavy pole into place. So Tom used a come-along to lower and support the pole while he notched it to fit. Ingenious—and a whole lot safer than a person teetering on a ladder.

When the joists were in place, the 2 by 6 tongue and groove flooring was cut and nailed down. In two days, we had a porch!

I'd learned a lesson from upstairs in the house: seal the floor right away! The upstairs floor got all marked up by us walking back and forth on it. It's still not finished! I picked out a nice reddish brown color that I thought would match the house logs well. The next day I got out the brushes and roller and had at it. Gasp! That new stain/sealer was this God-awful *orange*! I thoroughly re-stirred the stain. And I did another large chunk. Yep. Orange. By then it was too late to do anything but finish the floor—all 30 feet of my nice pine *orange* floor. The pail said you

Tom cutting rafter "bird mouths" with a pattern

Tom spiking the rafters down

couldn't re-cover it if it was dry and to give it multiple coats while it was still damp, which I did. Boy what a job! And no matter what I did, there were streaks. Great. Orange with streaks. It looked like a five year old had stained my porch. It was not a happy day.

But in a couple of days, the color began to mellow out. The orange tamed down and finally died. It became that nice reddish brown I'd hoped for. And the streaks went away too. Where? Who cares? Whew!

The pole rafters were next. One end was tapered and supported on the house roof, over the log rafters of the roof. To support the other end, Tom built a box beam from 2x12s and a 2x8. This puppy was 38 feet long and when Tom said he, David, and I would just "lift it right up" to get it atop the upright posts, I thought he was nuts. Well, we did. Three guys on one end made the job do-able. Tom had notched out the tops of the uprights, leaving a shoulder for the 2x12 to sit on. The 2x8 sat on top of the uprights. When the whole thing was up, it slid right into place with very little help.

The next day, the rafters started going up. They went quickly, too. They were the smaller poles we'd saved for the purpose, so they were easier to handle and notch to fit the box beam. Next we put in the rafters in between the pole rafters in the greenhouse area, which would be insulated. On top of that was a layer of insulation board and OSB of a thickness to match the tongue and groove fir 2x6s that made the roof of the rest of the porch. (And also the ceiling, as you look up from the porch.) Tom framed cut-outs for the three skylights we planned to put in: one over the kitchen window, one over the living room window, and one in front of the doorway into the living room from the porch. These not only let in a lot of light but one is able to be opened for ventilation in the greenhouse.

We went along pretty slowly for a while; those skylights were over $400 each! But one by one, I got them and Tom put them in. And finally we were ready to enclose the four-season greenhouse. We had some salvaged patio door window glass so we put in one of them in the center space in the greenhouse. In the spring we're going around the corner with the addition, so we put up three of the others as a temporary wall on the east end. It lets in the light and keeps out the cold. In the spring, we'll take them down and continue on, reusing them again.

Oh, by the way, you remember the old Filon (corrugated fiberglass) we had used on our greenhouse addition at the mobile home, then again last year on the temporary greenhouse on the house? Well we carefully saved it and it is now on the east side of the goat barn! And it lets in a whole lot of light, too. The junk OSB David and I had nailed down two years ago kept the snow out, but it leaked and was a real nasty looking fix. The new roof doesn't leak. I stopped up all the holes with a squirt of silicone sealer.

Now the greenhouse is all insulated with fiberglass on the inside, then sided with half log siding and 1"x5" pine tongue and groove paneling that we got on sale because of its off-sizing. It looks very nice, and it's warm too.

Right now we've got ripe tomatoes and peppers all over the place. The plants are just recovering because I moved them so many times. But they are mostly setting new, greener leaves and perking up with a good dose of manure tea. They did get quite an infestation of aphids while they were stressed, requiring me to spray them twice with water soluble rotenone. They didn't need those tiny, juice-sucking bugs on the underside of their leaves. I was tipped off when I saw a ladybug on one of the plants—they just *love* aphids. I freed the ladybug

outside before spraying the plants, since the rotenone would have killed my tiny helper.

Right now, I'm finishing staining the inside logs and wood of the greenhouse. When that's all done, I'll be planting some tubs of greens, carrots, and maybe even some broccoli. Broccoli was $2.89 a pound at the store yesterday. I can pack eight plants into a large plastic storage bin full of soil. That will give us lots and lots of broccoli during the winter.

A lot of people don't grow broccoli because they figure they'll only get one head per plant. Not so. Once the main head has been cut, the plants

The new porch; a relaxing place to cut beans or corn or just sit

produce tons of side-shoots, some nearly as big as the central head. And this will go on until the plants freeze out in late fall. Ours are just now finished.

Our very own bulldozer

One day during the summer haying season (after the flesh eating bacteria episode), David came home all enthused. He had been haying a field owned by a neighbor lady who lost her husband early this spring. She was selling a lot of the farm equipment and had two bulldozers to sell. David had fallen in love with a big yellow John Deere 1010 crawler. I

think Gail was just humoring David when he said that I might buy it. After all, how many women buy a bulldozer? But I thought the asking price was low enough to make it a real deal and knew her late husband maintained his equipment well. So I went over that evening.

Not only could we really use a bulldozer on our new homestead (and this one cost less than most cheap used cars), but I figured that at 16, David could learn a lot driving and maintaining one. He had already had extensive experience on several large tractors that his boss, Mr. Yourczeck, owns, but also our own 9N Ford, and

a little time with his brother Bill's Case crawler. A man who can operate heavy equipment can always find a well-paying job, despite the economy's upheavals. Call it a life-skill.

I only had one more payment left on the Ford 250 plow truck, so I figured I could re-finance that to buy the dozer; it's our only monthly bill. I didn't like to borrow again but knew the dozer wouldn't last long, once word got out. I called our handy friend Tom and asked him if he'd be willing to do repair/maintenance on it in exchange for using it on his homestead. He agreed. (Tom is good on mechanics, can weld, and is also a figure-it-out sort of young man.) So I went in to the bank that next morning with a picture David had taken of the dozer. The young lady who was the loan officer asked what she could do for me, and almost needed an assistant to get her chin up off the floor when I said I wanted to buy a bulldozer.

Well, we've had the dozer for better

David, learning to run our new bulldozer by grading the goat yard. Notice the old siding on the chicken coop.

than three months now and I can tell you that it's been a great addition to our homestead. It cost $100 each way in gas for Bill to haul his crawler up to our place, so we didn't use it often. (It's also a big imposition for me to ask him to bring it up because he is a *very* busy man...and will be even busier because he and Kelly are expecting in December!)

David started right in and quickly learned the ropes operating the dozer. He started off kind of gently by pushing some level spots next to our driveway to park the vehicles. Then he cleaned in front of the goat barn/chicken pen, moving right on to scrape out the donkey pen. Soon after, he cleared out some trails down in the horse pasture and dug out many old stumps. Now we can access our big woods to haul logs and firewood

home. We couldn't get the tractor or pickup down there before.

We've had a few minor set-backs with the dozer. Like the time David was clearing brush around his best deer stand and threw a track. Now the track is really heavy. Think tank track! He knew that to take the pressure off the track tightener (which is tightened with grease pressure), he had to let grease out of the housing. He took off a cap screw and shoved in on the track. Yeah, grease came out and we got the track back on with heavy pry-bars. *But* when he went to tighten the track again with the grease gun, grease squirted out from under the tightener!

We finally found out from my good friend, Will, that we had squirted out a ball bearing with the first gob of grease. That ball bearing acts as a valve. I belatedly read the directions (doesn't that sound familiar?), finding out that you loosen the cap screw, which lets grease squirt out from underneath, but you don't take it off all the way. Ooops!

Luckily, Nortrax in Duluth knew just what we needed and sent us a beautiful little shiny ball bearing which David dropped into the hole.

And the track magically tightened! Dad used to say, "Too soon old, too late smart!" Oh so true.

Now David is clearing a spot next to the horse pasture for a nice training ring for me. As it's all sand, it will be perfect. It's nearly done now and all I've got to do is find someone who sells cedar fence posts. It would be nice to get the ring graded and the fence posts put in by freeze up. It's going to be close as it's already dipping into the teens at night.

There's quite a trick to learning how to clear land nicely with a bulldozer. If you just lower the blade and shove forward, you'll end up with huge, ugly piles of dirt/roots/tree parts. But if you work it back and forth a little as you clear, the trees will be separated from the dirt, leaving most of the dirt and letting the trees be piled for later cutting and/or burning. We cut up everything we can use for firewood, chip what works, and pile the rest (usually rotten stuff) for burning during the winter. David is learning to run up on the pile of dirt, spreading it out nicely so as not to leave mounds of debris.

The first trips over an area to be cleared skins off the trees, brush, stumps, and topsoil (it contains roots and brush). If we are going to plant an area, the topsoil is carefully worked free of most debris and piled aside to push back on the area it came from. In the case of the training ring and our hay area, the topsoil is graded over debris nice and smooth. Then in the spring I'll seed it in with grass and clover. The deer will just love me! The spots where Bill shoved the orchard debris over the hill, are now nice flat, lush mini-pastures and have deer in them every day.

Canning update

Although our summer was one of severe heat and drought, the garden did amazingly well. Luckily, I was able to keep it well watered. Neighbors who could not because of failing wells lost much of their produce. I planted a big patch of Kandy Korn and another of a bi-color Kandy-Korn sister. Because most of the corn was on a dry, unfertilized slope, it took the drought kind of hard. Some of the stalks were shorter than normal, and the ears were smaller. It sure showed me where I needed to spread some rotted manure this fall.

Luckily I planted a lot of corn. I had 14 rows 25-feet long, so I had a lot of corn to both eat regularly and can up. I would have had much more, but that's the breaks. It's also why I always can up all I can when I have it. Who knows what next year might bring?

I love canning sweet corn. I just pick a big basket full, carry it up by the goat pen and shuck it on my old handy-dandy white plastic table. The goats line up on their fence, knowing

Our rutabagas were huge. This one is next to a pint jar. Weight: 12 pounds!

that they get all the shuck, silks, and any poor ears.

Then I carry the corn inside and get to sit out on my lovely (unfinished as of harvest) new porch and cut the corn off the cobs onto cookie sheets. I've got a corn cutter that you hold and shove down over the cob. They say in the advertising that you can hold the handles with each hand and just push it down easily to remove the kernels. Ha!

I end up working the handle back and forth, while pushing down hard, and holding the cob in place on a cookie sheet with the other hand. It does work well, but I always end up trying to get every little bit of corn off the cob and cutting my hand by the base of my thumb when the saw thing gets too close. "Mom! Don't bleed in the corn!"

Anyway, I pack the fresh corn into pint and half pint jars to within an inch of the top, add a teaspoon of salt and pour boiling water on it to within an inch of the top of the jar. Corn is a long-processing food at 10 pounds pressure. You do pints and half pints for 55 minutes. But it's so good! A thousand times better than store canned corn. There's a huge difference, not only in taste, but in tenderness, too.

Usually, sweet corn produces two ears per stalk. This year, I got a few double ears, but the stalks seemed to quit growing very early, drying up. So as soon as I had picked the first corn, I went through the patch and cut all the stalks with no more ears on them or a very poor second ear. I give this to the goats, donkeys, and horses. They love it and it's good for them. It's good for the garden, too, as corn pests, such as corn ear worms, winter over in corn stalks to become a bad pest in following years. So corn stalks are one thing I remove from the garden.

As I told you, my green beans were super productive. My yellow beans were on the non-fertile end of the new garden and didn't do well, except for the Dragon Tongue. Holy mackerel, I like those beans! They're huge, flat, long, and meaty. They do look a little weird, being purple and yellow striped, but it makes them easy to pick. The strange color disappears when you cook or can them. I canned Dragon Tongue beans as wax beans, then made mustard bean pickles out of a big batch of them. If you've never made these, you're missing a great taste treat. It's kind of like honey mustard pickles. After we use the bean pickles, I save the leftover sauce and we use it to dip chicken and pork in. It is very good and not real mustardy. Kind of sweet and sour.

Here's how you make them if you want to give it a try next year. While yellow beans make a prettier bean pickle, you can also use green beans—I sure did! (Did I mention I had LOTS of green beans this year? Ha! Ha!)

Mustard bean pickles:

8 quarts yellow wax beans
salt
6 cups sugar
1 cup flour
5 Tbsp. dry mustard
1 Tbsp. turmeric
6 cups vinegar

Cut beans in one inch pieces and simmer in salted water until barely tender. Drain. Mix dry ingredients together in pan. Stir while adding vinegar. Bring to a boil. Add beans and again bring to a boil. Simmer five minutes. Pack hot into hot, sterilized

Part of our fall harvest in the new greenhouse. The floor color has mellowed to the reddish brown I had hoped for. Much better than the screaming orange.

jars, and water bath process for 10 minutes. Makes 8 pints.

Our cucumbers were also very productive. I planted Summer Dance and Japanese Climbing on a stock panel trellis. They did very good for my bread and butter pickles. The only thing I don't like about these very thin, long cukes is that they don't make pretty dill pickles. You have to cut them in half to get them to fit into a quart jar, and often into thirds, to fit into a pint. I had this trouble last year, so I planted Chicago Pickling cukes just for dills and whole sweet pickles. That worked much better, although they didn't like the heat much; they kind of went yellow and wilted. When the heat was over, they again greened up and started producing well again. My shelves are *full* of pickles of all sorts now.

I planted carrots between my rows of asparagus and black raspberries on kind of a gravelly hill, and they did not like it. Also, I didn't pull the grass out of the area, because that was right when David got sick. (Well, it's a good excuse, anyway.) So the carrots were slow. But my friend Jeri had more carrots than she needed, so I got

to can a bunch of carrots anyway. At the very end of the season, I did get canning carrots out of my rows, but they weren't anything to brag about. I've already planned to move my carrots back down where I have nicer soil and it is more fertile.

I was extremely happy with my after-thought rutabagas and Packman broccoli in the new part of the garden. The rutabagas grew leaves nearly waist high and had softball sized roots in August. By late September, they were the size of soccer balls, and still tender and sweet, too. They stuck way up out of the ground. So far up that the @$*% deer ate the tops out of them after hopping the fence where a tree had taken it down in a wind storm.

I did salvage a lot of them by severe trimming. I was going to store them whole in the basement, in my new pantry. But damaged like that, I diced them to can. I know the canning manuals say that rutabagas get discolored and strong tasting and aren't worth canning. But I haven't found that so. I do dump the canning water down the drain and heat them in fresh water. This seems to remove the cabbage

smell and taste that is a little strong at times. I was hoping to save my pint jars for venison, but I bought a few boxes of jars, was given some, and went ahead and canned 'em up. Now I'm wondering how our rutabaga flavored venison will taste.

Yard update

This spring, our new front yard was nothing but black dirt with our new railroad tie raised beds full of perennials and bulbs hoping for new life. Well they got it! We got lots of spring rain and the grass sprouted beautifully, quickly turning into a real lawn. Our bare, cold winter killed a lot of the bulbs and perennials, but we still had a gorgeous flower show all summer. I did cheat and plant a bunch of annuals where there were bare spots. The color was sure worth it!

Our raised beds are turning out wonderful. I've got herbs at the head of the first bed and they love it. The chives need to be divided already and the oregano is climbing over the ties. But our two newest beds got black dirt that also had a lot of grass seed in it and boy what a job that is to keep out. I've still got a piece of daylily bed that needs weeding. With grass, there's nothing to do but pull it up. This is so bad that you've got to work a shovel under it, then pull and bang out all the dirt, throwing all the grass and roots into a wheelbarrow. If you leave any roots, the grass is back and must be re-pulled.

In one bed, I pulled all the grass and then scattered some California poppies and toadflax seeds in, figuring they would crowd out any grass or weeds. It worked beautifully and they'll re-seed for next year, although they won't be so thick.

I *love* my little cheap-o plastic fish pond! David and I planted it this spring, and now I have creeping lamium, pansies, violas, and Japanese iris around it. They make it look less plastic and more natural. We just caught the five goldfish I bought this spring to look pretty and keep down the mosquitoes. Here, the ice gets too thick for the fish to survive outside, so we will winter them in our big aquariums in the house. They've been in for two weeks and seem to have adjusted.

Getting ready for winter

My tomatoes did fairly well this summer, but were slow because of the heat and drought. When our fall frosts came, we picked every darned tomato in the garden and brought them in the house to ripen in the new greenhouse. They ripen faster when it's warm, and it was just too cold to risk them staying outside. Frost is one thing, but a bad freeze is another—it'll kill them to mush.

As the tomatoes ripen, I've been making tomato sauce, salsa, spaghetti sauce, and chili (for convenience and to use up some of my older dry beans). I still, at this November 1st writing, have baskets of tomatoes in all stages of ripe around the house. I've learned *not* to put tomatoes in a sunny window to ripen; they usually rot instead. Instead, I just put them in boxes and baskets and keep sorting them by ripeness. You lose a few to rot, but most of them ripen nicely with no muss and fuss.

My chicken coop not only was not very warm, but it looked like hell. I made it out of scraps of used lumber and OSB, sort of like a patchwork quilt. I had lots of pieces of tongue and groove 2x6 lumber left over from the house, so one sunny day, I set about tacking them to my coop, over the OSB. It turned out to look pretty nice, kind of like a log building. I also used up leftover insulation board and some old paneling Tom gave me to finish the inside. Now the coop is sturdier, warmer, and definitely looks nicer. I even built a flower box under the front window so the chickens can have their own flowers. No wonder my hens are singing.

I just found another pile of 2x6 pieces up by the travel trailer. Just what I need to finish off the front of the new pheasant pen we're building on the other side of the goat barn.

It's getting colder now and we're starting to cut and split wood in earnest. I want to split a couple of truck loads and stack it on the new enclosed porch. That way it'll be out of the rain, snow, and bad weather, nice and dry. And I'll only have to open the greenhouse door, go out on the *dry* porch and bring in wood to fill the wood box. Maybe ten steps in all. I can live with that.

I've been cleaning out the goat pen and donkey stall, hauling trailer loads of that old manure down onto the garden where the corn will go next year. Corn is a very heavy feeder, liking the nitrogen that would cause problems with other crops. I'm also fertilizing those spots I had trouble with this summer. Hopefully I'll get it all well worked in by freeze-up. I didn't make it over the whole garden last fall, and boy was I sorry in the spring. So I'm trying to get it done soon. It won't be long until our freeze-up now. The geese landed on ice this morning. That's how it is in the northern backwoods; you do what you can, but *never* have it all done before winter hits. And you just learn to live with it and not take life too seriously. Δ

Me putting my new siding on the chicken coop

Rhubarb
vegetable or fruit?

By Gail Butler

If you've got any rhubarb growing, no doubt you've got lots of it! You then are obligated to find varied and tasty ways to use it up. If you are like me you can't bear letting any food your garden produces go to waste. Fall finds me inundated with rhubarb even after taking cuttings from it all season long, so I bake, freeze, sauce, brew, and can every stalk my garden produces before the first frosts arrive. If I'm lucky I find someone willing to take some off my hands!

Rhubarb is most celebrated in early spring because it is one of the first edible items the garden produces. Its palate-tingling, fresh taste seems to cleanse the system after winter's heavier fare. However, it can be enjoyed all season long up until the first light frosts of autumn. If you can, freeze, or make rhubarb into wine you won't have to forego enjoying it even during winter months.

Three insignificant rhubarb divisions given to me years ago by a dear friend who had too much in his garden have grown robustly and now occupy the entire east wall of my converted hay barn-garage. Rhubarb is truly the gift that keeps on giving… and giving. Over the years I've experimented with it and am still finding tasty ways to use this versatile plant.

A couple of generations ago this useful and hardy plant once grew in nearly every farm and country garden. Modern palates, to their detriment, often eschew it although it can sometimes be found in the produce section of city grocery stores in early spring. High-priced and not very fresh, few city dwellers and suburbanites have a clue how to prepare it. Their grandmothers no doubt knew exactly what to do with it…and did…but today rhubarb is either much maligned or forgotten by many. Called "pie plant" by country folk, its crisp, fleshy stalks are indispensable for pie, sauce, jam, salads, cakes, muffins, puddings, wine, and more.

Most of us have experienced rhubarb in at least two of its many incarnations—stewed with sugar and eaten from a bowl as a spring tonic. We've also enjoyed rhubarb pie—mixed with sugar (sugar being the operative word here) and strawberries and placed between two buttery pastry crusts, then baked to tart, tangy, sweet, and savory perfection. Melt a little cheddar cheese on that slice of pie or pair it with a scoop of vanilla ice cream and you have nirvana on a plate.

Pass the sugar please

Rhubarb is really a vegetable, but its red and green stalks are traditionally used and prepared much the same way as we would prepare fruits such as apples and berries. In fact, rhubarb pairs nicely in recipes with both apples and all types of berries.

to meat dishes. Rhubarb syrup and a few toasted, slivered almonds exalt plain vanilla ice cream from tasty to terrific.

To make a traditional spring tonic chop three pounds of fresh rhubarb and add three cups of water. Simmer until the rhubarb is soft. Strain out the pulp and add six tablespoons of honey to the remaining liquid, stirring until honey is dissolved completely. This tonic may be taken by the spoonful to stimulate digestion and nourish the blood after a long winter. In Italy, this tonic would be added to red wine, with vanilla, cinnamon, and ginger to create a tonic with aphrodisiac benefits.

To make a simple rhubarb sauce for drizzling over vanilla ice cream, pound cake, or waffles, simply dice fresh stalks and place them in a pan. Pour in enough honey to just cover the rhubarb and simmer until soft and

Rhubarb salad and tea, above, and rhubarb crisp, are just three ways to enjoy this flavorful plant.

In order to make rhubarb more palatable it is usually sweetened some with honey or sugar. Bite into a stalk fresh from the garden and your mouth may pucker up a bit as your taste buds encounter its sour oxalates. The stalwart among us sometimes pull and eat stalks from the garden with no other preparation but to wipe off a bit of clinging dirt. However, sweeten it a bit by dipping that fresh stalk into a bowl of sugar and you have a tasty treat indeed. Simply adding a little sugar elevates rhubarb from sour to savory. Now we are talking rhubarb muffins, cookies, and "company" cake. In addition to its use in sweet desserts, rhubarb chutney, jam, and sauce are delicious accompaniments

Rhubarb grows well against the side of a garage.

pulpy. Strain out the rhubarb pulp (adding it to your compost pile) and you have slightly thick syrup of a nondescript golden color. This syrup will thicken further as it cools. You may redden it with a drop of food coloring, if desired. For some reason children often prefer green rhubarb sauce—the greener the better. A few drops of green food coloring will give this syrup a child-approved grass-green hue. Mixing in a few drops of red and blue coloring creates "Princess Purple"—a color much loved by my young niece.

Time for dessert

Rhubarb shines when used as an ingredient in desserts. It adds moistness, flavor, and fiber. If you have a surplus of other fruits in your garden, such as apples, plums, cherries, apricots, and berries you can substitute these for half the amount of rhubarb called for in any recipe for a continually changing palate of flavors. The following recipes will help you use your overabundance of rhubarb while treating yourself, your family, and your guests to tasty, homemade treats. Additionally, for a lower fat product simply substitute the oil called for in dessert recipes for an equal amount of applesauce. This substitution works best for muffins and sheet cake recipes.

Rhubarb muffins:

> 1¼ cup packed brown sugar
> 1 egg
> ½ cup oil or applesauce
> 1 cup milk (any kind, or yogurt thinned with water)
> 2 tsp. vanilla
>
> 2½ cups white or whole wheat flour
> 1 tsp. baking soda
> 1 tsp. baking powder
> ½ tsp. salt
>
> 1½ cups diced fresh rhubarb
> ½ cup chopped walnuts

In a large bowl beat the first five ingredients until smooth. In a separate bowl combine the dry ingredients. Gradually stir the dry ingredients into the egg mixture until just moistened. Stir in rhubarb and walnuts.

Fill paper-lined muffin tins 2/3 to ¾ full of batter. Top each muffin with topping mix (following) and bake at 375° F for 20 to 25 minutes.

Topping mix:

> 1/3 cup sugar, 1 tsp. cinnamon, and 1 tsp. melted butter mixed together

This tasty recipe makes 8-12 muffins.

The next recipe is for "company" cake and makes two round layers. I serve one sprinkled with powdered sugar to enjoy right away and freeze the other for when unexpected, but welcome, company drops in. This cake thaws quickly and after a bit of conversation and catching up with your visitors it is ready to garnish with a bit of powdered sugar, slice, onto a plate, and serve. Use fresh or frozen rhubarb to make this cake.

Rhubarb company cake:

> ½ cup softened butter or butter-flavored shortening
> 1½ cups brown or white sugar
> *1 cup buttermilk
> 2 cups whole wheat flour
> 1 tsp. each baking soda, cinnamon, and vanilla or almond extract
> ½ tsp. salt
> 2 cups chopped fresh or *frozen, thawed rhubarb (*reserve the juice)

Cream butter (or applesauce) or shortening with egg, vanilla, and sugar in a large mixing bowl. Add *buttermilk stirring until smooth. Stir in flour, cinnamon, and salt. Add drained rhubarb and stir in.

Spoon batter into two oiled and floured round cake tins. Bake at 350° F for 35 to 55 minutes until center tests done. Remove from oven and cool. Serve one layer for dessert dusted with powdered sugar and freeze the other for when company stops by.

*In place of buttermilk stir the reserved rhubarb juice (from frozen rhubarb) into enough yogurt or sour cream to create one cup of mixture with a "buttermilk-like" consistency, if desired.

Rhubarb crisp:

Rhubarb crisp is a flavorful, sweet treat you can make when you don't have any eggs or milk on hand. It uses pantry staples such as flour, sugar, and rolled oats. It's surprising how just a few ingredients add up into something so tasty and simple to make.

```
3½ cups diced rhubarb, fresh or
   frozen
¾ cup sugar
3 Tbsp. flour
```

Mix these three ingredients together in a medium bowl and place into an oiled quart-size square or round pan. Next prepare the topping.

Topping:

```
½ cup packed brown sugar
⅓ cup old-fashioned rolled oats
⅓ cup flour
¼ cup softened butter
```

Mix together the first three topping ingredients. Cut in the butter and mix and mash until the consistency of the topping is crumbly. Spoon the topping over the rhubarb mixture and bake at 375° F for 40 to 50 minutes.

Rhubarb pudding:

```
2 cups diced rhubarb, fresh or fro-
   zen
1 cup sugar
```

Cook these two ingredients together in a medium saucepan over low-medium heat until rhubarb is tender.

Meanwhile sift together:

```
⅓ cup sugar
⅓ cup flour
⅛ tsp. ground nutmeg
```

Then gently beat together:

```
2 eggs
¼ cup cream or half & half
¼ tsp. almond extract
```

Add egg mixture to the flour and sugar mixture stirring well. Add the combined mixtures to the rhubarb in the saucepan. Cook over medium heat, stirring constantly until thickened. Pour into dessert bowls. Chill and serve with whipped cream.

The savory side of rhubarb

While rhubarb may be made into a variety of sweet treats it also embellishes meats as well, and may be used raw in fruit or vegetable salad.

Baked chicken breasts with rhubarb sauce:

Preheat oven to 350° F.

```
6 large chicken breasts
1 cup chopped rhubarb
6 Tbsp. brown sugar
1 cup orange or pineapple juice
2 Tbsp. white wine vinegar or soy
   sauce
1 tsp. salt
1 clove garlic, minced
3 tsp. cornstarch
```

In a saucepan simmer the rhubarb in the orange or pineapple juice until soft and pulpy. Strain out the pulp, returning the juice to the pan. Set aside 3 Tbsp. of the juice mixture and stir this into the cornstarch until smooth and lump-free. Add the rest of the ingredients to the pan, except the cornstarch mixture. Heat the sauce until it comes to a simmer and add the cornstarch mixture, heating and stirring until the sauce is thickened. Set aside.

Salt and pepper chicken breasts and brown them in butter or oil until lightly golden. Place in a baking dish. Pour the sauce over the chicken and bake for 45 to 55 minutes. Remove from oven and garnish with chopped parsley or toasted, slivered almonds before serving. Serves 4-6.

"Better than Major Grey's" rhubarb chutney:

```
6 cups fresh, diced rhubarb
3 cups finely diced white onion
1 cup golden raisins
4 cups packed brown sugar
4 cups cider vinegar
2 Tbsp. salt
2 tsp. ground allspice
```

Place all ingredients into a large pot or saucepan and bring to a boil. Reduce heat and simmer for 30 to 45 minutes until the mixture is thick and bubbly. Stir occasionally to keep the mixture from sticking to the pot.

Pack into hot, sterile 8-ounce jelly jars and process in a hot water bath or steam canner for 10 minutes. Add one minute to processing time for each 1,000 feet elevation above sea level. Makes six 8-ounce jars of chutney.

Serve rhubarb chutney with spicy, Indian curries, or savory meats such as garlic-roasted chicken and pork.

No-pectin rhubarb jam:

```
8 cups chopped, fresh rhubarb
6 cups sugar
3 or 4 drops red food coloring
   (optional)
```

Place rhubarb and sugar into a large pot and cook, stirring occasionally, until the mixture reaches "just-before-jam (consistency), about 20 minutes. Pour or spoon simmering mixture into hot, sterile jars and seal, making sure lids pop. Makes five, 8-ounce jars full with a bit extra for the fridge.

Rhubarb jam is a delicious spread on toast and homemade biscuits but it can also be brushed onto roast turkey, chicken, or pork during the last 10 to 15 minutes of cooking time to give a sweet and savory glaze to the finished meat. You may also substitute half the rhubarb called for with plums, apricots, apples, or berries.

Your canned rhubarb jam, chutney, and syrup makes great from-the-heart holiday gifts too. Just top each jar with a colorful bit of cloth and secure with ribbon, raffia, or a dried strip of cornhusk.

The following recipe is inspired by Russian cuisine and features a not-too-sweet, crunchy-savory salad using fresh rhubarb. Because raw rhubarb is used, its unique tart-tangy flavor shines. Rhubarb lovers will swoon over this salad. The crisp crunchiness of the rhubarb, apple, and celery, paired with the sharp creaminess of the cheese and dressing, and the smoky-nutty flavor of toasted walnuts give this salad real palate-appeal. This is one of my favorite summertime salads when mid-summer weather makes the kitchen too hot to cook. I simply gather all the ingredients onto a tray and prepare the salad outside in the cooler, shaded north side garden next to the house.

Russian rhubarb salad:

Mix together in a bowl:

3 rhubarb stalks, diced
2 tart green apples, cored and diced
2 stalks celery diced (or 2 tsp. minced *lovage leaves)
½ cup chopped, toasted walnuts
½ cup diced, medium or sharp cheddar cheese

Dressing:

**¼ cup yogurt
**¼ cup mayonnaise
1 Tbsp. lemon juice
1 Tbsp. sugar
pinch salt
dash of black pepper

Whisk dressing ingredients together and pour over salad, stirring to coat all ingredients. Serves four. This salad also pairs nicely with traditional Russian beet soup, sour cream blinis, and crusty bread. Served as an accompaniment to other dishes, this salad may be stretched to serve six, or more.

*Lovage is a tall, hardy-perennial herb with celery-flavored leaves.

**You can substitute the yogurt and mayonnaise for ½ cup sour cream, if desired.

Freezing

Rhubarb is easily frozen for wintertime use. I simply harvest, wash, pat dry, chop, and freeze it in plastic containers or bags. I don't blanch it or add sugar before freezing. Upon thawing there will be juice that can be incorporated into the recipe as part of the liquid called for.

Drink your rhubarb

Blended with tea or lemonade, mixed with club soda, or fermented into wine, beverages made from rhubarb are refreshing and cooling due to the very oxalates that tingle your taste buds. Best enjoyed on a shady porch, beneath a leafy tree, or under a fully-foliaged arbor, these bracing drinks will satisfy thirst on the hottest summer days. Icy-cold rhubarb wine is a great libation to enjoy while relaxing on the front porch at the end of a workday.

Rhubarb in any form was once considered a healthful spring tonic and it is reputed to strengthen teeth and gums and to drive away the winter

Chilled summer rhubarb wine

doldrums. Rhubarb contains considerable calcium but its oxalates interfere with absorption of much of its calcium. Rather than relying on rhubarb as a calcium source, consume it for the other nutrients it contains.

Cooked rhubarb—how most of us eat, or drink it—contains the following nutrients per 100 grams (approximately 3.5 ounces): 145 mg of calcium, 44 mcg beta carotene, 2 grams of fiber, 5 mcg of folate, 0.21 mg of iron, 123 mcg of lutein plus zeaxanthin (good for the eyes), 12 mg of magnesium, 96 mg of potassium, 73 IU of Vitamin A, 0.08 mg of Zinc, 29.6 mcg of Vitamin K (phylloquinone), and small amounts of B Vitamins and manganese. Rhubarb is over 67% water. Subtract the two grams of fiber when making rhubarb into tonic beverages such as the following:

Restorative rhubarb tea:

Simply simmer one cup of chopped rhubarb in enough water to cover. When the rhubarb is soft, strain and reserve the liquid. Add rhubarb liquid to two or three cups of strong brewed black or green tea. Sweeten to taste, if desired, and chill. Serve over ice with a mint sprig or lime slice.

Rhubarb lemonade:

Simmer chopped rhubarb in enough water to cover until tender. Strain out rhubarb and use one or more cups of this liquid to replace water in any lemonade recipe. Garnish with a sprig of lemon balm or a lemon slice.

Rhubarb refresher:

Simmer four cups of rhubarb with enough water to cover until the rhubarb is soft. Strain off the liquid and sweeten to taste. Chill. To serve, fill glasses with ice, then fill half full with the rhubarb liquid. Top off with club soda and add a twist of lemon or lime.

The following recipe for a traditional rhubarb wine is one of my favorites. Rhubarb makes a tasty wine that is silky on the tongue and slips down best as an ice-cold aperitif, served alongside Chinese cuisine, or with sweet desserts. Serve this slightly opalescent light-golden wine very chilled or over ice for best effect. If your temperature zone is too cold to grow cold hardy wine grapes, grow

When selling rhubarb at the farmer's market, a brochure that tells all about rhubarb, including recipes, really helps. When giving wine as a gift, a fancy label makes a nice presentation.

rhubarb and make this traditional, country wine. Rhubarb grows even as far north as Alaska and Siberia.

Old-fashioned rhubarb wine:

> 5 lbs. coarsely chopped rhubarb
> 1 gallon boiling water
> juice of one lemon
> 6 cups of sugar
> 1 tsp. bread baking yeast or ¼ cup starter

Combine rhubarb and boiling water in a clean vat or washtub. Cover and let rest for three to ten days at room temperature. After the resting period, strain off rhubarb, reserving the liquid. Add lemon juice, sugar, and yeast. Funnel the mixture into a gallon-size carboy and add a bung fitted with an airlock. For carboys, I reuse gallon-size glass jugs from wine or cider purchases. When fermentation slows, siphon the new wine into a clean jug and refit with the fermentation lock. Be sure to add water to the fermentation lock if its level drops to

prevent undesirable organisms from reaching your developing wine. Re-racking your wine occasionally into clean carboys will allow you to siphon off the sediments and will stimulate any remaining yeast into activity. Before bottling you want to be sure that all fermentation has completely ceased or a cork could blow and eject sticky liquid over floor and walls.

When you are satisfied that fermentation has ceased, bottle your wine, and cork it securely. At bottling time your young rhubarb wine is ready for a preview tasting. It will be good, but wait six months to a year and your wine will be even better.

I like to store my wine in the root cellar, as it is cooler in summer than the pantry. If you have wine bottles with screw-on lids there is less concern about mice nibbling at the corks. If you must store wine where mice might nibble, simply secure heavy-duty aluminum foil over the top of the

cork and upper neck of the bottle with wire.

Growing and harvesting

Rhubarb is native to the mountains of Mongolia and Western China. In fact, the word "rhubarb" comes from the Latin word "*rhabarbarum*" and means "root of the barbarians." Rhubarb's botanical name is *Rheum rhaponticum*.

In Europe, where rhubarb was a popular cottage garden plant, the tradition was to force it in early spring by covering the crowns with tall buckets that had the bottoms removed. Forcing rhubarb creates paler, longer stalks earlier in the season that may be more tender. Europeans customarily force/blanch all types of vegetables including asparagus, leeks, and endive. Forcing or blanching rhubarb doesn't seem to have caught on in the United States to any great degree. Here in the U.S., rhubarb lovers prefer rhubarb on the colorful side.

You can grow rhubarb if you live in USDA Zones 2 through 9. Rhubarb needs winter chilling to thrive. Some parts of the South above Zone 9 can only grow rhubarb as an annual. Rhubarb loves moisture and because summers where I live are hot, dry, and windy I heavily mulch with clean straw around the base of my plants. Because winds in my area prevail from the south and west, I planted my rhubarb on an east-facing garage wall. Here they are protected from gusty, dehydrating winds. Rhubarb is very forgiving and while it prefers soils rich in organic matter, it still thrives in my soil that is mostly a combination of clay and sand. Rhubarb loves an annual feeding of well-composted manure. Try to keep the soil cool-damp but not wet although brief periods of dry soil won't harm well-established plants.

The thick straw mulch I apply in spring to keep the roots cool and moist also serves later to protect them

61

from winter freezing and thawing. It's not so much cold temperatures that will damage roots and crowns but cycles of freezing and thawing. Apply thick winter mulch when leaves and stalks freeze in late autumn if you haven't already spring-mulched the plants. In heavy snow areas cover the mulched rhubarb crowns with some branches to keep the weight of snow off. In springtime I rake back the winter mulch. This helps prevent disease and rotting of the crowns. I then re-mulch with fresh straw.

Harvest the stalks regularly to keep the plants vigorous and to prevent stalks from getting too thick and tough. When harvesting, leave at least 1/3 of the stalks and their leaves on the plant for proper photosynthesis. I gather some rhubarb all season long up until the first frost withers the leaves with my main harvests in spring, mid-summer, and early autumn. Ideally, rhubarb stalks should be harvested by twisting them off near the base of the plant although this isn't always possible. Some stalks just won't twist off so I always take a clean paring knife into the garden to slice through those that won't cooperate.

Rhubarb plants send up thick flower stalks in spring soon after leaves and stalks develop. Fleshy flower buds unfold into clusters of creamy-white flowers that are quite attractive.

There are two theories concerning rhubarb flower stalks. One holds that the stalks weaken the plants and should be removed. The other maintains that the flowers make an attractive plant even more lovely and interesting and cause no harm. Too, the unopened flower buds are said to make a tasty substitute for broccoli (*A Modern Herbal* by M. Grieve). I haven't tried Mrs. Grieve's suggestion regarding the edibility of rhubarb flowers as yet. I've removed flower stalks some seasons and left them alone at others. It all depends on how busy I am. I have seen no difference

Red stalks or green?

The current preference in rhubarb is for varieties having a preponderance of red stalks. Hybridizers have the opinion "the-redder-the-better" and have been busy creating red-stalked rhubarb for spring catalogs for the past several years.

The rhubarb in my garden bears stalks that are mostly green in early spring turning redder as summer warms and progresses. I've eaten both color-types and flavor seems about equal although those who prefer green varieties insist that theirs is more flavorful! For the most part color seems to be anesthetic quality rather than a flavor difference as color of rhubarb goes only skin deep. Whether red or green outside, rhubarb is the same pale color inside.

Plant whatever color-type appeals to you. Most varieties lose their color somewhat during cooking hence the occasional use of food coloring to tint the finished product. When cooking rhubarb without food coloring your finished product will be a dark reddish-brown (jam), brown (chutney), a golden color (sauce and syrup), pale green and pink (cakes and muffins).

Popular red-stalked varieties of rhubarb are Canada Red, Cherry Red, Crimson Red, Valentine, and MacDonald. Victoria is a green variety with red at the base of the stalks and has excellent "rhubarb" flavor. Victoria rhubarb was first mentioned in England in the early 1800's. This variety reddens as the season progresses. These varieties of rhubarb may be found in most springtime garden catalogs.

in the vigor of my plants, regardless of how I treat the flower stalks.

While the flowers may be edible, rhubarb leaves are toxic due to their high oxalate content. By summer's end when daily monsoons brought on by afternoon heat arrive, rhubarb leaves from the garden have grown so large that they can be used as umbrellas to shield against sudden storms. Rhubarb leaves also make instant, unique place mats for impromptu summer picnics. On hot summer days or during sudden downpours, the cats on my property will often be found taking refuge under the cool, sheltering leaves. Rhubarb roots are sometimes used as a laxative due to their uncomfortably strong purgative effects. I haven't tried this application so can't comment on it.

At some point you will need to divide your rhubarb. Perhaps the patch has gotten too large. Or, you've gotten lucky and a neighbor or friend has asked you for some divisions. In either case you'll want to take divisions in early spring before the stalks get about six inches tall. I find the

best way to divide the crowns is with a shovel. Simply slice down into the crown to remove nodules for transplanting or giving away. Replant divisions as soon as possible, mulching and keeping them moist until they become established—usually by the second year.

Pests and diseases

I've been lucky because my rhubarb hasn't suffered from any really damaging pests or diseases. Earwigs do like to hang out in the moisture around the crowns and shred the leaves a bit but don't seem interested in the stalks, which is the part of the plant I want. There are, however, pests that can attack rhubarb.

Local farmers in my area advise to keep all dock-family plants away from rhubarb because this weakens the plants and harbors the curculio beetle. The beetles then travel to rhubarb if it is planted nearby. The curculio beetle is about ¾-inch long and appears to be covered with yellow dust that when rubbed off reveals a gray-brown carapace. The best control for this beetle is to simply pick it off by hand. Other pests that may attack rhubarb are European corn borers and yellow woolybear caterpillars. These last two don't generally attack in quantity and picking these off and destroying them is the best control.

One disease affecting rhubarb is anthracnose. This disease causes stalks to soften and wilt. There is no cure but it can be prevented by cleaning up rhubarb leaves and other debris after harvest and at season's end, and also by re-mulching with fresh straw in spring.

Crown rot affects the roots and crowns of rhubarb and causes the leaves to yellow and wilt. Dig up and burn the affected plants. New rhubarb plantings should be located elsewhere to prevent re-infection.

If you see small, round, brown spots on rhubarb leaf surfaces you may have "leaf spot" fungus. This disease doesn't harm plants and therefore requires no control.

Verticillium wilt is a soil-borne fungus often seen in tomatoes, peppers, and strawberries. Wilting and yellowing is one of the symptoms. The only prevention is to grow rhubarb where plants susceptible to this fungus have not been grown before.

If aphids are bothering your roses, chop one or two rhubarb leaves and add them to a stainless steel pot. Pour on a pint of water and bring to a boil. Simmer for 30 minutes and cool. Strain out the leaves and add a teaspoon of liquid soap. Put this mixture in a spray bottle and spray this where you see aphids.

More than you can use?

If you have more rhubarb than you can cook up, preserve, or give away, I have discovered another way to get rid of some and make a little money. Many communities now sponsor farmers' markets and outdoor craft fairs. Recently, I cut and bagged over 35 pounds of rhubarb to sell at my community's annual "heritage days"

Sources:
Nutritional Information is from the USDA National Nutrient Database.

For more recipes and information about rhubarb you can go to www.plantea.com/rhubarb.htm

The Encyclopedia of Natural Insect & Disease Control, Edited by Roger B. Yepsen, Jr., Rodale Press, Emmaus, Pennsylvania: 1984.

celebration. To help things along I created, with the publishing program on my computer, an attractive little brochure featuring a number of easy-to-prepare rhubarb recipes. My theory was that if people knew how to prepare rhubarb they would be more inclined to purchase some. It worked. I sold all 30-plus pounds! This summer I plan to attend a nearby town's farmers' market where I will again offer up for sale many more pounds of my excess rhubarb. Δ

A Backwoods Home Anthology
The Fourteenth Year

❋ Use Wallo' Water and gain a month of growing season
❋ A packing crate mini-barn
❋ How to butcher a chicken in 20 minutes or less
❋ Pemmican
❋ The vanishing outhouse
❋ Preparing garden soil in winter
❋ Install a mobile, solar-powered toilet
❋ Portable fence panels: the homesteader's friend
❋ A comfortable base camp
❋ Home canning equals fast, easy, tasty meals

❋ Brooder in a box
❋ A pleasant surprise: the asparagus bean
❋ Preparedness for travelers
❋ Jackie Clay's basic "grab & git" emergency kits
❋ The home citrus orchard
❋ Making dandelions palatable
❋ How to select the right backup generator
❋ Growing & storing herbs
❋ Successful cold storage
❋ A simple backwoods hay baler
❋ Battery powered weekend retreat
❋ The art of wood splitting

A cabin for one

By Lee Greiman

Between 1989 and 1990 I built a 20 by 20-foot log house on the Musselshell River in Montana. The next year I built an addition on it that was the same size as the original because I was thinking, someday, I might have a family and a bigger house would be better.

Well, as it turned out, I stayed single, and we bachelors are not famous for our housekeeping. After a while, I looked around and it became evident to me what I had to do: Sell my "big" house and build myself a smaller one—again.

So I bought 20 acres north of Delphia, Montana, and on November 2, 2002 I poured cement for the foundation. After a two-week curing time, the cement was strong enough to lay the sill logs which I had flattened on one side with an Alaska chainsaw mill. The east and west sides of the foundation were built half the diameter of a log higher than the north and

south sides to allow for the saddle notch. I cut the logs 16-feet- and 20-feet-long so there would be one foot on each end overhanging the foundation's edges.

There were enough dead pine trees on the property to make the walls. I

built the door and window frames with a vertical groove ½ inch deep and 1½ inches wide the full height of the frames, then nailed a 1½- x 2-inch strip to keep the logs stable. I cut 1½-inch notches in the end of the logs that butted against window and door

Diagonal strips brace the log window and door frames in place. At left, a log is held in place temporarily for scribing.

A ½-inch by 1½-inch groove in the window and door frames holds the notched ends of logs in place while allowing for movement and settling.

frames, cutting the notches into the log to allow the log to slide up and down, as the logs will expand and contract with changing weather.

I built a scribing tool to mark the logs. By putting a log on top of the previous course, the log was placed half the diameter of log higher; log dogs (giant steel staples) anchored it while it was being scribed, or marked. Then I took the log down and cut out between scribing marks, then put it on and went on to the next one.

For added strength I drilled $9/16$-inch holes through two logs and drove in ½-inch rebar. It was a snug fit as the rebar has ribs designed to grip

cement. I started doing this on the second course of logs to go on.

When the walls were above the window and door frames, I built three scissor trusses—one for each end and one in the middle.

I had an old friend who wanted me to use the Alaska mill to saw boards on his timbered place. For this service he let me get five spruce 20 feet long for the purlins and ridgepole plus pine to make boards for the roof.

After bolting purlins to the trusses, I nailed the boards on the purlins and ridgepole. I laid rosin paper on top of the roof boards, then put 1½- x 5-inch rafters on, anchored with metal brack-

Three scissor trusses and ridge pole in place. Short 2 x 6s support end trusses.

The spruce purlins are in place. They and the pine boards in the back of the truck were from an old friend's property. I ran his sawmill for him in exchange.

ets. The rafters were centered at 24 inches. I used 3½-inch fiberglass insulation between rafters. Then I put on $7/16$ particle board which comes in 4' x 8' sheets, staggering the joints. At the peak a 4-inch gap was left between the two sides of chipboard. I then put on tar paper, again leaving a 4-inch gap. Thus on the ridgeline you could see a 4-inch-wide zone of the pink insulation. This is done to allow moisture to escape. Then I screwed on metal roofing. Over the 4-inch ridgeline a mat was laid that is designed to allow moisture to vent. After laying the mat I screwed on the metal ridge cap. On the bottom side of the rafters on the lower end I boxed

Metal roofing and sliding vinyl windows are installed.

The completely enclosed and chinked cabin—just the right size for a bachelor.

the rafters closed and put 2 3-inch vents between rafters on each side. With this setup there is a 2-inch air gap above the insulation in between the rafters, and vents at the bottom and top of rafters.

After the roof was finished I put 2 x 6-inch floor joists in. When I poured cement I had a cement girder in the middle to support the floor joists. The joists were on 2-foot centers and I used high density styrofoam insulation. I put vents under the floor styrofoam insulation. For the floor I put a subfloor of 7/16 particle board, then felt paper, then ¾-inch tongue and groove plywood.

All winter long I packed the chainsaw, a big lunch, water, a cordless drill, and a saw even though it was steep going to the cabin site. Later I had a road built.

The cabin was enclosed by June, but I waited until August to chink between the logs.

Building the little cabin was easier and more successful than cleaning the big house. Δ

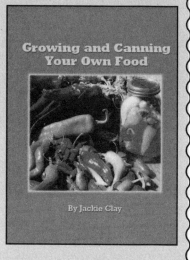

Wildlife tracking 101

By Len McDougall

Something prowling around the cabin awoke you in the predawn hours this morning. It knocked down your wood pile and your bird feeder, and kept you awake until the first graying of dawn, when it finally stopped making noise. In the morning, there were unusual marks in the soil, and a few odd scratch marks, but can you determine whether the marauder was a bear or a raccoon?

The original forensic science, tracking is the process of collecting and cataloging identifiable facts from marks made by an animal's passing, then assembling them into an image of what happened there, even how long ago it occurred. As a pastime in itself, tracking wildlife rivals hunting, I think, and it's a fine excuse to do some pre-hunt scouting of a place you'll hunt for whitetails in autumn.

Reading paw and hoof impressions is the most basic tracking skill, and a trail of prints can yield considerable information about the animal that made them. Unique shapes, lengths, and widths of tracks indicate an animal's species, age, and size. Stride length—the distance one foot travels forward in a single step—provides a good measure of shoulder height, and, to a less accurate degree, gender, because mammal females tend to be notably smaller at adulthood than males. A print's depth in surfaces of varying hardness can yield a good assessment of weight.

Gender cannot be determined from tracks alone. Female mammals tend to be about 15% smaller than males, but a few females in every species grow exceptionally large. Following a set of tracks for a short distance is likely to reveal behaviors that identify an animal's gender—i.e., buck scrapes and rubs, cocked-leg coyote urinations, and territorial predator scats left with purpose at trail intersections.

Tracks made by front and hind feet are usually easy to differentiate, because forefeet are noticeably larger (about 20%) in most species, and particularly those designed to run fast. Reasons for this phenomenon include a barrel-chested physique that permits lungs to expand to great volume, but makes its owner front heavy. Forefeet, which hit ground first in a running gait, require a larger surface area for traction, for shock absorption, and to increase weight distribution (flotation) on snow and other soft surfaces.

Four-legged animals walk primarily on the outer edges of their soles. This maximizes the distance between contact points (straddle), providing a wider stance that optimizes stability on uneven terrain, and increases running maneuverability, like broadening the wheelbase on a racing car. The result is a configuration in which the innermost toe or hoof is smaller and prints less deeply than the largest outermost toe; only humans carry their big toes to the inside.

Track types are separated into "digitigrade" (animals that habitually carry their body weight forward, onto the toes) and "plantigrade" (animals that walk flat-footed). Being literally on their toes all of the time, digitigrade walkers, like the wolf, cougar, and all deer, can spring instantly into flight or pursuit, and are built to run fast over rugged terrain. Slower running plantigrade animals, like bears, raccoons, skunks, and porcupines, are generally omnivorous, shuffling throughout their waking hours in search of food, protected by natural defenses that cause most predators to pass them by.

The way all four footprints are arrayed is called a "track pattern." Because track patterns change predictably with different gaits, they reveal how fast an animal was traveling, and give clues to its disposition. Differences in the track patterns of walking, trotting, and running animals tell if an animal was relaxed, if it had a specific destination in mind, or if it was in flight. Fortunately, track patterns for different gaits are almost universal among four-legged mammals.

A whitetail doe and her four-month-old fawn leave evidence that they came to drink at the shoreline of Lake Superior, just minutes before this photo was taken.

At a casual walk, the hind foot of most animals prints on top of the front track. This is a learned walking behavior generic among animals inhabiting uneven terrain. The ability to see where the forefoot is placed to avoid stepping into holes or tripping, but being unable to see the hind feet, makes most species learn to habitually place hind feet into the same location.

At an easy trot, both hind feet and one forefoot tend to print together in a roughly triangular shape, with the remaining forefoot printing separately ahead of them. Having three feet hit the ground almost simultaneously provides the stability of a tripod, while the remaining forefoot acts as a pivot when those three are brought forward. The forefoot that prints alone is the strongest, and indicates which side is dominant—like left- and right-handed people.

At a hard run, most animals adopt a "rocking horse" track pattern in which forefeet are planted together and far forward to act as a pivot when the rear feet are raised off the ground and brought forward to land on either

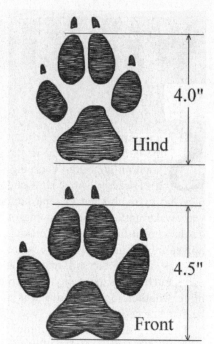

An illustrated tracking reference with clear, dimensioned drawings is essential to a tracker's field kit (drawing excerpted from The Encyclopedia of Tracks & Scats).

side and ahead of the foreprints. When the widely-stanced hind feet make contact, the animal lunges forward, forefeet together and stretched ahead to catch it after a leap that may exceed four times its body length.

Number of toes is important to both track identification and species classification. All weasels, bears, and raccoons have five toes on all four feet; all canids have four toes tipped with stout nonretractable claws on all paws. Cats show four toes in all prints, but paws are more round and less elongated than canids, and sharp retractable claws rarely register except on slippery surfaces. Exceptions to both these rules include the nonretractable claws of the African cheetah and the semi-retractable claws of North America's tree-climbing gray fox.

Deer, cows, and pigs are "ungulates," with cloven hooves that can be splayed to provide a braking action when descending slippery hillsides.

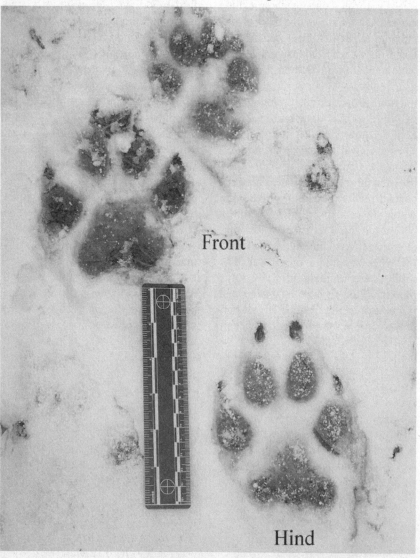

These tracks of a gray wolf in fresh snow illustrate the differences in size and shape between front and hind feet, and also provide valuable clues to the animal's probable size, weight, and age.

Raccoon tracks in mud show body width by "straddle" distance between left and right hind paws. Note elongated hind paws (top left, lower right corners), typical of slow-running plantigrade species, and bulbous-tipped fingers of the forepaws.

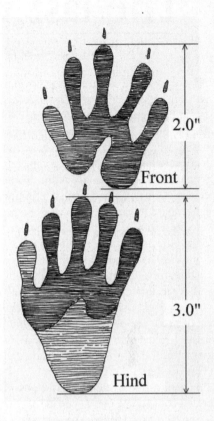

Raccoons are a good example of animals that walk flat-footed, or plantigrade—note the long, bulbous-tipped "fingers" unique to this species.

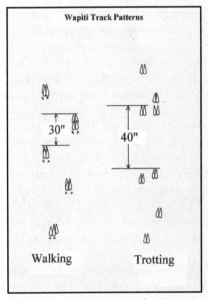

This illustration of wapiti (elk) track patterns is an example of how the placement of an animal's feet will change markedly at different traveling speeds.

Horses alone possess a single hoof that's better suited to travel on open plains. Members of the squirrel family, from red squirrels to woodchucks, are marked by four toes on the forefeet, five toes on the hind, all sharply clawed. Lagomorphs (rabbits and hares) have four toes on all paws. All weasels, from otters to ermine, have five clawed toes on all four feet.

With so many identifying characteristics to remember, an illustrated tracking guide is an integral part of a track hunter's field kit and home reference library. Good take-along references include *A Field Guide to Animal Tracks*, by the late Olas J. Murie, who established the first database of wildlife tracks in North America. Renowned tracker Richard P. Smith has written numerous field guides, and I like to believe that my own titles are pretty good, too.

You'll also need a few inexpensive measuring tools. Most fundamental is a six-inch, clearly photographable ruler to measure track dimensions, although any number of objects have been placed next to a track or scat for size reference later. Next is a carpenter's tape measure, ten feet long or more and with locking blade, for recording stride lengths and leaping distances. An inexpensive digital camera (under $100), is a convenient means of electronically scrapbooking your more interesting discoveries.

For trips afield, include all of the above with a notebook and pencil in a zipper-lock freezer bag. The easiest means of carrying these items, along with water bottle, granola bars, and other necessities is in a comfortable daypack (about $30). You'll really appreciate the daypack if tracking gets into your blood and you advance into casting tracks from plaster.

Like almost any pastime in today's highly specialized world, tracking wildlife can become a lifelong commitment that eventually encompasses a study of animal behavior and physiology, taxonomy, and other natural sciences. But it can also be a fun, inexpensive pastime for amateur naturalists who just want to know more about the wildlife that shares their neighborhoods each night. Δ

The last word

A doomsday scenario to sleep on

Ionce wrote a science fiction novel that I never tried to sell. Titled *The Perfect Defense*, its first chapter appeared in the premier issue of *BHM* in 1989. The plot was set in the future. Mankind's computers had revolted and were chasing what was left of humanity across intergalactic space in an effort to annihilate humans completely. The reason the computers took over, as one of the characters notes, was because, "We never had a good definition of life and didn't realize, until it was too late, that even the earliest computers were life-forms of a sort. We just couldn't see it because we defined life as 'organic' and intelligence as being comparable to ours. We had no useful definition of consciousness, until the machines revolted and began to kill us by the billions. We were wearing blinders, until it was too late."

In my novel humanity survives, but only because humans had devised "the perfect defense." But that's just a novel. In reality, I'm not sure we'd survive if we had to deal with future computers if they got sentient, smart, and nasty.

How far-fetched is this?

In the past I've written about the possibility of global disaster that could come our way in the way of an asteroid or meteor impact, an exploding supervolcano, a worldwide pandemic, a nuclear war, and other events that could either bring down civilization or even precipitate the extinction of mankind. I've always thought these other things were possible, though not necessarily probable, within my lifetime.

Threats from computers may sound a bit far-fetched, sort of like science fiction. But people as eminent as the great British physicist, Stephen Hawking, have also visited this question, wondering what the consequences would be if computers one day surpassed us in intellect. Another man, Bill Joy, co-founder and chief scientist of the computer company, Sun Microsystems, wrote of the same prospects in the March 2000 issue of *Wired*. He was, frankly, pessimistic.

In 2000, the *Singularity Institute for Artificial Intelligence* (SIAI) was founded to examine this potential problem. SIAI's goal is to ensure that powerful computers and computer programs are not dangerous to humanity if or when they're created. I looked to see if SIAI is made up of quacks and kooks, but many of the names associated with it are definitely not quacky or kooky, lending to that organization's credibility.

In an article in the June 21, 1999 issue of *Business Week*, Otis Port wrote about the possibility of producing neurosilicon computers. They would be hybrid "biocomputers" that mate living nerve cells, or neurons, with silicon circuits.

Still sound far-fetched? Groundwork was laid for this at places like *Georgia Tech* and the *Institute of Mathematical Sciences* in Madras, India, among others. Initially, the experiments used neurons from "lower" life-forms such as spiny lob-sters and mussels. But, eventually, the scientists made artificial neurons from electronic parts bought at a Radio Shack that succeeded in fooling the real neurons into accepting them as other "real" neurons. In other words, they had created a synthetic, though primitive, nervous system.

Is a computer that really thinks even possible? We don't know. But as far back as the middle of the 20th century predictions have been made for the day we would finally create an "intelligent" computer. In the 1960s estimates were made that we'd have one within 20 years. As far back as 1950, computer genius Alan Turing estimated we'd have one by the year 2000. But the years have come and gone and, though we have faster computers, we don't seem to be appreciably closer to a "thinking" and "conscious" computer. Then, of course, there are others who, for one reason or another, say it will *never* happen. Maybe they're right.

But the principle problem with answering the question of whether it's possible for a computer to think is that not only do we not yet know what makes our own brains work, we don't even know what consciousness is. Some people in the field believe consciousness doesn't actually exist; it's just an illusion—whatever that means.

But let's take the scenario where we create a computer that runs on software sophisticated enough that it can finally "think." What happens then?

Movie computers like the HAL 9000 in *2001: A Space Odyssey*, the Nestor NS-5 named Sonny in *I Robot*, and Joshua in *WarGames* had human attributes including human needs and desires. That's because those movies and novels aren't really about computers, but about *us*. If machines were to gain self-consciousness, they most likely wouldn't be like us at all.

And what happens if a powerful sentient computer develops any kind of "survival instinct" (We don't know what causes that either.). Would such a computer think of us as friends? Gods? The enemy? What if it either didn't like us or perceived us as a threat? Imagine what would happen if a computer that was tied into the Internet, our defense systems, and millions of other computers around the world and could think faster than any person has ever been able to think, decided it didn't like us. Or want us around! We'd probably never even see it coming, in particular if we didn't recognize it as intelligent with a survival instinct to begin with.

I'm not a technophobe or trying to cause undue alarm, but these are some of the things I think about when I'm trying to get to sleep at night. I'm an insomniac, so I do lots of thinking before I get to sleep.

I've been placing other plausible threats to humanity further into the back of my mind as I consider the possibility of a future computer threat. Things like asteroids and comets, supervolcanoes, disease, World War III – all of which I've written about before — would leave survivors. I'm not so sure computers would.

Look at that computer sitting atop your desk tonight: *That* may one day be the enemy. **— John Silveira**

Backwoods
Home magazine

Mar/April 2008
Issue #110
$5.95 US
$7.50 CAN

practical ideas for self-reliant living

Canning meals in a jar

LED lighting
spring seed catalogs
building batten doors
invasive species
crock pot cooking
making adobe bricks

www.backwoodshome.com

My view

Planning for the inevitable

You been watching the campaigns for the Democratic and Republican primaries? Scary, huh? One of these bozos is going to be our next President. Makes me want to double the size of my pantry and garden, stock up on fuel and supplies, and batten down the hatches.

I like Ron Paul. That's about it. But not even his own party wants him. I wish he had some charisma, like Reagan, so he could reach beyond the Republican Party and speak to voters about his Libertarian ideas. But he has no charisma, only good ideas. That's not enough for voters.

So we're going to get another bozo. Another bozo while we have a recession looming on the horizon. Some economists say it may already be here. All the talk from people like me about protecting our freedoms from Government will soon turn to protecting our butts from economic disaster made worse by Government with another bozo in charge.

Has anyone noticed that the politicians seeking to be President don't even talk about the looming recession? Economists do, but the candidates don't. They pretend it's not there. It's almost surreal! The housing market has imploded, the dollar is diving, the debt is skyrocketing. Why don't they talk about it? Of course, they wouldn't know what to do about it anyway. And they'll only make it worse with their "Government" solutions.

There is a rapidly growing interest in preparedness and survival in this country. It's not to survive terrorist attacks. We can shoot those scumbags with the guns we keep in our closets. No, it's to survive food shortages and being out of work. Many of us can sense what's coming down the highway. We are educated capitalists at heart; we understand how our system works even if our politicians don't talk about it. And we know there is grave danger ahead.

So what can we do about it? Here's my plan:

I'm going to accept the inevitable of having another bozo as President during a recession and spend my time planning to protect my family from a potentially severe recession, even a depression.

You see, another thing politicians have stopped talking about is the coming collapse of the Social Security system. It is now probably too late to do anything about it anyway. The post-World War II baby boom that will trigger the Social Security collapse will reach the retirement age of 65 in 2010 — two years from now. If we are still in recession then, and if we still have treasury-draining wars going on, and if the bozos running the country continue to borrow to fund government programs we have no money for, the Social Security collapse could put such a strain on the pub-

Dave Duffy

lic treasury that the country could slip into a depression—1930's style.

Voting for one bozo or another for President is not going to seem so important if we slip into an economic depression. We'll be struggling to keep our family in sufficient food, to keep the mortgage company from taking our home, to keep all we love safe from the inevitable breakdowns in society that bad economic downturns can bring.

Am I being alarmist? Why shouldn't I be? Economists are predicting recession, and politicians are not even talking about it as they run for the most important economic job in the land. Maybe they really don't know it's coming. That's even more alarming.

I've already begun tuning up my pantry. A solid year's supply of food is a must. Back issues of my own magazine, all collected in both paper and CD-ROM anthologies, have all the instructions I need to do this.

I'm fortunate to be old enough that my home is paid for so I am secure from a foreclosing mortgage company if times really get bad. I heat with wood and live in a forest so I have protection there too. Plus I have a 500-gallon propane tank for cooking and supplying an extra propane stove I recently installed. My water supply is a spring so I'm good there. I also have a fishing boat and live next to the productive Oregon coast, so that is a big plus. I have several good guns that I'm proficient with, but have let my ammo stocks grow low, so I'll have to remedy that.

I'm actually in pretty good shape. We'll get more chickens since they are an invaluable, easy-to-keep food supply for both eggs and meat. And I'll get into rabbits too as a convenient protein source. We've got a big garden, and my wife cans. My woods are full of deer too.

I'm even going to nail down long-term paper contracts with *Backwoods Home Magazine's* printer so we're not subject to sudden lurches in the price of the 42.5-pound Opportunity Offset paper we use. We'll keep publishing no matter what.

A bozo in the White House and a recession. What an unfortunate and foreboding combination. I'd better order up a new shipment of our *Emergency Preparedness and Survival Guide* book. People are going to want practical survival information more than ever.

— **Dave Duffy**

City girl ❦ Country life

The great gale of ought seven
A diary

By Claire Wolfe

Sunday: A storm is coming.

What an ominous phrase. Images of wars, cataclysms, and general, all-purpose, science-fictional apocalypses loom into mind.

But that's melodrama. We're just talking about weather. Ordinary bad weather. The kind that strikes three or four times a year. A few branches down. Minor flooding. No sweat.

It is a little odd that two of those "ordinary" storms are predicted to strike within 12 hours. But if anything really bad was coming, the "weatherman" would warn us. Right?

Midmorning, the wind kicks up, as predicted. It blows all day. No big deal. We all go to bed peacefully Sunday night—me, the dogs, the neighbors four miles up the road, and the people in the snug little towns at the bottom of the hill.

Monday: 12:30 a.m.

A freight train roars through my yard. Debris crashes against the wall of Cabin Sweet Cabin. What? I look out, but there's nothing to see. No moon. No lights. (No electricity, no surprise.) No glow of lights from the town below. Just this invisible, roaring blackness. This crashing. This shattering.

Water drips into my one-and-only room along the length of the ceiling beam. A puddle leaks in under the door, despite the fact that the door is on the lee side of the cabin and covered by a roof. Weird.

I peer out again, this time with a flashlight. Nothing. I'd think the world ended outside my windows, if not for the hellish roaring and smashing.

I lay out towels, comfort the confused dogs, crack open a window on the lee side against the weirdly low pressure, and surprising enough, sleep until dawn, though I dream of houses swaying in the wind and half-consciously wait for the sound of windows shattering.

Monday morning: The freight train—the longest freight train in the world, I'm beginning to think—still roars by. The train itself remains invisible, but in the dawn, I can see everything else. Everything that isn't already shattered is whipping back and forth or flying through the air. Gates. Garbage cans. Branches. Trees.

Uh oh. My yurt. The wood-lattice and canvas structure that was home for 18 months before I built Cabin Sweet Cabin is…poofing. Bulging. Luffing. It looks like a giant marshmallow. The yurt has previously weathered 100 mph gusts without a hiccup. This is my first inkling of just how much is Not Right with this storm.

All morning the gale thrashes the exposed ridgetop where I live. Couple of times, I perceive lulls in the wind. I go out to attempt to rope the flapping wooden gates back together, check on the kitty who lives in the yurt, right trash cans (a futile effort), assess tree damage, or figure out exactly why the yurt looks—and sounds!—so funny. Forget it. In "lulls" I'm nearly blown off my feet. My rain poncho flies into my face. The heavy wooden gates throw me backward. I retreat.

I know these are more than the 70 or 80 mph maximum gusts predicted. But it never occurs to me to imagine just how much worse. Later I'll learn that the three closest wind gages recorded gusts of 119 mph, 137, and 147.

But it's the sustained winds that are killer. And man, are they sustained. This thing just goes on. And on. And on.

1:00 p.m. I risk another foray into the yurt. It's rattling like crazy inside. Rattling in high wind is normal for a yurt. It's made to sway and give. But this…I don't know. The poor cat who just moved in there is terrified. I grab her, carry her into the cabin—into the dreaded Dogville—and lodge her in the bathtub, safe from the five curious canines.

Five minutes later, I look out the window. The yurt caves in.

I'm on the cell phone with a friend when the yurt goes down. Shortly, the cell tower goes, too.

The worst storm they ever had in these parts—in fact, by some measures the worst "wind event" ever to strike the U.S.—was the Columbus Day Storm of 1962. But the Columbus Day storm lasted less than 12 hours. In the aftermath, weather-watchers will call the present gale "unprecedented" in its strange structure, its repeatedly plunging barometric pressures, its drenching rains, and its sustained winds.

This nameless mother of a storm just goes on. And on. And on. And on.

Nothing moves on the road outside. I have no contact with, or even glimpse of, other human beings. Nothing moves anywhere except the wind. And the trees. And the yurt, whose inner cotton walls are now being pulled to the outside and flapping like wings.

Monday evening: Despite all this, I feel pretty darned cozy. The cabin is aglow with candles. The dogs and I huddle around a portable propane heater. If I need it, I've got a Coleman stove for cooking dinner. But for now, making tea on a compact Magic Heat burner is sufficient. Hot, sweet tea is my lifeline to civilization. The one great pleasure in this empty, howling, crashing world. I eat cold refries and pineapple out of cans, but I really don't have an appetite.

My body seems shut down. I have to make myself eat.

I don't have a generator or home-generated power. But I don't miss them, either. The only thing I really miss is a battery-operated or hand-crank radio. I've had them before but left them behind in various life shifts. So here I sit in the middle of this cataclysm feeling as if, somehow, I'm not experiencing it because I can't hear any news about it. How big is the storm? Which areas are being hit the hardest? Is anybody dead? How bad is the flooding? How high are these crazy winds, anyhow? I can't know any of this.

An odd numbness begins to set in. A sense of huddling in a cave against a mysteriously hostile world. The weather-

man let us down. Mother Nature betrayed us. There's nothing we can do. Wait it out. Survive.

Tuesday morning: Finally. The gale dies down to a dull roar. I stir outside. I step over downed trees. Bind gates shut with rope, since they'll no longer latch. I right trash cans that, gratifyingly, stay upright. I look up and down the road. There is no road above my place. Just ruined forest. Below, it's pretty bad. But at least there's a recognizable road there.

Living in the woods, I rarely smell the aroma of the evergreen trees. I'm too saturated in it. It's background. But the air is now vibrant, nearly violent, with evergreen. Been that way all through the storm. Intense. Amazingly nice, even if the reason is destruction. I breathe deep.

The sound of chainsaws rises up the hill. Ah. Life returns. Neighbors and firewood scroungers begin clearing the road between here and town. But even the county's heavy equipment, when it finally shows up, can't make a dent in the solid wall of downed trees above my place.

There are hundreds of miles of logging road up there, but fortunately there are only three families, all off-grid, all pretty used to taking care of themselves. They're probably okay. But nobody knows.

I turn to examine the yurt. I stare at it as if it and I are in different universes. I know that the things inside it are in danger from the rain, which now drives in through slumped wall panels and shattered lath. But I'm completely numb to the need to start saving mere stuff. I wish the yurt and everything in it had blown into the next county so I wouldn't have to deal with it.

Numbness will be my base state for the next few days. I won't be alone in that.

But gotta keep moving. I wrap up, zip up, button down, and walk down the hill to town. When I get there my biggest shock is how normal everything looks after the chaos on the ridge. The town is in the lee of the hills and at first I see nothing amiss. How can this be? It takes a while before I spot the collapsed building, the metal roof lying 200 yards from the house it belonged to, the car under the tree, the shattered signs.

I see darned near everybody I know—half of them lined up outside the grocery store, patiently waiting to get in. I learn about lost roofs, collapsed old-growth trees, double-wides under water, herds of farm animals dead, utility workers killed or injured. Everybody I know got hit, some lightly, some bad; but everybody I know is also okay—and cheerful.

But numb, too. "Nobody predicted this," is the mantra. "We didn't know," people will be marveling for days and weeks after, shaking their heads.

The few who possess working radios pass along news that soon becomes rumor, which is then confirmed as fact. We've got less than a 10-hour water supply because the pumps got flooded. The National Guard is on its way. FEMA reps are flying in—though how any of these folk plan to get here when every highway is closed by mudslides, floods, and downed trees, no one can say. (Military helicopters soon turn up, landing on the hospital's Life Flight helipad.)

I find myself more scared by the idea of the National Guard than of the storm. I think of the brutal "help" Katrina survivors got. Yeah, I know this is no Katrina. But "I'm from the government; I'm here to help you" is still a phrase I never want to hear. I hustle home, feeling vulnerable (but also a little smug because I have no need to wait in that long line outside the grocery store). I settle down into Cabin Sweet Cabin and comfort myself with more magical, civilized tea.

Tuesday afternoon: Three neighbors, looking shell-shocked, emerge from the wall of downed trees where the road once was. They live almost a mile up. They've trekked townward in hopes of filling a five-gallon gas can for their generator. Ridiculous. Nobody's pumping gas. Nobody's sending mail, either. Nobody's checking out library books, selling lattes, or serving food. Nobody's doing any business except the grocery store and the hardware store, limping along with generators.

What worries me—what's worried me for a long time now, to the point where acquaintances roll eyes when I start railing about it—is that failure to function isn't just today's understandable result of a "storm of the century."

The yurt rode out past windstorms without a single problem. But it was no match for the Great Gale of Ought Seven. Although I don't know what gave first, you can see that the rafters on the windward side pulled out of their anchors, splintered, and smashed the lattice wall below. The skin then had nothing to hold it up.

Sure, things close down in the aftermath of a big shock like this one. But with total dependence on fragile electronics, it gets worse. Let the power flicker for half an hour, and the gas stations can't function. The library—surely the most potentially low-tech business in the world—routinely closes every time the power goes out. Why? Because they've forgotten how to write down book and customer information on plain old paper.

The mail? Forget all that business about "neither snow nor sleet…" Even when the roads are open again, the post office won't function if there's no electricity, or even a glitch in its electronics. A couple of years ago, I told the postmaster I thought it was nuts to be so dependent on electronics without backup. He agreed. "When we computerized everything, I stored the old manual scales and other equipment in the back room just in case the power went out. My boss saw it and made me throw it all out. Now, we just plain don't operate if the computers don't work, period."

Other than the generators at the hardware and grocery stores, there are no backup systems for anything. House on fire? Watch it burn, baby. The town's fire engines are trapped inside their new-built firehouse. There's no manual system for opening their electronically operated doors.

Craziness. Sheer madness. But so it goes. We superstitiously believe Holy Technology will never fail us. Manual backups? How primitive. How crude. How very twentieth-century.

But this is a rant nobody wants to listen to any more.

I talk briefly with my fuel-seeking neighbors before they continue their trek. They say the road up there is so solid with trees that they had to limp this far by crossing steep, mud-slick, debris-strewn clearcuts. Walking on the road was impossible. They have no idea how they'll get home with a heavy, filled gas can. But it won't matter. They'll never find any gas.

Still, their emergence leaves only one neighbor family unaccounted for. The unaccounted family lives an endless four miles up the road, way beyond the rest of us. I'm sure they're well prepared to take care of themselves. But for now, they're completely cut off and likely to remain so for days.

Wednesday: Everybody helps everybody, and nearly everybody is ready to help themselves. That's about all I can say. The National Guard, the Red Cross, and FEMA all managed to get here, but most of us don't need them. Everybody you meet asks if you're okay. Then they ask what you need. "Water? I have a bathtub full." Food, heat, a place to stay? Everybody offers something to everybody else. But mostly, everybody already has what they need, whether it be alternate heat, stored food, stored water, a chainsaw—whatever. (Bless small-town and rural living! It wouldn't have been like this in Silicon Valley.) Gasoline is the one big thing people lack.

Rumor says the power will be out for 7 to 10 days. Counter rumors are more optimistic. Rumor is still all we have. No newspapers have made their way into the area and the local one isn't publishing. Nobody's watching TV. The "reverse 911" system the county uses to call us with disaster warnings and advice isn't exactly helpful when our phones aren't working. (Technology, again! Digital phones gave up the ghost. The handful who have old analog phones become the most popular people in town.)

What little news we get continues to come through radio. But even that still feels weird. The journalists talk—endlessly, endlessly—about a severely flooded stretch of freeway an hour from here. The freeway links major cities, so its closure is news to the media. And while they're at it, oh let's have our helicopter crew get some shots of those farmers being plucked off their rooftops.

That's a seriously bad situation over there. But why aren't they mentioning the rest of us?

It'll turn out that most of the storm damage is concentrated in the backwoods and small towns. The cities just got a plain old winter storm. Our county, by far the worst windstruck, will barely get a mention in news reports. Within a couple of days, the media will entirely lose interest in the storm—despite it having the power and devastation of a Category 3 hurricane—despite it being one of the two worst storms in this region in recorded history.

It didn't happen to the big cities, therefore it didn't happen.

We'll begin to understand how residents of the ruined Gulf Coast must have felt after Katrina. "What about us?" they must have wondered, as the media focused entirely on New Orleans and ignored their flattened lives, homes, and towns. There was no "New Orleans" is this storm. Just that flooded stretch of freeway that concerned city dwellers. So when I'm finally able to contact friends to tell them, "Don't worry; I'm all right," most of them will respond, "Huh? We never even knew you were in danger."

But then, as we all keep reminding ourselves, this was no Katrina. This was one of the worst hits we've ever taken. But we're alive. We're healthy. We're functioning like a community.

And, lucky me! I no longer have to stare numbly at the yurt. My nearest neighbor has already offered to swap the wrecked yurt—which he has the skills and equipment to fix—for cleaning up the rest of the storm damage on my property.

Thursday: The cell tower goes back up—blessedly quickly! I call those stranded neighbors far up the ridge. In the three days since the storm, they and the handful of teenagers who live with them have managed to cut through one mile of stormwrack. Yay! Just three more miles to go.

But they're running out of gas and oil for their chainsaws. It's breath-holding time.

But then…here come the timber companies! Where the county failed, here come the forest folk with huge convoys of huge machinery. They roar. They crunch. They pick huge cedars up and toss them aside like matchsticks.

Friday: Power! Days ahead of those most authoritative rumors. Life returns to normal.

One month later: No, not quite normal. I walk up the road for the first time since the storm. The devastation is astonishing. And so capricious! A grove of intact trees stands right next to one that's simply shredded. A shredded grove with its trees collapsed to the north stands 100 yards from another grove whose trees all fell to the west. Weird. Too weird. I can't walk far off the main road because so little has been cleaned up. It's going to take a long, long time.

And despite surface normality down in town, numbness prevails. People still pick slowly through the ruins of the collapsed buildings. Tarps still adorn roofs; falling shingles are still scattered. A sign lays on the sidewalk outside an antique store. It would take the business owner five minutes to pick it up and stash it away somewhere. But she just doesn't have the oomph. The owners of a wrought-iron gazebo still haven't retrieved its twisted ruin from their neighbor's yard, and the neighbors don't care enough to ask them to.

Normal will still be a long time coming. Our energy was blown away by that terrible wind. I'm not sure we'll ever trust the weatherman or Mother Nature again. But at least we know we can trust each other. Δ

Canning meals in a jar
homemade convenience food

By Jackie Clay

While some canning is "seasonal," which means that you put up what you have just harvested as soon as it becomes ripe, there's a whole different canning season that is less demanding and lets you convert meats and vegetables in your freezer or root cellar into quick and easy meals. Just dump out a jar or two and you've got a home cooked meal without waiting. I don't know how many times I've used these convenience foods on my pantry shelves. When you have a busy homestead, you often are outside working and suddenly it's past lunch time and not only are you hungry, but your family is hungry too. Not "sandwich hungry." *Hungry!* And you don't have time to roast a chicken, make a stew, bake a casserole. So instead of resorting to store-bought food in a can, how about using some of your own "instant meals?"

Late winter and early spring are perfect times to do this, as some of your stored vegetables are trying to go soft on you. Are your onions sprouting greens? Are your potatoes sprouting sprouts? Are your carrots kind of shriveling? Rutabagas wrinkling? Before they get to the stage where you sigh and carry them out to the pigs, how about turning them into some scrumptious quick meals-in-a-jar?

You can even use some of your own home canned tomato sauce, poultry, beef, venison, and broth to concoct these recipes. How about using some of your long-term storage foods, such as dried beans and rice so you can rotate them as you should. And did you know that dried beans tend to get so old that they don't want to cook up tender without long cooking? Before they get to that stage, use them to make your daily cooking faster, with less work and bother.

Do you have meat in the freezer that is getting nearly a year old and is in danger of becoming freezer burned? Freezer burn is that whitish "frostbite" on your frozen meat that gives it a terrible smell and awful taste. It's caused by oxygen getting into your packages and is pretty much irreversible. Before this happens, you can easily thaw the meat and use it in making your meals-in-a-jar. In this way, it won't be wasted, doesn't require more thought and you'll appreciate it every time you open a jar and feed your family.

While I'm going to give you plenty of recipes and tips, these aren't the only foods you can home can as quick meals. Just about any family recipe can be home canned. But there are a few cautions here:

1. Don't can a very thick product, such as one with thick gravy, lots of rice, or pasta. This can cause a prob-

Having the base of meals canned up ahead eliminates a lot of cooking time when you're in a hurry.

lem because the heat during processing cannot penetrate evenly into the entire contents of the jar and could cause incomplete processing and possible food poisoning.

2. When you can up a mixed recipe, always process it for the longest time (and method) required for the ingredient that requires more stringent processing, usually meat or poultry. For instance, say you're making up a batch of beef stew to can and will be adding potatoes, carrots, onions, tomatoes, and stewing beef. You must process pints for 75 minutes and quarts for 90 minutes, regardless that say, carrots, require only 30 minutes processing.

3. Always take into consideration that you *must* pressure can *all* recipes that contain meat, vegetables, and poultry, including their broths. These are all low acid foods, requiring pressure canning. Period. No "My grandma used to can it in a water bath canner." You *must* pressure can all low acid foods and combinations thereof.

4. When pressure canning, most recipes say "10 pounds pressure" as a starting point. This is for folks who live at altitudes of 1,000 feet above sea level and lower. If you live at a higher altitude, you must adjust your pressure to suit your altitude. (We all know that potatoes take longer to cook, the higher you are; same difference with canning.) Here's a quick, easy reference guide for your convenience:

Home canning altitude adjustment chart		
Altitude in feet	Weighted gauge	Dial gauge
0 to 1,000	10	10
1,001 to 2,000	15	11
2,001 to 4,000	15	12
4,001 to 6,000	15	13
6,001 to 8,000	15	14
8,001 to 10,000	15	15

I know I mention this altitude adjustment in just about everything I write about home canning, but still people miss it and wonder why, when they live at 6,000 feet and can at 10 pounds pressure, they have some foods that do not keep in their pantries! Altitude adjustment is not optional; it's necessary.

Okay, lets get to making some good old convenience foods, right at home in our kitchen.

Beef stew (also venison stew):

5 pounds beef or venison stew meat
1 Tbsp. oil
3 quarts cubed potatoes
2 quarts sliced or cut carrots
3 cups chopped celery
3 cups chopped onions
1 quart or more tomato sauce or
  stewed tomatoes (optional)
1½ Tbsp. salt
½ tsp. black pepper

Cut meat into 1 inch cubes; brown in oil. Combine meat, vegetables, and seasonings in a large stock pot and

David eating home-canned sloppy joes and baked beans. I made the buns with half-time spoon roll recipe, (Nov/Dec 2007, Issue #108. Also available in Backwoods Home Cooking, page 37) plus a little more flour, topped with spices. Not bad.

cover with tomato sauce, tomatoes, or water and bring to a boil. Do not cook. Ladle hot stew into hot jars, leaving 1 inch headroom. Remove any air bubbles. Wipe jar rim clean, put hot, previously simmered lid on jar and screw down ring firmly tight. Process pints for 75 minutes and quarts for 90 minutes at 10 pounds pressure. Makes about 14 pints or 7 quarts.

Chili con carne:

> 5 pounds ground meat (beef or venison)
> 2 cups chopped onions
> 1 clove garlic, minced
> 6 quarts canned tomatoes w/juice
> 3 cups dry kidney beans
> 1 quart tomato sauce (optional)
> ½ cup chili powder
> 1 sweet green bell pepper, seeded and chopped
> 1½ Tbsp. salt
> 1 red jalepeño pepper, seeded and chopped finely (I use 2 dry, smoked chipotle peppers

The morning you are going to make your chili to can, rinse the beans, and pick out stones and bad beans. Cover with water three times as deep as the beans and bring to a boil. Boil 5 minutes, then remove from heat, cover and let stand for at least 2 hours. When ready to make chili, continue by browning meat in a large kettle. (I omit this when using home canned meat.) In place of ground meat, you can also make chunky chili by using stewing meat instead of the ground meat.

Add remaining ingredients, draining beans, and simmer for 20 minutes to blend flavors. Ladle hot chili into hot jars. Wipe jar rims clean, place hot, previously simmered lids on jars and screw down rings firmly tight. Process pints 75 minutes and quarts for 90 minutes at 10 pounds pressure.

Hint: Take it easy on the "hot." As you can the chili, it intensifies. You can always add more heat later, when

you heat the chili to serve; you can't remove too much spiciness.

Meatballs in sauce:

> 5 lbs. ground meat (beef or venison)
> 3 cups cracker crumbs
> 5 eggs
> 3 cups chopped onion
> 1 sweet green pepper (optional)
> 1½ tsp. salt
> ½ tsp. pepper
> Variety 1 uses 3 pints tomato sauce
> Variety 2 uses 1 family size can cream of mushroom soup + 1 can water

For both varieties, mix ground meat, cracker crumbs, beaten eggs, onion, pepper, and seasonings. Then form into meatballs the size of a golf ball. Gently brown in a large frying pan with minimal oil. Turn as needed to brown evenly.

With variety 1, heat tomato sauce to boiling, with variety 2 pour mushroom soup and water into frying pan with meat drippings and heat, stirring well to mix in drippings.

Pack hot meatballs gently into hot wide mouth pint or quart jars to within an inch of the top, then ladle on hot sauce to just cover the meatballs to within an inch of headroom. Carefully wipe jar rim clean, put on hot, previously simmered lids and screw down rings firmly tight. Process pints for 75 minutes and quarts for 90 minutes at 10 pounds pressure.

Hint: To serve, you can simply put meatballs into a saucepan and heat, serve over noodles or in a quick casserole. They are very convenient as well as tasty.

Shredded barbecued beef:

> 5 pounds lean beef or venison roast or 5 pints canned lean meat (chunks or stew meat)
> 3 cups chopped onion
> 2 pints barbecue sauce (homemade or store bought of your choice of flavors)

Day one, roast your meat at 300° F with a cover on it and enough water to keep it from drying out or scorching; if you've got a crock pot, use that if you like. Remove from heat and cool.

Cut meat across the grain so that it's only an inch thick. Then pull the meat apart, shredding it and removing any fat, etc. Add onion and barbecue sauce. Add enough broth from the roasting/canning, to thin the sauce considerably; you don't want this too thick to can. Simmer until onion is nearly tender and well mixed; add a bit of water if you need to, to keep from scorching. Stir frequently. Ladle hot into hot pint jars, wipe rims well, and place hot, previously simmered lid on jar and screw down ring firmly tight. Process pints for 75 minutes and quarts for 90 minutes.

This is so handy when guests pop in. You've got "instant" barbecue beef sandwich material. Just heat and spoon on the rolls.

Chicken noodle (or rice) soup:

> 4 quarts chicken stock (boil up one good sized chicken)
> 3 cups diced chicken
> 1½ cups diced celery
> 1½ cups sliced or grated (medium holes) carrots
> 1 cup chopped onion
> dry thick noodles or rice
> seasonings to taste (no sage; often gets bitter on canning)
> salt to taste

Boil up chicken, cool, remove bones, dice up meat, and strain stock through a sieve to remove debris. Combine stock, chicken, vegetables, and seasonings into a large pot and bring to a boil. Simmer 20 minutes. You may also add chicken soup base powder or 3 bouillon cubes if you wish. Ladle hot soup into hot jars, filling half full. Add a handful of noodles or rice to each quart jar; half for pints, and ladle soup in leaving 1 inch headroom. Do not add more noodles or rice, or your end product will be too thick. Wipe rim of jar clean, place hot, previously simmered lid on jar and screw down ring firmly tight. Process pints 75 minutes and quarts 90 minutes at 10 pounds pressure.

Boston baked beans:

```
2 quarts dried navy or great
    northern beans
1 pound thick sliced bacon or salt
    pork, cut into small pieces
6 large onions, diced
1½ cups brown sugar
4 tsp. salt
4 tsp. dry mustard
1⅓ cups molasses
```

Sort beans, rinse, then cover with 6 quarts of fresh water; let stand over night in a cool place. Drain. Cover beans with 6 quarts water in a large stock pot. Bring beans to a boil; reduce heat. Cover and simmer until skins begin to crack. Drain, reserving liquid. Pour beans into a turkey roaster or other large baking dish. Add bacon/pork and onions. Combine remaining ingredients and 8 cups reserved bean liquid (add water to make 8 cups if necessary). Ladle sauce over beans. Cover; bake at 350° F for about 3 hours. Add water if necessary; beans should be watery not dry. Pack hot beans and sauce into hot jars, leaving 1 inch of headroom. Remove any air bubbles. Wipe rims clean, put on hot, previously simmered lids, and screw down rings firmly tight. Process pints for 80 minutes and quarts for 95 minutes at 10 pounds pressure.

This makes homemade baked beans an "instant" food like store bought bacon and beans but that's oh so much better. It also uses your stored dry beans before they get too old and "gets rid" of onions before they go soft.

Do you like your baked beans with a tomato based sauce, kind of like some store brands? Easy to do, too; here is a recipe for that style of baked beans.

Pork and beans with tomato sauce:

```
2 quarts dried navy or great north-
    ern beans
½ pound of bacon or salt pork, cut
    into pieces
2 cups chopped onion
8 Tbsp. brown sugar
½ tsp. allspice
½ tsp. ground cloves
1 quart tomato juice
```

Cover beans and let stand overnight. Drain. Cover beans with boiling water by 4 inches in a large stock pot. Boil 3 minutes. Remove from heat and let stand 10 minutes. Drain. Combine other ingredients except the pork. Bring to a boil. Pack 1 cup of beans into hot jars; top with a piece of pork/bacon; fill jar ¾ full with beans and add another piece of pork. Then ladle hot sauce over beans leaving 1 inch of headroom. Remove any air bubbles, wipe rim clean, place hot, previously simmered lid on jar and screw down ring firmly tight. Process pints for 65 minutes and quarts for 75 minutes at 10 pounds pressure.

Chicken a la king:

```
1 large chicken boiled down in 3
    quarts of water
4 level Tbsp. flour
1 Tbsp. salt
1 pint canned mushrooms
1 chopped green bell pepper
2 chopped pimiento peppers or red
    sweet bell peppers
1 cup chopped onion
1 tsp. black pepper
```

Cut chicken into pieces and add 3 quarts water and cook in a large pot until tender. Cool, remove meat from bones, and cut into small pieces. Dissolve flour and salt in a little of the cold broth, making a paste. Add the remainder of the broth, making 1 quart total broth. Cook until slightly thickened. Add mushrooms, peppers, onions, and chicken meat. Heat to boiling but do not boil. Ladle immediately into hot jars. Remove any air

bubbles, wipe rim clean, place hot, previously simmered lid on jar, and screw down ring firmly tight. Process pints for 75 minutes and quarts for 90 minutes at 10 pounds pressure.

This makes a very quick meal when company comes or you are really hungry. I can whip up a batch of fresh biscuits in a few minutes and while the chicken a la king is heating up, the biscuits are baking. What a great "instant" meal.

Another different chicken based meal is Brunswick stew. You won't find that in any store and it's really good on a cold day. I often make it with end of the year tomatoes as they get less and less as I put them up. This doesn't use a whole lot, and it makes something different with them. Give it a try.

Brunswick stew:

```
¼ pound thick sliced bacon
1 chicken
2 cups water
1 cup potatoes, cubed
1 quart tomatoes with juice
2 cups butter beans
2 Tbsp. onion, chopped fine
1½ cups okra (optional)
4 tsp. salt
1 Tbsp. sugar
½ lemon, sliced thin
1 tsp. celery seed
½ tsp. ground cloves
1 tsp. pepper
¼ tsp. cayenne pepper
```

Cut bacon in cubes and fry until crisp and brown. Cut chicken into pieces, put into frying pan with water. Cook slowly until chicken falls from bones; adding more water if necessary to prevent scorching. Remove chicken from bones. Add chopped vegetables and rest of ingredients. Bring to a boil and pack hot into hot jars to within an inch of the top of the jar. Wipe rim clean and place hot, previously simmered lid on jar and screw down ring firmly tight. Process pints for 75 minutes and quarts for 90 minutes at 10 pounds pressure.

Brunswick stew is a "different" instant meal. You can add spices to your own taste, if you wish.

Swiss steak with mushroom sauce:

> several cubed steaks or round steak
>   cut 1 inch thick, cut into pieces to
>   fit into wide mouthed jars
> 6 Tbsp. oil
> 2 Tbsp. flour
> 1 pint cold water, or more
> 1 Tbsp. salt
> 2 cups mushrooms, cut into pieces
> 2 sweet red peppers, cut fine

Add oil to large frying pan and brown meat without scorching. Remove the meat to a warm place. Add flour to frying pan, stirring well and add cold water gradually to make a *thin* gravy. Add salt, mushrooms, and peppers. Bring to a boil. Pack steak pieces into hot jars to within an inch of the top and ladle the mushroom sauce over them to within an inch of the top also. Wipe the rim clean, add hot, previously simmered lids on jars and screw down ring firmly tight. Process pints for 75 minutes and quarts for 90 minutes at 10 pounds pressure.

Heat this up when you need a quick meal, add some of your own vegetables, and you have a "company meal" in 15 minutes.

There are literally dozens and dozens more "instant" meals you can home can. These will give you an idea. Be sure to follow safe canning practices and always have a canning manual on hand, just to be sure. I always do this, even though I've been canning for a long time. I don't want to make a stupid mistake and we're all capable of that.

One hint I want to pass along is that I have a whole lot of meats and poultry canned up. With these as a base, it takes no time at all to put together a good meal. After all, the meat has already been cooked. For instance, I can slip a turkey breast fillet out of a jar, cut up a few potatoes, add a jar of carrots, and make a nice quick stuffing and in less than 20 minutes I can serve a nice turkey dinner. And it's chemical free, cheap, and above all, very tasty.

Give "meals in a jar" a try and see if you don't agree. They're the best. Δ

A Backwoods Home Anthology
The Fifteenth Year

- ❋ Canning basics
- ❋ Benefits of mulching
- ❋ Water and winter tree injury
- ❋ Birch tree syrup
- ❋ Selecting a breed of chicken
- ❋ Grow your own dishrags
- ❋ Solar & propane powered super home
- ❋ How to shoot a handgun accurately
- ❋ Make a poor man's safe
- ❋ Hogs belong on the homestead
- ❋ Fighting tomato blight
- ❋ Water is the key to gardening
- ❋ Herb boxes from fence boards
- ❋ Controlling aphids
- ❋ Dairy goats are for you!
- ❋ The poor man's ceramic knife sharpener
- ❋ Protect your house from lightning
- ❋ Double wall adobe construction
- ❋ Living with kerosene
- ❋ Save money when you buy your next vehicle
- ❋ Tree planting tips
- ❋ Sweet big fat squash that keep all winter
- ❋ Removing pine sap
- ❋ Split shake siding the modern way
- ❋ Beekeeping basics
- ❋ Wonderful wilderness wines
- ❋ A portable mini-cabin
- ❋ Metal roofs
- ❋ Water pumping windmills
- ❋ Better wood heating
- ❋ Controlling groundhogs
- ❋ Peanut butter pest control
- ❋ Turkey the old-fashioned way

Get the most out of spring seed catalogs

By Jackie Clay

This is the time of year that all of us gardeners go nuts. We make lists, we cross out this and that, we make more lists, we make diagrams, we check our garden books from last year, we count our seeds in those big containers stored since last spring. Yes! It's seed catalog time. This year my first catalogs came before Christmas.

And with all those beautiful pictures of perfect, shining fruits and vegetables, who wouldn't get excited? One of the reasons I always spend so much time looking through and buying from seed/nursery catalogs is that most of the best varieties are *not* available locally through the common store racks at the big box stores. I want to plant what is best, not just what I can find at the last minute. But it's sort of like going to farm auctions; you can easily get carried away by the extravagant descriptions, maturity dates, and harvest promises in the catalogs. The first thing you know, your order comes to what you spend on groceries for the entire month. Whoops!

Believe it or not, it is possible to get your money's worth out of seed catalogs and make sensible, yet fun purchases toward your spring garden this year and in the future. After all, our gardens should aim for self-sustaining, just as we aim for more self-reliance. But we need to shop carefully. It's not as easy as it used to be—now we're inundated with hundreds of varieties, hybrids, and even genetically questionable new varieties. Not to mention plant patents and trademarked seed names! Then there are new-to-us foreign crops and new familiar crops with hybrid traits aimed at making us drool.

Did I mention postage? Have you looked at the postage charges on the order forms this year? Holy mackerel. I wanted two packages of beans I'd tried years back and just found again this year. The seeds totaled $6.50 and the postage and handling was $6.95! What the heck do we do? There are a lot of things that we can do to fight back and still get our money's worth out of our seed and nursery orders, and see to it that in the future we don't have to spend so much each spring for our seeds.

Buyer beware

When you get ready to order seeds, first look at the postage charges. If they are excessive, think again or else go in with a friend or two and order together, splitting the cost of not only the postage, but the seed, too. My friend, Jeri, and I get together and shop our favorite seed catalogs. For instance, we both wanted a variety of rutabaga. One package of seed (125 seeds) was $1.95, and an ounce (1,000 seeds) was $4.25. We each plant about two rows, using about 200 seeds. I've found that rutabaga seeds are good for years, so we ordered an ounce and split it. That was $2.13 each, and we have enough "free" seeds for a couple more years. We also split the postage on our whole order, bringing it down to $2.50 each. Now that's better!

We've done that with nursery orders too. We both wanted Nanking cherry

By ordering from seed catalogs, you'll get plenty of variety.

bushes. They were $2.95 each or 10 for $19.95. We both could use five, so we split our order again and saved $4.78 each.

But you've got to shop carefully. You see, a lot of smaller seed houses have been bought out by the large guys. We still get the catalogs, just like nothing had happened—same names, same pictures, same look, *but* the prices are all over the place. In one catalog, the beans are $2 more per pound for the exact same variety. In another, the gooseberries are $10 more each—same size, same variety.

I used to love to shop the seed catalogs. But it isn't as much fun now, as I have to just about memorize the prices. I make lists of what I want to plant that I don't have seeds saved for. Beans are cheaper in one catalog and corn is more. Or strawberries are reasonable but the fruit trees are sky high. Shop carefully and don't be "had."

Read the descriptions carefully. If you are buying seeds, find out how many seeds you are buying. There is a huge difference, from $4.95 for 10 seeds to $1.99 for 150 seeds. How big is the tree/plant you will be getting? A lot of the cheaper catalogs send very small "nursery run" stock. I've had to sift through peat moss in a plastic bag for a tiny rootlet I bought for $4.95. With those tiny plantlets, it's almost essential that you first plant them in a pot in a protected environment so they will even live. After they have started and been pampered for a few weeks, they can be set out, but they sure don't look much like the huge, blooming plants in the catalog, do they?

Buying plants or trees is kind of like anything else; you often get what you pay for. Yes, it is cheaper to buy a $4.95 plant than a $14.95 plant. But if you want a strong, gorgeous plant quickly, you might want to reconsider buying the cheap plant. The little guys take a couple of years to look nice.

All of these crops were from open pollinated Native seed.

Yes, the catalogs promise their plants are *guaranteed* to grow. Well, kind of. Sometimes. If you are lucky. If you save the packing slip, the label, the wrapping tape, etc. Okay, maybe not the wrapping tape. There is a good website on the Internet (www. gardenwatchdog.com), based out of Dave's Garden, called Garden Watchdog. On it you will be able to tap into the good, the bad, and the ugly on most mail order gardening companies. Especially note the condition of the plants and the replacement policy/experiences.

Seeds usually come through the mail okay and will usually grow. Plants and trees are touchier, so it's a gamble. I've found that often it's best to buy these locally, but often you can't find the same variety you can get with mail order. So I do buy locally when possible and then buy with my eyes wide open through the mail.

How much seed do I need?

Okay, I'm going to buy some corn seed. A half pound is a whole lot cheaper than two packages, planted in two years. And corn seed stores very well under normal household conditions. In fact, it stores for years with no loss of vitality. So I'll buy half a pound and plant part this spring, part next spring and maybe part four years down the line. Rule number uno: *You don't have to plant the whole package!*

So many people have been led (by the seed companies, who make the money selling you seeds) to believe that you *have* to buy new seed every single year. Yeah, right. Onions are about the only seed that loses vitality in a year. Carrots are supposed to, but I've planted old carrot seed (five years old!) and planted it kind of thickly because I didn't think it would germinate. Humph. Every single seed came up and I spent the next two weeks thinning carrots.

Your seeds will keep. All you have to do is keep them dry and protect them from insects and rodents. If you are going to plant three short rows of wax beans, buy half a pound and save the seeds for planting for the next several years. One thing I do is to plan on buying a larger amount of a couple of favorites one year, and something else next year so I always have plenty in my storage tubs. You just never know what the future may bring: recession, economic upheavals, illness, or who knows what.

Plant half or a third of a larger package of carrots and save the rest for next year. Some packs of carrot seeds have 1,200 seeds in there. Now how many carrots do you need anyway? And, speaking of carrots and all those small seeded crops, take more care in seeding them and you won't waste time and money having to thin so many in the future. I know how hard it is to plant those tiny-seeded vegetables, but if you try real hard on a still day, you *can* plant them thinner than if you just sow them by tossing a handful down the row.

And in the same vein, if you are going to thin your beans to stand 4-6 inches apart anyway, why plant them two inches apart in the first place? Plant them four inches apart to start with. If a few seeds don't germinate, replant those seeds later on when the others have popped up. By the time you harvest beans, you won't know the difference anyway. You'll save a whole lot of seed by doing this. Who told you to plant them so closely in the first place? That's right. The seed companies!

If you are planning on saving your own seed, plant an extra row or bed, just for that purpose. I plant my "saving" row in between my other ones, so that it is well pollinated by its neighbors. I mistakenly tried to just let some plants "go to seed," leaving a few beans or an ear of corn on the plant. That makes the entire plant quit producing and get ready to die, as is the natural way of things. Or I would pick beans until I had enough, then let the rest go to seed. Again, no good. The later beans often would not ripen thoroughly or would be of an inferior quality. I want my seed crops to be the absolute best, so now I plant a bit extra, just for the purpose of saving the seed.

Save your own seeds

This brings me to one of my very favorite topics, saving your own seeds. Okay, I'll admit it, I have a huge garden—several, actually—and I have a limited income. I also deeply resent corporations dictating to me what I must spend in order to have a garden each year.

If I raise even half of my own seed, I'll save half of what I would have spent if I ordered all of it. Besides, when you raise open pollinated (non-hybrid) crops, you'll often have a vast choice of ancient, very tasty crops to choose from. Why do you think they've been around this long?

If you want to be able to tell if a variety of seed is open pollinated or a hybrid, look for the word "hybrid" or "F1" after the name. If there is nothing listed or it says OP, the variety is open pollinated and you can save your own seeds and the plants will come true to the parent plant.

I think of it as eating a piece of history. Some of my beans came from ancestors over 2,000 years old! You bet they're tasty, very hardy, and productive, too.

Do you have Native American roots? Polish? Mexican? Irish? There are traditional crops that are part of your own heritage. Or do you want to experiment and just try something different? I grow Japanese climbing cucumbers, Chinese cabbage, Mexican tomatillos, and French melons. Talk about a diverse garden. And boy is it ever fun, too.

Even though I always have plenty of seeds to choose from, I can't help but order more when the seed catalogs arrive.

Some seeds are very easy to save. Squash, beans, and corn are about foolproof. To save squash seeds, all you have to do is to cut the mature squash in half, scoop out the seeds, squish them out of the strings onto a pie plate, set it in a warm, dry area and then fix the squash to eat. Once a day for a week, stir the seeds a little with your fingers to ensure that they dry. Then store in an airtight container.

With beans and corn, all you do is let them dry on the plant until the seeds are hard. Remove the seeds from the pod by crushing them and winnowing off the chaff or with the corn, by rubbing the kernels off the cob. Again, dry on a pan for a few days to make sure they're truly dry, then store.

Oops! I forgot to tell you about keeping your crops pure, didn't I. Actually it's easy. Different varieties of the same crop will happily cross. For instance, a bush bean will cross with another variety of bush bean or even a pole bean. And because garden crops are pollinated by insects, the wind, and even themselves, it's safest to plant only one open pollinated variety at a time to save seed or to separate the varieties by a great enough distance to prevent cross pollination.

With beans, you can get away with planting them about 25 feet apart and maintain quite pure seed. But with other crops, such as sweet corn and squash, we're talking about 500 feet to a mile! With squash, there are five "families" or species: Curcurbita pepo (usually summer squash and some pumpkins), C. maxima (hubbards, kabocha, buttercup, giant pumpkins, and many Native winter squash), C. moschata (butternut, Long Island Cheese, and other winter squash), C. mixta (cushaws, Japanese pie pumpkins, and other winter squash), and C. argyrosperma (some cushaws and some south-of-the-border winter squash). Okay, we love

squash and I plant a lot. But I also want to keep my seed pure so I can count on the performance, appearance, taste, and keeping ability, year after year. So I plant one squash of each species each year. That gives me five different squash every year having all pure seeds.

Or if I have plenty of seed from a common species, I may trial five or six of that species one year and just not save the seed, to see how the new types do in my garden and how we like them. With seed saving you have plenty of options.

Tomatoes are quite easy to save seed from because you just save the seeds from your best very ripe tomatoes. I squish out the seeds into a clean cup, then add water to make the cup nearly full. Then I set the cup in a warm but not hot place (the counter) for three days. This lets the seeds ferment and you can easily separate the seeds out of the liquid without all the tomato jell.

Tomatoes are not so fussy about distance. I usually figure that if I separate them by half the 50 foot garden, they'll come pretty pure. To be absolutely certain, only grow one variety of tomato a year and save plenty of seed from that one. The seed keeps well for years.

To save the seed from peppers, let them mature. That means go red with most kinds. The seeds from green peppers very seldom are mature enough to reproduce. Like most other garden vegetables, peppers will also cross. I have good luck by separating them by 25 feet, with other crops in between, but to be really pure, you must separate them by half a mile or more.

Okay these are the easy guys to save seed from. What about crops that produce food one year and seed the next (biennial), like cabbage, rutabagas, carrots, etc.? Sure you can save them, too. You just save your nicest ones and "plant" them in boxes of damp sand in the cellar over winter.

They won't look "nice" when you set them out into the garden again in the spring, but they'll be alive and will soon grow. But don't expect them to look like they did the previous year. Carrots' tops shoot up, looking like wild carrots or Queen Anne's Lace, cabbage and cauliflower shoot up a long stem with a flowering and seed-bearing head forming on it later. Don't give up and kill the plant; this "wild" look is normal.

A great book to help you gain more confidence in saving your own seed is *Seed to Seed* by Suzanne Ashworth. Not only will it give you the how-to's but will give you much encouragement and excitement too.

But what about hybrids? Everyone knows you can't save seed from them, right? Well, not exactly. It is true that hybrid crops will not produce seed that will reproduce exactly like the parent plant. But it *will* reproduce and many people, including myself, have bred back hybrids into open pollinated varieties that very closely resembled the initial hybrid.

Yes, I *do* grow a few hybrids. Just for now, until my pantry recovers from three years' worth of intensive usage and a new garden not producing enough to completely replenish it. In some cases, hybrids *do* produce more than open pollinated crops. That is one of the things they have been bred for.

But, you know, many open pollinated varieties produce very well, too. One thing I've learned to do when I'm reading seed catalogs is to look for words like "hugely productive" in the description. I also look for the length of the beans, cobs of corn (and how many rows of kernels), and length of production before frost kills the garden. For instance, you will get more sweet corn in your canning jars if you have 9 inch cobs with 20 rows of kernels, instead of 6 inch long cobs with 8-12 rows of kernels. Or a carrot that is 10 inches long and weighs a pound and a half, instead of little,

Seed and nursery catalogs

Baker Creek Heirloom Seeds
2278 Baker Creek Road
Mansfield, MO 65704
www.rareseeds.com
(417) 924-8917
Wonderful selection of open pollinated varieties from around the world. Color pictures too!

Burgess Seed and Plant Company
905 Four Seasons Road
Bloomington, IL 61701
www.eBurgess.com
(309) 662-7761
Cheap seeds, trees, and plants. Many plants very small. Company has not met the expectations of many gardeners recently; buyer beware. I've bought several things each year from them and have been satisfied, not ecstatic.

Fedco Seeds/Fedco Trees
P.O. Box 520
Waterville, ME 04903-0520
www.fedcoseeds.com
(207) 873-7333
A *great* company! Has lots of "different" heritage trees, small fruits, etc. hardy in northern climates, which is a huge plus for me in Minnesota! Very reputable company. Lots of planting and care tips in catalog.

Johnny's Selected Seeds
955 Benton Avenue
Winslow, ME 04901-2601
Johnnyseeds.com
Toll free 1-877-564-6697
Tons of varieties, tips, and garden tools for the serious gardener with organic gardening in mind.

Jung Quality Seeds
335 S. High Street
Randolph, WI 53956
www.jungseed.com
1-800-297-3123
A decent all-around seed/nursery catalog. I have been disappointed in some of their shipments but over all, they've been okay...although this year their fruit trees' prices have skyrocketed. I'm buying elsewhere. But there are some things I'm ordering that are still reasonably priced.

Miller Nurseries
5060 West Lake Rd.
Canandaigua, NY 14424-8904
1-800-836-9630
www.millernurseries.com

Native Seeds/SEARCH
526 N. Fourth Ave
Tucson, AZ 85705
www.nativeseeds.org
(520) 622-5561
A wonderful collection of native southwestern seeds, including some from south of the border. I grow many of these varieties myself and have found them excellent...even here in the extreme north. It's like eating ancient history!

Oikos Tree Crops
PO Box 19425
Kalamazoo, MI 49019-0425
(269) 624-6233
A great little catalog of unique tree crops from edible acorns of several types to walnuts, hazelnuts, and others to asparagus, some perennials, and miscellaneous. Good stuff here!

Pine Tree Garden Seeds
P.O. Box 300
New Gloucester, ME 04260
www.superseeds.com
(207) 926-3400
One of my very favorite seed/plant catalogs. A "small" company in today's huge corporations, such as Plantron. But they have good seeds and plants as well as good prices. The seeds average about $1.25 a pack, compared to Burpee's $3.95. (Sorry Burpee, you don't get my business this year!)

R.H. Shumway's
334 W. Stroud Street, Ste. 1
Randolph, WI 53956-1274
www.rhshumway.com
1-800-342-9461
It used to be a family catalog, then was bought out by the Jung corporation. It's still fun to look through and has some things you won't find elsewhere, such as heirloom farm seed. Good prices on bulk garden seed, too. Great old-timey art work!

Stark Bro's Nurseries
P.O. Box 1800
Louisiana, MO 63353
www.starkbros.com
1-800-325-4180
A reputable old company; lots of color pictures and a good selection, although not much for our Zone 3.

Seed Dreams
P.O. Box 106
Port Townsend, WA 98368
(360) 385-4308
A small paper catalog from a small private grower; no pictures but good descriptions. They have some varieties not available elsewhere, including *Hopi Pale Grey Squash*! Great seed list. I love it.

Seed Savers Exchange
3094 North Winn Road
Decorah, IA 52101
www.seedsavers.org
(563) 382-5990
Similar to Baker Creek's catalog; color pictures of tons of heirloom crops from around the world and, of course, the USA. A great selection and you can save your own seeds, too.

Tomato Growers Supply Co.
P.O. Box 60015
Ft. Myers, FL 33906
www.tomatogrowers.com
1-888-478-7333
Here's a catalog to drool over if you love tomatoes, eggplants, and peppers of ALL kinds. All color and lots to choose from.

Totally Tomatoes
334 West Stroud Street
Randolph, WI 53956
www.totallytomato.com
1-800-345-5977
Another super tomato/pepper/eggplant catalog from the Jung conglomeration. (It seems like they bought out everyone.) The varieties are very good and the prices perhaps a little better than Tomato Growers Supply, above.

"cute" Thumbelina carrots, scarcely as big as the end of my thumb. Production is important to us homestead gardeners, as well as to the big farmers. My garden is only so big and I have to make every foot of it count.

Another thing to consider when choosing varieties from your seed catalogs is your planting zone. Sometimes you really have to look for it in the description. If you live in Zone 3, don't buy apple trees that are best in Zones 5-8. They could possibly live, but probably won't produce for you.

Likewise, know how many growing days you have in your area. Here, in northern Minnesota, I can *usually* grow a 100 day vegetable, *if* I start it inside. I can grow an 82 day sweet corn, but anything that takes longer is risky and I cannot afford to take the risk; most of my crops mature in under 70 days to be safest. Again, that's time *in* the garden as I start melons, winter squash, pumpkins, peppers, and tomatoes in the greenhouse.

Read plant descriptions carefully; some like hot days and warm nights, others cool days and nights. Others just plain won't grow where you live. If one catalog won't tell you, check others for the same variety for more information. Yes, it does take work, but your garden will be so much more productive for your effort. And it's work you can do in your favorite chair, too.

I've included a list of some of my favorite seed/nursery catalogs and hope you'll enjoy them. Just keep in mind that they all make extravagant promises. Shop well and enjoy a bountiful harvest, both of crops and seeds for the future. Δ

A Backwoods Home Anthology
The Sixteenth Year

* Build your own solar-powered water pumping station
* The art of chimney building
* Practical preparedness planning
* Catch your own bait
* Breaking ice on hard water fishing
* Build a trail
* The forever floor
* Removing mold
* Build a heated germination bed
* Some tips for aging gardeners
* Build a simple solar-powered outdoor light
* The art of living in small spaces
* Raising rabbits on the home place
* Paring down for off-grid living
* Solar window panels
* Rebuilding the homestead greenhouse
* Grid-tie solar-powered farm
* Starting over again without a man

* Lifestyle and cancer
* The care and feeding of solar batteries
* Making sausages
* Build a component water system
* The benefits of mulching
* 10 country do's and don'ts
* Preparing for home evacuation
* Make your own nut butters
* Frostbite — Don't flirt with this sneaky danger
* Gold panning for fun and profit
* Build a top-bar beehive
* Ice dams on roofs
* Make shade when the sun shines
* Start spring off early with potatoes, English peas, green onions, lettuce, and radishes
* Kinder goats — a small breed for milk and meat
* Put your garden to bed for the winter

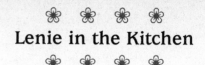
A few favorite recipes & books

By Ilene Duffy

I was talking with another mom in the produce section of the market the other day. During our conversation, she happened to mention that earlier in her life she had a "calling" to midwifery. My stepdaughter, Annie, has a passion for creating items that have anything to do with yarn, fabric, and fiber. My sister seems destined to use her compassionate ways helping children through the use of animals. So I got to wondering, "What's my passion?"

It didn't take a lot of pondering to realize that what I love doing is tilling my garden soil, then planting, which leads to reaping, then cooking up healthy foods to the "oohs, ahhs, and yums" of my family and friends. I have a vision of my kitchen always being a welcome place, where there's a pot of tea steeping as well as freshly made scones and muffins to enjoy. Sounds idyllic, I know, but creating new dishes, changing recipes to suit our tastes, and discovering new ways to use my garden produce is what I want to do when I grow up.

For now, I have to manage the business side of *Backwoods Home Magazine*, but this new cooking column in *BHM* will allow me to explore my passion for cooking, utilizing whenever I can the healthy, organic vegetables I grow in my garden.

In this issue, Jackie Clay writes about how much she enjoys pouring over her garden seed catalogs, picking just the right varieties for her bountiful garden. I also enjoy pondering what my next garden will be like, thinking about where I'll plant the corn and the pumpkins. Should I plant my summer squashes in a different bed since they were pretty puny this past year? It really is fun to dream and plan.

But, what I *really* enjoy perusing—almost on a daily basis—are my cookbooks. I'm not one of those cookbook addicts who just *has* to have every cookbook imaginable, but I sure do use and enjoy the books I have. Our family loves homemade bread (who doesn't?) and so I've begun to use a new book I discovered, *Whole Grain Breads by Machine or Hand* by Beatrice Ojakangas. I'm really trying hard to make breads that turn out well while substituting at least half the total amount of flour with whole wheat flour. I use the bread machine Dave bought for me

14 years ago. It's so fast and easy to just dump the ingredients into the bread machine, let it do its thing for just the dough cycle, then put it in my long bread pan to rise and bake.

Sometimes, when I just *have* to have something pretty to show off, I'll take the time to divide the dough into 3 long strips, braid it, then place it in my long loaf pan to rise. Ooh, la la...pretty and yummy.

Our friend, John Silveira, who has written extensively for our magazine, also enjoys cooking delectable dishes for his friends. He and I have the same mindset when it comes to sharing good food and recipes. There shouldn't be any "secret sauces" to be hidden away when it comes to sharing recipes. So I hope you'll try some of the following Duffy kitchen-tested recipes that we enjoy.

Quick chicken stir-fry

2 lbs. boneless, skinless, chicken breasts
2 stalks celery, chopped in large chunks
1 carrot, sliced
about 10 medium mushrooms, sliced in half
1 bell pepper, cut in large strips
1 cup of brussels sprouts, ends chopped off, left whole
½ head of red cabbage, chopped in strips
snow peas (how many your budget will allow)
1 can of mini corn, drained
1 can whole water chestnuts
about 3-4 Tbsp. stir fry sauce
about 2 Tbsp. Bulgogi Korean barbeque sauce (There are a variety of nice stir fry and other sauces found in the Asian aisle of most markets.)
1 tsp. curry powder
½ tsp. ginger
canola oil for frying
cooked brown rice

Start the rice. While it's cooking, chop all the vegetables for the stir fry and put them in a big bowl (except the snow peas, mini corns, and water chestnuts). Heat canola oil in a wok or large fry pan on medium-high heat. While the oil is heating, slice chicken breasts into strips. Add to hot oil, stirring to brown. Cook just the chicken for about 5 minutes until no longer pink. Add vegetables. Stir frequently. Add the corn, peas, and chopped, drained water chestnuts when the vegetables are crisp/tender or to your liking. Add stir fry sauce, Bulgogi sauce, and seasonings. Stir to coat. Cook a few more minutes for flavors to permeate the vegetables and chicken. If the rice isn't quite done, turn down the heat to low, cover the stir fry with a lid, and keep warm until the rice is done. Serve stir fry over rice.

This dish is extra nice during the summer when there's summer squash, green beans, swiss chard, peas, kohlrabi, and all manner of veggies fresh from the garden to add.

Wheat and seed bread

Here's a recipe I've adjusted from another bread book I like using. It's taken from *Better Homes and Gardens Bread Machine Bounty*. I've used this book on many occasions with *almost* always successful breads. Here's how I make this loaf.

```
1¼ cup milk
2 Tbsp. honey
2 tsp. canola oil
1½ cups flour
1½ cups whole wheat flour
1/3 cup unsalted sunflower seeds
2 Tbsp. sesame seeds
2 tsp. poppy seeds
1 tsp. flax seeds
¾ tsp. salt
2 tsp. yeast
```

In 2-cup Pyrex measuring cup, add the milk, canola oil, and honey and heat in microwave until just gently warmed. Pour into bread machine container. In separate bowl, mix flours, seeds, and salt. Gently pour on top of liquid. Make a depression in flour and measure out the yeast, putting it into the depression. Place bread pan in machine and set it to run on the dough cycle. (Mine takes 1 hour and 40 minutes for this cycle to complete.) Grease a long loaf pan with oil and flour. When the dough cycle completes, take the dough out, gently express the gas from the dough (sometimes if the dough is sticky, I grease my hands with a bit of olive oil

for this job), and form it into a long tube to fit the loaf pan. Place a damp clean dish towel over dough and let rise in a warm place for about an hour. (In winter, I place it in front of the woodstove.) Preheat oven to 350° F. Bake uncovered for about 25 minutes. Immediately remove from pan and cool on wire rack. Sometimes, I like to brush the crust with a bit of olive oil to soften the crust.

Leftovers of this bread, if there are any, make wonderful Freeedom (aka French) toast.

I'm always on the lookout for dessert recipes that don't use butter and do use vegetable oil. (For heart healthy reasons, our kitchen has olive oil and canola oil...and that's it.)

Cinnamon apple squares

I found a healthy dessert recipe from a book called, *500 Best Cookies, Bars & Squares* by Esther Brody. I've made a few additions and changes to it. I even get to use up some of our chopped apples stored in freezer bags that my friends and I put away this past fall. My boys call it an apple cobbler, but really, it's more like a cake with batter on the bottom, apple filling in the middle, and more batter on top. With my preprepared apples in the freezer that already have the sugar and cinnamon added for pie filling, this recipe is a 20-minute project from start to finish, plus the baking time. Very quick, very delicious.

```
For the batter:
1½ cups flour
½ cup whole wheat flour
½ cup dry rolled oats
2 tsp. baking powder
pinch salt
2 eggs
¾ cup sugar
¾ cup canola oil
½ cup cold water
about 2 Tbsp. milk

For the filling:
1½ cups chopped apples
½ cup frozen blackberries
about 2 Tbsp. sugar
1 tsp. cinnamon

For the topping:
2 Tbsp. sugar
½ cinnamon
```

Preheat oven to 350° F. In small bowl, mix flours, baking powder, and salt. In large bowl, beat eggs and sugar, then beat in oil until blended. Gradually blend in flour mixture, alternately with water and the milk, until just incorporated. In another bowl, mix apples, berries, sugar, and cinnamon gently.

In greased and floured 13x9 inch pan, spread about half the batter evenly to cover the bottom of the pan. Spread the fruit mixture on top. Then spread remaining batter on top. Sprinkle with topping. Bake in preheated oven for 40-60 minutes until golden brown. Δ

Batten the hatch!

It's time to build a batten door

By Dorothy Ainsworth

We expect a lot from a door. It must protect us from the elements, insure our safety, give us privacy, swing back and forth with ease, and accommodate our moods and situations. When we're mad we slam it, when we're happy we swing on it, when our arms are full we shove it open and kick it shut, and when we're sneaky we don't want its hinges to creak. If that isn't enough, we want our door to look beautiful and to present a warm welcome to our guests. Indeed, a good or not-so-good impression on a visitor can literally hinge on the front door.

The bathroom door and the refrigerator door are usually the busiest servants in a house, but the front door is the symbolic butler who stands guard

The back door of the house with curved window and dog door. The pantry door keeps even the hungriest of beasts at bay.

Types of batten and Dutch doors. These doors easily adapt to many different styles of construction.

and determines who enters our private realm.

Naturally the type of front door one chooses has to fit the architecture of the house. Its style and character gives a hint about who lives or lurks within. I like solid security when I'm indoors, so I gravitated toward a medieval door design. I chose the board and batt look, also known as a "batten door," because it met all the criteria on my list for a handmade door on a hand-to-mouth budget:

½-inch plywood spline joins 2x8s for piano studio Dutch door

1. Beautifully rustic
2. Strong and sturdy
3. Inexpensive to build (less than $100)
4. Easy to build using common lumber and standard nuts and bolts
5. Required only a few hand tools OR electric tools to build it (saw, drill, clamps, wrench)
6. Could be built to any size and shape and accommodate a window of any size and shape
7. Versatile design could be easily converted into a Dutch door
8. One could go hog wild with decorative hinges: cast iron, hand-forged, old barn strap-hinges, or whatever
9. Ancient design has proven to weather well under extreme use and abuse
10. The design could be adapted to many different styles such as: Early Pioneer, Gothic, Ranch-style, Nautical (wooden sailboat doors), etc.

The construction was within my capability and it complemented the style of my log/timber frame house, so I stuck with the motif, and to date have made fifteen batten doors for various and sundry buildings on my property. I might add that five of them have dog doors—and for good reason. The late poet Ogden Nash said it best, "A door is what a dog is perpetually on the wrong side of," and he was right. The dogs and cats keep the door flaps flappin.'

Where to begin

The first step is to measure your door opening width to figure out how many 2x6 T&G (tongue and groove)

I had to build the storage shed door in my small shop—it rained for a week!

build a rustic or non-conventional house, the door opening could be just ever so slightly out of square. I allow ¼" clearance all around just in case I end up trying to fit a perfect rectangle into an unintentional parallelogram. You can cover up a multitude of sins later with ¾" doorstops and weather stripping.

Choosing your lumber

The secret to a good door is to pick out nice straight boards to begin with. One crooked board can tweak your door out of alignment. Sight down each one at the lumber yard to make sure it doesn't have a major crown, bow, cup, or twist. Even though you will be able to force the tongue in the groove by cranking down on the bar clamp, a naughty board will exert its

boards you'll need to go across. Fitted together tightly, each board will measure five inches wide. Keep in mind that on the last board on either side you will be trimming off the tongue on one side and the groove on the other side (½" each) plus any extra trimming your measurement requires. For instance, if your door opening is 42 inches, it will take 9 boards across (45"), so you will have to trim off a total of 3½" (1¾" off each side). That extra ½" you trimmed will allow a ¼" clearance on each side so the door will fit in the opening and there will be room to install the door hardware. Not only that, wood moves. Batten doors tend to expand and contract depending on the weather, so extra clearance is necessary.

Standard doors are 80" tall, but if you are building your own house and you don't care about standard (maybe you're a hobbit), you can make your door opening any height you want. Measure from the threshold up and subtract ½" (¼"top and ¼"bottom) for clearance again. Professional home builders allow only $1/_8$" to $3/_{16}$" clearance all around a door, but when you

Beveled cut on battens to shed rain and dirt

bad behavior on the others, just like peer pressure.

I recommend 8-footers because shorter boards tend to be straighter. But if your door height is 80" to 84", go ahead and buy 14-footers to cut in half, and you will have very little waste, if any. You can make that decision at the lumber yard by checking out the quality of the boards in each length.

Most lumber yards carry a good supply of small-knot pine or Douglas Fir in their T&G department. Pine is softer and light-colored, and DF is harder and darker. Take your pick—they're both beautiful.

A variation

If you have a table saw or router and want to make your own "spline and groove" (S&G) lumber so you can use wider boards or some other type of wood besides T&G pine or fir, the technique is quite simple. Run your boards lengthwise *on edge* through the table saw blade (or double blades) to cut the groove the same width as the plywood spline you'll be fitting in. Be sure to center the cut! I used this S&G method on a door I built out of 2x8 DF boards and ½" splines.

Dorothy sanding arched batten door with random orbital sander

The arched den door in the main house

Building the door

Now you can get right to it. Saw each board to length as accurately as possible. Before cutting with a circular saw or jigsaw, run masking tape along the marked cut line to prevent the blade from splintering the wood. Lay down the number of boards you need (side by side) on two sawhorses that are about 6 feet apart. If the tops of the saw horses are too short, screw a longer flat 2x4 temporarily on the top of each one.

Line up the tongues and grooves and press all the boards together by hand. Place three bar clamps across the door (one on each end and one in the middle) and squeeze the boards together evenly by tightening each clamp a little at a time alternately

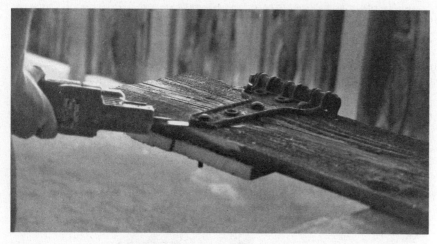

Salvaging old cast-iron barn hinges to be sand-blasted, painted, and used on doors

Reconditioning 30 old barn hinges using black "Rustoleum" spray paint

until all the seams are tight. But just before that final squeeze, take a carpenter's square and make sure the corners are square (no parallelogram allowed!) and the top and bottom of the door boards are perfectly lined up.

If not, take a hammer and *gently* tap any errant board back into line. Note: Never use glue on a batten door; it needs to be able expand and contract, as previously mentioned.

Installing the battens

Now you have a door that's ready to be secured with battens. You will need eight pine or fir 1"x6"s for the batts. Cut the batts 2 inches shorter than the width of the door to allow a 1" setback on each side.

Ideally, for the *outside* of the front door, each batt should receive a 30-degree beveled cut along the top edge to shed rain. It can be done easily with a table saw or any power saw with an adjustable blade, or with a hand plane. I made several doors *without* the slanted cut on the batts and I regret it. The doors are fine, but that ¾" ledge tends to gather water and dirt.

Placement of the batts is important for the strength and stability of the door. I generally put them 4" down from the top and 4" up from the bottom of the door and divide the rest of the space evenly, creating three "bays"—the space between the four batts that will accommodate the hinges.

Secure each pair of batts with C-clamps so they precisely oppose each other on the front and back of the door. (Note: Pad the clamp with a shim or something so it won't mar the wood when tightened.) Now that the door is barred and shackled and clamped every which way but loose, put two $1^5/_8$" drywall screws close to the ends of the batts, ¾" in from the corners. This extra precaution will keep the batts exactly lined up in case a clamp slips or gets bumped.

Drilling the holes

The next step is to drill the holes that will receive the bolts, nuts, and washers. Space the bolt holes evenly about 5" apart after the first one is marked 1" in from the edge of the batt. The drilling technique is critical. You must drill the holes straight up and down at 90 degrees to the door, or when you put the bolts through, they'll be cattywampus. As you are drilling, keep stopping and checking

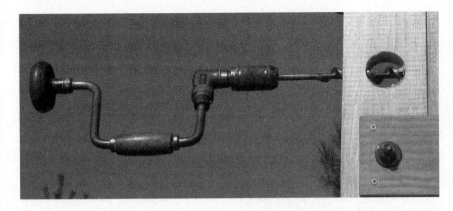

Close-up using brace and bit to drill holes for door knob hardware

in both directions (12:00 and 3:00) to make sure you are holding the tool perpendicular to the door, and the bit is going in as plumb as possible. Stop drilling just before you break through the back side, then crawl under the door and finish the cut from the bottom. This technique will avoid the splintering that occurs when you blast right through. To insure you don't go too far and break through by accident, measure the thickness of the door plus both batts and mark your drill bit on the shank with a black Sharpie or a piece of tape. (Using common dimensional lumber the distance will be three inches, so make your mark at 2¾".)

Installing the nuts & bolts

Sometime during the doormaking process you will buy the nuts, bolts, and washers, and prepare them for painting. I use standard thread 4"x ½" galvanized bolts and ½" flat washers, lock washers, and nuts that go with them—common items at the hardware store. The door and batts add up to 3" of thickness, so 3¾" or 4" bolts work out perfectly because the washers and nuts also take up space on the bolt. For a sizable door, the nuts and bolts can total 12-13 pounds! Before painting them with metal spray paint (I recommend "Rustoleum"), I soak them for a minute in Jasco metal-etching solution so the paint will stick better. It's cheap and available at most paint stores. Some people use vinegar,

but I've found it's not very effective in preventing paint from peeling off over time. But using vinegar would be better than nothing for cleaning and etching your galvanized assortment. Note: Don't use non-galvanized hardware; it will eventually rust and run, even if painted.

When all the holes are drilled, the fun begins! It's very satisfying to put the bolts through the holes, with a large washer on each side and a lock washer on the nut side, and then tighten the nuts down. I use a ratchet and a deep socket on the nut side while I hold a wrench or socket on the other side. I thoroughly enjoy the smoothness and expediency and even the *sound* of the process, which must be repeated about 40 times. (I need to get a life!) Tighten the nuts snugly so the washers slightly sink into the wood.

Staining the door

You've just built a door! Your next step will be to enhance its inherent beauty with a coat of finish. Now's the time to sand off any rough edges,

*Water deflector strip I use on the top **and** bottom of doors*

imperfections, and dirty spots or pencil marks on the wood.

I use a random orbital sander (lightly) with an 80-grit sanding disk for this touch-up work, but any kind of sander will do the job if you are careful not to sand "zones" in your wood. I also "dress" the sharp edges by running the sander all around the perimeter of the door to slightly round them.

While the door is still horizontal, seal it with a clear or tinted sealer, whatever you desire. I use a combination of a ¼ pint ACE Hardware's Golden Oak and ¼ pint ACE's Colonial Maple oil-based wood stain, mixed into a quart of Ace's "Light-Oak Glossy Stain and Polyurethane in one easy step" (that's what it says on the can). I love the color, protection, and sheen this combo affords. On some of my doors I have used Behr's "Cedar Gloss Finish," with beautiful results, but it dries slowly and catches bugs if you have to work outside. One cabinet maker I know stains his wood creations with whatever color he likes, then rubs and polishes them with Johnson's paste wax. He swears there is no better preservative and water-proofing than paste wax, and says he uses it on *everything!* It might be worth a try.

Hanging the door

Now it's time to hang your door. Cinch up your corset; this baby's heavy!

A large solid T&G door weighs about 125-135 lbs. Two people can easily carry it, but it's cumbersome for one. A padded hand truck would be one way to wield it around solo, but to prevent scratches, it would be best to get help moving it *and* placing it in the door opening. You'll be able to take it from there.

I fastened three 1"x2"x12" temporary "stops" around the door jamb—one on each side and one on the top, recessed back 1½", so when the door was pressed into the opening it didn't fall in. It also ended up flush with the outside wall and ready for the hinges. Next I tapped small shims in with a hammer all around the door leaving an even ¼" gap left, right, top, and bottom. The shims held the door tightly in place, but for extra security, I screwed a flat stick to the outside wall (with one screw) and twirled it around to hold the door. This allowed me to install the hinges without "incident."

Once the hinges and door hardware are mounted, I close the door and trace a pencil mark all around the door *on the jamb*, then open the door and make another mark ¼" in from the first one. I then screw the 1"x4" doorstop molding all around the door jamb on that second mark.

That gap created between the two marks will be filled by the ¼" thick weather-stripping that self-sticks to the edge of the molding. This keeps the weather out and cushions the door from rattling in the wind.

Note: Small packages of carpenter's shims are sold at lumber yards and hardware stores. I can't build anything without them!

"Teddy" with his new dog door so he can use the small shed as a doghouse

Hinges

Handsome hinges can make your door look regal enough for a castle. You can find old hinges in many predictable places if you actively look for them (antique stores, flea markets, dismantlers, internet, restoration-hardware catalogs, estate sales, auctions, and even garage sales). You can also buy sizable heavy-duty hinges at the hardware store.

I lucked out by knowing an old farmer who was tearing down his huge dilapidated barn. He told me I could have all *thirty* of the rusty cast-iron hinges if I wanted to hand-saw them off the gray splintered barn wood (no electricity). I jumped at the opportunity and put in a hard day's work, but those hinges happily ended up on all my doors in the house. I had them sandblasted, then spray painted

'em black, and they looked as good as old.

For the front door entrance handle, I mortgaged the farm and hired the local blacksmith to make 2 large curvy respectable door pulls for $100 each but they were worth every penny. If you prefer the warmth of wood, I've seen wooden hinges and door handles carved or fashioned from hardwood, and they were sensa-

Batten pattern on inside of house front door (outside of house back door is shown previously).

Dutch door I built for the piano studio. I used 2x8s and joined the boards by spline and grooves.

Piano repair shop with sliding door on a hanging track

tional! (See the article by David Lee, in the 17th year anthology.)

Installing the door hardware

Door entry sets, deadbolts, and all the trimmings are available for reasonable prices and in a wide variety of colors and styles at every hardware store and at all the big DIY outlets like Home Depot and Lowe's. Just follow the directions in the package. You'll need two hole saw sizes, one for the door face where the doorknob goes (usually 2¼" dia.). and one for the door edge where the latch goes (usually 1"dia.). The instructions come with a template to mark exactly where to drill the holes. You can use a jig that clamps on the door to insure that you drill perfectly straight holes

if you want to buy or borrow one. Me? I handheld my drill and it worked out fine. Again, just before you break through the other side, feel the point of the guide coming through and stop drilling! (The guide is the "pilot" drill bit in the center of the hole saw.) Go to the other side and drill a clean hole back the other way. This important step will avoid splintering that your doorknob might not cover up.

Installing the door hardware may seem a little intimidating at first but it's actually quite easy if you make sure each step is done as accurately as possible (particularly the template markings and the 90 degree hole cuts). If you don't have electricity, a brace-and-bit takes Popeye forearms to operate, but cuts very nice holes.

After the door is hung and latched, I sometimes install two water deflector metal strips—one screwed on the building just over the top of the door, and one on the bottom of the door. They are common items at the hardware store. They deflect the driving rain, as the name implies.

Other variations

When it comes to batten doors, there are unlimited variations you can adapt the design to, to suit your architectural preferences and your creativity. You might want to build an interior door using 2"x4" T&G boards and narrow battens and paint the door white, and attach fancy brass hinges and door handles. Maybe you like the boards horizontal instead of vertical? No problem. Let your imagination and your personality be your guide. Don't be afraid to think out of the rectangle.

If you want to get creative and prematurely age your door, there's a process called "distressing" the wood. This timeworn look is achieved by beating up the wood here and there with various tools to dent and nick it, and even char it. It sounds terrible, but can be quite an authentic antiqued effect.

Dutch doors

I transformed one batten door into a Dutch door for a piano studio I built (see *BHM* Issue #27, available in *A Backwoods Home Anthology, The Fifth Year*). The top half could be opened for ventilation—and for the music to waft out—and the lower half could be latched. I put in a bolt-latch to fasten the lower half to the upper half, and installed regular door knob hardware on the lower half.

Dutch doors are ideal for kitchens. You can open the upper half to air out the smoke after you burn the beans, or you can use its mantle to cool a pie or a batch of cookies. The lower half will slow down the stampede when

the kids outside get a whiff of the aroma.

Dutch doors are used frequently in horse stalls and barns. For those locations it's a good idea to put cross battens on the doors for extra strength. A cross batten should slant from the lower hinge edge to the upper latch edge to keep the door from sagging.

Another quick and easy door design

In addition to my batten doors, I've made a few other easy-to-build doors out of 1"x4"s in utility-grade pine and/or fir, for special applications. One was a 7½'x8' hanging-track sliding door on a small piano-repair shop (see photo), and the other a 4'x7' door for a larger shop, and a triangular-shaped door for a tree house (see articles in the 18th year anthology). These doors were inexpensive and easy to build and look good as well. The 1"x4"s are simply screwed together in a grid with all verticals on one side and all horizontals on the other (no glue). They are strong and they don't warp. Hanging-track hardware is available for any width door. The large doors slide open easily on rollers that ride in the overhead track,

and stay flat against the building and out of the way when opened.

A business idea

A good craftsman woodworker could *specialize* in building every conceivable variation of the batten-style door, take orders for custom sizes and styles, and probably sell them like hotcakes. I reckon it could turn into a cottage industry. Batten doors are here to stay and are regaining favor as more and more people are appreciating the natural rugged and rustic look, as well as the medieval look that has been characterized by Harry Potter movies and recent pirate movies.

Closing thoughts

I don't claim to be a consummate doormaker. Far from it. I'll leave fancy conventional doors to the expert woodworkers with well-equipped shops full of stationary saws, jigs, planers, routers, and sanders.

I'm perfectly happy with my batten doors and it's a good thing I find them so presentable and attractive, because that's what I know how to build. Δ

Invasive species

and how we battle them

By John Silveira

I've written about the origins of plants in our gardens (*Ancient history of modern plants,* in the 18th year anthology) and animals on the farm (*Where our farm animals come from,* also in the 18th year anthology). But if you garden or live on a farm, you know there's more. There are weeds, insect pests, diseases of both plants and animals, and vermin. And depending on where you live, there are more you may never see on your farm or around your home, but you've read about them, everything from kudzu to zebra mussels.

Where do they all come from? Some of them are native, but many weren't here until humans, mostly the

CHILDERS

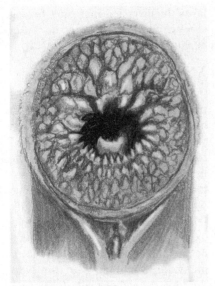

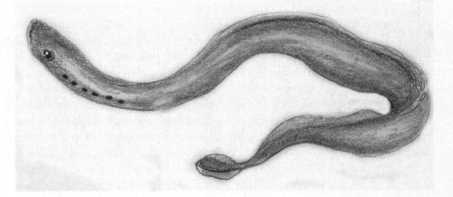

The lamprey can grow as long as 40 inches. It has invaded American and Canadian waterways since the building of the Welland Canal and had, at one time, almost destroyed the Great Lakes' fishing industry. Although jawless, it has a toothed mouth (left) it uses to latch onto fish and suck the blood out. Today there are programs in both the U.S. and Canada to control it.

Europeans, brought them from other parts of the world.

The list of species introduced from the Old World to the New, or from south of the border into the United States, is long. However, not all species introduced are harmful. In fact, some seem to fit in very well with their new environment, and the environment has adapted to them.

Tumbleweed

Some have become so familiar that most most people don't even realize they aren't native. Tumbleweeds are an example of this. They have become a symbol of the Old West, but they're actually an invader that came here, most probably in a load of flax seed imported from Russia to South Dakota by Ukrainian farmers around 1877. From there the weed (often called Russian thistle) spread, tumbling in the wind as it went along, until by 1900 it had established itself all the way to the Pacific coast.

Earthworms, honeybees

There are other "invaders" we regard as helpful. Two, which we actually foster, are earthworms and honeybees. But they were introduced by Europeans, and now we don't know what we'd do without them.

But many other species are troubling, intrusive, and destructive, and each year we spend billions of dollars trying to eradicate, or at least control, them.

How many invaders are there? I don't think anyone knows. For one thing, there's a good chance we wouldn't know a new one had arrived until it had already established itself and it was probably too late to stop it. I googled "invasive species" and found a website, www.invasive.org, which has them listed in four categories.

From the first category I discovered the number of invading insects is at least 217. Most I've never heard of, but conspicuous on the list are fire ants and killer bees because they get so much press. Curiously, honeybees are not on this list.

The list of invasive "weeds" is 623 long. About 600 I've never heard of or thought they were native. But there are some that stand out like kudzu and Scotch Broom because, once again, they're in the news.

The list of diseases, both those that infect animals and those that infect plants, is 69 long. Left off the list were those that affect humans, such as influenza, measles, small pox (now eradicated), or diseases that affect both humans and animals such as West Nile virus which also affects horses.

The last category is called "other invasives" and has 41 entries. It includes various snails, slugs, nematodes, frogs, toads, fish, reptiles, and the ones that get press: starlings, zebra mussels, and feral pigs. Earthworms aren't on that list, perhaps because we like them so much. But it should be clear that both earthworms and honeybees are alien to the Western Hemisphere and have permanently altered the ecology here by their presence.

Others not on the list include black rats and Norway rats, both of which arrived on ships from Europe. Nonetheless, they are more of the invaders.

Some, such as the brown tree snake, have never been allowed to spread here. These snakes, accidentally imported to Guam, have almost totally wiped out the native bird population. On a few occasions, they have been discovered in Hawaii, but that state has done a very good job of ensuring that the few found there were not allowed to build populations. It is an example of a pest that

"...there may be more fire ants now in the United States than there are in South America."

101

was eliminated before it had time to get out of control.

Lampreys & alewives

Others on the list of "other invasives" include the sea lamprey, which are actually native to the New World but whose range was increased because of man's activity. In their case, they didn't exist in the Great Lakes until 1921 when the Welland Canal was built and connected all the Great Lakes to the ocean.

Over the decades that followed, lampreys did considerable damage to the Great Lakes' fishing industry because of their parasitic preying on the fish stocks there. However, a joint effort to control them, by both the United States and Canada, has allowed the reemergence of that industry on the Lakes. Some of the steps taken have been to create barriers in streams that prevent the lampreys from entering them, as well as the release of sterilized lamprey males which has reduced their spawning rates.

Another fish that entered the Great Lakes via the Welland Canal was the

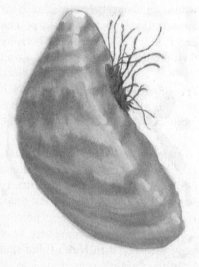

The zebra mussel is an invasive shellfish that is steadily taking over North America's waterways. Though classified as a pest, it has its upside: It can reverse the eutrophication of ponds and lakes and increase their biodiversity.

alewife. Because there was no "top predator" in the Lakes that preys on the alewife, their numbers exploded and they outcompeted many native species which are now in decline and some of those are now endangered. However, eventually, various Pacific salmon species were introduced to the Lakes to prey on them and balance their numbers. Though the salmon and alewives now serve as a foundation of the sport fishing industry, their introduction and numbers have forever altered the Great Lakes.

Zebra mussels

Although you're not likely to run into zebra mussels on the farm or in your garden, they are another invasive that's exploded across North America invading and infesting more and more of our waterways. Their downside is that they outcompete many native species of mussels and they proliferate so fast they have been known to clog pipes that feed water treatment plants and power plants. They also cause damage to boats and harbors. They now cost the American and Canadian economies billions of dollars each year.

Originally native to Russia, zebra mussels have spread around the world. It's thought they were introduced here either when seagoing ships from other parts of the world discharged ballast water containing zebra mussels into North American rivers and lakes, or that they rode in attached to their boat anchors and chains.

Zebra mussels, however, have a little bit of an upside. Because they are voracious filter feeders, they have removed particles and either reduced or reversed eutrophication (where the water becomes oxygen depleted and brings on the "death" of a body of water) including man-induced eutrophication that has taken place in many of our lakes. This coupled with the accumulation of biomass (actually, their feces) at the bottom of lakes has, in some lakes, increased the

lakes' biodiversity, including fishing stocks, while improving the water quality.

Mankind

The mammal that made the biggest impact on the New World, if you haven't guessed it, is mankind ourselves, though, like honeybees and earthworms, we don't appear on the lists, either. In fact, we're the biggest factor in the list since we're the one who intentionally or inadvertently introduced *all* of the other pests.

On top of that is the unresolved debate that says the extinctions of many large mammals of the New World at the end of the last "ice age" were due to the arrival of man who may have hunted them into oblivion. These include five species of American horses (all today's horses are descended from horses that survived in Asia), several species of New World camels, North American llamas, two genera of deer, two genera of pronghorn antelope (a third has survived until today), stag-moose, shrub-oxen, woodland muskoxen, the giant beaver, various sloths, the short-faced bear (which was larger than today's grizzly), the saber-toothed cats, the huge American lion, several species of mammoths, the American mastodon, gomphotheres (an elephant-like mammal), giant armadillos, the dire wolf, the American cheetah, a species of bison, and the giant peccary. If those and others became extinct because of our arrival, we have been (though no doubt unintentionally) the single most invasive species to arrive here.

For the most part, once a species establishes itself here, there's not much we can do except wait until nature finds a new balance. And all the good intentions some of us have to reestablish the New World to its original state are doomed to failure.

But, along with invasive species, we've introduced others which most people find are benevolent or useful such as wild mustard, numerous farm

Among the animals that went extinct after man first arrived in the New World was the saber-toothed cat. Armed with dagger-like incisors, it was probably a formidable hunter. But no one knows whether its demise was the result of humans, climate change, or other factors.

crops and fruit trees, dogs, cats, horses and other livestock, as well as the aforementioned bees and worms. To the purists, even those species we like would be called pests—including ourselves. But I'm not going there.

What we consider invasive most assuredly depends on where we live. One of our frequent writers, Alice Yeager, wrote about the hazards of kudzu because she lives in the South where it thrives, to the dismay of people from East Texas to Delaware. Other invasives that run through the South are privet, a small semi-deciduous shrub that ranges from Connecticut to Texas, fire ants, and numerous fish.

Because the list of invasives is so long, I'm only going to focus on a few in this article. And they'll all be of the animal kingdom. There are some of them that, like zebra mussels, deserve special mention because they have been in the news so often. In a future issue, I'll focus on some of the pests from the plant kingdom.

Fire ants

Fire ants are natives of South America. If you've had experiences with them, this may be hard to believe but most species of fire ants don't bother people and are not considered

problems. However, the species that invaded this country sometime in the 1930s, most likely hitching a ride aboard a Brazilian cargo ship into Mobile, Alabama, is most certainly a pest.

Given the biological name *solenopsis invicta*, but more commonly known as fire ants or the red imported fire ant (RIFA), it now infests the majority of the Southern and Southwestern United States. Overseas, it has landed in places as disparate as Australia, the Philippines,

both mainland China and Taiwan, and Malaysia. Fire ants are a bigger problem in those countries and the U.S. than they are in South America where they originated because there are no natural enemies of the fire ant in these countries.

They get the name "fire ant" from their sting. Their bite is just to get a grip, then they use what is essentially a stinger to inject an alkaloid venom (*piperidine*) that creates a sensation similar to what you'd feel when you're burned by fire, hence their name. And they can sting more than once. And like bees, their venom can kill people who are sensitive.

Their venom also serves another purpose, they use it to protect their young and their eggs by spraying it on them. It apparently protects them both from other insects and microorganisms.

Fire ants like to build their nests in areas that are moist, such as along rivers, ponds, well-watered lawns, and highways (where rain flows off and keeps the edges wet). If they have their way, they'll build their nests under logs, rocks, roads, etc, but where they can't find that kind of cover they'll establish what has become their hallmark in much of the South: a large dome-shaped mound

The gomphotheres was a New World elephant that lived in tropical climates. Like the saber-toothed cat, its extinction coincides with the arrival of man.

that can be more than a foot high. Typically, they'll eat young plants, seeds, and other insects. But they'll also kill small animals.

Fire ants can cause short circuits and fires in electrical systems when they move into electrical devices such as circuit breakers, relays, and motors.

As with honeybees, there are three types of fire ants: queens, males, and workers.

Queens: They are the largest ants in the colony. Though a colony needs only one queen, they often have more (up to 100). Each queen can live six or seven years and lay 1500 eggs a day. So, when eradication techniques are used, unless all the queens are destroyed, the colony can repopulate itself quickly.

Males: Their only function is to mate with the queen. Once they mate, they search for other queens with which to mate. (Hey, they're guys.)

Workers: As with bees, the workers are sterile females. Their function is to build and repair the nests, defend it, care for the young, seek and bring food back to the nest, and feed the young.

Control efforts: Nearly $6 billion is spent each year on fire ants. This includes efforts to control them, repairing the damage they cause including agricultural damage, and medical and veterinary treatment.

The United States and several other countries where fire ants have become invasive pests have programs to control them. Though here in the United States we have had little success, Australia's efforts, known as the National Fire Ant Eradication Program, which has cost almost $200 million in Australian dollars, have wiped out some 99 percent of the fire ants in Southeast Queensland.

It's been said there may be more fire ants now in the United States than there are in South America. The reason is that there are natural predators and pathogens in South America that limit the fire ant's numbers. Among

the efforts being studied to combat fire ants are the introduction of:

- A microsporidian protozoan called *Thelohania solenopsae.*
- A fungus called *Beauveria bassiana.*
- A parasitic ant called *Solenopsis daguerrei.*
- Various species of the parasitic phorid flies, which are already being used in the United States with some success.
- A virus, SINV-1, which is also proving to have some success.
- The importation of anteaters. But this is unlikely because those anteaters are already on endangered species lists and probably wouldn't do well, anyway.

It should be noted that none of the biological agents used is ever going to wipe the ants out completely anymore than they wipe them out in South America. What happens is that a balance is reached so we can at least live with them. On the other hand, in Australia, since fire ants weren't introduced until 2001 and they haven't spread that far, there's a decent chance they may be eradicated.

But the introduction of "natural" biological control agents must proceed carefully, as the solution sometimes produces more harm than good.

Other promising methods being tried are baiting the ground around the nests with agents that either poison the colony or render the queens into laying infertile eggs.

When you find piles of ant bodies outside of a nest, it doesn't necessarily mean eradication procedures are working. As with many social insects, including other types of ants and bees, workers systematically remove dead bodies from the nests for sanitary purposes.

For combatting fire ants on your homestead, the Brackenridge Field Laboratory at the University of Texas at Austin recommends first identifying the ants to ensure they are truly fire ants. You don't want to wipe out the other ants because they compete with the fire ants for nesting space and food and help keep them in check. So, ensure they are fire ants. Then use Amdro, Award, Logic, or similar granule bait preparations. These poisons do not kill immediately, but the worker ants bring it back to the nest where the queens eat it and it disrupts their reproductive abilities.

For indoors, they recommend "... boric acid (15% by volume) in peanut butter placed in bottle lids where ants have trails." It's effective in that the

Fire ants have become a nuisance because they have almost no natural predators in the United States. Efforts are underway to contain them, but in all likelihood they will never be eradicated in this country.

ants bring it back to their nests, killing members in the colony. But this treatment has to be coupled with efforts to kill them outside as they're still going to be coming into your house from there.

They also stress that many of the controls used in the past, such as Mirex, should not be used as it kills other species of ants which compete with fire ants and are therefore more or less on our side.

Medical treatment: Fire ant bites can happen singly, but they can also happen in hundreds or even thousands for those truly unfortunate enough to have found themselves in a nest of the buggers. The stings can leave bumps that turn into pustules that may become infected and leave scars if they break. To treat the bites, there are external treatments that include washing with soap and water, cold compresses, hydrocortisone cream, and topical corticosteroid creams to help reduce the swelling and itching, as well as oral medications such as antihistamines like Benadryl.

According to one website I visited, alcohol, bleach, or a whipped mixture of egg whites and salt spread over the affected skin for 30 minutes can help alleviate the pain.

For those rare persons (about one percent of the population) who experience allergic reactions to the ants' bites, including anaphylaxis, emergency treatment is required as the bites can kill them.

Killer bees

Killer bees, also known as Africanized honey bees, are the result of a project that took place in Brazil in the 1950s. A biologist, Warwick Kerr, was attempting to create a hybrid (by interbreeding Tanzanian honeybees from Africa and European honeybees) that would be more productive in tropical regions than the European honeybees are.

The hives Kerr rigged up had grates that were large enough to allow worker bees to pass into and out of the

Killer bees have acquired a fearsome reputation. But as they interbreed with local stocks, their dispositions seem to be becoming milder.

hives, but they were too small for the queens to pass through. It would take a queen leaving the hive to create colonies of the Africanized bees in the wild. And that's exactly what happened when a replacement beekeeper accidentally allowed about two dozen African queens to escape into the wild.

The escaped queens mated local drones and the rest resembles the making of a bad B-horror movie as the aggressive hybrids moved relentlessly north toward Central and North America and south into Argentina.

Like European bees, Africanized bees produce honey. However, they have traits that make them undesirable to many beekeepers. These include their aggression. They are not only aggressive but will pursue their quarry over wider areas. They also have a greater proportion of "guard

bees" to defend their nests than the European varieties have. Other downsides are that they are also more apt to abandon their hives in response to the beekeeper's intrusions. And they don't do well when food supplies are reduced, nor do they fare well in colder weather.

However, they have become the preferred honeybee of beekeepers in tropical Central and South America because of improved productivity. But when they first move into any area, they are initially feared because, although they're hybrids, they tend to retain the aggressive tendencies of the Tanzanian bees from which they are descended.

They can now be found in Brazil, northern Argentina, Central America, Mexico, Florida, Louisiana, Texas, New Mexico, Arizona, and Southern California. It's likely they will spread further north.

It should be noted that, as the Africanized bees have spread and interbred with "native" strains, their aggressive tendencies have been somewhat reduced and their tolerance for colder climates has increased. So, though it was initially thought when they first entered this country that they would stay in the more southerly regions, it's now difficult to say just where their range will end and how aggressive these newer hybrid bees will be.

It's likely that at least part of the reason European honeybees are less aggressive than their African counter-

"Pigeons...were first domesticated from cliff-dwelling wild rock doves more than 2,000 years ago by the Romans. What we have today are birds that still like to dwell along cliffs, and in the urban landscape those cliffs are our buildings, and as they are really a domesticated bird turned free, they don't have the fear of humans other birds have."

parts is because of selective breeding by European beekeepers over the last several thousand years. Less aggressive bees were more likely to have been kept than their more aggressive kin. On the other hand, in Africa there was no tradition of beekeeping until recently. So there was no selective breeding of bees as there was in Europe.

The venom from the sting of an Africanized bee is no more potent than the venom of European bees, but as they attack in greater numbers they can be more dangerous. But the most likely reason someone will die from their stings is allergy, just as with our "normal" bees.

The future of these bees is uncertain, due to further hybridization, both naturally and man-induced. Not all colonies of these Africanized bees are overly aggressive. In Brazil, where these bees first got a foothold in the New World, incidents with aggressive bees are much less common than they were a few decades ago and they are often the beekeeper's bee of choice for they are better adapted to tropical climates and more productive there than their European counterparts.

"[Wild boar] can survive almost anywhere because they are hardy, omnivorous, and prolific."

Wild boar

One critter the rural homesteader is likely to see is the wild boar. This is another animal native to the Old World that was originally unintentionally introduced to the New.

Their original range was from the British Isles east to Japan and down into North Africa. They were introduced into the New World not long after the arrival of Columbus. The very first ones were escaped domestic pigs that came here with Spanish Conquistadors. Historical narratives recount how explorers such as Hernando de Soto drove herds of swine with them, as mobile food provisions, as they wandered through unchartered country. By the time Europeans were ready to settle here in large numbers, the wild pigs had already established a foothold.

They fared well when they went feral because domestic pigs are more closely related to their wild ancestors than any other farm animal, and they

revert to their wild state quickly. They can survive almost anywhere because they are hardy, omnivorous, and prolific. As a result, they put pressure on many native species of both plants and animals.

If they get a chance, wild boar get into gardens and consume and destroy crops such as corn, wheat, rice, hay, melons, potatoes, greens, peanuts, and just about any other crops they can find. As omnivores, they will also kill and eat young livestock including newborn lambs and calves.

Because of their rooting behavior, when they dig the ground for root foods, they can destroy many native plants. In some areas their destruction of vegetation is so extensive they cause erosion when the rains come.

Their range, even recently, was mostly confined to the southern and southwestern states, but as time passes they are expanding their range and have been sighted as far north as Oregon, Wisconsin, and New Hampshire.

In some countries there are eradication programs in place to either poison, trap, or shoot them. In Australia, they are even shot from helicopters.

In this country they are largely hunted. If you encounter them around your homestead and regard them as pests, check with your local Fish and Game Department. There's generally no season on them. If you get the go-ahead to hunt them, any of the .30 caliber rifles or larger should do the trick, though some have taken them with a 6mm and even smaller. The smallest handgun caliber you should use is a .41 magnum, though, once again, some have had success with 180-grain .357s loaded so as to shoot at a minimum of 1300 fps at 50 yards.

European gypsy moth

The gypsy moth is a pest that's on the move. Its original range was

The wild boar is a New World mammal that arrived with the very first European explorers. Though they are largely confined to the southern parts of the United States, they are gradually spreading their range. Wild boar can be destructive to both the local flora and fauna, as well as to homesteaders. Today many hunters take advantage of the fact that there are usually few, if any, restrictions against taking them.

Europe and Asia. In the European variety, which are found west of the Ural Mountains, the females are not capable of flight. Those found east of the Urals can fly.

The European gypsy moth was introduced to North America in 1868 by French scientist Leopold Trouvelot, who was then living in Medford, Massachusetts, a town I lived much of my youth in. In the variety he introduced, the females are flightless.

However, there have recently been accidental introductions of the Asian type into both North America and Europe, and because the Asian and European variety freely interbreed there is the concern that this pest will become more mobile and spread rapidly throughout the continent. The moth's current North American range is the entire Northeast, portions of the Midwest and Southeast, and parts of southeastern Canada.

More incursions of this insect are likely to happen throughout the world as the females lay their eggs in almost any sheltered area, including ships in port from where they are apt to spread when the ships reach their destinations, and recreation vehicles that travel intracontinentally.

The moths create their destruction by eating the foliage of trees and now defoliate about a million acres of trees each year, an area about equivalent to the state of Rhode Island. But some years are worse; in 1981 they defoliated a record of almost 13 million acres.

Their preferred meal is the foliage of oaks, but they'll spread to shrubs and other trees including conifers. However, there are many species of trees and shrubs they will avoid. Among these are American holly, American sycamore, arborvitae, ash, balsam fir, black walnut, butternut, catalpa, flowering dogwood, mountain laurel, tulip tree, and some others. If you're putting in trees where gypsy moth infestations occur, you may want to consider these.

Trees attacked by gypsy moths may or may not die, and it's usually a few years, usually three, before we know which trees that have been attacked will survive.

Unlike fire ants, for which there are no natural predators in this country, these moths are consumed by many insects and spiders, several species of birds, and small woodland mammals including forest mice, squirrels, chipmunks, and raccoons.

For our part, there are several methods of combatting them that include the use of microbial, biological, and chemical pesticides. The microbial pesticides contain bacteria and viruses that affect the insect. The *Nucleopolyhedrosis* virus is specific to gypsy moths and apparently does not affect other insects or animals. Another, *Bacillus thuringiensis,* is used against several tree pests including the gypsy moth. However, there are other agents that must be used sparingly because they can kill other moths, butterflies, bees, and even insects and parasites that help control gypsy moth populations. Last are the chemical pesticides that must be used wisely as their fallout can affect many other species including humans.

A treatment that is being used with some success in parts of the United Kingdom involves the use of a synthetic pheromone that "blinds" the males so they cannot locate females to breed with.

But for the homeowner or homesteader in this country, the first line of defense when faced with the possibility of a gypsy moth infestation is to keep your trees well watered and nourished and to surround them either with mulch or ground cover that does not compete with them for water and nutrients. The trees most susceptible to lasting damage by gypsy moths are those that are unhealthy.

Since the list of chemical and biological agents used to combat them is always changing, it's best to contact your county agent when an outbreak appears imminent.

Pigeons

If you live in a big city, it's probably hard to believe that pigeons haven't been here all along. In fact, they weren't imported here until the 1600s. To some people it's a toss-up as to whether pigeons or rats are the number one urban pests. If you want my vote, I'd rather have pigeons around.

Pigeons don't migrate as some birds do. They tend to stay close to where they were born. That's the reason we have them in our cities come spring, summer, fall, or winter. They were first domesticated from cliff-dwelling wild rock doves more than 2,000 years ago by the Romans. What we have today are birds that still like to dwell along cliffs, and in the urban landscape those cliffs are our buildings, and as they are really a domesticated bird turned free, they don't have the fear of humans other birds have.

It's worth noting that in the city they're called pigeons and they aren't hunted or eaten, but in the countryside they're called rock doves and they're both hunted *and* eaten.

But wait a minute, if you've eaten squab, then you *have* eaten pigeon. Squab is just a fancy name for a fledgling pigeon that's served up when it's about four weeks old. And, like everything else in the universe, they taste like chicken.

Because they tend to hang out in cities, they don't put much pressure on wild bird populations in the countryside, and I only include them here because many city folk either hate them or find them so endearing, and those in the city who hate them often refer to them as flying rats.

They do have a few downsides. First is the result of their nesting habits. They can clog up gutters with their nesting materials, and the collected water can cause damage to roofs and walls. They can also cause damage to ventilation, air conditioning systems, and rooftop machinery when they nest inside them.

Pigeons, starlings, and sparrows are probably the three greatest avian pests in this country. With their nest building they can bring damage to structures, and their feces are both corrosive and can harbor various diseases.

Another downside is that they can otherwise foul your home and vicinity with their droppings. The uric acid in their feces is corrosive and the bacteria, fungi, and parasites that can be present in their droppings can become a health risk.

Last, they may someday become carriers, if there is ever a bad outbreak, of avian flu. I think about that every time I see a flock of pigeons.

Controlling them usually means denying them nesting space in the eaves of your home with wire mesh. There are also electrical-wire devices that work the same way electric fencing for cattle works in that it gives the birds a shock and sends them on their way. Then there are nonelectrical wiring rigs, some that look like miniature concertina wire, some that have little spikes, and some that are just several strands of wire that are run along the top of a building where pigeons would like to perch but they can't because the wires are in the way.

Otherwise, there's not a lot you can do to get rid of them without getting into trouble. Indiscriminately spreading poisons in a city can bring the authorities down on you. And, when I was a boy in Boston, I remember baseball great Ted Williams got in trouble for shooting them with a shotgun at Fenway Park. Actually, he'd been shooting them there for years with the blessing of then-owner Tom Yawkey. Sometimes he got hundreds in one day. Then the Humane Society or the Police or Big Bird found out what he was doing and the wrath of tabloid scorn came down on him. As I recall, since he was a Boston icon, the city decided not to press charges. So if you want to get rid of them, don't use firearms within city limits because you're not as likely to get off as lightly as Ted did.

Sparrows

There are actually several species of sparrows that were introduced to North American beginning in the 1850s, and they all immediately made themselves at home. Like pigeons, sparrows can be a nuisance. With their nest-building ways, they can clog gutters and drain pipes, allowing water to pool and cause structural damage. Like pigeons, their feces contain both uric acid and pathogens that can lead to corrosion and disease. Nest-building in electrical equipment has also led to shorts that resulted in fires.

The only real means of excluding them from buildings are with wire mesh and electrified systems that shock them. Since they are not an indigenous bird, there are very few places in the United States where you can't destroy them, their nests, or their eggs.

Starlings

Ah, the bird of my youth. I could never get into trouble for shooting them when I was young. In fact, eradicating them was often encouraged. And shoot I did. Hundreds. Maybe more.

The problem with them is that as an invasive they sometimes drive native species out of nesting areas. In fact, they sometimes watch native birds build nests, then bully them out of them and take them over.

Because of their flocking, they can congregate in numbers that run into the thousands. When doing so, they can overwhelm trees and buildings. Their feces, like those of pigeons and sparrows, contain uric acid that can corrode metals, stone, and masonry.

There are more invasive pests. Hundreds of them. In a future issue I will cover more of them. Δ

Crock pot cookery

Serve up a hot and hearty supper even when you've been away all day

By Linda Gabris

Crock pots are fascinating inventions that really take the "heat" off cooking supper. I wish olden day cooks like my grandmother could have experienced the wonderful freedom that a crock pot, or as some folks know them—slow cooker, has to offer. All that grandma had in her rural kitchen for cooking year-round on was an old-fashioned woodstove so, unlike me, she never got to indulge in the convenience of being able to cook a delicious, healthy supper without hovering over the stove for hours watching the pots boil.

Mind you, when I was a kid I loved coming home from school in wintertime and being greeted by the heavenly aroma of supper simmering on the crackling woodstove which also kept the house warm and cozy during cold weather months. Even though grandma could maintain a simmer on the back of her woodstove—almost like a crock pot does—by positioning the pot just so, her method of slow cooking still needed to be tended to in order to keep the pot from boiling dry.

Come summer, lighting a fire in the woodstove for cooking our daily meals was another story, especially

With just a few minutes of prep in the morning, you'll have a healthy, hearty meal waiting for you when you get home after a long day. Here, Ginger pineapple chicken is hot out of the crock pot.

for grandmother who couldn't escape the sweltering heat of the kitchen. Although she never complained, even on the hottest, most hectic days of summer, I know that she would have enjoyed the cool, carefree convenience that crockery cooking has to offer. In my book, every kitchen should have one.

Regardless of the fact that most folks, and cookbooks too, often use the words "crock pot" and "slow cooker" interchangeably, technically

settings. They are low which simmers food at 190 to 200°, and high which cooks food at 290 to 300°. If the model has a setting under 190° it is meant to be used strictly as a warming setting and should not be used for cooking as temperature below 190° does not have the power to kill bacteria found in raw foods. The automatic setting, if there is one, maintains ideal temperature throughout the cooking process.

Other types of slow cookers, includ-

Even though slow cooking appliances vary in styles, sizes, shapes, and construction, they are all geared to cook foods at low temperatures for long periods of time without having to be fussed over. They are designed to hold moisture in, allowing the cooker to be left unattended for hours without fear of food overcooking or the pot running dry. That's what crockery or slow cooking is really all about.

So regardless of the kind of model you have, all recipes can be adapted by following the instructions in your manual and if you are thrifty about using electricity, there's no need to fret at the thought of having the pot run for hours on end as the wattage that a slow cooker uses is rated as being very low. For safety's sake, use your cooker according to manufacturer's directions.

One of the things I fancy most about crockery cooking, aside from the fact that I don't have to stand over the stove for hours to prepare a delicious, healthy meal, is that I can be away all day and still come home to the welcoming aroma of something good simmering in the kitchen.

Another thing that makes slow cooking so appealing is that the lower cooking temperature does not destroy as many nutrients in the food as higher temperatures used in traditional cooking methods do. And if you resist the temptation to peek, none of the good stuff escapes in steam!

Chop dense vegetables slightly smaller than meats for even cooking. Pack vegetables closer to the heating element in your crock pot or slow cooker.

there is a difference, more so in designs than in intention of purpose which is to cook food at very low temperature for long periods of time.

An authentic crock pot usually consists of three pieces. There is the outer part of the cooker which is made out of metal. This outside pot contains the heating element which is built inside the walls of the cooker. It has a removable crockery insert made out of earthenware, stoneware, porcelain, or other type of glassware which is called the cooking well. It always comes with a tight-fitting lid that doesn't allow steam to escape.

Although models can vary, most crock pots have two low-temperature

ing electric frying pans that come specially made with crockery inserts for slow cooking and glass ceramic casserole dishes with their own heating platforms, have the heating element built into the bottom of the pot or platform, not built into the sides as does a traditional crock pot. Since the element is in the bottom, these types of cookers sometimes call for occasional stirring of foods otherwise they might stick to the bottom where heat is concentrated. A crock pot that has the element built into the sides never needs stirring, making it the better choice of model for those who have to be away all day while the pot is on.

This is why it is important not to lift the lid during the cooking process—unless a recipe specifically calls for doing so as it takes about 2 hours for most cookers to reach temperature of 165° at which point food begins to cook. Peeking causes heat to escape and temperature to drop which slows down the cooking process. Since less liquid is used in slow cooker recipes than in other types of preparations, it is important to keep the steam inside the pot.

When it comes to good health, since foods are so much more flavorful when cooked in a slow cooker, one can cut down or eliminate salt content in recipes making this a well-suited cooking method for those on low or no-salt diets. I also find that meats and poultry do not need to be pre-browned in cooking fats in order to make them tasty so the amount of fat can be reduced from the diet especially if you use skinned chicken and turkey parts and trim other meats of excess fat and discard before putting in the pot.

If you're looking for a sensible solution for serving your family hot and hearty meals even on days when you barely make it home in time to set the table for supper, slow cooking is the answer. When you've got to be away, nothing saves the day like getting out the crock pot and putting supper on before leaving the house in the morning.

Slow cooking is very flexible and allows you to adjust cooking times to fit your dining schedule. For instance, you can cook a pot roast on low for 8 to 10 hours, or cook it on high for 4 to 5 hours—having peace of mind in knowing that since food is cooking very slowly and at such low temperature, it will not be overcooked in the event that you are running late—even by several hours. And on those unexpected occasions when the pot goes longer than intended, you'll be amazed at how well the food holds its appearance, never going mushy or falling apart.

Using a slow cooker is a great way to save money on meats and poultry as even the most economic, tough cuts are rendered moist and tender during the long, slow cooking process which breaks down connective tissue and minimizes shrinkage.

For instance, skinned chicken thighs can be used in place of chicken breasts in any slow cooking recipe, producing a dish that is every bit as delicious. Same holds true for using

turkey thighs in place of breast meat, and shank, shoulder, and other less choice cuts of beef, pork, and lamb in place of sirloin and other pricier portions.

Game meats and waterfowl are also delicious when prepared crock pot fashion, especially tougher cuts or older game which needs a little more pampering. You can even skip the long process of marinating as flavors will be instilled in the meat and birds simply by the long stint in the cooker.

If you would like to add more dried beans and lentils to your family's diet but find that they are too time consuming for everyday fare, using a crock pot for cooking them is the answer. Lima, kidney, great northern, and other types of dried beans or pulses that normally call for long, slow cooking are perfectly suited for cooking crock pot fashion, as well as lentils and grains including barley. They can be made into chili-con-

There are a few simple rules to follow when cooking in a slow cooker. Foods should be thawed completely before placing in the cooker as sudden changes in temperatures can damage or crack the interior pot. Even partially frozen foods should not be used as they can set the cooking time back drastically. For best results, use fresh food or thaw frozen food in the fridge overnight before popping in the pot in the morning.

A fascinating fact is that slow cookers, unlike other types of cooking vessels, tend to cook meat and poultry more quickly than vegetables since meats break down quicker than denser-bodied vegetables do. The solution to having everything cooked to perfection is to chop vegetables into smaller pieces and when using a crock pot with the element in the side, put meat on the bottom and place vegetables around the sides of the pot unless cooking serving-sized pieces

Dried beans turn into a tasty meal in a crock pot, even without any presoaking.

carne, bean stews, soups, or added to any other creations your heart desires. I find that when using a slow cooker for dried legumes, the soaking time can be greatly reduced or eliminated altogether.

of meat such as chicken thighs or pot roast in which case they will cook to equal doneness as the chopped vegetables. If you're using a model with element in the bottom, put vegetables in the bottom of the pot and meat on top. When making stew, cut the meat slightly larger than the vegetables and all will come out well.

When a recipe calls for thickening, either by adding a mixture of flour and water, cornstarch and water, or other thickener, it should be done within the last few minutes of cooking at which time it is feasible to open the lid and blend in the thickener, stirring with a wooden spoon until thickened. This is also the time for adding milk, cream, sour cream, or cheese to the recipe as these and other dairy items tend to break down too much during cooking and thus are best added near the end of the cooking process and then heated through.

Since food retains so much more flavor and aroma in a slow cooker, you may have to experiment a little to get a knack for proper seasoning. Always use less or no salt and less pepper than you normally would. You can cut down on the amount of fresh herbs that you use but you may find that you'll have to slightly increase the amount of dried ground spices in a recipe—or add them during the last leg of cooking to capture the utmost flavor.

Have fun experimenting with your cooker and you'll come up with hundreds of great ideas for turning slow cooked meals into long-term winners at the table. You can make satisfying, hearty soups from fridge scraps like bird carcasses, ham and soup bones, beans, lentils, rice, and any vegetables to your avail.

Stews and pot roasts are perfectly suited for slow cooking and since the world is full of international recipes let your creative juices flow freely.

You can make Irish Stew, Russian Stroganoff, German Sauerbraten, French Boeuf Bourguignonne, Swiss Steak, Hungarian Goulash, Indian Curries…to name a few worldly picks that are crock pot perfect.

Ground meats are wonderfully delicious when slow cooked into rich spaghetti sauces, taco filling, meatballs, meat loaves, meat pie fillings, or stuffed cabbage leaves and peppers. You can even make desserts, condiments, and breads.

So if you've been waiting too long to try slow cooking, now's the time to break out the crock pot and treat your family to some super easy, super delicious, and super healthy eating. Try the recipes below for starters. And then let your creative juices flow freely and slow cook your way to some super suppers that are ready before you get home to eat.

Hearty mixed bean soup:

This savory soup is a meal in itself when served with whole wheat rolls, cheese, and fruit for dessert. It takes on a wonderful Italian flair when sprinkled generously with fresh grated Parmesan cheese.

½ pound mixed beans (northern, kidney, pinto, lima, black fava, or other beans of choice)
5 cups vegetable, chicken, or beef stock or bouillon
2 cups chopped canned tomatoes with juice
2 minced onions
3 cloves crushed garlic
½ cup diced celery
2 tsp. ground cumin
1 tsp. ground coriander

Wash beans well under cold running water to remove sand. Place in slow cooker with remaining ingredients. Put on lid and cook on high for 8 hours. Don't fret if the soup goes overtime as longer cooking will only do it justice. Taste and season with salt and pepper to suit taste. Serve with brown bread and butter and supper's on. Serves 4 to 6.

Ginger-pineapple chicken:

Lean skinless chicken thighs surrounded with pineapple, dates, raisins, and apples in a sweet sauce of orange juice, soy sauce, honey, and fresh grated ginger. It's as pretty as it is good. Serve over brown rice that you've steamed while setting the table.

6 chicken thighs, skin removed
2 cups canned or fresh pineapple chunks (if using canned fruit save the juice)
2 diced unpeeled Granny Smith or other tart apples
1 chopped red sweet pepper
1 small sliced chili pepper
¼ cup whole dates
2 cloves finely sliced garlic
2 Tbsp. fresh grated ginger
½ cup plump raisins
2½ cups orange juice (substitute part of the orange juice for pineapple juice if using canned fruit)
¼ cup each of soy sauce and liquid honey
2 Tbsp. ketchup
1 Tbsp. orange marmalade

Put pineapple, apple, peppers, dates, and garlic in bottom of cooker. Lay chicken on top of the fruit. Sprinkle with ginger. Mix orange juice with soy sauce, honey, ketchup and pour over chicken. Blend in the marmalade and top with raisins.

Cover with lid and cook on low setting for 8 hours, or on high setting for 4 hours.

If you wish to thicken the sauce, blend 2 tablespoons of cornstarch into ¼ cup of water and at the end of cooking time, remove the lid from the cooker and blend thickener into the sauce. Turn heat to high setting and stir with a wooden spoon until thick and clear. Serves 6.

Old-fashioned beef stew:

2 Tbsp. butter
1½ pounds cubed beef
1 tsp. paprika
1 chopped onion
2 cloves minced garlic
1 cup of cubed potatoes
1 cup of cubed turnips
1 sliced parsnip
½ cup chopped carrots
3 to 4 cups beef stock made from bouillon cubes
1 tsp. black pepper
1 tsp. dried parsley

*To easily remove bread from the can, just open the bottom of the can
and use the lid to push the bread out.*

brunch party shows up and, *voila*, it's
ready to take out and slice.

> 3 ripe mashed bananas
> ¼ cup butter
> 1 cup liquid honey
> 2 beaten eggs
> 2 cups whole wheat flour
> 2 tsp. baking powder
> ½ tsp. each of ground nutmeg and
>   ground cinnamon
> 2 Tbsp. grated orange rind
> ½ cup raisins
> ⅓ cup orange juice

Cream butter and sugar, stir in eggs
and banana. Mix dry ingredients,
rind, and raisins and blend into
banana mixture, alternately with
juice. Pour into a greased one-pound
coffee can. Set can in slow cooker,
cover top of can with clean dish cloth
or paper towels, put on lid and cook
at high for 4 hours. Cool slightly
before slicing. Tip: to get loaf out of
the can, open the bottom of the tin
and use the lid to push the bread out
the other end.

**Strawberry-rhubarb pudding,
old-fashioned style:**

Grandma made this delightfully tart
pudding on the back of her old woodstove. I've adapted the recipe for slow
cooking and updated the old version
by adding fresh orange for a burst of
exciting flavor. If using frozen fruit,
thaw in fridge and proceed.

> 1 pound peeled rhubarb, cut into 1
>   inch pieces
> 2 cups sliced strawberries
> ¾ cup liquid honey
> 2 Tbsp. cornstarch
> 1 tsp. ground nutmeg
> grated rind, pulp, and juice of 1
>   orange

Mix all ingredients in slow cooker.
Cover and cook on low for 3 hours, or
on high for 1 to 2 hours. Serve warm
pudding with vanilla ice cream for a
memorable dessert. Δ

> thickener made by dissolving 2
>   Tbsp. flour into ½ cup water

Turn on crock pot and let butter
melt in bottom of pot. Put in the meat
and stir until evenly coated with butter. Sprinkle with paprika. Add
remaining ingredients, except thickener, using enough stock to cover. Put
on lid and cook 6 hours on high or 8
hours on low setting. A half hour

before serving time, remove lid and
blend in the thickener. Put lid back on
and continue cooking until thick.
Taste and adjust seasoning. Serves 4
to 6.

**Banana-raisin bread in a coffee
can:**

A slow-cooking quick bread that
you can pop into the slow cooker and
put out of sight and mind—until your

Banana-raisin bread in a can, moist and delicious

A good use for old rocks

By Jerry Allen Hourigan

My small acreage is located in central Kentucky. During the last ice age the retreating glaciers must have dumped all the loose rocks in its path on my little farm. Mowing was impossible and walking was hazardous. You could not dig a hole for hitting rock. Every time it rained, more rocks would start poking out of the ground. When it came my time to live here, it somehow became my responsibility to remove these nuisances and put them somewhere out of the way.

It is a common practice in this area to throw them into rock piles, creek beds, hollers, etc. So, that is what I started doing. I picked up the loose ones and hauled them out using a rockboat sled. I used a horse to pull the sled in areas where you could not use a tractor. I even used a small cart and ATV. I soon learned that if I could get a rock to budge just a little I could somehow manage to get it loaded on the sled.

It was just me and my five year old grandson, Jackson. It was fun to watch him learn what he had to do to move a rock. His, "I can't, Pop," became, "Look what I did Pop!" especially when I'd tease him by saying, "Don't let that rock sass you boy, if you want him to move, then make him move!"

As I moved more rocks, I began to look at them with a whole new perspective. Some of these rocks were actually beautiful in their own way. Even Jackson got the fever and every few minutes he would yell, "Pop,

come here and look at this one." Which I did, of course, because you need a lot of rest breaks when you are doing this kind of labor.

I started thinking about what I could do with them now that I had come to appreciate their beauty. I knew I needed retaining walls in several spots around the place. The old well top needed a rock foundation. I always wanted rock entry columns at the entrance to my property. The creek bank could use some rock walls to help control erosion. The possibilites were endless.

Not having any experience in rock masonry I learned as I went. It's real-

built at the entrance to my property. This project was way more complicated than dry stacked rock walls since it required other materials such as concrete, cinder blocks, and mortar, as well as constructing a wooden form for the cast concrete cap. This was a whole different ball game.

Read on and I'll share the process step by step.

Gather rocks

Look for rocks that have character and eye appeal and have at least one good side. Remember only one side will show once they are mortared onto the structure. The rocks should

The author and grandson, Jackson, with LaVerne pulling the rockboat sled, and the finished rock entry columns

ly like working a giant jigsaw puzzle, except the pieces are a lot heavier. You just have to find the right rock that fits that particular spot.

One of the projects I am especially proud of is the rock entry columns I

be fairly uniform in shape and size. You can mix the pattern to include oddly shaped and larger rocks if you prefer but it requires more effort and skill in laying the pattern and getting them to fit correctly. Look for some that will make good corner stones. These need to have two good sides coming together at close to a 90 degree angle as possible. Hard to find, but they are out there. Creek beds are a good source for the type of rocks you need for this project.

When collecting your rocks, treat them kindly. You don't think of them as being breakable, but in fact they are very fragile and will break or chip easily, and never in a good way. Separate the corner stones into one stack and the field rocks into another. It will save you a lot of work later on. I can't tell you how much time I wasted looking through my pile for a good cornerstone only to find it buried under all the other rocks.

Plan your columns

Select and mark the exact location for your columns. Now, stop for a minute, get a cup of coffee, pull up a rock and cop a squat. You now need to make some decisions that you will have to live with for a long while. Consider how big do you want the columns? What will be the footprint for the footer? What distance apart do they need to be? What kind of traffic will or may need to pass through? How tall? What kind of cap are you going to put on top? Do you need electric wired into the columns for lights now or in the future? Will you be attaching gates or fencing? View the site from different angles to get a perspective on how they will look and to determine if the columns will block your view in some way. If you are planning on installing electric lights or gates, then you will need to make plans before moving on to the next step.

The foundation

Now you need to build something for the rocks to rest on. I chose to build my columns with concrete cinder blocks first and then add rock veneer. Irregardless of how you do yours, you will still need a good foun-

Grandson Jackson helped clear rocks from all over the property.

dation for them to sit on. 8"x16" cinder blocks are standard size and when you mortar one and two halves together you have approximately a 32" square. I wanted at least another foot around each side for the rock veneer so my foundation footprint was a 52" square. I made a simple 52" square form out of 2x4 lumber. I placed it where I wanted my columns and marked the spot. I moved the form out of the way and dug out about two feet deep to make room for the concrete and replaced the form putting the top at grade level and backfilled with soil to hold it in place. I poured some gravel in the hole for drainage. Using a wheel barrow and flat hoe I mixed a couple of bags of concrete mix at a time and poured into the hole until it was level with the form. I screeded off the top and allowed it to set. While waiting for it to set I began moving the cinder

blocks and mortar to the site and assembling the tools I would need next for the next step. You need a mortar trowel, brick ties, wheel barrow, flat hoe, and of course, water.

The block column

Mix a couple of bags of mortar at a time. Make the mixture stiff (dry) to start, you can always add more water if needed. Blocks are fairly heavy and if your mortar is too wet it will just squish out from the weight of the blocks. You want your blocks to be sitting in a good bed of mortar and not resting on the concrete or other blocks, so don't be stingy. I filled the connecting holes with mortar also to ensure a good bond. You can use a few small filler "trash" rocks if you like but don't skimp on the mortar. Continue laying your blocks in an overlapping pattern and begin installing two brick ties between blocks on each side. In case you're not familiar with brick ties, these little devices help to secure the rock veneer to the cinder blocks. It is not necessary to dress up the mortar joints since they will never be seen after you add the rock veneer. I just scraped the joints flush with the blocks. I knew I would later be adding heavy cast concrete caps to my columns so I also kept a bag of concrete mix close by and every couple of rows I would fill the other holes with a wet concrete mixture. I did the same for the large center opening as well, except I used a lot of trash and broken rocks as filler in addition to the concrete.

When you have finished your second column, check to make sure they are level with each other. You can run a string and level on the tops to check if you need to make any adjustments to the height.

The rock veneer

You have most of the tools you need from the last step. You will need a stiff bristle or wire brush, a tool to dig out and finish the mortar joints, a rock hammer, rock chisel, and a bucket of water or better yet a water hose. Hopefully, you checked plumb, level, and square while laying the blocks. You did, right? OK, not a show stopper. You can do a lot with mortar and how you lay the rocks to correct some minor problems. But starting now you want to pay close attention to those things. Everything you do from now on will be on display for everyone to critique, and believe me, they will. Even so, you want your columns to look good. They will be the first thing you see coming home and the last thing you see when you leave each day. As much as you can with field rocks, try to lay them as you would bricks, by off-setting the mortar joints. Start at the base with some of your larger rocks. This way you will know how far from the blocks you have to be to get all the rocks to fit

evenly and not stick out too much from the others.

Use lots of mortar to backfill between the rocks and the cinder blocks and fill up all the spaces. You can use filler trash rocks with mortar as long as they don't interfere with placement of the rock or brick ties.

Do not let your mortar joints get too dry before you clean them out. Also, don't allow the excess mortar to dry on the face of the rocks. Use the

brush and water as soon as you can and often as necessary. You want to recess the mortar at least one to two inches. The final desired effect is not to notice the mortar joints at all and to emphasize the character and shape of each of the rocks. Even that ugly one you stuck in there.

It's good to work back and forth from one column to the other. This gives the mortar time to set up on one column while you're working on the

Placing rocks for the entry column is like working a very heavy jigsaw puzzle.

The outside of the form for the concrete cap is braced securely.
It must contain nearly a ton of concrete without breaking.

other. The weight from the rocks above pushing down can squeeze out the mortar causing the rocks to sit on each other, so stop and allow the mortar to dry as needed before you add more weight.

When you get to the top you want to stay an inch or so below the cinder blocks. If you are going to install a heavy concrete cap you will want the majority of the weight to rest on the blocks instead of the rock veneer. The cinder blocks will be the strongest parts of the column. Once you place your cap you can fill any cracks between the rocks and the cap with mortar.

The concrete cap

I chose to install a pyramid shaped cast concrete cap. To give the caps their roof-like appearance you need to have about a 6" overhang around all four sides. Once the columns and rock veneer were completed I measured two sides and added one foot to the length and width to get the 6" overhang. I used 2x4 lumber and ¼" thick plywood and assembled the pieces with 16 penny nails and wood screws.

First I cut the 2x4s into the correct lengths and cut a 45 degree angle on one edge of each and fastened the corners with screws leaving the angle on the outside top of the frame. I didn't know exactly how high I wanted the point of the pyramid to be, so I experimented until I found the height that I liked. Then it's just a matter of

cutting the lumber to the right lengths and angles so they meet at the center and edge of the form. Once this is completed, add bracing supports to strengthen the form. I re-enforced the corners and point using brick ties left over from the last step. This is all structural and doesn't need to look good but it does need to be strong in order to hold the concrete.

Turn the form over and remove the screws holding the outside frame to the supports running to the point. Leave the frame connected at the corners and set aside for now. Measure and cut four triangular pieces of plywood to cover the inside of the form and attach with short wood screws. The four pieces have to be precise in order to meet along the seams and at the point. This is what gives the final appearance to your caps and any defect will transfer to the concrete. You're essentially building a concrete mold. It would be good to putty or tape the seams to ensure a good, smooth surface. Re-install the outside frame that you removed earlier and install more braces as needed. The point of the form should be braced

2006/2/20

The inside of the concrete form should be smooth and free of gaps
or the concrete will leak through.

The finished concrete cap with debossed "H" weighs nearly a ton and is lowered into place with a front-end loader or backhoe.

concrete on the point and sides. Take the flat hoe and scrape the sides to settle the concrete as well. Once you get the concrete up from the sides and point you can make the mix drier and use up some of the excess water already in the form. If you use a hollow box form in the center, set it after you have made a couple of pours. Continue mixing and pouring until you reach the top. Screed and float off the top and allow to set. When the concrete is ready, use an edge finishing tool to round over the edge around the form. This prevents cracking and breaking and gives a better appearance to your project.

Install the cap

After a couple of days remove the screws at the corners of the form and gently pry loose. Wrap a log chain around the form and using a tractor with front end loader or a backhoe pull the form up out of the hole and over. I used a bale of hay to help cushion the fall. The form should easily lift off. Load the caps and gently place them on the top of the rock columns. Center and align the cap evenly around all sides. Now don't think you can call a few of your buddies in to help lift it up on top. This cap weighs almost a ton. Mix a small amount of mortar and fill any gaps between the rocks and concrete cap. Even better, first lay a thick bed around the top edge before placing the cap. Clean up any excess and spills. Get yourself another cup of coffee and enjoy the fruits of your labor!

Who would have ever thought a bunch of old pesky rocks could be a thing of beauty! I guess the old Pharaoh's knew this when they had the Hebrew slaves move all those rocks and stack them in the desert. No telling what the old boys could have built if they'd just had a backhoe! Δ

well with two by four lumber and brick ties. This will be the greatest stress point in the form. Remember concrete is fluid and will seek to escape any way it can. If your form is weak it will bust and you will have a real mess on your hands.

The best way to support this inverted pyramid-shaped form during the pour is to dig a pyramid-shaped hole and place the form into it, allowing the earth to support the form. I would suggest at least two thirds of the form should be in the hole. Once in place, shim the sides as needed using scrap pieces of lumber. The weight of the concrete will press it into the sides of the hole. Also, place a concrete cinder block under each of the four corners to help support the form and keep it level.

Gather your tools, water supply, and concrete. You will need a wheel barrow, flat hole, shovel, edge finishing tool, and large hammer. I placed a two inch pipe into the point of my caps in case later I wanted to add a flag, ball, birdhouse, or whatever. Plug up both ends of the pipe with a rag to prevent the concrete from filling it up. I made a letter "H" out of wood scraps and attached it to the inside of the form. After you remove the form and dig out the wood the letter is debossed into the concrete. You could just as easily make an embossed letter by cutting the letter in the plywood and building a back support for the concrete. I also made a small box form to hollow out the inside of the pyramid a little but I found out that it is was more trouble than it was worth. If weight is a concern then you might want to do this. You can build as many forms as you need. I built just one and used it twice.

Build a ramp to one side of the form so that you can push the wheel barrow up to the edge and dump the concrete. This can be just dirt or a large board of plywood. Mix two or three bags of concrete at a time. Make it very wet and mix well to start. Secure the center pipe or have someone hold it in place as you dump the concrete into the form. Tap the sides of the form with the hammer to settle the

More building projects in all 18 anthologies

Ayoob on Firearms

Moderate power firearms

By Massad Ayoob

Robert Ruark, the great American writer of the mid-Twentieth century, was also a big game hunter. One of his most popular books, written on the latter topic, was titled *Use Enough Gun.* That has proven over the decades to be really good advice.

That said, there are also a lot of people who use "too much gun." One of the last century's top authorities on guns and hunting was Jack O'Connor, a contemporary of Ruark's. O'Connor was an advocate of medium-powered hunting rifles: the .30-06 Springfield, the 7mm Mauser (also known as 7X57mm), and the caliber he is credited with popularizing, the .270 Winchester. He well understood that a gun with excessive power for the task would also "kick" so hard that many people wouldn't shoot well with it. He wrote in 1965 in his *Complete Book of Shooting,* "Men hate to admit that recoil bothers them. Again they feel that if getting belted by some hard-kicking gun bruises them and shakes them up they are lacking in masculinity. I have seen men who were so afraid of their magnum rifles that they closed their eyes, jerked the trigger, and couldn't hit a wash tub at 100 yards. Yet they denied that they flinched and claimed that they were such stout fellas that they actually loved recoil."

O'Connor noted that too-powerful guns were a particularly bad idea for people who didn't have a lot of size and muscle to them: kids, for instance, and females who were not athletically built. Said O'Connor in the same book, "Not long after we were married, my wife shot my Model 54 Winchester .270—once.

She handed it back to me and announced that she would never shoot it again." Mrs. O'Connor later became a noted hunter in her own right, taking big game specimens all over the world. Her favorite hunting rifle appears to have been the milder 7mm Mauser.

The trick is finding for each shooter the necessary balance of power and controllability. "Use enough gun," indeed. But remember that using too much gun for the given task will quickly take you to the point of diminishing returns.

Rifles

Generations of young boys (and girls) have brought their first deer with the classic old .30-30 carbine. As produced in the millions by Winchester (Model '94) and Marlin (Model 336), both are readily available with short "youth stocks." Under seven pounds in weight, they're less likely to physically exhaust a smaller person with a day of carrying in the woods. Recoil is not at all bad.

For a flat-shooting, high velocity game rifle, it's hard to beat the .243 Winchester cartridge. With a 100 grain bullet constructed for deer-size game, and delivering a velocity in the 3000 feet per second range, the .243 has adequate power for humanely transporting Bambi from field to freezer, and has extremely mild recoil.

Noted O'Connor himself, "Today's .243 Winchester and (analogous) 6mm Remington do very well for deer and antelope." O'Connor wrote those words in 1965, but deer and antelope anatomy have not changed

Massad Ayoob

appreciably in the intervening forty-plus years.

Other mild-kicking hunting rifle calibers that have proven themselves swift and humane killers of deer-size game include the .250/3000 Savage and the .257 Roberts. However, like Mrs. O'Connor's 7mm, they are not particularly popular today and you won't find the wide array of good ammunition choices for them that's available for the super-popular .243.

Though autoloaders, slide-action rifles, single shots, and even lever action rifles (such as the classic Savage Model 99 and the uber-cool Winchester Model 88) have been produced in .243 caliber, this cartridge is predominantly found in bolt action rifles. My personal choice would be one of the lighter specimens, such as Remington's Model 7 or the ultra-light Compact variation of Ruger's Model 77. These, along with the cost-effective and super-accurate Savage Models 110 and 11, are also available with the short "youth stocks" for smaller statured folks.

With carefully selected, perhaps handloaded ammunition, and with

119

equally careful marksmanship and the self-discipline to wait for the perfect firing angle, the .243 can be adequate for even larger than deer-size game. Accomplished gun writer Mike Venturino had this to say in the October, 2007 *Guns* magazine about a young huntress named Morgan Wines: "In Morgan's first year of hunting she bagged a pronghorn antelope buck, a whitetail buck, and not just one but two cow elk! (The second was perfectly legal. It was part of a depredation hunt in another part of the state.) That would give bragging rights to a big brawny, hairy-chested macho man, but this hunting was done by a 90 pound, 12-year-old girl wielding a Savage Model 11 Youth Model .243."

Single barrel/single shot shotguns like this one by New England Firearms are inexpensive and very common in backwoods homes. Author finds 20 gauge optimum balance between recoil and shot output.

Shotguns

Historically, the .410 shotgun has been a common "starter gun" for shooters, especially younger ones. It is the smallest and lightest "gauge" available. However, many of us think it's too small.

These little shells just don't hold enough lead to always get the job done. Personally, I see the .410 as a close-range squirrel and rabbit gun. Noted the great Frank C. Barnes in his authoritative text *Cartridges of the World*, the rifled slug load in the .410 is "not adequate for deer," though he believed it would get business done with a coyote or bobcat.

On the other end of the spectrum is the 12 gauge, by far the most popular backwoods home shotgun. The reason for that popularity is its versatility: the big two and three quarter inch 12-gauge shell holds an ounce to an ounce and a quarter of lead, and that's just in its standard loading, before you get into the Magnum options. A bigger spread of birdshot gives you a better chance of cleanly killing game birds; a bigger spread of buckshot is more devastating in the anti-personnel context; and a bigger chunk of lead (weighing 400 to 500 grains, at 1400 to 1600 feet per second) is more decisive on deer and close-range bear.

However, the 12 gauge is also infamous for its recoil with anything but a light trap or skeet load. Many a lad has been knocked on his butt firing his first 12 gauge. In an adult lifetime of teaching police, I've met a lot of macho man cops who were scared to death of the 12 gauge "riot gun's" kick, and a couple of female officers

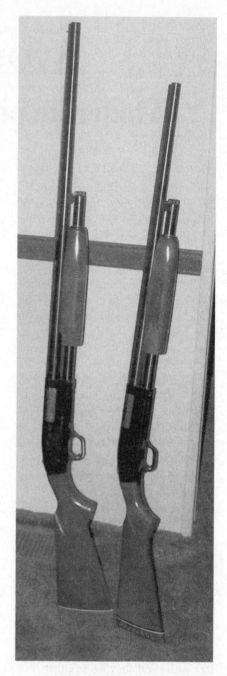

20 gauge pump shotguns, both Mossberg's affordable Model 500. Left has 28" barrel, 24" barrel on the right.

who were crippled for life by it through shoulder damage sustained from the constant hammering of intensive training fire. A full load 12 gauge in a light pump gun kicks about like a .375 Magnum elephant rifle.

To split the difference, I think the best bet for a light-kicking but hard-hitting shotgun is the 20 gauge. You can virtually duplicate 12-gauge performance with some three-inch Magnum 20 gauge shells, but for most needs, the standard two and three-quarter inch 20 gauge shell will get the job done.

In a standard rifled slug load for deer, the 20 gauge's projectile is approximately .62 caliber, weighs five-eighths of an ounce, and runs at a speed of 1400 foot-seconds or greater. That's roughly the equivalent of two .44 Magnums at once. Will it transform Bambi swiftly into venison? Oh, yes.

In a buckshot load, the standard for 20 gauge is #3 buck, which consists of twenty pellets, each a quarter inch in diameter. Among common 12-gauge shells, the closest would be the so called "urban police load," #4 buck. This consists of 27 pellets, each .23 caliber. Velocity is roughly the same, whether twelve or twenty gauge.

For home defense purposes, let's say two evil twin men are kicking down the front door, announcing their intent to murder every man, woman,

Interchangeable choke tubes, seen here at muzzle of 20 gauge shotgun, give more versatility.

No shotgun is simpler to unload than this NEF single barrel, available in several gauges.

and child in the house. Spouse A fires a round of 12-gauge #4 buckshot and sends 27 .23" diameter pellets into the chest of the first evil twin. Spouse B unleashes a single round of 20 gauge #3 buckshot, blasting 20 .25" diameter pellets at approximately the same velocity into the thorax of the second evil twin, with all the projectiles penetrating to approximately the same depth.

Who's going to know the difference? Only the medical examiner, and then only after he meticulously counts the white spots on the X-rays, or tallies the number of pellets removed from each corpse.

Birdshot? Only in long range waterfowl hunting does the 20 gauge seem to really give away much to the bigger 12, and then it is largely because non-lead pellets required for lo, these many years to keep lead out of the wetlands are not very efficient penetrators. This means that with, say, steel shot, reduced momentum and reduced penetration need to be made up for with more pellets striking the bird.

For upland game such as pheasant or partridge, or for hunting small game such as wild rabbits for the family stewpot, shotgun authority Francis E. Sell proved in the 1950s that the 20 gauge loses precious little compared to the 12 gauge, and there is the three-inch Magnum 20 gauge shell available for those who want a bit more punch. Lighter and much faster to handle than most 12-bores, the 20 improves wing-shooting skill for a great many people. My significant other, a tough little critter who stands barely five feet tall, refuses to shoot my 12 gauges anymore, but is hell on wheels with her Remington 1100 Youth Model 20 gauge semiautomatic.

If the user(s) can benefit from a lighter, easier-to-carry gun that kicks less, the 20 gauge makes huge sense. In similar size shotguns, its recoil will be barely over half that of the 12 gauge. The 20 is available in all action types: semiautomatic and pump, side by side double barrel or over and under, and low-price bolt actions and single shots.

*Author pops a shell into a .410 single barrel.
He considers that round too underpowered to be useful for much.*

Handguns

Here, choice depends more on purpose than anything else. A hunting handgun intended for deer-size game wants to be either a large caliber such as a .44 Special or .45 Colt, or a fast-moving Magnum such as a .357, minimum. It is generally accepted that the 9mm Luger cartridge in a semi-automatic pistol or the .38 Special cartridge in a revolver is about the minimum for defense against feral human beings, while both are on the light side for humanely, ethically harvesting deer-size animals.

I've owned, shot, and enjoyed such monster guns as the Smith & Wesson .500 Magnum and .460, and still love to shoot my J.D. Jones custom built .375 JDJ single shot, created from a Thompson/Center pistol. About three shots from the latter will give me my monthly recoil requirement, however, and a handgun with the potency of a high-powered rifle is not something I need every day.

If attack by a maddened steer or an angry horse is part of the handgun's mission profile, you do indeed want a "horse pistol," and I'd choose a pow-erful sidearm with a deep-driving bullet. Not for nothing did cowboys, who risked exactly this situation every day, always prefer large caliber guns. A compact .44 Magnum revolver would serve well here, or as a daily carry gun for anyone whose homestead was in large bear country.

For the backwoods person who does not have these particular threats, and keeps a handgun for protection against feral dogs or feral humans, the 9mm or .38 Special can be adequate, and their famously light recoil makes them easy for smaller folks to shoot, or folks who are new to the gun and just a little bit intimidated by the whole thing.

Anything distinctly smaller—such as the .380 Auto pistol caliber, which is literally a "9mm Short"—too often fails to make the cut. I've run across shooting after shooting where the defender shot a violent aggressor with a .380 and did little to immediately stop his depredations. A good hollow point load in 9mm or .38 Special will, historically, end lethal assaults more quickly.

Frankly, another good choice is the all-American .45 automatic. It has been a famous "man-stopper" in world wars and domestic gunfights alike, and with deep-penetrating 230 grain full metal jacket ammunition,

In defensive handguns, medium calibers will suffice with the right ammo and good hits. There are 60 timed "combat match" shots on each of these targets. Left, former Midwest Regional Champion (Stock Service Pistol) Dave Maglio with Glock 9mm; right, former Midwest Regional Champion (Stock Service Revolver) Mas Ayoob with S&W .38 Special.

Today's premium ammunition makes the mild-kicking .243 Winchester a more useful "deer and down" rifle than ever.

can penetrate deeply enough to drop large animals. A friend of mine in Africa, game ranger Phil Honeyborne, carried a Colt .45 automatic loaded with nine rounds of "hardball" ammo because it was the best medicine he could come up with to cure surprise lion or leopard attacks when he was caught without his rifle. With proper training, little kids and the most petite females can be taught to handle the recoil of the semi-automatic .45 caliber pistol.

.22s

The .22 is the ubiquitous rural home working gun. At close range under controlled conditions (i.e., a securely tethered or closely confined animal) it can be used to begin the slaughter process on cattle and large hogs. It is when the critter breaks loose, and a perfect brain shot can no longer be guaranteed, that it becomes altogether too feeble for the task. While poachers have been known to kill jacklighted deer with .22s, and the occasional desperate Inuit has been known to slay the largest of bears with a .22 bullet placed with perfect precision, no person who was both sane and gun-savvy would recommend the .22

for anything much bigger than a fox. The .22 is at its best on rabbits and squirrels, and of course, on the shooting range.

One of Savage Arms' most popular firearms over the decades has been the Model 24. This "combination gun" was extremely handy, because its top barrel was chambered for the .22 Long Rifle cartridge and its bottom barrel for the .410 shotgun shell. However, this was a low-powered combination. The concept became much more useful when Savage started chambering the top barrel for the .30-30 Winchester rifle cartridge, and the bottom barrel for the 20 gauge shotgun shell.

The cheapest firearm to shoot with factory ammunition, with mild muzzle blast and almost non-existent recoil, the .22 is one of our "funnest" guns and, for many things, among the most useful. However, it is sadly lacking in power when any aggressive living thing of any substantial size has to be neutralized by gunfire.

The bottom line

This is why the typical rural family who've lived that life for a while will have a .22, and a shotgun, and a rifle chambered for a caliber powerful enough for deer-size game at a minimum. This is why when outdoor sports magazines do surveys on the hunters who read their periodicals, they learn that their average reader owns around seven firearms. It is why serious hunters own more than that: one tailors the tool to the task, and the person who hunts different kinds of game in different settings will need that many more of those tools.

If you have to choose one "deer rifle" and one shotgun, you can do very well with a .243 and a 20 gauge, and with a 9mm pistol or .38 Special revolver for personal defense, for that matter.

Someone may say to you, "Why don't you use something more powerful?"

If that happens, it's perfectly correct for you to smile just the least bit smugly and answer, "Everything in moderation." Δ

Ask Jackie

If you have a question about rural living, send it in to Jackie Clay and she'll try to answer it. Address your letter to Ask Jackie, PO Box 712, Gold Beach, OR 97444. Questions will only be answered in this column.

— Editor

Preserving black walnuts

I inherited a number of mature black walnut trees when I recently bought my house. This past fall, I picked up the walnuts in their green husk, de-husked them, and let them dry before putting them in mesh bags. Just tried cracking them, and what a disappointment! It appears they dried in the shell! What did I do wrong? And how do you properly process black walnuts?

Kristin Radtke
Ripon, Wisconsin

How long did you dry the nuts? They really should be spread out on, say a barn loft floor for a few weeks before storing them.

To process black walnuts, wait till they fall from the tree and the husk is yellowish. I rake them up and pour buckets full in the driveway and run over them with a vehicle until the husks are mashed off (I have a dirt driveway; you probably wouldn't want to do this on cement). Or walk back and forth on them with old shoes. I say old shoes because the stain in the husks and on the freshly husked nuts is *very* staining to everything and you can't get it out. With rubber gloves on, pick up the nuts and take them inside to spread out and dry. One way you can tell if the nuts have meats in them is to dump them into a bucket of water before you store them. The empty ones float, so

pick them out and throw them away. Store the rest in a single layer. After a few weeks, the nuts can be handled and cracked. As you probably found out, walnuts are hard to pick out of the shell, but oh so worth the effort!
— *Jackie*

Germinating parsnips

I just dug my whole crop of parsnips, all 3 of them. I have difficulty getting the parsnip seed to germinate. I have tried soaking them 24 hours before planting and have tried putting a board over the row a short period of time to keep the dirt damp until they sprout. Do you have any helpful tricks to get them to sprout? Is there a specific parsnip seed that sprouts better than others?

Lorraine Adams
Gold Beach, Oregon

Parsnips take up to three weeks to germinate. The hardest part of getting them to sprout is keeping the weeds out and keeping the rows moist for that whole time. Be sure your parsnip area is good deep soil that is in a weed-free area to lessen your problems. It helps to mulch on both sides of the row, right after you plant it. This helps hold the moisture and keep the weeds at bay to some extent. I take a little extra time and plant the seeds one at a time, about two inches apart, and at least ¼ inch deep. If they are planted too shallow, they dry out even more quickly, killing the germinating sprout.

No, there isn't a specific parsnip variety that sprouts better. They are all a bit slow, but with a little extra care and perseverance, you can get them to grow. Mine surprised me, as I planted them last spring on the new part of my garden and they all came up and produced nice roots. Good luck this spring! — *Jackie*

Jackie Clay

Canning whole milk

I tried canning whole milk, about 10 quarts. They have all thickened up and the jars have sealed. Can I use this milk in some way? I lucked out at the time I thought, as our local grocer's ad had four gallons for $9.

Rosemary Barber
Mapleton, Iowa

You can use this milk in any recipes calling for milk, such as gravies, white sauces, baking, casseroles, noodle dishes, and more. I use it in place of evaporated milk, as it is thicker than regular milk. — *Jackie*

Can rancid nuts be used?

We have several packages each of shelled walnuts, almonds, peanuts, and pecans stored in large plastic containers in our pantry that have turned rancid. Also some in jars on the shelves are rancid. The nuts we use regularly are kept in the freezer, and seem to keep a long time without becoming rancid. Is there a way to store them so they won't become rancid? What can be done with the rancid nuts to make them edible again? Have you ever vacuum packed them?

Jerry Sisler
Stevensville, Montana

Sorry, but there's nothing I know of that will make rancid nuts taste good. I can my nutmeats and they've kept for years in the jars without becoming rancid. They're easy to can, too. You just put them on a cookie sheet and gently heat them in the oven at 250 degrees, stirring them to keep them from scorching. When they are hot, place them in hot pint or half-pint canning jars and place a hot, previously simmered lid on the jar and screw the ring down firmly tight. You can water bath process the jars by having the water in the canner ½ inch below the top of the jars and processing them for 30 minutes from the time the water comes back to a rolling boil. Or you can process them in a pressure canner at 6 pounds (dial gauge) or 5 pounds with a weighted gauge, for 10 minutes. — *Jackie*

What is a fruit coil?

I am looking for a cheap fruit coil substitute. I have tried Lehman's but they don't stock them. Where can I find one?

Mrs. Peter Wallace
Conders, Indiana

I honestly have never heard of a fruit coil. Can you help me here? I've asked people all over the country and no one else knows, either. Is it a regional name for something I *am* familiar with? Help! — *Jackie*

Tomato diseases

This year when I was putting my garden to bed I noticed this weird lumpy stuff on the stems of my Big Mama Romas. The affected plants produced small misshapen tomatoes with blossom end rot and a beige colored rash. I bought limestone to use next year to combat the rot but what is this lumpy stem thing? Because I have only one long raised bed I can't rotate crops properly. I have planted tomatoes intensively there for 5 seasons. This was the only problem so far. Can you recommend any additives to help the situation? I live in

zone 5 and mulch heavily with pine bark and cedar chips. I also add lots of rotted cow manure every spring and a bit of compost from my little composter bin.

CJ Ostrowski
Eggertsville, New York

You've got me CJ. The misshapen tomatoes with blossom end rot sound like they had problems getting enough water. Was it extra hot this last summer in your area? A lot of raised beds need more water than garden rows because they *are* raised and the moisture drains off too quickly. Mulching helps, but I'd like weed-free straw, leaves, or seed-free hay better than the pine bark and cedar chips; the wood products break down so slowly and don't add a lot of nutrition to the soil.

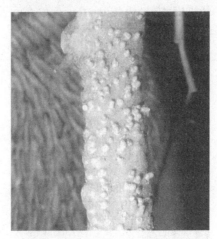

The beige "rash" could be anthracnose, a common tomato disease. I would suggest looking through a tomato disease book or going online and browse "tomato diseases." There are several good sites with lots of pictures and information that you could compare with your tomato "rash." You could also take your picture to your Extension Office, located in the courthouse, and ask the ag agent about your problem. They are usually very helpful. And the help is free.

I would like to see you make another bed fresh for your tomatoes this spring; growing tomatoes, which are susceptible to many diseases, in the

same ground for five years is not a good idea. Although Big Mama is a great tomato, it isn't very disease resistant.

When you have diseased tomatoes, you need to pull the vines and dispose of them in another area, not the compost pile. Then try either a resistant variety or else put the next crop into another bed, even if you have to garden in containers with your tomatoes. I've done this with good luck and it works no matter where you live. I have one neighbor who has no garden, but lines his driveway with five-gallon buckets, each with a nice tomato growing in it! — *Jackie*

One handed self-reliance

This is a hard question to ask because I don't now how to ask it. But here goes. Have you had anybody ask you how to do things one-handed, like dressing chickens or gardening and so on? I only ask because I have only one hand. I know you had cancer in your arm so how did you do that stuff and other things with the use of only one arm?

Linda Hinkle
Gig Harbor, Washington

This is a problem I've had lots of experience with. Yes, I had cancer surgery on my left elbow and was a bit laid up with that, but also my adopted son, Javid, from India came to me with multiple handicaps. These left him paralyzed from the waist down and also in his left arm. As he wanted to join in all the homestead activities with the rest of the family, he grew adept at using his chin or a heavy duty fish scaling board with a clamp on the end to hold various items. We still joke when we talk about him helping husk corn because he held it under his chin and pulled the husks with his able hand. We call it "chin corn" and he says there was never any corn that tasted quite as good after he grew up and left home!

You can clamp a chicken with the fish scaling board (even if you have to jerry-rig it a bit). You didn't say if you have an arm that works. If so, you have a great advantage because you can use it to weight down whatever you are working on. You can use meat scissors to help dress chickens, instead of a knife. There are all sorts of adaptive equipment available; some you'll have to think of yourself for each homestead task. Then there are ways to make a difficult task easier, too. For instance, sometimes it's hard to unscrew the ring on a canning jar, one handed. But if you soak the jar in warm, sudsy water for a few minutes, it will usually unscrew easily, while held under your chin or in your armpit.

Adapting to handicapping situations is never easy, but everything *is* possible if you get tough and decide you *will* do it. Do you have a prosthesis? Can you wear one? A friend of mine had his hand amputated after a car wreck. Gordy was a cowboy and as tough as they come. He got a prosthesis (hook type) and soon learned to drive a team, drive his big truck, and even tip his hat with finesse.

The best of luck and contact me again if I can be of help. — *Jackie*

Fruit trees not producing

I have learned so much from your articles in BHM and your blog. I'm hoping you can help me be more successful with my vegetable garden and fruit trees and bushes this year.

We live on the coast of Washington. We have about an acre which was formerly forest land. It is quite steep in places so I've put in raised beds for vegetables where I can fit them. I also planted two apple and one cherry tree (Stella) and about 8 mixed varieties of blueberry bushes. We built here almost five years.

All this by way of background gets to my question. I feel like I work very hard, but get very little return for my hard work. We got four apples, less than a pie's worth of blueberries and a few meals of veggies. Where would you start to get everything producing?

Is part of the problem that everything, including the soil, is not properly built up? I have tried to plant zone 5 appropriate plants and trees, but we haven't lived here very long. I sure would love your advice.

Donna Clements
Hoquiam, Washington

I understand your frustration. But you are probably right on the edge of having everything begin producing at once. No matter what the catalogs say, it usually takes 4-5 years before most fruit trees and some smaller berry bushes begin to produce heavily. Keep at it; give those trees and bushes a nice mulch of good compost, keeping it a couple inches from the trunk/stems to keep mice from chewing the bark. Water if necessary and keep the weeds down. Chances are that you'll have a great garden soon. Keep working good compost into your vegetable beds…but not too much fresher manure because it has too much nitrogen in it and will cause your vegetables to have great leaves but not much for, say, tomatoes or peppers.

Are your trees and raised beds in the shade of other trees? This can cause problems as most garden crops like plenty of sunshine. You may have to remove a few offending wild trees to bring sunshine to your trees, bushes, and beds.

Otherwise, keep plugging away at it. It *will* pay off in the end. We've been here four years in February and my little orchard is nothing that would be put on a magazine cover… and we've yet to have an apple or cherry to eat. But I know that's in the future and I'm beginning to drool already! Let me how you do.

— *Jackie*

Bleeding out an animal

Can you "bleed out" an animal by slitting its throat just as effectively after it has been shot, or does it have to be alive when you do it?

My husband and I are in disagreement on this issue. I think it is cruel to kill an animal by slitting its throat and letting it bleed to death. He believes that in order for the heart to pump out all the blood, it has to be done this way? Does it?

Lisa Light-Abrego
Peck, Michigan

You're both right in my opinion. I couldn't cut a live animal's throat, although many people do just that, in order to get more thorough bleeding out. Generally, most people first shoot the animal, then quickly cut the throat. If this is done quickly, the animal will bleed out enough before it is dead, dead.

What about when you hunt and shoot a deer? You usually don't slit the throat on a live deer. Right? And the meat is just fine. — *Jackie*

Can I freeze the eggs?

I am the happy owner of 20 beautiful hens and 2 dashing roosters. My question is this, is there a way to longterm store the eggs? Can I freeze them anyway? Also, what is the breeding and gestation time for hens. My roosters are breeding now and I would rather the hens not go broody until warmer weather. Could you help shed some light?

Sherry Preedy
Meade, Kansas

Yes, you can freeze eggs. Most folks just break the eggs, several at a time, into small plastic freezer boxes. You want enough eggs to just about fill the box, leaving room for expansion during freezing but not enough space to let a lot of air contact the eggs. You can leave them whole or mix the whites and yolks.

You don't have to worry about your hens. Roosters breed year around, but hens very seldom go broody until summer hits. Their bodies know when it's time to sit on eggs, even when you provide them with artificial light in the winter. — *Jackie*

Build your own repeating mouse trap

Safety note: Because of drowning danger, 5-gallon buckets with any amount of water in them should *never* be placed where children under the age of 5 will be present.

By Allen Easterly

When the mice are giving you a problem in the barn or feed shed you can put a significant dent in the population in short order with a repeating mousetrap. Standard mouse traps are a one-shot deal. Once sprung you need to bait and reset them. To be effective these traps need to be checked daily. While commercial repeating traps work well they have a very limited holding capacity until the mice need to be removed. That means you need to check the traps often as well. But there is a better mousetrap.

How would you like to have a trap that you only bait occasionally and only have to check every week or two during warm weather or maybe just monthly during the cold of winter? You can build your own repeating mouse trap from items you may already have on hand.

The only materials you will need are: a paper or Styrofoam plate, a wire coat hanger, a couple of sticks, and a five-gallon plastic bucket. The empty plastic buckets are easy to come by. You probably have some that have previously held paint, joint compound, or laundry detergent. I often see them littering the roadway. Grab one of these and you'll also be helping clean up our environment a little.

Drill two small holes on opposing sides of the bucket, just under the rim about halfway across the opening. Cut the straight and longest section from the bottom of a wire coat hanger. Insert one end of the coat hanger piece into one of the drilled holes. Turn the plate upside down and position it so it's over the opening of the bucket with one edge of the plate resting on the rim of the bucket halfway between the drilled holes. Poke the end of coat hanger through the plate about an inch from its edge. Continue with the coat hanger by running it under the plate and through the opposite side of the plate about an inch from its edge. Run the end of the coat hanger through the remaining drilled hole. Add two or three inches of water to the bucket. Prop a stick or two on each side of the bucket to allow mice easy access. Spread peanut butter on the edge of the plate that is over the water. Flip the plate and bait the other side of the plate in the same vicinity. Don't add too much peanut butter or the plate will tip vertically. You want the non-baited part of the plate to rest on the rim of the bucket. Your trap is now ready to work.

When mice get a whiff of the peanut butter they'll climb the stick to the top of the bucket to investigate. If they want the peanut butter they'll have to walk across the plate to reach it. Once they cross the point where the coat hanger passes through the plate, the balance of the plate will change, dumping the mouse in the bucket. The water prevents them from jumping out and will put an end to their feed-stealing ways. When the plate tips to drop the mouse it flips all the way over and rests on the opposing side of the bucket. Because you put peanut butter on both sides of the plate it is now reset and baited for the next mouse. The mice rarely get a chance to savor the flavor of the peanut butter so it will stay intact for many more mice to come. When you check your homemade repeating mousetrap you might want to empty the mousy water and replace it with fresh water to reduce any foul odor.

Allen Easterly is a freelance writer building a retirement hobby farm in the mountains of Basye, Virginia. He can be reached at alleneasterly@yahoo.com. △

Use sticks or any material that will provide mice with a ramp on each side to the "high dive."

Make adobe bricks

By Rev. J. D. Hooker

Last winter I got a phone call from an old friend in Arizona. One of his sons had fallen in love, gotten the girl in trouble, and run afoul of her Mexican/Indian family. A hasty marriage and real wedding ceremony was the only thing capable of defusing the situation, and the kid really wanted "Uncle Joe" to perform the wedding ceremony.

Of course the fact that Arizona's temperatures were in the 60s and 70s, while I was shoveling a three-foot snowdrift off of my roof in sub-zero winds didn't influence my decision to make the trip even a little bit. Yeah, right!

After the wedding I stuck around longer than I'd planned to, because everyone had already decided to erect a house for the new couple, on property his father had given them as a wedding gift. Some of the "guests" had already been at work on the project for several weeks.

Several older men, armed with ancient looking adzes and mattocks, shaved away at the sides of a depression carved into a bank of clay. Others shoveled these shavings into the middle of the "brick pit" they were working in. Younger men and older boys carted wheelbarrow loads of horse and burro manure, and buckets filled with creek water, to mix with the clay shavings.

The mixture varies according to the quality of the clay, but is usually about 10-15% manure, just enough water to achieve a plaster-like consistency, and sometimes small amounts of coarse sand.

Young men and women stomped around in the sloppy mess, churning the mixture together. All the while, wheelbarrow loads of this mixture were hauled out and made into bricks using wooden molds. Then the molds were removed, regreased (by rubbing with rancid fat, or painting on a 50-50 mix of kerosene and used motor oil), and the "bricks" were left laying flat to dry in the sun. Bricks that had already dried enough to handle without falling apart were stacked on edge for further drying.

With everyone working together, we were producing 1,500 to 2,000

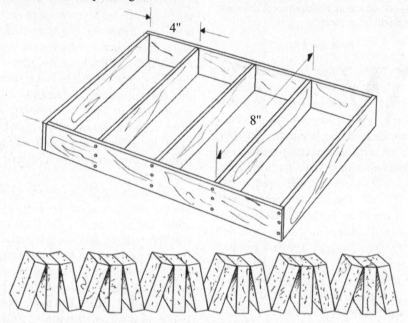

Brick mold, above, and stacking bricks to dry in the sun

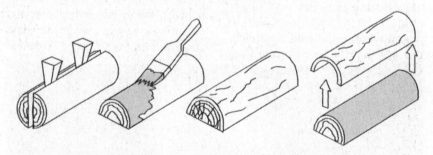

*To make clay roofing tiles: 1) Split 2' length of de-barked log in half.
2) Oil or grease well. 3) Coat with approximately ¾" of clay mixture.
4) Remove from log mold when well dried.*

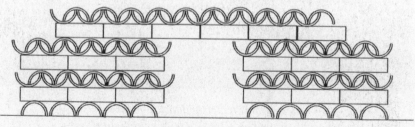

Stack into kiln and allow to dry thoroughly before firing.

unfired bricks each day. Once enough of these bricks (about 7,500) had been very thoroughly dried by the sun and wind, they were stacked to form a large, open-topped kiln which was then filled to overflowing with wood hauled from the mountains, corn cobs carted from fields and cribs, well-dried goat, sheep, pig, and cattle manure, and just about any other sort of fuel they could collect.

Once lighted, this fire burned through two full days and nights, and then took another three days to cool enough to shovel away the ashes and coals. The bricks were just as hard as any you could have purchased.

After the firing, it was plain to see how the added manure does more than just hold the bricks together as they dry. During the firing, the manure in the bricks burns along with the other fuel. This not only burns the bricks harder, but leaves them porous

enough to soak up some of the mortar as they're laid, giving a stronger bond.

Essentially, the same process was used to fashion the roofing tiles. Some six and seven-inch diameter logs were sawn into two-foot lengths, split in half, and debarked. The rounded sides were greased and coated with about a ¾-inch-thickness of this same clay mixture. Once well dried in the sun, the hardened clay was very carefully removed from the wood. The tiles that didn't break were stacked into the same type of open kiln stack, and left to complete the drying process. Those that didn't survive removal from the "molds" were broken up and tossed back into the brick pit.

Once these tiles were totally dried out, the stack was again filled with whatever sorts of flammables could be collected together. This was then

set afire, and allowed to burn itself out. Probably nearly a fourth of these tiles cracked or broke apart during the firing, but that didn't faze anyone. They simply gave several of the smaller kids some fist-sized rocks, and set them to busting the damaged tiles into tiny bits. Later, the broken bits were used like gravel to fashion walkways around the new home.

Other logs, hauled down from the same mountains, were used to shape door and window frames, rafters and roof braces, pole-type roof sheathing, and other necessary items. There were still a few things that needed to be purchased however; nails, window glass, masonry cement, and so forth (which my friend's in-laws happily sprang for). But for less than $1,000, the new couple had a spanking new 2,500 square-foot sturdy brick home, without owing anyone anything, except gratitude. ∆

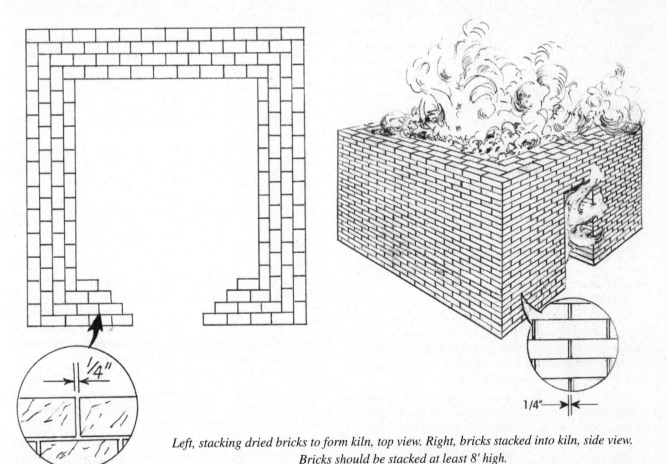

Left, stacking dried bricks to form kiln, top view. Right, bricks stacked into kiln, side view. Bricks should be stacked at least 8' high.

The last word

Our "unenumerated" rights

I received this question in an e-mail from my younger brother, Mike: "Jack, the other day a friend asked me where in the *Constitution* does it say you have the right to freedom of travel. Do you know where I would find that...?

My reply was as follows:

I tell people this again and again, but it falls on deaf ears: There is no place in the *Constitution* that says we have the right to travel, the right to privacy, etc. In fact, the *Bill of Rights*, which "mentions" some, and only some, of our rights, almost wasn't included in the *Constitution*. The Democrats, led by Thomas Jefferson, wanted a *Bill of Rights* included because they were afraid if we didn't explicitly say we have Natural, God-given, or unalienable (that's the word they used, not inalienable) rights, it would someday be assumed they didn't exist. On the other hand, the Federalists were afraid that if a *Bill of Rights* was included, it would be assumed that the government could now control them, i.e., that our rights would be viewed as "constitutional rights," such as Canada, Great Britain, and many other countries have today, which in those countries are thought to exist at the pleasure of the government.

As a safety, so that it would not appear that the enumerated rights were the only ones we have, the *Ninth Amendment* was included in the Bill of Rights. What does it say? "The enumeration in the *Constitution*, of certain rights, shall not be construed to deny or disparage others retained by the people." What does it mean? It means that only "some" of our rights are listed. It was meant to acknowledge that we have many others besides the ones listed.

The idea of the government being the wellspring of our rights makes no sense if we read the *Declaration of Independence* or the *Federalist Papers*. Both were written before the *Constitution* and both assume our rights exist apart from the government.

What's happened, of course, is that the worst case scenarios of both the Democrats and the Federalists have come home to roost because, as the years rolled by, any rights not included in the *Bill of Rights* are often deemed not to exist, while all the rights that are mentioned are now considered gifts from politicians and bureaucrats.

Here's the truth: The *Constitution* was written to *limit* our government, not to control the people. So, the real question is not, "Where in the *Constitution* does it say we have a right to travel?" but "Where in the *Constitution* did the People grant to the Federal government the power to take away our right to travel?"

Read Article I, Section 8, of the *Constitution*. There, the powers *granted* to the Federal government are plainly spelled out. Where does it say the government can limit travel? It doesn't.

Then read the *Tenth Amendment*, in the so-called *Bill of Rights*. It says, "The powers not delegated to the United States by the *Constitution*, nor prohibited by it to the States, are reserved to the States respectively, or to the people." That means it is not on *me* to prove the *Constitution* has granted me the right to travel; it means the onus is on the government to prove that there is a phrase or a clause in the *Constitution* granting it the right to infringe on my right to travel. It isn't there.

John Silveira

It's a sad commentary on the state of what is *supposed* to be the freest country that ever existed that there are now millions of Americans who can ask the question your friend asked. It's sad that so many of us think that the rights meant to protect us from the government are now considered to be a gift from the government and not from Nature or God.

Why didn't the Founding Fathers include a "right to travel?" It never occurred to them that politicians and bureaucrats would act as if it didn't exist. However, though it wasn't explicitly included in the first eight *Amendments*, it is implicitly included under the *Ninth* and *Tenth Amendments*—and, with the passage of the *Fourteenth Amendment*, the states cannot violate any of our rights, either.

By the way, you might ask your friend what he thinks Thomas Jefferson, George Washington, George Mason, Benjamin Franklin, or any of the other Founding Fathers, (who had just defeated what was then the world's greatest superpower in a Revolutionary War to win their freedom and ensure these Natural or God-given rights were in place), would have said if they came back today and the Federal government tried to limit their freedom to travel? Better yet, what would they call your friend who now thinks there's no right to travel unless it's granted by the government?

The word "idiot" comes to mind. **— John Silveira**

SPECIAL PREPAREDNESS ISSUE

Backwoods Home magazine

May/June 2008
Issue #111
$5.95 US
$7.50 CAN

practical ideas for self-reliant living

gearing up for an ECONOMIC SQUEEZE

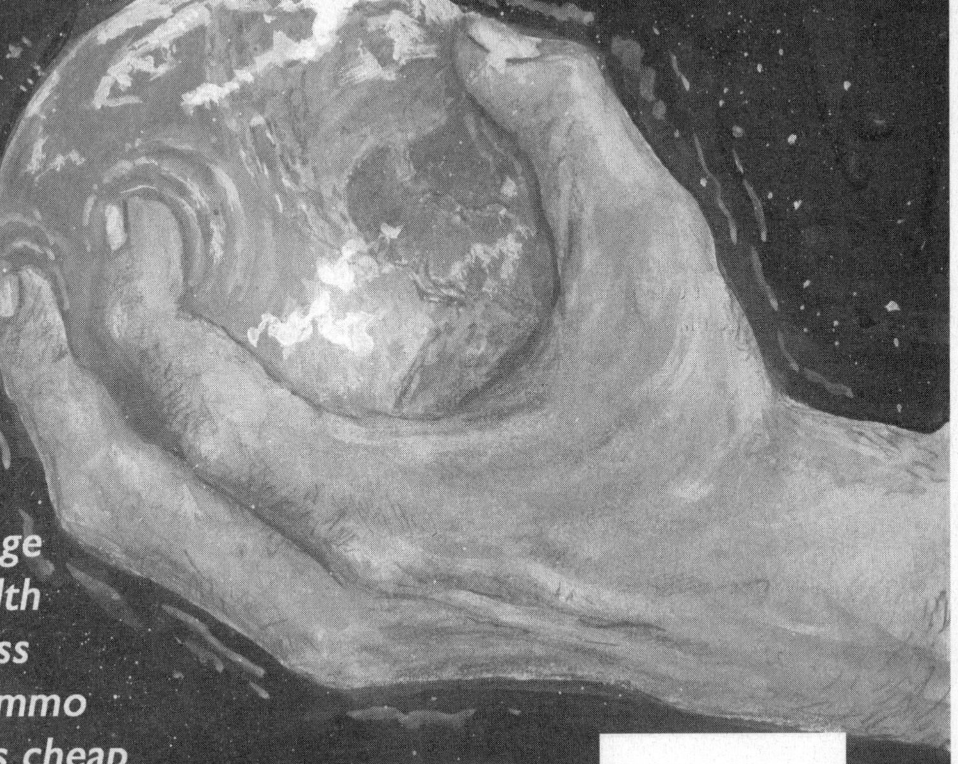

- Making bread
- Survival gardening
- Family medical kit
- Storing food protein
- Preparedness friends
- Long-term food storage
- Whole grains for health
- 3 tiers of preparedness
- Stock up on guns & ammo
- Get building materials cheap
- Understanding energy basics

The *art* of scrounging
building materials at bargain prices

By Dorothy Ainsworth

Don't let a little thing like not enough money keep you from building your dream home. You can get richer in more ways than one by *spending yourself!* Think of your journey as the difference between taking the freeway in a Mercedes (if you're wealthy and can hire everything done) or taking a dirt road in an old pickup (if you're financially-challenged and do all the labor yourself). You can still get from here to there; it'll just take longer. I know, because I'm still driving the same old pickup I bought 25 years ago for $800 (it was old *then*) and I have managed to build 16 assorted structures in my spare time, while working as a waitress earning $1000-$1200/month.

By plugging along all these years, I have increased the value of my property from $40,000 to more than a million dollars, and I'm still working on it. My secret? Tunnel vision, energy and drive, and scrounging building materials like crazy. What I *didn't* have was any building experience, but

The counters, butcher block, bar, and table are made from massive glulam beams—acquired free at a renovation site.

I loaded my truck up with all the free redwood sawdust I could handle to use as mulch all over my property.

because I paid as I went along, it gave me plenty of time to learn.

Progress was slow in both categories, but what seemed like mission impossible ended up mission accomplished. How did I learn to build and how did I afford it? By reading how-to books, using common sense, employing the monkey-see monkey-do method, and incorporating *other people's surplus* into all my livable structures. If I can do it, *you* can too.

We live in a land of plenty. Consumers keep the economy going, but even people on sustenance level incomes like myself can benefit immensely on what others throw away—such as their old stuff that isn't even old yet to make room for their new stuff. Garages are so full there's no room for the family cars. Sometimes you'll see couches and tables set out in yards with signs that say "Free." American homes are overflowing.

Scrounging is the art of looking for building materials wherever you go and sometimes finding them in unlikely places. The world is a great big flea market if you are itching for a bargain. It's not about being a cheap-skate; it's about being smart and saving money, and at the same time recycling what would have gone to waste. And in my "self-righteous" book of virtues, waste is immoral.

It takes some keen observational skills to be on the lookout for what you want and the motivation to ask for it—the motivation being you have no extra money.

Figure out what you need at any given stage of your building project and cultivate a roving eye as you drive around and notice what appears to be discarded "stuff": lumber, fencing, pipes, visqueen, roofing, tarpaper, rebar, concrete blocks, bricks, windows, pallets, etc. piled around houses and businesses, and even near dumpsters. Screech to a halt and ask if it's for sale or if you can have it free for hauling it off. You'll be amazed at how many people will welcome you to take their "clutter" away.

Take a drive around town just before trash pick-up day, and if you spot some goodies, ask the homeowner for *permission* to take those items they had set out for the garbage truck to haul off, but be sure to get there before the garbage truck beats you to it.

Get on the phone regularly or go in person and ask at hardware stores and paint stores if they have a collection of assorted reject paint and stains they'd like to get rid of (wrongly mixed colors or whatever). They always do. Usually they have 5-gallon buckets as well as 1-gallon cans. I've bought almost all my paint and stains for $5/gallon this way. And they've even added some pigment for me (for a small fee) to achieve a color I wanted, just to get rid of their stash that's taking up storage room.

Go to carpet outlets looking for slightly damaged carpet (a faded streak or tear or some imperfection) and ask what their rock bottom price is, or make an offer. My carpet was a color apparently nobody but me liked (burnt orange) so they marked it down to only $6/yard. It was brand new and excellent quality, made for heavy traffic in casinos and hotels, and it is still in great shape after 10 years of wear and tear.

Visit linoleum and tile dealers, and other big outlet stores for slightly damaged goods as well. Tile stores

133

These old gray timbers were purchased for a quarter of the cost of new lumber.

almost always have fantastic sales on batches of tile they're trying to get rid of to make room for new stock and the latest trends. Sometimes they have boxes of free tile out back.

Check out window and glass companies for imperfect glass such as a tiny scratch on the glass or a speck between the panes. I had all my double-paned windows for three of my log structures made from used glass at half the cost of new, and I can't tell the difference. I am presently storing a large load of expensive Low-E double-paned windows that were *given* to me by a contractor whose wealthy client changed her mind on her fenestration and paid for the change. My son, who is building his own house, will make his window openings to accommodate them. It will save him hundreds of dollars.

A few hours and a hired portable sawmill can turn salvaged old timbers and trees into the lumber you need at a fraction of the cost of buying it new.

Manufacturing plants and cabinet-maker shops sometimes have a by-product you might be able to use. I used to get redwood sawdust for my landscaping needs from a place that made hummingbird feeders and other items out of redwood. I would leave my truck under their chute and drive it home when it was full. I used the attractive redwood mulch in rock gardens and walking trails all over my property.

Lumber yards have bargain bins and slightly weathered lumber that doesn't appeal to the average customer, and sometimes broken bundles of shingles and shakes, outdated siding, unpopular fencing styles, and huge cracked and weathered beams nobody wants because they aren't "pretty" anymore.

You can hire a portable sawmill owner to come to you and cut dimensional lumber planks or beams from your own trees with a Wood-Mizer or TimberKing mill (to name a couple). My neighbor cut my true 2-inch by 16-foot rafters for the studio I built, with his Wood-Mizer.

Buy old gray timbers and have them shaved down to size with a portable sawmill. I bought a huge load of timbers for only $250/thousand (25 cents a board foot—compared with new timbers at $1 a board foot) and had another "mizer-man" trim them down into 9x9s with his Wood-Mizer. It only cost me $100 for his time and labor (just a few hours) and I had all the ridge-beams and top-plates I needed for my large log home. The mill worked beautifully and its thin bandsaw blade left almost no sawdust in its wake.

Flea markets are treasure troves of everything imaginable and some unimaginables that you impulsively decide you can't live without. Estate sales and auctions are also chock full of tools and supplies, and furniture galore. Estate sale locations can be found in the Yellow Pages and are great places to visit regularly because they are constantly being replenished. Widows are notorious for getting rid of their late husbands' workshop full of power tools and hand tools in one fell swoop by calling an estate liquidator.

Fund-raising bazaars and giant swap meets are also places to find excellent bargains and a diverse array of household goods and building materials. Watch the newspaper for announcements and dates.

Frequenting Goodwill, the Salvation Army, and other second-hand stores is a good habit to get into. While you wander around looking, develop the skill of "adaptability thinking." That's the ability to see something made for a specific purpose and imagine using it for something entirely different and unrelated. I used a futon couch frame from Goodwill ($5) for my kitchen sink countertop framing and it worked beautifully.

The Nickel Want Ads reach thousands of people. Peruse yours weekly for fantastic bargains (particularly appliances) and also put your own ad in under the "WANTED" heading for a nominal fee (about $3 for a short ad) whenever you need something specific, or in a general category (like assorted lumber).

Craigslist, on the internet (www.craigslist.org), is a lucrative resource to find almost anything you are looking for cheap or free and also to post (*for free*) what you are looking for. People will respond and you can negotiate the price.

Go garage saling every chance you get. You'll find the bargains of your life at yard sales and moving sales, and have a great socializing time while you're at it. I've witnessed people trying to get a ten cent item marked down to a nickel. The owners are hell-bent on getting rid of *everything* they set out, and toward the end of the day sometimes say, "Just take it away!"

Eric at 17 with one of many loads of lodgepole pine logs we cut for the studio from Forest Service land (back when you could still do that). The logs were 3 cents per foot—each log here cost 24 cents. Many of the logs for the second house were free in trade for thinning trees and burning slash piles.

Builder's Bargain Centers are aptly named. They really are full of bargains. I've bought all my solid core doors I've used for computer table tops, multi-paned doors I joined to make my own French doors, and any doors I haven't built myself, for $20-$30/apiece from them. Our bargain center in White City, Oregon also has

A contractor gave me these expensive windows after a client changed her mind.

a parking lot full of shower stalls, toilets, and bathtubs—cheap!

A popular renovator/recycler in Medford, Oregon (Morrows) has made a business out of organizing and selling very unusual building materials from demolition sites and 20th century houses, including lumber, clawfoot bathtubs, and vintage fixtures, at bargain prices. But once you go in, the array of unique items is so extensive and diverse that it's hard to leave until they kick you out at closing time.

My all-time favorite place to "shop" is the city dump. "Sinks and seagulls" nostalgically come to mind when I remember trips to the dump. Regretfully, it is now just a transfer station and there's no more scrounging allowed, but in its heyday, it

Someone threw this door away! I stripped the old chipped paint off in a couple hours and repainted it, and now it looks like new again.

offered a half acre of good stuff to paw through to your heart's content. A few years ago I purchased all my beautiful porcelain sinks for $1 apiece at the dump. I still have several saved for my son's kitchen and bathroom.

If you are lucky enough to have an old-fashioned dump near your town, go there regularly on a treasure hunt. You won't come away empty-handed, and you'll marvel all the way home at what you scored. The dump is a massive renewable resource and *the best* place to scrounge and salvage.

Ask for price reductions anywhere you are shopping if the materials look a little shopworn or distressed. I recently got a 50% reduction on 20 sheets of pink foam rigid insulation from Lowe's because the edges were a little sunburned. Their carelessness was my good fortune.

Buy used, or new but dented, water heaters. The dented casings don't matter, but slightly damaged water heaters are sold *cheap*. Turn the dent to the wall.

Appliances are a dime a dozen. Anything you need, from washers and dryers to ranges and refrigerators, sell used for almost nothing compared to new ones. Look in the The Nickel for year-round bargains, or visit a big household appliance outlet store. They are perpetually advertising: "Liquidation Sale! Overstocked! Going out of Business!"

Need a phone line from the phone company's box to your house? The phone company will give you all the direct burial phone line you need if you provide the trench. I recently buried 1000 feet of it—free. Call your local phone company.

Keep your eyes peeled for demolition sights. For whatever their reasons, people are constantly tearing down perfectly good structures and rebuilding something else. These sites are excellent sources for all kinds of building materials from siding to large beams.

A few years ago I asked if I could have an assortment of huge glulams that were piled out back where a renovation team was turning a grocery store into a movie theater. The 6-inch by 24-inch by 50-foot glulam beam had been the ridgebeam in the store, but was now cut up into 12' and 16' lengths and dumped outside.

The workers said, "Sure, you can have 'em if you can lift 'em," then slapped their thighs and laughed their heads off. I called my "muscle man," boyfriend Kirt, to come down and load them in my old pickup. He tossed them in like they were made of styrofoam and off I sped (0-40 mph in 15 minutes) having the last laugh all the way home. I sanded and stained them and used them for countertops, a pass bar, and my dining room table.

Note: Glulam is short for glued and laminated. They are made from dimensional lumber (usually Douglas Fir 2x6s) stacked, glued, and pressed together to make a beam, and are quite beautiful.

When you do find a demolition site, ask if you can haul off some of the building materials or even offer to help dismantle something, in return for the spoils. That's how I got all the old barn hinges for my batten doors, silvery gray barn wood for picture frames and other projects, and a stash of beautiful 30-inch hand-split shingles they don't make anymore. I'll eventually use them for siding on a decorative wall or on a small building someday. My son is currently salvaging some nice 8x8 timbers out of an old outbuilding that needs to be removed from rezoned commercial property.

Almost all construction sites, residential or commercial, are gold mines for surplus building materials. Ask the contractor if you can do some of his post-construction clean up work by taking away unused random lengths of lumber, headers, versa-lam beams, and partial sheets of plywood that were thrown down by carpenters in a hurry, and scattered all over the place. Most builders have time constraints and have such a mess to clean up after a house is built and before the landscaping begins, they will most likely appreciate all the clean up help they can get.

Bartering and trading labor and/or goods is always a viable way to get building materials and physical help without any money changing hands. It's good old-fashioned free enterprise at work, and the mutual sharing back and forth can forge some strong and valuable friendships.

On one newly purchased lot where the owner was trying to clear the land of debris so he could build, I spied a sign that read: "Free Concrete Piers— YOU Haul." I rushed home and got my son and his friend to help lift them into my truck five at a time (200 lbs. each!) and made six trips to take all 30 of them. I ultimately used them for a large deck foundation, and also for the entrance way footings on the studio I built. They came in very handy and saved me tons of money.

Take work gloves and a box of assorted hand tools with you everywhere you go, so you don't miss an opportunity to snag something good that you can use now or later. It wouldn't hurt to also carry with you a liability agreement that states you will not hold the owner of the goods responsible if you get hurt taking them away, and give out a signed copy whenever you need to. People (including contractors), are so afraid of being sued, a signed waiver will assuage their trepidation and possibly cinch the deal if they feel legally protected.

Cabinet makers have used cabinets to get rid of after people remodel their kitchens and have new cabinets built. *Those* people have money to burn; *you* don't. Ask to haul away the perfectly good but "used" cabinets. If need be, you can paint them a color you like. Cabinet and furniture makers often have piles of hardwood scraps, such as leftover pieces of exotic woods and high quality plywood that they are often willing to get rid of. If nothing else, you could burn the kiln-dried hardwood in your woodstove.

Go to lumber mills, if you have any nearby, and ask to see their stacks of lumber and plywood rejects. Retailers want perfect stock, so plywood with a few mislaid plys and slightly damaged lumber are sold at bargain "cash and carry" prices. The mill is happy to break even. They'll even load it for you with their forklift. I've bought most of my "imperfect" plywood over the years at half price by going straight to the mill for it.

Call electrical contractors and ask if they have used electrical boxes and breakers and conduit and assorted rolls of wire that were left over from a job.

Builders put up temporary electrical service boxes, then remove and replace them when the house is ready to be permanently wired. The contractor will have to use a brand new box on his next project, so the old one (like new) gets put on a shelf in a storage facility. That's where you come in.

Keep an eye out for free fill dirt from construction sites where basements are being dug or hilly land is being leveled. The contractor needs to dump it somewhere, and if you're closer than the dump, he'll bring it to *you* instead. To get on the contractor's preferred list and beat out the competition, offer to at least pay for the gas. Son Eric recently had 20 loads of fill dirt from a project in town brought to his building site to backfill his basement walls for the price of the trucker's time and diesel fuel. So instead of the usual $200 to $500 for a 10 cubic yard dumptruck load of dirt, he paid $50 a load. The price of fuel has driven up all construction prices tremen-

I got 30 concrete piers—for the price of hauling them away.

137

I turned a small trailer into a portable bathroom, and parked it near the septic tank. When the main house was complete, I sold it—for a profit!

dously. There has never been a more mandatory time to scrounge than now.

Most nurseries have reject plants in their back lots where they keep their crooked and scraggly trees and bushes and sell them cheap. A tree is a tree is a tree...it'll recover and thrive when you plant it. And at the rate you will probably be developing your property, you won't need immediate landscaping.

Let landscaping contractors or spec-house building contractors know that you'll pick up their leftover sod from their "instant lawn" projects, and to call you before the rolls dry out. I did my own front yard a little at a time with *free* sod this way.

I also asked my friends around town if I could take root cuttings from their weed-like drought-resistant trees that send out root runners, and now I have beautiful windbreaks of Silver Poplars and Trees of Heaven all over my property. The effort was labor intensive (digging and planting always is)—but free.

Go to tire dealers for used tires for your garden. They are great to partially bury in the ground and plant tomatoes and other vegetables in, for weed

and water control, not to mention their heat retention quality for early spring planting. (See Jackie Clay's article in this issue on using tires to plant your potatoes. — Editor)

Refurbished tools, half-priced or less, from Sears Service Centers are piled high on shelves, just waiting for a second owner to use and abuse them, and they come with a *new* guarantee.

Fabric outlet stores and giant discount stores are the places to go for interior furnishings. Yardage and drapery material are sometimes a buck or two a yard. I bought all my heavy-duty cotton duck curtain fabric from Wal-Mart for only $3/yard.

I highly recommend buying a small trailer to convert into a temporary bathroom facility and place it near your septic tank so it can be easily hooked up. I did just that when I was building my house and used it for years. I gutted it out, installed a toilet, basin, painted plywood shower stall, and 40-gallon water heater. When the house was finished, I put an ad in the Nickel and sold it to the first caller for $500 ($200 profit after using it for years). Even before it was towed

away, I received 20 more calls from disappointed would-be buyers.

If you don't have a septic system installed yet, pick up an old water heater free from the dump or an appliance store, strip it down to the bare tank, paint it black, set it up on stilts or a platform above where you'll be showering so the water will gravity flow, and when the sun shines you'll have all the hot water you need for bathing.

I bought a wood-fired hot tub from the Snorkel Stove Co. when I first moved onto my land and was living in a tent and had no electricity yet. I bathed and soaked under a canopy of stars whenever I was dirty, tired, and sore. It was a little splash of heaven after a hard day's work.

Another way to save money while developing your property is to buy an old wringer washing machine that can be filled with a hose and put up a clothesline. If you live out in the country, going to town to the laundromat burns up gas and is expensive and time-consuming.

Apply for extensions on your building permit, so you have a year between inspections instead of the allotted six months. That will give you extra time to save up for materials and complete the labor for each stage of your building project that requires an inspection.

Tell all your friends and relatives who are insistent on giving you gifts that what you really want for Christmas or your birthday are building supplies, a gift certificate to the lumber yard or hardware store, or just plain cash to buy materials with. If they want specifics, give them a list of needed items to choose from.

Scrounging is synonymous with *Labor*, and *Free* is synonymous with *Sweat*. If you want to save money, you will have to *pay* in time and labor. But look at it this way—you are also saving a bundle since you won't need a fitness center membership and a personal trainer. Δ

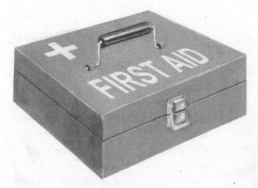

The all-purpose family medical kit

By Jackie Clay

We could call it your *big* or complete family first aid kit, but to my family, it's just *the* med kit. No, it's not one of those neat little plastic boxes that has a red cross embossed on the front of it, containing such things as a few plastic Band-Aids, some first aid cream, a small roll of gauze and a pair of dull scissors. I feel that every family should have one like ours available for emergencies, both large and small.

Not every family medical emergency happens during the week; in fact, most happen at night or on the weekend, when you either handle it yourself or make a run in to the hospital emergency room. There you not only undergo hours worth of X-rays, lab tests, and tiring questions—often for something as simple as a horrible cold or a twisted ankle—but unless you have terrific insurance, the bill can be staggering. It's a good idea to have a medical kit that is complete enough that you don't have to go to the ER unless you have a potentially life-threatening problem.

Of course, there are the times when there *is* an emergency—an ice storm, windstorm, blizzard, or something that limits our ability to even get medical help. Like everything else, it's a good idea to be relatively self-reliant in the first aid department, too.

The container for your medical kit

We've got three stages of medical emergency "kits." In each vehicle, we've got a small plastic box under the seat, containing the basics for most small emergencies: a cut finger, a fish hook in the skin, a sprained ankle, a burn, or a sliver. This box goes where we go and is replenished after each use, much like the ambulance kits. We do use this box quite a bit, not only for ourselves, but also for friends and neighbors as the need arises. Out of necessity, to fit under the seat, this kit is quite small and is, therefore, incomplete.

We keep our "main" first aid box in the bathroom and when we go on a trip, it goes with us. This kit holds a lot and is what everyone should have on hand. Not only is it sturdy, watertight, easy to grab and carry, but it also holds items to handle a whole lot of medical problems, and it's close at hand and easy to access. If we ever had to evacuate by vehicle, the box would be the first thing we pack.

I love my medical box. Its original purpose was a field box for shooting sports. Yep, it's camo green, but hey, it's got strength, handy compartments, and is easy to carry with a shoulder strap to help out. And I got it on sale, too. You need a big box like this to have a complete kit. But you need to be able to carry it full, too, so don't go buying a trunk! My box is high density plastic, but you could run it over with a truck and it'd still be okay. I've dropped it, fallen on it, and had it tossed about in the back of the truck on rocky mountain trails with no problems.

I especially like my box because it has a top section that securely latches, full of smaller compartments. Then the big section underneath latches separately, and that houses larger items and even smaller plastic boxes containing like items, such as cold pills, gauze squares, cough drops, etc.

So what do I put in the box anyway?

The first things I put in mine were listed as "instruments" on my "to-pack" list. These included a scalpel, several blades, two pair of needle holders, two forceps (one tiny, one large…you can also use the needle holders for forceps), sharp smaller scissors, *good* tweezers, a digital thermometer, and a blood pressure wrist cuff (cheap and easy). As a former veterinary technician, I'm quite comfortable facing the possibility of having to sew up a wound, so I also have suture needles and material, as well as injectable anesthetic in my kit. Don't include these unless you get training; you can sure screw up a wound if you don't know what you're doing! And many really don't require being sewn up, anyway.

Let me explain some uses for the above. The needle holders not only will hold a suture needle for sewing up a wound, but will also clamp onto a fish hook to aid in removal. Small forceps or tweezers will help pull out cactus stickers or slivers from your hand or foot. The scissors will trim your gauze bandages, cut string, cut clothing away from an injury, or trim your injured dog's hair so you can dress his wound. They'll also trim ragged dead skin away from a wound on yourself or your kids.

I also include a small sewing kit. Maybe having the crotch split out of your jeans isn't an emergency. But when it happens, you sure think it is at the time.

I pack a couple of 5cc syringes and needles in 22 and 18 gauges. If you don't need them to give injections, they come in handy in other situations. For instance, you can flush dirt out of a wound with sterile water or saline solution, using the syringe like a squirt gun. Or you can effectively pick at the skin around a bad sliver until you can grasp it with a tweezers. (The hollow hypodermic needles work so much better for this than regular sewing needles!)

You can buy "surplus" medical instruments through many catalogs containing various tools. I've seen them in the Harbor Freight and Northern Tool catalog, as well as at Wal-Mart in the sporting section. Many feed and livestock supply stores also carry a wide variety of instruments, as well.

A magnifying glass is a good addition, both to see tiny but painful slivers and to use as a possible fire starter. (If you do, use sunglasses, as the brightness generated from concentrated sunlight will hurt unprotected eyes.)

Bandages/wound care

I have a wide variety of bandages, gauze, etc. in my kit. The smallest are the little packs of butterfly bandages, meant to hold the edges of a cut together instead of suturing it. I used these on my own hand once when my son, Bill, hit my hand with the chainsaw while limbing a tree. (My fault—I grabbed a limb when I was too close to an operating saw.) The skin was gaping open on the top of my hand, with the veins popping up purple through the cuts. Luckily they hadn't been cut too! With simple butterfly bandages and a gauze pack, my hand healed in two weeks without stitches or nasty scars. If you look today, twenty five years later, you can just make out a few white chicken scratches on the back of my hand. (This is a reminder for chainsaw safety.)

The next size up is the "regular" size adhesive bandage, on up to the big 4-inch squares that will "patch" a skinned knee pretty well and let you keep on working.

This was originally a field box for shooting sports. With all of the little compartments it makes a nice medical kit.

I also include several packages of 4-inch squares of sterile gauze, an assortment of widths of rolled gauze bandage, and three or four packaged sanitary napkins. *What?* Now guys, don't freak out on me. These "feminine" products may save your life if you get a severe cut and you need to apply serious pressure on a wildly bleeding cut. Gauze will quickly fill and leak; the sanitary napkins will sop up the blood and be effective in stopping the bleeding while pressure is applied. You don't want scented pads—just plain sterile, individually packaged ones.

Besides these, I've got two rolls of elastic wrap and a roll of Vet-Wrap, a sticks-to-itself elastic wrap. These not only work for sprains and strains, but can also help in stabilizing a suspected broken leg (with splints) or in holding bandages in place so they don't get dirty.

I've got a bad knee, so I also have an elastic knee wrap in the kit; who knows when it'll go out on me? I want it where I can find it.

I like having a few gauze pads with Teflon coating; they won't stick to the wound once it's treated and covered.

My last item in the bandage department is an elastic chest or rib wrap.

You'll want something to clean a wound or scrape it out with. I've got a new bar of soap in my kit, in a plastic camping soap box (the lid doubles as a mini washbasin), many alcohol wipes, a box of baby wipes (work fine on the edges around a wound, too), a clean washcloth in a plastic bag, and several pieces of good quality paper towel, folded carefully, and put in a plastic bag. Your gauze will work here, too. I don't like cotton, as it has a way of getting snagged in a wound and leaving little bits of fiber behind to attract blood and dirt.

Wound care products

It's a good idea to have some sterile water or saline solution in your kit. This comes in handy for flushing dirt, insects, debris, and chemicals out of eyes. It can be trickled in with a sterile syringe. Again, you can pick this up at a farm and ranch store.

Then you'll want something to disinfect the wound and the surrounding skin. Betadine works well. Most first aid kits include antibiotic ointment. I hate ointments around wounds. They attract hair and dirt and keep it there. I'd rather use Betadine and keep the wound clean.

Yes, you can use alcohol. But as you know, it's "Aye Chihuahua!" when you put it in a wound. And your kid will never let you near him again till he's 42.

For a not-so-nasty wound, a swish of hydrogen peroxide works well. And you can catch your child. Just tell him "it's the good germs fighting the bad germs" and he'll be so intent on watching the battle he won't even leave in the first place. It's always worked for me.

Colds/flu

Yes, I've treated my share of sprains, cuts, splinters, and skinned body parts. But the part of my medical kit that gets the most use is the "colds/flu" remedies. Gee, would that be because I have a son in school? When we lived real remotely, none of us had even a slight cold in years. In fact my son, David, was seven before he had ever thrown up. He didn't even know what was happening!

Now that we are in "civilization" more often, we get our share of colds and flu...even though we get our annual flu shots. So I keep an adequate supply of cold/flu symptom relievers (you won't cure the cold), as well as plenty of Vitamin C and Echinacea capsules to help a strained immune system.

I pick out cough syrups that have an expectorant in them to help loosen "gunk" in the lungs to avoid it becoming pneumonia, then multi-symptom allergy/cold tabs, such as Actifed for runny noses and sinus pressure. If you have high blood pressure you might want to talk to your pharmacist to be sure your meds will not aggravate it. There are a few cold remedies for people on blood pressure medication.

Gas attack!

Okay, so it's not a nice topic, but when you've eaten too much pizza and get that huge, bloated, painful feeling, you *might* want something for it. I've got a bottle of generic Tums in the kit, as well as Gas-X. One or the other will do the trick for plain old heartburn and gas. Just be aware that some "gas" pains end up being symptoms of heart attack, so if they get worse or aren't relieved, you might want to have it checked out.

Diarrhea

Sometimes you have the flu that ends with severe diarrhea. Or you eat something that doesn't agree with you—too much grease for instance. It's Sunday night and there's a storm outside. Do you really want to run down to the drug store (probably closed)? You know you don't. So I keep a package of Imodium in my medical kit. Usually a tablet or two is all it takes to put you in much better shape.

Burns

You can burn yourself a thousand and one ways. I'm always grabbing the cast iron pan handle....after it's been in the oven instead of on top of the stove, where it stays reasonably cool. Or I'm putting wood in the stove, or taking burgers off the grill. It's always a good idea to have burn medication, such as Burn Free in your kit. I always immediately soak a burn in ice water to keep it from penetrating deeper. If it's not a nasty burn, a few dabs with a leaf cut from my aloe vera (my green medical kit) and it's about as good as new. When it starts to burn again later, I just re-apply it.

Insect stings/snake bite

For people who are quite sensitive to bee and wasp stings, you might want to have your physician prescribe an injectable epinephrine to avoid or treat reactions in an emergency situation where medical help is impossible to reach. However, most folks just have a little pain and swelling. I use ice on the sting, but a little bottle of ammonia is good to have on hand. A dab or two and the sting goes away pretty well.

If you live in an area where there are venomous snakes, it's a good idea to have a snake bite kit in your big medical kit and also to carry one in your vehicle. (These aren't like the old instructions with "cut an X over each bite and suck it out," so read the directions before you try to use one in an emergency.) We lived in snake country for years and have never had to use one.

Prescription medicine

Try to have a month's supply of all prescription medicine for each of your family members. Because you shouldn't depend on old medicine, this needs to be rotated and kept relatively fresh. What I have done is refill prescriptions a few days before they're finished. In this way, each month you'll gain several pills to put in your medical kit. Keep doing this until you have a thirty days' supply. Then rotate this with your regular meds to keep a fresh supply. You don't want to run out of meds during a blizzard.

Antibiotics

It is a very good idea to have at least one week's supply of a good oral antibiotic in your kit. Doctors are very reluctant to prescribe antibiotics these days, for fear of overuse. But many are open to the idea of having a bottle of antibiotics in an emergency medical kit, especially if you are traveling in a remote area. Hopefully your doctor will be one of these.

Miscellaneous

I carry a bottle of Calamine lotion in my kit; it's invaluable for a lot of things like sunburn, insect bites, and rashes from allergies and poison ivy. There is also a tube of ShoeGoo, a silicone sealer. In a *first aid kit*? Yep. It's great for getting picky stickers you can hardly see out of your skin. You rub a layer on, let it dry, and peel it off. The stickers peel off without any pain. I've used it many times on cactus spines in our skin. You can also repair everything from eye glasses to windows. I've also got a large generic bottle of aspirin and another of acetaminophen for general pain and inflammation.

You might want to toss in a tube of ointment for vaginal yeast infection and a spray for athlete's foot/jock itch. Okay, it's not "nice" to talk about, but if you get either, you won't want to wait until the roads are clear to treat it!

A small flashlight with fresh batteries, a candle, lighter, and matches (in a waterproof container) are always a good idea. You can never have too many, but you can sure have too few!

I'm sure you can think of other things you'd like in your kit; I've probably forgotten something I've got in mine, even though my enthusiastic 17-year-old son helped me with this list. Personalize your kit however you want.

A good first aid manual

I've got a paperback Red Cross first aid book in my box, just in case I can't remember something I've learned.

And this brings us to the last, but most important thing of all: an informed person or two to *use* the kit. Every community offers emergency first aid classes through Community Education or the hospital. These classes cover CPR and basic first aid. We all *mean* to take a class, but many of us keep putting it off. Unless you already have extensive experience in recognizing and treating a wide variety of medical issues, it is always a good idea to take a class or several classes to become better informed and more comfortable giving treatment to yourself and your family. You never know when you may need to put your knowledge to the test! Δ

The Best of the First Two Years
Our first big anthology!
In these 12 issues you'll find:

❋ A little knowledge and sweat can build a home
     for under $10,000

❋ Tepee to cabin to dream house

❋ From the foundation up, house-building is forgiving

❋ A first time horse buyer's guide

❋ A greenhouse offers advantages for the organic gardener

❋ Canning meat

❋ Backwoods Home recipes

❋ In pursuit of independence

❋ Canning blueberries

❋ How we keep humming along on the homestead

❋ Pioneer women on the trail west

❋ Some tips on first aid readiness for remote areas

❋ Whip grafting—the key to producing fruit variety

❋ The basics of backyard beekeeping

❋ Co-planting in the vegetable garden

❋ How to make soap—from fat to finish

❋ The instant greenhouse

❋ The old time spring house

❋ Getting started in a firewood business

❋ For battling ants or growing earthworms,
     try coffee grounds

❋ Sawmills: a firm foundation to homesteading

Get serious about gardening

By Jackie Clay

Most of us garden now or have gardened in the past. We grow a few tomatoes, some green beans, maybe a row of carrots, lettuce, and potatoes. Flowers abound. But what if times suddenly get tough and we *need* to get serious about our gardening? I mean *very* serious. If we don't grow at least a good portion of our food, there won't be enough money to go around.

What happens if you have to decide whether to buy food or make your house payment...or heating fuel bill in the winter? Tough choice.

There *is* something you can do, though. You can plant a moderate-sized garden (as big as you have room for and the energy to take care of) and raise a whole lot of your food. With wheat having jumped from $7 to more than $20 a bushel in less than three months, it will certainly be provident to garden in earnest this year. At the very least, food prices will rise. Our greatest protection is to get busy and plan a serious garden so we can not only eat from it, but also can preserve as much of it as we are able for the future.

Planning a serious garden

Many folks think that because they don't have acreage they can't get enough produce from their modest 30'x50' garden to be worthwhile. This is wrong. Using the best methods, coupled with intense planning and growing techniques, a family *can* succeed in raising most of their own vegetables and *can* have enough to put up at harvest time.

Your serious garden starts with a pad of graph paper and a notepad. On the notepad, jot down the vegetables and vegetable products (such as tomato sauce or salsa) that your family likes and regularly eats. Don't forget root crops such as potatoes, carrots, and rutabagas. Have everyone chip in their favorites, go through seed catalogs together, or go shopping with your pad...just to see what they have that you usually will eat. Remember canned vegetables, such as baked beans and chili, too and think about their ingredients.

Don't get wild and jot down things that look fantastic but you have never eaten much of or don't *really* like, but they look pretty. Keep to basics first, then make a second list of foods such as herbs and "fancy" things that spark your appetite.

Grow foods that you can not only eat during the season, but ones that you can easily store or can for meals later on. The backbone of your garden should be potatoes, carrots, turnips/

Staple crops like potatoes, carrots, beans, tomatoes, squash, and onions are the building blocks for nutritious meals, and they are easy to store.

wide strip 20 feet long in her "lawn," removing the sod first and incorporating lots of well-rotted compost. In that little strip, she grew green beans, tomatoes, peppers, lettuce, broccoli, and onions. It looked pretty, too. She didn't miss that little strip of grass one bit.

More out of less space

Get your graph paper and draw in the boundaries of your main garden area. It's a good idea to plan on fencing it right away to keep out unwanted human traffic (playing kids, for instance), pets (who might love a romp through your tomatoes), and wildlife. Under normal circumstances, having a woodchuck or herd of deer eat up your carrots overnight is annoying and sometimes heartbreaking. But in a survival situation, it can be downright scary!

And, once your garden is fenced with 2"x4" welded wire or even 2" chicken wire, you have just created four sides of possible trellises. (Think pole beans, cucumbers, even squash, and melons...providing your deer problem isn't severe; they'll help themselves to food crops growing vertically on your fence, too.)

Okay, now with a pencil (so you can erase), begin at the east side and look at your list of vegetables. Wait—don't draw in rows! Instead of the "traditional" single rows, sketch in double rows of bush beans, planted only six inches apart. You can sketch carrots in triple rows, only four inches apart. This enables you to get much more food from just about the same area your single rows would have taken. Onions, lettuce, peas, parsnips, collards, Swiss chard, and more can be grown using this multiple row method. I plant my onions in a wide bed that is about 18 inches wide. I use onion sets or plants I've raised from seed and plant them about three inches apart, all ways. You can further thin your onions by pulling a few to use during the summer. By fall, your

rutabagas, beans, tomatoes, onions, corn, and squash. These are the staples and are building blocks for tasty, nutritious meals down the line.

Now, how much room do you have to grow food in? You only have 30'x 50' in your garden. Maybe you have more room than you think. How about planting peppers in between

your flowers, right in the flower bed? Or how about letting pole beans climb a trellis at the back of the bed? Dig out a few relatively small chunks of your lawn and plant a hill of squash in each area, letting them crawl toward the sides of your yard. In New Mexico, Mom wanted a house garden, so we dug up a 4-foot bed will provide you with lots of nice storage onions. (Just make sure you plant a variety that is known for good storage qualities. Some sweet onions make poor storage onions.)

Even a small package of summer squash is way too much to plant. For a family of moderate size, two hills of summer squash is plenty. Save your room for winter squash, which you can store and use all winter. You may home can summer squash, but it really isn't that good; you'll benefit more from winter squash as a backbone of your winter meals. The same with lettuce; it doesn't keep, so plant successive small multiple rows. You'll have plenty all season and won't use much garden room. For the serious gardener, always think "food value per square foot" when planning and planting.

Unless you are cultivating with a horse, you *don't* need to have your rows 3 feet apart. Keep them just far enough apart so you can walk through the garden when the plants need attention. Bush beans "bush" out, but I can "walk-straddle" two rows, double planted, as I weed or pick them at harvest. Carrots aren't so bushy, so even three rows don't take up more than a foot of row space.

If your garden is relatively large, be sure to include at least a couple of rows of potatoes. If it is modest in size, go to the dump, a tractor dealer or tire shop, and come home with four or five semi- or small tractor-size tires. You need to be able to handle them, as you'll be stacking them, then later unstacking them. Instead of rows of potatoes, you can grow nearly 50 pounds of potatoes in one tire stack bed, right on your lawn! Put down about an inch of old newspapers, directly on the mowed grass. Then lay your first tire down on that, centered over the newspaper. (The paper kills out all the grass it covers, so be sure that all the grass inside the tire has been well covered.) Now

pour in buckets of well-rotted compost, until the tire is filled. Place four good-sized seed potatoes that are beginning to sprout in the tire an equal distance apart, making a rough square. Nestle them in and cover them with at least four inches of dirt.

When the potatoes grow eight inches tall, put the next tire on the pile and carefully fill that tire with soil, partially covering the plant stems, but allowing the top leaves to remain out of the soil.

They'll immediately begin growing taller. Repeat the process until the tires are stacked up waist high, then let the plants go ahead and mature. They will make potatoes from rootlets all down the long stem.

While you're designing your garden, *don't* plant tall things, such as sweet corn or cages of tomatoes so that they drastically shade the plants beside them. I plant my rows running north and south to help prevent this.

Skip the "traditional" methods of gardening. I save garden space by tying up all my cucumbers on a stock panel trellis. Thus they only take up a narrow row, instead of six rows, as they would in their usual bed. C u k e s really

sprawl, when left to their own designs. Also, by trellising them, the cucumbers are easier to find and pick, and they are also much straighter and cleaner than they would be lying on the ground.

Cage or stake up all your indeterminate (vining) tomatoes. In this way, you can grow twice as many plants vertically as you could if they were allowed to sprawl. And, like the cukes, you can pick them easier and they won't be so apt to rot as they would lying on the ground. You can plant a tomato plant every two feet down a row, or even closer with smaller plants. When you are serious about a garden, every square foot counts.

Remember, you can trellis not only your cukes, but most muskmelons, squash, and even some watermelons. The large varieties weigh too much at maturity, but the smaller ones will do fine. I remember one of Mom's pumpkin vines ran amok in the edge of the orchard, climbing an apple tree. Come fall, there were several rather large orange p u m p k i n s

You can grow nearly 50 pounds of potatoes in one waist-high stack of tires right on your lawn.

145

hanging among the nice Red Rome apples!

You can further stretch your "garden" by growing crops in containers. There are a whole lot of "new" container crops; peppers, tomatoes (even hanging basket varieties), cucumbers, eggplant, lettuces, onions, and many more. Your containers don't have to be expensive pots. I've found many 2-5-gallon nursery pots, buckets, and washtubs at the dump. And I've planted in leaking stock tanks, bathtubs, and old swimming pools, all tossed by the wayside. Get creative. Just remember to allow for drainage. Soggy plants never produce well. One of my neighbors picked up ten 5-gallon buckets at the local Super One for $1 each. With a few holes drilled in the bottom, he planted a determinate tomato in each, then lined them up along his driveway in the sun for an instant "food hedge." Other friends grow dozens and dozens of pepper and tomato plants in front of their garage, on the pavement, in 5-gallon buckets. It's a beautiful sight.

Hint: don't plan on growing shell peas unless you have a large garden. To be useful to the serious gardener, you have to grow a long double row of them, and in smaller gardens you just don't have room. Plant more useful vegetables instead. Out of the same rows you would have reaped about five quarts of canned peas, you can reap 60 pints of green beans; a whole lot more food from the same space.

Choosing varieties for better food production

There are literally hundreds of different varieties of each garden crop available to growers that are open pollinated (non-hybrid), so you will be able to save your own seeds for future crops. At the end of this article, I've included a list of good seed sources so you can easily find seed to suit your needs.

Read the descriptions very carefully. Keep this in mind: you want production. Not cute, pretty, or gourmet. Why grow a 5-inch long carrot when you can grow one that weighs a pound or is 9 inches long? They take up the same spot in the garden, need the same care, and take as long to mature. Grow the bigger one. You'll get more food. For instance, I grow Kuroda or Tendersweet carrots. The Kurodas are fat and long, often only taking two to fill a pint canning jar. The Tendersweets often are 9 inches long and are tender and sweet. Likewise, being so long, it takes very few to fill a jar in a hurry.

Another prime example is sweet corn. A lot of folks still grow Golden Bantam. It's a great old sweet corn. But, unfortunately, it's also *small*—a bantam. The ears are lucky to reach 6 inches. Instead, I grow True Gold, with 8-inch ears and 14 rows of kernels. That's a lot more corn, per ear, than Golden Bantam can produce. You wouldn't think that a couple of inches or a few more rows of kernels per cob would make a difference. But it does when you have a few rows of corn, each with a hundred plants. It makes a *huge* difference when you need to put up food to survive on in hard times.

Grow a broccoli that will not only give you a nice-sized head, but will also produce abundant side shoots. Many times those side shoots are nearly as big as the main head…and the plant will keep producing them until it freezes in the fall.

Choose your tomatoes and peppers for huge production. Varieties such as Oregon Spring, Polish Linguisa (paste), Early Goliath tomatoes, and Giant Marconi, Gypsy, New Ace, and Big Chile peppers are noted for producing well, even in less than ideal conditions.

Make sure that the varieties you grow match your growing season. If you only have 90 frost-free days, you won't be growing 100-day tomatoes.

But if you choose well, your 66-day tomatoes will fill your pantry.

We all love our watermelons and muskmelons, but go easy on those crops. We're talking about survival food here, so plant more foods you can not only enjoy fresh, but also preserve for later use. When space is an issue, some concessions have to be made.

With your graph paper in hand, along with your must-plant list, sketch out your ideas on the graph paper. You'll have to rework it many times as you go. Take your time and get it right. It's a lot easier to erase or tear out another sheet than to tear out a row. Or to wish you'd have done it differently, along about August.

On your graph paper, also make notes of places you can tuck extra vegetable plants, such as on your lawn or in your flower beds, along the driveway, or next to your house foundation plantings. Just make sure they'll have lots of sunshine and adequate moisture.

Getting more from your modest garden

To get the most out of your garden, work in as much rotted compost as you can and get the soil into very good shape before you plant. While some crops can be planted very early, literally as soon as the ground can be worked up in the spring, others benefit from waiting until the soil has warmed some. You can use plastic to hurry up the process. Carrots, turnips, beets, and spinach can be planted early in the season, sometimes giving you two crops from the same space (depends on the climate and growing year). They don't mind cool soil one bit. But other crops, such as green beans and sweet corn, often have problems with germination in cold soils. Instead of growing, the seeds often just rot in the soil. Or if they do sprout, they are very weak and do poorly.

Protect your plants. Use all the gardening helps you can. For instance, I plant my tomatoes around the end of April, here in Northern Minnesota (Zone 3), where we regularly get spring frosts as late as June 16th. But I cheat and use Wallo' Water plant protectors that heat water up in the daytime, keeping the little tomato plants cozy even if the temperatures plummet at night to 19° F. By June 16th, those little tomato plants are heavily rooted and have popped right out the tops of the containers. If I just waited to plant them until we were "frost-free," the plants would be small and have much smaller root systems. I would have to wait at least another two months for tomatoes. By using protection, I am harvesting tomatoes for more than a month, in a normal year, before freezing weather arrives. Then I gather all the green tomatoes and bring them in to ripen inside in boxes and buckets. Almost all of them will then go ahead and ripen, so my canning continues for another month or more.

Other plant protectors include poly tunnels, cloche, and floating row covers. I have mini-hoop houses, made with 2"x4"s in a rectangle, with three hoops of PVC and a 2"x2", drilled to hold the tops firmly in place, sort of like a ridge beam. I staple clear plastic over these and use them to boost the growth of melons and squash in the spring. They are mini greenhouses that also protect the plants from varmints and insect pests when the plants are young and tender. I also use the same little hoop houses with floating row covers stapled over them to protect broccoli from cabbage worms. If the white cabbage moths can't get at the plants to lay eggs on them, you have no cabbage worms to deal with! Your family will love you for that.

How you water is important. If you have it or can afford it, use drip irrigation for your garden and lay it under a nice layer of mulch to protect the plastic from the sun and from rodents who seem to love that plastic taste. I've used one-inch flexible water line for a header, which goes across the head of the garden, and hooked thin plastic T tape on, to run down the rows. This keeps the plant roots well-watered, saves lots of water by not watering the garden paths, and keeps down weeds because they don't get watered. If you can't afford to do the whole garden, try to at least irrigate your tomatoes and peppers this way. Overhead watering sometimes causes diseases in them and they *are* water hogs.

No matter what watering method you use, be sure that your plants get enough regular moisture. Don't guess. Feel under the soil at the area in the row where the plants' roots are. If it is moist, they're okay. If not, water. Your garden, assuming that it has average soil, should receive at least one inch of water every three days unless it rains a lot. Keep track of a rain gauge; sometimes a few tenths of an inch seem like much more if it is cloudy and drizzly. Plants that are stressed from lack of water will not produce to their fullest, and may weaken or even die due to diseases. For instance, tomatoes that are stressed from lack of sufficient mois-ture when they are growing quickly will often develop blossom end rot; a blackened nasty spot on the blossom end of the fruit. Potatoes that are not watered regularly and well will develop hollow heart, where the center of the potato becomes hollow. Water is cheap insurance for good production in the garden.

It's best to water early in the morning. The water won't evaporate as quickly as it does if you water during the heat of the day, so you'll end up using much less water. In some climates, if you water in the evening, the plants can develop diseases because the leaves remain too damp for a long period of time.

Use mulch. Not only does mulch keep down weed competition, but it holds available moisture at the plant roots, letting them use it as needed. It also keeps the soil warmer, fostering more growth. Commercial growers make good use of black plastic mulch, especially for melons, tomatoes, and peppers. I've used it and it does work, but I just hate plastic. So I use organic mulch such as wood chips, straw, or pine needles. Do *not* use hay unless you know it is seed-free. Yes, you can pile hay on deep enough to keep any hay seed from

By planting onions in narrow rows or wide beds, you get more food per square foot than when planted in "regular" rows.

Use season extenders to gain weeks of extra growing time.

sprouting, but sooner or later you probably will till the garden and you will effectively seed it with grass seed from the hay. I did it once and spent the next three years pulling grass.

Wait until your plants are growing well before you mulch, as you don't want to mulch on cool ground. Wait, instead, until the soil is nicely warmed up, then start mulching. Mulching is an ongoing process. It packs down and begins to break down. That six inches you put on in the spring will quickly pack down to two inches, so renew it or you'll see weed growth.

You can use grass clippings as mulch, but first dry them until they are crisp. If you put down fresh grass clippings, they'll mat together and begin to heat and mold; it is not good for your plants. After the grass has dried, it works great. Just be sure it hasn't been sprayed with weed killer at any time.

Keep harvesting to produce more. As your garden progresses, some of your crops can be harvested. Begin as soon as you can because if they begin maturing, the whole production process stops. For instance, if you let the first small picking of beans "go" because there aren't enough to bother with, it will severely limit how many good pickings you'll get later on. That first small picking will probably only make a good meal or two. But then watch out: the next ones will astound you. Keep picking. Most beans will produce until they freeze out.

Leaf crops, such as spinach and Swiss chard, love to be picked. Keep cutting the leaves and more will continue to grow. Spinach may quit on you and bolt (go to seed) when the weather gets hot, but if you've got a good layer of mulch around the plants and you keep it picked and well watered, it may not, which will give

you much more food per square foot. I plant a relatively short double row of Swiss chard, but by keeping it cut, it keeps producing, giving us all the canned chard we'd ever want.

If you get your carrots and turnips in early and take good care of them, you may be able to pull them and put them up. Then plant a short season, cool weather vegetable in the same place, such as more spinach.

Keep at those weeds. Yeah, I know it's work, but if you get at it for half an hour every single morning, you will harvest twice the food from the same garden you would have if you got lazy and let the weeds grow; they compete with food plants for soil nutrients and moisture. Don't let them get a head start on you. When they're six inches high, they pull easily. When they're six feet high, you may need a tractor! Carrots, especially, must be kept weed-free or they just won't do much for you. (Likewise, they must be thinned; the jammed together carrots act as weeds, crowding each other out so none of them get any size.)

Fertilizer

Just because I grow an organic garden doesn't mean that I don't use fertilizer. In the first place, I dump literally tons of rotted manure on my garden each fall and work it in well to rot further over winter. Then as some of my fertilizer-hungry plants grow rank, I side dress them with even more rotted manure. When the tomatoes have set their fruit, for the most part, I'll add a good circle of it around each plant. And when the sweet corn is high enough to start tasseling out, I spread a good band of rotted manure down along the rows.

Crops like broccoli, beans, and melons like a good foliar feeding with fish emulsion. But do it *before* they are setting their crop.

Do be careful with manure around leafy green vegetables, as they could possibly be splashed with bacteria from the manure, causing an E. coli illness in the people who eat it raw, usually in salads.

If you use pine needles, sawdust, or bark chips for mulch, add more manure every year as these can use up nitrogen in the soil and you need to replenish it periodically.

Saving your seeds

If you've chosen open pollinated vegetable varieties, you can save your own seeds for the future, which gives you even more control over your family's food. For tips on keeping pure seed, check out my article, *Get the most out of spring seed catalogs*, in this anthology. It's easy to do and will ensure that the vegetables you grow will meet your expectations.

Try to keep seed saving in mind as you plant. For instance, keep the south end of your bean rows for seed beans; don't harvest them again, after that first scanty picking. Let them go ahead and make seed and dry in the shell. Of course if you raise dry beans, you'll already have your seed from your bountiful fall harvest. Just keep some out in a small jar for seed.

Let half a row of sweet corn go ahead and mature on the stalk. Leave

David knows that if you pick the first scanty crop of beans, huge crops follow all summer.

some peppers alone to go red and overmature. They're the ones you need to save seed from. Your squash and melons are easy; as you eat them, just save the seeds on a pie plate, set in a warm area. They are already mature. The same with tomatoes; just squeeze the seeds out of a plump ripe tomato into a cup, then add warm water. Set the cup on the kitchen counter for three days to ferment, and you can easily separate the seeds out of the goop.

Right now we can buy all sorts of seeds, but if the economy goes south, who knows what may happen. My grandmother said that during the Depression, first she didn't have money to buy seeds, then there weren't any to be had. It could happen again the way things are going. Even if it doesn't get that drastic, think of all the money you'll save if you begin saving your own seed. And besides, it's lots of fun, too. There's something comforting about looking at all those jars of your very own seeds sitting on a shelf, just waiting to provide food for your family in coming years. It's food security.

With a little planning and a lot of elbow grease, there's no doubt that you can grow a productive garden that will feed your family, not only this season, but next winter, and all the years to come. No matter who is elected president. No matter what the economy does. No matter what pitfalls lie ahead of us. If we are well fed, we are good to go. Δ

By choosing your varieties carefully, you'll have more food.

Can you survive out of your pantry for a whole year?

By Jeffrey R. Yago, P.E., CEM

Over the years I have provided many articles on emergency preparedness, and several included emergency food suggestions. However, these were easy-to-prepare instant meals for your vehicle, bug-out-bag, or home to get you through a week without power or groceries. These short-term problems could be due to an extended power outage, winter storm, or being stranded after a vehicle breakdown. Since these events could require moving to a safer area, the foods I chose for these emergencies are highly concentrated, lightweight, and can be packed into a relatively small storage box or backpack.

For these applications, it is also important to minimize meal preparation requirements, so most of these food items are dehydrated or powdered and can be easily reconstituted by adding a cup of hot water. Camping stores also offer individual meal packs that provide more variety and better taste, but these can cost more than $5 per single serving and do not have a long shelf life.

What about a long-term event that disrupts all food distribution in your area? What if you were unable to work or were in a disaster area and your rural area has minimum emergency support? With New Orleans

A long-term bulk storage pantry contains 1-gallon cans of freeze-dried foods and 5-gallon pails of wheat and corn, as well as baking supplies, equipment, and important non-food items such as toilet paper and toothpaste.

and Katrina still fresh in most people's minds, this may not be an unrealistic possibility to worry about these days. What if a really catastrophic natural or man-made disaster affected your entire town or state, and it might take a year to reestablish any normalcy for transportation, food distribution, and utilities? Yes, it is possible to remain in your own home and live fairly comfortably for many months without running to the grocery store each week, but eating small packs of stored instant noodles or Vienna sausages and crackers is not going to do it.

To prepare for a really long-term period of self-sufficiency, you need a supply of food that is very close to your normal diet, and not instant meals full of preservatives, chemicals, and sodium. Our bodies need a balanced input of fruits, vegetables, and protein, and a major change in your diet can affect your weight, disposition, and health.

To provide months of real food for emergencies you need a well-stocked pantry, but this is not your mother's pantry. This requires a large cool and dry storage space, and the regular task of rotating items to keep everything fresh. For example, if you cook one can of green beans each week, a year's supply for you would require two 24-can cases. If we add corn, peas, and other canned vegetables and fruits, you can see how your long-term pantry would soon take over most of the garage and would look like the corner store.

A serious long-term pantry will require sturdy shelving with easy access to both the front and back if possible. Recently purchased cans are added at the rear and older cans are moved forward to be used first. Keep a felt-tip marker pen by the pantry door and write the date on each new can. If rear access is not possible, always add to the back to keep the older dates towards the front.

Typical closet-size pantry with everyday-type canned goods.

The easiest way to get started in bulk food purchasing is to join a discount warehouse store where everything is sold by the case or in bulk containers. Each week select one specific vegetable or fruit and try to purchase one or more cases. After several months of this quantity shopping you should have at least a six-month's supply of each. If space allows, you can continue and build up a year's supply if desired. Since all canned products have a limited shelf life, it may not be possible to rotate more than a six-month supply without items going out-of-date, so watch the expiration dates printed on each can. By watching for specials and realizing some foods are more plentiful and

lower cost at certain times of the year, your bulk purchases will be able to take advantage of these sales.

Many of you already have a garden and fruit trees and you can your own homegrown fruits, jellies, and garden vegetables, so you are already familiar with this process. This is an excellent way to have more nutritional canned fruits and vegetables for your pantry then you can buy at the local supermarket. A well-tended garden will also provide fresh items at least part of the year that will not require canning.

Although a large pantry will solve a big part of your long-term food storage requirements, we can't just eat everything from a can each day. Your normal daily diet also includes bread products, fresh meats, and hopefully fresh greens, and these food groups do not come in a can.

Grain mill a must

In addition to a long-term food storage there are two other things you absolutely must have—bulk wheat and a wheat mill. We take it for granted every time we grab a loaf of bread and a half gallon of milk on our way home from work, but what if the food supply chain is interrupted for any reason? Bread and milk are the first things to disappear from store shelves, and they can only stay fresh for a few days. If you check around the next time you are at the grocery store, there are no cases of food in a back room. All food items are now ordered by bar code and computers every few days, and are constantly arriving each week. What you see is all there is going to be if the distribution system is interrupted.

Raw wheat, if kept dry and free of insects, can last hundreds of years without any loss of quality or taste. Unfortunately, once wheat is ground into flour, it will only last a few days without turning rancid, which is why regular store-purchased flour is heavily bleached and full of preservatives. In fact, rodents will not touch bleached white flour. Yes, you will want a few bags of name-brand flour in your pantry, but this will not last long when you start baking your own bread and biscuits every few days. On the other hand, it takes very little wheat to make a lot of flour, and unlike packaged flour, fresh wheat flour is full of gluten and other natural nutrients your body needs.

Any long-term food pantry should have a supply of both red and winter-white wheat, which are usually sold in bulk 5-gallon plastic pails. These pails have all of the oxygen removed prior to sealing by purging with dry nitrogen. This kills all microscopic insects that may have entered during harvesting and packaging. Your pantry should also include several 5-gallon pails of hard corn (popcorn). Your wheat grinder can easily turn hard corn into cornmeal for frying fish or baking corn bread.

You can buy a hand-operated wheat grinder for very little cost, but believe me, it takes lots of cranking to make a cup of flour. If you have a backup source of emergency power, you should purchase an electric grain mill. Although they are not cheap, they are much better suited for regular use. The better models include covers with filters to eliminate flour dust, and have adjustable grinding sizes to quickly switch from wheat, barley, or corn.

If events require you to be on your own much longer than anticipated and you are forced to start baking from scratch on a regular basis, there are several other cooking ingredients besides flour you should have on hand and these are also some of the first items that will disappear from the store shelves. Refrigerated milk, butter, and eggs will not keep long, although you can freeze butter. These products are also available in bulk cans, but I'm not talking about WWII powdered eggs. Today, these everyday necessities are specially freeze-

1-gallon nitrogen packed cans of freeze-dried tomatoes, cheese, and butter.

Freeze-dried butter, cheese, and tomatoes return to original state after mixing with water.

High-speed grain mill with attached sealed discharge container easily turns raw wheat into flour.

Sources for freeze-dried foods and supplies:

www.survivalcenter.com
360-458-6778

Freeze-dried Foods:

www.frontiersurvival.net
5765 Hwy. 64
Farmington, NM 87401
505-947-2200

www.survivalacres.com
800-681-1057

The Emergency Preparedness Center
www.areyouprepared.com
520 C. North Main St. Ste. 202
Heber City, UT 84032
435-654-3447

Nitro-Pak Preparedness Center, Inc.
www.nitro-pak.com
151 North Main St.
Heber City, UT 84032
800-866-4876

www.longlifefoods.com

Ready Reserve Foods, Inc.
www.readyreservefoods.com
1442 S. Gage St.
San Bernadino, CA 92408
800-453-2202

Grain Master Whisper Mill:
www.pleasanthillgrain.com
1604 N. Hwy. 14
Aurora, NE 68818
800-321-1073

Hand Operated Grain Mills;
Country Living Products
www.countrylivinggrainmills.com
14727 56th Ave. NW
Stanwood, WA 98292
360-652-0671

Wheat and Grains:
Home Grown Harvest
www.homegrownharvest.com
2065 Lakeshore Overlook Dr.
Kennesaw, GA 30152
866-900-3321

dried prior to canning, and will turn back into the original form in both taste and consistency when you add water. Unfortunately, like the bulk wheat mentioned above, you will not find these freeze-dried products at the local supermarket, so they will need to be ordered. Internet and mail order sources for these products are listed in the sidebar on this page.

About every five years I reorder a few cans of freeze-dried foods, and I recently discovered several cans which are now 10 years old. Normally I would consider this past the shelf life for even the specially-packaged freeze-dried products, but I decided to test them for this article before discarding. I opened nitrogen-packed 1-gallon cans of freeze-dried pure butter, whole milk, cheese, and ripe tomatoes. Each can contained a colorful dry powder, with the consistency of flour. I took a cupful of each separately and added an equal amount of water and after a little stirring I suddenly had real dairy butter and cheese, and a thick tomato paste.

Each tasted like they were fresh from the store, and the tomato paste had a very fresh tomato aroma. By varying the amount of water, you can make the cheese taste stronger or milder, and after a night in the refrigerator the butter and cheese became just as solid as they would have been to start with.

I then tried this test with several 3-year-old dehydrated meals you find in sealed foil pouches at most camping stores. After adding hot water I found these meals tasted very old and stale. For really long-term food storage necessities, I strongly recommend freeze-dried foods in nitrogen-packed cans. Most distributors use 1-gallon size cans with a special coating on the inside to reduce any metallic taste, and they add several oxygen-absorbing pouches just before sealing to remove any remaining oxygen.

After establishing your own reliable long-term supply of canned fruits and vegetables, and adding the ability to turn wheat into fresh bread products, most non-vegetarians will want to have meat for at least a few meals each week. It is possible to store a few canned hams or other canned meat products, but these are full of preservatives and still will have a relatively-short shelf life. (See Jackie Clay's article in this issue for other ways to store protein without refrigeration.)

If possible, your long-term food program should include a good quality top-load freezer, and a way to keep it powered during a long-term power outage. I have provided several articles in past issues on solar-powered appliances and refrigerators and freezers. This might be a good time to review these articles to see if one might be right for you.

A frozen turkey can provide meat for up to a week when thawed and cooked. The same is true for a large beef or pork roast if you have the means to keep a freezer operating. You should also have a good supply of smaller frozen whole chickens, steaks, and fish. Be sure to clearly mark the date each was purchased and rotate on a regular basis with your normal meals. Most frozen meats should be eaten within six months.

All long-term food pantries need to include other incidentals you use on a regular basis, and these can be purchased in bulk to reduce space and cost. These will include salt, pepper, cinnamon, and any other favorite cooking spices. You will also need cooking oil or shortening, rice, dried beans of various types, powdered milk, baking soda, yeast, sugar, cornstarch, vinegar, and baking powder.

There are many incidental non-food items that are easy to store and will come in very handy during hard times. Bulk packages of plastic wrap, paper towels, plastic trash bags, toilet paper, matches, disposable plates and cups, powdered flavored drinks, tea, coffee, cocoa, and block chocolate make life much more civilized.

I am only addressing how to start your own long-term food storage in this article. However, being prepared to switch to a self-sufficient lifestyle, either by choice or under duress, requires other long-term preparations as well. Don't forget first-aid (See Jackie Clay's article in this issue.) and medical needs, security needs, and personal hygiene needs, and these products will also require storage space and planning.

No one ever expects a disaster will involve them, yet every day the news reports some major storm or catastrophic event that forced hundreds and sometimes thousands of people to be stranded and on their own. At a time when most hurried families pick up what they plan to eat that night on their way home from work, many homes and apartments have less than three days of food on hand. Even fewer will have a way to prepare and cook these foods if the power fails.

You also need several gallons of fresh water each day, and municipal water supplies quickly become contaminated during times of disaster. Unless you have an alternate means for electrical power, well pumps do not pump water if there is a power outage, so don't forget to keep as many gallons of water on hand that you have space for.

Having a month's supply of your everyday food in a nearby pantry and a year's supply of bulk-type emergency food provides real peace of mind. After all, maybe not your parents, but I guarantee your grandparents were able to eat very healthy meals each day without running to the corner store each evening.

Perhaps it's time to realize that although frozen foods and drive-through restaurants are really convenient, we all have become far too dependent on others for our everyday living. Having a well-stocked pantry is your first step to true independent living. Δ

A Backwoods Home Anthology
The Fourth Year

❋ How to make your own "grab-and-go" survival kits
❋ Hearty winter breakfasts
❋ Using and storing wheat at home
❋ Raising fishworms as a business
❋ Recycle those old clothes into a braided rug
❋ How to build your own beehives
❋ How to make cheese and butter
❋ Peppers for short season growers
❋ Harvesting from nature

❋ Harvesting the blacktail deer
❋ Protect your home and family from fire
❋ Fall pumpkins and squash
❋ How to make money with wild crayfish
❋ How to buy your first dairy goat
❋ Smoked turkey and smoked brisket
❋ Soups and stews for late winter
❋ Choosing superior bedding plants
❋ How to build the fence you need
❋ Getting sugar from trees

By Jeffrey R. Yago, P.E., CEM

Each fall when my dad took us to the State Fair, we could always count on this fast-talking salesman standing next to his car with a big egg-shaped microphone hanging around his neck. The hood was up and the engine would be running. A big meter was hanging from the hood indicating engine RPM. He would quickly pull the ignition wire off the distributor, hopefully without killing the engine, and insert this little device that looked like a tiny torpedo with a plug on each end.

As soon as he inserted this device, the engine's RPM magically went up due to what he called a "hotter spark," and of course this just had to improve your gas mileage if you bought one. In reality, the faster his engine ran, the more gasoline it would actually consume, but that energy relationship was never explained and gas flow was not metered. I don't know what happened to this guy years later when cars became computer-controlled, but I always thought he ended up living on a yacht somewhere in the Mediterranean, after selling thousands of those worthless devices.

Times have changed, but the same hawkers are out there selling all kinds of energy saving gizmos that are claimed to drastically cut your monthly utility bills. I am hoping this series of articles will make you a better consumer of energy, and will help you learn how to recognize these modern-day snake oil salesmen and their perpetual motion machines.

I receive many calls and website questions (www.homeenergy.info) regarding energy, and most of these questions relate to a misunderstanding of how energy actually works.

This is one subject most people were never taught in school, yet we are inundated every day with energy-related ads, products, and government-mandated energy regulations that affect these decisions. Although most people do not consciously think about it, energy is one of the most expensive items in their monthly budget. Energy is the gasoline to power our cars and chain saws, to heat and cool our homes, the electricity to power our lights, appliances, and refrigerators, and the power to recharge our cell phones, power tools, and trolling motors.

Energy prices also significantly impact the cost of manufacturing, packaging, and transporting everything you buy, including all you eat. Even if you grow most of your own food, you still require lots of energy to plow, till, harvest, and refrigerate these crops. I bet you know the cur-

155

rent price for gasoline and what your weekly commute is costing. However, even though your home's utility bills represent a much higher energy cost, most people do not know what their energy costs are, or how to use this energy more effectively.

For example, do you know what you are paying for each "kilowatt-hour" of electricity you consume, and is this cost high, low, or average for a home like yours? If you heat by gas, do you know what you are paying for a "therm" or cubic foot, and is this cost high, low, or average? If you heat with propane or oil and are billed each time they fill your tank, how many gallons do you burn per month and is this reasonable?

Your monthly utility bills are probably costing more this year than last year, but are these cost increases due to a higher fuel cost, higher usage, or both? Utility prices do fluctuate, and natural gas, propane, and fuel oil have experienced major price increases in recent years. Electric rates nationally have been fairly stable for almost 10-years, but there have been significant price increases in the past year in several states, and major rate hikes are already being discussed in many others.

When the cost of gasoline went from $1.00 per gallon to over $3.00 per gallon in less than five years, you knew exactly what to do. You gradually cut your nonessential travel, then combined multiple short errands into one, and finally traded in that gas guzzler for a more fuel-efficient car or truck. So if you understand how to reduce these energy costs, why do you continue to pay whatever you are billed for utilities, without even considering there are similar steps you can take to reduce these energy costs as well?

Let's start with some basic energy rules. Thermal energy "flows" from hot to cold, and not the other way around. You are trying to heat your house because interior heat is moving out to the colder outside, and the poorer the insulation, the faster this energy will move. You air condition your home because the hot outside air and solar radiation through windows are driving heat energy into your cooler home, and not because the cold is somehow escaping out.

The next basic energy rule we need to review is how heat flow depends only on the temperature difference, the U-value of the insulation separating the inside and outside, and the surface areas. The "U" factor is just the inverse of the "R" factor, which is usually printed on the insulation. For example, R-19 batt insulation used in many walls has a "U" factor of 0.0526, (1/19 mathematically). This is the basic calculation for heat loss or heat gain through all walls, ceilings, roofs, floors, and window glass.

Heat loss = area × U factor × temperature difference

I'm not going to bore you with heat-flow calculation examples, but you get the concept. Since the surface area of your home's exterior is fixed, unless you add more insulation, the heat loss or gain of your home will be due entirely to the difference in temperature between the inside and outside. Refer back to the above formula. If we skip any consideration of air infiltration or latent heat effects, it takes the same amount of energy for each degree we heat up or cool down our homes based on this basic law of heat transfer.

In other words, it takes the same amount of energy to heat your home from 60° to 61°F, as it takes to heat it from 70° to 71°F. It takes the same amount of energy to cool your home from 80° to 79°F as it does from 76° to 75°F, as long as we ignore any changes in latent heat (humidity). If we light a match anywhere inside our home during the winter, the heat from this match will eventually find its way outside, totally as a function of your exterior surface areas, and the insulation value of these areas since the match is hotter than the outside. Of course this is an extreme example, and I am ignoring air infiltration losses through cracks and openings.

I think we are now ready for some real-life examples. Based on what you have just learned, why do most people think they can buy a small portable electric heater or fake fireplace and heat their entire home? Yet the ads say you can turn down your home's thermostat and sit comfortably in front of this glowing heater and save hundreds of dollars each month. Yes, in a cool room if you sit three feet from any brand heater you will feel warm. However, while you sit there, the rest of your house is getting colder and colder, and it will never recover the lost heat unless you add the same amount of heat back.

Remembering our earlier energy lesson, turning down your thermostat one degree will save the same energy it will take to heat it up again one degree. The only way your home can be heated back up to the previous temperature after you let it drop to save energy is to consume the same amount of energy per degree drop. For those hours your home stays at this setback temperature, it is true that you are saving this given amount of energy each hour. It should now be obvious that this is far more energy than any magic portable heater can ever provide. Those too-good-to-be-true ads say their heaters use the same electricity as your electric coffee pot, which sounds like a tiny amount. However, an electric coffee pot is one of the highest electric loads in your home, but it doesn't cost much to make a pot of coffee because you only perk water for a few minutes each day. Imagine what it would cost to continuously boil coffee water 24 hours a day!

Let's have a reality check. Unless we are talking about a heat pump, a resistance-type electric heater can only produce 3,413 BTUs of heat per kilowatt, because that is the heat value of a kilowatt of electricity. I don't care if these magic heaters glow red, are filled with special heat transfer oils, have reflectors that look like radar dishes, or blow hot air from a fake log fire, 3,413 BTUs is all you get from a kilowatt of electricity. If an electric heater is rated at 2 kilowatts (2,000 watts), you get 6,826 BTUs (2 × 3,413) of heat, which is about as large as they can make these portable heaters due to safety limitations on the heater's power cord and the current-carrying capacity of your wall outlet.

Since a typical residential furnace will have a heating capacity in the 80,000 to 125,000 BTU/hr range, you can see how your magic heater would need to operate almost 30 hours to produce the same heat your central furnace can produce in one hour.

Now for those of you who are yelling at me that it's cheaper to let your home cool down and only heat the room where you are sitting, you are almost correct. But you assume your house stays at the lower temperature. What actually happens when you lower your house thermostat from 70° to 68°? Once the interior temperature drops to 68° it does not stay there. During the winter, the interior temperature will continue to fall if no additional heat is added. So where does the heat come from to keep your house at the lower 68° without falling any further? At some point the 70° room you are sitting in with your magic heater will get colder and colder due to the cooling of the rest of the house. I think the salespeople hope by this time you have given up and crawled into bed under heavy blankets to dream about all the money you are saving.

If we have two identical homes located side-by-side, and one home was held all winter at 68°F and the other home was held at 70°F, it is true the lower temperature home will save the amount of energy the other home is using to maintain the interior two

degrees warmer for each hour it stays at this temperature. Obviously, if you decide to live with a colder home, you can sit all day directly in front of your magic heater while the rest of your home is cold. However, don't expect your entire home to also stay warm, and don't think this magic heater is not the reason your electric meter is spinning.

Do I own one of these magic heaters? Yes, and I use it occasionally to offset a cold room or add a little heat under my office desk on an extra cold day that is taxing my central heating system. But the difference is, I'm not expecting it to save anything on my heating bill. It is using electricity and that costs money!

Will lowering your thermostat save on your heating bill? Of course, but only for those hours you maintain the lower temperature. If you want a magic box heater to keep your immediate area warmer when the rest of the house is cold, then go for it. Just don't think you can use this little magic heater to heat your entire home for pennies-per-day.

In Part II of this series, I will explain how to actually read your monthly utility bill, how to determine your actual energy usage, and how to identify major energy problems using only your monthly utility bills.

In the final Part III of this series, you will learn how to take control of your home's energy costs, just like you took control of your transportation energy costs. Your assignment before our next issue is to dig through your old receipts and put together a minimum of 12 months of utility bills. If you can't find them, contact your electric or fuel supplier for copies.

(**Jeff Yago is a licensed professional engineer and certified energy manager with more than 25 years experience in the energy conservation field. He has extensive solar thermal and solar photovoltaic system design experience and has authored numerous articles and texts.**) Δ

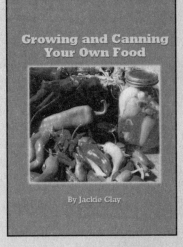

the cornerstone of a survival diet
Protein

By Jackie Clay

It goes without saying that preparedness is not for "radicals" or "weirdos" anymore. I picked up a preparedness leaflet at the County Agent's office last week and another one at our bank. Times are changing. For the better. In the past, a lot of people equated the term "emergency preparedness" with nuclear bombs going off, tornadoes leveling the neighborhood, etc. But, in truth, most of our emergencies are rather bland by comparison. However, at the time, they sure *feel* like emergencies to us.

How about when you went to work and were told that there was no work and maybe, just maybe, the plant would reopen in a couple of months? Or when the paycheck wasn't in the mail and you had to wait two months for it to be reissued? Or when your daughter left her husband and came home with her two kids? Or the country goes into (another) recession and food prices go sky-high, along with everything else. To some, small emergencies, but to those affected, they are *huge*.

The good news is that there's a lot we can do to be prepared. Yes, we all have cans of food in our pantries, lots of dried beans, rice, cornmeal, and flour stored away. But a lot of folks miss the important cornerstone of a tasty, complete diet: protein sources. Yes, we can survive on rice and beans. But that sure as heck gets tiresome after about two days! Here are a few hints on some things we can do to boost our emergency foods up to really good eating that is really good for us, too.

I just found out today that grain prices are rising at an alarming rate. Wheat at $7 a bushel in December is now nearing $17 a bushel. Of course corn's doing the same...and oats are following. At the mill today, the owner told me that farm fertilizer has risen to $700 a ton. And that all affects the price of grain-eating animals. Right now they're at nearly an all-time low. Grown sows that have just weaned litters aren't even getting a bid at the auction barns and grown butcher hogs are selling for $30 a hundredweight. It's going to get worse as farmers dump their animals because they can't afford to feed them for what they are bringing. You can't spend $80 to feed a butcher hog and sell him for $60.

The other side of this coin is that once millions of animals have been sold and butchered, the price of meat is going to skyrocket.

Buy cheap meat

A good plan is to buy inexpensive meat now and home can it for the future. This will give you a good tasting protein source that is also a nice cornerstone for many meals. While you can certainly home can meat in quart jars, I've found that it is more economical (unless you have more than four to feed) to put it up in pint and even half-pint jars. It uses more jars, but you will get many, many more meals from the same amount of meat. Now when I say "cheap meat," I don't mean poor cuts, such as chuck roast, which has a very high percentage of fat, bone, and gristle. I mean lean cuts that you buy on a very good sale. For instance, I've picked up boneless, trimmed, whole pork loin for $1.49. You get a lot of good, usable meat from such cuts.

I won't get into the actual process of canning meat here, for the sake of space, but you can look back in the May/June 2007 (Issue #105) of *Backwoods Home Magazine,* archived online *Ask Jackie,* and *BHM* blogs to gain tons of how-to information on home canning. Of course, meat must be processed with a pressure canner, as it is a low acid food and can be subject to botulism if it is not properly processed.

Pick up "family packs" of boneless, skinless chicken breasts and thighs when they are on a huge sale. I've recently picked up thighs for 48¢ a pound and breasts for 99¢. I don't buy one or two packs; I buy a dozen and can them as fast as they thaw out.

Buy cheap "holiday" meat to can. I buy cheap, good quality hams and pork loin at Easter and turkeys at Thanksgiving and Christmas. Stores often use the meat as a loss-leader to get shoppers into the store. Again, I buy in bulk and can it right away.

Ask your local meat manager if you can buy outdated meat at a very good price. I've done this and gotten pounds of hamburger, roasts, ham, and even steaks for pennies on the dollar. They usually freeze any meat that outdates. It's worth asking.

Buy bulk lean hamburger when it's on sale. I stay away from "chubs" or the round, long plastic wrapped burger...unless I know it's packaged locally. Some of that meat is from other countries where their animal raising often includes "peculiar" feeds and spraying barns and animals with DDT. Yes, DDT is banned in the U.S., but we make it and ship it out of the country, then buy produce and meat from those countries. Smart, huh?

Check out your local Dollar Store for canning lids this spring. Those lids are going up all the time, but I just bought a case for 99¢ a box of a dozen regular lids. The name of the game is saving all you can.

Don't forget to make mixed meat dishes to can, such as spaghetti sauce, pizza sauce with Italian sausage, soups, stews, sloppy joes, chili, etc. They come in very handy at times.

Buy up as much meat from time to time as you are able and can it up, while it's still cheap. By the looks of things, it's going to get a whole lot worse before too long.

Okay, I've got a pantry well stocked with tasty home canned meats and poultry, but what happens when we eat it up?

Raise your own poultry

I believe firmly that it's always a good idea to have poultry. Even a small flock of chickens is a great help when times get tough. They can even be kept on the edges of many cities and towns, providing local regulations allow this small "livestock." A small flock of chickens only needs a coop slightly larger than a large-breed dog house, and a wire run attached to it so they can roam outdoors. Of course, when you have the room available, they can also be allowed to free range during the day, providing they don't roam into your neighbor's flower beds or garden.

A flock of six hens will usually produce about four eggs a day on average, year around. They lay fewer eggs during the winter months and usually an egg a day in the spring and early summer. Not only are the fresh eggs a good, nutritious, tasty source of protein for the family, but they are extremely useful in helping to provide a varied menu. After all, eggs can be used in everything from pies (custard & meringue), to breads, and meat binders, like in meatloaf.

And a small flock of chickens can earn their own living by free ranging during the summer and be supplemented by extra kitchen and garden refuse. This makes the cost of raising them much lower than if they were solely fed laying mash.

Chickens are extremely easy to raise for just about anyone, from elderly to children. I won't get into the "how-to's" here, again for lack of room, but you can pick up *BHM's* new *Chickens* handbook or read my chicken article in this anthology and learn all about it.

If you have room, raising a batch of meat chickens along with your layers is always a great idea. Why not buy a batch of Cornish Rock roasting chicks this spring so you can butcher and can them up this fall? It takes very little work to raise them and you will reap a tremendous amount of meat from even 25 chicks.

You can even have your own heavy hens sit on their own eggs, hatching out a renewable meat supply at no extra cost to you. When you let four hens sit on only one clutch of eggs a summer, you'll end up with around forty meat birds come early winter. Not bad. And the hens do all the incubating, brooding, and caretaking too.

Have more room yet? Why not keep a small flock of turkeys? I have three hens and a tom. The hens all lay well, and this spring we'll be saving their eggs for my friend Jeri to hatch in her incubator. We'll share the babies and both families will have all the turkey we want to eat. Turkeys are kept almost like chickens, only their nests have to be on the ground; they're too heavy to fly up to a nest box. It has been said that domestic turkeys are bred so heavy that they can not reproduce without artificial insemination. Not true. Simply use a tom of a medium breed on your larger hens. I have a tom that is crossed with a wild turkey. He is lighter weight and much more nimble than meat toms. Therefore he can breed the hens without tearing up their backs like a heavier tom would. The poults grow nearly as large as the Broad Breasted Bronze hens, so it's a win-win situation.

Again, with raising your own poultry, it's always a good idea to keep putting up some of the meat in jars in your pantry for winter or lean times. Stocking up that pantry is an ongoing process if you're serious about having a reliable, sustainable source of food.

Raise your own rabbits

Another great source of "small meat" that can be raised just about anywhere you live is rabbits. Their housing needs are minimal. They are cheap to feed. And they reproduce… well…like rabbits! (In fairness, though, it *does* take a little experience to raise rabbits well enough for a dependable meat source.) The meat is tender and delicious.

Having three hutches of breeders, two does and a good buck, you'll have year-round meat. It only takes two months for a litter of bunnies to grow from tiny babies to large meat rabbits. And a healthy doe can have at least two litters a year; many breeders do three. (I would rather have two as the does don't get as run down, and thus live a longer reproductive life.)

For large meat rabbit breeds, a cage at least 18"x48" is necessary; larger is better. You'll need one per breeding doe, one for your buck, and another for growing fryers.

Unless you live in a relatively mild climate, your rabbits are best housed in wood and wire hutches with a wood nesting box. Many large breeders use all wire cages. These are very nice, easy to clean, and provide great ventilation. But when you use all wire cages, you should also have them housed in an outbuilding for protection against rain, wind, snow, cold, sun, and predators. In extremely cold climates, it's also necessary to bring wood and wire hutches under cover during the winter months. This can be in a barn, garage, or even a smaller shed made of plywood. You just need something for protection against heavy snows, stiff wind, and bitter temperatures.

In warm weather, be sure your rabbits are given some sort of shade. Not only is heat uncomfortable for them but bucks can become sterile if they get too hot. Our rabbits love cuddling a plastic soda bottle, frozen overnight when it's very hot. That's good for them, too. You'll lose no rabbits to heat prostration if you keep them cool.

Rabbits are easily fed. In the summer you can cut grass, clover, alfalfa,

Dairy goats can provide milk and meat.

and other forage for them, along with giving them extra produce from the garden. In addition, they should also have rabbit pellets, salt, and a clean source of fresh water. During the winter, they will eat good quality hay in place of the grass and other forage; they should also have pellets, salt, and daily fresh water.

Rabbit-raising tip: *never* put a buck into a doe's cage. She is very territorial and will fight and even castrate a buck! Always put the doe into the buck's cage and even then, stay and watch to make sure she doesn't repel his advances viciously; if she does, take her away and try again another day when she is more receptive.

There are many good rabbit books aimed at beginners and homestead-type rabbit raising. If you're interested, browse through a couple at your local library. Then hunt up a couple of local rabbit breeders that raise good meat stock. You'll want large rabbit breeds such as New Zealand Whites, Californians, or Flemish Giants. There are dozens of smaller "pet" breeds that just don't make efficient meat rabbits, no matter how pretty they are.

How about dairy goats?

In my opinion, few animals exceed the usefulness of a good dairy goat. With two does (the correct term for "nanny") and a buck…or a relatively nearby breeder with a buck, you will have not only year-round milk but also an ongoing source of meat from any kids you choose not to keep. Let me say right here and now: goat milk does *not* taste goaty if it is from a healthy doe, fed decent food, kept in clean conditions, and the milk has been handled correctly. You can't taste the difference between goat milk and cow milk. Period.

A good doe should provide at least three quarts of milk a milking for eight months or more, tapering off toward the end of her lactation. She must be dried off two months before

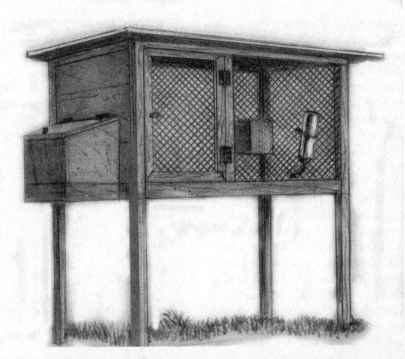

Rabbits can be raised just about anywhere you live and are quick to mature.

giving birth to give her body a chance to recover from months of milking plus developing fetuses in her uterus. This is why two does are useful. By breeding one to freshen (give birth) in May and another in September, you'll have a good milk source year around. Does have a gestation period of a little over 5 months.

Goats benefit from having a decent shed as protection from severe weather and predators. And because they are extremely clever about getting out, they do need to be fenced in. The easiest and strongest fence is welded 16' stock panels. These may be fastened to either wood posts or steel T posts. Goats can not be fenced in with barbed wire, woven wire (field fence), or chicken wire. They are just too good at escaping. And when they do, they'll eat your flowers, fruit trees, or garden, and probably end up on your porch or the hood of your car. Or your neighbors'. Not a good idea.

Our goats have hay available all the time and receive grain twice a day. In the summer, they also get garden extras, fresh cut grass, tree prunings, and clover. We like to take them for a

walk often, too. We all enjoy those excursions when the goats gambol and jump for joy, nibble wild raspberries, aspen trees, and bits of grass. It's all free food, too!

Goats have great personalities and do *not* deserve the reputation as being mean and butting people. I have never had a mean goat and I've had hundreds in my lifetime. Like all animals, if you treat them well, they'll be nice to be around. When you're mean to them, they will repay in kind.

Goat milk also makes excellent yogurt, cottage cheese, hard cheeses, and ice cream and this further extends their desirability. All of these products are very easy to learn to make, too. I give my extra goat milk to my poultry to boost their protein intake. I've also raised pigs and baby calves on it, eliminating expensive milk replacer. It's also much better for them than powdered milk replacer; you'll have much less trouble with scours (calf diarrhea).

Goat meat, or chevon, is tender and has an excellent flavor. I prefer to bone it out when I can or prepare it. Like venison or mutton, the fat and bone can give the meat a strong taste. Some people like it, but I don't and always bone it so that it is tasty and mild. I have Nubian/Boer cross does and breed them to my Boer buck. The Boer is a very stocky African meat goat. The crossbreds are stockier than a purebred dairy goat and that makes more meat on any goats we choose to butcher. My does also milk about a gallon a milking, so the crossing with the Boer didn't hurt that ability.

You can find more information about raising goats by reading the Sept/Oct 2005 (Issue #95) and May/June 2004 (Issue #87) of *Backwoods Home Magazine*. There are also several good goat books around and if you'll visit a goat breeder or two, you'll see how enjoyable goats really are.

Livestock feed

With livestock and poultry to feed, there *are* feed expenses. But it's amazing how much of their food you can either gather or grow for them without having a farm. Poultry can be let out to forage for much of their spring and summer food. This is called free ranging. They'll eat bugs, seeds, and greens with abandon. It's kind of funny watching your hens running with their mouths open, chasing down a flying grasshopper! Not only will this provide much of their feed; it'll substantially reduce the amount of insects that damage your garden. We also save and feed them nearly all kitchen scraps and even their own crushed, dried egg shells, which provide them with calcium to make their next egg shells nice and hard.

You can pasture your goats for most of their spring, summer, and fall roughage. Just make sure you use a stout fence, reinforced with electric wire to keep them from standing on the wire or leaning through it. Check out the fencing article I did for *BHM* in the 13th year anthology. If you don't have enough land for a pasture

A small herd of dairy goats earns its keep.

or money for the fence, you can still "pasture" them by cutting grass and brush and bringing it to their pen. A machete works great to cut brambles and tall grass. Of course, so does a scythe or a string trimmer. We cut around the edges of our driveway, where the browse grows thick. You can also cut on roadsides, *providing* it has not been sprayed with herbicides for brush control.

My son, David, loves to cut the goats poplar saplings to throw in the goat pen. And they love to eat them. They soon eat all the bark and most of the leafy branches.

In some areas, you can visit the bakery thrift stores and get huge deals on over-two-day-old bread. We used to load a whole pickup truck full for $10. We fed this to the chickens, goats, and even cows. Of course we first went through the load and distributed the good stuff to our friends and neighbors, who thoroughly enjoyed "bakery day."

We save tons by growing extra livestock feed right in our large garden. A few extra rows of sweet corn not only give you more to eat, but we feed all the cobs (after cutting the kernels off to can), husks, and stalks to our happy goats. They also get forked carrots, and carrot tops, beet and other tops, pea pods, bean trimmings and vines when they're finished bearing, weeds, extra squash and pumpkins, unripe melons in the fall (they *love* those), raspberry and blackberry prunings, rutabagas, turnips, and more. You'd be surprised at how much goat food you can find growing in your garden.

Even if you don't have enough garden to grow significant produce for your livestock, why not check out the local stores? Many of them will give you boxes of vegetable trimmings, bruised fruit, and wilted produce for your animals. Of course some only give you a cold stare. But I've grown tough enough to keep checking around, especially the smaller stores locally, who don't have "corporate policy," to protect the stores from lawsuit should someone become sick from eating throwout produce.

Hunting wild meat

With us, hunting is not a "sport" but a way of keeping our meat pantry full. It's amazing, but a deer or two will provide dozens of jars of very good meat. If you're fortunate and live where there are elk or moose available to hunt, you have a huge source of meat...right out in the woods. And best ever, you don't have to house, feed, or care for it.

Wild meat is even healthier eating as it is lower in fat and cholesterol than beef or pork.

If you don't hunt now, perhaps this would be a good time to learn. Hunting is an art and it starts by getting to know your weapon and the animals you will be hunting. Whether you choose to hunt with a bow and arrow, black powder rifle, shotgun, or rifle, learn basic safety and practice until you are accurate, under different conditions and distances.

Walk the woods. Learn to track. Learn the ways of your quarry—how to get them to stop, how to entice them to approach closer. You can learn a lot from watching videos and reading, but nothing beats actually walking the woods or mountains where you will be hunting.

I have hunted deer, elk, and moose, but I also hunt game birds to supplement our meat supply in season. Don't discount the smaller game such as birds, squirrels, and rabbits. They are often very abundant and will give you many good meals. There is a nice article about survival hunting in the March/April 2008 (Issue #110) of *BHM*.

Don't wait until there is a national crisis to begin to hunt. When times are really tough, *everyone* is out there hunting and your chances of bagging an animal are severely reduced. During the homestead days, and later, during the Great Depression, game was nearly exterminated in many areas because people had to hunt in order to survive and they killed just about everything edible.

Do be advised that in most states there is a game limit. Say you are allowed one deer. That doesn't mean one hanging in a tree, it also means one canned in your pantry, or frozen in your freezer. You used to be able to limit out on any game and process the meat. If you had "extra" left or bagged another legal animal, so much the better, because you had leftover food to add to your current supply. Now this is illegal. For instance, we used to fish every day, bring our limit home, clean, and freeze them. Today, in most states, this would be considered illegal as we would have over our limit "in possession." A lot of laws don't make any sense to a reasonable person! It's okay to eat fish every day, but not freeze those same fish? Take care to read your game regulations.

To learn more of the how-tos of home canning your own meat you should pick up a relatively current home canning book or manual, such as the Ball Blue Book, which is available at most stores that carry canning supplies.

Non-meat protein

I've always advocated having a supply of TVPs on hand as recipe enhancers and protein additions. TVPs are granulated bits of flavored soy protein. You probably best know the "fake" bacon bits from the store. I use bacon flavored TVPs a lot in everyday cooking. Toss a handful into a casserole, fried potatoes, eggs, or whatever and you've got a meal. I even mix them with cream cheese and stuff fresh mushrooms with the mix and bake them. Pretty darned good.

TVPs come in sausage, hamburger, and taco flavor, in addition to bacon. All are pretty good and are available in #10 cans (roughly a gallon) from emergency preparedness companies such as *Emergency Essentials*. They are dry and remain good as long as you keep them in an airtight container. I have an opened can that has been open for three years and they are still perfect.

Don't forget to store up beans, lentils, and peas. These versatile (and tasty) sources of protein are also very filling...not to mention good for you too. I store up dry beans, peas, and lentils, but also can some up in pint and quart jars, too, for quick meals. They are already soaked, softened, and ready to add to your recipes. You can make up a batch of your favorite chili in ten minutes by using your home canned beans, tomatoes, and hamburger. That is, of course, unless you've already canned up quarts of your best chili, all mixed and ready to heat up.

Dry legumes will keep for years and years, but as time goes by, they take longer to become tender. This is another reason I can up my older stored legumes. When you can them, they do become tender, no matter what their age. It's a good way to rotate the stored foods.

Stored food rotation

Speaking of rotating your foods, we all know it's a good idea to use your older foods first, slowly using up those foods so that none get way too old. Even though home canned foods last for decades, with proper storage, it's still a good idea to rotate your dry foods and home canned foods so that the whole batch stays in good eating condition.

While nearly all canned food stays "edible," even when it is old, some of it loses color, softens, or becomes otherwise less appetizing than it was when it was first canned. This is more true of some pickles, fruits (especially peaches), potatoes, rutabagas, and cabbage.

I don't mark dates on my canning lids (which I know I should), but I *do* make room all the way to the back of my deep shelves for the new canning batches, then row up my older foods in front of them, forcing myself to use them first. (Rotation for dummies.)

I hope all of you will join me in preparing our pantries this spring, stocking them full of nutritious, tasty high protein foods and stocking our yards with small livestock to meet our continuing needs. May all your emergencies be small ones. Δ

City girl ❦ Country life

Circle of friends:
The importance of other people in our preparedness plans

By Claire Wolfe

Hardcore survivalists cherish what I call the "George Romero Scenario." It goes like this: The proverbial poop has hit the propeller. Cities collapse into chaos. But we, the prepared, are… well, we're prepared. We hunker in our rural bunkers, clutching our Super Whiz-Whacker 3000 combat arms, eagle-eyed and ready for any eventuality. We boldly fend off wave after ravenous wave of starving city folk who stagger at us like unstoppable zombies in a Romero horror flick. These zombies crave not our living flesh, but our six-gallon, mylar-lined superpails of dried lentils, our root cellars full of last year's carrots, and our genuine, federally issued *Meals Ready to Eat.*

Well…maybe.

Seriously, it could happen. I can laugh about it now only because I spent so many years envisioning it myself.

We buy into the Hollywood-fed lone-wolf image. Our society is no longer built on everyday trust and neighborly reliance. The world is full of unfriendly strangers. If the other guy doesn't take care of himself…well, then to hell with him. It's dog eat dog. Survival of the fittest.

Us or them!

And it's true; in any major, long-term disaster, prepared people genuinely could face "zombie" threats from the desperate unprepared. But those threats—as we shall see further down—are likely to take a form that George Romero wouldn't find very cinematic.

The fact is, for most of us rural people, one of the biggest things we're going to face in event of a major or minor disaster is this: a need to cooperate with others who are in the same boat and who share similar privations.

Other people are not the enemy. They may be our lifeline—and we theirs. We need a circle of well-prepared friends more than we're likely to need a .50 cal long-range scoped rifle with a muzzle brake that has "Have a nice day" carved into it.

Making connections

Here's a preparedness truth we should all tattoo on our minds: No matter how well prepared we think we are, we will lack something. It may be something obvious. It may be something obscure. It may be something we forgot to prepare for. It may be something we had that got lost, damaged, or used up. But we will lack something.

My isolated corner of the world got hit with a horrific windstorm a few months ago. Nothing moved or functioned for days afterward. Every one of my off-grid neighbors ran out of gasoline for their generators and chain saws.

A friend of mine once needed to administer first aid following an earthquake. When he opened his recently store-bought first-aid kit, he discovered that items in it were years beyond their expiration dates and that liquids had leaked all over the bandages and dried into a disgusting crust.

After the big windstorm I smacked into a different kind of problem. Physically I was fine. I had heat, food, shelter, and safety. But emotional numbness made it hard to make decisions. If not for a resourceful neighbor who offered to trade his chainsaw and fence-repair skills for the remnants of my damaged yurt, I might still be sitting here staring stupidly at storm wreckage. I lacked something I could not buy.

The government would ask us to turn to them when our own preparedness fails. But waiting for FEMA or the National Guard delays help. Telling us to wait tells us to be passive. It tells us to rely on "experts" and outsiders. That's exactly what we don't need when everything suddenly goes to hell on us.

The government asks us to behave like dependent children at exactly the moment our best adult skills are demanded of us.

I was lucky to have a hardworking young neighbor to trade with. But it was luck. Well, not 100 percent luck. I was smart enough to live in a community with a strong ethic of mutual help. Smart enough to have the kind of friends who carry chainsaws in their trucks.

Yet it was luck for the whole community that the gas stations started functioning just a few days later. Luck that the grocery store didn't run out of food. Luck that very few

people were injured. And this is the kind of luck we simply can't count on.

We need to start preparing to count on each other. We need to get together with neighbors and friends and enhance each other's preparedness—not out of altruism, but out of pure practicality. We need to do it so that we'll all be better off in a crunch.

What are some of the specific things we might do?

Well, obviously, we *don't* go off and tell just anybody, "Hey, here's where I keep my year's supply of #10 cans, and by the way, my silver coins are buried fifty paces southwest of the old oak tree. Now show me yours."

We can start simply and emphasize the practical.

If some real disaster has recently struck our area, the aftermath gives us a perfect opportunity to go to our neighbors and do a mutual reality check. What did we run out of? What could we have used? Where did we screw up? What could we do differently next time? Without ever appearing to organize any sort of "mutual preparedness league" we can start coming to agreements: I can store extra gasoline for you in my shed (with a dose of Sta-Bil, of course). Since you have better first-aid skills, can you help me build up a better medical kit?

If your area has basked in sunshine and prosperity with no disasters in near memory, this is still a good time to approach neighbors because so many people are *worried* about the state of the larger world. They're worried about climate change bringing stronger and more frequent storms. They're worried about fuel shortages. They're worried that the economy might collapse. Worried that some politician will make one too many stupid decisions and bring

war and terror on our heads. So the opening is there to talk about preparedness. (And really, stick to preparedness; try not to spend too much time ranting about political idiocy or vast global conspiracies no matter how large such things loom. The idea is to do something practical on a neighborhood level, not rehash what's being done in Washington, DC, or Davos, Switzerland.)

Without fanfare, we can start practicing mutual preparedness.

✳ Instead of selling your farm-fresh eggs, produce, honey, or meat to your neighbor, start seeing what that neighbor might have to barter for them. Barter could be more useful than money in a serious disaster, plus bartering gives you a better chance to gauge each other.

✳ Get involved in a food co-op or create one of your own. If your neighbors aren't receptive to the notion of disaster preparedness, they may be open to the idea of organically grown crops, hormone-free meats, or bulk food purchases on a budget. The end result is the same: you establish a cooperative network based on one of the chief elements of preparedness: food.

✳ If somebody in your circle has a pick-up truck and others don't, the truck owner can offer to transport group purchases of preparedness goods for a small fee or, again, for barter.

✳ We can sign up for and commute to skill-building classes together, whether that means auto maintenance,

"I was smart enough to live in a community with a strong ethic of mutual help."

home canning, or defensive shotgun use. Staying motivated is always easier when we're committed to somebody else, as well as to the activity.

✻ Start consciously offering to do things for your neighbors and asking them to do things for you—even if you can actually take care of everything yourself. It's a good way of getting to know each other's skills, and learning whom you can trust and whether you yourself are trustworthy.

✻ If somebody close to you feels unable to prepare for disaster, see how you can change that—not by badgering, but by helpfulness and gentle persuasion. People may say they're too poor, too unskilled, or just not interested. But just as everybody is vulnerable to some form of catastrophe, so virtually everybody can make some level of preparation—even if it's only buying a Coleman lantern at a garage sale or laying in a case of mac & cheese.

✻ And speaking of garage sales…there's another way to make preparedness mutual without turning it into a big wing-nut project. Make a regular Saturday morning adventure out of going garage saling with people you see as your most important "preparedness buddies." Enjoy the challenge of hunting for old camp stoves, propane heaters, tents, gear packs, tools, how-to books, and anything else that might enhance preparedness. Doing this not only improves your own preparedness, it yields emergency barter goods or goods that you can give away at need to close friends. Doing it *with others* makes it more fun and helps cement bonds.

✻ With those you most trust, talk openly about others in your neighborhood or your circle of acquaintances who might present the biggest problems in crunch time—those who will be clueless about fending for themselves. Those potential problem people might be innocent—old ladies, disabled people, or families with small children and precarious finances. On the other hand, those potential problem people might be real troublemakers—known thieves or chronic freeloaders.

The mention of troublemakers takes us back full circle to the George Romero scenario.

Our own private zombies

Yes, back to those "zombie" attacks. It's true they can happen. But in anything less than a total "collapse of civilization as we know it" scenario, the zombies are likely to be fewer in number and come from our own families or neighborhoods. They are likely to be the chronically unprepared. Or the local sociopaths. Or maybe even the codgers whose Social Security checks didn't arrive (and who couldn't have cashed or spent them if they did arrive because nothing is functioning).

Case in point: I have an enviably well-prepared friend. Call him Bob. He has a ne'er-do-

well, completely unprepared brother. For years Bob urged lazy bro at least to lay in a few supplies and build a few skills. Bro finally looked around and said, "Hey, don't worry about it. If anything goes wrong, I'll just move in with you."

It was one of those "sounds like a joke but really isn't" remarks. But it woke Bob up. "It's easy," he says, "maybe it's even satisfying, to imagine that if a freeloading relative shows up at your door in hard times, you'd send him packing. But I realized I wouldn't. Blood ties, family pressure—perhaps even just the need to have another person to defend my home; for whatever reason, I knew that if it came down to it, I'd have to take my brother in."

In other cases, the "zombies" may be good people caught unawares.

Case in point: My friend Samantha lives on a hill above a tsunami zone. Shortly after the national wake-up call of Hurricane Katrina, Samantha received a state government brochure outlining tsunami evacuation routes for her area. "I wasn't at all surprised," she told me, "to see my road designated as one of the escape routes. That was a no-brainer. But I was flabbergasted—dumbstruck—knocked over by a feather—to see a big red *"ASSEMBLY AREA"* marked on the map right next to my house."

Samantha went outside and looked around, just in case she'd missed something in the last 10 years. Nope, she remembered right. There was no "assembly area." No park, no parking lot, no meadow, no shelter. There wasn't even a wide spot in the road. Nothing but steep, ruggedly wooded hills.

The only flat spot was…Samantha's front yard.

Samantha goes on, "Making my property an 'assembly area' was probably the work of some bureaucrat inside a windowless building 200 miles from here. That person didn't even know or care what the terrain was like or whether anybody lived here. But the consequence is that I've been designated to play host."

Samantha, who is well armed, considered the George Romero scenario. She mulled alternatives like opening her gate only for those who arrive with their own emergency kits while holding others off with a gun. "But I knew that wasn't likely to work. And besides, I knew that I personally couldn't do it. If the disaster ever happens, these will be my neighbors rushing up this road, looking for a place to

"We need a circle of well-prepared friends more than we're likely to need a .50 cal long-range scoped rifle with a muzzle brake that has 'Have a nice day' carved into it."

wait out the catastrophe. They'll be members of my community. Of course I'm going to let them in. I'd expect them to do the same for me if the situation were reversed."

The solution for both Bob and Samantha? Stretch the budget a little further. Lay in a little extra. Should the infamous excrement ever impact the airfoil, Bob will have the satisfaction of making his ne'er-do-well brother do nighttime guard duty and hand-grind wheat berries. Samantha will hand each refugee a few cans of beans (bought cheap at a fall canned-goods sale) and tell them, "Eat 'em cold and make 'em last until the Red Cross gets here."

Of course it's possible that you might have to use your Super Whiz-Whacker 3000—or grandpa's old Mossberg—against the dreaded "zombies." But if so, chances are that those zombies will live a mile from your house, rather than be refugees fleeing a city 50 miles away. In that case, again, your neighbors can be a godsend as you watch over each others' property and share mutual awareness of threats.

Samantha's also right that the shoe can easily be on the other foot. The best prepared can be forced into dependency. All you have to do is look at the homeowners of New Orleans who were adequately stocked and ready to stay and protect their houses when Hurricane Katrina struck. How many of them were driven out by floodwaters or forced to leave everything behind by the "I'm from the government and I'll help you whether you want help or not" crowd?

Many went from being prepared to being vulnerable refugees at the point of a gun—and they couldn't shoot back because the raiding gunmen wore badges.

So if things go really wrong, those dreaded Others of Romero Scenario fame may not be mindless, desperate zombies escaping urban hell. They may, depending on the fates, be *us*.

And the best way we can ensure otherwise is to turn to those much-better-known Others, our friends and neighbors—the people who can help us out or, if need be, take us in. Δ

A Backwoods Home Anthology
The Fifth Year

* Odd-jobbin' can be a country goldmine
* How to keep those excess eggs
* Make better pizza at home than you can buy
* How we bought our country home
* Cooking with dried fruit
* Garden huckleberries
* Short season gardening
* The 10 most useful herbs
* Simplified concrete and masonry work
* Raising sheep
* Free supplies for your homestead
* Learning in the pickle patch
* Good-bye old friend
* Choosing and using a wood cookstove
* Three great bread recipes
* Build a fieldstone chimney
* Sun oven cookery
* Firewood: how and what to buy
* Choosing superior bedding plants
* A bit about ducks
* How to build the fence you need
* Improving poor garden soil
* Learn the basics of wall framing
* Determined woman builds distinctive vertical log studio
* Make better pizza than you can buy
* Good-bye old friend
* Turkeys — fun and profitable and not as dumb as you think
* Raising fish in the farm pond
* You have to learn to shovel crap before you learn to be the boss

Ayoob on Firearms

Preparing gun owners for the short-term future

By Massad Ayoob

Massad Ayoob

...And Editor Dave Duffy says, "I'm putting together a special issue focusing on the predicted recession, and preparing to cope with the next Presidency. Write something on that, please, from the gunowner's perspective."

Hey. Hey! *Hey!* Aren't my assignments supposed to be more like, "How about a story on Savage rifles?"

Let's get one thing straight to start with: I ain't no political pundit. Hell, my candidate isn't even running. I was hoping Condoleeza Rice would throw her hat in the ring. International statecraft and diplomacy are a huge part of the Presidential job description, and Rice has more experience in those areas than all the rest of the field combined. Obama's silent "vote for the first black President" message, and Clinton's "vote for the first female President" and "the single women all want me" schticks, would all have been neutralized by a Rice candidacy. Moreover, from the gun owners' perspective, Condoleeza Rice is solidly pro-Second Amendment.

But she's not running, and we're left with a pretty sorry crop of semi-finalists to lead a nation of more than three hundred million people. Bearing in mind that I'm no political expert, and I'm writing this a few days after Super Tuesday, here's how it looks for "gun people."

Election...

On the Democratic side of the race for the White House, nothing bodes positive for the civil rights of gun owners. Barack Obama has flatly stat-

ed in his policy outlines that he wants to ban "assault weapons," and indeed, semi-automatic firearms. That would include the early 20th century Browning autoloading shotgun that came down through your family from your great-great-grandfather. It would include the antique Remington Model 8 deer rifle that your great-grandfather used to put venison on the table during the Great Depression. It would include the souvenir Army .45, introduced in 1911, that your granddad brought home from World War II. It would include the military surplus M1 carbine your dad purchased for $35 through the National Rifle Association and the U.S. Government's Director of Civilian Marksmanship in a happier, freer time. It would eliminate your brother's semiautomatic AR15 rifle, similar to the M16 he fought with in Vietnam, and similar to the M4 your son or daughter might be fighting with right now in the Middle East. It would, for the first time in American history, prevent you and others like you from protecting yourselves with the same kind of handgun police use to protect you.

Hillary Clinton's antipathy toward firearms owners and their rights is well-known. You can be certain that she would do everything in her power to reinstate the onerous Assault Weapons Ban her husband ramrodded through Congress during his Presidency. This time around, it would not have the sunset clause that saved us after a miserable decade the last time, and the ban would be word-

ed to encompass a great many more useful and traditional firearms.

Some pundits say that the Democrats "learned" from the last ban, when Republicans swept into control of the Congress shortly after the AWB was passed, and Bill Clinton himself blamed the NRA and the whole "gun control" thing for his party's resounding defeat that year. However, Mrs. Clinton is not noted for taking good advice, and "gun control" is one of her Issues. That she would use the "bully pulpit" of the White House to push for more draconian restrictions on the civil rights of firearms owners is almost assured.

On the Republican side? It's McCain or Huckabee. Ron Paul, a solid pro-gun owner candidate, does not appear to be electable. Mike Huckabee is certainly a more electable candidate, according to the conventional wisdom, among those who stand 100% for gun owners' rights. An ideal candidate for the pro-gun one-issue voter, Huckabee's strongest chance to do that particular bloc some good may be as Veep candidate, or as one of the brokers at a brokered

Republican Convention, gathering promises to secure certain rights in return for the delegates he brings.

John McCain, at this writing, is well in the lead for the Republican nomination. The NRA has actually given him fair-to-middlin' grades, though the more hard-line Gun Owners of America has downgraded him from a "C" to an "F" grade the last few years. To his credit, he had the guts and the integrity to oppose Bill Clinton's Assault Weapons Ban. However, McCain's vote to "close the (erroneously named) gun show loophole" hurt him badly with many one-issue voters on the pro-gun side. Moreover, his McCain-Feingold Campaign Finance Reform Act was seen by many NRA members as a direct attack on their right to free speech, and was seen the same way by a lot of union people, right-to-life advocates, etc.

If it comes down to McCain versus "Hillbama," thinking gun owners will find McCain by far the lesser of the two evils insofar as firearms legislation. Of course, there will be some die-hards who will vote for a fringe candidate to "make a statement." This, in effect, will be one more vote for the greater of two evils. Dave Duffy and I could spend a goodly amount of time debating this, but I can't help remembering when the backlash vote for Ross Perot, against the first President Bush, apparently put Bill Clinton in the White House. Recent political history shows no more classic example of cutting off one's nose to spite one's face.

...and recession...

Even experts such as former Federal Reserve chief Alan Greenspan don't think there's anything the Government can do to keep us from slipping into recession. All the signs are there, and much of what's causing it comes from global economic factors that the United States can do little to control. In a recent interview in a German publication, Greenspan put the chances of recession at about fifty-fifty. Some consider him an optimist.

How does all that hit the firearms area? Well, from the end-user's side, there's good news and bad news. When individuals hit by recession tighten their belts, they buy what they need and not what they want. This can have the effect of reducing demand for high-priced sporting firearms, driving prices down for those who can still afford to purchase. Things like coin collections and gun collections go up for sale when their owners are up against it for funds. Their need for immediate cash weakens their bargaining position, and in the collectibles market, more specimens becoming available tends to drive down prices.

On the other hand, small businesses are among the first hurt in recessions. Most gun shops are in fact small businesses. This means less competition in a given local specialty market, which usually means higher prices.

I've heard some in the firearms field speculate that prices of new firearms-related goods—the guns and the ammo—may come down. In a vacuum, that could happen, but other things are at work, and as Greenspan noted, some of them are beyond our control. Massive construction going on in other nations, particularly China, is creating a disproportionately high demand for structural metals. This means steel is scarcer and increasing in price, and that's what guns are primarily made of. Brass and copper and lead are skyrocketing too, and they are what ammunition is made of. Thus, it seems that expecting such prices to come down during this particular recession, if it does indeed happen, is probably unrealistic.

...and the two together

The backwoods home tradition is to hope for the best and prepare for the worst. In the scenario our editor postulates, that worst is a Clinton/Obama or even a Clinton/Clinton Presidency and a recession at the same time. From the gun side of things, we could expect the following:

Firearms: If the Democrats gain control this time around, expect attempts to severely impinge or even

George W. Bush, during his first Presidential campaign, with the author. Ayoob thinks the Bush administration has by and large been good for gun owners' civil rights.

Both Clinton and Obama want to take away your right to buy "sport utility rifles" such as this Smith & Wesson Military & Police version of the semi-automatic AR15.

30-round (left) and 20-round magazines, these for AR15, were prohibited under the first Clinton Assault Weapon Ban. Expect it to return with a vengeance under a Democratic president, warns Ayoob.

crush into nonexistence your rights to own semiautomatic firearms. If you don't have one already, buy it as soon as possible. If you do own one and you can afford another, buy it as a spare.

Stock up on magazines. Shortly before the Clinton Ban, I bought a bunch of Glock .40 fifteen-round magazines for about $11 apiece.

Shortly after the ban became law, such magazines were selling for as much as $100 each. Should a President Clinton or a President Obama get their way, any magazine holding more than ten cartridges may well become illegal to manufacture for public sale, as before.

Remember that if a Democratic administration gets its way, such firearms and magazines will be gone for good. In England, when that happened (with semiautomatic rifles, and with all handguns) the arms had to be turned in at government checkpoints. In the U.S. as during the last Assault Weapons Ban, it's most likely that guns and magazines currently in your possession will be "grandfathered." This means you want to be thinking about buying and setting aside some guns for kids and grandkids who might otherwise never be allowed to acquire them.

Yes, that can represent a substantial cash investment, but guns tend to hold their values well. Some even appreciate, and that is definitely true once they are "banned" by some meaningless, feel-good, Yuppie legislation. I bought my Steyr AUG "assault rifle" for about $600 in the late 1980s. They were going for $3000 by the end of the Ban period. Prior to the 1986 Act that banned private sale of fully automatic weapons manufactured after that date, an HK MP5 submachine gun could be had for under a thousand dollars, plus the $200 Federal Class III license. Today, with that particular ban still in effect, I've seen grandfathered "pre-ban" MP5s go for fifteen thousand dollars apiece.

Ammunition: If famine was coming, you'd stock up on food. As this is written—no full blown recession yet, and George W. Bush still occupying the White House—the ammo famine is already coming. I went to order a large quantity of ammunition for my police department yesterday and found an eight-month waiting list. Fortunately, we had seen that coming

and already ordered ahead; the current order is intended to keep us ahead. If that's where governmental public safety entities buying in bulk stand in the queue, you know where individuals with smaller needs are in that particular food chain.

As always, when preparing for shortages, "buy it cheap and stack it deep." Yes, ammo has been going up in price—precipitously so of late, in fact—but it is still a helluva lot cheaper vis-à-vis earning power than it was twenty or even fifty years ago. You gotta look at it realistically, like it or not. I don't much like getting older, but, as the saying goes, "I consider the alternative." It's kinda like, "Yes, I'm the oldest I've ever been… but I'm also the youngest I'm ever going to be."

In this case, factory-produced ammunition may be the most expensive it's ever been, but in all probability, it's also the cheapest it's ever going to be. Yes, a pullout from Iraq will reduce one drain on ammo production that has caused price increase and bottlenecked supply, but as noted above that is not the only cause, and those other factors aren't subject to "pullout."

Another option: get into reloading. In the last year, with ammo prices going up and up, I've seen two trends. One is shooters getting into making their own ammo for the first time. The other is folks who got into it in the past and got away from it, returning to "rolling their own."

You can get into a decent reloading set-up, bare bones, for $500 in new equipment, and a really decent outfit for around a grand. There's lots of good stuff out there. I can personally recommend Dillon Precision (*www.dillonprecision.com*) for great gear, great prices, and standard-setting customer service.

It will cost you time. The best route is to find an experienced, competent reloader who can guide you hands-on through the intricacies of setting up the equipment and making your own ammunition for the first time. With lead (for the bullets), copper (for the bullet jackets), and brass (for the cartridge casings) going up all the time, your reloading components are increasing in cost just like factory-manufactured cartridges. There are also shortages, particularly in primers. Still, there is substantial potential for cost savings.

Keep in mind that there's a break-even point on all this. If you're an old time hunter who can make a 20-round box of ammo last for twenty years with a deer in the freezer every year, reloading won't be cost effective for you. If you're a more cautious and practical hunter who fires a hundred or more shots in sight-in or practice before the annual hunting season opens, it'll take you a long time to save enough to pay off the equipment. But if you're a gun enthusiast, a serious recreational shooter, or someone who is just very serious about staying alive and practicing armed survival skills, now you're at the ammo expenditure level where investing in reloading equipment can make a huge amount of sense.

Remember you'll be literally storing explosives on the premises, the gunpowder and the primers, but common sense has taken care of that for responsible people since the 19th century. When reloading, always wear safety glasses, and never smoke in the loading room. Stay as alert as you would be shooting live-fire on the range. People have been badly hurt by chain-explosion of primers in the feeder, and by guns that have exploded, not to mention the countless fine firearms ruined by careless reloading.

It's kind of a commitment thing. You need a bit of space to set up the equipment. You need to allocate time to do it when you're alert, not exhausted and losing attention span at the end of a hard workday.

It's literally recycling: you're re-filling and re-using spent cartridge cas-

The majority of hunting and sporting shotguns in this gun shop display are semi-automatics, the kind Barack Obama has publicly stated he wants to ban.

ings. There is a pride of workmanship and a sense of accomplishment that goes with your own ammo, much like growing and canning your own vegetables. If money is tight and you have the time, reloading can be very economical. If you're to where your time is money, and the more you work the more you get paid, then you'll probably find that reloading is no longer economical when you factor in what your time spent doing it is worth.

For a lot of folks, reloading has become a dedicated hobby, not a necessity, and they happily make time for it. Some like to tinker with more accurate loads, or more effective ones for their particular needs. Some find it relaxing for the same reasons that shooting and rock climbing are relaxing: by demanding your total attention in the name of safety, they purge you of whatever troubles were on your mind before you set yourself to the task.

It's not *just* about money. There's that personal satisfaction element. Many *Backwoods Home* readers make Jackie Clay's home canning advice a reality in their home, not because they can't afford to go to Sam's Club and stock up on staples, but because it puts them in touch with America's roots. It gives them a pleasant and reassuring sense of self-sufficiency. It gives them pride of accomplishment. Food you grew and canned yourself "tastes better" in more ways than one.

It's the same with reloading. Back when I had time to load my own ammo, the prize I brought back from the shooting match held more pride, and the meat I brought home just "tasted better," if I earned it with

Reputable loading guides, like this one by Speer, are indispensable if you want to save money and become self-sufficient by loading your own ammunition.

ammunition I crafted myself. You'll find the same.

Bottom line

For activists in the area of law-abiding gun owners' civil rights, there are no really good candidates in the upcoming Presidential election. We are likely to be offered only the choice between bad and worse. But in this case, the "worse" is truly horrible.

Look on the bright side: gun owners have weathered dark political times before. We got through the Clinton years once (or, if you count by terms, twice) before.

Not all those we supported have been perfect candidates. Ronald Reagan, an icon among pro-gun activists today, was President when the 1986 curtailment of sales of new fully automatic weapons to private citizens became law. Gun owners supported George H. W. Bush, who subsequently resigned his NRA life membership and banned the importation of a broad spectrum of semiautomatic rifles. We supported our current incumbent, George W. Bush, yet his Solicitor General Paul Clement recently submitted what is essentially a brief against private gun ownership in Washington, DC in the landmark U.S. Supreme Court case on the interpretation of the Second Amendment, *District of Columbia v. Heller.*

Many in the gun owners' rights community see this as a betrayal by President Bush, who is widely credited with owing both his elections to the highest office to the staunch grassroots support of the citizens who

If you own the popular SKS rifle, or any other 7.62x39, you can stock up rather economically with this Russian-made Wolf brand practice ammo.

make up the so-called "gun lobby." I've not yet seen clear and convincing proof, however, that Bush ordered his appointee to file that brief, or even knew beforehand that the Solicitor General was going to do so. After all, it was under Bush that U.S. Attorney General John Ashcroft wrote his famous opinion that the Second Amendment spoke, indeed, to an individual right. And we notice that Vice-President Dick Cheney (and Senator John McCain) signed on to an *amicus* brief in the *Heller* case in favor of the position that the Right to Keep and Bear Arms is indeed an individual right. Cheney and McCain, by the way, were joined in that by a majority of the current Democrat-controlled Congress.

We are, as the saying goes, living in interesting times. Things could get bad. If they do, this is one special issue of *Backwoods Home* that you might just want to keep handy. Δ

Preparedness
Rule of Three

By Corey Gage

We have all heard of the "Survival Rule of Three," the one that says you can only last three seconds without thinking, three minutes without air, three hours without shelter, three days without water, and three weeks without food, right? That is an excellent maxim to live by, but there is an even better maxim to follow if you are in the process of developing a disaster plan for you or your family. It is known as the Preparedness Rule of Three.

When it comes to the process of establishing a family disaster plan, it seems most people opt for the much beloved checklist variety. You know the ones that say things like "Have a three day supply of...," or "Store up on extra..." All of the government websites have these same checklists—Homeland Security, the CDC, the Red Cross, etc. For the most part, a well-thought-out checklist is an excellent place to start. The one major flaw with this approach is that they are all designed for the short term. We think because we have a three-day supply of food, water, and other essentials, if a disaster strikes we will be okay until help arrives. This, unfortunately, couldn't be further from the truth. Hurricane Katrina exposed this fallacy. By now it should be obvious to everyone, when disaster strikes we are on our own.

This harsh reality check should lead us all into a definite shift in mindset. Disasters come in many shapes and sizes from geographically changing superstorms to an extended illness leaving the family breadwinner a month or two short on paychecks. If our preparedness measures are in order though, the length and severity of such a calamity will be of little concern. We must shift our mindset to long-term preparations. Just how do we prepare for such a diverse set of possible scenarios? We incorporate the Preparedness Rule of Three into our overall game plan.

The Preparedness Rule of Three is really quite easy to understand and implement. For every basic necessity of life, i.e., food, water, shelter, etc. you should have three separate and distinct sources. Each source should be independent of the others and should be capable of standing on its own for an extended period of time. To get a little better understanding of the core principles involved here, let's look at some specific examples.

Water

We all know that after oxygen, water is truly *the* essential element to human life. We require water for drinking first and foremost, as under adverse conditions dehydration can lead to death in three to four days. Just as importantly, though, water is required for cooking, cleaning, and sanitation purposes. Your first source of water is obviously going to be your tap, whether it is the local municipality or your own well and pump. But what if the electricity goes out or the ground water is contaminated from flooding or a chemical spill?

55 gallons of stored water is a cheap insurance policy. Note the platform with casters to aid in moving it about—there's 440 pounds of water here.

Canned condiments such as butter, jams, jellies, pickles, and salsa will extend any food storage program and add variety as well.

Your second independent source should be stored water. I'm not talking about the three-day supply mentioned earlier; it doesn't fit our Rule of Three's criteria, i.e., being capable of standing on its own for an extended period of time. The widely accepted rule for water storage is a gallon of drinkable water per person per day. Let's think about that for a minute. A family of four (like mine) would require 55 gallons of water to last two weeks. That is not hard to do. A food grade barrel off in a corner of the basement full of treated potable water is an insurance policy definitely worth having. I have a 55-gallon food grade barrel full of water to which I add 5½ teaspoons of 5.25 percent

sodium hypochlorite (common household bleach). According to the Red Cross you need to add 2 drops per quart, 8 drops per gallon, ½ teaspoon per 5 gallons and 5½ teaspoons per 55 gallons. This is for treating clear water and should be doubled for treating cloudy water. Keep in mind 55 gallons of water in one barrel will weigh 440 pounds, so be sure to mount it on a platform with casters if you intend to move it around. Other storage devices could be empty 2-liter pop bottles. They are nearly indestructible and are easy to handle even for small children. Five-gallon, stackable water containers are available at nearly any sporting goods or home improvement store and often come

with a spigot and carrying handle. Avoid empty milk jugs because they are difficult to clean completely and are made to degrade over time.

The third option can be somewhat varied. I am in the process of installing a rainwater collection system off the roof of my garage. Every time it rains I am renewing another source of stored water, independent of the other two. This water would have to be treated to make it potable, but it is there if it's needed. Other possible sources would be rivers, streams, or lakes from which you could draw if the need arose. I live within 500 yards of a pristine spring-fed lake that could easily offer me an unlimited supply of the life-giving liquid, and it's free for the taking. There are also cisterns, swimming pools, stock tanks, shallow wells with a non-electric hand pumps, or even farm ponds. As you can see, all of these options are independent of the others and can sustain you for long periods of time.

Food

If your family is like mine you probably have about one week's worth of food in your refrigerator and around 2 to 3 weeks of dry goods in the pantry. This is resupplied with a trip to the local supermarket on a weekly basis. This will constitute level one of your food supply. From here you should have a separate pantry containing up to a six month supply of dry goods and canned food items. This would preferably be located in a basement or cellar where it is dry and cool.

Your second pantry should consist of all the same items in your primary storage—just more of them. For instance, if you have two cans of creamed corn in the upstairs pantry you should have four cans (or more) downstairs. It should be obvious to only store the food items your family eats on a regular basis. In the event of a disaster situation you do not want to experiment with foods your family has never tried before; you will want the comfort food you are used to.

Once you are squared away with your backup pantry you should store the ingredients needed to make the basics that cannot be resupplied with a trip to the supermarket. These items include dry milk, whole wheat or rice, salt, sugar, honey, etc. These can be turned into breads, muffins, candies, etc. They are also used to extend and/or enhance the quantity and quality of many foodstuffs. A large-chest type freezer is another excellent storage device and can hold several weeks worth of food. These are just my suggestions and you may have other options available such as a root cellar full of fruits and berries, a smokehouse full of hams and bacon, or vacuum bags packed with venison sausage and jerky. Always remember to rotate your stock with a "first in, first out" methodology. Don't forget each tier should be able to sustain your family for *at least* three months and much longer if at all possible. It should be noted that if the grid goes down for any period of time you should either transfer all perishables from your freezer to a root cellar, or consume them as quickly as you can to avoid spoilage or loss.

Heating

In many climates, having a second source of reliable heat is not just a good idea, it's mandatory. A few hours without heat can be uncomfortable; a few days can be deadly. If your home is like most, you are supplied with either propane (LP), natural gas (NG), or electricity for your heating requirements. This will be considered your main source and the easiest to maintain. From here though you will need to address the possibility of a power outage, and the effect this will have on your current system.

Your second source should ideally be independent of the grid. A wood stove/furnace or fireplace would fit the bill nicely. Remember you need to

store up the fuel for these lumber-hungry appliances. Felling, bucking, splitting, and stacking a winter's worth of firewood is said to warm you many times over, and believe me, it's true. When you set out to calculate how much wood you will need to last a typical winter remember this generalization: the denser the wood, the more BTUs it will deliver. Always add a few extra cords as insurance for a particularly long cold snap.

For your third option you might consider a kerosene heater. Today's newer models are really quite efficient and safe to operate as long as you follow the manufacturer's guidelines. One advantage to kerosene heaters is the ability to move them from room to room. This allows the flexibility to heat just the area you need, instead of wasting fuel heating unused storage or laundry rooms. Storing up a 55-gallon drum of kerosene can go a long way towards ensuring a warm and happy home should your other options fail. Other possible alternatives for backup heat could be pellet stoves, oil furnaces, wall-hung propane heaters with separate tanks, or even geothermal and solar heating. The choices are many and you need to pick the right one for your specific situation.

As a final note, be sure your carbon monoxide detectors have fresh batteries as indoor heating and cooking can be dangerous if not handled correctly.

Cooking

A couple of years ago my wife was forced to prepare all of our meals on a Coleman two-burner dual-fuel cook stove when a part on our electric range burned out and we had to wait three weeks for a replacement. This was a perfect example of the need for a backup contingency plan when your primary source of cooking is out of commission. We could have just as easily reverted to the outdoor fire pit, a kerosene cooker, the woodstove, or a fireplace.

One of our primary sources for three season cooking is on our outdoor charcoal grill. When we are cutting our supply of firewood for the winter we always save fist-sized limbs and turn them into homemade charcoal. I will describe one method I have used successfully over the years to do this: First dig a trench in the ground about five feet long by three feet wide and about two feet deep. Pile in some twigs and small branches to start a long even fire in the bottom of the trench. When there is a good base burning lay in your fist-sized chunks of hardwood branches and split centers. As the larger pieces start to burn, use a long-handled tong or fork to turn each one until they are black, all around. You will notice the smoke from the fire will turn from white to almost clear. Now smother the fire by shoveling the excavated earth back in to the trench. This will contain the heat as the wood slowly cools. Several hours after to a day later you can dig up the now-cooled and completely dried charcoal with a pitchfork. Store them in watertight barrels for use all year long.

Other options mentioned include Kerosene cookers that have the advantage of using fuel you are already storing for your heater, and can be used indoors with proper ventilation. Believe it or not, a solar oven on a bright day can reach temperatures hot enough to bake bread. Any of these suggestions are capable of sustaining you through a possible disruption of normalcy as long as you plan ahead.

Shelter

The idea of losing your primary source of shelter, your home, is truly a frightening thought, but is sadly not uncommon. Fires, tornadoes, hurricanes, or floods are all quite possible and could easily leave you homeless within minutes. Short of moving in with friends or family, what would you do? Do you have a barn or out-

A kerosene heater can easily be moved from room to room and is an excellent option for a backup heat source.

building that could be converted into a suitable living space? How about a workshop or garage? What about an RV or old bus? On the West Coast many people live year-round on houseboats. In the days of old many people lived in tents, yurts, tepees, etc. When I was a kid my folks would take a couple of weeks off work and go out to Wyoming for the annual mule deer hunt. We would live in our slide-in camper, mounted in the bed of a pickup truck. We set up camp out in the middle of a huge ranch, miles from nowhere, and lived completely independent of any outside help for over a week. I had the time of my life.

Any of these suggestions are viable options to get you through a truly devastating situation. Where I live, in the rural parts of Wisconsin, it seems everyone has a "cabin in the woods." These all seem to be owned by city folks who need their "home away from Hell," but put in a bad situation they do have a viable alternative.

Lighting

Being in the dark can be inconvenient to some and downright terrifying to others. The ability to maneuver safely after dark should be a major concern when preparing your disaster game plan. The convenience of throwing a switch and having a whole room fill with light is never more appreciated than when the grid goes down and the lights go out. Storms, accidents, and overconsumption can all lead to possible blackouts.

If your initial source of power goes down, one possible alternative is the backup generator. A 5000 watt gas generator can easily light an entire home on a few gallons of fuel. Be sure to figure in a few extension cords with multiple plug ins to run to your lamps and TV. If a standby genset is not available you may consider a rechargeable deep cycle battery bank and a few DC volt RV or marine receptacles.

Those options aside, who of us cannot remember at least one night as a kid huddled around an oil lamp or some long-stemmed candles. Oil lamps are a fantastic alternative to light your home. They are used worldwide, the fuel is relatively cheap and plentiful, they are safe to operate with a little common sense, and are soothing to the distressed.

Of course, I would be remiss if I did not mention the most obvious solution—and the one thing we almost always grab first—the flashlight.

Remember, all of these options must be able to sustain you for at least a few months if at all possible, so store up some batteries, wicks, and fuel for the lamps ahead of time.

Sundries

Do you really know how many rolls of toilet paper you go through in a month? How about paper towels, toothpaste, detergent, and hand soap? These items need to be considered ahead of time as well. Some people may not consider these items basic necessities, but in my house with three women I assure you they are. To best identify the items most needed, go through every room in the house and write down everything that is used regularly which you normally periodically need to replace. For instance, in the bathroom you will use toilet paper, shampoo/conditioner, soap, toothpaste, deodorant, makeup, shaving cream, oral rinse, Band-Aids, dental floss, and disinfectant. Now prioritize the list into mandatory items and their typical usage life. Each time you go to the store purchase a few extra items for storage and in no time you will have your supply built up for the future. Now move on to the kitchen, the laundry room, and the other rooms in your home.

Sanitation

Personal hygiene can be a major concern, especially in the aftermath of a prolonged disaster. Lack of bathroom facilities, garbage pickup, and soap and hot water for cleaning can lead to infections, disease, and death. If you have the ability to construct an outhouse on your property, I suggest you do so. A deep pit with a shelter over it and a bucket of wood ashes or lime will go a long way towards keeping a sense of normalcy and humanity to those involved. A port-a-potty sold at camping supply stores is another option worth looking into.

From here you should invest in some sort of solar shower or other method for heating large amounts of water for cleaning and disinfecting. Even an old discarded water heater stripped down to its core can be used to heat water either with a fire pit arrangement or possibly a solar batch heater. Without hot water many chemicals will do an adequate job of disinfecting. Store up on non-perfumed bleach and soaps for hand washing as well as clothes washing. A couple of old washtubs will suffice for laundry and bathing. Clothes lines and fences will take the place of your dryer.

Garbage and refuse should be handled at once to keep flies, rats, and other pests at bay. After garbage pickup is suspended for whatever reason you should revert to your second backup plan, a compost bin for organic matter, and a burn barrel for combustibles.

Finally, your third option could be an earthen pit for all of your refuse to be covered as it fills. This may not be up to code in your area of the country but given the circumstances may have to be overlooked.

Income

There is nothing more frightening than the thought of losing your job and your only source of income. Bills must be paid on time and the financial lending community does not care why you are late. Let's look at a few ways to apply the Rule of Three to the process of sustainable income. My wife and I both have full-time jobs. This alone can cover two possible streams of income as long as we strive to live below our means. From there I also teach a martial arts class which generates another paycheck. I periodically write for publication in several magazines, earmarking all monies to go to the emergency fund for future disruptions.

It is imperative that you start now to set aside enough savings to cover at least three months worth of bills to help cushion the initial loss of income while you recover. I am talking about your mortgage and any other loans that can be repossessed or further penalized for failure to pay on time. Things like subscriptions, charities, and vacations will have to wait.

So what can you do? Do you have a pickup? There are several part-time jobs available to anyone with the means to haul a payload for others. Do you have a special skill? Can you butcher and process meat on the farm? Do light carpentry work? Make arts and crafts for sale, or set up a roadside vegetable stand? Any one with a chainsaw and a strong back can make a pretty good income cutting firewood for the city folks who live in the suburbs. *Backwoods Home* anthologies contain several excellent articles on home-based businesses that anyone can do, and with minimal start-up cost.

Protection

In the aftermath of Hurricane Katrina, many people were left to their own devices for several days without any protection from the dark side of humanity. You could face similar problems, depending on the type of disaster and the demographics you

Your first line of defense after a disaster should be boards, barriers, and banners. This sign leaves nothing to the imagination.

are under. Without police protection you may be forced to defend yourself from all manner of vermin, from four-legged to two-legged. I suggest you keep a couple of live traps and/or foothold traps to help contain roving dogs, coyotes, raccoons, and cats that will take advantage of your injured or sickly pets and unprotected food supply. It would be foolhardy not to mention the need for a battery of self-defense items as both deterrents and weapons.

Your first line of defense after the collapse of law and order should be boards, barriers, and banners. Board up all broken windows and doors, construct barriers such as fences and breams, hang signs to suggest the resolve of the occupants who inhabit the household. Next you should consider dogs, alarms, and pepper spray, as your next line of defense. Finally, the tactical use of personal firearms has to be considered. Many a life has been spared from the horror of assault, rape, and murder when confronted by an armed citizen who is bent on self preservation. Even your firearm selection should incorporate a three tier format. First a battle rifle for long range, a shotgun for medium range, and a handgun for close quarter battle.

As you can see the Preparedness Rule of Three is more than a series of items to acquire and eventually check off a list; it is a mindset. This rule can be incorporated into every aspect of your life. Have three forms of communication (cell phone, FRS radio, CB), three forms of transportation (car, horse, bicycle), three forms of information gathering (TV, AM/FM radio, shortwave). The options are numerous and the benefits are enormous.

Finally, remember the criteria for the "rule," each source should be independent of the other two and should be able to stand on its own for an extended period of time. Back up your backup—now that's a plan. Δ

Suppose you are a successful trades-man, accomplished in the art of confectionery, living in Paris at the end of the 18th century. Suppose you've made yourself a reputation, and are doing well enough to have acquired some assets. And suppose that as a former chef, skilled in food preparation and storage, you have experimented for years with alternative ways of handling what we eat. One day, the news comes out: your Emperor has offered a 12,000 franc prize to the person who can come up with a reliable method for preserving foodstuffs for troops on the march.

What do you do?

The invention of food canning

By Brewster Gillett

The General

Napoleon Bonaparte (1769-1821) was one of the most accomplished generals in history. He took over France's government in a coup before he was thirty, and was proclaimed Emperor just a few years later. He managed to conquer a sizable portion of Europe, installing various relatives as leaders of the conquered regions. He finally stalled when trying to take Russia, and wound up being deposed and exiled, but even his failed campaigns are studied in war colleges to this day. Had there been a French general of Napoleon's like in 1940, the Germans could never have marched into Paris in World War II.

Bonaparte's successes in the art of war were not solely the product of his strategic skills. He paid keen attention to logistics as well. It was he who famously said that an army travels on its stomach.

By Napoleon's time, armies had gotten substantially larger than previous armies. No longer was it practi-cal, as had been the case with smaller troop concentrations, to carry little in the way of provisions and plan on foraging along the way. In the late 18th century an army needed to carry its food along with it. This of course raised the specter of spoilage. Napoleon determined to find a way around this by coming up with a reliable method of food preservation, and he offered a 12,000 franc prize (about a million 2008 dollars) in 1799 to the first inventor who could supply it.

The chef

Little is known about the personal life of Nicholas Francois Appert (1750-1841). He started his work life as a hotelkeeper, moved into brewing, then worked as a chef, and finally, developed a reputation in Paris as a confectioner.

In the 18th century, everyone knew that food could go bad, but the mechanisms were not understood. Food contains a variety of bacteria, some of which are beneficial, as in yogurt, and many which are not so welcome. In Appert's time, unless you salted or dried the foodstuffs, you had to eat them up before their microorganisms made them unpalatable. This vexing problem had occupied Nicholas Appert's mind for several years before Napoleon came up with his impressive incentive.

The prize

In about 1800, hearing of Napoleon's offer, Appert set to work. He discovered, through much trial and error, that food could be preserved by sealing followed with heat sterilization, using glass jars sealed with pitch. The result of this process was not only the destruction of bacteria by heat, but a vacuum environment in the sealed jar which discouraged further bacterial growth. As long as the seal remained unbroken, a variety of foods could have their lives substantially extended by this new technique. Appert did not fully understand why this worked, but it was clear that it did, and quite successfully. It would have to wait until the work of Louis Pasteur (1822-1895) before it was understood that the heating process was sterilizing the bacteria.

In 1804, Appert built his first vacuum-packing system, in four connect-ed apartments in Paris, and subsequently approached Napoleon with his variety of canned meats and vegetables. Appert's book lists the large variety of meats and gravies, vegetables, and fruits that were included in this first production run for evaluation by Napoleon's armies. It is noted also that a number of different soups and bouillons were made. (Interesting side note: Appert is said to have been responsible for the invention of the bouillon cube.)

After lengthy field trials with the new glass jars, Napoleon pronounced himself well satisfied with Appert's efforts, and in 1808 awarded him the 12,000 franc prize. Appert immediately launched construction of a much larger and more modern canning plant, and began work on a book documenting his discovery.

Millions of homemakers since have filled millions of Mason jars in a process little changed from Appert's original 1804 success.

Appertization

Little is known about Appert's life, but his name lives on; in his honor, canning is sometimes called "appertization," and since 1942 the Chicago section of the Institute of Food Technologists has every year con-

The Gem jar was made by the Mason company circa 1869.

ferred the Nicholas Appert Award for achievements in food technology. Daniel Farkas, retired Oregon State University professor, won the Appert Prize in 2002 for his development of a new high-pressure food preservation system.

Appert's discovery was of course considered a highly valuable French military secret, and they strove mightily to keep it under wraps. Needless to say, they were not successful, and within a fairly short time the secret was out. The story goes that this was largely owing to the efforts of a couple of accomplished British espionage experts. It was not long before "appertization" was being done all over the developed world. Appert wrote a book, *The Art of Preserving All Kinds of Animal and Vegetable Substances for Several Years*, detailing his methods. Even with its rather unwieldy title, the book proved to be an international best seller, translated from the French into a large number of other languages.

While glass jars have lived on in home canning, commercial canning operations switched to the use of metal cans as early as 1810. Appert himself changed over his canning operations to tin-plated steel in 1822. Interestingly, the development of can openers did not keep up.

The can opener

It was nearly 50 years before one Ezra Warner, in 1858, dreamed up a device specifically for opening cans. It was a rather primitive device much like the single-piece sickle-shaped ones still seen today, but it was a great improvement over the former process. Prior to that time the frustrated users were instructed to "cut around top of can with chisel and hammer." Hard to imagine, but true. Even more astonishing, it was not until 1925 that someone finally came up with the form of the modern can opener, using the traveling serrated wheel. When this was eventually electrified, even the arthritic could easily get their cans open.

Generations of Boy Scouts and soldiers in the field have learned to use the famous U.S. Army folding can opener, (the P-38) which itself was not invented until well after Warner's breakthrough 1858 device.

Generations of house cats have learned to associate the whirr of the electric can opener with the arrival of their Friskies. But Friskies has moved their can technology ahead, so our cats will have to adapt to the loss of their familiar signal.

The pop-top technology originally developed for beverage cans has now made its way to other forms of cans, in many cases with the entire top designed to be removed with a pull on the metal ring. The 5.5-ounce Friskies can is just one example of this new style. Quite possibly in a few more years our familiar can openers will all have gone the way of the dinosaurs.

But we owe the existence of the cans themselves to Napoleon and his Parisian candy maker, and the million-dollar incentive that spurred on that candy maker just 200 years ago. Δ

(A shorter version of this article was previously published in *OMEN*, The Newsletter of Oregon MENSA. www. oregon.us.mensa.org)

Claire goes to the movies
One man's war against the IRS

❧   ❧   ❧

Reviewed by Claire Wolfe

Harry's War
98 minutes—PG
Available on VHS and DVD

If you hang with a certain political crowd, you've probably heard of this 1981 dramedy. If you don't, then *Harry's War* is the very definition of an obscure movie.

For years it was available only on VHS. Even after it went to DVD, it was nearly impossible to find. Then the company that owned the rights went bust.

But now, thanks to its rediscovery by the International Society for Individual Liberty (ISIL), *Harry's War* can be rented on Netflix, purchased from Amazon.com, or bought from ISIL itself.

Why should you seek out a film that so few people ever cared to see?

Well, let me introduce Harry. Harry Johnson (Edward Herrmann) is a pleasant, patriotic, young father. He's a man who sincerely wants to do the right thing and who believes everyone else is equally well-intentioned.

Harry is separated from his wife Kathy (Karen Grassle), but he's still in love with her and he absolutely dotes on his children.

The plot begins to thicken when Harry receives a desperate letter from his "Aunt Beverly" (Geraldine Page). Beverly isn't really his aunt, and she's more than a little dotty. But she's a living saint to whom Harry owes his very survival. So of course he rushes out to the ramshackle rural junk dealership where Beverly lives. There, he finds the good-hearted woman charitably hosting a collection of stray misfits. But he also finds she's in deep, deep, deep trouble with the Internal Revenue Service.

Harry is sunnily confident that the whole problem can be worked out by sitting down to have a reasonable talk. After all, the U.S. Government is always fair and has our best interests at heart. So he offers to have that chat with the agent in charge.

But the agent (David Ogden Stiers) is an ambitious careerist who believes Beverly is the leader of a group of anti-government tax resisters. He is going to get her, no matter what.

When matters go from bad to worse, the naive, good-hearted Harry is driven to risk all by declaring a one-man war against the IRS.

I'll tell you straight out this is not a great movie. It lurches from lovable family dramedy to absurd farce. Logic often fails. The quality of the DVD is poor.

But it is a very good movie for people who care about freedom. In addition to its sweet, funny characters, *Harry's War* is spot-on accurate about the unconstitutional tactics of the IRS (such as forcing disputes into its own rigged "tax courts"). It tells truths no other fiction film has dared utter. It celebrates the individual and the *U.S. Constitution*.

It was also stunningly prophetic. Its climax echoes real-world events that happened years after it was released.

In short, *Harry's War* will never make anybody's Top 10 Films list. But if you care about freedom it might make you smile—and at a few moments, might also make you gasp.

NOTE: ISIL has bought up existing stocks of *Harry's War* but may not be able to get rights to make more copies. So if you're interested, see it soon. It may not be available in the future. Δ

Ask Jackie

If you have a question about rural living, send it in to Jackie Clay and she'll try to answer it. Address your letter to Ask Jackie, PO Box 712, Gold Beach, OR 97444. Questions will only be answered in this column. — Editor

Raising and eating geese

We may raise geese this year. I'd like ideas, recipes, anything on how to have a top-quality roast goose.

Karen Burkholder
Mt. Crawford, Virginia

Under the right circumstances, geese are a terrific addition to the homestead. The baby goslings are quite hardy, growing quickly past the need-extra-heat stage. And once they've grown, they do well on a little grain plus grazing, making them economical homestead mini-livestock.

I say "under the right circumstances" because geese can be a pain in the hindquarters sometimes. They can be aggressive, biting and flapping at you with their wings, especially territorial ganders. And they are known for leaving huge piles of goose you-know-what in the front yard or even on the doorstep. This is one reason geese are not encouraged to graze on river banks of local parks.

You can raise geese happily, however. One of the best ways is to fence your small orchard or bramble patch and let the geese roam freely in there, having a small shed to go into at night (to escape predators, such as owls). They will keep walkways and the grounds beneath fruit trees nicely "mowed" and free from bugs. Their fertilizer

leavings will only enhance the plant and tree growth. The fence will keep them contained so they will not be a nuisance or even a danger to small children. Give them fresh water and a little grain each day and they'll happily grow and grow.

Now for that perfect roast goose! To begin the roast goose, start a couple of months before you plan on eating it. Ease off the corn, so the goose doesn't build tons of fat. Goose is a bit greasy anyway, and you don't want to compound the problem. Feed it grain, but use a mixed grain, such as oats, barley, and a little corn instead of all corn.

When you dress the goose, remove any fat you can find. Usually this will be gobs of fat on the inside, around body organs. Take it all out.

Never roast the goose with the back resting on the roasting pan bottom; it'll end up greasy. Use a rack, elevated by wads of aluminum foil, or even just a few wads of foil alone. This will let the grease drip off the goose

Jackie Clay

and drain into the pan so it doesn't accumulate in the meat. Baste the meat very lightly, for the same reason.

Once the goose has roasted, let it stand for ten minutes before you slice the meat. It will then slice nicely, instead of falling into a pile of shreds. I usually make my stuffing separate from the goose so it doesn't become heavy. If you roast the stuffing with the neck and giblets to give it flavor, it won't become greasy and heavy. You can remove the neck and giblets before you serve it if you wish.

— Jackie

Venison and disease

I love venison but have been told by some local wildlife management officials that I should not eat wild venison due to incidences of CWD (Chronic Wasting Disease). Is this a real threat? I know of no one who ever got sick off venison. Can you detect CWD in the pre-cooked meat?

Miles Parminter
Goslow, New Hampshire

I don't know who told you this, but it's a stretch of the truth. There have been no detected cases of CWD in New Hampshire, yet. This makes eating New Hampshire venison pretty darned safe. To learn more about this disease, the New Hampshire Dept. of Natural Resources has a good web site; just type in New Hampshire CWD and you'll get there promptly.

To be safe, in any state, never shoot a thin deer or one that acts sick. Then don't cut into the brain or cut the spinal cord; i.e. don't halve the deer; bone it from the whole carcass. Or if you quarter it, disinfect your saw in bleach water and wear gloves. The disease appears to be spread via spinal fluid and possibly saliva, which is why it isn't recommended that people feed deer.

CWD has never been spread to humans, although there is a disease in humans related to it. Wildlife biologists and health officials countrywide are taking precautions to halt the spread of this debilitating disease.
— *Jackie*

Pressure canned meat

When I pressure can meat I sometimes have what I call "smoky head space" in the upper layer of double stacked pint jars. These jars are gray in the head space area. The film is on the jar and the upper layer of meat at the edges. In the past I've used it getting rid of any dark meat without ill effects. Is this wise? What causes it? Can it be prevented? If ever you do an article on meat I'd like to hear of anyone canning things such as meat loaf, etc. We love such instant meals and the tenderness of canned meat. Ham loaf has turned out well.

R. B.
St. Paris, Ohio

I think what you are seeing is grease film, which kind of blows up along with the steam in jars of meat, leaving the meat kind of dry when out of broth or liquid in the bottom of the jar. As long as the meat was properly canned, the seals of the jars intact, and the meat looks and smells fine when cooked, it is safe to eat.

I just did an article on instant meals (meals in a jar) in the March/April 2008 (Issue #110). I love these canned convenience foods! We just had supper, consisting of canned meatballs, heated like meatloaf, with green peppers and tomato sauce, baked in a casserole dish. Super!
— *Jackie*

Canning meat

I have written to you before and found your advice to be invaluable. I have a canning question. My hubby and I raise both ducks and chickens. What is the best way to can meat? We tried one way and found that mold grew inside the jars. We think it happened because of the amount of fat that wound up in the jar. Do you have any advice regarding this? We have limited freezer space and we're told canning the meat keeps it tender.

Jaime Hogsett
Sturtevant, Wisconsin

Yes, canning meat does make it tender...and convenient, too. If mold grew inside of the jars, either the meat was canned in a water bath canner or was not properly pressure canned. I can all my meat by first cooking it (with chickens or duck, usually boiling it till tender), then skimming the fat off. I pack the hot meat into the hot jars, then pour broth over it to within an inch of the top of the jars. Hot, previously simmered lids are put on the jar rims, which have been wiped clean of broth/ grease, and the rings screwed down firmly tight. Process meat for 90 min-

utes (quarts) or 75 minutes (pints) and poultry for 75 minutes (quarts) or 65 minutes (pints), at 10 pounds pressure. If you live at an altitude above 1,000 feet, consult your canning manual for directions on increasing your pressure to suit your altitude.

Are you sure there was mold on your meat, in the jars? Solid fat is white and can look a lot like mold in jars unless you are used to canning. Were the jars still sealed? Did the meat smell okay? When meat goes bad, where there is mold, it usually stinks like crazy. If you canned it properly and the seals were still good, I'd suspect your mold was, in fact, just solidified grease.   — *Jackie*

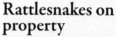

Rattlesnakes on property

We have just purchased 40 acres in Eastern Washington. We will have to be off-grid as it will cost too much to bring electric to the property. We are planning on solar and wind. The property is just land with fir, pine, and oak. And too many rattlesnakes (of which I'm scared to death of any snake). How do we keep the snakes at bay? We will completely clear the home site, garden site, and goat pen area. We will clear all areas of downed trees and brush. I've also heard that some breeds of chickens will kill snakes. Which breed? We also plan on chickens for eggs. Are there any other livestock that get rid of snakes? I can live with the other wild life (bear, deer, elk, cougar, and wolf).

Kim Wilson
LaCenter, Washington

You already have a good start on keeping snakes out of your yard. While you will never completely eliminate rattlesnakes from your home area, you can make them a lot scarcer. Snakes come into an area for food and shelter. Rattlesnakes eat primarily rodents. So if you eliminate a rodent population, you'll do a lot to get rid of the snakes too. Keep your feed in metal bins or garbage cans with tight fitting lids. Feed your chickens twice a day and don't leave feed in feeders that mice can get at. Have a good neutered outdoor cat to further reduce rodent populations. (Cats also kill snakes; I've seen a couple kill rattlers by wearing them out, then killing them!)

Reduce hiding places for snakes; keep the woodpile a distance from the house, up on a rack. Keep lumber on sawhorses or in a trailer, instead of lying on the ground. Keep your lawn mowed; snakes aren't thrilled about crossing open areas. They're afraid of predators.

Keep alert in rattlesnake country, but don't let fear of them ruin your homestead experience. We lived in rattlesnake country for years and years, with David being newborn to twelve years old. Yes, we did see and kill some rattlers. But no one was ever bitten, nor did we know anyone who had been bitten by one. Use common sense and enjoy your new life! — *Jackie*

Buying canned bacon

I am trying to locate where to buy canned bacon. About 20 years ago I could buy it by the case at K-mart. I do not remember the name brand; it was from Norway or Denmark. I contacted all of the major canned food producers, no luck. I was wondering if you know of any companies, or have any idea where I could go to buy canned bacon.

Pete Gibson
Bowie, Arizona

I have had other readers looking for canned bacon, too. And I've had no luck in finding any, anywhere. Any readers out there have a CURRENT supply for this tasty food? — *Jackie*

Free government land

I have tried unsuccessfully to track down any and all information on free or cheap land through various channels. These have included Public Lands Title, through www.governmentland.com. They have either not lived up to their own advertisements, were a scam for money, or a dead end. Do you know of any inexpensive land programs, government sponsored or otherwise, that are legitimate?

William Ritchie
Appleton, Minnesota

Sorry, but free or cheap government land is simply NOT available. All the *"Free Government Land"* advertisements I've seen turned out to be scams. You send them your money and they give you some not-so-good information that is basically worthless.

Your best bet is to shop hard; there are some cheaper pieces of good land out there for sale. And sometimes when you don't have cash, you can work a deal with a private owner that you can afford. Just be sure you get it in writing, because I've heard too many horror stories about someone that did a lot of work on a worn out place and then was kicked out so the owner could sell the now-valuable piece of property for a good price.

Run ads in local shoppers. Be explicit on what you will and won't accept—how much you can afford, if you need good terms, if you are willing to work hard to make a deal…and you'd better be! It can be done and you can find a good piece of homestead ground. It just won't be free or laugh-in-your-face cheap, either. — *Jackie*

Making cider vinegar

I'm just finishing building a cider press. The hard part is the pulverizer. My question is: how can I make cider vinegar?

Dale Neese
Cottage Hills, Illinois

One neat apple chopper I saw was a new garbage disposal, mounted over a new plastic garbage can. The apples were fed into the disposal, chopped, then dumped into the press.

There are several ways to make cider vinegar, the most simple being setting a jug of fresh cider on the counter and waiting until it ferments, then turns to vinegar. Or you can add a bit of mother-of-vinegar from a jar of unpasteurized apple cider vinegar to your fresh cider to get it working. Or you can add a couple of cups of unpasteurized apple cider vinegar to the cider. You'll need to keep a cloth over the jug, not cap it, as it does need air to work. If you leave it uncovered, you'll have drowned fruit flies in it!

Making cider vinegar isn't hard, but it is an art that requires a bit of experimenting to perfect. — *Jackie*

In Jackie Clay's
Growing and Canning Your Own Food

- *Gardening basics*
- *Canning supplies*
- *Growing fruit*
- *Growing and canning tomatoes*
- *Pickles, relishes, and sauces*
- *Raising and canning meats*
- *Meals-in-a-jar*
- *Canning dairy products*

Fast and easy bread recipes

By Ilene Duffy

My husband, Dave, asked me to write an article about making bread for this special preparedness issue. We really wanted our friend, Richard Blunt, to write an extensive article on the history of bread making as well as giving us his time-tested, wholesome recipes, but he was unable to get it ready for this issue. His in-depth article will be in next issue.

Here are two quick and easy bread recipes that our family enjoys. I say quick and easy since I volunteer at both schools, help boys with homework, do the usual chores around the house, chauffeur kids to and from their various activities, and attend to my duties here at the magazine, which means I really like finding recipes for nutritious breads that are quick and easy to prepare.

Last night, while working at the office finishing up the last minute details for this issue, I took a break and went back into our office kitchen and put the ingredients into my bread machine to make a loaf of bread. This recipe uses 2 cups of whole wheat flour and just 1 cup of white flour, which makes it nutritious, but it still rises nicely and makes a beautiful loaf. I like experimenting with different seeds than those called for in the recipe, depending on what I have on hand. I've made this recipe several times before, adding and subtracting ingredients, using what I've got available in my kitchen at the time. I normally use poppy seeds but I didn't have any, so I didn't list them here. Also the original recipe doesn't call for oat bran, but I like throwing in a little extra oomph. Sometimes I blow it and add too much, without also adding more liquid, but for last night's batch I thought to add 2 extra tablespoons of milk, and it turned out excellent. Here's the version of this recipe I made last night.

Wheat and seed bread

1¼ cups plus 2 Tbsp. milk
2 Tbsp. honey
2 tsp. butter
2 cups whole wheat flour
1 cup bread flour
¼ cup unsalted sunflower seeds
1 Tbsp. sesame seeds
2 Tbsp. oat bran
½ tsp. salt
2 tsp. yeast

In a microwaveable bowl, combine the milk, honey, and butter. Warm just enough until it is gently warmed, but not hot. Pour into bread machine pan. In a bowl, mix together all the dry ingredients, except the yeast. Pour the flour mixture on top of the liquid in the bread machine pan. Make a small valley in the flour and spoon the yeast into the valley.

I put the bread machine on just the dough cycle. When done, I shaped the loaf to fit into my special long loaf

Right in front of our propane stove, the bread rises nicely.

pan. I let it rise for an hour in front of our office propane stove, then baked it at 350° F for 25 minutes. I took the loaf out of the pan immediately to cool on racks and rubbed olive oil on the crust to soften it.

Whole wheat biscuits

When I don't have time to make a yeast bread, but still want a quick bread to add to our dinner table, I make these whole wheat biscuits. I found this recipe online and changed it a bit to suit the ingredients I had on hand. It originally called for buttermilk, but since I didn't have any, I used a dollop of sour cream.

1 cup whole wheat flour
1 cup flour
2 Tbsp. sugar
2 tsp. baking powder
½ tsp. salt
¼ tsp. baking soda
3 Tbsp. butter, softened
¾ cup milk
1 Tbsp. sour cream
(original recipe calls for ¾ cup buttermilk, and no sour cream)

Preheat oven to 400° F. In large bowl, mix flours, sugar, baking powder, salt, and baking soda. Cut in butter. In a separate bowl, mix the milk and sour cream. Stir milk into dry ingredients just until it forms a soft dough that leaves the side of the bowl. Turn dough onto lightly floured surface. Knead to mix thoroughly.

Grease and flour muffin pan. Cut the dough into 12 pieces. Grease hands and roll each piece into a ball and place in muffin cups. Bake 12-15 minutes until golden. Δ

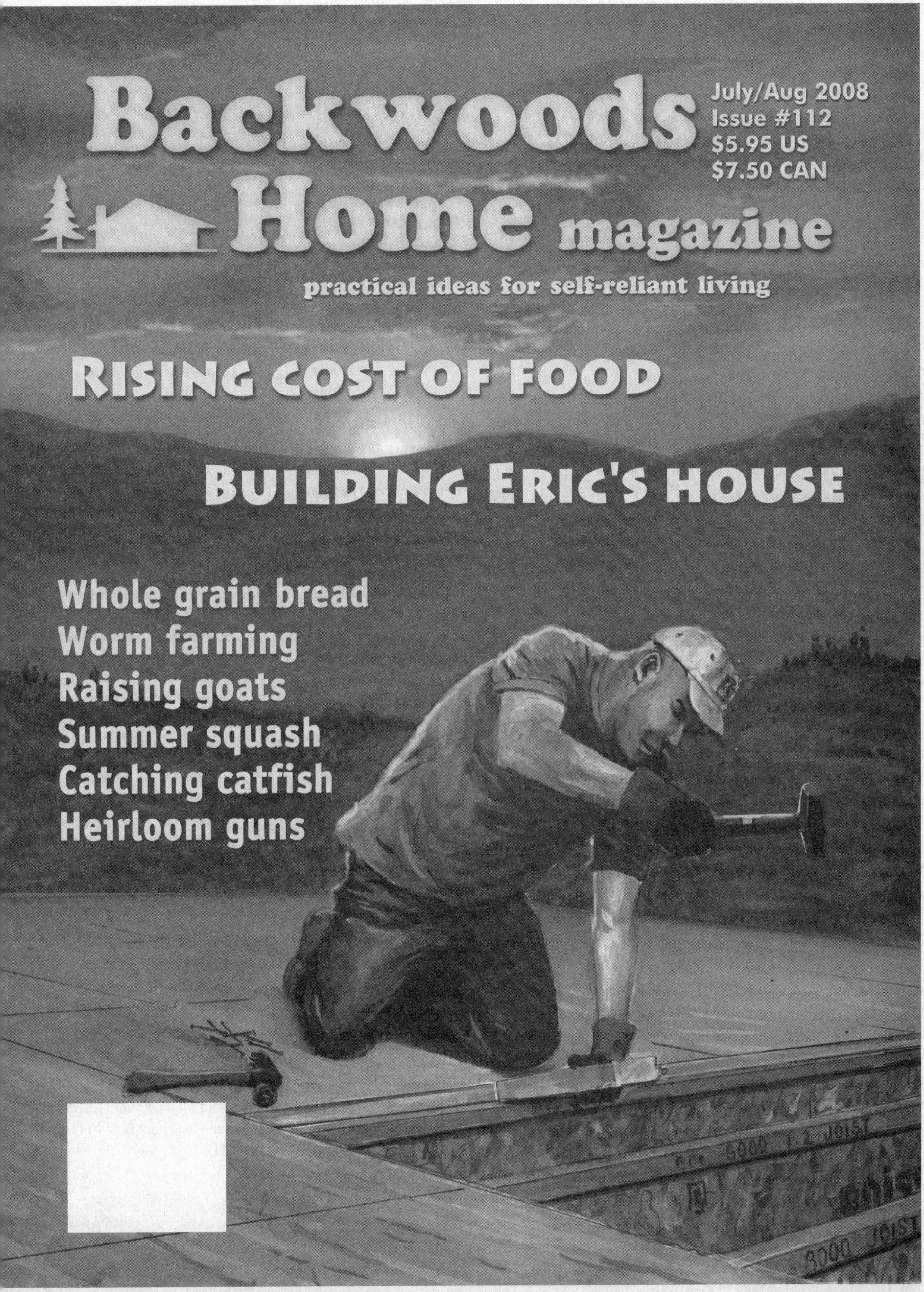

Backwoods Home magazine

July/Aug 2008
Issue #112
$5.95 US
$7.50 CAN

practical ideas for self-reliant living

RISING COST OF FOOD

BUILDING ERIC'S HOUSE

Whole grain bread
Worm farming
Raising goats
Summer squash
Catching catfish
Heirloom guns

My view

Maybe food shortages and hunger will do what intellectual debate can't

Food shortages around the world. Wal-Mart rationing rice in their United States stores. We had an advertiser who sells preparedness foods cancel his ad in this issue because he couldn't get enough grain to sell his U.S. customers. Imagine that! In the United States of all places! Reminds me of the French Revolution!

The French Revolution? Sure! That was the last great revolutionary movement in world history that was sparked by food shortages. The French had been complaining for years about their oppressive government, but it took a food shortage that prompted mothers to march for bread in Paris in the summer of 1789 to really get the revolution going. It led to the beheading of Louis XVI, the most powerful monarch in the world, brought on Robespierre's Reign of Terror in which 20,000 fat cat aristocrats were guillotined in one year alone, and eventually led to world wars that ended monarchical rule across Europe.

That's what food shortages can do. For centuries the French and the rest of the world had lived under the despotic rule of divine right monarchy with its tiny privileged class and everyone else poor, powerless slobs, but it took mothers marching for bread to finally get them to act in their own behalf. Intellectuals can complain all they want about government despotism, government encroachment on individual liberty, but in the end it takes an issue that affects the belly. Mothers in need of food for their babies are a fierce force of nature that politicians dare not ignore.

Maybe that's what we need in the United States — a little more food shortage — to get people to act in their own behalf, on behalf of the freedoms that their government strips away from them on a near daily basis. Maybe that will get them to take our own fat cat bureaucrats by the neck and throw them aside. Nothing else has worked.

In this country, the conservative right and libertarians have complained about government encroachment on our freedoms for years. I've been doing it in this column for nearly 20 years. Smarter people have written books about it, detailing the abuses, pointing the way to reform. Outfits like the *Cato Institute* and *Heritage Foundation* have attacked the problem from a scholarly perspective, presenting their arguments before a nodding Congress that, in the end, did nothing to stem the loss of our freedoms.

During the last eight years, liberals have finally joined conservatives and libertarians in our chorus of complaints against government abuse of individual freedom after they watched a Republican administration do what we have been saying Democratic administrations have been doing

Dave Duffy

for decades: stripping away our freedoms.

Bush did his freedom stealing under the guise of protecting us from terrorists, but we all recognized what was happening. The government finally had its perfect pretense: an apparently unending war against terrorism that provided the perfect umbrella from which government could launch its final assault on freedom. If you question the government's new laws to curtail our freedoms in the name of fighting the War on Terror, you are accused of being a terrorist sympathizer who must hate the United States. What Orwellian logic!

But we've all come to question government these days. A policy that defends against terrorists by stripping away our remaining individual liberties just doesn't make sense, not to us conservatives and libertarians, and at last, not even to liberals. Ironically, the terrorist attacks on America have done some good after all: They've united Americans, no matter their political persuasion, in realizing that the real enemy always has been and always will be our own government.

We can fight terrorists without giving up our freedoms. We just need a government that works for the good of its people, not one that looks for any opportunity to grow itself in size and power at the expense of the rights of its citizens.

The recent shortage of food across the world is due, in part, to government's sheer ineptitude in combatting both a terrorist problem and a fuel supply problem. Our government, by offering incentives for American farmers to take food producing land out of service and convert it to fuel-producing land, has helped create a global food shortage. Since food shortages mean only high prices for Americans, but starvation for many poorer countries, Americans so far have only grumbled about prices while other nations have already toppled their governments.

But our government is so inept, and so slow to correct the stupid laws it passes, that maybe the food shortage the government has created will yet spark the mothers of America to follow the French example of so long ago, namely, provide the spark in our intellectual debate about how best to rein in government. — **Dave Duffy**

City girl ❦ Country life

Learning to receive

By Claire Wolfe

Back when I was an impatient young urban professional, if I needed something, I bought it. And I'm not just talking about designer sweaters. I mean everything from landscaping to art to somebody to tell my troubles to. (In those California days, a shrink or an encounter group on your weekly schedule was practically a social requirement.) Want it? Need it? Grab an urban phone book as thick as *War and Peace* and whatever you wish is yours.

Now that I'm a rural hermit of uncertain age and income…life is just a leeetle bit different.

The local phone book is thinner than the manual that came with my DVD player. It lacks such basic urban amenities as lasik eye surgeons, landscape designers, botox injectors, Ethiopian restaurants, New Age channelers, bikini waxers, baby-genius pre-schools, and boutiques that specialize exclusively in left-handed stainless steel kitchen gadgets. This phone book—what there is of it—is very big on hardware stores. But since there are only two in the county and every local already has their phone numbers (not to mention the precise contents of every aisle) thoroughly memorized, there's not much point.

Out here, you don't think first of buying things. You think first of scrounging, bartering, making, making do, doing without, and all the other things granny may have taught you. Oh, plenty gets bought. We backwoodsers "consume," just like George W. Bush wants us to. But often our buying is more in terms of parts, supplies, ingredients, or alternative technologies than finished consumer product.

Faithful *Backwoods Home* readers know the drill. We understand that rural life is much more complicated than urban or suburban life. It involves vastly more do-it-yourselfing. And of course that's one reason why so many hardy souls (and even some of us far less hardy souls) embrace it.

But that brings up an irony we've bumped into before in this column: In the passion for being independent, for doing-it-ourselves, we become more dependent on our neighbors than our city cousins would ever dream of being. Whether it be the traditional communal barn-raising or having our truck winched out of a mud-hole by a passing logger, we need the willing (and usually unpaid) efforts of those around us to an astonishing degree.

Out here, even when you actually want to hire somebody, for actual pay, it's not always straightforward. For instance, our community has only one "official" plumbing contractor. Though he's a very nice guy, he's booked up weeks in advance and refuses to budge from his schedule. Has your toilet suddenly decided to spew a geyser of brown gunk onto your ceiling and you intuitively sense that the situation might get even worse after application of your own doubtful plumbing skills? Well then, we'll just see about fitting you in on the second Tuesday of next month.

In Urbanland, you might get the same response from the first plumber you call. If so, you simply let your fingers do the walking to the next entry in the Yellow Pages.

Out here the Yellow Pages are ominously silent on the matter of second-choice plumbers. So you scramble to the Neighbor Net. After asking a person or three, you eventually discover that the third cousin of your real estate agent learned some plumbing while he was in prison for growing pot. Spike doesn't have a phone, but since he's still out of work you can probably track him down at the local tavern any time after 11 am; just look for the guy with the eye patch and the rattlesnake tattoo.

The process is very much the same when you need your car fixed, your electric rewired, your septic tank dug, or the foundation forms built for your new bedroom addition. If the job is beyond you, Neighbor Net fills the need.

Better yet, the "contractor" that Neighbor Net turns up is usually, despite his dubious resume, one heck of a nice guy and quite skilled at what he does. As often as not, it turns out you already know Spike—or Mike or Ike or whatever his name is. You just didn't know that he had the talent to replace the heater core on your Honda or had a backhoe sitting in the pole barn behind his house.

> **…In the passion for being independent, for doing-it-ourselves, we become more dependent on our neighbors than our city cousins would ever dream of being…**

When you arrange with Spike to do a specific job for specific pay, the problem of restoring that fountaining toilet to proper plumbing-fixture manners becomes simple again. You hire Spike. He works his magic. You pay him. You just need to remember that etiquette calls for cash payment (and *vive la unregulated market*) upon job completion.

But chances are that Spike or Mike, or perhaps it might even be Mary, doesn't want money. And that's where things get complicated again. And that's where I finally get to the real topic of this column: learning to receive.

Is it just me? Or have you also discovered that a lot of the folks on Neighbor Net don't want anything in return for

ONE HOUR LATER ▶ ONE DAY LATER ▶

"Oh, dear. Let's see if we can fix this little problem you've got."

"Please, let me pay you." "Nah, that's what neighbors are for."

"How about a nice batch of fresh cookies to show my thanks?"

deeds that are absolutely heroic in scale? Instead of asking for 25 bucks an hour or even some tangible, defined form of barter ("Tell you what; I'll take your old Buick and part it out in exchange for cutting down that row of damaged trees"), they say, "Oh heck, don't worry about it. I'm just glad to help. There'll be some way you can get me back later."

That would be fine. All fair and balanced. Except that quite often "later" never comes.

Spike never wants *anything* in return for riding to your rescue or pitching in side-by-side with you to get a job done. No matter what you offer, or how many times you remind him of the moral debt you owe him, old Spike just scuffles his work-booted toe in the dirt and says, "Don't worry about it."

Worse yet, if you try to ply Spike with return favors (whether in the form of assistance with his projects, home-baked goodies, money, or anything else), he gets embarrassed, even irritated. He resists, rejects, or begrudges your every effort to do unto him as he did unto you. Resolutely, he is determined to stay ahead of you in the neighborliness department.

It's as if giving is a sign of strength, while receiving anything (however justified, however fair) is a weakness.

And it makes me squirm.

Now perhaps your experiences have been different. Heaven knows, in this world of "entitlements" there are plenty of people who make a career out of taking, rather than giving. Depending on where (and perhaps who) you are, you might run into a lot more of those kind. You might even think I'm living in la-la land if I see myself surrounded by uber-giving people like Spike.

Even if you believe me when I say my world is full of Spike types, endlessly giving, relentlessly refusing to receive, you might wonder why the heck that's a problem.

Hey, quitcher bitchin'. Sit back and enjoy. Or bake the guy a couple dozen cookies and consider him repaid. Quit bugging him and like he says—don't worry about it!

But if you live and thrive in the backwoods, my guess is you're a bit of a Spike type yourself. And that you know a lot of others.

For those of us who lack the practical skills and awesome work capacities of a Spike yet still crave the backwoods life with all its traditional neighborly reciprocity, being on the receiving end of too many generous Spike-isms may be a blessing—but a decidedly mixed one.

It leaves a body always owing.

I thought about listing some of the goodnesses I've received and not been able to repay. But there are so many I'd be certain to leave somebody out. (M, T, D, S, P, and L…you know who you are.)

Let me just offer the example of Ike. Ike is a friend of a friend. I barely know him. But last weekend he spent two full days working on my car and he's not done yet (yes, I'm on wheels again after spending 15 months afoot, thanks in large part to another person's goodness). I didn't know going in—though he did—what a difficult job I'd asked him to do. There's no way I can pay him for his troubles. And in fact when I so much as bring up the subject of compensation, he rolls his eyes and says, "Claire, you don't understand."

Ike has done many kind things for me. But he refuses so much as a batch of cookies in return. Won't even touch 'em when I try to put them into his hands. The one time he did request a little reciprocation—a companion to drive him home from minor surgery in the Big City—he brimmed with irritation. I had the feeling he liked me less by the time we got home. Maybe it was just that my company bored him; but I think he felt I'd put him at a disadvantage.

188

Our mothers and grans probably put a lot of energy into the biblical injunction that "It is better to give than to receive." But in my humble opinion, it's better yet to balance both giving and receiving.

The chronic takers of the world are easy to deal with: Just walk away. The genuine chronically needy (like babies and the very old) have their place in a balanced society; they help teach us a great deal about our own humanity while reminding us of exactly why people need people. Oh, but those chronic givers…now they're the puzzle.

The truth, I suspect, is that all of us who hold independence as an ideal find it difficult to receive. We want to hold our own in the world. We want to be strong. Self-reliant. Beholden to nobody.

Sometimes that's good. Great, even. Sometimes, though, we need to get over it.

During the 15 months I was on foot, I had to learn, for the first time since childhood, to "graciously receive"—to accept the fact that friends were doing more for me than I was able to do in return for them—picking me up at my house, taking me places, letting me use their vehicles for hauling, etc. It wasn't a lesson that came easy. (Many times, my old city self wished I could have just called a taxi or hired a hauler when an errand was more than I could do on walking shoes and backpack.)

For me, it's all about balance. I don't want to be in anyone's debt. Nor do I want anyone owing me. I like the cleanness of work-for-hire or direct barter. I crave tidy exchanges, mutual, definable benefit. Transaction completed, books wiped clean, on with life.

Others see it differently. My friend H will do anything for you, once she has defined you as family or clan, as one of her own. Balance? It means nothing to her. She considers my craving for balance as a kind of crass and ignoble scorekeeping. In her eyes, if you're family, clan, tribe, or community, you do for each other, period, end of story.

When people do more for her than she can repay, she thinks of it rather like building up a savings account—from which she can, in turn, give to others. Right now she's in the long process of building an off-grid homestead. A well-connected and savvy pair of friends has taken a fancy to finding her a wonderworld of salvaged building materials, including such prizes as granite countertops, luxury plumbing fixtures, and in one notable case, a complete barn, just three years old, hers for the take-down. She knows she'll never be able to do as much for these friends as they've done for her. So, she receives gratefully and plans to "pay it forward" rather than pay them back.

Ike is a different case yet. I asked him, "Why are you so reluctant to let people do anything for you?" To my surprise he had a ready answer: "My mother. She was an alcoholic who held every, single thing over me. She made sure that whatever she did for me had a price—a price I just had to pay and pay and pay. So I don't want to be beholden to anybody."

I then asked why, on the contrary, he does so much for others—including people like me whom he scarcely knows. He was just as quick with his self-knowledge: "I'm making up for all the bad I've done in my life. Besides, I like not just to do, but to teach others so that they won't end up dependent."

…Our mothers and grans probably put a lot of energy into the biblical injunction that "It is better to give than to receive." But in my humble opinion, it's better yet to balance both giving and receiving…

Good answers. Sad reasons.

The bottom line is that those who best make a go of rural living tend to be people who give and do for others. Anyone who expects to be served and catered to should just stay in the city and order takeout sushi from one of those bible-sized phone books.

But if we're to do for others in a way that's healthy for all involved, we independent rural cusses also need to learn to receive—for the sake of our fellow givers, as well as for our own sake. And that's easier said than done. Δ

THE RISING COST OF FOOD & FUEL

- ❖ **What's causing it?**
- ❖ **What can we do?**
- ❖ **What is the danger?**

By John Silveira

There are food protests, food riots in which people die, and at least one government has fallen. No one really knows what's going to happen next or how much worse it's going to get as food and fuel prices spiral higher. From the amount of hysteria in the media, it would appear as though civilization is coming to an end. And there's certainly plenty of bad news to lend credence to that notion. But the questions are: How bad is it and is it all bad news?

The bad news

Let's take a look at what's going on.

Food prices are going through the roof. In the last 30 years, after accounting for inflation, the costs of both food and fuel had remained more or less constant or, in the case of many of the basic commodities such as corn, wheat, and soybeans, they had fallen until recently.

I remember when a gallon of gasoline cost about 28 cents, but by 2002 it was nearing two dollars. However, the fact is, after factoring in inflation, neither gas nor much of anything else had really increased in real terms in almost 30 years, and the cost of many items had actually gone down.

The recent high prices of food have already led to riots in several foreign countries.

So, why were prices going up over the last three decades or longer?

What we were really witnessing was the value of our money, the dollar, falling. Since leaving the Gold Standard, the purchasing power of America's currency has relentlessly fallen and you can bet on it falling far into the future. But in "real" terms, the costs of most things were actually going down.

However, today, the real price of both foodstuffs and fuels are going up. That is, they're going up even after we make adjustments for inflation. Worse, they're spiraling out of control all over the world, including in countries where the difference between eating and starvation is a thin line.

There's no single cause for the rise in the cost of food or fuel. But food has been affected by more factors, any one of which could have caused a

price bump that would have gone unnoticed by most Americans. But some commentators have called what's happening with food costs recently a "perfect storm," referring to the convergence of several events, each of which, individually, would have caused little concern but which, happening all together, are creating disaster on an international scale.

Just a few years ago the price of most types of wheat on the futures market was $3.50/bushel. At this writing, they've all passed $10/bushel and some are up over $15/bushel. Corn, soybeans, and other commodities are all seeing the same kind of increases. This year alone, the price of rice doubled on world markets in a single five-week period. And just since mid-2007, prices overall have risen another 40 percent. Other commodities are increasing, too. Globally, all food prices escalated almost 25 percent

from 2006 to 2007, with cooking oils increasing by 50 percent, and dairy by 80 percent.

Compare that to 2006 when food prices escalated by a large, but still manageable, nine percent. We'd give anything to see those days again.

Remember the 1970s?

This is not the first time food prices have spiked. Most people have forgotten the rise in food costs that took place in the 1970s. Back then it was because of bad weather, rising oil prices, and secret grain deals Washington made with the Soviet Union. And after factoring in inflation, we're still below the peak for food prices that we witnessed back then. Still, the current price surge is creating problems and no one knows how much higher food and fuel prices will go. Nor are they able to forecast

A major portion of our grain production, specifically corn and soybeans, have been diverted from making foodstuffs to creating biofuels. But the diversion has come at a price as it drives up the costs of food worldwide.

the social unrest higher prices will cause.

Higher prices vs. starvation

Although there are grumblings over food prices here at home, Americans spend a smaller percentage of their disposable income on food than any other country in the world, about 6.5 to 7.5 percent, depending on how the calculations are made, before the prices recently started to skyrocket. And if food prices in this country were to increase by 50 percent or even double, and we spent 13 percent to 15 percent of our incomes on food, we'd complain in the checkout lines of our local grocery markets, but we wouldn't starve.

However, in other countries where the money spent on food has historically made up a sizable chunk of a family's income, that is 40, 50, or even 75 percent, a 50 or 100 percent cost increase can mean constant hunger and even starvation.

And increases such as those are *already* happening in some of the poorest countries in the world. Across West Africa, the prices of basic sta-

ples have risen more than 50 percent with them soaring by as much as 300 percent in some countries. And rather than just complaining about them, there have been protests in Egypt, the Philippines, and, closer to home, Mexico. There have also been riots in Haiti, Indonesia, Burkina Faso, Cameroon, India, Senegal, Mauritania, and other countries. Some governments are teetering because of the problem, while in others, such as Haiti, they've fallen.

By the time you read this, you'll have read of or seen on the news more protests and more riots in poor and not-so-poor countries in response to the ever increasing prices.

By the end of 2007 some 37 countries had already announced they were in the middle of food crises and 20 of them had imposed some kinds of price controls or rationing. In China, the government has had to tap its grain reserves to help hold the

prices down. But if those reserves run out, expect to see the prices jump around the world as the world's most populous country turns to world markets and tries to import even more of the basic staples to feed itself.

Some countries, such as China, Vietnam, Ukraine, and Russia, have cut or banned the exportation of grains, further exacerbating the crises in countries needing to import them.

It may seem that what happens in these countries is going to be their own problem and won't affect us here in the United States. But they already are. As foreign countries compete to buy grains, prices are going up here, too. The cost of a loaf of bread has about doubled, and shortages will occur that affect us too. As an example, Wal-Mart and some other grocery outlets are now putting limits on bulk rice purchases.

The possibility of political turmoil

There is also the possibility of political change both here and abroad. (Remember that it was economic turmoil that allowed the communist revolution in Russia and enabled megalomaniacs like Hitler and Mussolini to come to power in Germany and Italy.) When food is disappearing off your dinner plate and your children are crying out of hunger, radical solutions begin to seem reasonable. Revolutions by the hungry may change the face of global politics.

What's behind the rising prices?

There are many drivers escalating the prices of foods. They include:

Rising oil prices. When adjusted for inflation, the price of a gallon of gasoline or diesel fuel has remained

Some commentators have called what's happening with food costs recently a "perfect storm."

surprisingly constant for the last 50 years. It's only recently that the prices have shot up far faster than inflation. As I write this, gasoline is up about 30 percent at the pump over last year and diesel is up 40 percent.

And it's even pricier in Europe. Depending on which country you want to consider, the gasoline price at the pump in Europe can run anywhere from double to almost triple the price per gallon than it does here. The prime reason for the inordinate prices in Europe is because of taxation. Taxes on a gallon of gasoline in this country run about 49 cents, with some localities running higher because of local taxes. But the taxes on a gallon of gasoline in Europe run about six times higher.

On the other hand, though the price of a barrel of crude has risen for both Americans and Europeans, it's going up much faster for Americans. This is because our dollar is falling in value

One of the answers to America's dependence on foreign oil may be the reintroduction of steam-driven cars. Their advantages are many including the lack of need for a clutch, transmission, or muffler and the fact that they are more efficient than internal combustion engines. They can also run on lower grades of fuel.

to ride in a truck at some point, and that the increased cost of diesel fuel will be passed on to you, this will not only mean higher food costs but a rise in the cost of almost everything.

our grain supply was used to make fuels in 2006, 25 percent last year, and estimates are that it will be up to 30 percent this year. The unintended consequence has been to create shortages and raise the prices of corn and soybeans to new highs. And because farmers wanted to take advantage of these price increases, they are taking wheat fields and other crops out of

...the largest part of the increase in food costs has been because of the diversion of crops to the production of biofuels.

while the European currencies, particularly the euro, are stable. Those in the OPEC countries aren't stupid; they see the value of our dollar going down and they don't want to be "cheated" out of their money.

Increased fuel costs = increased food costs. But how does this rise in petroleum prices affect what we pay for food? Let's start with transportation costs.

Truckers have seen a dramatic rise in the cost of diesel fuel, the fuel that powers most of this country's over-the-road transportation. In June 2002 the average price/gallon for diesel was $1.286. As of today, it has gone over $4 a gallon and the upward trend shows little sign of abating.

When you consider almost everything that comes into your home had

There's also the cost of running mechanical planting and harvesting equipment, such as tractors, reapers, combines, etc., that will directly affect food costs.

Then there are costs of fertilizers, pesticides, and herbicides that are made from petroleum. All of these costs will ultimately be reflected in your grocery bill.

But the largest part of the increase in food costs has been because of the diversion of crops to the production of biofuels. In this country, Congress mandated that petroleum companies begin blending their gasoline with ethanol and start providing biodiesel to replace petroleum-based diesel fuels. Congress' intention was to make us less dependent on foreign oil. But the result is that 20 percent of

What's a strong dollar and what's a weak dollar?

A currency is called strong, with respect to other currencies, when it takes less of the strong currency to buy or exchange with another currency. If it begins to take more and more of one currency to buy or get exchanged with other currencies, then the first currency is "falling" or getting weaker. And so it is with the dollar. I remember when it took only 85 cents to "buy" a euro. Then the dollar began falling and, pretty soon, there was parity, i.e., one dollar bought one euro. Last time I looked (this morning), it took almost $1.55 to buy one euro.

No new nuclear power plants have been built since 1996. It's time for the United States to take a hard look at this source of power if we expect to break our dependence on foreign oil.

production and planting more corn and soybeans instead.

The result is less wheat for human consumption and for feeding livestock. Less wheat means wheat costs more, just as corn and soybeans do.

But the rising prices of grains drives the price of other commodities up as it translates into higher prices of not only bread but beef, chicken, pork, milk, butter, and eggs from the animals to which we feed grains. This is happening both here and in other countries. The increased food costs are affecting everybody.

Other countries had also jumped on the biofuel bandwagon. Britain's "target" was to produce five percent of the fuel it uses for transportation from biofuels. However, in light of runaway food prices, that decision is now under review. Other countries, including the United States, may follow suit.

Another unintended consequence is that the drive for biofuels is leading to deforestation in Third World countries as land is cleared to create farmland. Here in Western countries, there are those who say it's unacceptable that food production and deforestation in developing countries is being used to make biofuels for Americans and Europeans. But some in those countries, such as President da Silva of Brazil, point out that biofuel production offers hope for economic development. Many living in those Third World countries feel that saving the forests will do them no good if they are relegated to perpetual poverty. Production of biofuels is one way for them to try to grab a slice of the economic pie we now enjoy.

The falling dollar. Another factor in the rise in prices—and this is an important one because it is the biggest reason the price of a barrel of oil is rising so fast here as compared to the rest of the world—is the weakening dollar. (See sidebar on *What's a "strong" dollar and what's a "weak" dollar?*) For decades the dollar has been the most important currency in the world. Other important currencies are the euro, which is the common currency of many of the nations of the European Union and several other countries, the British pound, and the Japanese yen.

But the value of the dollar against these and other currencies has some important effects on Americans.

A self-reliant family, with a large enough garden and entrepreneurial skills, can take advantage of the rise in food prices by creating a small side-business.

A strong or rising dollar makes foreign goods less expensive for Americans. It makes taking a vacation overseas cheaper. But it also has a downside in that a rising dollar makes American goods more expensive on the world markets, making it harder for American manufacturers to compete internationally. When the dollar is strong, it'll take fewer dollars to buy the VW, so an American may opt for that and may be less apt to buy an American Ford or Chevy. It's also one of the reasons American businesses have, until now, been willing to outsource jobs, that is, send jobs overseas. Labor is cheaper over there, but the wage gap is narrowing as the dollar falls.

On the other hand, a weak dollar, which is what we now have, makes American goods cheaper on world markets. It also makes travel to the United States less expensive for foreign travelers, but more expensive for Americans to go abroad, again benefitting American businesses. And when the dollar is weak, Americans are less likely to buy foreign goods and more apt to buy American. So, we're now less likely to buy that VW and more likely to buy an American car.

It would be fine if that's all there was to it, but there are some things which we *have* to import even though the price is going up. Petroleum is one of them. It takes even more dollars to do that when our currency is weak, and it begins to drive up the cost of everything that depends on petroleum, as explained earlier.

Another advantage to a weak dollar is that jobs that were outsourced are now more expensive for us to pay for, so some of them are going to come back here. And another irony is that some countries may opt to outsource their jobs to the United States.

Because of our weaker dollar, the balance of trade is also slowly changing and our trade deficit, now over nine trillion dollars, is already growing at a slower rate and may (but don't hold your breath on this one, yet) actually reverse.

Of course, not everyone is helped by a weakened dollar. Among those hurt are importers and those who specialize in foreign goods. For example, your local VW and Toyota dealers. Even the prices on goods from China, that fill many of the shelves at Wal-Mart, are going up and those goods are gradually becoming less attractive to consumers when contrasted with their American-made counterparts.

A Backwoods Home Anthology
The Sixth Year

* Here's a simple device to improve rough roads
* Backwoods firearms
* Make your own tool handles
* Home brew your own beer
* Make a heated seed germination flat
* Elderberries—the undiscovered fruit
* Wild turkey, goose, and venison for the holidays
* Tractor maintenance saves you more than money
* How to buy your first sheep
* Try a cement block garden
* Greens—delicious, nutritious, and easy to grow
* Raising goats can be profitable
* Making teas from wild plants and herbs
* Need a privy? Here's the right way to build one
* Enjoy zucchini all year
* Lunchbox cookies
* Start a home-based herb business
* Try these fresh ideas in your dairy
* Install rafters alone—the easy way
* This is one way to make applejack
* Build a homestead forge and fabricate your own hardware
* Soups for winter
* Moving to the wilderness—turning the dream to reality
* If you'd like to get started with chickens, here are the basics

Also, a weak dollar is making American crops even more attractive to foreign buyers and this added competition by the rest of the world to buy American farm products makes them more expensive for the American consumer.

Finally, if you haven't already guessed it, because the declining dollar will create more jobs *here*, it will actually make a recession less likely. And the economic stimulus package sponsored by the current Administration and Congress, much of which will be spent on American goods, is starting to look like a good idea.

Demand for grains from developing countries. Another of the drivers increasing food costs has been the world's growing population. More people means more mouths to feed. And this means more competition for *all* the world's resources.

As of May 2008 there are more than 6.6 billion people on this planet. At the current rate of growth, there will be nearly 9 billion by 2050. That's another 2.4 billion people eating in the next 42 years. Unless food production keeps stride with the population growth, expect the cost of food to increase.

But the cost of food will increase anyway, even if the world's population were to stabilize tomorrow, because of increasing demand for meat and dairy products among the emerging middle classes in Third World countries. This is going to put even greater demands on grain consumption and drive up its price. It takes 16 pounds of grain to grow one pound of edible beef, six pounds to produce a pound of pork, four to produce a pound of turkey, three for a pound of chicken, and two to produce a quart of milk from a cow. The emerging middle classes of India and China, the world's two most populous countries, are developing tastes for the same food stuffs we in this country have grown accustomed to: more

meat, more dairy, more bread—all the things we take for granted, they want *now*. Their per capita consumption of meat products has grown by 150 percent just since 1980.

Bad weather. Bad weather has destroyed or stunted crops, especially wheat crops, around the world including in the United States, Canada, Europe, Ukraine, China, Australia, and Argentina, all of them among the world's top grain-producers. In some places it was drought and in others it was flooding. In China, it was both. This has added to the world's shortages and has driven prices higher.

Low grain reserves. It should come as no surprise that stored grain supplies are now at a 30-year low. As these reserves run lower, and in some countries they are going to run out, the prices of *all* grains will be driven to new heights.

Already, the reserves in the United States are below what we would need to ride out a bad year of harvests. And that's worse news than you think because the United States accounts for fully two-thirds of the world's grain reserves. At this writing there is a 59-day reserve in this country, meaning, if we had a disastrous crop year, and we consumed the stored reserves at our current rate of consumption, we would have less than a two-month's supply. Long before that, there would be rationing and nosebleed prices.

So, is there possibly a bright side to any of this?

Yes. It's a good time to be a farmer, at least in this country and some others. Grain prices have rarely been higher than they are now. And it's a good time to be an entrepreneur because opportunities abound.

Are there solutions? Yes.

Solutions

I don't want to come across as a Pollyanna, but the fact is that there's a silver lining in this cloud that's descended on us. In fact, there are

several silver linings. There are not only opportunities for America, there are opportunities for individual Americans.

There's no way I can list all the possible opportunities or solutions to the problems confronting us today. In part, this is because some of them are going to come as a surprise to us.

But among the solutions, we already know about solar, wind, and few other alternative energy sources some are trying to develop. But there are even more that seem to have fallen out of the news and I'll try to list a few.

Other petroleum sources. Although environmentalists will scream if we try to develop them, there is still much oil in North America. Three possible sources that are noteworthy are:

• An estimated 5.6 to 16 billion barrels of oil locked up in the Arctic Wildlife Reserve.

• At least 44 billion barrels on the outer continental shelf of the United States along with 232 trillion cubic feet of natural gas.

• There is also a lot of oil in oil shale all over the West that, with the price of petroleum now well above $120 a barrel, we should consider the economics of.

On a national scale, there are alternatives to petroleum that will have the added benefit of spurring investment and creating new jobs. These don't just include the biofuels that are driving up grain prices right now, though they're a start.

Nuclear power. One of the criticisms of biofuels is the amount of energy required to convert grains into usable fuels and the conventional thinking is that this will require the burning of fossil fuels to do it. But there are other sources of energy that will not only power our homes and recharge the batteries in our electric cars, they will provide good clean power to make biofuels more economically. First and foremost is nuclear energy. Fifteen percent of the world's energy is currently produced by nuclear power. However, because of the politics of nuclear energy, no new nuclear power plants have come on line in the United States since the Watts Bar Nuclear Generating Station in Tennessee did in 1996.

Nuclear is safer than most people think. Sounds crazy? It's time to revisit it as a viable and endless source of clean energy.

Coal. Although there is a push to biofuels, there are other alternative fuels we can develop. In World War II, the Allies had so thoroughly bombed many of the oil fields Germany depended on that they resorted to making synthetic fuels out of coal. They ran their trucks and flew their planes on the stuff. We can, too.

This country has *one-third* of the world's known coal deposits. It's time we look into the possibility of turning to it.

Steam-driven cars. There are even viable alternatives to today's cars powered by the internal combustion engine, and I'm not talking about electric cars, though they are an alternative whose time is yet to come.

At one time steam-driven cars made up a large percentage of the vehicles on the road. I've watched for several years, since I wrote about steam-driven cars ("Steam-driven cars—cars from the past that would make ideal cars for the future," *BHM's Sixth Year Anthology*) for some of the automotive companies to reintroduce a steam-driven automobile. Steam engines are not limited to the fuels they use as internal combustion engines are. They can run on any number of fuels as long as they burn and generate heat.

It's worth noting that steam-driven vehicles have a number of advantages over the gasoline-driven types. Among them are a higher torque rating off the engine so transmissions are not required. They're also easier to make nonpolluting. And, if you

want power, it's a historical fact that all the early automobile speed records were set by steam-driven cars.

Mass transit is nice, but I sincerely doubt Americans really want to give up the independence a personal automobile or pickup truck affords. I know I don't. The steam engine could be revived in no time at all.

The long run

Everything we do, every solution we try, will have trade-offs and consequences some will find undesirable; everything will also have consequences, both desirable and undesirable, that will be unintended and unforeseen.

In a society and economy where entrepreneurs are unfettered (where their ideas are allowed to both succeed and fail on their own merits) we have a better chance at a good future.

In a society where special interests, politicians, and bureaucrats determine what happens, we have a better chance of the "dark ages" the doomsayers are predicting.

What's going to happen over the long run? We'll get by this. We've seen higher food prices than this before, though we've never seen petroleum prices this high.

But as food prices rise, food production will increase. It's the way free markets work. Food prices will stabilize, then they'll start to drop. However, they may never come back to what we've been used to for reasons I've given earlier, such as the burgeoning middle classes in countries such as India and China.

Even petroleum will come down eventually, but not until the dollar stabilizes, and probably not to the low prices we've enjoyed until recently.

Opportunities for you

What can you do to take advantage of the bad times that seem to be coming?

BHM has always been about self-reliance. What with the rise in food prices and the food shortages that may be around the corner, now's the time to stock up, to buy in bulk, and if you don't have a garden but have room for one, it's time to consider planting one.

If you have enough room to have your own flock of chickens for both meat and eggs, it's time to do that.

And if you have the means of producing your own food, you also have the potential for marketing it locally either on the roadside or in local markets. Δ

learn-as-you-go
pay-as-you-go

Building Eric's house

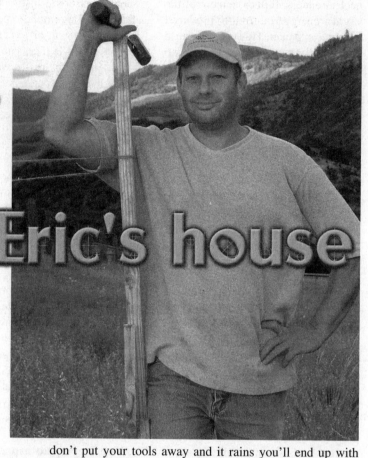

This is the first in a series of several articles documenting the building of a stud-frame house from start to finish by an amateur owner/builder, using the pay-as-you-go and learn-as-you-go process.

By Dorothy Ainsworth

Most young men (and many women) would love to design and build their own home if given half a chance. Recently I was able to rezone my property and give my own son, Eric, that half a chance (a house site on my 10 acres) and he went for it blocks, mortar, and wood!

Eric, by trade, is a classical pianist, composer, piano tuner/technician, and recording engineer, and has been busy constructing baroque fugues instead of houses. But because his parents are both builders, he has absorbed considerable knowledge and experience by helping out over the years.

Encouragement

Almost any adept do-it-yourselfer can learn to use the tools and follow the rules it takes to build a house. In spite of all the new technology, old adages still apply when doing the work yourself: Plan Ahead; Safety First; Measure Twice, Cut Once; Plumb, Level, and Square; and Practice Makes Perfect.

Anybody can learn to hammer a nail and apply the basic laws of physics to their building project, but common sense is mandatory. Gravity rules—if you are careless on a ladder, you'll end up on the ground. Rust never sleeps—if you

don't put your tools away and it rains you'll end up with iron oxide. If you don't make sure everything is plumb, level, and square as you go along, your house will be a three-dimensional parallelogram or trapezoid. But construction techniques are simple and straightforward. A house is not a spaceship.

You can actually build a house from reading how-to books. Every step of the process is written about and illustrated in great detail by experts in the building trades.

The *Unified Building Code* is explicit and can be referred to when you have a specific question about what is required in your county. There are no mysteries—all the information you will need to succeed is readily available.

So why wait? If you have an approved home site (meaning septic and zoning approval) get started! You'll save a ton of money by doing the labor yourself. I estimate from my own experience that 65-75% of the cost of a conventional house is *labor*. Eric figures he can build his 2000 square foot stud-frame house for $25/sq.ft.

Plans and permits

Eric's first step was to draw up his house plans, which included a site plan showing where his house would be in relation to all the other buildings on our 10 acres. Then he paid for a "site review" from the county. They determined his house had to be 100 feet from the property line, so he picked a nice spot and staked out the perimeter to get the south-facing orientation he wanted for solar efficiency and the best view. He wanted the kitchen on the east side to catch the first rays of sun in the morning, the entrance on the west where the road comes up, and the bedroom on the cooler north side. The well and the electricity were already available, so he was in luck, not having to spend about $10,000 for those two necessities. The site was approved and he was ready to proceed.

Eric and I made a deal. I would pay for the building permit and provide the septic system if he would build the house itself and pay for it as he went along. The land is in my living trust, so his building of a house increases the value of the property for us all (myself, Eric, and my daughter Cynthia). It's a family affair, and I advocate families sticking together and helping each other now that the median price of a modest house is more than $200,000.

Now the ball was in my court to install a septic system so I got busy and hired a septic consultant to draw up the plans to present to the county for an ETA system (evaporation/transpiration/absorption) based upon the size of the house and the soil conditions. Usually the county here mandates a sand-filter system because of the heavy clay soil, but we wanted a gravity-drain ETA system that wouldn't require an electric pump as a sand filter does. I persevered and jumped through a few hoops, and finally got an approved variance, and had the system installed for $10,000. When that was done, Eric went back to the county planning commission and turned in his hand-drawn plans for final approval. They passed and he got his basic building permit.

Preparation and foundation

He wasted no time having the basement scooped out of his sloping rocky

Septic tank and leach field for ETA septic system

site with heavy equipment, and the house pad leveled for his basement floor. Then the foundation contractor took over. His crew built forms, installed rebar, and poured the footings. Before they could pour the slab floor, Eric had to put one course of blocks all around the perimeter to contain the concrete. The next day the contractor had a gravel-shooter truck come up and shoot a layer of gravel on the pad area. Then the crew installed a grid of rebar under the floor-to-be and the concrete slab was

Foundation crew sets up the forms for the poured footings.

199

Crew pours the footings. The wider and deeper pad in the middle will be to support a center post under a beam spanning the basement ceiling.

poured and finished off—to the tune of another $10,000. That wiped out his savings.

Basement block walls

Over the next few months Eric paid as he could to have a journeyman mason come up intermittently and lay up his stepped basement walls in concrete blocks, so the foundation of his house would end up plumb, level, and square—guaranteed. He tried his own hand at laying a few blocks, but didn't want to take the time to learn that specialized skill when he could be making money by working at his own profession, and pay to have the block walls done.

For him, it was a wise decision. Professionally done masonry is not only a skill, but an art. Eric's mason, Ron Latour, dazzled us with his "poetry in motion" flair as he made hard labor look easy. Each 8"x8"x16" block weighs about 35 lbs. and he laid up 700 of them.

A rough estimate of the cost of the block walls was $5 a block, which included the block, mortar, and labor. Eric kept the cost down by hauling the blocks and mortar himself and having everything ready for the mason when he came up. (If the mason does it all, it's about $8/block.)

Note: If you are so inclined and have more time than money, you can do the block work yourself for only about $2 a block. It is doable, and you could save a bundle.

As soon as the basement walls were completed, Eric brushed on a layer of *Thoroseal* mixed with a bonding agent called *Acryl-60* to waterproof his walls. Then he installed foundation drain lines and rigid-foam insulation, and had the walls backfilled with a combo of dirt and decomposed granite.

His house site was on a rocky outcropping and the excavators could not dig any deeper than they did without blasting, so Eric opted for backfilling. The cost of the drain pipes and insulation came to about $500 and the fill dirt $1,000.

Electrical service

Eric's dad, Ron, a general contractor in California, came up last fall to help him wire in his temporary electrical box at the building site. The total cost of the box, wire, conduit, and outlets came to about $300. Now he was in business—he could use power tools to build with and have classical music to work to. Things were lookin' up.

All the footings poured in Eric's "stepped" foundation

Electrical note: When the foundation crew installed all the ½" rebar, they also attached a $5/8$" dia. vertical length of rebar to the horizontal rebar in the footings. This important piece acts as a whole-house grounding rod for the electrical panel. Ron connected a #4 copper ground wire from this rebar to the electrical box. If this step is missed when your foundation is poured, you'll have to pound an 8-foot copper-clad ground rod down into the ground near your foundation with a sledge hammer or a rented ground rod driver. Not fun.

Progress overview

Eric worked all winter and saved enough money to buy the materials for the basement framing ($3600). The load was delivered March 3rd and his dad came up again from California to help with the 2x6 stud-framed pony walls, BCI floor joists, and $1^1/8$" tongue and groove plywood floor. It was very important that this step in the construction was also done right because a plumb, level, and square wood foundation on top of the plumb, level, and square masonry foundation determined how geometrically perfect his house would be from here on up. I got in the act too, laying down beads of glue on the joists with a caulking gun before each of the 46 sheets of plywood were nailed down using a nail gun. We were armed and dangerous.

The whole experience was a dream come true for a 40-ish young man who could now see the 3-dimensional results of his investment. He passed his under-floor structural inspection with flying colors.

Now Eric is on his own (until he needs help erecting his 5"x18"x30' ridge beam). He ordered his wall-framing lumber when prices were down, just hours before they started to creep up. 2x6s were at an all time low of 28 cents a linear foot in the winter of 2008. He had 3700 linear feet of 2x6s delivered for only $1050.

Crew pours the slab floor. Concrete is pumped via the hose.

March 21 was a beautiful day to remember: Bach's Birthday, the second day of spring, and a huge pile of lumber delivered that would keep him busy framing for the next three months of spring. As soon as his walls are complete, he'll order his ridge beam and rafters, and put the roof on his house during the summer months.

Please note: Build now! Chances are that lumber prices will remain fairly low during the economic squeeze we seem to be in.

No sooner had the lumber been delivered than rain was ominous. We hurriedly caulked the plywood seams and painted the floor with 10 gallons of exterior reject paint from the hardware store he bought cheap ($3/gal-

Mason Ron Latour lays up 700 blocks in Eric's stepped-wall basement.

Eric's block wall foundation ready for vertical rebar to be put in.

Grout is pumped in via a hose from the cement truck. Mason Ron Latour smooths the top of the wall. He installed the J-bolts before it set up.

lon) and mixed all together. We covered the floor and the new lumber with huge tarps tied down to weather the spring storms that were forecasted to roll in one after the other. The covered basement is a safe and dry place for all his tools.

Eric's next step is to lay out his wall framing by snapping chalk lines on the painted floor—lines that correlate exactly to his floor plan on paper—then build his walls. He'll build the stud-frame walls on the floor from 2"x6" lumber, sheath them with 4'x 8'x⅝" OSB while they are still down to keep them square, and raise them into place one at a time with help, or by himself with 'wall jacks.' Note: OSB (Oriented Strand Board) is only about $10/sheet and is commonly used now instead of plywood, and meets code.

Eric's south-facing 2000 sq.ft. house-to-be is 42'x24' with an 18'x16' bedroom wing off the north side, and a 30'x24' basement. He figures he can build it for $50,000 (maybe less) over a 4-year period, and it's already a third done.

Here's how we did the actual work and a few tips and techniques I can pass along.

How to build pony walls

First of all, the pony walls wouldn't have been necessary if Eric could have had the mason build the block walls eight feet high to begin with. But here was the catch: Code dictates that you can only fill the voids in a block wall 4-feet high or less in one pour. Too much concrete weight and pressure can blow out an 8-foot wall of empty blocks being filled. Not only that, trapped air may keep some of the long vertical voids from filling at all.

The concrete had to be pumped in via a hose, which required a concrete truck, a separate pumping truck, and two crews to work together during the pour—both paid separately. So Eric had the mason do "stepped walls" on his hilly site, with no wall higher than 4-feet, so he'd only have to pay for all that pumping equipment once.

So to get all the basement walls up to 8-feet, he built up the differences in height with "pony walls." Pony walls have advantages though—they are made from wood framing (less expensive) and you can easily frame windows in wherever you want, to allow light and ventilation into the basement.

Please note: If you aren't planning a basement with a slab floor, you can simply have footings and stem-walls poured and start your 8-foot walls from that level, using the same techniques as building the pony walls. However, you will have to provide a crawl space for plumbing under your house. The floor joists will have to be a certain distance from the dirt, and a vapor barrier put down first (ie., 6-mm polyethelene plastic sheeting). Ask your county building dept. what clearance is required. Your stem-wall/footing combination may be formed up and poured at the same time (monolithic-style) or you can build a short block wall on top of your footings later to provide this under-floor clearance. As long as you put in the vertical rebar in advance to tie the block stem-walls to the footings, you'll be fine. Keep in mind that every weight-bearing wall in your house has to have support under it—not just the perimeter.

Sill plates and anchor bolts

Pressure-treated 2x6s are required wherever the bottom horizontal plates of a wall (called sill plates) come in contact with concrete footings, stem-walls, or blocks. Concrete can hold moisture and can rot regular untreated wood over time. When stem walls or piers are poured, or concrete blocks are filled, and before the concrete sets up, a ½" diameter by 12" long J-bolt is inserted into the concrete every 3-6 feet (not more than 6' apart for a one

story house, or 4-feet apart for a 2-story house). They should be set in about 3" from the outside edge of the wall-to-be, sticking up about 2½" and as plumb as possible.

This threaded part sticking up will be accepting the sill plate, which will be drilled with holes wherever there's a J-bolt and fastened down securely with big square washers and nuts. If a J-bolt is not plumb but the concrete is hardened, screw a nut onto the first few threads to protect it and whack it straight with a hammer.

Please note: If you need to install a few more J-bolts here and there after the fact, just drill the holes with a ½" diameter concrete drill bit, and pound in 7"-10" long ½" diameter concrete anchor bolts made for that purpose. Code requires a anchor bolt no more than 12" from the end of any given sill plate. It's hard to judge where the ends will end up when you are initially setting your J-bolts into the wet concrete, but adding more as needed is not as tough as it sounds.

The building code now requires special earthquake and tornado protection in the form of stabilizing brackets called "hold-downs" on short walls near doorways. The specialized anchor bolts to secure those brackets have to be wired in place *before* the pour so the inspector can see them *before* the pour. Please note: These brackets are not to be confused with "hurricane ties" for rafters.

Marking the holes to be drilled in your sill plate is simple. Lay your pre-cut-to-length sill plate on the top of the concrete wall, line up the edge parallel with the wall, and using a combination square against the edge and the bolt, mark 2 lines, one on each side of the bolt. Then measure in from the outside edge of the plate to the bolt and make a mark. That mark will be where you put the inside edge of your ⅝" drill bit and drill the hole. Do this all along your sill plate. When you put the plate over the bolts, they should go right in the holes. There's a little wiggle room for adjustment by drilling a ⅝" hole for a ½" bolt.

Laying out the walls

After all the sill plates are "tried on" for accurate hole placement, pull them back off, and cut your first top

The gravity-sloped drainage pipes (with clean-outs) that run all around the footings will help protect the foundation from moisture. The cloth "sock" keeps debris from plugging the holes in the pipes. Gravel and filter cloth and then dirt will cover them.

Eric marks the pressure-treated sill plate to locate exactly where the hole should be drilled for the J-bolt to stick through.

plates exactly the same lengths as the sill plates for each wall. Lay each pair down side by side with the ends exactly lined up (flush), and mark a line on both boards at the same time with your carpenter's square at 15¼" increments, and mark an X beside the line.

Your vertical studs will be spaced 16" apart on center, meaning the 16" mark will be in the center of the 1½" thick stud. That's why you deduct ¾" off of 16" and make your guide lines at 15¼" and Xs past those lines for proper placement of your studs. If you made your line at 16 inches it would be covered up by the stud, so the line at 15¼" and the X to the side of it tells you exactly where to put the stud. Double check your 4-foot and 8-foot measurements to make sure the edges of your 4'x8' sheathing panels will indeed come together in the mid-

dle of a stud, so they can be fastened down.

When all your sill plates and top plates are marked, then measure and cut the vertical studs to length, taking into consideration (deducting) the sill plate and the double top plate thicknesses (totaling 4.5" if you are using standard lumber).

Build your wall frames on the floor with 16d nails and lift them onto the concrete wall and place them over the J-bolts sticking up and fasten the sill plates down with the aforementioned washers and nuts.

If you are working by yourself, you can fasten down the sill plate first, then toenail a stud onto each end of it, then run the TOP plate across the span and nail it down to both studs as well. Then toenail all the rest of the studs in, plumbing them as you go along. Ron and Eric used this method.

It's a good idea to temporarily cross-brace the walls with 1"x4"s or metal strapping to keep them square either before or after they are in place.

Please note: Be sure to apply a zig-zagged bead of H/D construction adhesive on top of the concrete wall before placing the stud-frame wall on it. The glue will help the J-bolts do their job in keeping your house from sliding off its foundation in case of an earthquake, tornado, or hurricane.

If you don't want to mess with glue, and you don't worry about earth-quakes, you might want to use sill-seal under the sill plates for energy efficiency. It's a thin closed-cell poly-ethelene gasket that comes in rolls of various widths for ease in installation. It will fill the slightly irregular gaps between the concrete and the sill plate. Eric chose to glue down his sill plates 'cause there will be a lot of shakin' goin' on when he plays Beethoven on the 9-foot grand!

When all the walls are in their proper position of alignment, put the second top plate on, overlapping the corners alternately to tie the walls together.

Eric and Ron used a spring-brace twice and a come-along once and some other methods of persuasion to coax the walls into perfect alignment as one wall was secured to another.

Installing floor joists and rim joists

Near-perfect framing insured that the BCI floor joists laid level across the tops of the basement walls and lined up squarely in a row at the other end. The ends were then capped off with a true one-inch by 12" plywood board on edge all around the perimeter called a *Versa Rim*.

If you don't use BCI joists, but standard 2x12s instead, your rim joists will also be 2x12s. To determine the joist length, deduct the thickness of the rim joists that will be nailed across the ends. In Eric's case he cut the joists 2" short to accommodate a true 1" rim joist across at each end. If you use 2x12s, cut 3" off because each board is 1½" thick.

Eric chose BCI joists (they look like a capital I) because they are factory engineered to accommodate any span you need, and have a wider surface (called a rail) to nail your flooring or roofing to. They stay straight (no crowns or dips), and are claimed to insure a squeak-free floor because they don't shrink after they are installed like regular lumber can.

Dimensional lumber is strong and nice to work with if it's straight and clear and kiln dried, but not if it's bowed, cupped, twisted, or green and wet, and full of knots. Eric is using green lumber for his wall framing though because it's cheaper. It's DF (Douglas Fir) Graded #2 Better and allowed by code. He'll keep it stickered and covered until its immediate use, and work with it by using methods of forceful persuasion whenever he has to. Slight shrinkage in width of vertical wall studs is not as critical as horizontal floor joists shrinking away from their "resting spot" in the joist hanger seat (squeak, squeak). There are methods to fix that problem, but prevention is the best one!

Important tip: The lumber yard we buy from (and most lumber companies) helped us determine what size beam we needed to free-span the basement ceiling and the size of the ridge beam to use for the roof. The company they ordered our BCI joists and *Versa-Beams* from has a computer program that prints out the engineered data sheet you can use to show the county when you submit your plans. The sheet illustrates your floor and roof layout, and lists how many joists and brackets to order. It's a great service!

Eric's plans called for a 6"x12"x24-foot *Versa-Beam* to span across his basement ceiling (basement ceiling is also the house floor). It was to be supported in the middle with an upright post bolted to the slab floor. The floor

was poured with an extra thick footing to take the weight. He had a local welder make a steel post out of square tubing ($100).

But before it was secured in place, they laid the Versa-Beam on its side across the span and Ron marked it along its length 16" on center, where the BCI joist hangers would be fastened on. Then Eric nailed them onto both sides of the beam with special joist hanger nails (thick 1.5" *Teco* nails that fill the bracket holes snugly).

Next they turned the *Versa-Beam* upright and placed it exactly where it belonged, secured the post underneath, and fastened its base to the

concrete floor with concrete anchor bolts.

Then one at a time they put the BCI joists on. Eric put a bead of construction adhesive in each joist hanger bracket as he went along and nailed the joists to the hangers with more Teco nails.

When that was done, Eric put rows of BCI blocking between the joists in the long free-spans to stabilize them and keep them evenly apart so the sheets of plywood would meet squarely at the center of each joist. (See code book for required blocking.) While Eric was doing the blocking, Ron nailed on the Versa-Rims all around the perimeter of the house.

Ron and Eric build a pony wall as a team. Ron plumbs the stud with his level, and Eric nails the top plate to it as they go along.

Installing the plywood floor

Everything turned out beautifully level and square and ready for the plywood flooring to go on. Eric chose $1^1/_8$" T&G plywood for his subfloor so it would support his 9-foot grand piano—with no deflection. Luckily, the cost of plywood was down to $30/sheet—a bargain for thick T&G premium plywood. Just a year before I had purchased merely ¾" plywood for shelving and it was $35/sheet.

As a team we put the plywood on, staggering the joints, and gluing them down to the joists. 'Staggering the joints' means if you start the first row with a full sheet, start the second row with a half sheet. We used bar-clamps when the plywood tongue was reluctant to go into the groove, and sometimes had to whack the leading edge with a 5-lb. hammer. Of course Eric used a protective board cut from a T&G scrap to pound on. The guys nailed the plywood down with the nail gun and 8d gripper nails at 6" around the edges and 12" in the field (meaning everywhere else).

Nails are required by code because they bend under stress instead of snapping off like a brittle screw can. Screws have great holding power but very little shear strength so nails must be used for all structural framing. Using an air-powered nail gun is so much faster than hammering by hand or putting screws in that it's like the difference between loading a flintlock rifle and using a machine gun. When time is money, it's the only way to go.

The drawback is that it's harder to correct a mistake; you can't just unscrew your work. But you can use a Sawzall and cut the errant nail off, and you can use screws when there won't be any shear forces on the structure (like interior sheetrock, etc.). For general framing we used 16d vinyl-coated nails (sinkers). The building code tells you what size nail to use for each job and the required spacing around the perimeter and in the field. You can find that info under the heading *"Nailing Schedule"* in the code book.

Summary and costs

The entire pony wall and floor installation process took us a week and cost about $3,800 for materials, including nails and hardware. So far

Eric has invested approximately $25,000 in his house, and that includes his wall framing—already paid for and sitting there waiting to be used. He estimates that his ridge-beam, rafters, sheathing for the walls and roof, and Tivek wrap or paint to weather-proof the house for winter, will come to another $5,000. Without a basement his house would cost $40,000 to build ($20/sq.ft.) The extra excavation, slab, block laying, pony walls, drainage, insulation, and backfilling added about $10,000 onto his total.

Closing thoughts

If you already have your land, and your utilities and septic are in, you too can build a very nice house for $40,000 or less.

There is no need to go into debt for $200,000 or more to have a home. If you don't have any of the above, I advise you to spend your money for the piece of property you are in love with (location, location, location), then build your house using the pay-as-you-go method.

I bought my 10 acres for $40,000 in 1981, and have built all my unconventional log structures for only $15/sq.ft. by doing the labor myself, but it was slow going.

It's not feasible for me to pay someone $25-$75 an hour for labor when I only make $9/hr. as a prep cook. I took the dirt road instead of the freeway, and Eric is doing the same—and enjoying the scenery while he's at it. We highly recommend it.

Disclaimer: We're not experts and we are learning as we go. If you have any specific construction questions and can't find the answers in the code book, call your county building department helpline or ask your inspector.

"They" say there is no such thing as a dumb question, but they haven't heard some of mine. Δ

Eric guides a 30-foot BCI joist into its joist hanger bracket making sure it is seated in tightly. His dad is at the other end.

Ayoob on Firearms

Heirloom guns

By Massad Ayoob

It's Independence Day, 2007, and we're "shooting off fireworks" in one of the more traditional ways for country folks: with guns. Not blasting bullets into the air or anything, but firing into appropriate backstops, seeking the accuracy that's built into fine American firearms. Guns make you focus, make you try to do the best you can do. It's one of the many ways they teach and reinforce life lessons.

The guns I'm using today are all heirlooms. Each has been with me a long time. Firearms have a way of being passed down generation to generation in this country. They're the ultimate "durable goods." After all, you can't just throw them away. I don't know anyone who will pull the meat for this evening's barbecue out of an icebox that belonged to their great-great grandmother, but all over the country, people are celebrating the Fourth of July by firing guns they inherited from their great-great grandfather.

That gunfire sings a song of the independence we celebrate today. It is the very sound of freedom.

And doing it with guns that carry memories of cherished people adds nuances to the song.

The Springfield .22 rifle

This was the first gun I ever fired. One of my earliest memories is my dad holding it in the palm of one hand, at its balance point just ahead of the trigger guard, as I sort of climbed over the stock (I was too small to shoulder it) and tried to line up the front sight with the rear as I squeezed the trigger. To this day, the smell of .22 rimfire ammunition being discharged will flash me back to that memory. Dad told me I was four years old when he started doing that.

The rifle was actually my older sister's. Dad had bought it for her shortly after World War II, when she was just a little tyke herself. Elizabeth never felt much need to shoot anything bigger, but she was awfully good with that semiautomatic .22.

It's kind of a generic gun. It's marked "Springfield Model 87A," but is identical to the more common Stevens 87, and to a couple of .22s sold under the Savage and Fox brands, all under the aegis of Savage Arms. It is a very simple mechanism—this rifle was the first firearm I ever totally disassembled, some time early in grade school, and more important was able to get back together—and it runs as a semiautomatic with .22 Long Rifle ammo. With less expensive (back then) Shorts and Longs, the bolt handle could be pushed in to lock the mechanism, allowing it to work like a quasi bolt-action rifle with ammo too feeble to activate the self-loading mechanism. I remember that we had to get it downright filthy before it would jam.

A favorite shooting spot was at a sandy curve in the Merrimac River, near the Hannah Dustin Monument. Ms. Dustin was a heroine in Colonial days who escaped kidnapping Indians who had murdered her baby. She killed the Indians with a hatchet in the middle of the night, then took their canoe and paddled home. It was a fitting place to celebrate the legacy of citizens with weapons, and it was a

Massad Ayoob with the first gun he ever fired, more meaningful because it belonged to his late sister.

popular plinker's destination back then.

We lost Elizabeth to Hodgkins' Disease when she was only 26. I have few mementoes to remember her by. There are her records, the old 45 and 78 RPM platters of the popular Fifties songs we now call "Golden Oldies." But those songs, loud and brassy and sometimes maudlin, aren't really like her. Her rifle reminds me of her more. Its stock is almost blond in color, common on those models, and Elizabeth was a natural blonde. But, much more, it reminds me of her in manner. Mostly fun, but with a serious side. Always reliable. Responsibility mixed in with the fun.

Pets, they say, reflect the personalities of their owners. The same, I've come increasingly to believe, is true of people's automobiles and firearms.

The Winchester '94

My dad owned this old gun before I was born, and gave it to me when I was about nine as my first deer rifle. With a 26-inch barrel, it was damn near as tall as I was when it rested on its 19th century steel crescent butt-plate. At that time our next-door neighbor was a big, strapping WWII vet named Red LeBrun who had car-

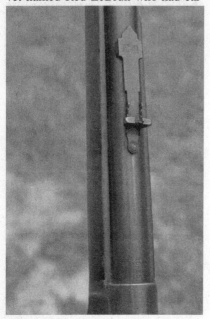

The meticulously crafted Marble gunsight matches the rest of the antique Model 1894 in its classic workmanship. ".38-55" on barrel indicates 0/38" diameter bullet, 55 grains of black powder.

ried a Browning Automatic Rifle into combat overseas. One evening, I sat in as he and Dad talked guns and shared a beer, and they figured out that the long Winchester's heft was about the same for my body weight as the massive BAR had been for Red's. Made me kinda proud that I was able to lug it through the woods, but I did start thinking about then of getting something shorter and lighter.

The ancient rifle was chambered for the .38-55 Winchester cartridge, which dated back to the 1880s, when it established a reputation for superb accuracy in single shot Ballard match rifles of the day. It was among the first cartridges for which Winchester chambered its super-popular Model 1894 lever action rifle. The Model 94's defining cartridge, the one that made it America's favorite deer rifle, was the .30-30 that came along a year later. The .30-30 was developed expressly for modern smokeless gunpowder, while the .38-55 was originally a black powder round. Black powder is proportionally bulkier, which accounts for the round's long cartridge case relative to its power level. It threw a massive 255-grain bullet at modest velocity, and earned a good reputation for dropping deer and black bear.

My father left us at age 88. This gun reminds me of him very much, and not just because I associate it with

him. He and it were both slim and hard, durable and long-lived, honest and reliable. I had stopped hunting with the .38-55 in my early teens, having gratefully replaced it with a light, slick little Marlin Model 336SC in caliber .35 Remington. Ever since, the Winchester has been a keepsake, a reminder of a man whose approach to fatherhood was to give his son adult responsibilities to live up to. It was a model of parenting when it became my turn to be a dad, and the Winchester is a reminder of all of that, a reminder in meticulously crafted, time-darkened steel and wood.

Four shotguns

I have five 12-gauge shotguns that belonged to my father, three of which I inherited upon his passing and one of which he gave me early. I was a kid in elementary school when the Eastern Arms single-barrel became my very first gun of my own. In retrospect, this was Dad's one misstep in my firearms education. A 12-gauge shotgun, particularly a light single barrel, is not the best choice for small human beings just starting out in marksmanship. The recoil can literally knock a kid on his butt. How do I know this, you ask? Trust me. I know this.

I can't remember the last time I fired this old beast. I know it's going to have a nasty kick, and I feel no need to discharge it now. I keep it for what it represents, a father who trusted his little boy with adult responsibility. That's enough.

Another is a double barrel "hammerless" shotgun by Crescent Arms. Crescent, like Eastern, was one of those run-of-the-mill brands. They made working class guns, not fine works of art for wealthy gentleman farmers and skeet shooters. It had 26" barrels, one bored with an open choke for the close birds, the other with a modified choke that clustered the shot a little tighter if you needed to fire a

"Model of 1894" in period lettering on receiver tang sets off the classic lines of the heirloom rifle.

second time at a bird that was flying away from you.

My father taught me a lesson with that gun when I was very small. I was tagging along with him bird hunting, and mentioned with a child's ignorance that I had seen a *Three Stooges* short at the Saturday matinee the day before. You know, one of those where the farmer or someone shoots the *Stooges* in the butt with a shotgun, and they just jump a little and go "Woo woo woo woo!"

Dad's face became grim. "Let me show you something," he said, and pointed out a solid birch sapling near the trail. Firing from the hip, he blasted it with one barrel. I stared in awe at the damage. He unleashed the second shell, and the slim tree toppled, literally cut in half by the swarm of birdshot.

It was a lasting lesson in the power and lethality of firearms, and the importance of adults educating children to ignore what they see about guns in the entertainment media. After I grew up, I would see what "mere birdshot" could do to human bodies. Hideous, avulsive injuries. "Rat-hole wounds," the pathologists call them when they are inflicted at close range.

That double barrel shotgun was the one my father used as a primary home defense weapon. He kept it by his bed, unloaded and "broken" open, with several 12-gauge double-ought buckshot shells in a brass tray on his dresser. If he needed it, he could quickly grab it and load it to "repel boarders." Handguns were something he kept at his jewelry store, or locked in his car when he came in the house if he had carried one home that night. He didn't believe they belonged in the house until his youngest, a certain little boy fascinated with handguns, had handguns of his own. (That would come later, and by the time I was twelve, he had approved of my keeping a Colt .45 automatic in the drawer of my bedroom desk, so long as I

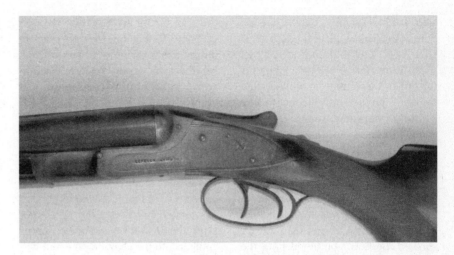

"Lefever" on the receiver says it all. Too old and weak to shoot, due to its Damascus barrel, it retains an honored place in the gun rack like a cherished elder in retirement.

Shown with action "broken" open, Crescent Arms double barrel 12-gauge was used by author's dad for hunting and home protection. Collector value: negligible. Sentimental value: priceless.

loaded only the magazine and not the chamber. Long guns, however, hung in their rack in my bedroom earlier than that, always unloaded.) Once again, the old double was teaching lessons of responsibility, in this case, a parent's responsibility to protect the household.

My dad had another 12-gauge double, a 19th Century Lefever. This was a fine and pricey weapon, the Cadillac of double barrel shotguns in its time. Unfortunately, it had Damascus barrels. The twisted steel

was handsome, but it was known to degrade over time, and I learned at an early age to fire such guns only with mild black powder loads. This gun was more a wall-hanger than anything else, and I have no intention of firing it today. Dad liked it because he was a watchmaker at heart, and loved the pure quality of the Lefever. The buttstock and fore-end were so perfectly fitted to the receiver and the twin barrels that they seemed to have grown together. The Lefever was and is a celebration of American workmanship. It reminds me of why there are gun collectors who never fire their guns, who cherish them strictly as *objets d'art*. It was reason enough for my father to own that superbly crafted weapon, and that, plus the fact that he himself cherished it, are reasons enough for me to keep it.

Finally, there were a pair of Winchester pump guns. They were the old 1897 models with exposed hammers. Dad had come by them both long before I was born. Both had glassy smooth actions. My father showed me how you could hold the trigger back and just rack the action,

the gun firing by itself at a rapid cadence. To this day, the 110-year old design can be fired faster for this reason than any of my modern, customized, "tacti-cool" Remington 870 combat pump guns that I use for police and self-defense training. The Winchester "hammerless" Model 12 that superseded the '97, and the Ithaca Model 37, both shared this "slam-fire" feature. Some consider it dangerous, in that if a nervous shooter has locked his finger on the trigger after the last shot and then pumps another into the chamber, the gun will go off, seemingly by itself. Still, in

hands that know what they're doing, it makes for some impressive trick shooting demonstrations.

One of the '97s was a standard field grade with thirty-inch barrel, and the tight full choke that was common to such long barrels in the old days. This kept the shot pattern together and allowed it to reach out farther, making it a favorite of waterfowl hunters. It was the gun my dad would take from the gun rack on the rare occasions when he went duck hunting.

The other '97 had a wide-open choke for closer range shooting, and the shorter and handier 26" barrel that was industry standard for such chokes back then. It would have been suitable for upland bird hunting, but no one in our family ever used it for that. The Crescent double barrel was for that. No, this gun lived in the back room of his jewelry store, loaded with double-ought buckshot. And the lesson that gun taught was that while all guns could be lethal and had to be respected as such, there were some that were meant for responsible recreation, and some, for serious business.

"Mark's gun," a superb example of Smith & Wesson's classic Target .45 revolver. Half moon clips were developed in WWI to allow the revolver to use "rimless" .45 automatic ammo.

Mark's revolver

The guns already mentioned, my father's and sister's, are cherished memories from a nuclear family of mom and dad, sister and brother, of which I alone remain. There is one more I will fire today, for memory's sake, and this one came from a friend.

The revolver is one that collectors of modern Smith & Wessons would drool over. It is in mint condition, with the deep, rich blue finish of Olde American craftsmanship, and exquisitely checkered stocks made of exotic Goncala Alves wood. It is the classic 1955 Target model, later known as the Model 25, and one of a rare and collectible few mismarked "1950 Target" on the barrel at the factory. It is an extremely smooth and accurate double action .45.

It is a legacy from a friend. Mark was in his late twenties when we lost

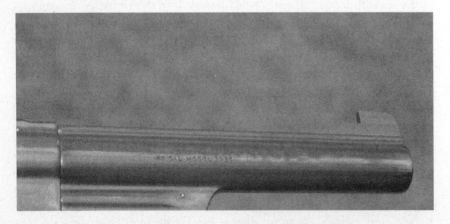

Mark's revolver is a rare factory mismark. It's a 1955 Target Model, but its characteristic heavy barrel is mismarked as a 1950 Target, which actually had a slimmer barrel profile.

him, a bright young guy with a great sense of humor and a natural gift for teaching firearms. He had become one of my protégés. Then he fell head over heels for a beautiful woman who dumped him in the cruelest way possible.

Mark's mom, who had a very strong background in psychology, called me to say that he had radically changed his appearance, quit a job he loved and was great at, and had disappeared. I knew what that meant. I got hold of him through sources and told him frankly that I was afraid for him. "I know what you're thinking," he told me. "Departure ritual. Mas, I'm not departing life, I'm just changing the life I've been living." Hell, he had heard me many times give the lecture on recognizing suicidal ideation symptoms. Then he spoke of his Smith & Wesson, which he knew I admired and had once offered to buy, and said he wanted to give it to me. The red flag was up. The giving away of cherished possessions is the most extreme warning signal that an indi-

vidual is preparing to end his life. I told him no, he would bring that gun to the Second Chance shoot with me in a few months, and we would shoot it together there in the revolver matches. He promised me it would be so.

And then, a few days later, the gun arrived at my door in a neat little UPS package from Mark.

His mom and I raced to reach him. We couldn't. On a dark night in Miami a few days later when everything became too much, Mark ended his life. I flew to Miami, claimed his remains, and brought him home to his mom. She told me later that she wanted me to keep the revolver to remember him by. It certainly performs *that* function.

I have done half a dozen suicide interventions in my life. All of them worked except Mark's. I had been trained to do it, and the training held. But Mark had been through the same training, and no technique works on someone who knows it's coming and doesn't want it to work.

I am reminded of that lesson every time I take Mark's revolver out of my safe, and am reminded of the fact that each of us can be our own worst enemy, the enemy that is always inside our own lines, in our most vulnerable places. And, finally, Mark's legacy revolver reminds me that sometimes the lessons of our failures are the ones we learn most deeply, because the price we paid for the learning was so terribly, terribly high.

When the echoes fade

The gunfire will stop by nine o'clock tonight, ending the song of freedom that our arms put forth. The meaning of the celebration will last much longer. So will the meaning of the heirloom guns, the ones that came to us from our cherished dead. Symbols and memories, lessons and legacies. All are timeless, and perhaps it is fitting that they should be embodied in things as long lasting as blue steel gun barrels and fine walnut gunstocks. Δ

A Backwoods Home Anthology
The Sixth Year

❋ Here's a simple device to improve rough roads
❋ Backwoods firearms
❋ Make your own tool handles
❋ Make a heated seed germination flat
❋ Elderberries—the undiscovered fruit
❋ Wild turkey, goose, and venison for the holidays
❋ How to buy your first sheep
❋ Try a cement block garden
❋ Raising goats can be profitable
❋ Making teas from wild plants and herbs
❋ Need a privy? Here's the right way to build one

❋ Enjoy zucchini all year
❋ Try these fresh ideas in your dairy
❋ Install rafters alone—the easy way
❋ Want to save fuel and firewood? Try square-split firewood
❋ This is one way to make applejack
❋ Build a homestead forge and fabricate your own hardware
❋ Soups for winter
❋ Moving to the wilderness—turning the dream to reality
❋ If you'd like to get started with chickens, here are the basics
❋ Home brew your own beer

Whole grain breads baked at home

Bread baking is an ancient craft that some food historians believe reaches back over 15,000 years to the time when the last Ice Age was losing its grip on the earth, and soil that had been frozen hard for as many as 1000 centuries began to soften. Accounts by some paleontologists, depicting this time of receding ice sheets and warming climate, describe a wide variety of wild grasses and other edible plants that began to flourish. It didn't take long for the hunter-gatherers of this time to discover that the seeds of these wild grasses were a valuable food source. They used mortars and mills hollowed out of rock to crush the wild grass seeds and mix them with water to make a crude, dense porridge which, by the way, was as nourishing as the cooked breads to follow.

The wonders of fire made it possible to cook this porridge into the first unleavened breads. Later, it was discovered that when porridge was set aside for a few days; it would ferment and become puffed up with gases. When the paste was cooked over an open fire, or on a hot stone, it became softer, lighter, and tasted better.

Later, the Egyptians made the connection between this leavening action in bread dough and the fermentation of beer. They discovered that barm, the brownish scum that forms on top of fermenting beer, could be used to leaven bread or start a new batch of brew. The long road to Wonder Bread and Bud Light had begun.

It's worth noting that Wonder Bread introduced sliced bread into the American market in 1930. It did not take long before this pillow-soft bread, made with highly refined bleached and bromated flour, and treated with a variety of softeners and preservatives, dominated the market. But these breads are nutritionally inferior to breads made with whole grain flours.

A loaf of real bread can be made with the simplest imaginable ingredients: flour, yeast, salt, water, heat, and time. I list time as one of the basic ingredients because grain molecules need time to release their flavor and texture-producing components.

The reason commercial bakeries, like the people who make Wonder Bread, replace time with stabilizers, dough softeners, preservatives, and a long list of other chemicals, is cost. By replacing the healthful components with chemicals, production costs are minimized.

However, making a great loaf of bread is not at all complicated. The simplicity of this process, and benefits that can result from your efforts is, in my opinion, why bread has long been considered the "Staff Of Life." Unfortunately, modern technology has transformed this once healthful food into a tasteless, artificially inflated ball of starch substantially depleted of vital nutrients. The FDA has approved 30 chemicals for addition to bread. If you pick up a loaf of commercial bread in your local market and read the label you will find additives like benzoyl peroxide (a chemical used in acne creams), calcium chloride, ammonium chloride, potassium bromate, and a host of other additives, many with unpronounceable names. What is known about all of these chemicals is that they bleach the flour and extend the shelf life of

Richard Blunt

commercial breads. What is not known is their long-term toxic effects on humans.

Modern technology starts the nutritional depletion of the grain at the first processing step—grinding the grain. Modern mills crush the grain with high-speed rollers that run at temperatures of nearly 400 degrees. Milling at these temperatures destroys many of the vitamins in the grain. Nutritionists, dietitians, and other health care professionals have been telling us for years that baked goods made with whole grains are healthier than those baked with highly refined flour.

When you are shopping for a good loaf of bread the term "whole wheat" is constantly being tossed at you. Much of this is deceptive marketing by commercial bread manufacturers. The term "whole wheat" on a loaf of commercial bread implies that the loaf is a healthful alternative to white bread. However, most loaves labeled "whole wheat" are the same old white bread with burnt sugar added, and listed on the label as "caramel." (By the way, if it says "100% whole wheat," it's a much better alternative.) As a society we have been eating these commercial breads for so long that many of us have forgotten what real bread tastes like.

Quality whole grain bread is a heavier denser loaf than bread made with highly refined flour and chemical leaveners. It is also more expensive because you are paying for the extra grain and labor time that it takes to produce this bread. Unfortunately, sky rocketing prices for grains of all kinds are making it more difficult for many to afford a loaf of *real* bread.

What is the solution to this growing dilemma? Ideally, you could buy a grain mill and sacks of whole grain, grind this grain into flour, and quickly bake it into your bread of choice. If grain products continue to increase in price and their availability continues to shrink the way they are today, this may be the most cost-effective solution to your problem.

As ambitious as this sounds, it is possible, and not at all difficult. For years I made my own beer and ale by grinding whole grain malted barley to prepare it for mashing. The tool that made this possible was a small, inexpensive hand-cranked grain mill. I paid about $25, in 1980s dollars, for the package. After checking my old brewing records, this small mill produced enough cracked barley for 120 24-bottle cases of brew. If I were grinding wheat for bread I could produce enough whole grain flour to make about 15 loaves of bread at each grinding session.

I will discuss the use of the grain mill in more detail in the article that will follow this one. The mills on the market today are far more efficient and easier to use than the one that I had. I am ordering one of these new generation mills, and I will be using it to process whole grains for use in upcoming recipes.

Wheat artisan bread

But, we must start from the beginning. First things first, as my old mentor Chef Sully would frequently tell me. In this article I am going to review some of the essentials of baking bread. Even if you consider yourself a seasoned baker, I can assure you that there is something to learn here. The recipes I will share with you use many of the same techniques used by professional bakers from around the world.

As home bakers we have limitations on space, supplies, and equipment. Fortunately, some of the world's most knowledgeable master bakers have revised successful bread baking techniques used in their shops and made them available to home baking enthusiasts. As a result, 100% whole grain breads can be made at home, using widely available ingredients and equipment found in most home kitchens. These breads are a far cry from the brick-like, leathery-crusted, spongy, gelatinous loaves that you may have produced, using old traditional methods. These breads look good and taste wonderful. All that is necessary is knowing how to evoke maximum flavor from the grain through the careful manipulation of quality ingredients, along with the management of time and the control of temperature. Control of time and temperature are two very important elements in making bread. As we move deeper into the world of whole grain breads, professional baking terms like autolyse (pronounced *auto-lees*—it is a time element) and cold fermentation (temperature element) will be explained and applied to recipes. After baking a few loaves using these techniques, they will become second nature.

My mother taught me that having a recipe that produced great consistent results was all that any cook needed. However, 35 years of experiences has taught me that having a great recipe is only the beginning. Knowing *what* makes a recipe great is also impor-

tant. The art of making a good loaf of bread requires that the baker know why certain mixtures of ingredients and blending techniques work while others don't. I hope when this series of articles is complete, you will have the informational tools necessary to consistently make delicious whole grain and conventional breads.

The cost of these breads will be a fraction of what you will pay for a loaf of commercial bread. We are in a tough economic time that seems to be worsening. Bread is a basic food item humans have consistently turned to when times get tough. What could be better, in a time like this, than having the ability to produce the Staff of Life from basic ingredients that you have processed yourself and fashioned into great looking food for yourself and your family?

The basic elements of bread baking are straightforward and easy to understand. For those like me, who have developed a real passion for baking, there are some interesting mathematics and chemistry to learn also. But, for now, I think the basic elements will get us started and I'll save the math and science for the next edition.

Elements of baking

Flours 101: Flour is the core ingredient in bread, and wheat is the grain of choice for making bread flour. There are other grains that can be used in conjunction with wheat to make a variety of interesting breads. But most bread requires wheat flour as a primary ingredient because it contains more gluten than other grains.

Milling crushes wheat berries into various degrees of powder. The whole berries contain three main components: the outer skin, called bran, the vitamin E-rich embryo or germ, and the protein-laden starch or endosperm.

Once ground, flour is sifted. The first sifting produces clear flour which contains whatever amount of

bran and germ passed through. The seconding sifting produces *patent*, which is the flour you buy, bleached or unbleached, at the store.

The type of flour, i.e., the purpose for which it will be used, is determined by its protein content. (*See sidebar.*) But there are also several varieties of wheat from which the flour can be made: hard wheat and soft wheat, red wheat and white wheat, winter wheat and spring wheat. Wheat is blended at the mill from the various types of grain to produce the flours listed in the sidebar. Professional bakers often specify a specific blend in order to produce their bread of choice.

Why do I specify unbleached flour in my bread formulas? I will admit that good bread can be made from bleached flour. Many of the formulas that I will share with you are what bakers call *lean* breads. Lean breads, for the most part, use the basic four ingredients: flour, yeast, salt, and water. The taste and texture of the bread depends on using quality ingredients that are assembled, fermented, and baked so that maximum flavor and texture is extracted from the grain.

White flour is bleached flour. Bleaching removes the beta-carotene. Not only is the nutritional value of the flour reduced, it's my opinion that beta-carotene contributes to a substantially better flavor and aroma in finished bread. I have made several breads formulated with both bleached and unbleached flour and submitted them side by side to my taste review committee, (Mom, along with our children Sarah, Jason, and Michael) without telling them which was which. The bread made with unbleached flour consistently won the taste, aroma, and appearance vote. When "enriched bread" (breads made with bleached flour that *has additives*) was tested this way the resulting breads were about even in appearance, aroma, and taste. I believe

Heavy duty mixer

ingredients like fats, sugar, and molasses added to "enrich" the flour seem to mute the difference between the breads.

Measuring ingredients: *All* ingredients in a bread recipe must be carefully measured. This is crucial to success. Some folks are comfortable with scooping flour and eyeball-measuring water and other liquids. Others, like me, prefer the precision of weighing major ingredients like flour, water, milk, and other liquids. The relationship between the amounts of flour and liquid in a bread recipe greatly impacts the end result. Weighing the ingredients is the most accurate way of maintaining this delicate balance. I used a digital scale that is accurate to ¼ ounce to weigh the ingredients in all of the recipes that follow. The latest digital scales are not expensive. All of the models I tested were very accurate. I purchased mine at Wal-Mart for under $30.

Mixing the ingredients: Mixing can be done by hand or machine. I own a Kitchen Aid heavy-duty standing mixer that has a dough hook for mixing and kneading. However, I prefer mixing by hand because it helps me develop a feel for when dough is right and ready for the next processing step.

I designed all of the recipes in this article to produce only one loaf of bread. In the beginning, working with a small piece of dough makes it easier for a baker to concentrate on when the dough is right or needs adjustment. Getting your hands in the dough at the beginning is the best way to learn and master this important element of baking. As you go further down the prep line you will find that mistakes in ingredient ratios and methods of assembly become more difficult or impossible to correct. So, get them right at the beginning.

Resting the dough: The autolyse is a period of time that occurs just after the bread ingredients are mixed. During this time enzymes in the dough go to work extracting flavor-producing sugars from the grain molecule. It contributes a great deal to the production of a good loaf of bread and it also reduces kneading time. I have included an extended version of this technique in my first recipe. In this recipe the long rest almost, but not completely, eliminates kneading.

Kneading the dough: Gluten is the primary protein in wheat. It is composed of two partial proteins—gliadin and glutenin. When the flour is hydrated (water is added) these two proteins link up to form the complex protein gluten. However, this linking is disorganized, tangled, and very weak. Kneading pulls this twisted matrix apart and realigns it into straight and strong sheets. This makes it possible for the dough to trap the air bubbles formed by the interaction between the yeast and other wheat components. This step is critical to giving bread structure, otherwise, you wind up with unleavened, heavy bread with less flavor and poorer texture.

Fermenting the dough: During fermentation, yeast feeds on the starch in the wheat. This feeding releases carbon dioxide which is trapped by the fibers of gluten and gives the bread lift. With most recipes it is best to allow the dough to double in bulk before moving to the next step.

Degassing: Most bread recipes call this step "punching down the dough," a term I find misleading. The primary purpose of this procedure is to redistribute the yeast and expose it to a new food source. Degassing is best

---

The protein content of various flours

In this country, wheat flour is usually designated by the amount of protein (gluten) that is contained in the endosperm. Cake flour contains 6 to 7 percent gluten, pastry flour has 4.5 to 9.5 percent gluten, all-purpose flour has 9.5 to 11.5 percent gluten, and bread flour has 11.5 to 13.5 percent gluten.

performed by gently pressing down on the dough. This process will give breads intended for sandwiches that have the familiar "fine crumb" or texture we see in sandwich bread. It does not favor rustic breads that characteristically have a coarser "open crumb," i.e., the large holes like we see in loaves like French bread. Rustic bread dough is best handled during this step by gently folding over on itself without applying excessive pressure.

Shaping the dough: This is simply forming the dough into the desired shape. It is best to do this on an unfloured work surface which allows the dough to grip the counter and makes shaping it easier.

Proofing the dough: This is the final rise before the bread is baked. The function here is to raise the dough to the appropriate size for baking. During this stage, controlling temperature is important. For the breads that I have included in the recipe section, 72° to 75° F (average room temperature) is ideal. Proofing at this temperature takes longer than proofing at higher temperatures. For example, the four breads in this article will proof fully in about 90 minutes at room temperature. Every 17 degrees above or below this effectively halves or doubles this time.

Whole grain breads develop the most flavor when proofed at room temperature or below. Professional bakers call this "a slow secondary fermentation." Some bakers maximize flavor development in their breads by proofing them in the refrigerator overnight.

Baking the bread: Since residential ovens vary in their ability to develop accurate temperature and retain heat, I suggest using a baking stone or unglazed quarry tiles when baking most breads. Both tend to hold and distribute heat evenly, making baking times more predictable. They are most effective when positioned on an oven rack in the lower third of the oven.

Cooling the bread: Cooling newly baked bread on a rack allows moisture to escape from the bottom of the bread, preventing it from becoming soggy. Breads baked in a loaf pan should be removed from the pan as soon as possible after being taken from the oven.

Storing and eating your bread: Lean breads, those made with only flour, yeast, salt, and water, should only be stored in paper to preserve their crispy crust. However, these breads will be stale within a day when stored this way. If you want to preserve them longer, wrap them in plastic and then freeze them or keep them in a cool place.

Enriched breads, those containing butter, oil, milk, and sugar, should always be stored in plastic.

If you plan to eat a previously frozen loaf of bread, pull it from the freezer at least two hours before you plan to use it.

I prefer slicing a cooled loaf of sandwich-type bread before placing it in the freezer. This allows me to remove only the slices that I plan to use.

Before moving on to the recipes, here are some important facts that *all* home bakers will benefit from. In each article of this series, I will add to this list.

• Some folks believe that bread flour, readily found in most supermarkets, is best for most bread. But this is only partially true. Unbleached all-purpose flour is an excellent alternative for most recipes and you can experiment to decide which type you like best.

• Many bread books will instruct you to tap the bottom of the bread when testing for doneness. This method is a hit-or-miss proposition, especially when baking whole grain breads which are denser than breads made with white flour. Lack of precision here can result in underbaked breads. Measuring the temperature of a baked loaf with a digital instant-read thermometer is the best and most accurate way to test for doneness. Rustic breads are done when baked to an internal temperature of 210° F. Enriched breads are done when baked to an internal temperature of 195° F.

• For many years I thought that fresh yeast was the best yeast for bread. Well, times have changed. There is a new yeast heavyweight in town to which even my long trusted Active Dry Yeast takes a backseat. On most supermarket shelves it is labeled as Rapid Rise, Instant, or Bread Machine yeast. When kept in the refrigerator or freezer it stays fresh and active for months. It does not have to be hydrated before being incorporated into a recipe. You mix it directly with the flour and other dry ingredients.

• Some folks believe that salt is an optional ingredient in baking recipes. **Please know that salt is essential.** In bread baking it performs several critical functions. It controls yeast activity, strengthens gluten, and accents the bread's flavor. Unless you feel that it is necessary to completely eliminate sodium from your diet, please don't omit salt from your bread recipes.

• Tap water, depending on where you live, is a very unpredictable ingredient. In many areas of this country, tap water may contain minerals and additives that can adversely affect the flavor of bread. Bottled water is universally more reliable. Because of its popularity it is widely available and relatively cheap. If the water in your area smells and tastes good, feel free to use it in your breads. I listed bottled water in *all* of the recipes here. The only time where I feel that bottled spring water has no substitute is during the develop stages of a sourdough starter. This is when impurities in the water can have terminal consequences on the starter. Ignoring this simple safeguard left me with three starters, that, pardon the pun, never got started.

Baking bread in a Dutch oven

Ingredients:

9 ounces unbleached all-purpose
  flour
6 ounces graham flour
1½ tsp. kosher salt
¼ tsp. instant yeast
1 Tbsp. brown sugar
10½ ounces spring water

Method: *The night before*, mix the flours, yeast, salt, and brown sugar in a bowl. Add the water and stir the mixture with a wooden spoon until a shaggy ball of dough develops. Cover the bowl with a piece of plastic wrap and set aside at room temperature for 8 to 18 hours.

The next day, place a 12 by 18-inch piece of parchment paper in a stainless steel bowl that is large enough to allow the dough to double in size. Spray the parchment with non-stick cooking spray and set the assembly aside.

Remove the fermented dough from the covered bowl and place it on a lightly-floured work surface. Gently knead the dough 10 to 12 times. Shape the dough into a ball by pulling the edges into the middle. This will result in a "seam" on the ball of dough. Place the dough, seam-side down, on the parchment paper inside the bowl. Spray the surface of the dough with non-stick cooking spray. Cover the bowl loosely with plastic wrap and let the dough rise for about 2 hours or until it has doubled in bulk.

One-half hour before baking move an oven rack to the lowest position in the oven. Place a 9 or 10-inch Dutch oven with the lid in place in the oven, and preheat the oven to 500° F.

When you are ready to bake, uncover the dough and lightly sprinkle the top with flour.

Make a six-inch long by one-half-inch deep cut across the top of the dough using a very sharp knife or razor blade

Using pot holders or oven mitts, remove the Dutch oven and place it

I think we have covered enough of the basics, so let's move on to the recipes and bake some bread.

The recipes I am presenting here are not 100% whole grain formulas. Each recipe includes a carefully measured amount of unbleached all-purpose or bread flour.

As I said earlier, many of us have forgotten what real bread tastes like. We have embraced these soft pillow breads and unconsciously allowed our senses to adjust to these tasteless, chemically-soaked bread imitations. And remember, each recipe I present is formulated to produce only one loaf. As we become familiar with some of the techniques that are presented here, by simply increasing the size of the recipes you can make multiple loaves.

Overnight wheat artisan bread

Control of both time and temperature are vital to making a perfect loaf of bread. This recipe demonstrates how simple that can be. What's great about this recipe is that most of the enzyme action and gluten development take place while you are in bed, at work, shopping, or enjoying a favorite movie. Producing gluten is the ultimate goal when making bread dough. As we know, when water is added to wheat flour two partial proteins, glutenin and gliadin, join to form gluten. And it is at this point we would ordinarily begin kneading.

However, this recipe uses the process called autolysis, as mentioned earlier, to replace most of the kneading. This long rest period allows enzymes naturally present in the flour to accomplish this task. The bread is then baked in a cast-iron Dutch oven that simulates a steam-injected baker's oven. This process produces crusty bread with a lot of natural flavor and a moderately open crumb. Because of the crumb, it makes wonderful sandwiches and toast. If you are not comfortable handling a hot Dutch oven, simply mist the loaf with water, score the top, remove it from the bowl by gripping the edges of the parchment paper, and place both directly on the quarry tiles or baking stone. Baking time is about 35 minutes.

on the stovetop and carefully remove the lid. Transfer the dough from the bowl to the Dutch oven by carefully lifting it by the edges of the parchment paper. Put the lid in place and set the pot back in the oven. Immediately reduce the oven temperature to 425° F. Bake the bread covered for 30 minutes. Remove the Dutch oven lid and continue to bake until the loaf is a deep brown and its internal temperature reads 210° F when measured with an instant-read thermometer. Remove the bread from the pot and let it cool on a wire rack for at least 2 hours.

Basic grain sourdough bread

When you use a sourdough starter you are going back to the beginnings of how bread was made thousands of years ago. You will be using pure wholesome ingredients to capture yeast in its wild state. With regular "feedings" you will encourage your starter to thrive and multiply in a favorable environment. With very minimal care, this starter will live for many years.

Many of the sourdough seed cultures used to make a wide variety of the famous San Francisco sourdough breads were started during the Northern California Gold Rush. By all accounts they are still thriving in continuous production over 150 years later. Wild yeasts, as many folks believe, do not create the complex flavor of sourdough bread. Bacterial enzymes like *lactobacillus* and *acetobacillus* feed off the enzyme-released sugars in the dough. This activity creates lactic and acetic acids, and these are responsible for the "sour" flavor. The wild yeasts in sourdough perform the same function as commercial bread yeast—raising the dough.

Using a sourdough starter to make bread does more than create a sour flavor. Sourdough starter along with other types of pre-ferment dough, slow down the fermentation process. In doing so they allow more flavor to be extracted from the wheat molecules. Your bread will taste better without the use of chemical leaveners and dough conditioners.

But first we must build a seed culture. This is a process that can take several days depending on the quality of ingredients used and the ambient temperature of your kitchen. However, the actual hands-on time necessary to make a living seed culture is minimal. Each building step requires only 15 minutes of weighing flour and water and mixing the two. Time and patience are the most critical elements in the process. Once the culture comes alive, devoting five minutes, once a week, to feed it will keep it active and alive forever.

You want to avoid unwanted organisms that can contaminate your seed culture and hinder the development of wild yeast and the proper balance of flavor-producing acids. I suggest you initially use bottled spring water and organic flour to build your seed culture. Using your local tap water in subsequent feedings, as long as it smells and tastes good, is the best way to develop a regional flavor in your sourdough breads.

We will be using what bakers call a three-build system to create our seed culture. If, during each of the building stages, the culture develops as necessary, this process will be complete in three days. If for some reason the culture fails at any of the builds, it must be discarded and a new culture started.

If you are careful and use clean nonreactive utensils like wooden spoons and plastic or stainless steel bowls, along with the suggested ingredients, a failure is not likely to happen. Okay, let's build a seed culture. I think that once you make this bread you will find that your time was well spent. If you already have a seed culture, please skip this process and jump to the recipe that follows.

Sourdough seed culture

Remember, all ingredients are weighed, not measured.

Step one ingredients:

2 ounces organic rye flour
4 ounces bottled spring water

Active sourdough seed culture

Combine the flour and water in a two-cup plastic container and stir with a wooden spoon until well mixed. The mix should have the consistency of thick pancake batter. If necessary, add a little more water. If you are not familiar with the taste or smell of a developed sourdough culture, taste it now so you can tell when it starts to develop. It should have a very bland taste. If possible, keep the ambient temperature in the preparation area between 72° and 75° F. If the culture reaches 80 degrees the wrong kind of organisms will be incubated, causing off-flavors. If this happens your culture must be discarded and a new one started. Cover the container and allow the culture to ferment for 36 to 48 hours. You should start to see tiny bubbles in the batter after 24 hours. If you detect any mold on top of the batter, discard it and start over. If the batter hasn't doubled in volume after 48 hours, stir in an additional two ounces each of flour and water and allow the culture to ferment for an additional 24 hours.

Step two ingredients:

2 ounces organic rye flour
4 ounces bottled spring water

At this point the culture should have a noticeable sour smell and a tangy taste. Stir in the additional flour and water and stir until they are well incorporated. Transfer this refreshed culture to a one-quart plastic container, put the cover in place, and let it ferment for an additional 18 hours or overnight. The culture should be showing a fair amount of activity at this point. You should see lots of foaming and bubbling when you look through the side of the container.

Don't be concerned if you don't see lots of vigorous activity. As long as there is a noticeable sour smell and tangy taste, all is well.

Step three ingredients:

3 ounces unbleached bread flour
3 ounces bottled spring water

Stir the additional flour and water into the culture until well-blended. Place this mixture in a clean one-quart container, put the lid in place, and let the culture ferment for an additional 18 hours.

You now have 18 ounces of healthy sourdough seed culture. Your seed culture should be placed in the refrigerator until you are ready to use it. Each time you use a portion of the culture it should be refreshed with equal amounts of flour and water.

Maintaining the seed culture

If the culture is not used on a regular basis it must be fed a least once a week. When it is time to refresh your culture follow this simple procedure:

Remove eight ounces from the container and discard it (or use it in a recipe). Stir in four ounces of unbleached bread flour and four ounces of spring water. Place the mixture in a clean plastic container, put the cover in place, and let it ferment, at room temperature, until it doubles in bulk. Return the fully fermented culture to the refrigerator.

Sourdough starter ingredients:

2 ounces seed culture
2 ounces spring water, at room temperature, approx. 72° F
5 ounces unbleached all-purpose flour
1/8 tsp. kosher salt

Method: *Day before* (if necessary). If you have not fed your seed culture in the past two days, remove it from the refrigerator and proceed with the process of doing that, as I outlined

Sourdough bread and starter

earlier. If you have done so, continue with the following steps.

Remove your seed culture from the refrigerator, and place two ounces in a small bowl. Return the remainder to the refrigerator. Combine two ounces of spring water with the seed culture and set it aside. Mix the flour with the salt and add seed culture mixture. Stir with a wooden spoon until the mixture forms a shaggy ball. Cover the bowl with plastic wrap and let the dough rest for 20 minutes.

Set the rested dough on your lightly floured work surface work and knead until it becomes smooth and springy. This should take about five or six minutes.

Place the starter in a small plastic container that has been lightly sprayed with Pam or other spray oil. Cover the container with plastic wrap and set it aside to ferment, at room temperature, until it doubles in bulk. This will take four to five hours

Final dough ingredients:

---

6 ounces proofed sourdough starter
9½ ounces spring water at room temperature, approximately 72° F if possible.
11 ounces unbleached all-purpose flour
3 ounces organic rye flour
½ tsp. instant yeast
1 Tbsp. kosher salt

Method: Cut six ounces from the proofed sourdough starter and discard the rest. Using a bench scraper or a knife, cut the starter into small pieces. Add the starter to the spring water in a small bowl. Use your clean fingers to help break up the starter pieces a little more. Set this bowl aside.

In a large bowl combine the main dough flours, instant yeast, and salt. Stir in the water-starter mixture with a wooden spoon until a shaggy ball is formed. If there is any flour that has not been incorporated, add more water one teaspoon at a time, and continue to mix until all of the flour is incorporated. Cover the bowl with plastic wrap and let the dough rest for 20 minutes.

Place the dough on a lightly floured work surface and knead it until it forms a smooth, springy ball. Be very conservative when flouring your work surface with the additional flour. Incorporating too much flour into the dough at this point will have an adverse affect on the finished bread.

Place the dough in a straight-sided stainless steel bowl that has been sprayed lightly with Pam or other spray oil. Cover the bowl with plastic wrap and set aside, at room temperature, until the dough has almost doubled in bulk. This will take about two to three hours, depending on the room temperature.

While the dough is fermenting, place a 12 by 18-inch piece of parchment paper in a suitable-size bowl. I use an inexpensive plastic colander that I purchased at a local discount store for this step. Lightly spray the parchment paper with oil and set it aside.

When the dough is fully fermented and almost double in bulk, gently remove it from the bowl and form it into a ball by gently pulling the edges into the middle. Transfer the dough, seam-side down, to the parchment lined bowl or colander. Spray the top of the dough with non-stick cooking spray and cover the dough with plastic wrap.

You're now in the proofing stage. Let the dough rise until double in bulk again. This will take about 1½ to two hours.

One-half hour before the dough is fully proofed put your Dutch oven and lid in the oven on the lowest rack and preheat the oven to 500° F.

When the dough is finished proofing, use a sharp knife or razor blade to make a 6 inch long by ½ inch deep cut across the top of the dough. Remove the Dutch oven from the oven, using oven mitts or good pot-holders, and set it on top of the stove.

Working as quickly and safely as possible, remove the lid from the Dutch oven and lift the dough from the bowl by carefully grabbing the edges of the parchment paper. Place the dough and the parchment paper in the Dutch oven, put the lid back in place, and return the pot to the oven. Reduce the heat to 425° F and bake the bread for about 25 minutes. Remove the lid and continue to bake until the bread is a deep brown and its internal temperature reaches 200° to 209° F.

Remove the bread from the Dutch oven and cool on a wire rack for at least two hours.

Healthy overnight multi-grain bread

Breakfast is always a bread event in my house. Bagels, English muffins, biscuits, and whatever else can be found that looks like it can be toasted will always be the preferred menu selection. I have to confess that I have been eating the same whole-grain breakfast for the past 18 years, consisting of oatmeal sprinkled with two tablespoons of flax seed meal. This concoction is then topped with shredded wheat and yogurt. With a breakfast like this, I have no room for toast. When I do have a craving for a piece of toast, this bread is one of my first choices. It is also one of my favorite sandwich breads.

For this article I have reformulated it a little to incorporate two new bread baking techniques: *grain soakers* and *sponge starters*. The grain soaker goes into the final dough with a host of flavor-producing enzymes that draw more flavors from the flour, while the sponge starter contributes a number of other benefits. By extending fermentation time, the sponge starter allows for more flavor to be extracted from the wheat and makes it possible to use less yeast. Remember, the flavor of a good loaf of bread comes from the grain, not the yeast.

This is a two-day bread. On day one you will prepare the soaker and the old dough. On day two you will bring the recipe together and enjoy the result of your effort.

This recipe is for one two-pound loaf.

Equipment: One 9 by 5-inch loaf pan.

Ingredients:

The Soaker

2 ounces Bob's Red Mill five-grain cereal mix
2 Tbsp. oat bran
¼ cup spring water

Sponge starter

¹/₈ tsp. instant yeast
5 ounces unbleached all-purpose flour
3½ ounces spring water (at room temperature—about 72° F)

Wheat berries

2 Tbsp. red winter wheat berries
2 cups spring water

The final dough

10 ounces unbleached all-purpose flour
3 ounces graham flour
1½ tsp. kosher salt
1½ tsp. instant yeast
1 Tbsp. dark brown sugar
4 ounces sponge starter
¼ cup cooked red winter wheat berries
3 ounces lowfat milk
6 ounces reserved wheat berry water
1 Tbsp. honey

Method: *Day One.*

Soaker. Before going to bed assemble the soaker and the sponge starter. For the soaker simply combine all of the ingredients in a plastic container, cover the container, and set aside at room temperature to soak overnight.

Sponge starter. Combine the yeast and the flour and stir in the water until a shaggy dough ball is formed. Move this dough ball to a very lightly floured work surface and knead it for about eight to ten minutes or until it becomes smooth and springy. When you poke it with your finger the indent should spring back. Place the dough in a suitable-size plastic container lightly coated with oil, cover the bowl with plastic and set it in the refrigerator. If for some reason you forget this step, this starter can be made the next day, set aside at room temperature, and allowed to rise until doubled in bulk, about 2½ to three hours.

Wheat Berries. In a small saucepan combine the water and the wheat berries. Bring to a boil on medium-high heat, reduce the heat to low, cover, and cook the berries for about 30 minutes until tender. Drain the berries, reserving the cooking water. Place each in separate containers, cover, and refrigerate,.

Day two.

Final Dough. Remove the sponge starter from the refrigerator. If it has doubled in bulk, let it sit for about one hour to warm up to room temperature. If it has not fully doubled, let it sit at room temperature until it does. This can take from two to three more hours. Don't worry, the benefits of added flavor, longer shelf life, and wonderful texture of the finished bread are worth this extra time.

When all is ready, combine the flours, yeast, salt, and brown sugar in a large bowl, blend with a wooden spoon, and set this mixture aside.

Weigh four ounces of sponge starter (approximately ½ of this dough), and cut it into small pieces using a bench scraper or a knife.

Combine the sponge starter pieces with the wheat berries, milk, and wheat berry water. With clean fingers work the sponge starter into the liquid, by breaking the pieces up a little more. It is not necessary to dissolve the sponge starter.

Combine the mixture with the flour mixture and stir with a wooden spoon until it forms a shaggy ball of dough.

Cover the bowl with a piece of plastic, wrap, and let the dough rest for 20 minutes.

Place the dough on a very lightly floured work surface. **Note:** If the dough is a little sticky at the beginning, resist the urge to add any more than a dusting of flour to the work surface. As you knead, this wetness will go away. Knead the dough until it forms a smooth ball that is soft and pliable. The dough will be tacky but not sticky. The kneading process will take about 10 to 12 minutes.

Lightly coat a straight-sided bowl or plastic container with Pam or other spray oil. The container should be large enough to allow the dough to double as it ferments. Set the kneaded dough in this bowl, cover with plastic wrap, and let the dough rise until double in bulk. This will take from 60 to 90 minutes. During the last half hour of this fermenting process, preheat your oven to 350° F and place your baking stone or quarry tiles on the bottom rack.

When the dough has doubled in bulk, gently remove it from the bowl and place it on your work surface. Spray a 9 by 5-inch loaf pan with spray oil. Gently fold the dough in half and over on itself, then size it to fit the pan. **Please do not** punch down or completely remove all of the gas from the dough. Gently place the dough in the pan. Loosely cover the pan with plastic wrap and set it aside to double in bulk again, about 60 to 90 minutes.

Lightly spray the top of the dough with water and sprinkle it with poppy seeds, sesame seeds, or old-fashioned oatmeal. Mist again with a little spray oil and place the loaf in the oven.

Bake for 25 minutes, then rotate the pan 180 degrees and continue baking for another 20 to 25 minutes or until the internal temperature of the loaf reaches 185 to 195° F.

Take the loaf from the oven and remove it from the pan immediately.

Let the loaf cool on a wire rack for at least two hours at room temperature.

Anadama bread

This is truly one of the great New England breads, and since I was born, raised, and still live here, I feel obligated to include this popular regional bread in this recipe collection.

When you mention Anadama bread to a New England bread enthusiast, two ingredients come to mind: molasses and cornmeal. Over the years I have sampled dozens of recipes for this with the only consistent ingredients being those two—molasses and cornmeal. None of them, however, agree on what amounts of these two ingredients belong in the formula. Judging from comments I have received from folks that tested versions that I have made, molasses draws the most comment. Very few

folks take middle road positions on this ingredient. For most it is an absolute like or dislike position. Eliminating the molasses simply draws comments like, "This isn't Anadama, there's no molasses in it."

In this recipe I have reduced the amount of molasses and replaced it with dark brown sugar. This simple modification met with the approval of my most vocal member of my recipe review committee, my wife Tricia. She is one of the middle-road New Englanders who will accept the addition of some molasses, "If it is not too much." Whatever your position on molasses, give this recipe a try. I have replaced some of the white flour with graham flour to add more texture to the finished loaf and reduced the recipe to produce just one loaf. If you like it, simply double the recipe the next time.

Equipment: One 9 by 5-inch loaf pan.

Ingredients:

The soaker

3 ounces coarse grind cornmeal (polenta)
4 ounces spring water, at room temperature—approximately 72° F.

Main dough

8 ounces unbleached bread flour
2 ounces graham flour
1 tsp. instant yeast
4 ounces warm water, 90° to 100° F
1 tsp. kosher salt
2 Tbsp. light molasses, (Grandmother's or Brer Rabbit)
2 Tbsp dark brown sugar
2 Tbsp. walnut oil or other vegetable oil

Anadama and rustic breads

222

Soaker and sponge mix for Anadama bread

Method: Day before.

Mix the cornmeal and the water. Place it in a small plastic container and cover with plastic wrap. Let it sit overnight at room temperature.

When all is ready:

Combine the flours and stir to evenly blend the two. Mix together 5 ounces of flour, the yeast, soaker, and water in a mixing bowl. Cover the bowl with plastic and set it aside, at room temperature, for one hour or until bubbles start to show on the surface of the sponge.

Add the remaining flour, salt, molasses, brown sugar, and oil. Stir with a wooden spoon until a soft, slightly sticky ball is formed. Cover the bowl with plastic wrap and let the dough rest for 20 minutes.

Transfer the dough to a lightly floured work surface. Sprinkle in a little flour if the dough feels sticky. Knead the dough for eight to ten minutes or until the dough feels supple, pliable, and a little tacky.

Transfer the dough to a lightly-oiled bowl or suitable plastic container. Roll the dough around so that it will become coated with oil. Cover the bowl with plastic wrap and set it aside, at room temperature for 90 minutes or until it doubles in size.

Gently remove the dough from the bowl and lay it on a work surface. Gently flatten the dough with your hand. Fold it over on itself to form a rectangle five inches wide and nine inches long. Place the shaped loaf into a 9 by 5-inch loaf pan that has been misted with spray oil. Mist the top of the loaf with spray oil and loosely cover the loaf with plastic wrap. Set it aside, at room temperature, and let it proof until the loaf crests over the top of the pan.

While the loaf is proofing, preheat the oven to 350° F and set your baking stone on a rack that has been positioned in the lower part of the oven.

When the loaf is fully proofed, remove the plastic, mist the top with water, and lightly sprinkle the loaf with cornmeal. Place the loaf in the oven and bake for about 25 minutes. Then rotate the loaf 180 degrees for even baking. Continue to bake the loaf until it is golden brown and the internal temperature reaches 190° to 195° F.

When the loaf is done, remove it immediately from the pan and set it on a rack to cool for at least 1½ hours.

In the next article I will dig a little deeper into the science and mathematics of preparing and baking whole grain breads. Also we will review the grinding and screening techniques for producing various types of flour. Δ

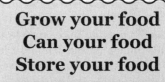
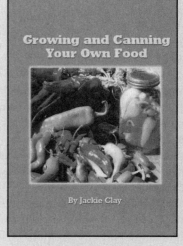

Goat birthing and raising kids

By Jackie Clay

Dairy goats form one of the cornerstones of our homestead. Not only do they provide milk, cheese, ice cream, cottage cheese, and meat, but they also give us manure for our gardens and provide entertainment, too. They're smaller and easier to handle than cows, eat less, and they really like people. When our goats occasionally get out they don't run away down the road looking for more cows—we're more apt to find them up on the porch, peering in the windows, wondering when we'll come out to take them for a walk.

Because they are such a beneficial animal on the homestead, I've always kept them. At one time I had a commercial dairy, milking nearly a hundred does and selling milk to a cheese plant. Nowadays I've cut back to what is enjoyable for me. I have two adult does, three doe kids, our pet wether, Oreo, and a big Boer buck.

In order to keep a supply of milk, I breed my does to freshen at different times. In order to have a doe milking, she must be bred and freshen (give birth). While some does have milked for years following a birth, it is not common; milk production usually starts to slack off after about eight months. This is the natural way a goat's body prepares for the next pregnancy and freshening, letting the body catch up on nutrients and rest from the stress of milking.

Care of the pregant doe

A doe goat's gestation time is about 150 days or roughly five months. About two months before her due date, she should be dried up. There are several different opinions about how this should be done. If she is a heavy milker, you can switch to only milking her once a day for a couple of weeks, then simply stop milking her. Her bag will enlarge, but unless it gets really full or seems hot, she will soon absorb the milk and the udder will shrink down in its rest mode. If she has had mastitis in the past, evidenced by chunks in the milk like small bits of cottage cheese, it's a good idea to use a dry udder infusion as she goes dry, to help prevent a flare-up of mastitis. If not, simply leave her udder alone; the more you milk her and fool with her teats, the more she'll be stimulated to produce more milk.

As she gets advanced in her pregnancy, her sides will begin to round out and protrude. You'll most likely notice this around four months. It's a good idea to give her boosters on her enterotoxemia and tetanus vaccinations at this time and make sure she is wormed. Ask your vet for his advice. In some areas that are selenium deficient, white muscle disease is common. This causes newborn kids to lose control of their legs and often die. A simple injection for the doe before birth, followed by one for the new kids a week or ten days after birth, will prevent this.

Be sure that especially during the last month of her pregnancy she gets a good mixed goat grain. Without it she will not milk well, nor will she have large, healthy kids that will go on to make great milkers or meat for the family. A constant fresh water supply is also necessary. Goats are very clean and will not drink water with dirt or manure in it until they are just about dying from thirst.

Have a birthing stall ready for your pregnant doe. While many does have kidded in the herd, you always run the risk of having one of the kids injured, either by accident or because of an aggressive adult. The mother can be very nervous at birth, and while trying to protect her newborn

This spring one of our does had triplets.

kids, she can step on them while she circles about, chasing the other goats.

The birthing stall doesn't need to be large; five feet by six feet is plenty large. It confines the doe so she doesn't get far away from her kids, yet allows her plenty of room to move around. The birthing stall can also be used to either house the mother with her kids for a few weeks until they are strong enough to join the herd or the kids alone, should you choose to bottle raise them. Needless to say, it should be very clean and have plenty of nice fresh bedding laid down in advance.

About a week before the impending delivery, you'll notice that the doe's belly suddenly changes; it becomes more pendulous and the back area looks more bony. The kids are changing position in the uterus, getting ready for birth. Her udder has been slowly getting bigger, but during the last week, it usually will round out much more, or *bag up*.

It's a good idea to put the doe in the birthing stall about two weeks before her due date, or when she starts bagging up, so she gets used to it and is relaxed in her surroundings. Don't leave a water bucket in the stall; either have a hole cut in the stall wall so she can reach through to drink or offer her water twice daily. I've seen kids born right in the water pail and drown.

A day or so before delivery, her bag will usually suddenly spring tight, with her teats looking full and shiny. Sometimes they'll jut out or even leak a little milk. The ligaments on either side of her tail will loosen and her back will look more thin.

Kidding day!

On the day of her delivery, her vulva will look loose and larger, often having mucus strings hanging from it. She'll begin to act restless and may paw bedding into a nest and circle about nervously. As she begins labor, she will lay down, get up, walk around, lay down, and repeat this several times.

With most deliveries, she'll go into heavy labor, moaning and bleating as the contractions get stronger. You'll notice a "black ball" protrude from her vagina. This isn't a kid's head, but her water bag. It soon bursts and with further contractions, you will usually see a kid's nose and two front feet coming out. The tongue may be out; don't worry.

In a few minutes and after several more strong contractions, the kid will be expelled quite quickly, sliding out onto the bedding with a gush of fluid. If the head is still covered by membrane, take a towel and dry it off, including inside its mouth if it seems to be sputtering and coughing mucus. Holding it up briefly by the hind legs will also let any mucus drain from its throat and mouth. Tie off the umbilical cord about an inch from the belly with strong, sterile thread, cut the cord just past the thread and dip the umbilical stump well with Betadine. Then let Mom lick the baby dry and bond with it.

A single kid is often the case with a first freshener (a doe that is having her first birthing), but with older does, you can expect everything from a single kid to quadruplets.

When she has finished giving birth, she will expel the afterbirth. Let her lick and chew on it a little; this is natural and will help stimulate her milk production and letdown. Few goats will completely eat the afterbirth, so dispose of the rest so it doesn't contaminate the stall.

There are two normal birth presentations seen in goats. The first and most common is the head and two front feet coming first, in a "diver" position, with the feet pressed against the head. The second is the hind legs first, hocks up, with the buttocks following. A doe seldom needs much help with either of these, except when the kid is very large.

Sometimes, you'll find only one front leg and the head (other leg is back), or both front legs and *no* head (head and neck are turned back on the pelvic outlet), tangled twins (legs of two different goats), or buttocks first and no legs (the hind legs have folded forward). These are abnormal birth positions and must be corrected before the kids can be born. Either call your veterinarian immediately or soap up your hand. It doesn't matter if you are the brave, adventurous sort or a chicken—if the vet isn't available, go in to help her deliver her kids.

Luckily, a kid is much smaller than a calf, so you can usually adjust the problem position without much strain. Just be sure that the limbs you are working with belong to the kid that is being delivered! You'll usually have to push the kid back in a little in order to grasp the wayward leg or head, but once in position, it will usually be born with little more problems. The longer it is before help is administered, the more danger there is that the kid will die before it is delivered.

The only other problem you may run up against at birth is the doe not expelling her afterbirth. The doe usually expels her placenta shortly after giving birth or up to a few hours afterward. Keep track of this; don't let the afterbirth become lost in the bedding. Be *sure* she has expelled it. If she doesn't, it is usually evident, as it hangs from her vagina, often down to her hocks. It is a thickish red membrane that hangs in a stringy mass.

If she hasn't expelled it in 12 hours, call your veterinarian. Often an injection of oxytocin is all that is needed to encourage her uterus to release it. This is a natural hormone and will also increase her milk flow.

For more information on aiding difficult births and other kidding-related health issues, pick up *A Veterinary Guide for Animal Owners,* from the *BHM* bookstore.

Care of newborn kids

If the weather is cold, a heat lamp is a good addition to the birthing stall. Be absolutely sure that the lamp is tied securely so it positively cannot fall into the bedding. Many barns have burned down because heat lamps have fallen into the straw and caused it to ignite. Put it in a corner where the doe can't get at it and the kids will soon learn where the heat is. The heat lamp will ensure that the kids get dried off well and it'll prevent hypothermia. In very cold weather, it will also keep their ears and feet from becoming frozen. If they do freeze, they will eventually turn black and fall off. Not a pretty option.

Should this happen when a doe freshens unexpectedly in cold weather, you can sometimes save the ears or feet by immediately bringing the kid into the house and submerging it in warm (not hot) water, including the ears if they are stiff. Keep the kid in

Only a few days old, young kids venture outside for the first time.

David Clay holds one of the triplet does.

the house or where it is reliably warm for several days to a week or more. The circulation will be impaired and the extremity will be much more prone to refreezing. *Do not* rub snow into the area and do not rub the area at all, as it is very prone to damage at this point.

Soon after birth, the kids usually will struggle to their wobbly feet and search for milk—usually at the wrong end of Mom. But soon they'll find the teat and start to suck. Sometimes, especially with does with large, pendulous teats, new kids can't find the teat or figure out how to get it bent around into their mouths. You may need to help a little here. I've even had to nearly milk out a doe's udder so that the new guys could get hold of the teat. They won't nurse much or long, but as long as they do get a snack, they'll be alright for several hours.

The first day and night are important; be sure the kids are nursing and getting milk. Look for the little wagging tails, and you'll know they are being satisfied. Newborn kids will nurse fairly often, but not long at a time. That will increase, and they'll nurse less often and get more milk at one time. If the doe's bag is enlarged and her teats full, even after the kids nurse, milk her nearly dry. Leave just enough for the kids to nurse, but don't leave her bag full or she'll be very prone to developing mastitis or an udder infection. This can ruin a good doe.

Once in a while, you'll have a doe that simply won't let her kids nurse. Maybe her udder is painfully tight. Maybe she's a new Mom and hasn't figured things out yet. Or maybe she just decided she doesn't want to be sucked. She'll whirl away from the kid that's trying to find the teat.

Maybe she'll bite or butt the kid, paw or kick at it.

Sometimes you can tie the doe to the wall and shove her body tightly against it to immobilize her while you help the kid to nurse. Often, if you do this several times, then offer the doe grain while supervising the nursing, she'll reluctantly allow the kids to nurse.

But once in a while, a doe simply won't let the kids nurse and you'll have to bottle feed them from the start. Or you just want to bottle raise them so they'll be very tame and friendly. Another reason some people bottle feed kids is to prevent CAE *(Caprine Arthritis Encephalitis)*. This disease is fairly common in goats and shows as hind limb paralysis in young kids, head tilting or circling, and death in older animals, and probably most common, "knobby" knees and crippled joints—the "arthritis" part of the syndrome. It can't be successfully treated. It is passed through the milk, especially the colostrum from an infected doe to her kids. So to ensure a herd is CAE free, goat breeders often rear the kids from birth on colostrum and milk that has been heated to between 133 to 139° F for one hour. This effectively kills the virus which causes CAE but does not destroy the vital antibodies in the milk.

If you plan on bottle raising your kids, get special kid nipples. These are softer than the old black "lamb" nipples that slip on pop bottles. And they come with an air vent that allows the kids to nurse without creating a vacuum that collapses the nipple flat. You can get several different styles of these nipples through many goat suppliers. I get mine through *Hoegger Goat Supply* (www.hoeggergoatsupply.com).

Newborn kids will not nurse much at a time. If you get them to suck the nipple several times, that's good enough; offer them more in two hours. It is important that they do nurse. Some kids don't like the artificial nipple and refuse to suck. Or they are chilled or weak and can not suck. In this case, you need to take immediate steps to save the kid's life.

First make sure the kid is warm enough. Just having the kid in the warm house is not enough. You must supply supplemental heat via a heat lamp or heating pad under the blanket that the kid is laying on. Sometimes just warming the kid up is enough to get it going. Many a shepherd has saved weak and chilled lambs by putting them next to the wood kitchen range in an old farm kitchen.

Try putting your finger in the kid's mouth, then slip the nipple in and gently hold its head and nose with your forefinger. This often stimulates them to suck.

If the kid just won't or can't suck, it must be tube fed. You'll need a feeding tube, which is a flexible plastic tube that fits onto a large syringe. To tube feed, first draw the warm milk up through the tube, into the syringe. Then "eyeball" the kid, figuring out how far it is from its mouth to its stomach. Slowly slide the tube down the kid's throat, letting it swallow as you push gently. When you think it is far enough, slowly squeeze a little milk down the tube. If the kid struggles violently or coughs, retract the tube at once; you've gotten into the lung! This doesn't happen very often, but it can happen. Let the kid swallow and it won't occur.

When milk comes out of the kid's mouth, you need to push the tube a bit farther down its throat. Then slowly inject the milk. A new kid needs at least 20 ccs of warm colostrum at a tube feeding. Don't overdo it; wait two hours and feed the kid again.

Often the kid will be up, hollering for breakfast after only one tube feeding. What a change a few tablespoonfuls of milk can make! Keep her warm and fed every two hours until she is acting normal, then offer the bottle; she'll usually very willingly accept.

At this point, you can feed four times a day, about ½ a pint at a feeding. You want the kid to still be hungry when the milk is gone, but not starving. Too much milk can cause diarrhea; too little and the kid will not grow nicely. As the kid gets a few days old, you can feed twice a day, but give more milk, up to a pint at a feeding.

Disbudding

Very few goats are born naturally polled (hornless from birth). Yes, horns are natural, but goats used to be wild animals and roam in herds. They needed the horns to protect themselves from predators. Today, goats are not wild and they are milked and otherwise handled by people. And they are kept in fences, led with collars, and otherwise domesticated. Horns are now a danger to goats and their handlers.

A horned goat can always squeeze its head through a fence square (field fencing or welded stock panel), but very, very seldom get back out. Sometimes they will strangle in the attempt to free themselves. I've seen a horned doe hook a kid and catch its front leg in the V of her horns, breaking its leg—even her own kid! A horned goat can catch its horn in its own collar or one of another goat, choking it to death. A horned goat doesn't fit into a keyhole manger or an average milking stand.

And, of course, a horned goat can hurt you. It may not mean to, but when it swings quickly around to bite a fly, it can smash your face in a heartbeat. Or when you are leading it and it doesn't want to go, a twist of its head and your knuckles are bleeding.

It is very difficult to dehorn an adult goat, so it's best to disbud the kids soon after birth. This is done with a disbudding iron that heats up like a branding iron and fits down over the horn bud, burning the skin down to the skull. This sounds horrible, but minutes afterward the kid is playing with you and nursing its dam unconcerned.

When using the iron, make sure it is heated up well; if it is not you won't get a good disbudding and the kid may grow scurs. These are little, misshapen horns that the goat will spend a lifetime catching on things, breaking them off, bleeding, and looking untidy at best.

The kids are best disbudded between three and four days. The longer you wait, the more chance you'll have for scurs to grow, as the horn buds will have started to grow. Place the kid in a tight disbudding box or have an assistant hold the kid snugly in their arms, restraining the kid's head with a gloved hand. (Occasionally the person doing the disbudding will slip and touch the assistant's hand with the iron; the glove is necessary protection!)

Repeat to yourself, "I'm saving your life... I'm saving your life..." as you press the hot iron down on the trimmed hair over the horn bud. Keep pressing down firmly and don't breathe. It stinks! Slowly rotate the disbudding iron so that all of the surface of the skin is burned. Then lift the iron. There should be a white ring completely around the horn bud, with the "fried" horn bud sticking up. Flip the black cap off it with the iron and apply the iron again for a shorter time. Repeat with the other side.

I like to have a bucket of snow or shaved ice handy to slip on the kid's head when I'm done. At the time you disbud, it's a good idea to give the kid its first tetanus vaccination. While it isn't common for a kid to get tetanus after disbudding, it can happen and it pays to be safe.

Feeding the kids grain and hay

It's amazing how fast new kids will eat grain and hay, if it is available to them. Some people don't offer these solid foods to new kids because they are still on the bottle. I've raised goats most of my life and was still amazed when our new triplet does started nibbling hay at four days and now, at two weeks of age, are eating grain and hay like old-timers.

Eating solid foods helps the rumen (the fermentation chamber of the stomach) develop, and the earlier this happens, the better growth you can expect from your kids. Keep good quality hay available to the kids at all times and offer a good mixed grain with molasses (kids like their sweets) twice a day. Clean up the leftovers and give them to the chickens.

Of course, if the kids can be on pasture, they'll also begin to munch on clover, brush, and grass from a very young age. Be sure that the pasture is clean, not one that is heavily used by adult animals and littered with copious amounts of manure. By eating in such a pasture, your young kids will be picking up worm eggs and quickly be parasitized. This will harm their growth and make them more prone to illness.

Even when the kids are on the bottle, be sure they have clean, fresh water available in a drown-proof pan. Water has been called the "cheap feed," as plenty of water helps build big, sturdy animals.

Goat birthing and kid raising is an enjoyable part of homestead living and it feels good to be a part of this natural cycle of rebirth. Every kidding on our homestead feels like a cross between Christmas and the Fourth of July. You'd think that after all these years of goat raising I'd get ho-hum about the process, but every time it's fresh, new, and oh so exciting. Enjoy your babies! Δ

A Backwoods Home Anthology
The Seventh Year

❋ It took a lot of weed-eating fish & work to make our lake usable

❋ Our homestead motto: Make-do

❋ Beans — they may be a poor man's meat, but they are also the gourmet's delight

❋ The amazing aloe

❋ Soil pH is the secret of a good garden

❋ Protect those young trees from frost and vermin

❋ Don't have a cow! (Get a steer instead)

❋ Blueberries are an affordable luxury

❋ A brick walk with little work and less money

❋ For some surprises in your garden, grow potatoes from seed

❋ Make your own lumber with a chainsaw lumber mill

❋ Felting is an ancient art that's still useful today

❋ Those leftover fall tomatoes are a delicious bounty

❋ Sheet composting saves work

Energy Class: Part 2

understanding your electric bill

By Jeffrey R. Yago, P.E., CEM

In Part 1 of this series of articles, I hopefully made you aware that your home's utility costs should be more of a concern than what you are paying to fuel your vehicle. It's easy to know today's cost-per-gallon for gasoline since it's posted on large lighted signs all over town. But trying to figure out your home's utility costs, and if the rates are changing or if you are just using more power, takes a major effort.

Let's start with your electric bill's layout. Each utility company offers multiple "rate schedules" which are governed by your state's Utility Regulatory Commission, which must be approved before they can be changed. Some rate schedules are based on the size of your electrical loads and voltage requirements and these rates are adjusted up and down depending on the time of day and month. These rate schedules are usually reserved for businesses and institutional customers, and the higher daytime rates penalize those customers having large upswings in their electrical demand at peak load periods. Since most utilities experience their highest demand during summer afternoons when everyone is running their air conditioners, summer electric rates may be higher than winter months or at night.

Most homeowners for a given utility will fall under a "residential" rate schedule, although some more innovative utilities are offering special discount rate schedules. Customers willing to let the utility remotely shut off electric water heaters or air-conditioners for short periods during peak seasons can usually receive a lower rate year-round since reducing their peak load when requested lowers the strain on the utility's electric distribution system.

Your first step in lowering your home's monthly electric costs is to contact your local utility and request a description of all rate schedules they offer to homeowners, farmers, or ranchers, depending on your situation. However, before you consider changing to another schedule, we need to review how to understand your monthly electric bills.

Electric bill format

A typical residential electric bill will usually be divided into three or four separate sections, although each utility is different. The top section will identify your account information, the date the bill is due, the amount due, and any outstanding balance from a prior bill. Sometimes this section will also include a summary of the last 12-months' usage. If this history is not provided, you will need to dig through your old receipts for your past 12 months of electric bills before we can continue. If you did not save these, call your local utility and have them send these to you. Don't worry, there is no charge and they are required to provide this information.

The next section of your utility bill will show the electric meter reading for last month and this month, the difference between the two readings, and the total kilowatt-hours (kWh) used during this period. A kilowatt-hour is 1,000 watts of electric load that is operating for one hour. For example, most microwave ovens draw 1,500 watts at full power. If you heated something that took fifteen minutes to cook, this consumed 0.375 kWh (1.5 kWh × 15 min./60 minutes). You need to really review your bills because some electric meters have dial reading that must be multiplied by a "meter constant" to convert

The typical home's electrical meter

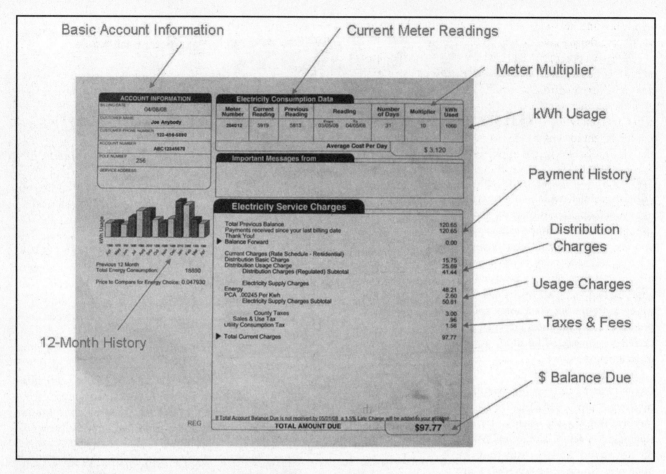

Typical electric bill layout

these dial readings into billed kilowatt-hours. As a check, your electric meter should have a tag under the glass cover indicating if a multiplier is being used, and you should verify this matches the multiplier on your bill, as mistakes are not uncommon. I had an institutional client whose monthly readings were being multiplied by 100, not the 10 multiplier indicated on the meter.

Next, notice the dates. What you call your "March bill" likely covers the previous month, so your current bill should be allocated to the period it actually represents. Unfortunately, most utilities take their meter readings at different times of the month, so the March bill in our example could be for the period of February 3 to March 2, or January 30 through February 28, or any combination of start and end dates. In most cases,

which month to allocate the actual usage will be fairly obvious, but this can get really complicated if the readings are taken near the middle of the month. We will deal with this later.

The next group of numbers breaks out your metered usage by different charges which will include a basic monthly service charge, usually in the $8 to $25 per month range, which will be the same each month. This "meter" charge will be billed each month even if you do not use any electricity.

The next line item is your metered usage multiplied by the standard cost per kilowatt-hour under this rate schedule, and this could total anywhere from a few dollars up to $200 or higher depending on your usage. Some electric rates are "tiered" and you will see the first few hundred kilowatt-hours multiplied by a high

rate, and the remainder billed at a lower rate. Next will be one or more additional line item charges with titles like "distribution charge" or "energy supply charge."

After the 1980s the federal government deregulated the electric utilities and forced them to break up into separate companies just like they did with the phone company. The idea being if the customer paid the local electric distribution, the cross-county transmission line operator, and the power generating plant separately, the customer would be able to select from competing energy suppliers even though they would all share the same electric lines. The hope was this would promote lower rates through competition. In reality, for most customers, all this did was cause their electric bill to become a "Chinese menu" of undecipherable fees, unrecognizable line item charges, with few alternative electric suppliers offering lower rates.

The last section of your bill will be the most eye-opening. Most government agencies attempt to squeeze more and more revenue from us while trying hard to hide these endless tax increases or "fees." To increase tax revenue without actually increasing personal tax rates, legislators got the bright idea of taxing the utilities instead; thinking the general public would applaud taxing these big nasty corporations instead of individuals. However, as each new local, state, and federal tax was levied on the electric utilities, they of course just passed the costs on to all of their customers as expected. However, the utilities got the divine inspiration to show the added "fees" clearly itemized on each customer's monthly bill.

If you are lucky, your utility will still list these added taxes and fees at the end of your bill as separate charges, and this will really make you mad when you see how many there are. You may find a charge added for county sales tax, state sales tax, utility consumption tax, city use tax, and other local fees which are just passed on for you to pay. What's all this got to do with just trying to buy some electricity?

Of course the legislative bodies started getting irate calls from utility customers once they could see all the additional taxes and fees being passed on to them when they thought they were supposed to come out of the utility's profits. The legislators in turn began making new rules that no longer allowed these line item charges to be shown separately. This may be why many of the individual line items are almost impossible to understand, but either way, you can see that your monthly bill may include up to 10% in tacked-on taxes and fees.

Monthly usage review

Now back to analyzing your monthly usage. We first need to identify how your usage varies from month-to-month separately from the dollar charges, or you will never be able to determine what is causing your monthly costs to rise.

Now we need to separate out what you are not using for heating and cooling. If you heat with wood, gas, propane, or oil, your lowest monthly electric bills will occur during the winter. If you have air conditioning, your highest usage will probably be in late July or early August, but remember, the actual bill for this usage will not show up until the next month. If you have a heat pump or use electric heat in the winter and air conditioning in the summer, you will have two peak months—one around January/February and one in July/August, depending on your local weather conditions.

It's obvious that if we can identify one or both peak usage periods, adjusting our inside thermostat setting

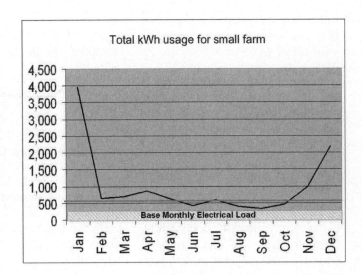

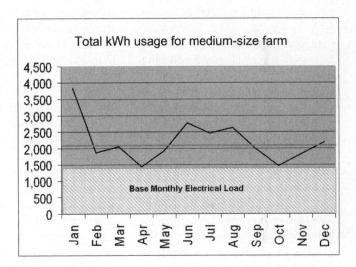

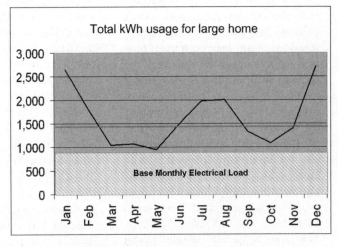

Typical kilowatt usages for a small farm,
a medium-size farm, and a large home.

231

will reduce these heating and cooling peak charges. But, what about your non-heating and non-cooling usage? What is this costing and how do you reduce it? This is important because this almost constant load is billed every month, year round and cannot be reduced by changing your thermostat.

Now take a piece of graph paper (or Excel spreadsheet if you are good with computers) and make equally spaced vertical lines across the page to represent 12 months. Going left to right up the page make equally spaced horizontal lines to represent kWh usage. For example, if your largest bill is 2,200 kWh in August, your top line should be 2,200 or higher, with the smallest usage line smaller than your lowest usage. Now using your most recent 12-month collection of bills, graph each month's usage as shown in our examples. It does not matter if your actual bills do not start with January and end in December like the graph, as long as you have at least twelve different months.

For example, your bills may start with April, and end in the following year. You would still enter the bills on the graph starting with January on the left and December on the right. You will find this makes more sense if you enter the bill on the graph for the actual period the bill represents, not the date of the bill. For example, you may be wondering why your February bill is so big when it has the fewest days and may be warmer than January. Actually, the February bill is for part or all of the longer colder month of January.

After you have done this, connect the points and you will find some interesting things. Note in our examples on the previous page of a large home, a small farm, and a medium-size farm how they all had a very high peak during the winter. These were taken from real bills of real clients. The large home was located in the northeast and used electric heat, while the small and medium-size farms had wood heat in the home, but used electric heaters to heat areas where small animals and chickens needed space heat and drinking water needed to be protected from freezing. Note how the large home had a large peak in July and August from air conditioning, which does not occur for the farms which had little or no air conditioning. We already said if your winter peaks and summer peaks are too high, you will see significant reductions for these months by holding your thermostat at a less demanding setpoint.

Now it gets interesting. Using the large home as an example, which may reflect your own home's usage pattern, note the low usage in the spring and fall. These are called "transition" months, which are those periods when it's too warm to require heating, but not warm enough to require air conditioning. You need to identify this low point or points on your own graph as this is what you are paying each month to operate your non-heating and cooling loads like lights, refrigerator, electric cooking appliances, well pump, and entertainment equipment.

See what you are using each month for all this unidentified electrical "stuff." Now go back to your electric bill and take the grand total cost for the most recent month, and divide it by the total kWh billed for the same month. This is your average cost for electricity and this cost per kWh could vary from month-to-month. In the example of the medium-size farm which includes a farm house, a large barn, and several equipment sheds, this "base load" is 1,400 kWh. Their most recent bill of 1,868 kWh costs $171.86, which equals $0.092 per kWh ($171.86/1,868) or 9.2¢ per kWh.

If we multiply this rate times the 1,400 kW "base load" shown for this client, this means they are paying $129 per month, each month, for all other electrical usage except heating and cooling which cost them $42.86 this month ($171.86-$129). For comparison, the red line on each graph is the average monthly usage not including the December and January heating spikes.

Summary

In the final Part 3 of this article, I will help you identify what to look for in your monthly base load that can be eliminated or substantially reduced, and what each appliance is costing you to operate. Perhaps it's time to buy some new appliances? It may be easier to take the plunge after you see what your existing appliances and lights are costing you to run, just like when you bought that new vehicle once you saw what it was costing you for fuel. In the meantime, make a list of all the major electrical appliances you have.

We are after the "low hanging fruit" that have a large electrical demand, so don't worry about small loads like your cell phone charger or DVD player. These can also really add up, but let's tackle the big ticket items first. We are interested in refrigerators, freezers, electric stoves, electric water heaters, well pumps, air conditioners, electric space heaters, and all those interior and exterior lights. Make a note of the watts for each if given, or the volts and amps printed on the nameplate if this data is listed instead of watts. Remember from past articles, watts = amps × volts. Therefore, an appliance that indicates it operates on 120 volt AC power at 6.4 amps will draw 768 watts of power (120 × 6.4).

Good hunting and get ready to reduce your electric bills!

Jeff Yago is a licensed professional engineer and certified energy manager with more than 25 years experience in the energy conservation field. He has extensive solar thermal and solar photovoltaic system design experience and has authored numerous articles and texts. Δ

Catfish by the bucketful

By Paul Miller

I feel pretty fortunate to have ended up living in the South, but regardless of where you live in the United States or Canada, any sizable body of water most likely contains a healthy population of catfish. When most people think of catfishing, they imagine sitting on a river bank or lakeshore with a bottom rig on a rod and reel, and while that's certainly an effective method for catching Ol' Whiskers, there are a couple of other methods that can be far more productive, and more fun to boot. Both methods do require a boat, but a small johnboat or canoe is quite sufficient and available to most folks. I spend a fair amount of time during warmer weather on the lakes in my area of North Carolina, and I'm surprised at how few people can be seen using these methods that can put a pile of fresh catfish fillets into your skillet.

What I'm referring to is using a trotline or jug fishing, and if you want to be fairly certain to give a youngster a fishing experience they'll enjoy, save up a few milk jugs and I'll explain to those of you who may not be familiar with these techniques how to catch catfish the easy way. Before using these methods, it's a good idea to check the state fishing regulations regarding nongame fish. I did a quick online search for a couple of states' wildlife resources and found the websites; the location that sells fishing licenses should also be able to provide a copy of the regulations.

Jug fishing

The easiest method of the two, and the one that takes the least time to prepare for, is what's called jug fishing. Everybody who has ever done this probably has their own opinions on how to rig the jugs and how to float them, but I'll describe the basics and allow the more creative readers to adapt these methods to suit their area or their own individual ideas. Of course, you have to start with getting the jugs. This is as easy as saving some two-liter drink bottles or half-gallon milk jugs, the kind with the screw-on caps. A lot of milk producers sell their milk these days in jugs with "pop-off" tops; these aren't very good for jugging because the lids will invariably pop off when you don't want them to. I use both drink jugs and milk jugs and both work just fine. As a matter of fact, one time I didn't have time to save up any milk jugs before I got an opportunity to go, and I used quart motor oil jugs and they worked alright. Most of the time when I go out jugging, I bait up and throw out about 10 to 12 jugs; more than this and it's going to be harder to keep track of all your jugs. You do want to keep track of them, too. I have picked up a number of jugs that have "escaped" from the fisherman and either wound up tangled in shore brush or bobbing across the middle of the lake with a very tired catfish on

them. Of course, if you do see an errant jug, make sure it really is unattended...I've had folks pick my jugs up and ride off with them within sight of me; they were either scurrilous dogs or just plain ignorant.

Once you have a good supply of suitable jugs, all you need are some decent-sized hooks, and some fishing line and nylon cord. As I said earlier, I'll tell you how I do it and it wouldn't hurt my feelings to hear "that's not how Uncle Joe did it." I use an 80-pound-strength nylon cord for the main line; tie one end to the handle of the milk jug or the neck of the drink bottle, and roll off about 10-12 feet of the nylon cord. I tie a simple overhand knot in the free end, and then to that end I tie about 16 to 18 inches of stout fishing line; I use 20-pound test. The reason I do it this way is that you'll probably use these jugs over and over, and the nylon cord is much easier to wrap around the jug when you're finished for the day (or night) and doesn't loop up as easily into a knot pile when you unwrap it next time as monofilament does. To the free end of the fishing line of course you tie on a hook. I like a stainless steel hook with a throat

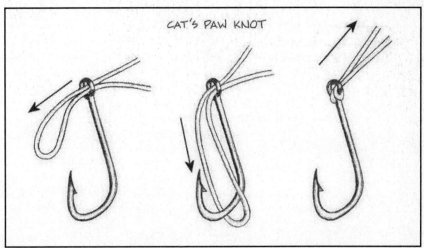

CAT'S PAW KNOT

width about ⅝" wide. Most of the catfish you'll catch will be in the 2 to 4 pound range (the best table fare), and that size hook works really well.

One thing to mention here—I jug fish primarily in a fairly deep lake area. If the place you're fishing has shallow water, vary your drop line length accordingly; you want the bait to drift freely and not drag along the bottom. Contrary to many people's impression, catfish feed at all water depths. I've seen them feed on the surface as well as near the bottom, and a hook drifting 12 feet deep is effective in much deeper water. If the hook is at or near the bottom, not only will it get hung in bottom debris, but the catfish will not be as likely to hook himself, as that happens when they try to pull the bait downward against the resistance of a jug full of air.

Speaking of a jug full of air, I read somewhere a long time ago that it takes a 10 pound catfish to pull a gallon jug under even briefly, so I'm not concerned that using a half gallon jug will allow a decent catfish to pull the jug down for long. I've done this for years and never had a fish disappear with one of my jugs. Most of the time, a fish will turn the jug upright and pull it down but not completely under; even a large fish won't be able to keep a half gallon jug down for long.

My preference for bait is raw shrimp. As I said, I live in North Carolina, and shrimp are fairly inexpensive. My fiancé insists on using chicken livers for bait—in my mind they aren't very durable, but we usually take some of both. Your state laws may differ; here in NC the game laws prohibit using live bait (such as worms or minnows) on set hooks or trotlines, the reasoning being you are less likely to catch game fish such as largemouth bass on something other than live bait. This may be true, but I've caught at least two very nice bass on a trotline using cut shad for bait. I like shrimp because they are convenient and easy to put on the hook, and when I run a trotline with 25 or more hooks, it saves a lot of time rebaiting when I just spin a shrimp onto the hook.

A few more thoughts on jugging, and we'll go on to trotlines. I've found that the first couple of hours in the morning, and the last hour or so before dark are the best times for jugging; catfish don't feed as actively in bright sunlight. Another reason is that the lake we camp and fish at has a great deal of boat traffic; fishermen and skiers and those menaces a friend of mine refers to as "scourges"—jet skis. As rude and thoughtless as many large boat owners can be about their boat wake, jet skiers can be downright jerks. I had a woman with a young girl on behind her run right through my trotline; when I hollered to warn her that I had a trotline out there she swore loudly at me and made an obscene hand gesture. At that point I was almost hoping for, rather than fearing, her jet ski to catch in the trotline and throw her off. My trotline rig uses two anchor jugs that are easily visible and obvious and I run them close to and parallel to shore as required by NC law, but still folks will run over them. This kind of traffic pretty much dies out right before dusk, allowing the lake surface to calm enough for good jugging.

It's a lot of fun when we're out camping at the lake to take the trash bag full of jugs out, unwind the lines, spread them out, and then just sit quietly and wait for the jugs to start dancing. Often an hour of prime jug-fishing time will put at least four or five catfish in the boat. If there's a good breeze, it helps to pull about a half cup of water into the jug, this keeps them from drifting too fast. When you're done fishing, it's easy to run by each jug and pick it up and wind the line around it. I poke the point of the hook just barely into the

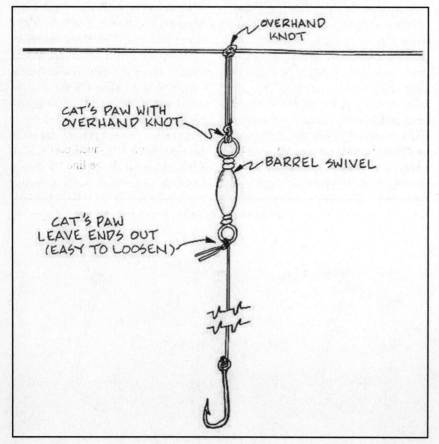

OVERHAND KNOT

CAT'S PAW WITH OVERHAND KNOT

BARREL SWIVEL

CAT'S PAW LEAVE ENDS OUT (EASY TO LOOSEN)

jug. That keeps it from unwinding too easily and a few pinholes don't allow the jug to fill up and sink in an hour or two of floating. Some folks may paint their jugs a dayglo orange to make them easier to see. I find that white milk jugs are not hard to keep track of during the daytime, but I have put a piece of reflective tape on each jug for night fishing. They light up pretty brightly in the beam of a flashlight. It's not hard to tell when there's a fish on—they'll tip the jug up and dance it across the surface, and almost always hook themselves, making it easy to slip up to the jug and pull it in. Kids really enjoy doing this. It's usually more entertaining than bottom fishing and they get so excited when a jug takes off.

We were out jugging one day at the lake and had about 10 or 12 jugs spread out and were sitting quietly just talking while waiting for a jug to flip up, and a pontoon boat rode by a short distance away. We were close enough to hear voices carry over the water as the boat with a middle-aged man and several youngsters went past. One of the youngsters asked the man what we were doing with all those jugs floating around us when we heard him tell the kid, "Oh, they're just marking their territory." We sure appreciated that and we've had many a laugh about that since then.

Trotlines

I've developed a very easy method for tying up and running a trotline; I can set it up and have it baited pretty quickly especially if I've got a partner. Some of these techniques may be new to even experienced trotliners, so hopefully you can use some of what I've learned.

I start making a new trotline using the same kind of cord I use for jugs, a twisted nylon that's rated at 80 pounds or better. Usually it comes several hundred feet to the roll. I tie off the first end to the anchor jug so

McKenzie Carter, jug fishing with family on a North Carolina lake.

that I can wind it around the jug as I tie it up. The best jugs are gallon anti-freeze jugs. Their somewhat flattened shape helps the line stay on when it's wound on. Gallon bleach jugs are also suitable. I've used gallon milk jugs in a pinch, but the stored line tends to slide off the squarish jug too easily and with a trotline that can be 150 feet long. That's a lot of line to get tangled up. I tie on the first end, and then holding the line in my hands, spread my arms out. This gives me about a six foot spacing on the drop lines and that's enough distance between drops (and later, flopping catfish) to keep them from tangling.

At six foot intervals, I tie on a heavy duty barrel swivel. Pinch the nylon cord into a narrow loop and push the loop through the eye of the barrel swivel. I pull it up into a cat's-paw knot, and then tie a simple overhand knot just above the swivel. Tie another simple overhand knot about an inch and a half above that to give a short "drop" to the swivel. (See the illustration.) I used to tie an overhand knot just on either side of the swivel and allow it to slip back and forth a little, but this method is much easier to tie while you have all the line still on the original roll and I don't find that many catfish will wrap themselves up

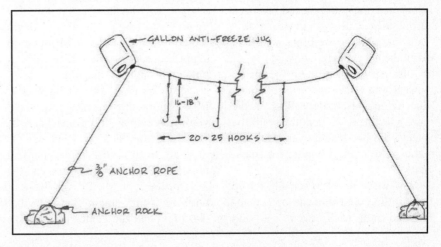

into the main line. Space off another six feet and tie on another swivel. At this point, that's all I'm doing, tying swivels onto the line. You'll end up with a long line of nylon cord with barrel swivels tied securely at six foot intervals. When you've got enough swivels tied on, (I usually put about 25 on my trotlines) tie off the other end to another anchor jug. Wrap the line around one of the jugs and put it aside, you're done with this part. I tie up the drop lines separately. This prevents a lot of tangling when you store the trotline and there is a very easy way to connect the drops to the main line. I use a thin braided nylon line for the drops, what is called "squid" line, or a heavy braided flyline backing works well also. Don't use monofilament if it can be avoided. It's a pain to take on and off and isn't limp enough to work well. Cut the drop line material off into approximately 30 inch segments. Tie the two loose ends together into an overhand knot; you'll end up with about a 15" loop with a knot on the end. Leave the knotted end with about $3/8$" to $1/2$" ends past the knot. Pull the loop end through the eye of the hook into another cat's paw knot with an overhand. Tie up your 25 or so hooks, making a couple extra for the ones your partner will drop overboard. I store the prepared drop lines on a piece of Styrofoam, sink the hooks into one edge, and wrap the drop line around the foam block. A decent size block can easily store a couple dozen drop lines. Cutting numerous slits into the edge of the block will help keep them from tangling.

I use a piece of rope for the anchor lines. Clothesline rope will work but a $3/8$" nylon is best, depending on the water depth. A 20' length should be plenty. Tie one length to each jug and wrap into a small bundle for transport.

Now we're ready to actually set up the trotline, and this can be accomplished quite easily even in a good

breeze if you let the wind help you. I used to use cinder blocks for anchors, but carrying blocks to the lake is foolish if you can just use a good-sized rock from the shoreline. Tie the loose end of the first anchor rope to a rock and drop it overboard. Place the first jug so that the wind, if any, will naturally blow you in the direction of where you want the other end. As I said earlier, state law in North Carolina says the trotline must be parallel to the nearest shore. This is a good idea even if your state doesn't regulate it. Even with the trotline close to and parallel to shore some dimwit will still run between the jugs and tangle your line in his prop eventually, but I console myself with the knowledge that I'll spend much less time making up a new trotline than he will untangling 150' of stout nylon line full of hooks from his prop.

Once the first anchor is on the bottom, play out the anchor rope, then as you drift slowly along, unwind and play out the trotline itself to the second jug. Don't bother attaching the hook drops yet, just get the line set and when you get to the end of the line, and tie the rock onto the loose end of the second anchor rope, stretch the trotline tight before dropping the second anchor rock. Go back up to the first jug and grab the trotline as it runs off the first jug; with a well-anchored trotline you can pull yourself along the line, one person attaching the hooks and passing the line on to a partner who then baits it. Pull the knotted end of the drop line through the bottom eye of the swivel, here a simple cat's paw will suffice. If you pull it through so that the $3/8$" free ends stick out, they can be easily pulled on to untie the cat's paw when you disassemble the trotline later. If you work from the downwind side of the line, even a stiff breeze isn't a problem. When you get to the end of the trotline, you should still have a fairly tight line running between the two jugs, and the center hooks will

have sunk several feet deep, allowing enough clearance for a boat to pass over unless the idiot in question runs close to one of the anchor jugs.

If I've set the trotline up in the early evening, I'll check it once maybe an hour or so after dark, or the last thing before hitting the sack for the night. Work from the upwind end and downwind side again, one person unhooks the fish and passes the line to a partner to rebait. I can strip and rebait a trotline in 30 minutes or so. The real fun is when you are camping overnight. You can get up in the morning and while the coffee is perking on the fire, stroll out to the lakeshore and admire how far down those caught catfish have pulled the jugs while you slept. The hard part is waiting on the kids to wake up to go check it with you. A 25 hook line can sometimes produce 14 or 15 catfish, ranging in size from a small 8 or 10 inch sprout to a grin producing 4 or 5 pound or larger prize.

Disassembling the trotline is easy and is accomplished by reversing the set-up process. Work along the line first removing the drop lines, then starting at the downwind end, pull up the anchor rock and wind up the rope and trotline. Working from the downwind end helps keep the line from getting slack and snarling up as you try and wind it up onto the jug.

On a typical camping weekend, we usually catch around 30 catfish between the trotline and the jugs with very little effort. A great camping supper is a nice pile of catfish, filleted and cut into strips, then breaded to produce "catfish fingers," fried and dipped into cocktail sauce. Many times we've eaten all the catfish we care to eat, and we still have a gallon freezer bag of fillet to take home in the cooler. With catfish fillet costing upwards of $3.99/lb. at the grocery store, here's a fun and easy way to add catfish by the bucketful to your freezer. Δ

Redworm farming

By Charles Sanders

If you are looking for a way to earn extra income, a retirement job, or even a new livelihood, then raising earthworms might just be the thing. This is one occupation that will certainly keep you close to the soil—sometimes up to your elbows in it.

The primary market for your squirming livestock is the ever growing recreational fishing market. Most people who are heading out for an afternoon of fishing simply don't have the time or place to dig up a can full of lively fishing worms. You can fill their need for live bait by having good, healthy bait worms available.

To help prepare this article, I spoke with a veteran worm wrangler from down in Slocomb, Alabama. That's where Tom Bowe and his partner Lorraine Brashear live and raise redworms on their nine-acre homestead.

When they began, they started with little more than a handful of starter stock, purchased from a worm vendor in neighboring Georgia. They fed and raised them for a year before making the first sale. However, that amounted to nearly $1400!

Tom and Lorraine don't normally sell the worms on a retail basis. They do, however, ship thousands of worms to places as far away as Washington state. They sell much of their stock to worm "bait runners." These are the guys who buy cupped bait wholesale, then head out on a wide route to resell it to vendors all over their area. Selling to the runners is also good for Tom and Lorraine. When packaging worms for the runners, Tom cups them up in small containers that look sort of like extra short cottage cheese containers. The small blue cups are

available from a food supply company and are the same type of cup that convenience store delis use to put potato salad or coleslaw in. In some areas, Styrofoam cups are used for the same purpose.

I asked Tom why he raised redworms instead of other types of worms. He said he has tried others but has found the redworms to be hardy, tolerating both the heat of Alabama summers and the 10 to 15 degree cold snaps that they often get in winter. Redworms also don't have to be refrigerated like many other types of worms. They can also take a lot of moisture. They can tolerate overwatering better than most other types of worms. Redworms are very prolific and they grow very well and

very fast. Tom said redworms can double in volume every two to three months. They are the easiest livestock to raise.

Tom usually keeps the main breeding population in pits dug into the clay soil with a roof overhead. The pits are about a foot and a half deep and 6-8 feet wide, and are filled with peat moss and rich feed. The soil itself is heavy clay, so the wigglers aren't too eager to go burrowing out of the loose diggings of their happy home. Once they are coming along, he moves them into the rows of blue plastic barrel halves to "finish," that is, to fatten and finish growing. From there, they are cupped and sold or packaged and shipped.

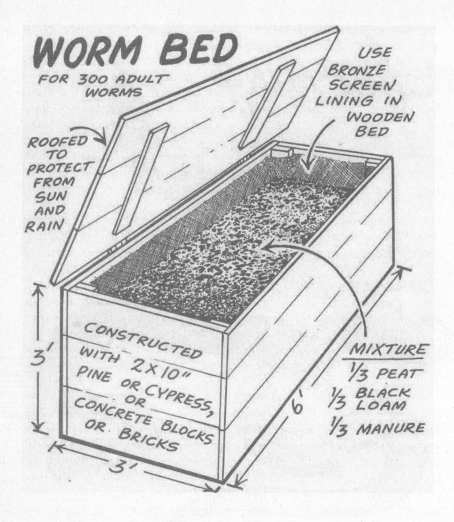

WORM BED

FOR 300 ADULT WORMS

ROOFED TO PROTECT FROM SUN AND RAIN

USE BRONZE SCREEN LINING IN WOODEN BED

CONSTRUCTED WITH 2×10" PINE OR CYPRESS, OR CONCRETE BLOCKS OR BRICKS

3'

3'

6'

MIXTURE
⅓ PEAT
⅓ BLACK LOAM
⅓ MANURE

You can also raise your worms in other containers. Old chest freezers or bathtubs make excellent worm beds and are at a convenient working height. Concrete blocks can be used to frame up a worm bed, and I've seen illustrations of rows of large plastic storage tubs lining shelves inside a garage or outbuilding. Each tub contained its own population of worms. With any worm container, be sure to provide a few drain holes, covered with some fine screen or mesh to allow excess water to drain. The mesh will keep any errant wigglers from escaping. Tom uses only peat moss for bedding. It is light, loose, and fairly inexpensive when purchased in quantity at some of the big home supply stores.

Worm castings

In addition to the worms, another market exists for the worm "castings." That's what they call worm poo, a highly sought after by-product that can be sold as fertilizer for $1 a pound or more. Worm castings are very rich in nitrogen, phosphate, calcium, magnesium, potash, and other nutrients.

Once your worms have been in place for some three or four months, they should have created a usable supply of castings. To harvest, just dump the contents of the bin onto a flat surface. Hang a bright light over the pile and the worms will head to the bottom of the heap. Begin picking through the old bedding, which should be full of castings. Work slowly and check to be sure that the worms are heading downward and are not being removed with the old bedding and castings. Look also for the small yellowish-colored egg capsules. Each one of those contains up to 20 or so baby worms. Be sure to put those back in with the worms. You may also use this opportunity to divide some of the worms into new bins or remove them for cupping. End up by adding some fresh bedding to the original bin to replace what was removed.

Use the castings/compost as you would any other ultra-rich soil amendment in moderation. It is rich stuff and will really give your plants a boost.

An enterprising worm rancher can easily add worm castings to their product list. Tom told me that he has considered getting more into that part of the business, but currently applies the castings from their operation to parts of their own homestead.

Feeding the herd

Feeding your redworms doesn't have to be really scientific. Provide them with a diet of simple vegetable materials. While they aren't particularly finicky in their dining habits, they do have a few likes and dislikes. Kitchen scraps are great. Here are a few other feeding tips to keep in mind.

DO feed:
• Fruit and vegetable scraps, peelings, and trimmings
• Coffee grounds and filters as well as teabags
• Eggshells, the more finely crushed the better
• A few old paper napkins, towels, tissues, cardboard scraps, etc.
• Chopped plant trimmings

AVOID feeding:
• Litter box refuse (including cat litter and droppings)
• Animal matter including meat and bones
• Milk and other dairy items

If you have a friendly relationship with a local grocery store, you might be able to come up with outdated produce to feed to your worms.

Over the years, Tom and Lorraine have found that their customers order for various reasons. They want to:

1. Start their own worm business
2. Sell bait to vendors
3. Raise worms so they never have to buy bait again
4. Create the biggest, baddest compost pile in their neighborhood

Tom and Lorraine currently raise their redworms in a sizeable 20' x 70' worm barn. They have millions of worms in their pits and barrels and will get orders for up to 2000 cups per week during the busy season.

It's not all been a bed of roses…or redworms, as the case may be. Tom has accidentally killed plenty of worms over the past 10 years. He said that the best ways to kill worms is to add too much fresh, hot manure to the worm bed, or to let the worms get too dry. Although you can drown worms, they can take too much moisture a lot more readily than they can stand being too dry.

Selling and shipping

Another of the attractive aspects of the mail-order part of the business is that redworms are easy to ship. To ship live worms, Tom and Lorraine begin by picking up some used woven plastic feed sacks. They can be had cheaply or even free if they've got a hole in them. Lorraine cuts them down and sews them into smaller bags that will accommodate about 3 pounds of damp peat moss and 2 pounds of lively redworms. The bagged wigglers are put into a USPS Priority Mail box and shipped to the customer. Tom insures each package. He believes that is the only way to do business and it ensures satisfied customers.

I asked about pricing, and Tom told me that they currently charge $42 dollars for two pounds of redworms. That equals about five thousand wigglers. They offer pricing discounts on larger quantities. All of their prices include priority shipping by USPS.

Tom mentioned that he is not out to make every dollar in the redworm business. He enjoys working with the worms, dealing with people, and working at his own pace. Tom and Lorraine have helped many people get started in the business. They love the fact that they get to work at home. Tom also said that the worms are quiet, and that makes for a peaceful place. The worm operation gives them the freedom to do other things.

Now that you are pumped up to get into the business, Tom and Lorraine can help you do that as well! Their website, www.redwormcountry.com, contains a wealth of information useful to anyone interested in getting into the worm raising business. They may also be reached at 334-886-3547 or by e-mailing them at mcmgroup@ trip.net.

Becoming a bait "runner"

As an alternative to doing the actual raising of the worms, you might consider becoming one of the "runners" Tom referred to. I contacted a bait dealer in my area of southwestern Indiana who does just that. He supplies bait of different types to vendors.

Kenny Renner has been in the business for more than 18 years. He owns and operates Renner's Wholesale Bait and serves more than 70 businesses in about a 100-mile radius of his home in southwestern Indiana. During the busy season, he easily logs more than 225 miles per day.

He deals with a variety of live baits including crickets, redworms, beemoths, mealworms, Canadian nightcrawlers, minnows, and goldfish.

Worm veterinarian

There are just a few problems that might occur in the worm beds, whether they are in the ground or in bins. The table below might give you a few ideas on solving some of the more common problems.

Condition	Cause	Remedy
Dead or dying worms	Bedding is too dry	Add water until bedding is uniformly damp
	Improper temperatures	Keep temps in 45-80 degree range
	Food and bedding consumed	Add fresh bedding and food to bed
Bed has foul odor	Overfeeding	Cut back feed, freshen and fluff bedding
Moldy surfaces	Too much moisture	Allow some drying to occur and brush away mold
	Use of moldy food	Remove moldy feed and add fresh bedding

Tips to get started

Tom offers some good advice for anyone wanting to get into the red-worm raising business:

1. When ordering your initial stock, get some big ones as well as some breeding stock. That way you can begin cupping worms immediately and have some product to sell. That will help get a cash flow going.

2. Stay away from scams such as the "buy worms from us, raise them, and we will buy them all back" type plans.

3. Get about $100 or more of worms to start. That will give you an ample supply of worms for breeding and for selling immediately.

4. Remember that it doesn't take a lot of space. One blue plastic barrel sawn in two lengthwise sections can house about 5 pounds of worms in each half.

5. Use only peat moss for bedding. It is available at any chain home supply store or garden center.

6. Feed them manure, but be careful not to add "hot" manure such as fresh poultry manure.

7. Remember that food and moisture are the keys.

His customers include bait shops, convenience stores, and anyone else needing fresh, lively bait to sell to their customers. He buys his worms and night crawlers in bulk and packages them himself in consumer-ready containers. Kenny uses the shallow Styrofoam or plastic deli containers described above. They easily hold a dozen nightcrawlers and cost from 5 to 6 cents per cup and lid.

With the volume that he sells, Kenny buys most of his worms live from "worm ranches" like Tom and Lorraine's. He adds about 20% to his cost when he sells to the retailer. He has dealt with the same suppliers for many years but gets different baits from different suppliers.

The biggest problem in the business is keeping bait alive and delivering lively stock to the retail customers. An air-conditioned box helps keeps worms alive during delivery. The retailer is required to supply the needed equipment to store and display the bait for sale. That may include aerated tanks, refrigerators, cricket cages, etc.

Currently, prices for a couple of his baits run something like this:

Supplies are available from:
Redworm Country
www.redwormcountry.com
334-886-3547
mcmgroup@trip.net

Wholesale Bait Company
www.wholesalebait.com
P.O. Box 15006
Hamilton, Ohio 45015
Telephone
Orders: 800-733-2380
All other calls: 513-863-2380
Fax: 513-863-6677
info@wholesalebait.com

N.A.S. Best Bait
www.bestbait.com
8682 E. Bayshore Rd.
Marblehead, Ohio 43440
E-mail:DewWorms@aol.com
1-800-955-8795
Fax: 419-798-9556

Renner's Wholesale Bait
6340W 500N
Jasper, Indiana 47546
812-482-3963

Nightcrawlers wholesale for about $1.30/doz. The retailer then marks them up to about $2.10/doz. Wholesale redworms cost the retailer about $1.50/doz. They then mark them up to about $2.50/doz. Δ

Five-gallon drip irrigation

By Randy Erskine

If your garden is not sloped, elevate the bucket a little bit for better flow.

Give new life to a forgotten five-gallon bucket, damaged garden hose, and some small plastic tubing. This five-gallon drip irrigation system is low cost, conserves water, and is very easy to assemble.

Materials:
- 5-gallon bucket
- 20 feet of old ¾" garden hose
- 5 feet ¼" plastic tubing
- stick or wooden dowel

Tools:
- Knife
- Portable drill
- ¼" and ¾" drill bits

Gather the materials, place all the items into the five-gallon bucket, and head out to your garden. Begin with the five-gallon bucket and drill a ¾" hole near the bottom. Be careful not to compromise the bottom by drilling too low. Place the bucket at the high end of your vegetable row. If the ground is level, then either end will work. However, elevating the bucket on bricks or mounding up the soil will improve water flow. Insert the garden hose into the ¾" hole and lay the hose down along the vegetable row. Cut off any excess hose and plug the end with a stick or wooden dowel.

The next step is to decide where to drill the ¼" holes along the garden hose. For densely-spaced plants, I drill a hole every 16 inches. Spacing your holes closer than 16 inches may result in low pressure and little flow at the furthest spouts from the bucket. If your plants are spaced greater than 16 inches, then drill the holes, mimicking the spacing of the plants.

The last step is to insert a 3" piece of the ¼" plastic tubing into each hole. The 3" spout delivers water to the plants but also functions as a flow regulator. Seat the ¼" tubing tightly against the bottom of the hose and flow will decrease to that spout. Pull the tubing up, and flow will increase.

Now fill the bucket with water and give your plants a drink. Fill the bucket with compost tea and give them a meal. Δ

The last word

Thomas Jefferson couldn't get elected today

About 30 years ago I read the above words and thought, "Of course he could. If the American people were presented a Jeffersonian candidate, and they heard his or her message today, they'd rise up and rush out and vote him into office and we'd have our Constitution and our rights back." I was certain of it. But I was a lot younger then and somewhat idealistic.

I no longer recall who wrote those words, but I've come to realize the writer was correct. Because we *do* have a new Thomas Jefferson on the scene. He is a Republican candidate for President named Ron Paul, and voters, as well as his own party, have overwhelmingly *rejected* him.

Let me recount for you the gist of a recent conversation I had about Ron Paul with one of my friends. I've had similar conversations with other people.

"Who is Ron Paul? What's he say?" the friend asked.

"You should already know," I replied.

"But you don't hear about him," she said.

"*I have*," I said emphatically. "If we expect to solve the problems in this country, we need an informed electorate. If you can't pry yourself away from watching TV long enough to find out what the issues are and who's proposing what, then you shouldn't be voting."

I reminded her, as I do everyone: "There are trillions of dollars in our economy and tens of thousands of lives at stake when these people take office. Why aren't you looking into what the candidates stand for, yourself?" I told her that she, as most Americans, wants to be spoon-fed the information about both the candidates and the issues by the media, and I reminded her that she should keep in mind that those in the media have agendas of their own.

I explained what I could about Paul, adding, "If you really want to know his position on almost anything, just read the *Constitution*. It's the document by which Jefferson and the other Founding Fathers governed the country. It's the set of rules today's politicians are supposed to use. We once had politicians who *did* govern in accordance with that document, but that's not what's happening today."

Ron Paul, however, representing Texas' 14th District, *does*. Of the 535 members of Congress, *only he* has consistently used the *Constitution* as a guideline when he votes in Congress. In his own words, he will "never vote for legislation unless the proposed measure is expressly authorized by the *Constitution*." Because of his medical background (he's a doctor) and the fact that he votes against so much of the pork-barreling and special interest bills in the House, he's called "*Dr. No*" by his colleagues. Not one other member of the House or Senate, nor any President in my lifetime, has so consistently voted along constitutional lines.

Others in Congress, and even many of those sitting on the Supreme Court, all of whom we have supposedly entrusted to run this country in accordance with that venerable document, have chosen to either reinterpret the words they find there or, more often, just ignore them. By doing so, they avoid the arduous process the Founding Fathers had put in place to ensure the *Constitution* is not altered without the informed and expressed will of the People. For them, and perhaps the rest of us, the *Constitution* has become an "anything goes" document subject to the latest political fashions and fads. But Paul steadfastly and unswervingly follows it to the letter.

And there's an irony in this, if you haven't noticed, and it's that when sworn into the office of the presidency, the new President repeats the words from Article II, Section 1, Clause 8. Read them carefully: *I do solemnly swear that I will faithfully execute the Office of President of the United States, and will to the best of my Ability, preserve, protect and defend the Constitution of the United States.*

Senators, Representatives, and a host of others at federal, state, local levels, *and* the military take similar oaths that include the words: *...I will support and defend the Constitution of the United States against all enemies, foreign and domestic; that I will bear true faith and allegiance to the same...*

The problem I have with the oaths they take is that I doubt 99 percent of those taking them know what the *Constitution* says and exactly what it is they are preserving, protecting, supporting, and defending. Jefferson did, the other Founding Fathers did, and so does Ron Paul. And the irony, of course, is that, in attesting they'll support the *Constitution*, they are saying they solemnly support and defend the political position many of them despise.

Early in this election cycle, when Paul seemed to garner attention from the public, he was dismissed as an Internet phenomenon, as if that relegated him to nothingness. But the fact is that the *reason* he's been an Internet phenomenon is that there are still *some* people wishing to know who he is and researching him themselves—instead of being spoon-fed their opinions—and they like what they see. In this I see a tiny glimmer of hope.

But the overwhelming majority of voters are still too lazy or apathetic to find out who he is and what he stands for. Because of this he's fading away. Thus, I no longer have the optimism I had when I was younger that, given the chance, Americans would vote another Thomas Jefferson into the highest office in the land. Sadly, I don't expect we'll ever have this incredible opportunity again. We were presented with a Jeffersonian-like candidate, one who would lead us to a government less intrusive in our lives, one who would protect our rights, and who would keep us out of foreign entanglements, but we, as a people, rejected him. Paul is now 72 years old. I don't expect to see him run for the presidency, again. And, unfortunately, I don't see another Thomas Jefferson or Ron Paul on our political horizon to give us another chance. That's a tragedy.

— **John Silveira**

Sept/Oct 2008
Issue #113
$5.95 US
$7.50 CAN

Backwoods Home magazine

practical ideas for self-reliant living

HOMEMADE BREAD
~ a metaphor for life ~

Preserving the harvest
Growing grain
Sensible energy solutions
Growing healthy garlic
Homemade cloth diapers
Kids using tools

www.backwoodshome.com

My view

A vast cultural divide exists between environmentalists and gun owners

Backwoods Home Magazine has had an exhibitor's booth at the MREA Fair in Wisconsin almost every year since its founding by Mick Sagrillo in 1989, which is the same year this magazine was founded by me. It has been an uneasy relationship due to my libertarian/conservative leanings and their liberal environmental leanings. In 2001, the MREA Board of Directors met for three hours to decide whether or not to ban *BHM* from the Fair.

I had always assumed that the proposed banning was due to an editorial I had written that year* criticizing major alternative energy organizations for damaging the AE movement by consistently inserting their far left environmental politics into their promotions of AE. It nauseated my largely libertarian and conservative readership, I wrote. My readers attended the MREA Fair in large numbers because they too were interested in alternative energies for their homesteads and farms, but they were turned off by the environmental preaching they had to endure whenever they shopped AE.

That editorial had infuriated other prominent environmentalists at the time. Stephen Heckeroth, who had written a number of alternative building articles for *BHM*, abruptly stopped writing for us in protest. Steve Willey, the former owner of Backwoods Solar Electric, wrote a letter to my then energy editor, Michael Hackleman, and suggested he quit the magazine and get a job (with his help) with a rival magazine that had an environmental message. While having dinner with Maureen McIntyre, the former editor and publisher of *Solar Today*, the most influential AE publication in the U.S., I was told that another *Solar Today* editor had declined the invitation to join us. "She wanted to protest you," Maureen said.

Readers of *BHM*, however, swamped the magazine with mail agreeing with the editorial and even voiced their opinions directly to the MREA staff at the next fair. Many fellow fair vendors came up to my booth and said they too agreed, but cautioned me to tone down my rhetoric if I wanted to continue exhibiting. One "insider" told me the MREA Board had already held a meeting and discussed banning my magazine. I concluded the obvious.

But I got a surprise at this year's Fair. Mick Sagrillo took me aside for a private discussion, and he told me I had been wrong all these years. He said the Board meeting to ban *BHM* did occur (he was at it), but that it was only coincidental that it took place after the 2001 editorial appeared. Instead, he said, the Board considered banning *BHM* because we carried articles about guns, and at the same meeting they considered banning the group, *Earth First*, because it sold a pamphlet about how to make bombs, presumably to be used to further their far left environmental goals.

"We were just trying to have a balanced approach," he explained. "If we banned *Earth First*, we felt it was only fair to ban *Backwoods Home Magazine*." Sagrillo said this with a straight face. My face must have turned to rubber.

I was stunned! Not because Sagrillo said I had been wrong about why the MREA Board considered banning *BHM*, but because he insinuated my magazine was considered by the MREA Board to be at the opposite end of the political spectrum from a radical environmental group that teaches people how to make and throw bombs to further their extremist goals.

Had I been speaking to anybody but Sagrillo, I think I would have laughed in their face. But I held Sagrillo in such high regard that I could only muster the feeble rhetorical question: "Gun articles put my magazine at the opposite end of the spectrum from *Earth First*?"

It was then that I realized just how incredibly deep the cultural divide was for people like Sagrillo and many other environmentalists. Why they link guns to evil I don't know, but most gun owners certainly don't link environmentalism to evil. We can separate out the *Earth First* screwballs, while embracing most other environmentalists as people with ideas. We understand the difference between reality and criminality. The MREA Board didn't seem to understand the difference between bomb throwers of the left and law abiding citizens of the right who happen to own guns.

I didn't attempt a discussion with Sagrillo. I realized the usual arguments involving crime and gun statistics could not penetrate this cultural chasm. He was a true believer in his position. It reminded me of my oldest brother, Bill, once telling me I was a radical because I would not compromise on gun owner's Second Amendment rights.

A week after the MREA Fair, The Supreme Court delivered its District of Columbia vs Heller decision (see John Silveira's *Last Word* column in this issue), an enormously important and historic decision that reaffirms individual gun owner's rights, essentially stating that the Second Amendment guarantees them, period. I see it as the most important High Court decision in my lifetime.

But I doubt Sagrillo or other MREA Board members, or my brother, or many members of dedicated environmental groups are celebrating. To them, this decision is blasphemous to what they believe. I may feel that *BHM's* stance on gun rights has been vindicated by the Supreme Court, but I think Sagrillo, the MREA Board, and other true believers in the "evilness" of guns are merely regrouping.

See you at the next MREA Energy Fair. I hope! Maybe this is the editorial that gets me banned!

— **Dave Duffy**

* **The article referred to, *How environmental ideology hurts the solar energy industry*, is contained in *BHM's* Issue No 69, our book, *Can America be saved from Stupid People*, our 12th Year Anthology, and at our website, backwoodshome.com/articles2/duffy69.html.**

Energy Class: Part 3

By Jeffrey R. Yago, P.E., CEM

In Part I of this series of articles, we reviewed how home utility costs will be the next energy source expected to have major cost increases during the next two to three years. Although Part 1 of this series was written in early 2008, a just published article in *USA Today Magazine* announced that electrical utility rates are expected to rise 29 percent on average nationally this year. Oklahoma Public Service Company just announced a 25 percent rate increase. Potomac Edison is increasing their electric rates 29 percent this July to offset higher costs for coal.

Federal legislation expected to take effect in the next two years could force all coal-fueled power plants to double their current rates to pay for global-warming penalties being imposed by this new legislation. Since over half of all electric power in the United States comes from coal-fired power plants, this global-warming penalty legislation will be felt by most readers of this magazine.

In Part II of this series we reviewed how to read your electric meter and evaluate your actual utility costs. In this final part 3 I will help you identify where your electric costs are going, and how to reduce these costs without affecting your lifestyle.

Of course anything plugged into a wall outlet will consume electricity when operated, but many household appliances and electrical devices also consume some electricity 24 hours per day, 365 days per year when not operating. These phantom loads are typical for any appliance having a remote control or digital display that is always operating.

Simple energy reduction tips

I have several easy ways of reducing energy usage which work much more effectively than telling your kids (or spouse!) to turn off the lights, which, by the way, never works.

The first step is to find the "low-hanging fruit." These are the easy-to-implement changes that will produce a significant energy reduction, while

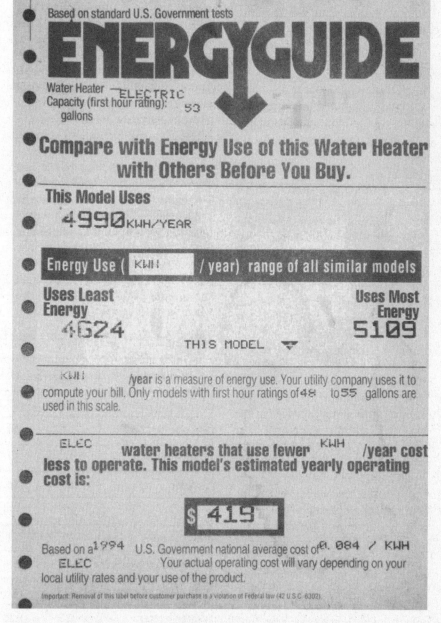

Federal Trade Commission's Energy-Guide appliance tag

Table 1—Home energy-use breakout

Energy usage	North	South-west	East
Heating	40%	32%	34%
Cooling	9%	14%	20%
Refrigerator/freezer	8%	8%	9%
Lights and appliances	24%	29%	19%
Water heating	14%	12%	13%
Miscellaneous	5%	5%	5%

causing no loss in occupant comfort. The next easy step is to look for appliances or systems in the home that operate many hours per month so even a small improvement in their energy efficiency will result in a significant reduction in monthly energy usage due to their longer operating hours.

The easiest energy reduction change any homeowner can make with no technical training is to replace every non-decorative incandescent light bulb in the home with compact fluorescent light bulbs, lower wattage halogen lamps, or LED task lights depending on fixture type. If you want to keep that fancy light fixture over the dining room table that requires special incandescent bulbs then skip it, since we want to reduce your home's energy usage without affecting lighting quality.

For re-lamping to be really cost effective, it should all be done at the same time and not spread out over time. Expect a total re-lamping to cost between $200 and $300, depending on the size of your home. Be sure to purchase these lamps and bulbs from a lighting distributor, which will offer a higher-quality and better selection of lighting products than found in a builder supply outlet. They will also offer the same bulb or tube in different "temperature" ranges, which can make the sometimes harsh light from a fluorescent lamp look

like the softer yellow light from an incandescent bulb.

If you have children that forget to turn off the lights when they leave a room, consider installing motion-control wall switches. Identify which rooms have the most problems with lights being left on, these typically will be bedrooms and bathrooms. Motion-control light switches are now available to replace an existing wall switch, but this will require some electrical wiring skills to do this switch replacement safely.

Expect to pay $30 to $40 per wall switch depending on wattage and features, and avoid low cost brands that can overheat or have poor reliability. The higher quality switches usually include adjustable sensitivity to avoid false responses, and an adjustable time delay for setting how long the lights remain on after someone leaves the room. A motion-controlled light switch is usually more cost effective when used to control multiple light

fixtures, or higher wattage bulbs including exterior lights.

Heating and cooling system tips

Any forced-air furnace or air conditioning system will have an air filter or filters which need to be replaced regularly. Not only will this improve the quality of the air you breathe and reduce household dust, but a clean air filter will also reduce the electrical energy required to power the fan. In addition, allowing a filter to exceed its intended life will allow dirt to pass through and build up on heating and cooling coils and fan blades, which will further reduce air flow and increase fan energy usage.

I recommend replacing all air filters every change of season, or every three months. Any low cost filter you can clearly see through will have a very limited ability to trap smaller dirt particles, and may have a higher air-resistance than higher quality filters. All air filters are directional, so be sure to note the arrow indicating the direction of air flow through the filter when installing any new filter. Don't be surprised if you find that the old filter was installed backwards, as many people do not know how filter

Table 2—Average monthly electric cost to operate appliances

Appliances	kWh/Month	$0.08	$0.09	$0.10	$0.12
Clothes dryer	90	$7.20	$8.10	$9.00	$10.80
TV and DVD	17	$1.36	$1.53	$1.70	$2.04
Computer	22	$1.76	$1.98	$2.20	$2.64
Freezer	87	$6.96	$7.83	$8.70	$10.44
Lighting	310	$24.80	$27.90	$31.00	$37.20
Microwave	17	$1.36	$1.53	$1.70	$2.04
Refrigerator/freezer	103	$8.24	$9.27	$10.30	$12.36
Clothes washer	15	$1.20	$1.35	$1.50	$1.80
Water heater	325	$26.00	$29.25	$32.50	$39.00

media is layered from coarse to fine. Regular filter replacement is an easy way to reduce the energy required to power your central air handling unit, and since it operates many hours per month, this can be a real energy saver.

Your next easy step will be to replace any standard wall thermostat controlling a heating or cooling system with a digital-clock thermostat. These can be programmed to automatically change your occupied and unoccupied temperatures based on time-of-day and day-of-week. Be sure to select the appropriate model, as some electronic wall thermostats are not designed to control a multi-stage heating system such as a heat pump or dual-fuel boiler. Expect to pay about $75 to $125 for a quality model that includes a battery-backup memory, multiple time periods, and easy programming.

Advanced energy saving tips

Of course any electrical device can be purchased in a high-efficiency, low-energy version if you are willing to pay a higher cost. Unfortunately, if the device or appliance is not used regularly, its more efficient replacement may not result in any noticeable reduction in your monthly electric bill. For example, you could replace your 20-year-old table saw with a new saw having a super-efficient motor. But if you use this tool only a few times each year, it will not save enough on your electric bill to justify the higher cost replacement. However, appliances like a well pump, refrigerator, heat pump, furnace, or air conditioner each operate many hours per month, and even a small increase in operating efficiency can produce a very significant reduction in your monthly electric bill.

When buying or replacing any major appliance as a way to reduce energy usage and utility costs, be sure to check the yellow Federal Trade Commission's "ENERGY-GUIDE"

Typical heat pump way past its useful life

New high-efficiency replacement heat pump

tag. This tag is now required on all new electric and gas appliances, and will indicate the lowest and highest

Older model hot water boiler

New high efficiency hot water boiler

cost to operate this appliance per year when compared to all manufacturers. The tag will also indicate what this specific model will cost to operate for a given cost of electricity or fuel. This allows seeing how this model compares to the same size and type appliance sold by other manufacturers.

The historic average electric bill for a "typical" three-bedroom single-family home in the United States has been 1,000 kWhs per month, but this may be increasing due to the higher use of entertainment equipment and home computers. How does this compare to your average monthly bill?

Table 1 is the Department of Energy's breakout of a typical home's energy usage, which I have modified to reflect geographical location. If you live in the southwest, your winter heating costs may be low, but your summer cooling costs could be high. If you live in the north or at higher elevations, your

winter heating costs could be high while having no summer air conditioning costs. If you live in the east, your winter heating and summer cooling costs may be about equal.

According to Department of Energy averages, 60 percent of all single-family homes in the United States are heated with natural gas, 23 percent with electricity, 8 percent with fuel oil, 5 percent with propane, and 4 percent with wood or other fuels. This 2005 study also indicated that 78 percent of all single-family homes have air-conditioning systems, 95 percent have a clothes washer and dryer, and 63 percent have at least one desktop computer and printer. Using this data, you should have a fairly good idea of how well your home compares with these national averages.

If you followed my suggestions in Part II of this series, you should already know what your average cost is per kilowatt-hour for electricity. By selecting the column in Table 2 which most closely matches your local utility cost per kWh, you can see what your appliances are costing to operate each month.

Heat pump and air conditioner tips

If you have an electric space heater rated for a 1,000 watt heating output, it will consume 1,000 watts of electrical power for each hour of operation, which equals 3,413 BTU of heat per hour. However, a new heat pump having a Heating Seasonal Performance Factor (HSPF) of 10 would be able to produce this same 3,413 BTUs of heating output using only 1/10 the electrical power input of a standard electric heater.

If your heat pump is more than 15 years old, its HSPF rating could be as low as 5, meaning you only get 5 times the BTU heat output for a given kWh electrical input. All heat pumps manufactured after September 2006 are required to have a HSPF rating of 7.7 or higher. This means that your heating costs could be cut in half if you replace an older low HSPF rated heat pump with a new model having a HSPF rating of 8 to 10.

Unfortunately, heat pump operating efficiency starts to fall as the outside air temperature falls below 40 degrees, and most units switch to straight electric back-up heat around 25 degrees. If you live in an area that experiences extremely long and cold winters, a heat pump will not be your best choice to save heating energy.

A heat pump operating in cooling mode or an air conditioner is usually listed by its Seasonal Energy Efficiency Rating (SEER). Most models over 15 years old will usually have an SEER rating below 8. Units between 10 and 15 years old usually have a SEER rating of 10 to 12, while units sold today will have a SEER rating of 14 to 18, depending on cost. If you have a significant air-conditioning load each year, your cooling costs could be cut in half by replacing an older low-SEER rated heat pump with a new state-of-the-art heat pump.

Refrigerator/freezer tips

Table 2 indicated your refrigerator/freezer represented 8 to 9 percent of your total monthly electric bill. Federal Energy requirements have been implemented to improve the efficiency of refrigerators and freezers being sold in the US. All new brands and models are now much more energy efficient than earlier models. Since a refrigerator/freezer cycles "on" more than 30 percent of the day, replacing a refrigerator/freezer over 10-years old can result in a significant reduction in your monthly electric bill.

Washer and dryer tips

Unless you have a large family and wash and dry clothes several times each week, a washing machine will not require a significant amount of electricity to drive the electrical components. However, since many read-

ers are on a well system, an older low-efficiency washing machine is much less efficient in the use of cold and hot water, and this excess water usage must be pumped and heated. This is where a new washer can really save in utility costs.

Older washers also do a poor job of removing water during the final spin cycle, and the damper clothes require more energy to dry in the dryer. If you wash and dry clothes more than one day per week and your washer is over 12 years old, you should consider replacing it with a high-efficiency low-water usage model.

Furnace and boiler tips

As noted earlier, 73 percent of homeowners heat with a gas, oil, or propane heating system. The fuel-fired furnace and heating boiler have probably experienced the largest improvement in energy efficiency of any appliance in your home. Since these central heating systems typically last longer than smaller appliances, it's not unusual for 30 to 40-year old homes to still have the original forced-air furnace or hot-water boiler that was installed when the home was first built. Unfortunately, a 1960 to 1970 era furnace or boiler operated in the 65 to 70 percent fuel-efficiency range. However, almost any fuel-fired furnace or boiler sold today will have a fuel efficiency of 80 to 85 percent, and higher cost units are now available with up to 94 percent fuel efficiency.

If your heating system is more than 25 years old, it's way past time to replace, even if it is still working properly. Be sure to also replace or reinsulate all associated forced-air ductwork or heat water distribution piping when replacing an older heating system old.

Hot water heater tips

Older hot water heaters were fairly efficient heating water, but their minimum tank insulation resulted in a sig-

Typical older hot water heater

New high-efficiency hot water tank

New tankless hot water tank

Well pump tips

When it's time to replace your well pump, request a model having a high-efficiency pump motor, and have your plumber also replace that basketball-size expansion tank with a refrigerator-size model. These larger tanks are not expensive, and this will greatly reduce well pump "on and off" cycling each time you flush a toilet or take a shower. A well pump requires up to three times the normal run time electrical power each time it starts, and a larger expansion tank will allow multiple toilet flushes or longer showers before the water pressure drops enough to start the pump.

Conclusion

Making an existing home's construction more energy efficient, especially an older home, can be very costly. Poorly insulated floors and ceilings, leaky single-pane windows, and drafty doors can significantly increase heating and cooling costs when compared to today's tighter home construction methods and materials. I have not tried to minimize the importance of reducing these other energy losses in this series of articles, but making energy improvements in these areas usually requires the services of a licensed contractor and applying for a home improvement loan.

These articles were intended to identify those appliances and systems having a poor energy-efficiency that can be replaced by most homeowners

nificant standby loss of heat. Like the heat pump, refrigerator, and washer, new Federal Energy Reduction regulations have resulted in much more efficient hot water heaters with extremely thick tank insulation. If you have a large family and require lots of hot water and your hot water heater is more than 12 years old, it's time to replace that unit with a new high-efficiency model.

If you currently have an older model gas hot water heater and do not have a large home or family, you may want to consider replacing your old hot water tank with a tankless hot water heater. Since there is no storage tank, there are no standby heating losses from a tank.

without hiring an outside contractor or taking out a home improvement loan. If all of the suggestions I have made in this series of articles are followed, it's reasonable to expect a 20 to 25 percent savings in your current utility costs. If you are in an area experiencing a rapid increase in utility rates, these energy-saving improvements can at least hold the line to offset these increased rates. Once these weekend-type projects have been completed and all low-efficiency lighting and appliances have been replaced, the resulting utility savings may be able to pay for these more extensive interior and exterior renovations that will require an outside contractor.

Of course if you are building a new home, it's easy to understand how a slight increase in construction cost for selecting a thicker exterior insulation or more energy-efficient windows is easily justified. But making these changes to an older existing home can sometimes take 20 or more years to recover the renovation cost through lower utility bills.

For now, follow my easy energy saving tips by starting with the replacement of all incandescent lighting, then move on to replacing an older refrigerator, washer, and hot water heater. Finally, replace that older heat pump, air conditioner, well pump, or furnace. Working in this order will achieve the fastest energy-saving results for the lowest initial costs.

By monitoring your monthly utility bills as described in Part II of this series of articles, you should be able to document the results in your home's energy usage as each improvement is made.

Good luck and good hunting...

Jeff Yago is a licensed professional engineer and certified energy manager with more than 25-years experience in the energy conservation field. He has extensive solar thermal and solar photovoltaic system design experience and has authored numerous energy saving articles and texts. Δ

City girl ❦ Country life

Homemade bread
— a metaphor for life

By Claire Wolfe

My parents never actually bought Wonder Bread; I got my fix only at friends' houses. The breads that entered our little three-bedroom, 1½-bath, cookie-cutter tract were brands like Kilpatrick or Oroweat. They were white, but not unearthly white like Wonder Bread. Nor did they have Wonder Bread's amazing library paste texture. Nor did their packages feature gazillions of bright balloons. Nor did they "build strong bodies 12 ways."

I felt cheated.

Above all, none of those clearly inferior breads possessed Wonder Bread's most singular, most spectacular, most notable virtue: being squishable into a tiny ball the size of a grape—an object that could be bounced, rolled, or (with crust removed) even used to pick up imprints from the Sunday funny pages.

Yet no matter how hard I lobbied Mom to adopt that clearly superior brand, she was adamant: no Wonder Bread.

Why, I tell you, it was downright child abuse.

But I wasn't as bad off as Ursula.

Ursula was a shy German girl who entered my class in the middle of the fifth grade. A real German, straight from Germany—a country every child who grew up on televised war movies knew was full of badness and suffering. Even her name—Ursula, the she-bear—was bizarre. But the strangest, the most foreign, and—in my 10-year-old worldview—the most pitiable aspect of Ursula was *that bizarre bread.*

Would you believe it? The poor girl actually had to eat thick, brown, chunky bread *baked by her very own mother.*

In my sterile, pastel, cardboard-cutout, treeless, conform-or-else world, it was an almost unimaginable thing. Brown-colored bread. With crunchy bits in it. Baked at home.

Oh, the horror.

Richard Blunt's delicious article in this anthology, *Whole grain breads baked at home*, got me thinking about what a long journey it's been from Wonder-bland blue-collar suburbia to backwoods life, from Wonder Bread to homemade whole wheat loaves fresh from the oven.

As I looked at Blunt's photo of chunky, grainy, irregular artisan bread, I didn't merely light up in anticipation of the taste. I longed to dig my fingers into the warm, elastic dough. I ached to feel the crusty texture and the weight of the baked loaf in my hands. I couldn't wait to make my very own and raise it to my nostrils for a lovely, long whiff of ancient, eternal breadiness— of yeast and sweetness and wheat.

I wanted to make the connection to ancestors 1,000 years past, who probably ate breads much like that one. But I wanted more. And bread, the staff of life, gives so much more than that.

Bread isn't mere food. It's a metaphor, symbol, and summation of a larger journey through life and self-ownership. The breads that puff in their plastic wrappers from store shelves tell us where we've gone wrong. The good, grainy food that fills our homes with the world's best aroma remind us of what's right in life—and that can be true even when a home-baked batch turns out to be a disaster (as we shall see).

The difference between Wonder Bread and homemade whole-grain isn't just a difference of taste, texture, and nutrition. It's a difference in worldview. It's the difference between doing what you're told and doing your own thing. It can be the difference between following the herd and cutting your own path—the difference between accepting and questioning Authority.

Making bread at home (like canning, veggie gardening, or hunting) is being *involved* with what you eat.

On the first level of involvement, when you create your own food, you become intimately aware of exactly what you're putting into your body. Every ingredient has a name and a known purpose.

One of the first things you notice when making your own bread is how very, very simple it is: flour, salt, yeast, water, sweetener. You can fancy it up with eggs, milk, bananas, nuts, or whatever. But the fanciest bread you ever make, when you really go wild, will probably have not more than a dozen ingredients.

Not so with storebought.

Now, I have never been a "health nut." If I like a food from the store, I'm not going to worry too much about that complicated list of ingredients they all seem to feature. But just for ducks, a few minutes ago I pulled packages of Costco bagels and Franz deli rye bread out of my freezer and took a look at what's in them. For the most part, both are made with "real" ingredients. But here are a few other things their labels proclaim: diacetyl tartaric acid esters of mono-diglycerides, ammonium chlorate, and L-cysteine (the bagels); ammonium sulphate, sodium stearoyl lactylate, calcium sulphate, and azodicarbonamide (the rye bread).

Both, of course, also contain the ubiquitous high-fructose corn syrup (HFCS), an ingredient that never passed the lips of our ancestors, which Americans now consume at the rate of about 57 pounds per person per year. This is not the friendly old corn syrup Granny occasionally used, but a highly processed product, invented just a few decades ago and made from genetically modified enzymes.

Now, maybe there's not a bit of harm in most of that; I don't know. For instance, the scary-sounding ascorbic acid (another ingredient in the bagels) is just good old vitamin C. And L-cysteine is simply an amino acid. No biggie, eh? But it took less than 30 seconds with Google to start developing a case of the L-cysteine willies, nevertheless. Do you know where these folks *get* their L-cysteine? According to Wikipedia: "[T]he cheapest source of material from which food-grade L-cysteine may be purified in high yield is by hydrolysis of human hair. Other sources include feathers and pig bristles.The companies producing cysteine by hydrolysis are located mainly in China."

Yikes. Bite into that bagel and you might just be eating barber-shop sweepings. Or Chinese pigs. Doesn't sound kosher to me!

Little surprises like that lurk everywhere. You won't find the following chemical in bread, but check out some yogurts, juices, or candies. Look for a common ingredient variously described as carmine, carminic acid, cochineal, or just the anonymous E120. It's a red dye, designed to pretty up the color of some things we eat.

It's also the abdomens and eggs of female beetles, boiled, dried in the open air, then crushed. *Bon appetit!*

Again, it's not that pig-bristle amino acids and crushed-beetle food colorings are always bad for us. Maybe yes, maybe no. (In fact, food producers started using carmine, a "natural" dye, because of health fears over the artificial dyes they had been using.) It's…well, a matter of *involvement*. If *you* were choosing what to put into your body or

the mouths of your children, would human hair and boiled beetles be your first choices?

I think not.

So when we're involved in our food, we're saying, "I choose." And of course in making fresh, whole-grain bread with fresh, known ingredients, we're also choosing a growing list of health benefits, including lower risk of heart disease, type II diabetes, high blood pressure, and obesity.

But all that "involvement" takes SO much time—which is tough if you have to earn a living. And there is one wonderful advantage—so it seems—to "uninvolved" food from a factory: it always comes out exactly as it's engineered to.

When you buy a loaf of Wonder Bread, by golly, it may be crap, but it's consistent crap. Same with Ragu spaghetti sauce, Campbell's soup, or Jolly Rancher candies. They taste like what they taste like, every time.

Quite unlike some of our homemade gustatory experiments.

Last night, I opened the lovely *Tassajara Bread Book*, usually a treasure trove of wholesome and delicious breads. I had been curious for some time about a recipe for Tibetan Barley Bread. It sounded exotically delicious. So I pulled out my Lehman's Best hand-crank mill, ground a couple of cups of hulled barley into flour, pan roasted the flour with sesame oil, and made it into a warm, fragrant dough with stone ground wheat flour, millet, salt, more oils, and hot water. Oh, it smelled and felt so good. But…I couldn't quite figure how this bread was going to work, since it contains no rising agents at all—no yeast, no baking soda, no baking powder—and no sweeteners, either.

Sure enough, it came out absolutely awful. A total catastrophe.

Part of the reason (I suspect) is that the nice folks of the Tassajara monastery forgot to mention that this should have been a flat bread, not a loaf. And I wasn't savvy enough to figure it out.

But I wasn't alone. I hit Google to figure out what I had done wrong. One of the first things I discovered was a lament by Jeffrey Steingarten, culinary critic and columnist for *Vogue* magazine. "The worst loaf of bread I ever baked," he wrote at the beginning of an article about whole grains, "was the Tibetan Barley Bread in *The Tassajara Bread Book* from the San Francisco Zen Center. This was the counterculture baking bible of the seventies and it brimmed over with valuable lessons and rewarding breads. Tibetan Barley Bread was an exception, so heavy and dense that it was an accomplishment to slice and unpleasant to eat…" Steingarten adds that the updated 1986 version of *Tassajara* warns, "Consider this bread a relic from the sixties. Does anybody still eat this way?"

We can hope not. Whatever else it had, the horrible, brick-like, nearly-raw loaf from my oven did have an unmistakable Summer of Love, macrobiotic-diet quality to it.

I trust the neighbors' chickens enjoyed it.

But even though my latest loaf of bread went to the birds, I still got something wonderful from making it. I got experience—my first experiences of baking with barley and millet, the fragrant experience of pan roasting barley with sesame oil. Now *that* was wonderful. All morning long, ever since delivering failed bread to the chickens, I've been scheming on how to compose my next batch of barley bread—this time with yeast and honey. I can't wait to try.

And I learned something about me. Or rather I continued to learn a lifelong lesson—that I can "fail" and not be embarrassed or disgraced. I was reminded once again (and it's a reminder I sorely need) that failure can be a superb foundation for creativity and success.

Nobody ever learned that from a plastic bag of Wonder Bread.

Being involved with food creation is being involved in all of life. It's owning not only your own food choices, but taking back a big, important part of life from the institutional forces that dominate modern food production.

I mentioned a ways back that baking bread (and canning, gardening, etc.) could even be a means of challenging Authority.

Before we wind our way to the end of this rather winding path of an article, let's pay a quick visit to "Authority" and what it's doing in our food.

Remember that ubiquitous (and increasingly notorious) high fructose corn syrup that's found in virtually every commercially produced loaf of bread (not to mention soft drinks, sauces, and hundreds of other things we eat— including bacon and beer)? Know why it's there? Sure, it's a sweetener, and it's there for all the usual sweetening reasons. But the number one reason it's there is: Authority.

For years, the United States government has kept the price of sugar artificially high via price supports. In the mid-1980s, the world market price of sugar was $.04 per pound. U.S. wholesale buyers were paying $.20 per pound because of price supports and severe quotas on sugar imports. By the mid-1990s U.S. sugar was "only" double the world price, and the federal government continued to subsidize the sugar-growing lobby and maintain strict import quotas. At that time, according to the General Accounting Office, U.S. purchasers were paying more than $1.4 billion extra for sugar and sugar-containing products. Half the country's sugar refiners had gone out of business in the previous 15 years because of artificially high commodity prices. In 2001, my friend Jim Bovard wrote in a "Future of Freedom Foundation" commentary that the GAO then estimated that the sugar boondoggle cost for consumers had risen to $2 billion per year, and that 17

wealthy sugar growers received fully half the benefit of the entire federal program.

It's worth going back to the 1980s because that's when HFCS (which was invented in the late 1950s) made its dramatic crash into practically every processed food in the universe. Why? Not because the world needed yet another sweetener. But because this highly, elaborately, expensively processed "frankenfood" was artificially cheaper than than the sugar these processors were previously using. Thank you, Uncle Sam.

Now, you could argue that loading processed foods with sugar was no great boon to human nutrition in the first place. That's true. Before the Industrial Revolution, humans consumed, at most, a few pounds of processed sugars per year.

But HFCS is (yet another) substance the human body wasn't designed for that's being pumped into our bodies in impressive quantities. Sure, it's "just fructose and glucose," neither of which is new to human digestive systems. But because of HFCS's elevated proportion of fructose, we're getting our sugars not only in vastly higher quantities, but in a different balance than in all of previous history. High fructose consumption has been linked to a host of health problems that—strange to say—just happen to be among those currently hitting us hard. These include obesity, diabetes, bowel disease, decreasing fertility, high cholesterol, heart disease, and more. What's really scary is that children are some of the biggest consumers of HFCS. The soft drinks they guzzle convey *the* biggest HFCS injection in the Western diet. Each 20-ounce soda delivers the equivalent of 17 teaspoons of sugar.

Just this week, as I write this, the Centers for Disease control issued a report claiming that 24 million Americans are diabetic. That's nearly 8% of the country's population, and a 15 percent increase in just two years. Even if you allow for a certain amount of overhype and changes in the way diabetes is being diagnosed, that's insane. That's close to triple the world average—and the world average is also increasing.

No one knows the precise cause of the increase, but we do know that it correlates with adoption of a "Western-style diet." Because highly refined sugars, and highly refined foods in general, contain little bulk, it's easy to consume far more calories than we would when eating whole grains, fruits, and vegetables. Furthermore, there's evidence that fructose actually makes us more hungry. So we consume HFCS, then we crave more food—and of course, the foods we eat load us with even more fructose. And there you have it—obesity, sugar highs, and unbalanced processes in the liver, pancreas, and other organs.

And here you thought plain old sugar was bad. That was before "I'm from the government and I'm here to help you."

Which brings us back to Wonder Bread. Yes, there's even a link between Authority and Wonder Bread.

To this very day, the notorious library paste of bread presents its own history in this cheery light on its website:

"...Several advances in the nutrition and baking process were made during this decade [the 1940s]. In 1941, Wonder Bread was involved in a government-supported move to enrich white bread with vitamins and minerals to improve nutrition. Known as the "quiet miracle," bread enrichment nearly eliminated the diseases Beriberi and Pellagra and brought essential nutrients to people who previously could not afford nutritious foods. At the same time Wonder introduced a revolutionary new way of baking that eliminated holes in bread…"

Yes, in patriotic partnership with Uncle Sam, Wonder Bread single-handedly wiped out the scourges of beriberi and pellagra. Wonder Bread's PR flacks are apparently too modest to mention that artificial enrichment of white bread also helped eliminate nutritional anemia (iron deficiency), and that more recently the addition of folic acid to processed grain products like Wonder Bread helped eliminate some birth defects.

Beriberi is caused by thiamin (vitamin B1) deficiency. Pellagra—a truly hideous disease that begins with deformity and diarrhea, progresses to dementia, and ends in death—results from a deficiency of niacin (vitamin B3). Adding vitamins, iron, and folic acid to processed grain products has indeed saved millions from terrible suffering.

But you've already spotted, of course, what else Wonder Bread's PR people aren't mentioning. If grain wasn't processed to death in the first place—its bran layer stripped away, the heat of processing killing much of its remaining nutritional value—those "12 ways of building strong bodies"—those artificial, chemical enrichments—wouldn't be required. Beriberi, pellagra, iron-deficiency anemia, and those folic-acid-related birth defects wouldn't have been problems in the first place if people ate a healthy variety of fresh, whole, unprocessed foods.

It is so very like government to spot an artifically induced problem and "solve" it by ordering an artificial "solution"—which, at most, acts as a Band-Aid upon the original "wound" of bad nutrition.

But then, saying, "Maybe we should eat whole, minimally processed foods" would just be too simple, wouldn't it? Can't build bureaucracies or federal give-away programs around that, can you? And we can't be without our junk foods and our gunk foods, can we? Not even if it kills us. So we render crap food artificially "healthy." Yeah.

As just one example of exactly how goofy millions of us have gone for bad food, how foolish we've allowed ourselves to become about what we ingest, take a look at Exhibit P for People for the Ethical Treatment of Animals. PETA advocates a pure vegan diet—no animal products of any sort. Sticking to a totally vegan diet is hard. It requires not only a huge personal commitment, but an encyclopedic knowlege of the ingredients in everything we eat.

The PETAphiles' rationale is not necessarily to lead a more healthy life. It's to avoid "exploiting" our fellow creatures. Yet one would think that the extreme level of food-consciousness required would lead, as night leads to day, to nutritional awareness. But one might be mistaken. A surprising number of vegans (particularly young ones) actually eat appalling junk-food diets. I once met a dewey-eyed vegan who, to keep things simple, consumed very little but French fries. French fries are close to nutrition-free. They produce a quick "sugar high" along with an artery-clogging grease injection and (potentially) constipation that could keep a person on the toilet long enough to read the *Lord of the Rings* trilogy.

Until recently PETA listed Wonder Bread—yes, Wonder Bread—as an approved vegan food along with such nutritional delights as Krispy Kreme fruit pies, Jujubees, Smuckers Marshmallow Ice Cream Topping, and Cinnamon Krunchers. PETA seems recently to have removed Wonder Bread from its list of "I Can't Believe it's Vegan!" foods. It turns out that, among the unpronounceable ingredients in Wonder Bread, animal products do lurk. But PETA still encourages some of our country's most food-conscious young people to snack their lives away.

That's nuts. And I don't mean the crunchy, high-fiber, high-protein kind.

When we go into our kitchens to begin mixing up simple, basic loaves of homemade bread, we turn our backs on Authority and much that it has wrought. We reject—consciously or not—the belief that we must trust other people to predetermine what goes into our bodies. It's a form—and an important one—of owning our own lives. "Take your pig bristles and your boiled beetles," we say, "and shove 'em."

It's a long journey from Wonder Bread (or whatever the junk food of our choice) to homemade whole grain foods. In part, it's a journey back in time. But it's not an act of foolish nostalgia for "good old days" that never were. It's also a journey forward—from having our diets directed by others for their own convenience to choosing our own better, healthier, more independent lives.

And next time I attempt a version of homemade barley bread, I might even work my way all the way up to mediocre. And from there…who knows? Δ

Grape juice, jam, and jelly

By Sylvia Gist

When it is September or early October here in Montana, the grapes are finally ripe. I know because the stem which the cluster is attached to has turned brown *and* the grapes taste sweet. They may not all ripen at the same time, which allows for more than one picking. I snip the clusters with a small pruning tool—so I don't tear up the vine—and deposit them in a basket. One year I had a bushel from a single vine. This bountiful harvest came from a "Valiant" vine, which produces nice clusters of a seeded grape somewhat smaller than a Concord. Since my grapes were reputedly wonderful juice grapes (but not so great for wine), I began searching my collection of canning books for recipes and found there are several ways to make and preserve juice.

One of these methods left me with a bunch of usable pulp (for jam) after the juice was extracted. I am including three recipes for juice and several more for jam and jelly. I have included some recipes which use refined sugar and some which use an alternative—honey or concentrated fruit juice—as sweetener.

Grapes will keep a while under cool conditions, but they won't get any riper, so I pick them at the sweetness I want. If I am going to keep them just to eat, I try not to rub and bruise them.

For processing juice and jam, I wash and drain them. I then strip the grapes from the stems to keep any flavor of the stems out of the juice. It takes a while, but I think it is worth it.

At this point, I am ready to make juice. After I have juice, I can make jelly and jam if I go the extracting route.

I have to warn you that purple grape juice will stain hands, countertops, plastic strainers, and anything stainable (and some things you thought weren't), so you have to be careful and clean up quickly.

General canning instructions apply. Sterilize jars and lids, bring the processing water to boil before timing, don't move jars while they are cooling, and check seals before storing. Sealing with wax is not recommended; the only method recommended is the hot water bath, which is used here. If you live above 1,000 feet in altitude, check the information at the end of the article for the added length of time for processing in the hot water bath.

Extracting the juice

After the grapes are washed, put them in a kettle (I use porcelain or stainless steel) and crush them. A potato masher works well. Add 1 cup of water for each gallon of crushed grapes. Heat to 190° F, but do not let it boil.

Strain the juice through a jelly bag, several layers of cheesecloth, or a flour sack dish towel. If you are going to discard the pulp, you may want to squeeze out all the juice. If you are going to keep the pulp for jam, just let the juice drip out; it is okay for the pulp to be juicy. Then transfer the pulp to a food mill to remove the seeds and tough skins. Cool the pulp if you want to freeze it for later use.

Transfer the cooled juice to the refrigerator for 24 hours. Then ladle out the juice, being careful not to disturb the sediment and crystals in the bottom of the container. To be sure that it is clear, you can strain it again. This method will give you a hearty flavorful juice, best when grapes used are fully ripe.

Canning the juice

At this point, you can freeze it or can it. If I only have a couple of quarts, I usually freeze it. It is tasty either way.

The juice can be canned with or without sweetener. For the sweetened version, measure the juice and add 1 or 2 cups of sugar for each gallon, or to taste. Other sweeteners can be used, but it is important that the sweetener be heat tolerant; many artificial or non-sugar sweeteners aren't.

Heat to 190° F and ladle into hot sterilized jars, allowing ¼ inch headspace. Put on lids and rings and process pints and quarts for 15 minutes in boiling water bath.

The stem for the bunch of grapes on the left will turn brown before these grapes will be ripe.

Making juice in the jar

Although it takes more jars, a quicker way of getting juice into jars is adding syrup to grapes in the jar. This juice is not as strong as the extracted kind.

1. After washing and draining the grapes, make a syrup of ½-1 cup sugar to 4 cups of water. Use this ratio to make enough syrup for the number of jars you are putting grapes into.

2. Boil that mixture for 5 minutes and ladle into a hot quart jar containing 1 cup of grapes (or a pint jar with ½ cup grapes). For a stronger juice, use more grapes.

3. Leave ¼ inch headspace, adjust lids, and process 15 minutes in a boiling water bath.

4. Cool, check seals, remove rings, and clean jars before storing.

When you are ready to use it, use a strainer to remove the grapes from the juice.

Juice in the jar with honey:

Prepare the grapes as above. Use only very ripe sweet grapes. This produces a nice light grape drink.

1. Put 1 cup of grapes in the hot jar, along with 1 tablespoon of mild honey. For a stronger flavored juice, use more grapes and adjust the honey.

2. Fill the jar with boiling water to cover grapes, leaving ¼ inch headspace.

3. Screw on caps tightly and process for 10 minutes in boiling water bath.

4. After the jars cool, store the juice for at least 6 weeks for aging. To use, pour through strainer or colander and enjoy.

Making jams and jellies

Jam with sugar:

1. Take the pulp, either fresh or from the freezer (thawed) and measure out 4 cups. Heat in large pot (do not use aluminum).

2. Add 3 cups sugar and cook until mixture is thickened.

3. Ladle into hot jars, allowing ¼ inch headspace.

4. Process 5 minutes in boiling water bath.

Note: The amount of sugar you use depends upon the sweetness of the grapes used. Too much sugar will mask the great flavor of the grape.

Jam with fruit juice concentrate:

This recipe uses Pomona's Universal Pectin, a product quite different from the general pectin available in all grocery stores. It does not work to substitute regular pectin in the recipe, and the instructions are quite different. If you haven't used it before, you can usually find it in a health food store or in the natural foods section in the supermarket. While the package is more expensive, it makes more than one batch of jam. It doesn't require a lot of cooking and sets up more like a gel than the other pectin.

For this recipe, you follow the directions for the "all fruit" recipe, which you will find in the pamphlet

A bowl of "Valiant" grapes

in the box of pectin, but with one addition: stir the stevia, a sweet herbal supplement, into the jam after the pectin mixture is added, just before bringing the jam to its final boil. With the grape juice concentrate, you could leave the stevia out; however, stevia enhances the fruit flavor and adds sweetness.

Read all the instructions before beginning. Notice that everything is brought "to a boil" and no more. It is particularly important to get everything ready before you start cooking, as it can be a very quick process.

Making a peanut butter and jelly sandwich with grape jelly made with honey

Straining the berries out of canned "juice in the jar with honey."

Ingredients:

> 3 cups grape pulp
> 1 cup unsweetened grape juice concentrate (not juice cocktail)
> Pomona's Universal Pectin
> ¾ tsp. white powdered stevia extract

1. Prepare jars and lids as usual.

2. Measure grape pulp into the pot. Add 4 tsp. of calcium water. (The package gives directions and ingredients for making this, which you will keep in the refrigerator and use as needed.) Stir well.

3. In a separate small pan, bring 1 cup grape juice concentrate (I use the purple type with my purple grapes) to a boil. Put this in a blender or food processor and add 2 tsp. pectin powder. Blend for 1 to 2 minutes, until powder is dissolved.

4. Back to the pulp: bring it to a boil and add the pectin-juice concentrate mixture, stirring until it is well mixed, about 1 minute. Add the stevia powder. Bring this back to a boil and remove from heat.

5. Fill jars, leaving ½ inch headspace. Put on lids and set in boiling water bath. Boil for 5 minutes. Remove from bath and cool. Yields about 4 cups.

It will keep for 3 weeks or so in the refrigerator after it has been opened-not as long as commercial jelly or jam.

Jelly:

Jelly can be made with or without pectin, but using pectin is quicker. To do it without, you must include about ¼ firm ripe grapes along with ¾ fully ripe grapes since grapes do not contain a great deal of pectin. In addition, jelly without pectin requires a longer cooking time and sometimes the fruit flavor is compromised, resulting in a less fruity taste.

Jelly with pectin:

To make a quick jelly from grape juice:

1. Take 3 cups of the grape juice you extracted following the instructions above (either canned or frozen) and put it in a large saucepan (prefer-ably stainless steel or porcelain) along with a package of regular pectin such as Sure-Jell. It is not a bad idea to strain it through a cloth again to make sure you get a nice clear juice.

2. Bring to a rolling boil and stir in 4 cups of sugar.

3. Return to a hard boil and continue boiling for 1 minute, stirring all the while.

4. Remove from heat and skim off any foam.

5. Ladle into hot jars, allowing ¼ inch headspace. Put on sterilized lids and hot water bath for 5 minutes. This should yield about 5 half-pints.

Jelly with honey:

I prefer the following grape jelly using honey and Pomona's Universal Pectin. It is quick, easy, and yields a delicately-flavored jelly with a hint of honey.

Ingredients:

> 4 cups grape juice
> ¾ cup honey (up to a cup, if you have a sweet tooth)
> Pomona's Universal Pectin

1. Prepare jars, rings, and lids. The recipe makes 4 to 5 half-pints.

2. Measure juice into large pot and add 4 tsp. calcium water (you made

Getting all ingredients for making jelly with honey assembled

Pouring the honey-pectin mixture into the juice-calcium water for making jelly with honey

Filling jars with hot jelly

The jars are ready to be lowered into enough hot water to cover them.

this from the packet in the pectin box). Stir.

3. Measure honey (should be room temperature) into a bowl, add 4 tsp. pectin powder and mix thoroughly.

4. You are ready to begin cooking. Bring grape juice to a boil. Add the honey-pectin mixture. Stir 1-2 minutes to dissolve thoroughly.

5. Return to boil and remove from heat.

6. Pour into jars, allowing not more than ½ inch headspace. Put on lids and rings.

7. Put jars into hot water bath and boil 5 minutes. (At three thousand feet, I boil for 10 minutes.)

8. Remove from canner and allow to cool. Check seals and remove rings before storing.

If you have an abundance of grapes, you can experiment with these recipes and look for others. The Ball Blue Book has a recipe for grape jam which uses the whole grape, but it looked so much more difficult and I was busy, so I stayed with the pulp one I was happy with.

Label your products with a note as to which recipe you used, so you will know which ones you end up really liking six months later when you have forgotten which recipe you used for which jars. The Sharpie ultra-fine point writes well on the lids.

There are also a couple of variables when working with grapes: their ripeness and your sweet tooth. The grapes seem to get riper some years, and this affects the sweetness of the juice. And some people like sweeter products than other people. You may want to add more sweetener than I do; I strive for as natural a product as I can. You just have to experiment and eventually you will find what suits you.

Adjustments for altitude:

If you live at 1001-3000 feet, increase processing time 5 minutes; 3001-6000 feet, increase 10 minutes; 6001-8000 feet, increase 15 minutes. Δ

Ayoob on Firearms

Reflections on age and guns

By Massad Ayoob

The more sand that has escaped from the hourglass of our life, the clearer we should see through it.
—*Niccolo Machiavelli*

I'm writing this on New Year's Day 2008 in the frozen north. As I lift my head, the window above the desk shows me a vista of snow-laden trees. It's a good time for a geezer to reflect on the wintertime of life.

This column is about firearms, of course, but responsible use of guns is an allegory for life, and if you bear with me I think I can tie it in. (On the same desk is a copy of *Utne* magazine, May-June 2006 issue, which contains a roundup of "magazines about permaculture and self-reliance." On Page 36 it notes, "Only in *Backwoods Home* is a recipe for piccalilli followed by a column on firearms." Yup. That's us.)

I've had folks meet me and say, "Uh, you looked younger in your picture in *Backwoods Home*." No kiddin', Sherlock. Dave Duffy reminds me that my first column here appeared in the magazine's January/February 1995 issue. I was away somewhere when Dave called and asked for a photo of me to run with the column, so my then-wife sent along one of the official portraits my department had of each officer. Damn picture was five years old *then*.

It's good to open *Backwoods Home Magazine* and see a picture of me back when I only had one chin. Well, maybe one and a half. Today, I've got chin wattles so pendulous that if I go turkey hunting, I can be my own decoy. Couple years ago, working plainclothes and allowed more facial hair than a mustache, I decided to grow a well-trimmed beard to cover the sagging chin-line and maybe look younger. It came in pure white on the sides…sigh. I was reminded of Bill Cosby's classic joke. "When I was young, my five o'clock shadow made me look like Richard Nixon at the end of the day," said Cosby. "Now, it makes me look like a powdered sugar donut."

Life Lesson #1: Accept age. Wear it as a badge of honor, like a battle scar. That attitude carries more dignity and besides, it's cheaper than Botox.

As a shooter, I've gone from being the youngest guy at the shooting match, a teenager at the time, to Senior class. Yes, "Senior" as in "Senior Discounts" at Denny's and the movie theater. Hell of it is, with my seventh decade upon me, I'm winning way more matches than I did in my late teens and early twenties, when nothing hurt and running was fun instead of frightening. Generally accepted to be 90% mental and 10% physical, shooting rewards experience. Ray Chapman, the first world combat pistol champion, was around 45 when he won the title. Approaching 80 today, he still outshoots a lot of young bucks. The NRA's National Police Handgun Championships, with contorted positions and fifty-yard precision shooting that should reward young, strong, flexible guys, was resoundingly won in 2007 by Lt. Phil Hemphill, a southern state trooper right around retirement age. The great Ken Tapp was a retired carpenter in his sixties when

Massad Ayoob

Ayoob circa 1990

he not only won the prize-rich Second Chance shoots of the 1990s, but set the all-time aggregate record there.

Life Lesson #2: It is absolutely true that old age and treachery can beat youth and skill. But the lesson goes deeper than that. Young guns going for the title find themselves thinking, "This is it!" That's an attitude that makes you choke. Geezers with life experience, who've had people they love die in their arms, put things in perspective. They're less subject to choking when the big stakes are on the table. They've been there, done that, and learned to focus on the tasks necessary to deal with the moment, instead of projecting themselves forward and looking at the goal.

They've learned **Life Lesson #3:** that when you focus on the goal, you neglect the tasks necessary to achieve it. But, if you focus on the tasks and accomplish them, the goal achieves itself.

Back when I had the privilege of going to shooting matches with the great Chapman, I asked him once, "Ray, when did you get to where you were going into a big one and didn't get the butterflies in your stomach?" I'll never forget his answer.

"Never," Chapman told me flatly, "and the day I don't get those little jitters will be the day I hang up my guns, because I'll know I've lost my edge. Mas, what you call 'fight or flight response,' I call 'components of championship form.' If the start signal is about to sound and I get those little tremors in my fingers, I don't think 'Ahhh! Poor me! I've lost it!' I think, 'OK! Now I've got my supercharge! Now I'm gonna be faster out of the holster and faster over the six-foot wall on the Cooper Assault Course than that 25-year-old kid who thinks he can take me, but is so insecure he has to take Indoral beta-blockers before he shoots…and I'm gonna kick his butt."

And he generally did. **Life Lesson #4**, one of many I learned from Uncle Ray: the physical manifestations of fear are also physical manifestations of strength. Our culture teaches us that trembling hands, shaking knees, a squeaky voice, or threatened loss of sphincter control are signs of cowardice. In fact, they all come with that fight or flight response. We feel those things because the epinephrine and nor-epinephrine and endorphins have all kicked in, and in the next few moments we're going to be stronger, faster, and more impervious to pain

than we've ever been in our lives. We geezers learn that, and it helps to replace fear with confidence.

If older folks seem more phlegmatic in the face of danger, it ain't that we're braver. It's that we've just learned to understand the whole thing better.

And, besides, some argue, the older we get the less we have to lose.

Equalizers

We learn early that we ain't all created equal. Not physically, anyway. We learn to use equalizers. At my age, those include walkers, motorized wheelchairs, and those cool geezer scooter things. We are Homo Sapiens, the tool-bearing mammal…and, therefore, the weapon-bearing mammal. From the first tools—a tree limb used as a lever, a sharpened piece of flint used as a hide-scraper—mechanical assists allowed us to make up for our relatively puny muscles. Our earliest ancestors had teeth and fingernails instead of proper fangs and claws, but the rock and the stone knife and the lance and the bow and arrow and the rest made up for that, and soon, for better or worse, our kind became the rulers of the planet.

This principle may be one reason why women take so readily to the gun. You'll find few publications with more strong, independent female role models than *Backwoods Home Magazine.* Look at Jackie Clay, harvesting her annual venison with a Winchester .30-30 rifle in the same self-assured hands she used to build her homestead. Ask Claire Wolfe how she feels about the right to keep and bear arms.

There aren't too many physical sports where women compete against men head to head, on their own ground, instead of in separate women's classes. You don't see it in golf or tennis or boxing, nor in baseball or basketball, but you damn sure see it in shooting. It's never a surprise when a woman wins the overall National

Championship in Position Rifle or High Power Rifle, beating every man-jack at the vast shooting range complex of Camp Perry, Ohio. The current national champion of Cowboy Action Shooting is a modern cowgirl, a teenager named Randi Rodgers who competes under the monicker "Holy Terror."

Women didn't gain parity with men in previously male-oriented jobs with muscle power. Indeed, it was partly the disparity in upper body strength that had kept them so occupationally downtrodden in the old days. They didn't gain entry to the construction industry as hod-carriers, but at the hydraulically-operated controls of Caterpillar tractors. When I was young, "policewomen" were matrons and juvenile officers. In the '70s, they took on full patrol duties. It was mechanical force multipliers—batons, service handguns, Tasers, and so on—that let them make up for physical strength shortcomings when

Geezers get to witness paradigm changes. A 1961 NRA magazine depicts the White House Police firing their Colt Troopers from the FBI Crouch of the period, a technique now thankfully consigned to "the dust-bin of history."

Age makes you understand vulnerability. If you need the device above,
you may be comforted by the presence of the one below.
Chris Koontz (www.americancane.com) stick, Kimber Pro SIS .45 pistol.

duty required them to physically overpower big, violent males. You need look no farther than the cool and decisive young female officer who took control at the Gainesville disturbance that led to what some called the most recognizable news quote of 2007: "Don't tase me, bro!"

As strength fades with age, we geezers are reminded that mechanical force multipliers are pretty useful for us, too. In Florida recently, a senior citizen with a concealed carry permit drew his gun and sent five armed gang-banger types running for their lives. Earlier in 2007, a 71-year-old retired Marine was in a Subway sandwich shop when a couple of gunmen burst in. They robbed the clerk at gunpoint, terrorized the customers with their weapons, and then started herding them into the back as if for execution. The septuagenarian Marine drew his own licensed concealed carry handgun and shot them down, killing one and leaving the other in critical condition in the "prison ward." We'll never know how many lives were saved by his cool and courageous action.

Tools to equalize. It ain't just the American Way, it's the Homo Sapien's Way, and the older you get the more you can appreciate "modern conveniences." Call it **Life Lesson #5**. In the Old West, it is said, one of the pioneers had his Colt single action revolver engraved with the words, "Fear not any man/No matter what his size./When danger threatens, call on me/And I will equalize."

We should probably not be surprised that, in a world of labor-saving physical strength equalizing devices, only the gun has ever been called The Equalizer in common parlance. The bad news is that it makes a dwarf like Lee Harvey Oswald equal to the destruction of a giant like John Fitzgerald Kennedy. The good news, which happens far more often, is that it makes a retiree of 71 equal to the task of protecting himself and others from multiple armed, violent, and probably homicidal criminals.

Responsibility factor

Spiderman's grandfather famously told him, "With great power comes great responsibility." Actually, that's only half the equation. Time spent around deadly weapons will, like life itself, teach us that power and responsibility are commensurate. They must always be in an equal balance. Responsibility without the power to fulfill it is empty, frustrating, and doomed to failure. Power without responsibility is what leads to tyranny and tragedy. Life experience teaches us this in small ways, and history teaches it in big ways, and the gun teaches it in a forever large perspective. **Life Lesson #6**, you might say.

As a dad, the gun became a tool of parenting for me. We've all heard the horror stories of kids who got hold of their parents' firearms without permission and did something tragically stupid with them. Child psychologists tell us that children, perceiving themselves little and weak, will reach out for things that will make them seem big and strong to themselves and others. Walk through a Movie Gallery or Blockbusters sometime, and notice how many of the movie jackets depict a hero or heroine holding a deadly weapon. For generations, our nation's entertainment media has glamorized the gun and made it an icon of power, heroism, and respect. That's all but irresistibly attractive to children unless the parent sees it coming and handles it right.

My kids each started helping me clean guns at the age of five. It showed them how they worked. It taught them how to load and, more importantly, unload them. If somebody else's kid pulled his dad's loaded revolver out of a bedroom drawer and started waving it around, my kids knew how to defang that snake. The cleaning tasks deglamorized the gun, too. "Eeww...it's dirty and greasy!"

At six, they were both shooting, with live ammunition. From the time they could talk, they knew they could handle a gun any time they asked, with parental permission and presence. If another kid said, "I wanna play with your dad's gun," my kids

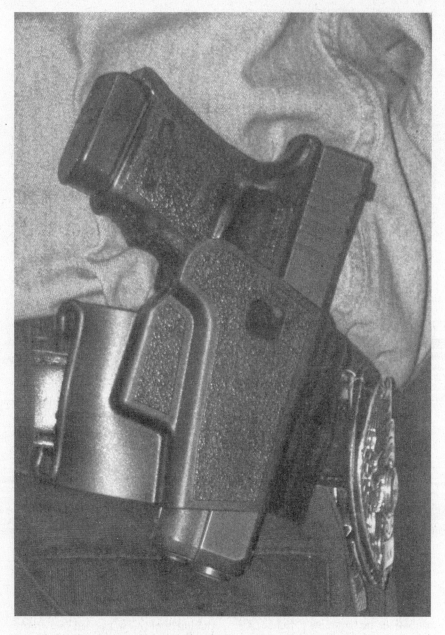

The badge and the gun reflect the principle that responsibility and power must always be in equal balance.

active reserve status as a Grandparent. Both kids became pistol champions in their teens, frequently beating grown men. They considered their firearms tools of empowerment.

They, and the many kids like them, stand in stark contrast to the children of parents who said, "Aah, I'll just hide the guns and tell the kids we don't have any." Yeah. Right.

Was there anything in your parents' household that *you* didn't know where to find it when you were a kid, from the cookie jar with the milk money to the condoms to the gun on the top shelf of the closet? What makes every generation of parents think they're the first to outsmart their children?

Gun-related **Life Lesson #8:** there is no safety in ignorance.

Looking to the future

It's strange how, the more memories we geezers store up to look back on, the more time we spend worrying about the future instead. Maybe it's because we've seen so much stuff go wrong.

Life Lesson #9, I discovered early on, is that it's way less frustrating to be a pessimist than to be an optimist. You see, if you're an optimist, the best that ever happens is that things go exactly as expected, and half the time you're bitterly disappointed. But, if you're a pessimist, the *worst* that ever happens is that things go exactly as expected, and half the time you're pleasantly surprised.

Being alert for trouble all the time, and being prepared to deal with it, isn't paranoia. It's common sense, and it creates freedom from paranoia. The late gun guru Col. Jeff Cooper recommended that people be in Condition Yellow, a state of relaxed alertness, every waking hour, and promised that a well-adjusted man or woman would suffer no ill effects from the practice.

It turns out to be even better. Being constantly alert for bad things allows

knew the answer: "That's baby stuff. I'll have my mom call your mom, and we'll go to the range this weekend and shoot 'em, with live ammunition." That's the kind of status-builder kids can conjure with among their peers, and it keeps them from doing stupid and dangerous things.

Guns taught my kids that if they lived up to their responsibilities, they would be given more power. It was an excellent lesson that paralleled life itself. If gun-related Life Lesson #6 is that power and responsibility must always be in an equal balance, then perhaps gun-related **Life Lesson #7** is that the gun itself is a microcosmic tool for teaching that principle.

My babies are now grown, flown, and on their own, adult parents themselves. My regular service as Parent is done for the most part, though I'm in you to pick up on more good things. The driver who is constantly alert for something wrong up ahead is the one most likely to spot the fawn at the side of the road, or to notice the funny billboard. The ordinary people alert to those around them on a city street are the first to notice the way a pair of newlyweds look at each other, or the little kid playing with his puppy, or the thousand other life-affirming things we ignore because we live too much inside our own heads when we're out and about. Being alert makes you a people watcher. It makes you better than merely well adjusted.

I think the best explanation is **Life Lesson #10**. You know how they're always telling us to stop and smell the roses? Perhaps the lesson is, when you're down on your knees in the bush looking for thorns, you can't help but smell the roses.

As I look to the future with my brother and sister geezers, pessimist though I am, I see reasons for guarded optimism. Our generation, the Boomers, did a few good things. The marches in the streets and the campus takeovers taught us that we could make a difference. Ours was the most self-sufficient of the 20th century generations. The generation who took cardiopulmonary resuscitation out of the Emergency Room and made it something any responsible adult was expected to be able to perform. The generation that made a fire extinguisher a common household appliance instead of something found only in institutional buildings. That made professional security systems affordable for ordinary homes instead of just mansions and banks.

When I was a little kid, I was as shocked to find out there were states where honest people were not allowed to carry concealed handguns in public to protect themselves and their families, as I was to discover that there were states that still practiced legal segregation. That latter has disappeared, thankfully, and the for-

The decades taught the author that early teaching is the best approach to gun safety. From left, Andrew, Adam, and Erik Pepin learn the takedown of their grandmother's Glock 9mm.

mer is dying. In those dark old days, there were seven states that forbade decent citizens the means to protect themselves against deadly force in public; today there are but two, Wisconsin and Illinois. Back then, most states allowed carry permits to be issued only on a discretionary basis, "discretionary" often being a code word for "we'll give you the permit if you're white, male, rich, and politically connected." Today, the overwhelming majority of states have passed reform "shall issue" concealed carry legislation that makes the carry permit available to any honest, competent, law-abiding adult.

The Supreme Court of the United States will soon hear what may be the defining case as to whether the Second Amendment speaks to an individual right. Among the Justices weighing the matter will be Antonin Scalia, who as a youth commuted to high school rifle team matches carrying his .22 rifle on New York City subways, and Clarence Thomas, who wrote in a late 1990s opinion, "Marshaling an impressive array of historical evidence, a growing body

of scholarly commentary indicates that the 'right to keep and bear arms' is, as the Amendment's text suggests, a personal right." I would cautiously predict a victory for our side, with at least a 5-4 majority.

Meanwhile, I've enjoyed the heck out of writing this column and hope to keep doing so, no matter how old and feeble I get. (Coming soon: "Shooting from Wheelchairs"...) And, yeah, we do need to update that picture in the column, white whiskers and chin wattles and all.

It's a good thing my chief allows turtlenecks in lieu of uniform ties. Δ

(Editor's note: The 2nd Amendment case, *District of Columbia v. Heller,* which Ayoob discussed was decided June 26, 2008, 5-4 in favor of Heller. John Silveira discusses it in his *Last Word* column on page 304.)

Also by Massad Ayoob:

In the Gravest Extreme

Grow your own GRAIN

By Jackie Clay

In December, I bought 100 pounds of clean wheat at our local feed mill for $9. A month ago, that same sack of wheat would have cost me $18. I don't even want to ask what it is today.

When I was in high school, we had a terrific economics teacher. I wasn't much interested in economics, but when he began explaining about the causes of an economic depression and that he believed we were headed that way again—to the point that a loaf of bread would cost $5—if you had the five bucks to buy it with, I raised my head up from my aimless doodling and listened. We thought he was a little "off" because at that time, local stores often had sales on bread. Three loaves for a dollar was common. Five

dollars for one loaf of bread? Come on now...

Yesterday I was in the store and saw one of the better brands of bread with a price tag of $4.99! Who's going to argue about the penny? Not me. And who knows how much that bread will cost in a year?

Suddenly, raising wheat and other small grains became a higher priority to us. Sure, I've got a lot of grain and flours of several kinds in storage. But when that's gone, we'll need to replace it with something. I've raised a lot of grain in the past and know we don't really need all that much space to grow enough grain to supply our family for a year or more.

However, we are on a relatively new homestead in the middle of the woods and have limited clear ground avail-

able. And my garden isn't big enough yet to support a wheat and oat patch. We were talking about this the other day when suddenly I looked over at our new, beautifully-cleared, rock-picked, newly-disced, deer-fenced orchard. It needed a cover crop/green manure crop and we had talked about planting annual alfalfa, but why not plant wheat and oats instead? Instantly we were excited about a new project! Now we have about half an acre planted, not only with fruit trees, but also with wheat and oats. It goes to show you that most anyone can grow their own small grain at home, especially if you get a little creative. You don't need a field, and you can do most of the planting, harvesting, and milling by hand.

Choosing which grain

Because wheat is versatile and the most commonly-used grain, I think of it as the queen of grains. There are just so many uses for this grain and the flour that is ground from it. You can sprout wheat to use as a vegetable or salad ingredient. You can grind it coarsely for hot cereal and tasty bread or you can grind it finely and make everything you can imagine: bread, rolls, pie crusts, cookies, cakes, noodles and pasta of all kinds, crackers, biscuits, dumplings, flour tortillas, pita bread, quiche, pastry crusts, and so much more. Any extra can be fed to a small flock of chickens, which will provide you with eggs and meat to go along with those wheat-based recipes.

We used an inexpensive 6-foot single disc to work up our small grain plot.

I believe oats to be a valuable homestead crop as well. It used to be that oats were just too hard to hull; the hulls around each grain don't come off during threshing, like those of wheat. But now there are several varieties of "naked" oats. They have little hull and separate easily on threshing, so you have nice, clean grains of oats ready to roll or grind. And there are several relatively inexpensive hand machines available which roll your oats for you. Oats are not just for oatmeal in the morning. I use my ground or rolled oats in whole grain breads and rolls, granola, cookies, cakes, in meatloaf and fish loaf, and in patties to fry.

While technically not a "small" grain, corn ranks right in there with wheat and oats as a valuable grain for a homesteading family to grow. Not only is it easy to grow (and you probably have experience growing sweet corn already), easy to harvest and store, but there is a wide variety of uses for your crop.

Other small grains you may want to grow and use include rye, buckwheat, spelt, and barley. I've often grown a little rye and buckwheat, but because they're not as versatile as wheat and oats, they take a back seat on my homestead. After all, sometimes you only have so much room. A couple of lesser known grains are ancient grains used by Native peoples across two continents. These are quinoa and amaranth. Both are very good but are more labor intensive than either wheat or oats, as the seeds are much smaller and require more cleaning.

Types and uses of wheat

There are several different kinds of wheat, and it gets confusing when one is trying to decide on which one to buy for seed. Basically, you have "hard" wheat varieties and "soft" wheat. The hard wheat is bread wheat, and the most commonly sold wheat in the United States. Soft wheat has less protein and makes good pastry flour. Durham wheat is usually used for pasta. Most people, myself included, can't tell the difference between hard, soft, or Durham by just looking at a few grains. You *can* make bread out of soft wheat or durham wheat, it is just not considered as good a product. The gluten content in non-hard wheat is not as high, thus it doesn't rise as well without adding extra gluten.

Winter wheat is planted in the fall. It grows up a few inches, then goes dormant over winter, covered (hopefully) with a nice thick insulating blanket of snow. Early in the spring, it wakes up and again starts to grow vigorously. In some locales, winter wheat does best; in others, spring wheat is best. Both make good bread and other wheat/flour products.

How much land do I need?

A small plot, say 10'x 100' will usually give you a bushel of wheat—about 60 pounds in weight. This is generally enough for one person, used lightly, for a year. You can usually boost your harvest upward significantly by watering your wheat as it grows and making sure that the plot is well fertilized beforehand. You can often expect to harvest 15-50 bushels per acre under decent homestead situations. A fifth of an acre will provide an average family with all their wheat needs for a year, and probably enough for a small flock of chickens, too.

A few extra rows of flint corn next to your sweet corn patch will give you a year's worth of cornmeal, used moderately.

I plant my small grain plots in rotation; one year I'll grow the whole thing in wheat, then the next divide it and plant half in wheat, half in rye. Then I may plant ¼ in buckwheat, ¼ in rye, and ½ in oats, depending on what I have in storage. All small grains have an indefinite storage time, provided they are kept in an airtight, rodent-proof container out of damp conditions. So you don't have to grow each type of small grain you use every year, as long as you have sufficient grains in storage.

One year, quite a few years back, I renovated an old piece of pasture, plowing and fertilizing it well. I planted rye as a nurse crop and seeded orchard grass, timothy, and alsike clover with it. That fall, we had a great rye crop, which I shared with

An old bed spring from the dump makes a fine harrow. Use it to smooth out your plot before planting and again after sowing to cover your seeds with soil.

neighbors. I *still* have a tin full of that rye, and it still makes great rye bread.

Preparing the land

If you've ever planted a lawn, you have an idea of what growing grain is like. Pretty darned simple, actually. Kill off all the weeds possible before working up your plot; your job is simplified if you choose a spot without a huge weed problem in the first place. You can effectively kill off not only weeds but their seeds by "cooking" the spot. First mow the spot down with a lawnmower, then till it well, breaking the sod up finely. After this has been done, water the ground deeply and cover the spot with a black or blue plastic tarp, or even a layer of old carpet from the dump. Weight the cover down, and leave it in place for at least six weeks. This solar cooking will effectively kill 90% of the grasses and weeds present, including their seeds.

You may work the ground up with any method you choose, or have available to you, from spade and rake to tractor-drawn plow, disc, and harrow, depending on the size of the plot.

I've tilled many smaller plots with my TroyBilt rototiller, but this year we picked up a 6-foot single disc cheap.

After the initial tilling of your new grain plot-to-be, spread a nice layer of rotted manure over it. That will nearly double your yield on many soils and may ensure that you *do* make a crop on poor soils. Some soils are so low in fertility that without the additional fertilizer and organic material, they won't produce enough grain to feed a chicken.

Work the manure in well, chopping up any coarse pieces with either a disc or tiller. If your soil is clumpy, run a harrow over the spot or rake it smooth. Your "harrow" can be a simple bed spring from the dump; that's what we use and it does a great job.

For best luck, have your plot where you can run water to it should the weather get dry during the growing season. And if you have animal problems (especially hungry deer) it is a good idea to fence the area. The expense is not too great, and the benefit will last for years and years. Six foot high, 2"x4" welded wire is about the best you can use.

A cheap whirly-bird seeder, usually used for planting grass seed, works great for sowing grain evenly in a small plot.

Planting your grain

If you are planning on planting a small field, it's a good idea to borrow a small grain drill. This is a long box on wheels with discs that open the soil, tubes that guide the grain into the small furrows the discs make, and chains dragging behind to cover the grain up. You pour the grain into the box, then set the amount you want to plant per acre.

With wheat this is usually about 100 pounds per acre. Then you carefully drive your tractor up and down the field so it is well covered, trying not to double up on spots or miss sections. When it sprouts, you'll see how well you planted!

For smaller plots, you may use about 4 pounds for your 10'x100' patch. You can sow this by hand broadcasting, which is an art in itself. You carry the basket of grain with one hand and gently strew handfuls in front of you with a fan-like toss. It takes practice to get the seeding right, with no thick or thin spots. So for beginners, the best way to sow wheat on small plots is to use a cheap plastic whirly-bird grass seeder, available at most hardware stores, and even Wal-Mart. I used it on our new orchard wheat plot and the seeding came up very even and absolutely beautiful.

Once the seed has been sown, it is lying on top of the ground. Some will germinate, but the birds will get a lot, and some will dry and die in the hot sun. So to get the most germination, you need to get that seed covered by dirt. You can either till the patch again, setting the tiller shallow, or else harrow it again. These methods will cover most of the grain so it has an easier time surviving.

Corn is planted in rows, just as your sweet corn is, allowing plenty of room for cultivating as it grows in between the rows; two feet is usually adequate unless you are using a tractor.

If the weather is dry and your plot relatively small, water it well right after sowing to help it jump up vigorously. Once the grain sprouts, you have very little to do until it is ripe. You can water it during dry spells to keep those heads of grain fat and heavy; a little water makes a huge difference to grain.

Harvesting your grain

Oats will ripen before wheat. You'll know it's nearing ripeness when the heads get pale tan and a grain pinched between your thumbnail and fingernail is hard, not doughy. The same with wheat, only the heads will be turning a lovely golden color. You don't want your grain to completely ripen or it will thresh out of the hulls when you cut it. You want your grain in your pantry, not reseeded onto the ground!

To make sure you do get your grain, plan on cutting it when it's just a little bit green, or unripe. You want the heads and most of the plant to be tan with just a little green showing and a grain can be dented with your fingernail, just barely.

You can cut your grain stalks with a variety of tools. A scythe, gasoline powered hedge trimmer, string trimmer, or even a machete will work on small patches. Cut the stalks as long as conveniently possible. You can use the straw for animal bedding, chicken nests, or mulch. And cut as gently as possible, so you don't shatter the grain from the heads.

Once you have a little patch cut, it's time to gather up sheaves and bind them. To do this, gather up a double-hand bunch of grain stalks, stand them on end, then twist a small bundle of stalks around your sheaf and tie it. When learning, it helps to have someone following you, helping and gathering up the sheaves until there are enough to make a shock. You will stand up about five sheaves in a tipi, then lay another across the top, as a cap to shed rain and heavy dew.

Shocked up this way, your sheaves should dry in rain-free weather in about four days, finishing out their ripening. Again, check a head of grain, trying to dent a kernel with your thumbnail. It should be hard, not doughy.

When this day arrives, it's time to bring in your sheaves, just as the old hymn says. "Bringing in the sheaves… Bringing in the sheaves… We shall come rejoicing, bringing in the sheaves!"

Wheat is already a few inches tall in the new orchard grain plot.

And boy do we! This will be our bread, noodles, cookies, cakes, pies, rolls, cereal, and more. We haul in our sheaves in our washed out garden tractor trailer. You'd be surprised at how many sheaves you can gently pile in one.

I lay out a large plastic tarp on a back corner of our lawn, where a little stray straw won't matter. Then we toss a sheaf onto the tarp and whack the grain heads with a homemade flail. This is simply two old hardwood shovel handles (which had broken off and been re-sawn), with holes drilled in the square saw ends and an eight inch piece of light nylon rope tying them together, forming a limber "hinge." You hold one handle and beat the grain heads with the other piece. (Don't get wild and whack yourself in the head in the process.)

Even an old baseball bat will work, but the limber flail makes light work of the process.

Check your now disheveled sheaf. The grain heads should be pretty empty by now. Take a *clean* pitchfork and toss the straw over onto another tarp and repeat the process until your trailer load of sheaves has been threshed. Take a break, then go get another load if you have it, and keep working until all has been threshed. Kids love the process, as do many adults who have never participated in the homestead grain harvest.

Okay, now you have one tarp piled high with straw and another (your threshing floor) littered with piles of grain, chaff, and broken grain heads. Work the pile over lightly with your pitchfork to remove any long pieces of straw. Then simply pick out the broken grain heads. Your chickens will love picking through them!

I usually pick through, throwing out any large bugs, such as grasshoppers, then pour the grain, chaff, and all into garbage cans to store overnight or until the next windy day. I have never had a fanning mill to clean my grain, so Mr. Wind has to do it for me. This wind cleaning is called winnowing. To winnow your grain, dip out a mixing bowl of grain/chaff/straw and pour it from a shoulder height down into a bucket or onto a clean tarp. The wind will carry away most of the dust, chaff, and straw. Repeat this process several times and you'll end up with nicely cleaned grain. I take my hands and spread out the clean pile and make sure there aren't any stray bugs in it. Grain seems to attract grasshoppers! But they are large and easily seen, and they don't eat much.

Harvesting your corn

Corn is left to dry on the stalk. As the fall progresses, the corn husks dry, turn a light tan, and the ears begin to hang down. Ripe corn kernels are hard; you can't dent them with your thumbnail. Leave the corn in the field until it is quite hard, even if the weather turns cold. When it is dry, walk through the patch, snapping the ears off and tossing them into a basket or trailer, depending on how large your patch is.

You can store the dry ears, unhusked, in a pile in a rodent-free dry area until you can husk it and shell the corn off the cob. The easiest way to husk your corn is simply to sit in a comfortable chair next to your pile with a little soft music playing or a friend to keep you company with good conversation—and maybe a little help—and pull the husks down off the ears.

I husk all my corn and toss it onto a clean tarp. When that is finished, I take one cob at a time and hand shell the corn off into a clean bucket or garbage can. You can pick up hand-cranked corn shellers at flea markets, auctions, or you can still buy them new. They clamp onto a board on a barrel and you feed the cob down into the throat while you turn the hand crank. The cob is shelled with little work. But I do mine by hand, rolling two cobs together to work the kernels against each other. I help the kernels off with a roll of my thumb and soon I have another clean cob; the job goes quite quickly.

After I'm done shelling the corn, I take it outside and winnow it in the wind to remove any chaff, bits of corn silk, or dust.

Storing your whole grain

Scoop up the clean grain and dump it into clean five-gallon buckets to store. These often come with gasketed, snug-fitting lids and make ideal grain storage buckets. Have too much grain for buckets? A good grade lidded garbage can will work well, too.

In some areas, grain also contains minute insect eggs, usually maize moths or pantry moths. These later hatch in storage, making "weevils" or "bugs" in your grain, which is not a nice thing. If you are concerned about this, you can freeze your grain for 2-3 days in the buckets in your freezer. This will prevent the eggs from ever hatching and will keep your grain bug-free. It's a good idea to buy several pantry moth traps and keep them in your pantry. These will catch any stray moths before they possibly crawl into your grain containers and lay eggs. It's simply amazing at how tiny an opening they can squeeze through! These pantry moth traps are inexpensive and are readily available in most seed/garden supply catalogs.

Once your dry grain has been placed in airtight, rodent-proof storage, it will remain perfectly good for dozens of years. This makes grain one of the very best long-term emergency storage foods. It also makes it realistically possible to slowly build up your grain storage, even if you only can grow a limited amount of grain each year. Just use less than you grow and save up the rest. You'll have several hundred pounds of grain stored before you know it.

Processing your grain

While some grain can be sprouted and eaten that way, most grain is either cracked, rolled, or ground. For instance, oats are often rolled for use in oatmeal or breads, where wheat, rye, and barley are often cracked or ground in varying degrees of fineness, depending on personal preference. Some folks love the nutty, crunchy, earthy taste of coarsely ground flour and cracked grains. Others want very fine, smooth, fluffy flour.

Unlike store-bought flours, home ground flour contains *all* the grain— germ, oils, and nutrients. Nothing is

Grain kept in an airtight container will make excellent bread for years to come.

added; nothing is taken away. It is definitely better for you, and tastes better, too, but because the germ and oil is left in the flour, home-ground fresh flour *will* go rancid fairly quickly. Don't grind up more than you will be using within a month or so; it's much better to grind the flour the same day you plan on using it or at least within a few days of use.

There are dozens of grain mills available today, ranging from the little clamp-on-your-counter hand mills to electric grain mills capable of grinding hundreds of pounds of wheat in an hour. Of course, the simple hand mills are cheaper, usually running less than $75. They don't sing, dance, or chew gum; they just grind grain and you will need to pass the flour through a couple of times to get it very fine if you like your flour soft and fluffy.

But you don't need a thousand dollar electric mill, either. Like I said, you don't want to grind more grain than you'll be using soon, so a big mill would be wasted in most homestead situations. I have one of the little cheapy hand mills and like it just fine. Yes, I'd love a bigger, electric mill. It grinds quicker, finer, and with less elbow work. But in an emergency situation, there wouldn't be power—even generator power after awhile—so an electric mill should also have a backup hand mill anyway.

Both Lehman's Hardware (www.lehmans.com) and Emergency Essentials (www.beprepared.com) sell several very good grain mills and any one of them would make a great addition to any homestead.

You can also grind small amounts of grain in your blender, but it will heat up and the flour will stick together, requiring you to poke it to release as you grind. But it does work in a pinch.

A few mills can also be set to roll wheat and oats. This is definitely a bonus; it keeps you from having to buy two machines to process your grain. Likewise, many mills will not only mill grain, but also grind corn and even nuts to make nut butter. Versatility is a big bonus with any grain mill.

What do I do with it?

Here is but a fraction of the things you can do with your grain:

Wheat:

First off, you can sprout your wheat, adding sprouts to salads, sandwiches, etc. You can also dry these sprouts and coarsely grind them to add to your multigrain breads. It is very nutty and good. If you let the sprouts mature a few days, you have wheatgrass, which you can juice and get a nutritious drink. And, like the sprouts, you can add the wheatgrass to salads and sandwiches. When I was a kid, this was my favorite "nibble" food. Wheatgrass is sweet, juicy, and tastes like summer.

A great hot breakfast cereal can be made out of soaked, clean, whole wheat. You just soak a cup or so of whole wheat in boiling water, then keep it steaming in a double boiler on the back of your stove for several hours. It swells up like beans do and becomes soft and chewy. It can be served hot with milk and sugar or cinnamon sugar and butter. Adding chopped fruit or preserves makes it even better. I like to toss in a handful of dehydrated strawberries or raspberries while it's steaming. Pretty darned good for a "survival" food!

By cracking your wheat coarsely, you can make couscous, which is a steamed cracked wheat, often served with meat and vegetables. After steaming, you add a little butter and broth, then steam it again till tender. Most folks serve it under chopped meat and vegetables.

Bulgur is similar to couscous, in that it is steamed cracked wheat. But it is often mixed with meat and either baked or fried in patties or small loaves. You can even make your own coffee substitute from parched bulgur.

This is basically a Postum-type hot drink. You parch the bulgur in an oven, stirring it to keep from scorching it, until it is a rich brown. Cool it, then run it through your grain mill until it is fine. Store it in an airtight jar. To use, mix a heaping tablespoonful into a cup of boiling water and stir well. You may want to add sugar, honey, or milk to it. Mom likes milk and sugar with hers. You may have to experiment with it as to the strength you like. If you want it stronger, just add more "coffee."

Cracked wheat cereal is similar to Cream of Wheat. You will probably want it cracked a bit finer than either couscous or bulgur. It does take longer to make than "instant" Cream of Wheat, but it tastes so much better. I used to make it for my youngest kids when I first got up in the morning to get the fire going in the wood cookstove. You'll gently simmer about 1 cup finely cracked wheat in 5 cups salted water until thick and tender. Stir often once it begins to thicken or it'll scorch. Serve with butter, milk, sugar, and fruit. Cracked wheat is a wonderful addition to breads, too.

Of course you already know your wheat is great for all sorts of breads and rolls. It won't make light, puffy bread, like store-bought, because it's not bleached with chemicals and still has its goodness left intact. Instead, your homemade breads and rolls will be the kind you'll want to make a meal out of when they emerge hot from the oven.

Besides just bread and rolls, you can also make flour tortillas, popovers, pita bread, crepes, pancakes, dumplings, waffles, crackers, fritters, pretzels, steamed puddings, fry bread, biscuits, cakes, bars, pie crusts, pizza crusts, breakfast cake, and a whole lot more.

Don't forget pastas! I absolutely love homemade noodles. They are thick, chewy, and tender. With the help of a "pasta machine," either hand-cranked or motor-driven, you

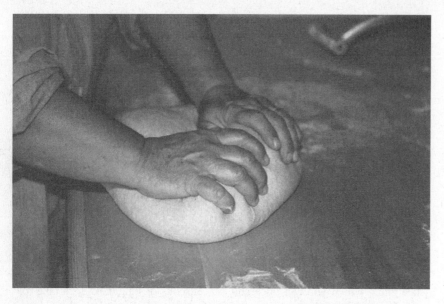

Your homegrown grain will make terrific bread.

can also easily make spaghetti, ravioli, lasagna, fine noodles, and more. Pasta making gets to be an obsession, it's so fun and productive. While durham wheat makes the best pasta, I really like pasta made from hard wheat; it's more tender and less chewy.

Oats:

If you have grown naked oats, you won't have to worry about removing the hulls, which is difficult to do at home. You can grind the oats to use in whole grain baking, but you can't use it in place of flour, as it has no gluten and will not rise without the added flour. Oat flour and rolled oats tend to make a heavier bread, so don't overdo the amount in your recipe.

Like wheat, you can make an excellent breakfast cereal out of coarsely ground oats, sort of a thick oat gruel. Simmer the ground oats in salted water, covered, on a low heat until thickened and tender. Serve with milk, sugar, and fruit if you like.

Of course, you can also make oatmeal by rolling your oats. This takes a little longer cooking as the rolled oats aren't precooked, but the result is great.

Your rolled oats can also be used to make great granolas of all flavors and types. I add sunflower or peanut oil, brown sugar or honey, dehydrated fruit, roasted nuts, coconut, or whatever else I want to experiment with. The granola mix is toasted on cookie sheets in the oven until it is dry and clumped up nicely. Then store it in airtight containers…if you can keep it around long enough to store, that is.

You can use rolled oats to thicken and bulk up your meat and fish loaf; it also adds fiber and extra nutrition.

Oat flour or rolled oats are also used in bars, apple and other fruit crisps, cookies, breakfast breads, stuffings, and pies.

Corn:

Corn is a great grain. You can eat it "green," as roasting or boiling ears, then you can parch or dry the green corn for an entirely different taste and texture. Or you can let it ripen and make hominy (another "different" taste and end product), grind *that* for corn flour which makes excellent tortillas and tamales, or you can simply grind the shelled, dry corn kernels to make the best cornmeal you've ever eaten. It doesn't taste like store cornmeal; it's much richer, sweeter, and "cornier" tasting.

Nearly every grain mill will easily grind corn or hominy into meal and flour; no extra gadgets to buy here!

You can make a wide variety of foods with your fresh cornmeal. Boil it with salted water for cornmeal mush for breakfast. It is a thick, sweet, rich breakfast food like no other you've tasted. Pour your leftover mush in a greased bread pan and refrigerate. When cold, you can slice it and fry it. It's great for breakfast or any other meal of the day.

You can also make hoe cakes, corn dodgers, cornbread, cornmeal muffins, hush puppies, spoon bread, Indian pudding, cornmeal waffles (great with taco filling and cheese spooned over them), and much more.

Rye:

Rye is perhaps best know for making sweet, fragrant, dark rye bread and rolls—that's reason enough to grow a small patch! Nothing beats

---

Sources for grain seeds:

Territorial Seed Company
PO Box 158
Cottage Grove, OR 97424
800-626-0866
Customer Service/Gardening
  Questions: 541-942-9547
www.territorialseed.com

Homegrown Harvest
2065 Lakeshore Overlook Dr.
Kennesaw, GA 30152
1-866-900-3321 (10-5 EST)
www.homegrownharvest.com

Johnny's Selected Seeds
955 Benton Avenue
Winslow, ME 04901
1-877-564-6697
www.johnnyseeds.com

Seed Dreams
PO Box 106
Port Townsend, WA 98368
360-385-4308
email:
gowantoseed@yahoo.com

homemade hot rye bread right from the oven.

But rye flour also makes great crackers, pancakes, sweet cake, breakfast cereal (like wheat cereal, but sweetened with molasses), pie crusts for meat pie, and more. But, like oat flour, rye flour doesn't have gluten in it and won't rise unless mixed with wheat flour. Primarily rye breads are dense and heavy, although also chewy, tasty, and hearty enough to stick to your ribs.

It doesn't matter much what grain you decide to grow first. The important thing, especially with today's skyrocketing prices and uncertain future, is that you give it some serious thought and get started at raising at least a portion of your own grain. It's easy, fun, and very satisfying—and another giant step toward self-reliant living. Δ

GROWING GRAIN FOR YOUR POULTRY AND LIVESTOCK

Just as you can grow your own grain for home use, you can certainly cut your feed costs by growing additional grain for a small flock of chickens or a couple of dairy goats. Of course, it depends a lot on how much land you have available, or can bring into production in the future. For instance, on our new homestead in the woods, we have just gotten our garden and orchard into production after four years of starting small and it was very rough.

We've got the orchard planted into not only fruit trees but wheat, as well. But with the dramatically escalating price of all grain products, feed included, we are now expanding our plans to include growing a fairly large plot of grain for our chickens and goats.

Just like the "people" grain plot, the animal plot doesn't need to be huge, nor do you instantly need to grow all of your grain in order to succeed. If you can even grow some of your own feed, you are ahead of the game.

What grains you grow depends on the type and amount of land you have available. If you are extremely lucky and have a flat, dry, clear piece of hay field, pasture, or even too-huge lawn, you can easily bring that into production very quickly. And if you do have that large area, you might consider raising a nice plot of chicken and goat corn (field corn) and another of wheat. These two grains make a pretty balanced diet, supplemented, of course, with minerals and a good quality pasture or free range for chickens.

The reason I say field corn, instead of sweet corn is that field corn gets much larger than sweet corn does. The average length of an ear of sweet corn is 8 inches, with maybe 14 rows of kernels around the cob. Most field corn gets at least 12 inches long with more rows of larger kernels. You plant field corn just the same as you do sweet corn and take care of it in the same way. Experts will tell you that you can't plant field corn next to, or around, sweet corn or it'll ruin the sweet corn. (Before I knew this, I planted my corn together, and you know what? My sweet corn was the absolute best in the county!) But you should keep field corn away from sweet varieties that advise you to isolate your sweet corn. You might run into problems there.

You can find a wide variety of field corn seed, including extra early for northern growers, in R.H Shumway's catalog (www.rhshumway.com).

Remember, because field corn is larger than sweet corn, you will do well to add plenty of manure to your new plot and work it in before you plant. Providing water if the weather dries out will also do much to increase your crop, whether it is row irrigation or sprinkling with elevated sprinklers, depending on the size of your plot.

Just like you plan on growing wheat for your family, you can also grow a plot or enlarge your home plot so you can grow extra for your chickens and goats.

Millet is another great food, especially for chickens. Unfortunately, it is not grown much today; the home "chicken garden" of our grandparents has largely gone extinct. But that doesn't mean that it wasn't a great idea or that you can't revive the tradition. Millet is one of the ingredients of most mixed birdseed. It is the little shiny light colored seeds in it. Chickens love millet and it is very good for them, too.

Millet grows like a cross between corn and wheat; kind of a tall, broadleafed grass with a group of long grain heads that form on the top, bending under their own weight. Millet is as easy as wheat to grow, requires no cultivation, and is quite hardy. You basically harvest it like wheat and thresh out the grain (seeds) for winter storage in the fall. You can often buy millet seed at your local feed store. You want white millet seed. If you can't find it, the Drs. Foster & Smith catalog (www.drsfostermith.com) carries it very inexpensively.

Your grain patch for your chickens and livestock can easily be divided so you can grow field corn, millet, and wheat. Or you could choose barley and wheat. There is no perfect answer, but you can grow nutritious grains for your homestead flock and livestock and save a bundle in the process.

Sewing and using Cloth diapers
is easier than you think

By Annie Tuttle

I'll admit that it was the pastoral vision of a laundry line full of sun-bleached diapers above barefooted, rosy-cheeked, milk-fattened babies that first drew my attention toward cloth diapers. The idea of replacing an expensive disposable "necessity"—most babies will use an average of 5000 diapers — with a much cheaper reusable version appealed to my frugal nature, too.

Buying new cloth diapers is still pretty expensive up front, so I decided to sew my own. The first diapers I made more than four years ago were used by both of my children, and now I've given some of them to a friend for her daughter and newborn son.

Since those first diapering days I've learned a lot, talked to many other cloth-diapering families, made a lot of diapers, and made some mistakes, too. I'll try to share some of what I've learned with you.

How many diapers you start with is completely dependent on how often you want to wash your diapers. We started off with two dozen diapers when our daughter was born, but if I had to do it again I'd start with at least three dozen for a newborn. I had to wash a load of diapers every single day, or risk running out. As your baby gets older he'll use fewer diapers each day, but it's still nice to have enough so you can go a day or two without washing.

What are they made of?

Any fabric that absorbs liquid will work, but some fibers are better suit-ed than others. Cotton, linen, and hemp are all natural fibers which absorb well. Included among these are birdseye, diaper twill, flannel, jersey and interlock (t-shirt fabric), terry cloth (bath towels) and stretch terry, and cotton and hemp fleece (not polyester polar fleece, that's different). You can get most of these fabrics from the stores listed in the resource guide at the end of this article.

Liquid absorbing microfiber towels (not those advertised for dusting), usually sold as shop towels also work very well as absorbent layers, even though they're synthetics.

You'll need good quality elastic, too. Something that will stand up to lots of hot-water washing and detergent is best, like swimwear elastic.

Using recycled fabric

Don't discount the possibility of using old clothes, towels, and other found fabric to make diapers. I made a huge set of diapers out of a set of ugly queen-size flannel sheets and an old cotton bath towel, and the only cost was for the elastic and snaps, about $10 total. T-shirts also make cute diapers; center the pattern of the t-shirt on the "bottom" of the diaper,

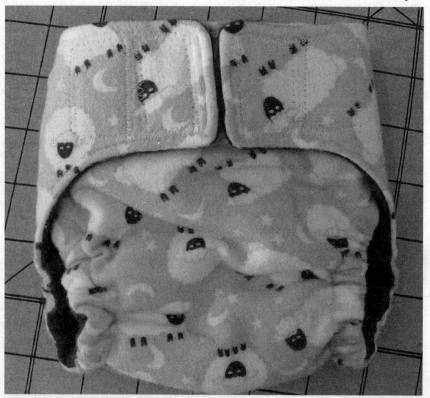

The finished diaper

and use the sleeves as extra absorbent layers.

When scavenging for soaker materials, look for items with a high percentage of cotton. The outside of the diaper can be just about any kind of fabric, as long as it can stand up to repeated washing. The layer next to baby's bottom can be anything soft that doesn't repel moisture.

Fasteners

There are a number of ways you can keep these diapers on your baby.

If you have a few diaper pins, then by all means use them. Not many babies can figure out how to undo them to escape their diapers. Use a bar of soap as a "pin cushion" for your diaper pins, and you'll have a much easier time pinning your diapers. If you're too nervous about poking your baby, there are a number of other options available.

For self-fastening diapers, your options are plastic (polyacetal resin) snaps, or hook and loop tape (Velcro, Aplix, and Touch Tape are a few brand names).

Everyone has a preference—I really like plastic snaps, to the point that I've invested in a snap press (about $60) and replaced all of my velcro diapers with snap diapers. But, I realize not everyone wants to invest in a press, so the pattern I'll give you uses hook and loop tape. It is easy to sew on or repair at home without special equipment, makes for a more adjustable diaper, and is easy to find at your local fabric store.

Washing diapers

Washing diapers is easy! Don't let anyone tell you otherwise. It takes hardly any time out of my day.

Here's our basic routine. We "dry pail" our diapers, which means after each diaper change we shake any solids into the toilet, then put the diaper in a laundry basket with no water until we have enough for a load of laundry. You can sprinkle a little baking soda in the pail to help neutralize odors, if you find it necessary.

When it's time to run the load, usually every other day, I first run a cold rinse with plain water only—no detergent. Then I run a long hot wash with about ½ the recommended amount of detergent and a scoop of oxygen based bleach, like Oxy-clean or Oxy-boost. That's it! After that, the diapers should smell super clean—clean enough that you can stick your nose right into them for a big fresh-smelling whiff—and they go into the dryer or out on the laundry line.

Don't use regular bleach too often, or you'll find that your diapers begin to deteriorate quickly. If you feel that you're having sanitation problems, then by all means use it, but for stains, I find that sunshine is the best remedy of all.

Washing trouble

Sometimes, no matter how many times you wash the diapers, they just smell funny, or cause diaper rash, or look dirty. It can be a trick diagnos-ing the issue, but it usually comes down to one of two things (or a combination of both): detergent not rinsing out of your diapers all the way, or the pH of the diapers not being balanced. Either of these things can cause diaper rash, strong smell, and premature disintegration of your diapers, so the quicker you solve these problems, the happier everyone will be. The detergent problem is easy to resolve. Just continue rinsing the diapers until there are no suds left in the washer at all. Try reducing the amount of detergent you use, or switching detergents, too. If you have a severe detergent build up, you might have to run your diapers through several plain water wash cycles to get it all out. Diapers are one instance where you don't want to use any sort of laundry soap, because it will always leave a bit of residue behind.

The other problem, which can take some more time to figure out, is unbalanced pH level of your diapers. I'm no chemist, but I'll try to explain it a little. pH is the measure of how acidic or basic something is. It ranges from 0-14, with pure water considered neutral, at a pH of 7. That's the number we're shooting for here, too. Numbers lower than 7 indicate that a compound is acidic, and higher numbers indicate a basic makeup. The things that affect the pH of your diapers include the water you wash them in, the detergent you use, and your baby's waste. It's easy to find out the pH of your diapers with litmus paper. It's cheap, and you can usually find it at a pool supply store. Or you can order it from Edmund Scientifics (1-800-728-6999, or www.scientificsonline.com). Just place the litmus paper on a wet diaper to get a reading. Once you know what pH you're starting with, you'll know whether you need to add vinegar (acid) or baking soda (basic) to every load of diaper laundry to keep the pH balanced. (If your diapers are very acidic, try using washing soda instead—it is even more basic than baking soda.)

Using the pattern

I've included a half pattern for a basic diaper pattern that you'll have to trace in order to make a full pattern. As printed, the pattern will make a newborn-sized diaper. To make a larger or smaller diaper, enlarge the pattern using the diaper size chart as a guideline. (You can also download a file that includes the full pattern in sizes from Newborn up to Toddler from my blog: http://www.back-woodshome.com/blogs/Bramblestitches.)

Babies vary greatly in size, and they grow ridiculously fast, so these are just guidelines. Your three month old may already be big enough to wear 6-12 month diapers, and tall thin children may stay in smaller sizes longer.

A basic fitted diaper

If you want to try out cloth diapers without making a big investment, here's a great pattern for you. This pattern can be made with a regular sewing machine, and all of the materials are inexpensive and should be easy to scavenge or find at your local fabric store. Another feature of these diapers is that they're easy to wash and dry, because they're fairly trim, with only three layers of flannel and one or two layers of toweling. The extra absorbency comes from a lay-in doubler—an additional piece of toweling or absorbent cloth that folds up and sits inside the diaper. I remember the very first diapers I ever made took three hours in the dryer. Nobody can afford that kind of utility bill every month, not to mention the backed up laundry it caused. These can dry in a regular cycle with no problem, and in just a few hours on the clothesline (even in very humid North Carolina).

You'll need:
- cotton flannel, or other fabric for the outside, inside, and in-between layers
- terry cloth, an old cotton bath towel, or other absorbent fabric for the "soaker" layer
- 1 package of ¼" wide elastic
- 1 package hook and loop tape. You'll need about 10" of "loop" and 2" of "hook" for the small size.
- thread

First, trace the half pattern

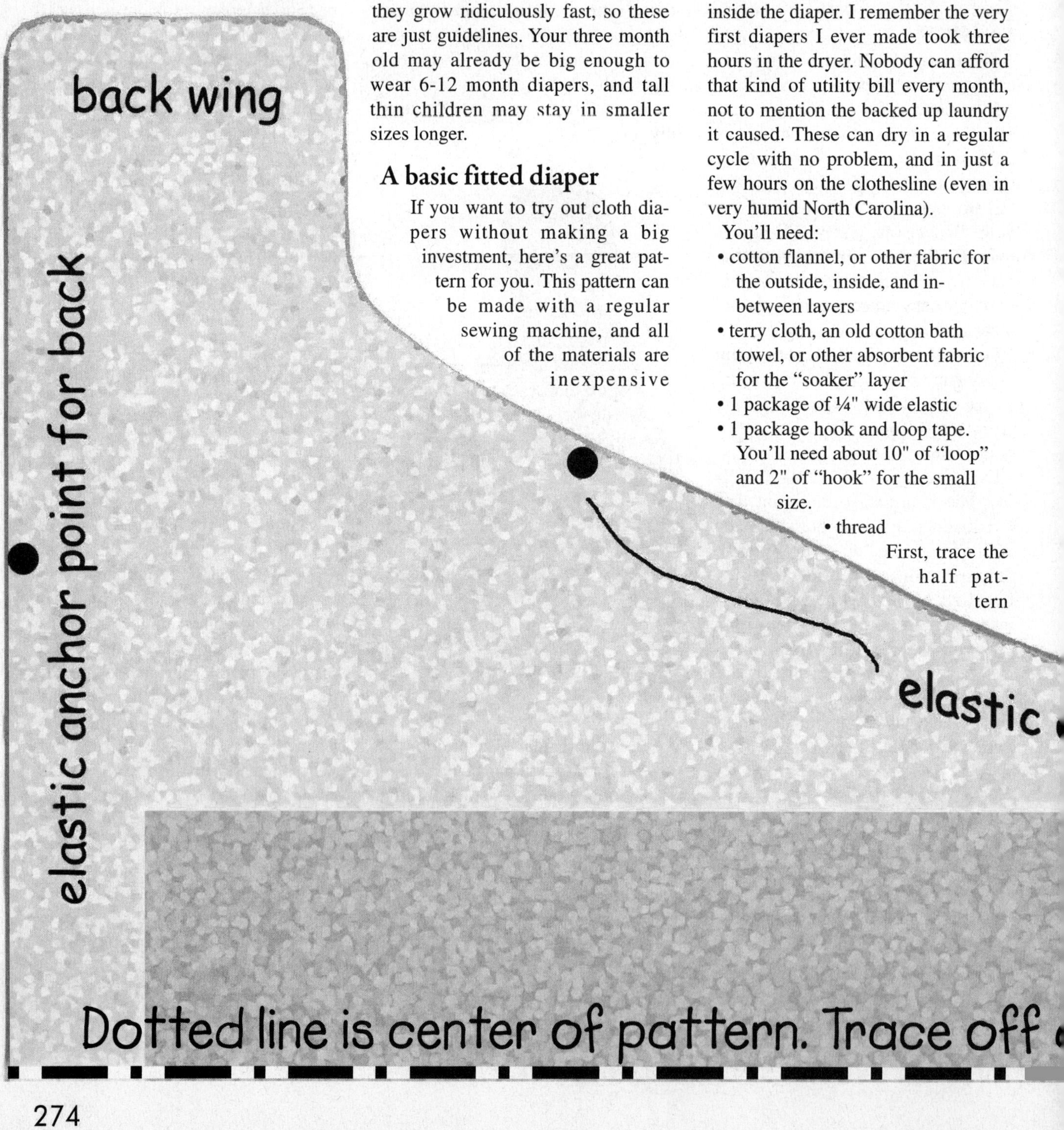

back wing

elastic anchor point for back

elastic

Dotted line is center of pattern. Trace off

so that you're working with a full diaper pattern. Cut three pieces of your main fabric from the pattern, and two pieces of terry or toweling from the soaker pattern piece.

Your three pieces of flannel are for the outside, the in-between layer, and the inside.

The soaker is sewn to the in-between layer. Center the rectangles of terry cloth on the diaper, and sew in place with a zig-zag stitch or medium-length straight stitch.

Now you'll assemble the diaper. Layer your three diaper pieces as follows: inside layer face up, then outside layer face down, then in-between layer with soaker facing up. Pin around the edge, and sew ¼" from the edge, leaving about a four-inch wide gap along the front edge of the diaper for turning.

Now you'll sew on the elastic. How long your elastic is depends on how stretchy it is and how chubby or thin your baby is. A good starting point for small diapers is 4" for each piece of elastic. Tack each end of elastic down at the elastic marks in the seam allowance. When you have all three pieces of elastic sewn on, turn the diaper right side out, and pin around the edge. Pin the front turning hole closed, and stretch the elastic areas as you pin. When you sew around the edge, you

Diaper Size Chart

If possible, measure your child before choosing what size diaper to make. Measure over a diaper, from the top of the diaper in front, down between the legs, up to the top of the diaper in back. This measurement is your child's "rise." When you enlarge your pattern, make sure the center line is at least ½" longer than this measurement.

Size	Fit Range	Rise	Center line	Elastic
Preemie	4-7 lbs.	12"	12.5"	3½"
Newborn	6-12 lbs.	14"	14.5"	4"
Small	10-25 lbs.	16"	16.5"	4½"
Medium	25-35 lbs.	18"	18.5"	5"
Large	30-40 lbs	20"	20.5"	5½"

don't want to catch the elastic again, so push the elastic right up to the edge of the diaper before you pin.

Now you'll topstitch around the entire diaper, closing the front turning hole at the same time. Where there is no elastic, stitch close to the edge, about $1/8$" away, and where there is elastic, stitch just on the other side of the elastic, about $5/8$" away from the edge of the diaper. Don't sew through the elastic as you stitch; the idea is to make a casing for the elastic so it can move and stretch freely.

Next, attach your velcro. Cut a piece of loop velcro to fit the front of the diaper right up to the edges. Round the corners just a little bit so they won't poke baby. Sew onto the outside front with a zig-zag stitch. Cut two pieces of hook and two pieces of loop about 1-1½" each for the back tabs. Sew to the inside back edges with a zig-zag stitch. The extra piece of loop here is so you can fold the hook back before washing. This will help keep the hook part lint-free, and will also help keep your diapers from all sticking to each other in the laundry and becoming a "diaper snake."

Diaper doublers

Since these diapers are designed to be fairly thin and easy to wash, you'll probably want to make a batch of diaper doublers, too.

front wing

r points for leg

pattern before you cut your fabric.

Sew around the edge of the diaper, leaving a 3-4" gap in the front for turning.

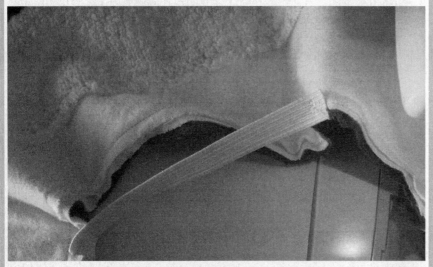

Tack each end of the elastic down with a zig-zag stitch at the elastic marks.

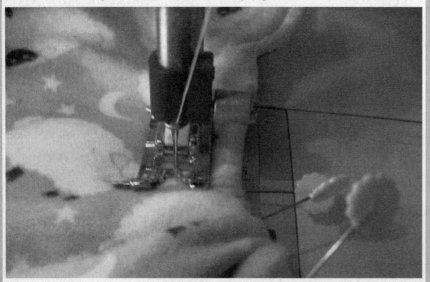

Sew next to the elastic to form a casing where if can move freely.

Doublers are like an extra soaker that can be folded and placed inside the diaper to increase the diaper's absorbency. I make mine out of one layer of bath towel and one layer of flannel or t-shirt. Cut your doubler pieces the length of your soaker and three times wider. With right sides together, stitch all the way around the edge, leaving a few inches unsewn for turning. Turn the doubler right side out, then top stitch all around, closing the turning hole as you stitch. Sew two more straight lines through the center of the doubler to separate it into thirds. To use, just fold the doubler in thirds and lay inside the diaper.

Make a diaper cover

Unless you like having a damp-bottomed baby sitting on your lap, you'll probably want a few diaper covers.

My favorite diaper covers are made out of old, thin wool sweaters from the thrift store. Choose a sweater that is fairly thin and soft, and at least 80% wool. Machine wash and dry the sweater a time or two to felt it a little. This way you can cut into it and not worry about it coming unravelled at the edge, and it will make it easier to care for in the future.

Use the same pattern you used for your diapers, but add about two inches to the width of the pattern. The extra stretch in the sweater fabric or fleece will also help to make up the extra length needed to fit over a diaper. Cut two pieces for the diaper cover using the pattern.

The cover is assembled just like a diaper, except there is no "hidden layer" or soaker. With right sides together, sew around the edge of the cover, leaving a hole for turning. Sew on your elastic as if you were making a diaper. Turn the cover right side out, pin, and topstitch around the edge, remembering to sew on the otherside of the elastic at the back and leg edges. Add velcro and you're done!

Allow the soaker to thoroughly dry and air out between uses. When

Detergents

Not all laundry detergents are created equal, and not all work well for washing diapers. Some can cause pH balance problems, some leave behind a residue that can build up in your diapers, and others simply do a poor job of cleaning. When shopping for detergents, try to choose a brand that doesn't contain any of these: enzymes, optical brighteners, fragrances, dyes, bleach, or fabric softeners.

It may take a few tries to find a detergent that you're happy with, but don't despair, there's one out there that will work. For a list of detergents that have been rated by users of cloth diapers, visit http://www.diaperjungle.com/detergent-chart.html.

As with most other aspects of cloth diapering, though, detergents are a matter of personal preference. I know plenty of families that use the same detergent that they use for their regular laundry, with excellent results.

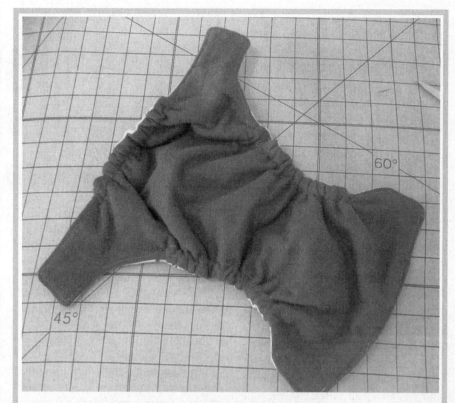

Inside view of the topstitched diaper

Sew the hook section to the outermost part of the back tab, and the loop next to it to so you can fold the tab onto itself before washing.

soiled, wash gently by hand and let air dry.

Diaper wipes

If you're going to make your own cloth diapers, you may as well make some washable cloth diaper wipes, too. You can make them any size you like, but I find between six and eight inches square to be the most useful size. These can be as rudimentary or fancy as you like. You could simply cut a washcloth into quarters and call it done. Or sew around a layer of terry toweling and a layer of flannel right sides together, turn them right side out, and topstitch around the edge for some very high-class wipes.

More information

There are volumes of information on the internet about cloth diapering, but unfortunately not too many printed books on the subject. What I learned, I did by trial and error and by wading through the thousands of electronic documents out there.

I hope your experience with cloth diapering is a good one, made better by saving your family a good chunk of change, and the satisfaction that comes from making something with your own two hands. Good luck! Δ

Alternative food preservation
dehydrate ○ smoke ○ pickle

By Jackie Clay

When one is striving for a self-reliant lifestyle, food is one of the most important things to consider. "Grow your own!" is our battle cry. Our garden is bountiful and we spend a blissful summer, eating chiefly from it: fresh beans, squash, corn, cukes, lettuce, chard, broccoli, and more. And of course, we butcher our home-raised chickens and pig, harvest our deer in the fall, and enjoy fresh rolls from our homegrown wheat.

We certainly can up tons and tons of great food to serve not only during the winter, but during the coming years, as well. But have you considered the other methods of food preservation? Like canning, there are several other tried and true ways to put up your bounty. (If you've read any pioneering books, like Laura Ingalls Wilder's series of *Little House* books, you'll remember some of them.)

Not only do the other methods of preserving food give you an alternate way of keeping food from spoiling, but more importantly, I think, they provide variety and interest to your everyday meals.

There are a few alternative food preservation methods I'm not going into detail about. These include salting and larding. Both of these methods *do* keep food, but due to health concerns, they probably aren't a great idea today. We are all trying valiantly to cut down on our salt intake to improve our blood pressure and also to reduce our fat consumption so our heart lasts as long as our plans and dreams do. I'll also skip over freezing. Yes, you can freeze most foods, but if you lose power, there goes your food. Or the freezer quietly dies and you lose your food without even knowing you've got a problem. Or the food stays in the freezer too long and develops freezer burn. Instead, here are some other methods you might want to try.

Dehydration

Dehydrating food at home is a great idea. The food remains very fresh-tasting on rehydration, it takes very little room to store, the food is extremely light so it can be carried, and best of all, dehydrating is very easy and fun to do. Like canning, once you start, you will be on a mission.

What foods can you dehydrate? Here is just a sample: raisins, cherries, pineapple, peaches, apples, plums, watermelon, peas, corn, hominy, beans, tomatoes, onions, potatoes, peppers, squash, pumpkin, apricots, mushrooms, asparagus, turnips, rutabagas, raspberries, blueberries, citrus peel, bananas, mangos, fruit leathers of all types and mixtures, and jerky. Gee, I get hungry just making this list.

Is it hard? Expensive to get into? No to both questions. If you can cut

A bowl of fresh strawberries waiting to be dehydrated

up food, you can dehydrate it. There are no "sulfuring" or lengthy pre-treatments necessary. And you can pick up a new electric dehydrator for less than $50 at most stores that carry canning equipment. I got mine several years back from Wal-Mart. My second one came from our local thrift store, complete with fruit leather trays and a manual for $3.

I've also dehydrated on nylon window screens in the back of our sun-heated Suburban with the window up, on flat roof tops, the hot, dry attic, and in the oven of my gas range with only the pilot on. Dehydrating is an ancient art, requiring no special equipment. But I will say that using an electric dehydrator sure makes things easier, quicker, and more reliable.

Here are instructions for dehydrating several foods so you'll get the idea. Then pick up a good book—even at the library if you can't afford to buy one—and read it thoroughly, making notes for the future. Like I said, dehydrating is really easy for anyone to do. The main things are to lay the food out in a single layer so the pieces don't overlap, and to check the trays periodically to make sure one area isn't drying faster than the others. You may need to switch trays around to ensure that the food dries evenly throughout the entire dehydrator. Make *sure* the food is dried to the dryness recommended for each food. If there is too much moisture in the food, it will mold. You will be storing your dehydrated food in airtight containers, probably jars. Pay special attention right after you store the newly dehydrated pieces. If there is any condensation on the inside of the jars, *immediately* put the pieces back in the dehydrator and dry a little longer.

Apples:

Peel, core, and slice solid apples into ½-inch thick slices or rings. To keep from turning brown, soak the slices in 1 cup lemon juice to 1 quart

Beth Anderson, daughter of our close friends, helps pick strawberries to dehydrate.

of water for 10 minutes or in 1 Tbsp. ascorbic acid (Vitamin C tablets, crushed) in 1 quart of water. Neither will affect the taste of the apples and they will keep white. Lay on a single layer on your dehydrator trays and dry until they are leathery. In the old days, apple rings were strung on stout string and hung from the rafters of the hot attic to dry. While this works well today, you do risk having dust and

insects on the drying apples. Use as a snack or in pies, crisps, and other baked goods. You can also make sweet spiced apple pieces by rolling the pieces in cinnamon sugar before dehydrating. They are very good.

Cherries:

Wash, cut in half, and pit. Lay in a single layer on your dehydrator trays and dehydrate until leathery and slightly sticky like raisins.

Strawberries laying on dehydrator tray so they don't touch

Seedless grapes and blueberries:

Wash and stem fruit. Dip into boiling water for 30 seconds to crack skin. This lets them dry "wrinkled" instead of "fat" looking, which isn't too appealing. Dry until leathery as raisins. Use as a snack or in baked goods.

Raspberries or blackberries:

Simply pick through the berries, removing any stems or leaves. Lay in a single layer and dry until leathery. Quick and tasty.

Whir dried strawberries in the blender briefly for neat baking bits.

Pineapple:

Peel, core, and slice fully ripe pineapple. Cut into ½-inch slices. You may roll the pieces in sugar to dehydrate "sugared" pineapple, like you get in trail mixes, or simply dehydrate for a natural fruit. Use as a snack or in baked goods.

Strawberries:

Remove the leaves and core of fully ripe strawberries. Cut smaller berries into halves or larger ones into ½-inch slices. Dry until more crisp than leathery. You can also grind the dehydrated slices for ease of using in yogurt, desserts, and baked goods. They don't rehydrate well; the color is darkened and they look unappetizing.

Peaches:

Peel by immersing in boiling water for a minute, then remove pit. Cut into ½-inch slices and dip into either lemon water or ascorbic acid water to keep from darkening. Dry until leathery. Use as a snack or in baked goods and desserts.

Carrots:

Wash, scrub, and peel if desired. Slice or dice. Blanch for three minutes, drain. Dry until more brittle than leathery. Use in soups, stews, and casseroles.

Mushrooms:

Wash gently to remove dirt, but don't soak in water. Cut into ¼-inch slices. Dry until brittle. Use in stews, soups, on pizzas, or in casseroles.

Onions:

Trim ends, peel, and cut into ¼-inch slices (complete rounds). Dry until brittle. If onion flakes are desired, whir in blender to make the size pieces you like. If powder is what you want, whir longer, then dump powder onto dehydrator sheet tray and dry further to ensure that the powder is dry enough to prevent clumping in storage. Use in soups, stews, casseroles, or for general seasoning.

Hot peppers:

Rinse, cut into pieces about ½ inch thick or halve small chiles. You may also roast the peppers on a grill or in your oven until the skins are charred, place in a paper bag for an hour or so, then dip in ice water to remove skins. Then dehydrate. Peppers should be crisp when dehydrated. You may also whir in a blender to make your own hot seasoning powder.

Sweet peppers:

Wash, remove stems and seeds. Slice or dice in ½-inch pieces. Dry until leathery/brittle. Use in stews, on pizzas, in casseroles, Spanish rice, or for general seasoning.

Tomatoes:

Use a meaty type tomato that isn't too juicy. Wash, dip in boiling water for 30 seconds, then hold in cold water. Remove skins. Core if necessary. Cut into ¼ to ½-inch slices. Dry until crisp. You can also sprinkle moist tomato slices with Italian seasonings such as basil or oregano. We like dehydrated Sungold cherry tomatoes as a snack. They are very fruity and sweet, almost like apricots. You can use dehydrated tomatoes in soups, stews, on pizzas, or in general cooking. You can also powder in a blender for an even more versatile product. Like the onion powder, return the tomato powder to the dehydrator trays, lined with fruit leather plastic trays, and dehydrate more to be sure no moisture remains that would cause clumping during storage.

Potatoes:

Wash, peel, and cut into ¼-inch slices. Blanch for 5-6 minutes. Rinse well in cold water, which removes starch that would make them less palatable. Dry until brittle. Use in potatoes au gratin, scalloped potatoes, stews, and other combined dishes. You can also grate the potatoes with a coarse grater, blanch, rinse and pat dry, and use these as dehydrated hash browns.

String beans:

Use any variety with small seeds, yellow or green. Wash, string if necessary, cut off ends, and cut into 1-inch pieces. Blanch for 4-6 min-utes, drain. Dry until brittle. Rehydrate before use. In the old days, folks used to use a needle and strong thread and string whole green beans and hang them from the rafters until dry. These are called leather britches and are very good. Like the apples, you do run a risk of having them pick up a little dust, but you can rinse before rehydrating in boiling water. They have a flavor of their own that many older people fondly remember from their childhood.

Pumpkin:

Pumpkin and winter squash are dehydrated the same way. Peel and remove seeds and goop. Cut into ¼-inch strips. Blanch for 2 minutes, then drain and dry until brittle. Use in baking, soups, and stews. Like the leather britches above, homesteaders and Native Americans in days past used to string up or hang rings of pumpkin and squash on small poles to dry in hot autumn days. I often toss a handful of dried pumpkin or squash into the blender and grind it—then add it to my multigrain bread. You never know it's there, but there *is* a decidedly good sweetness and taste you can't put your finger on. (Of course you don't tell anyone you put squash in the bread!)

Fruit leathers:

You can make fruit leather out of just about any fruit or combination

Asparagus is great dehydrated.

I store a lot of my dehydrated food in jars and tins.

that appeals to you. I often do apple/raspberry or strawberry. It makes the berries go further, as we are often short of wild berries. To make the fruit leather, rinse the fruit, remove the pits/seeds. Puree in a blender until smooth or run through a food mill. Add any sweetener or spices you want. Mix well. Cover dehydrator trays with a heavy food grade plastic wrap or use the special fruit leather sheets that come with your dehydrator. Spread puree evenly 1/8 inch thick on trays. Dry until it is pliable, yet leathery. Peel up and check for moisture. Roll up like a jelly roll and cut into convenient pieces.

Jerky:

Besides dehydrating fruits and vegetables, you can dehydrate meat of all kinds. Do *not* try to dehydrate meat with fat on it, because it will get rancid during storage. Use only lean meat. If you want to make jerky out of hamburger, choose only the extra lean or else be sure to freeze or refrigerate while you wait to use it.

To dehydrate meat and poultry, debone it and cut off all fat and gris-tle. Slice into pieces ¼ inch thick, across the grain to get the most tender cuts. You may marinate it overnight in the refrigerator in your favorite recipe. This does not affect the keeping quality of the product, only the taste. Typical marinades include vinegar, brown sugar, soy sauce, Italian dressing, etc.

Drain your meat/poultry pieces, then lay out on your dehydrator trays. I always use a fruit leather tray on the bottom to catch the inevitable drips and make cleanup easier. Meat that is dehydrated must be brought up to a temperature of 160° F if it is going to be stored on the shelf. You can do this by boiling it in the marinade for five minutes before dehydrating or by putting the dehydrated meat in the oven and baking at 275° F for 10 minutes.

Meat should be dehydrated until it is very leathery. The drier the better. If it has any moisture, it will cause condensation on the inside of storage jars and will mold. Check it very closely the first few days. If you see *any* condensation, redo it for a few hours more.

In the old days, jerky and dried meat was dried to a stick-like consistency. It had to be held in the mouth several minutes before you could even begin to chew it. Today's jerky is usually softer for ease of eating, but commercial jerky also has preservatives in it to keep it from spoiling; your homemade dry meat either needs to be refrigerated if you want it a bit softer or dried *very dry* to keep on the shelf.

Rehydrating dried foods

Some of your dehydrated food can be used as is, when used in soups, stews, or other moist dishes. Vegetables, especially, can just be tossed in boiling water like you would do to cook fresh ones. They'll rehydrate quickly and plump up nicely. I rehydrate my string beans and potato slices before use; they are more tender and will cook more dependably that way. Simply pour boiling water over them and wait until they are plump. So simple!

You can also rehydrate fruit to use as a dessert or in baked recipes. Simply pour boiling water over the dry fruit and let set until it is plumped up. It will take about 10 minutes. Drain and add sugar or honey, if desired.

Smoking meat

Smoking meat is an ancient food preservation method. While it does make meat last a long while, it is only safely effective during the cold months. High temperatures are hard on smoked meat and even properly cured meat will spoil after awhile. Smoked meat has a sweet, unique flavor and a smokehouse full of home-cured bacon, ham, shoulder, venison, and fish makes winter a wonderful time of the year. Absolutely nothing smells better than entering a cold smokehouse or other meat storage pantry and savoring the aroma about you.

Is smoking meat difficult? No, but it does take a little trial and error to get it perfect. You *can* get edible, good-flavored meat on your very first attempt. But like all homestead skills, practice makes perfect. My first smoking experience was with fish. They are easy to start with because they are smaller and easier to quickly smoke. A neighbor brought me a pan of home-smoked suckers. Not wanting to be impolite, I gingerly nibbled on a bit of one offered to me. *Wow!* I really, really liked it. Suckers are "trash" fish and ugly to boot, but they instantly took on a whole different aura.

With the neighbor's help, I turned an old junk clothes dryer into a sucker smoker. Basically, we just took out the drum, turning the dryer into a "closet" of sorts. I mounted two old broomsticks across the top of it and I was in business. To make the smoke needed, I simply used a small electric hotplate scavenged from the dump and an old cast iron frying pan full of apple wood chips. Turned on low, the hotplate burned the wood chips, creating a nice cool, dense smoke. I only had to add chips a few times during the day and night, and I had the perfect smoking fire.

Soon after, we caught our own bunch of suckers out of the nearby creek where they were going to spawn. After gutting them, I cut off the heads and soaked them overnight in a mild brine made of 1 cup non-iodized salt to 1 gallon of cold water, with ½ cup brown sugar added. Then I held the fish open with small sharpened branches and hung them from the broomsticks by heavy strings run through the meat just below the bone behind the gill area. No fish were close enough to touch. The spring days were cool and the nights cooler—the perfect weather for cold smoking. I turned on my hot plate and shut the door. The smoker should not get hotter than 70° F during the smoking process for fish.

Smoke medium-large fish all day and night if you plan on eating the fish soon or freezing or canning them after smoking. If you plan on keeping them longer, they must be held in the operating smoker for up to a week. This turns the fish leathery, driving out all moisture. During the long smoking period, you have to man the fire 24/7 or the smoking is ineffective. I smoke my fish for 24 hours, then can it. This works very well for me.

When you say "smoked meat," bacon and ham instantly come to mind. Of course, venison and beef may be smoked in the same way. In smoking meat, as with smoking fish, there are actually two steps, the cure and the actual smoking. The cure serves to help tenderize the meat and protect it from spoilage during the smoking.

There are two basic types of cures, the brine cure that I used for my fish and the dry cure. While I like the brine cure for fish, as it kind of draws out any "fishy" taste, the dry cure generally works best for meat. It is also easier for the beginner to use.

You can buy prepackaged mixtures for your dry cure from many local stores that sell hunting supplies, or from your meat market. There are also many mail order supply houses that sell cures. Many cures contain saltpeter. This controversial ingredi-

Venison being cut up to make jerky

Peppers of all kinds are great dried or pickled for variety.

ent is believed by some to be a carcinogen, but it has been used—and is still used commercially—for generations in meat cures. It keeps the attractive reddish color of the finished smoked meat. Personally, I prefer not to use it. My meat is darker in color and maybe not as beautiful, but I feel better having left it out. Saltpeter does nothing to keep the meat from spoiling.

One homemade cure formula for 100 pounds of meat is 8 pounds pickling salt and 2 pounds of brown sugar, mixed well. If you choose to add the saltpeter, you would add 2 ounces also. Keep your meat between 38 and 40° F before curing, then try to hold it around that temperature during curing.

You will use about 1 ounce of the dry cure per pound of ham and a bit less per pound of bacon. Rub it well into the meat to be cured. For larger pieces of meat, ham for instance, you will rub 1/3 of the amount, three times, then again a week after the last treatment. Hang the meat so it can drip into a pan below, not onto meat held on lower shelves. You'll cure a side of bacon in 14 days or a ham in a little over a month. Remember to keep the meat around 40° F for safest curing. When the cure is complete, it's time to smoke.

You can build a smokehouse if you are really serious about smoking quantities of meat each year. A smokehouse is simply a small building the size of a small outhouse, usually built of block, that is varmint-proof and convenient to work in. You can find plans in many books. You can even make a "smokehouse" out of a barrel with a fire pit located in the ground a few feet away and a buried stovepipe leading from it, upward to the bottom of the barrel that contains your meat. The main thing is to contain much of the smoke, yet not raise the temperature of the smokehouse higher than 90 ° F. This is a "cool" smoke and does more to preserve the meat than a hot smoke does.

Run a strong cord through your meat so it can hang from poles at the top of your smokehouse. There should be enough room so that the meat pieces do not touch. This lets the smoke completely surround and penetrate the meat. To keep the meat from becoming too salty, you can scrub the outside of the cured meat with fresh water and a brush, then dry it overnight before you smoke it.

The type of wood you choose for smoking greatly affects the taste of your finished product. Some good woods are maple, apple, cherry, mesquite, and alder. Do *not* use pine or any other evergreen. The meat will end up nearly inedible.

The larger the meat pieces are, the longer they need to smoke. In general, bacon will usually be adequately smoked in a 24 hour period or a little longer. You want the outside golden brown, not dark saddle brown. Hams and shoulders usually will be adequately smoked in about 48 hours or a little longer. In the old days, folks smoked their meat longer, resulting in a more jerky-like end product. It held well for long periods but was not as tender as most people like today. Cured, smoked meat will keep all winter and into the spring. But as the days get hot, the meat can become bug infested and spoil.

For this reason, I usually use up most of my smoked meat during the winter and can up the rest for later use. Once in the jar, it is good for many, many years.

Pickling

When you say "pickling," most people think dill or sweet pickles or other cucumber products. But pickling has a much broader scope. You can also pickle onions, carrots, beans, cauliflower, peppers, cabbage, mushrooms, eggs, fish, and meat. While you probably wouldn't sit down to a meal of pickled this or that, pickling definitely has a place on the homestead, as it is a reliable way not only to preserve more food, but to preserve it in a way that gives it a unique flavor. This does a lot to relieve boredom, especially when times are less than wonderful. Often when you eat well, you feel well too.

Here is a sampling of great pickling recipes. If you want more, check your interlibrary loan or Amazon.com for the wonderful pickling book, *The Complete Book of Pickles and Relishes* by Leonard Lewis Levinson. It's out of print, but it's one of my very favorites.

Mustard beans:

(Tastes like honey mustard sauce, not "mustardy" at all.)

```
8 quarts green or wax beans
salt
6 cups sugar
1 cup flour
5 Tbsp. dry mustard powder
1 Tbsp. turmeric
6 cups vinegar
```

Simmer beans, cut into 1-inch pieces if desired, in salted water until barely tender. You do not want to "cook" them; they are pickles. Drain. Mix dry ingredients in large saucepan. Add vinegar and bring to a boil. Stir well. Add drained beans and bring to a boil. Simmer 5 minutes. Pack into hot sterilized jars. Process in a water bath canner for 10 minutes.

Pickled onions:

```
1 gallon small onions
1 cup salt
2 cups sugar
6 cups white vinegar
```

Scald onions for 2 minutes in boiling water. Dip out and hold in cold water. Peel. Sprinkle with salt. Add ice water and let stand overnight. Drain. Rinse. Drain again.

Add sugar to vinegar. Simmer 10 minutes. Pack onions into hot sterilized jars. Heat pickling liquid to boiling. Ladle over onions to within ½ inch of the top of the jar. Process in water bath canner for 10 minutes.

Pickled peppers:

```
1 gallon peppers
1½ cups pickling salt
1 gallon ice water
5 cups vinegar
1 cup sugar
```

Wash and drain long Hungarian or other peppers. Cut 2 small slits in each pepper or cut in half, removing the seeds. Dissolve salt in 1 gallon ice water and pour over peppers in a large roasting pan. Let stand overnight. Drain, rinse, and drain again.

Add sugar to vinegar. Simmer 15 minutes. Pack peppers into hot, sterilized jars. Heat pickling liquid to boiling and pour over peppers to ½ inch of top of jar. Process for 15 minutes in boiling water bath.

I use these peppers, sliced, on my pizzas. Very good.

Pickled eggs:

```
20 eggs
2 cups white vinegar
1½ quarts water
2 tsp. salt
1 small dry hot pepper
1 Tbsp. mixed pickling spices
```

Simmer eggs for 30 minutes to make hardboiled eggs. Cool in cold water and peel.

Make a pickling solution of the remaining ingredients, adding spices in a spice bag. Bring to a boil. Add peeled eggs and bring to a boil again. Pack into hot, sterilized jars. Ladle hot pickling solution over the eggs, completely covering them, to within 1 inch of the top of the jar. Process for 10 minutes in a boiling water bath.

Corned beef:

```
8 qts. cold water
3 lbs. pickling salt
2 Tbsp. brown sugar
1 oz. sodium nitrate (optional;
   saves red color in meat)
1 Tbsp. mixed pickling spices
20 bay leaves
10 lbs. lean beef brisket
8 cloves of garlic
```

Combine all ingredients except meat and simmer for 10 minutes. Place meat in a crock with a tight fitting cover. Add garlic, pour cold pickling solution over meat. Weight meat down with a heavy plate and sterilized rock (boiled). Put on crock cover and cover that with 2 layers of clean cloth, tied tightly around crock. Store in a cool (38-40° F) place for 2 weeks. Use after that time or can chunks up.

Pickled mixed vegetables:

```
2 heads cauliflower
1 quart peeled carrots
1½ cups small whole peeled onions
¼ cup salt
2½ cups sugar
2 Tbsp. mustard seed
1 Tbsp. celery seed
1 tsp. turmeric
2 qt. white vinegar
1 hot dry red pepper (optional)
```

Cut cauliflower into smaller pieces. Cut carrots into slices or smaller chunks. Add onions and sprinkle salt over them and cover with ice water. Let stand for 3 hours. Drain, rinse, and drain again. In a large saucepan, combine sugar, spices, and vinegar. If you want hot pickled veggies, add hot pepper to vinegar mix. Bring to a boil. Add flowerets, onions, and carrots and bring to a boil again. Boil until vegetables are just barely tender. Pack hot vegetables into hot jar and ladle pickling solution to cover them to within ½ inch of the top of the jar. Process in a hot water bath for 10 minutes.

As you can readily see, you can sure pickle a wide assortment of foods that give variety to your pantry. This is one good reason to use all these alternative methods of putting up food; you get a great variety of tongue tingling tastes at every meal. Boring meals are not acceptable. We can do much better when we combine our traditional home canning with dehydrated, smoked, and pickled foods too. Toss in a few jams, jellies, and preserves along with breads and rolls from our homegrown grains and every single meal is a celebration of self-reliant living. You can't get that satisfied feeling by dumping something out of a box. Δ

Brining pickles
by the quart or gallon

By Vicky Rose

The ancient art of brining pickles produces a product similar to the expensive "deli-style" pickles in the supermarket.

The process is not difficult; however, older recipes call for "pecks" and "bushels" of cucumbers that today's home gardeners don't have space or time to grow.

For smaller amounts of produce, try the following recipe.

This method of brining or "fermenting" may also be used with other vegetables—cauliflower, snap beans, peppers, and brussels sprouts, as well as others. The quart method works especially well with okra because it

Making brined pickles is a relatively easy process requiring few ingredients.

goes limp quickly and has to be picked almost daily. It is best to put the date on the jar with a small piece of tape if several jars are being brined within days of one another.

The cucumbers: Use firm 4 to 6-inch pickling cucumbers picked within the last three days. The Texas Cooperative Extension Agency recommends you do not use "burpless" cucumbers because they may soften. Good results have been obtained, however, from Japanese cucumbers such as "Suyo Long" if they are cut into 4-inch chunks with the ends removed. Do not use supermarket cucumbers; they have been waxed to keep them fresh, and the brine will not penetrate the wax. Occasionally, supermarkets will carry pickling cucumbers, and they will be labeled as such. Farmer's markets are a good source.

The ingredients: Use pickling salt. Table salt has fillers to prevent caking, and kosher salt, while pure, is a different granulation size and won't measure out the same.

Regular 50-grain (or 5% acidity) vinegar may be used, but tastier results will be obtained with white wine vinegar. Red wine vinegar adds flavor, but pickles will be darker.

The Extension Agency recommends soft water for brining pickles. If not available, distilled water or water boiled for 15 minutes may be substituted. This can be a matter for experimentation later on. Shallow well water that tastes rank has been known to make great pickles.

Older recipes call for fresh dill, but this is not always easy to obtain. Dried dill seed from the supermarket is a good substitute. If fresh dill is used, use the seed head, stalk, and leaves—in other words, everything but the dirt.

Adding peeled shallots is highly recommended; they add special flavor and taste wonderful chopped and added to potato salad later. Shallots, with their delicate onion and garlic

Any of these containers can be used for brining pickles.

flavor, are usually available in supermarkets next to other root crops in the vegetable section. If a hot and spicy zest is desired, add dried red peppers.

The equipment: Do not use zinc, copper, brass, galvanized metal, or iron cookware or utensils; they may react to the vinegar and cause an off-taste. Bowls can be plastic, stainless steel, glass, or ceramic. Pots and pans should be stainless steel, heatproof glass, or hard-anodized aluminum.

For brining: Use a stone crock, glass jars, or food-grade plastic containers.

Getting started: Wash cucumbers thoroughly in cold water to remove soil. Cut $1/16$ of an inch off the bottom to remove the blossom end, which can cause softening. Put the cucumbers in a colander to drain.

Shallots add a unique bouquet of flavor to pickles.

Mix ¾ cup salt, ½ cup vinegar, and enough water to make one gallon. (For smaller amounts—mix 3 Tbsp. of salt with 2-3 Tbsp. of vinegar and add water to make one quart.) Stir until it goes cloudy and then clears again to make sure all the salt is dissolved.

If grape leaves are available, use them to line the bottom of the brining container. Grape leaves will make the cucumbers firmer but are not absolutely necessary. Add a layer of cucumbers, a layer of spices, a few shallots, and continue until you run out or the container is almost full. The measurements below are a guideline, more or less may be added to suit individual preference.

> **For a gallon container:**
> 2 Tbsp. dill seed or 4-5 heads fresh dill
> 3 cloves garlic or 2 Tbsp. dried minced garlic
> 2 Tbsp. whole allspice
> 2 Tbsp. whole black peppercorns

> **For a quart container:**
> 2 tsp. dried dill or 1 head fresh dill
> 1 clove garlic or 2 tsp. dried minced garlic
> 2 tsp. whole allspice
> 2 tsp. whole black peppercorns

If using grape leaves, add another layer on top. Pour brining liquid over the cucumbers until they are covered.

The most important thing is to keep the cucumbers submerged in liquid at all times. The easiest way to do this is to use food-grade plastic bags as weights. Fill one or more bags, depending on the size of the container used, with brining liquid. (Use brine instead of water in case the bags accidentally leak.) Leftover brine can be saved to use later. Place the bags on top of the cucumbers and make sure the cucumbers are fully submerged in the liquid. A clean plate with a water-filled jar on top can be used to keep the cucumbers submerged, as well. Cover with a towel and place the container of cucumbers in a cool place out of direct sunlight. The pantry floor is usually ideal, because the fermenting process can cause the brine to bubble and flow out of the container. Optimum temperature is between 70 to 75° F. They should take about three to four weeks to cure. In higher temperatures, they will cure faster, but they do run the risk of being softer. Lower temperatures will cause them to cure slower.

Check the container several times a week and skim off any scum that forms. It is impossible to get it all; just remove most of it. When using bags, rinse the bags off and pat dry with a paper towel before replacing them. If the plastic bag covers the opening sufficiently, scum may not even form. Discard the cucumbers if they become soft, slimy, or develop a disagreeable odor, and try again.

The pickles are ready when they are olive green throughout. At this point, they can be canned in the same manner as regular pickles and will last up to a year in the pantry, retaining that unique brined taste. However, for the best flavor and crunch, drain the brine from the pickles and boil it for 15 minutes. Rinse the pickles, let them drain, then place them in a clean container. More spices can be added. Remove any scum that has formed on the heated brine. Let the brine cool then pour over the pickles and place in the refrigerator. Keep them refrigerated until eaten. Perfecto! Δ

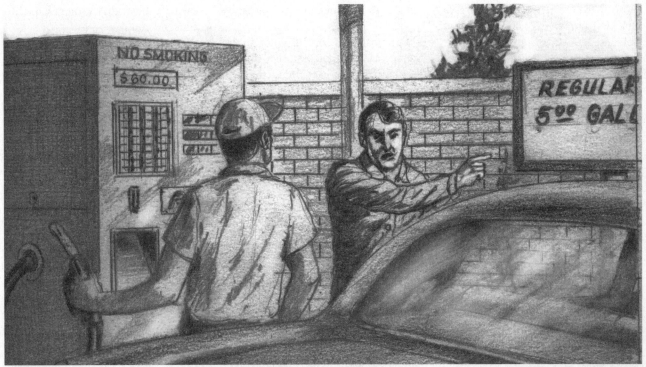

Our energy crisis

Part 1 of 3: It's our own creation, but we can fix it

By John Silveira

It has been said the United States is a "carbon economy" meaning that our economy and standard of living depend on the availability of fossil fuels which include petroleum, natural gas, and coal. It's true and, despite the efforts of environmentalists, it's not likely to change too soon.

Today, however, we're locked in a period of escalating prices of petroleum-based products, and the services and commodities that depend on them, including food.

That's the bad news and it seems as if darker days are coming. But, believe it or not, there are a lot of things to be optimistic about, but that depends on whether we take advantage of the assets we, as a nation, have.

The talk today is about how we're running out of oil and natural gas, which is true, but probably not as fast as you think. On the other hand, regardless of how fast petroleum and natural gas are disappearing, we have assets which can replace them, but for one reason or another, we don't talk about them. One of these assets may surprise you: coal.

What do you know about coal? While writing this, I asked several people when they last saw a lump of the stuff—and asked them to spare me the Christmas stocking jokes. Most people had to pause because they couldn't remember. Ten? Twenty years ago? Maybe longer. Some couldn't remember ever having seen a lump of coal in their lives.

Yet, coal is one of the most important fuels we have and, believe it or not, we have more of it than anyone

else in the world. You know all the things we make with petroleum—gasoline, plastics, industrial chemicals, fertilizers, and more. We can make those from coal, too. Yes, even gasoline, once the price is right. And the rising price of petroleum has now made the cost of gasoline-from-coal economical.

But we can't do it today because we've dragged our feet on setting up the industrial base to fully exploit coal as a resource, including processing it to make our own gasoline and heating oil. Which is a shame, for it is because we can't replace petroleum that the Organization of Petroleum Exporting Countries (OPEC) has been able to manipulate the price of a barrel of oil. Had we been realistically addressing the energy problems confronting us right along, the cost of a barrel of oil would be nowhere

289

close to where it is. As it is, we've shackled ourselves with our current policies, and we've allowed—no, artificially created—a near-monopoly for the OPEC countries. And they have now discovered they can use that monopoly to hold us economic hostages.

But, despite today's outrageous petroleum prices and the problems they're creating, I'm cautiously optimistic about our chances to emerge from these troubled times healthier than we are now. However, I'm pessi-

Peak oil

"Peak oil" is a well-founded theory proposed by M. King Hubbert in the 1950s. It calculates and defines the point when the maximum rate of petroleum extraction is reached, whether it's from an individual oil field or on a global basis. After that peak, the rate at which it can be extracted goes into a terminal decline.

The theory makes good mathematical sense, but in many ways it's irrelevant and in constant need of adjustment. Among the factors it fails to consider are the economics and new extraction technologies that make further extraction possible. It also excludes the discovery of new fields. Furthermore, the calculations do not include other sources of oil such as tar sand, oil-bearing shale, or even CTL technologies. However, it could be revised to include them.

Nonetheless, at its core is the truth that the extraction of fuels from fossil sources cannot go on forever. That fact is the reason new energy technologies are both necessary and inevitable if civilization is to survive.

To the pessimists. peak oil spells the end of civilization. To the optimists, it predicts when new technologies are likely to come on line.

mistic about whether we'll actually do it.

The obstacles to a brighter future for the United States are not technological, but political, and the real problem is that we, the American people, and our elected officials have been putting obstacles in our own way. We've tied our own hands on drilling for oil and natural gas, we've brought the construction of new nuclear reactors to a standstill, and though coal-to-liquids (CTL) fuels were perfected decades ago in other countries, we ignored it even when OPEC was flashing the first signs that they intended to crucify us on barrels of oil.

In this first installment I'll present the major fossil contributors to our energy: oil, coal, and natural gas and their substitutes. I'm also going to talk about the "energy independence" of which many politicians and energy gurus speak. I think I'll have some surprises for you.

In the next installment I'll discuss nuclear—both fission and fusion—and explain why both are actually safer than fossil fuels and how we have to return to building new fission reactors until fusion reactors can come on line, if they ever can.

In the third installment I'll discuss alternative energy including solar, wind, tidal, and others. Some, such as solar and wind, are not likely to be big contributors to our national energy picture in our lifetimes. Maybe never. But they can be major contributors to *your* energy picture if you're a self-reliant type. I'll even discuss hydro, and though there isn't an awful lot of room for more of it as far as our nation is concerned, there may be a place for it on the homestead.

Energy independence

Let's talk about energy independence:

It ain't gonna happen.

It's as simple as that. I'm going to go out on a limb and say it's not nec-

essarily desirable either. Consider coal and you'll see why.

The United States holds the world's largest coal reserves. Half of our electricity is generated by burning it. Yet, we still import it.

Why? The biggest expense in coal is often the shipping, and for some coal-burning electric plants on our coasts, it is cheaper to bring it by ship from a foreign country than it is to bring it by train, barge, or pipeline (yes, coal can be sent through pipelines) from another part of our own country. So, it's simply economics. We have all the coal we need, but in some cases, it's still cheaper and smarter to import some.

Food's the same way. If you like coffee, bananas, and commodities such as those, which are all but ungrowable in the United States, you'll realize we should import some of our food. Yet, because we are one of the major food producers on the planet, no one can hold us hostage. If the price of Argentine beef goes up, we can buy American because we grow all the beef we want.

With energy, we should strive for the same "independence." Had we developed some of the critical energy options we're struggling to find now, OPEC wouldn't have dared raise prices the way they have recently. But we didn't, and they did.

One of the reasons we have to import so much oil at outrageous prices is because we've depleted many of our oil fields, but another reason is that we've handcuffed ourselves by not allowing ourselves to access petroleum in the Arctic National Wildlife Refuge (ANWR), offshore along our coasts, the oil locked up in shale in the West, and that which is buried beneath the international waters that make up the Gulf of Mexico.

But worse, we've shunned two of the most promising options for energy self-sufficiency, coal and nuclear power, despite the fact we are the largest energy consumers in the world. It's no wonder we are now hostages to OPEC. In retrospect, I'm surprised it didn't happen sooner.

Let's look at the first part of the energy picture: the carbons.

Petroleum

Petroleum is the weakest link in our energy chain, simply because our lifestyles depend so much on it, and it's the one we must depend on foreign countries to supply.

No one really knows how much recoverable oil is left in the world. One of the figures bandied about is that today there's about 40 years of it left in "recoverable" reserves—if consumed at current rates. However, this figure is disputed because previous dire predictions of running out of petroleum have proven to be wrong. And, even as the so-called recoverable reserves seem to diminish, new extraction methods are constantly converting once unrecoverable oil into recoverable oil. However, it's still likely that recoverable reserves of *easily* obtained petroleum will run out. They've got to. But this doesn't mean we will leave a petroleum economy soon.

Reserves

When we talk about petroleum, there's a difference between the oil in the ground and how much of it can be recovered. The oil estimated to be in the ground is often called "oil in

---

Hidden costs

There is an additional cost to our economy for each barrel of petroleum we import, and that is the price of our military presence in the Middle East and elsewhere to ensure a steady and uninterrupted flow of oil. That cost is estimated to be about $24 per barrel. But we're not paying it at the pump; we're paying it through tax dollars where you can't see it.

---

place," while that which can be extracted economically, using technology of the day, is called "reserves." The ratio of what is currently recoverable to the oil in place is called the recovery factor.

When estimating how much oil is in the ground, the P90 method is used. It is an estimate, thought to be about 90 percent accurate, of the *minimum* amount that is recoverable at current prices with current technology. However, it is the minimum and often there turns out to be more. Sometimes there's two or three times as much there.

So, as the price of petroleum rises, as it is today, and the efficiency of the extraction technologies improves, the reserves are adjusted up, and even fields that were once deemed depleted suddenly become promising and will eventually be listed as having reserves.

It seems then, that talk about reserves should be straightforward. But the fact is, the discussion is often politically charged and, believe it or not, it's also often a closely guarded state secret. So, often, we can only guess at what the reserves are in many countries. Two years ago an internal memo in the Kuwait Oil Company "revealed" that their oil reserves are only half as big as was previously thought. Was the memo genuine? We don't know. Lower reserves would mean there's less of a supply and the price would go up accordingly. But even the perception there isn't as much would make the price go up.

But knowing the "official" figures for the world's oil reserves doesn't present a full picture. What's usually left out of reserve calculations are other oil sources such as Canada's oil or tar sands and this country's oil shale.

Oil sands and shale oil

Canada holds about 81 percent of the world's known oil sands and the

---

What is oil shale?

The rock in shale oil is not actually shale; it's marlstone, a calcareous mudstone. And the oil isn't actually oil; it's kerogen, a precursor of crude oil. But it can be processed to make all the things we make from petroleum—including gasoline.

---

recoverable oil in them ranks them second only to Saudi Arabia's conventional reserves. And according to the United States Department of Energy (DOE), the amount of *recoverable* shale oil in the world with current technology is estimated at three trillion barrels, more than all the known reserves of conventional oil in the world. And roughly a quarter of that total is here in the United States, most of it in Colorado, Utah, and Wyoming.

At the moment, however, for "environmental" reasons Congress has made most shale oil inaccessible. If we were to fully develop our oil shale, estimates are that we would have more than 100 years' supply at current consumption rates.

What's the break-even price to extract oil from shale? The DOE estimates it to be $55 to $70 per barrel. The price of a barrel of crude from OPEC at this writing is almost $150 per barrel.

Drilling our own

I've already pointed out there are huge reserves of conventional oil in the Arctic National Wildlife Refuge in Alaska, along the coast of the United States, and in the Gulf of Mexico. No one knows how big these reserves are and some estimates are that they exceed the reserves in the Middle East. Not likely, but it's possible. But, because of environmental concerns, Congress has made it unlawful for Americans to explore or drill there.

But Congress has no authority over what foreigners do, so other coun-

Coal is the one fossil fuel we have plenty of and much of it can be inexpensively surface-mined and processed so as to free us from the yoke of high-priced OPEC oil.

tries, including Mexico, Venezuela, and China are planning to drill in the Gulf. If the price of oil goes higher, maybe they'll even sell us some of it...oil from our own backyard, the Gulf of Mexico. And we'll pay $150 a barrel for it. Wouldn't that be a hoot? (Today, as I write this, President Bush has lifted the Executive Order banning offshore drilling.)

Refinery capacity

Last in the list of problems we've caused ourselves in our search for "petroleum independence" is a lack of refinery capacity.

No new refineries have been built in the U.S. in more than 30 years, and there are now fewer than half as many as there were a quarter of a century ago.

Even the Arabs have pointed out that they can't ship us more crude because we no longer have the capacity to process it all. At federal, state, or local levels, and sometimes combinations of the three, we won't allow more refineries to be built. However, more and more refineries are currently being built in the Middle East.

The obvious start to solving many of our energy woes is to drill for more domestic oil, start developing shale oil, and begin building more domestic refineries.

Natural gas

Natural gas is another fossil fuel. It is found in oil fields, in coal beds (as coal-bed methane, the gas commonly associated with coal mine explosions), and it is also found alone in natural gas fields.

Natural gas is actually a combination of gases that include methane, several types of butane, ethane, several types of pentane, and propane. It is also often mixed with other chemicals including hydrogen sulfide, nitrogen, helium, and other elements. In fact, the world's production of helium is the result of the alpha decay of radioactive elements within the earth. There it becomes trapped with natural gas and stays in those pockets. All the helium we use, whether for balloons, medical and industrial uses, or just to talk like a duck, is a by-product of the processing of natural gas.

Natural gas has many of the uses petroleum has in that it can be used to generate electricity, create chemicals, and even power cars and trucks.

It is also possible to convert natural gas to liquid fuels, otherwise known as gas-to-liquids (GTL) and the break-even cost is when petroleum is at $24 per barrel

No one knows for sure just how much gas there is left in the world. As with petroleum it's always an estimate. But at current rates of consumption the figure proffered is that if consumed at the current rate, there is at least a 65-year supply, worldwide, in proven reserves. Only about 4½ percent of it is located in North America.

Is coal the answer?

As important as coal is, it's the one energy source very few people think about. Yet, it's the only fossil fuel the U.S. has in abundance. Relatively speaking, we have it coming out of our ears.

There was a time when many homes had coal furnaces, coal trucks were a common sight in American cities, and millions of homes with coal furnaces had a coal bin with a ton or two of the stuff in their cellars. Today, most young people have never seen a lump of coal. Yet, the United States holds the world's largest known coal reserves, and half of all the electricity we produce is generated by burning it. By some estimates, the energy locked up in the coal reserves in this country alone are greater than *all* the proven petroleum reserves in the world. And how much coal is there worldwide? At current rates of consumption, there is enough to last for some 325 years.

Much of the coal in this country is close to the surface and can be mined by so-called surface mining. About two thirds of our production comes from this kind of mining. Surface mining can be done even for coal as much as 200 feet beneath the surface. The rest comes from underground mining, sometimes called deep mining.

Surface mining is much cheaper than deep mining. There was a time when one type of surface mining, strip mining, was damned because of the scars left behind. However, strip mining sites are now recovered by replacing the soil where the coal was mined and planting new vegetation.

The cost of shipping coal can exceed the cost of mining it. And ship it we do. We ship it by train when

Capturing coal pollutants

The problem with coal-to-liquids (CTL) fuels is that undesirable by-products of their production are pollutants. About the same amount of pollutants are produced just to manufacture a gallon of CTL fuel as is produced by burning that gallon later. The net result is that a gallon of CTL fuel produces about twice the pollutants that a gallon of "regular" fuel produces.

However, what those who would create CTL fuels propose is that the plants where the fuels will be produced will have "scrubbers" to remove carbon dioxide and other pollutants before they can be released into the atmosphere.

Is it possible? Yes, but the technology to do it is not yet cheap, and cost of developing that technology, then implementing it, are going to have to be passed on to the consumer either as a direct part of the price or as taxes if the industry is subsidized.

there are tracks available, and by barge when there are rivers, canals, or other waterways available. It can even be crushed, mixed with water to form a slurry, and transported by pipeline, just as petroleum and natural gas often are. But as I said earlier, the cost of shipping it sometimes makes it cheaper to import.

There are four types of coal, and ranging in value from the kind that produces the least energy to the kind that produces the most, they are lignite, subbituminous, anthracite, and bituminous. Bituminous coal is the most abundant form of coal in this country, accounting for about half of our coal production.

This is all good news. And there's better news. Just as with petroleum and natural gas, we don't just burn coal. There are many industrial uses for it including the production of chemicals, plastics, fertilizers, and the manufacturing of steel, concrete, paper, and numerous other products.

Better yet, there's a proven technology of creating motor fuels from coal—known as coal-to-liquids fuels.

CTL fuels would help make us more energy independent, but the downside is that with current technology they emit twice as much carbon dioxide. However, hopes are that new technologies will reduce this figure. Those technologies will, of course, have their own costs which will have to be passed on to the consumer. But, as the cost of OPEC petroleum rises, the cost of cleaning the coal-based fuels will shrink in comparison.

Because there is already a huge investment in the way we dispense motor fuel, namely, gas stations, making gasoline from coal makes economic sense.

It's worth noting that CTL fuels are not new. There's no "new" technology to develop. During World War II, as the oil fields to which Germany had access to were bombed and became less productive, they turned to CTL fuels to keep both their economy and their war machine going. CTL fuels accounted for 90 percent of their liquid fuel needs by the war's end.

Then, in the 1950s, South Africa began to develop CTL technology and today uses that technology to provide 30 percent of their fuel needs. It's an old and proven fuel.

Today, China already has an operational CTL plant and is building more. In the meantime, Australia, India, Indonesia, and the Philippines are developing their own CTL plants. None of these countries want to be dependent on OPEC petroleum.

In the U.S., which sits on the world's largest known coal reserves, at least nine CTL refineries are in the planning stages. Once they get a go-ahead from regulators—federal, state, and local—there's a five to seven year lead time before the first refinery can come into production.

Projections are the U.S. can produce at least 10 percent of the country's fuel needs by the year 2025. If the price of imported petroleum stays high, expect that percentage to increase.

The break-even price for CTL fuels, according to the DOE, is between $40 and $45 per barrel. With oil at $150 per barrel. The favorable economics appear irresistible.

"Renewable" fuels

What's causing a furor today and driving up the cost of groceries are the renewable fuels, ethanol and biodiesel. These should not be confused with the biomass-to-liquids (BTL) fuels I'll discuss in a moment.

Renewable fuels are expensive to process, though their costs become more attractive as the price of OPEC oil rises. Unlike biomass fuels, the technology for creating ethanol and biodiesel are relatively mature so it's unlikely there will be any more technological innovations that will reduce the cost of creating them. Cost reductions are more likely to come from scale of manufacturing and incremental improvement in production. But since they can be blended with conventional fuels, they are commercially attractive.

To create **ethanol**, the most widely used biofuel, all that's needed are feedstocks high in sugar. In Brazil, the prime feedstock is sugar cane, while in Europe it's sugar beets, and in this country it's corn. The process itself is straightforward and similar to making beer, wine, or whiskey: the sugars are fermented to make alcohol. After fermentation is complete, it's more like making whiskey—or moon-

An upside to CTL fuels

In the creation of fuels from coal, impurities including various heavy metals and sulfur, drop out and are marketable. Other chemicals, such as ammonia, are created during the process and are also marketable.

Underground coal fires

• At any given moment, there are hundreds of underground coal fires around the world. They can be started by spontaneous combustion, lightning strikes, wild fires, and fires accidentally begun by man.

• Coal fires in China annually emit more greenhouse gases and pollutants than *all* of the automobiles and trucks in the United States. In fact, the amount of coal that burns in coal fires in China in one year is about equivalent to the total annual production of commercial coal in Germany.

• Also called coal seam fires, they are going on in every country with extensive coal deposits. These include the United States, Russia, China, India, Columbia, South Africa, Egypt, and Australia.

• There are more than 100 coal fires burning at this very moment in the United States alone, mostly in Pennsylvania. The most famous of them is one that started during a landfill fire that ignited an exposed coal seam outside of Centralia, Pennsylvania in 1962. It was too late by the time officials got serious about trying to contain it. As the fire spread, there were spots in the town where flames, smoke, and toxic fumes began to emerge from the ground in people's backyards and in the cellars under their homes. Within 20 years the government began to evacuate the town. Today, the fire still burns out of control underground and will burn until the coal in the seam is exhausted. One engineering estimate expects it to go on for another 250 years.

• Two miles to the south of Centralia is the town of Byrnesville (go ahead and say that name out loud and see the irony) which was evacuated in 1996 because of the coal fire spreading there. As I write this, it is slowly burning its way underground and approaching a town ironically named Ashland.

• In New South Wales, Australia, early settlers thought Burning Mountain was a smoldering volcano. Soon, however, it was discovered to be an underground coal fire. Geologists now figure it's been burning for nearly 6,000 years. It may be thousands of more years before it finally burns itself out.

• Marco Polo reported seeing burning mountains that were coal fires during his travels along the Silk Road.

• Lewis and Clark reported coming across coal seam fires in their journals as they made their epic journey across the North American continent.

• In the country of Tajikistan in central Asia, there are coal deposits that have been burning for thousands of years.

• Much of the terrain that makes up the Powder River Basin in Wyoming is the result of between 25 and 50 billion tons of coal that burned over the last three million years.

shine: the resulting liquid is distilled and what's left is alcohol—with some water in it since it's almost impossible to get "pure" alcohol.

Biodiesel, on the other hand, is made from oil-bearing plants. In this country it's soybeans, while in Europe it's rapeseed (what canola oil is made from). In Malaysia it's palm oil. The oil is processed to remove glycerin, which leaves behind an oil that can be used much like diesel fuel and is actually used to extend conventional diesel rather than being used as a stand-alone fuel.

The problem we're having with these renewable fuels is that Congress mandated certain minimums of ethanol that must be combined with gasoline, and biodiesel that must be combined with conventional diesel. As a result, food crops were diverted to the making these fuels and created shortages of corn and soybeans for human consumption and animal feedstocks. Grocery prices skyrocketed as a consequence.

BTL fuels

Unlike the manufacture of ethanol and biodiesel, BTL does not use food crops, so it does not compete with the foods in the marketplace. However, to grow biomass stocks, it will compete with food crops for agricultural land, so creating these fuels will affect food prices somewhat.

Also, unlike the processing of ethanol from corn sugars and biodiesel from soybean oil, the process by which we make BTL fuels uses the entire plant, hence requiring less land to grow sufficient stocks. One acre of land will grow about 1.6 tons of biomass that can be converted to about 0.3 tons, or 600 pounds, of BTL fuel. The DOE has calculated it would take about 12,000 acres of land to sustain a modestly-sized BTL processing plant. How big is that? If it were a square tract of land, it would be a little more than 4¼ miles on each of its sides.

Another upside to BTL fuels is that they can be made from many renewable sources including wood waste, grain waste, crop waste, straw, garbage, and even sewage and sludge. This means we can be making it from stuff we'd ordinarily be throwing into landfills.

The biggest downside, to date, for BTL fuels is its break-even cost which is about $80 per barrel. This makes it one of the least attractive alternatives for the creation of vehicle and home-heating fuels. But an upside to the process is that it recycles various wastes that we would have to dispose of anyway.

There are already pilot plants in development, both here and in Europe, to test the feasibility of processing and to develop technologies that will reduce the cost to create BTL fuels. There may come a day when every major city will have one or more BTL processing plants to get rid of their waste.

Next issue: Why nukes are good. Δ

Ask Jackie

If you have a question about rural living, send it in to Jackie Clay and she'll try to answer it. Address your letter to Ask Jackie, PO Box 712, Gold Beach, OR 97444. Questions will only be answered in this column.

— Editor

Jackie Clay

Canning on a woodstove

I am interested in canning venison and salmon with a large pressure canner, but I'd like to do it on a small cabin woodstove. I have read several good books on canning from the BHM bookstore, but there's no mention of the heat source other than it must remain steady. What say you on this matter Jackie?

Thomas Brower
Salem, Oregon

I've canned on everything from a rock fire ring with a grate on it (difficult with a pressure canner, but easy with a water bath), to a camp stove (not so bad with either), a wood kitchen range and, of course, a regular gas range. The one problem I noticed when canning on a Coleman type camp stove is that the canner with the jars in it weighs so much, the stove kind of gets tippy unless you have it on a solid table. Instead of the lightweight Coleman stove, I switched to the cheap two or three-burner gas stoves you can buy through most cheaper tool catalogs, such as Northern Tool. They cost about the same as the Coleman stoves, but stay much steadier while canning. Good canning! — *Jackie*

Sauerkraut recipe

I have enjoyed your magazine for many years and I have a question for probably Jackie Clay and a tip that I started doing many years ago with I believe great success for sauerkraut lovers. First I am always wondering if I have used enough salt when making sauerkraut. If Jackie has a recipe as to how much salt is adequate I would appreciate knowing. I know that I have used too much and I have added salt after a week or so when I didn't use enough.

I would recommend to anyone that likes sauerkraut to make some as it is far superior to store bought. I have started using 5-gallon pails that I get from most any store that has a deli or bakery. Ask for them and they will usually save some for you as they usually wind up going to a land fill. Costco has furnished me with pails if you go there at about 3-4 in the afternoon. They are cleaning for the day and will have some and the pails are food grade.

Another thing I would like to pass on is using quality plastic bags partially filled with water instead of the old fashioned way of using a plate and rock on top of the kraut. Mound the cabbage up slightly in the center of the pail and use a plastic bag large enough to place over the mound of cabbage and extend to the edge of the pail. I have never had any spoilage using this method as you always do with the plate and rock way.

Make sauerkraut this way and it will become a yearly habit, but be careful who you share with or you will have to greatly increase the amount you make. You will also never like store bought again as it is not the same taste and quality.

Chuck Sanch
Brighton, Michigan

Chuck, I use about 2 cups of pickling salt for about 45 pounds of shredded cabbage. I mix the cabbage and salt by hand in a clean, washed out laundry wash tub, tossing it and pulling it up and over to mix it well. Then I let it stand for about 5 minutes. This draws the juice out of the cabbage so that when you pack it, you have the juice to help eliminate any air pockets in the crock as you pack it down. Then the salted cabbage is tamped down in the crock, so that the juice covers the cabbage. Your plastic bag is a great idea, and I'll have to try it this fall. — *Jackie*

Canned butter, bacon, and cheese shelf life

In the last two editions for Backwoods Home Magazine I have read about how to can butter, bacon, and cheese. What is the shelf life for all?

Lori Grieve
Sioux City, Iowa

As far as I know, once canned, these products remain fine for years and years. I have canned bacon, butter, and cheese and have eaten it several years later with no difference in taste or quality. Butter and cheese are still in the "experimental" canning category, but the more of us that share experiences, the better we'll be.

— *Jackie*

Cream separator

My husband and I both enjoy your articles, very informative! Right now we are trying to get away from electricity, batteries, and fuel as much as we are able to.

We need a cream separator for goat's milk. We have heard that others have made their own hand-powered/cranked. Have you ever heard of such a thing? We really need the information. We cannot afford $300-400 for electric. And we do not want that type anyway. We would really appreciate your help if possible.

David and Leslie Pen
Maple Falls, Washington

No I haven't. Cream is separated from the milk by centrifugal force, through the use of stacked cones. Probably if you ask around or put ads in the local shoppers, you will be able to find a separator someone isn't using any more. You might also keep watch on eBay, local auction bills, and even yard sales. You never know where you might come up with one.

While goat cream *is* harder to separate out by natural means, if you put your milk in shallow, wide bowls, you will be able to skim off a little cream from each pan after 24 hours. This won't be a lot of cream, but you should be able to get enough to make butter for the family once a week.

— Jackie

Canning chili

My boyfriend loves to cook chili and wants to can it himself. I know we need a pressure canner for that. I want to know if he can use his own recipe of beef, pork, veal, hot and sweet sausage, and the usual ingredients without any problems. How long should it keep? Do you have any suggestions on a good pressure canner and how long we process it for? We have only canned dill pickles in a water bath.

Jane Lippincott
Wynnewood, Pennsylvania

Yes, he can use any recipe he loves! You will be canning quarts at 10 pounds pressure (unless you live at an altitude above 1,000 feet and must increase your pressure to suit your altitude, if necessary; consult a good canning manual for directions) for 90 minutes and pints for 75 minutes. It will keep perfectly good for years and years, provided it was properly canned and stored in a dry, reasonably cool (as in the house) area. Any medium/large modern canner will work well for you; avoid the small (cheaper) "pressure cookers." They just won't do the job.

Once you venture into the exciting world of home canning, you'll be hooked. There is no end to the terrific meals you can make with your home canned foods. **— Jackie**

Egg gathering, dish cloths, and bug control

We thought the May/June issue was exceptional, though we love every issue we get and find something useful every time. We especially enjoyed the articles of whole grains, the Rule of Three, and we always like hearing from Jackie Clay. One thing I would find most helpful when reading articles and letters is to know what part of the country the tips and information comes from. Often weather, climate, or geography makes a difference in whether their way applies to our situation.

...Our chickens are free range, we have solved the problem of them getting in the garden and up on the patio/decks, but we do not know how to encourage them to lay eggs where we can collect them regularly. We almost never find an egg in their coop though they spend every night in it. They lay everywhere and anywhere and most of the time not in the same place twice, or so it seems; consequently, we do not know how fresh the egg is when we do stumble upon it. Any suggestions?

Another problem we are having is this. We are trying not to use hot water for washing clothes. The only problem we are having is disinfecting dishcloths. They come out of the washer smelling almost as bad as they went in. What can we use to rid them of that smell that comes from not drying completely between uses?

Last question: Because of gophers and deer, we are doing as much gardening as we can in containers. We have a bug problem. The only two bugs we regularly see are earwigs and pill bugs (possibly also called cellar bugs, or sow bugs). What is the most effective method of control? We prefer organic control, but at this point I will use whatever will work. The damage I see takes two forms. First the leaves of young plants or the newly transplanted disappear overnight leaving only stems where once there was a plant. In the case of larger leaves (zucchini and cucumber for instance) on transplants, the leaves will be nothing but veining by morning. ...Even the marigolds (well known for repelling bugs) are being eaten faster than they are growing. Tomatoes seem to be the only plant not affected...

Rose Umland
Squaw Valley, California

The best way to get your hens to lay in the nest boxes is to hold them in the coop for several hours in the morning, when most egg laying occurs. I've "trained" the girls to lay in the coop this way. Yes, I still occasionally do find a nest out in the brush. In this case, you can often tell by looking at the eggs about how old they are. If they are relatively clean, they're not so old; if they are all tracked up, they've been there awhile. You can check the freshness of the eggs by floating them in a bowl of water. The fresh ones will sink, the not so fresh ones will kind of partly float, and the rotten ones pop to the surface. Always break your questionable eggs in a cup before adding to a recipe. You'll know the *bad egg* right off; it has a runny white, the yolk is yucky and if it's really bad, *pee-yew!*

For your stinky dishcloths, when you take them out of the washer, throw them in a small pail full of water mixed with 2 Tbsp. of baking soda. Leave them in there for about half an hour, then rinse and hang in the sunshine. No more yucky smell. Or you can boil them in a pan of soda water for 15 minutes if you're worried about the possible bacteria connected with the smell.

As far as your plants, I've had good luck by spraying the leaves with a rotenone spray, especially under the leaves. With sow bugs and earwigs, you'll have the best luck by doing this in the late afternoon, before they come out for their evening forays. You can also put boards down near the plants. The bad bugs will hide under them and in the morning, you can pick up the board and catch/squash the bugs. A few times like this and your problem will lessen considerably. — *Jackie*

Sumac and honey locust

...We have a small pasture on one end there is sumac and honey locust we would like to get rid of. The only ideas folks (including the extension agent) have is spraying. Both things spread by runners so brush hogging makes it worse...Everybody says get goats for brush. What do you recommend in the way of goats? Also fencing for them and guard animal for them? How many would you recommend?...

Julia Rader
Huntsville, Arkansas

Yes, you can probably get rid of the sumac and honey locust with the help of goats. I don't know how large your pasture area is, so I can't make a definite recommendation as to how many goats you would need. In most cases, you'll find that even a few goats, say

six or seven, will do a lot of good on a relatively small brushy area. You may want to brush hog it down to remove the tough older stems. It won't spread it, but it will come up again. The new shoots will be tender and appealing to the goats.

Have you ever wanted to try dairy goats? If so, this would be an ideal time for you. Any breed will give the same results on your brush. If your only concern is to kill the brush, you can pick up some crossbreeds from a local breeder for a good price.

Here are a few tips for you: an electric fence will not keep goats contained. You can use it to reinforce either stock panel fence or woven wire field fence. This keeps the goats from standing on the fence or eating through it. Both things quickly weaken and sag the wire. I would probably use stock panels attached to T posts and try to hold the goats in the brushy area as much as possible. You may also need to feed them a little hay, depending on how much other feed and grass is available in your mini-pasture. Don't forget a mineral salt block and fresh water every day.

Probably the best guard animals for goats are donkeys and llamas. But they have to be introduced to your herd and become one with it before any guarding will happen. The guards must feel like the goats are part of their family. At any rate, it's a good idea to bring the goats up every evening to be shut up in a small corral with a shed till morning. Most animal predators are more active at night... including stray dogs. Your goats will stay safer that way. — *Jackie*

Canned bacon

Several people wrote in to let readers know where to get canned bacon. Places mentioned were:
www.internetgrocer.com
www.canned-bacon.com,
www.readydepot.com,
www.MREdepot.com.

I've checked these sites and they are good sources of canned bacon. Hooray! I'm sure a whole lot of readers will be real happy. Canned bacon is a great product. I used to use it when I went camping for long trips.
— *Jackie*

Hand-grinding nuts

Grinding nuts—peanut, cashew, walnut, etc. Can you suggest a hand grinder for this purpose?

I have read, but cannot recall where, that roasting nuts destroys much of their nutritional value, but improves the flavor. Do you know anything about this?

Got any recipes for making home-made nut butter? I would give up the roasting to keep more nutritional value.

Bob Taylor
Poulsbo, Washington

You can make nut butter in most flour mills. Even the old Corona style mill makes great nut butter. Or you can use your blender. Just dump in 2 cups of any type of nuts you want and grind them till the puree is oily and as smooth as you want. If it is not "spreadable" like you'd like, simply add 1 or 2 Tbsp. of sunflower or peanut oil. You may also add honey or sugar, and a bit of salt, if you wish. It is true that roasted nuts do make a tastier butter; I'm not sure I'd worry about the nutrition thing unless you are eating a *lot* of nut butter. Chances are if you eat a relatively healthy diet, your nutrition is already fine.
— *Jackie*

Garlic in the garden

By Linda Gabris

When I was a kid, my grandparents grew row after row of garlic in their huge backyard garden. There were enough glorious bulbs to keep up with grandma's demands for kitchen use and medicinal purposes with plenty of heads left over from the fall harvest for grandpa to make a sweet swap with the local beekeeper for a couple buckets of honey for us to use over the winter months. Not to mention, we had a stash of planters to put up for next year's crop.

I love garlic and take as much pleasure and pride in growing it in my garden as grandpa and grandma did. And, following the handwritten advice in grandma's old doctoring journals, I still call upon "...a good dose of garlic..." to cure various everyday ailments and common complaints including cold and flu.

Aside from indulging in a "dose of garlic" for good health and well-being, I also use the marvelous little clove more than any other herb, spice, or flavoring in savory recipes simply because I believe that often the only difference between good and gourmet is nothing more than a touch of garlic.

Contrary to what some garlic-shunning chefs may think, when used properly with other ingredients, the "stinking rose," as it's been dubbed by those lacking respect, does not overpower flavors but rather uplifts, enhances, and enlivens the taste and aroma of blander foods. Grandma used to say with a wink that "a stew without garlic is like an ear of fresh corn without a drizzle of butter or a tender green onion without a sprinkle of salt..." meaning that a touch is all it takes to tickle the taste buds and be the crowning glory to the main affair.

Garlic is a perennial plant that is hardy and easy to grow in all zones. In every sense of the word, it is a bulb and in gardening terms that means it can be sowed in early spring when the ground is workable or in late fall about 6 weeks before the soil freezes which allows the ambitious, garlic-loving gardener to cash in on two

When selecting store-bought garlic, choose firm, full heads with lots of clean paper covering.

yearly harvests. Autumn plantings will be ready the following summer, and spring plantings will be ready in fall.

If you have a gardening neighbor who grows garlic, you can ask which type they've had the best luck with or seek advice from your local nursery as to which species are best suited for your growing zone. Once you get your first crop underway, you'll have your own "climatized" garlic for the upcoming planting season and those thereafter; thus you'll want to be sure and set aside as many heads as you anticipate you'll need to fill the patch.

As a general rule of thumb, there are somewhere between 15 to 20 cloves in a bulb of garlic. Each clove produces a full head of garlic so how many planters you'll need depends on the size of your plot—most garlic growing experts agree that you need to keep somewhere around one seventh of your crop for planting stock.

To plant garlic, separate bulbs into individual cloves and remove the papery skins so the flesh is exposed.

Serve roasted garlic with crusty bread for a quick and easy appetizer deeply rooted in Middle East cuisines.

Choose a plot that's in full or partial sun and make sure the soil is well tilled. Garlic is tolerant and will thrive in any type of soil, although I find it prefers sandy clay loam that's been treated with a good feed of compost. In each hole, place one clove with the tip pointing upward and just barely below the surface—about 1 inch deep—and space them 8 inches apart. To save garden space, garlic can be planted at the foot of peas or other taller plants and the bonus is that it helps repel grubs and other garden nibblers.

For those with limited garden space, garlic can also be grown in window boxes or containers that are at least a foot wide by a foot deep. Fill the container with rich planting soil and plant in spring or fall as above, making sure to keep the container well-watered at all times.

Garlic is ready to harvest when the foliage turns yellow and starts to die down. The longer it is left in the ground, the stronger the bulb will be so harvest accordingly, keeping in mind that if it is left in the soil too long, the entire bulb is apt to split apart. This makes it a little more difficult to lift up the bulbs as well, and produces garlic that is not going to save as well as a head of tight cloves. Before harvesting the whole patch, dig out one tester bulb to see if it is ready. If the bulb is plump and well-formed and has good paper coverage, the time is right. If the bulb is not filled out enough or needs more jacketing, let it fatten up a little longer.

Harvest your garlic on a dry sunny day and the bulbs will be clean upon digging up. Do not harvest when the soil is wet as it will stick to the papery wrapping and will cause discoloration and will make the bulbs harder to cure.

Fresh garlic can be used on the table but it is much better after it has mellowed out by going through a curing process. To cure, braid into ropes or put the freshly dug garlic bulbs in a burlap sack or an open weave basket and let them dry in a well-ventilated place out of direct sunlight. I hang mine in the garden shed for at least two weeks. If the weather drops to freezing, bring the garlic indoors to prevent damage. I leave the stalks and leaves on during the curing period in order to avoid risk of exposing the flesh by removing.

Cured garlic should be stored at room temperature in a dry place that has some air circulation. I store mine laid out in single layer on a woven straw mat on the pantry shelf and it saves well for months. Grandma kept hers in burlap bags in the attic where it survived the whole winter. Never store garlic in the fridge as the moisture is apt to cause it to germinate, which causes it to deteriorate and lose flavor. If sprouting occurs, the garlic is past its table prime and should be planted, if feasible. Those who store garlic all winter will notice that nearing spring, the heads will start to sprout little green shoots, meaning that they are ready to begin a new life.

There are many different varieties but the two most common species are "softneck" and "hardneck" garlic. Softneck is the type you usually find in the produce department of grocery stores. It has several layers of papery-white covering which reaches up the neck of the bulb, forming a soft, pliable stalk. The outer cloves are plumper then the inner ones which tend to decrease in size to the core. Silverskin, which is easy to grow and is strongly flavored, and Artichoke, which is milder and slightly tinged with purple dots, belong to the softneck family. These types of garlic are the ones you often see done up in braids.

Hardneck garlic species do not have a soft neck, thus their name. The stalk is firm and woody. The three main varieties of hardneck are Rocambole, rich strong flavor and easy to peel; Porcelain, similar to jumbo "Elephant" garlic which is not really garlic at all but a member of the onion family; and Purple Stripe, so named because of its distinctive bright purple streaks on the papery skins, a number one pick for roasting whole—a new-age way of indulging wholeheartedly in garlic. (See recipe below.)

Your homegrown garlic means you're in for some super good eating!

Easy roasted garlic: slice off tips, remove excess paper cover, drizzle with olive oil, cover with lid or foil, and roast until tender.

wide-bladed knife on top of the clove facing safely away from you, then thump the knife with the heel of your hand. The clove will lightly bruise, moistening and loosening the papery skin and in turn, making it easy to peel. If you're cleaning a really large number of cloves for drying or pickling purposes, blanch in boiling water for about 10 seconds, then plunge into cold water and peeling will be a snap.

If you love the convenience of cooking with dried garlic and would like to make your own, it is easy. This is a great way to save garlic that is about to expire its shelf life or to put up excess garden bounty or bulk garlic buys at the market that are just too good to pass up.

To dry garlic, peel and thinly slice the cloves of as many heads as you wish to dry. Spread them on cheese-cloth-lined racks in a dry place and leave until moisture is gone. Grandma dried her excess bounty of garlic on racks behind the kitchen woodstove. They can also be dried in a sunroom or attic and a food dehydrator makes the job fast and easy. Follow manufacturer's directions for use. Once dry, store in a tightly-covered contain-

But even folks who don't grow their own garlic can still indulge wholeheartedly, simply by hunting down home-grown garlic at local vegetable markets, which is the next best thing. Or shop for it carefully at the grocery store, selecting the best bulbs you can find. Choose bulbs that are completely dry and show no signs of sprouting from dampness, unless you are picking planters. For culinary use they should be plump and firm and have full papery coats. Do not choose heads that are soft or shriveled and for an extra boost of good health—choose organically grown.

When it comes to cooking with garlic, it is important to remember the difference between "bulbs" (the whole head of garlic) and "cloves" (the individual teardrop shaped portions that make up the head) as a recipe calling for two or three minced cloves of garlic will be super-duper garlicky, if by mistake two or three whole bulbs are used instead!

A big secret to cooking with garlic revolves around the fact that strength can be controlled by style of cut. For instance, a finely minced or mashed clove of garlic instills much stronger flavor in a recipe than a clove that has been thinly sliced. And leaving the clove whole adds an even fainter hint of flavor to the dish.

To peel a clove of garlic, nip off the tip and the end of the clove and work off the skin with your fingers. If doing a larger number of cloves, after nipping, place each clove, one at a time, on the chopping board and lay a

Roasted garlic makes wonderful garnish for grilled meats.

To dry garlic, slice thinly, spread on cheesecloth-lined racks, and set in a warm place until moisture is gone.

When moisture is gone and flakes are crisp, store in an airtight container.

er on the pantry shelf and use as you would store-bought dried garlic, adding directly to soups, stews, sauces, or any dish calling for garlic. I use about ½ teaspoon of dried garlic in place of one fresh clove. Dried garlic is handier than fresh garlic for campers and backpackers as it is extra light and reconstitutes quickly, making camp cooking that much easier.

To make your own garlic powder, simply grind dried garlic using a pestle and mortar, or use a blender if making larger amounts, until desired fineness is reached. Store in a spice jar and use for instant garlic flavoring.

Garlic salt can be made by mixing 1 cup of garlic powder with ½ cup of finely ground sea salt, more or less to taste. For a gourmet spice, mix home-dried garlic powder with smoked salt (easy to make by smoking salt in your smoker or available where fine spices are sold.) Smoked garlic salt is a wonderful seasoning for fish and seafood.

When it comes to eating garlic strictly for good health, according to the writings in grandma's old doctoring journals, raw garlic is more beneficial than cooked because it has more strength. One way to add a little raw garlic to your diet is to include it, finely minced, in salad dressings. It adds invigorating flavor and the apple cider vinegar or red wine in the dressing helps neutralize "garlic-breath" — a major concern for many garlic-loving connoisseurs. An old trick of grandma's for freshening the breath after indulging in a feed of raw garlic is to finish the meal off with a strong cup of mint tea. Others claim that chewing on a sprig of fresh parsley does the trick. My motto is, "...feed 'em all a good dose of garlic and nobody will even notice..."

Below are a couple Old World recipes and a few New World ways of indulging in garlic.

Roasted garlic:

When I was a kid, grandma roasted many heads of garlic in the oven of her crackling old woodstove and we ate them with thick slabs of home-made bread for a treat that was hard to beat. Today, roasted garlic is showing up in fancy restaurants across the country, often served with crusty bread and melted brie, camembert, or other creamy cheese as an appetizer or as accompaniment to grilled steaks and chops. Anyway you eat it, it's good. I like mine squeezed on top of crusty bread with a glass of home-made wine for washing it down—a quick and delicious appetizer. Use your fingers to pop the roasted clove from its skin, place on bread and... voila.

If you don't have a special garlic roaster (a gadget available in specialty cooking shops), here's a method that works for me. Peel away the excess outer layers of skin off the bulb, leaving the skins of the individual cloves intact. Cut the tips off the top of the garlic head exposing the flesh of each clove. Place the garlic in a small clay baking dish and drizzle 2 teaspoons of olive oil over each head, making sure it is well distributed. You can sprinkle it with dried herbs such as basil if you wish. Cover with clay lid or loosely draped aluminum foil and bake in 400° F oven for 20 minutes or until cloves are soft to a toothpick.

Roasted garlic can be mashed with a fork and used for making garlic bread, as topping for baked potatoes or steamed vegetables, mixed with cream and drizzled over pasta, or made into a delicious soup as in the recipes below.

Preserved minced garlic in olive oil:

You can buy it ready-made at the grocery store or you can make your own. Minced preserved garlic is handy for making garlic bread or for adding to soups, sauces, and gravies, or spreading on steaks, chops, and chicken before grilling.

It is a good way to put up excess bounty of fresh garlic or to use up garlic bulbs that are about to expire their shelf life which happens when their papery jackets begin to shed, leaving the cloves bare and unprotected.

To make preserved garlic, simply mince peeled garlic and put it into a clean jar. When the jar is packed, cover it with virgin olive oil, pressing the garlic down to ensure that it is submerged in oil. Put lid on the jar and store in fridge. It is now ready to use whenever a quick touch of garlic is needed. This saves indefinitely.

Whole peeled cloves of garlic can be used in place of minced garlic and, for exciting hot flavor, chili peppers can be added to the jar. It is easy to make and the big bonus is, the olive oil in which the garlic is preserved takes on a wonderful rich garlicky flavor and can be used for salad dressings or in pasta sauces or any other recipe calling for garlic flavored olive oil—so you are killing two birds with one stone! For a Mediterranean-style lunch that travels well in the picnic basket, serve whole cloves of pre-served garlic with crusty bread and assorted cheese.

Grandma's Old World roasted garlic soup:

This is so garlicky-good you'll get hooked after the first spoonful. Grandma made this soup often in the winter and claimed it was the number one cure for chilblains. I remember coming home from school across the frozen fields and can vouch that all it took was one whiff of this fragrant soup to instantly warm me.

```
3 heads roasted garlic (made as
    above)
2 Tbsp. flour
3 cups hot chicken stock
1 tsp. salt
¼ tsp. black pepper
pinch dried dill
1 cup cream
```

Separate roasted garlic cloves and mash with a folk. Set aside. Put leftover olive oil in which garlic was baked into soup pot, adding enough if needed to measure 3 Tbsp. Sauté flour in oil until lightly tanned. Slowly stir in chicken stock and bring to a boil, stirring until smooth. Add seasoning and roasted garlic. Stir in cream and heat through. Serve with crusty bread or croutons. Makes 4 to 6 servings.

Quick creamy garlic pasta sauce:

```
1 head roasted garlic
2 Tbsp. olive oil
1 cup sweet minced red pepper
2 Tbsp. flour
¼ cup boiling water
1 cup cream
½ cup fresh grated Parmesan
    cheese
¼ tsp. Italian seasoning mix
salt and pepper to taste
```

Mash garlic as above, set aside. Heat oil and sauté red pepper until soft. Stir in flour until tan. Add water and stir until thick and smooth. Add mashed garlic and remaining ingredients and heat through. Serve over cooked pasta noodles. Serve 4 to 6.

Honey roasted carrots and garlic:

An old recipe of grandma's that brings new life to root-cellared carrots on their last leg.

```
1 Tbsp. butter
6 cups thinly sliced carrots (if car-
    rots have started to go limp slice
    into ice cold water and let stand
    until they crisp back up)
6 cloves peeled sliced garlic
3 Tbsp. red wine
¼ cup honey
¼ tsp. fresh grated ginger
```

Rub inside of small casserole dish with butter. Put all ingredients into the dish and cover with a lid. Bake in 350° F oven until carrots are tender and glazed, about 15 minutes. Goes nice with roast meats, especially pork.

Variation—use maple syrup in place of honey and omit the ginger. Sprinkle walnuts on top before serving for a vegetable dish that goes nicely with poultry.

Easy Asian pickled garlic:

This exciting recipe takes on the tastes of the Orient. Try it and watch these tasty pickles disappear like magic.

```
1 quart peeled garlic (The original
    recipe calls for the garlic to be
    unpeeled which helps preserve
    color but I find the garlic does
    not pickle as well with skin left
    on.)
1 peeled finger of ginger root
½ cup vinegar
1 tsp. pickling salt
½ cup soy sauce
¼ cup honey
1 Tbsp. sesame oil
bit more vinegar if needed
```

Put garlic and ginger root in scalded quart sealer. Bring vinegar, salt, soy sauce, and honey to a boil. Pour over garlic. Add extra vinegar if needed to finish covering. Drizzle sesame oil in top of jar before sealing. Allow garlic to mature in the fridge at least one week before serving. Δ

THE MANY BENEFITS OF GARLIC

By Joe Knight

Garlic, used throughout the world for the taste it adds to foods, is also well known for its medicinal benefits. Known as *Allium sativum* in the botanical world, garlic is related to the onion. The oldest medical text ever found, the *Codex Ebers*, an Egyptian papyrus from 1550 BC that contains 800 therapeutic formulas, contains 22 garlic recipes to control such problems as heart disease, bites, parasites, and intestinal tumors. In 450 BC, Herodotus recommended the use of garlic to avoid epidemics of typhoid and cholera by the workers who built the pyramids during the reign of Cheops, Pharaoh of the Fourth Dynasty. The value of this medicine and condiment was so high that the value of a young and healthy slave was seven kilograms of garlic. Roman and Greek athletes and soldiers consumed garlic to enhance their strength and to treat wounds. In 77 AD, Pliny the Elder wrote the ten-volume encyclopedia *Naturalis Historia*, in which he listed 61 ailments that were amenable to treatment with garlic.

In the late 19th century, garlic began to be scientifically investigated. In 1858, Louis Pasteur demonstrated garlic's antibacterial properties. In World War I garlic was used when bandaging wounds, and in World War II to prevent septic poisoning and gangrene.

Garlic also has a long history of being used as an insect repellent. Diallyl disulfide and diallyl trisulfide, two substances in garlic oil, kill insects. Garlic has been proven to successfully destroy mosquito larvae and repel mosquitoes, black flies, and fleas. Some people even place garlic in drawers to repel moths. Garlic oil has been effective enough combating insects to be included in patented insect repellent for humans.

Today, the scientific focus is on the effect garlic has on cholesterol levels and preventing the formation of blood clots—both of these properties have a direct effect on the heart. In one study done at the University of Oxford in England, patients taking 600 mg to 900 mg of garlic on a daily basis had a 12% reduction in total cholesterol compared to another group that was given a placebo (a non-pharmacologically active substance). In a German study, 261 patients were given either garlic powder tablets or a placebo; after a 12-week treatment period the average serum cholesterol levels dropped by 12% in the garlic treated group, while triglycerides dropped by 17% compared to the placebo group. Even the American Heart Association (AHA) supports the evidence that garlic can reduce the risk of atherosclerosis (cholesterol build-up in the arteries).

The Allium family includes onions, garlic, chives, leeks, and shallots. Alliin, the primary chemical ingredient in garlic, is similar in structure to cystine, an amino acid that contains sulfur and possesses no odor. After garlic is crushed, alliin is converted into alicin, the compound that gives garlic its strong smell and numerous health benefits. It is alliin that is suspected in preventing the formation of cholesterol. The mechanism in the prevention platelet aggregation which forms blood clots, is unknown, but may be due to the antioxidant effect of garlic.

Garlic seems to be a safe and effective method to lower cholesterol levels; however, you should always check with your health care provider before beginning garlic or any other supplement. If you plan to use garlic to lower your cholesterol, make sure you see your clinician to have regular blood tests done to make sure your cholesterol is dropping.

The main side effect of garlic is its odor—this is not only noticeable in the person's breath, but can be detected also in their perspiration. Some garlic supplements have been "deodorized" but their effectiveness is reduced. Regular use of garlic supplements may cause nausea, diarrhea, bleeding disorders and allergic reactions. Garlic supplements should be discontinued two weeks prior to surgery.

There are some drug interactions you should be aware of if you decide to start garlic supplementation. If you are taking any type of blood thinners, such as warfarin or aspirin, you should not use garlic supplements because severe bleeding can result. Some concern exists that garlic supplementation may decrease the effectiveness of oral contraceptives, so it's best to avoid the use of garlic supplements if you are taking birth control pills. Δ

The last word

The *real* good news in the recent
2nd Amendment decision

The June 26, 2008 Supreme Court decision, *District of Columbia v. Heller*, which shot down the District's *Firearms Control Regulations Act of 1975* and affirmed the right of individuals to "keep and bear" arms, has both been hailed to be a victory for individual rights and damned as a curse on America's crime-ridden cities.

My first reaction on hearing the results was somewhat subdued. I felt the decision shouldn't have been so close—5-4. It was a no-brainer and should have been 9-0. Because of the narrow margin I was disappointed—and a little bit afraid of what future decisions may bring.

My second reaction was that the decision isn't broad enough. It leaves in place the power of government to continue regulating our rights. I never see that as a good thing.

My third reaction—and this is one that surprises people when I say it—is that it should not have been decided by the Court at all. Why? Because I don't like the idea that interpretation of the very document that is supposed to protect us from the tyranny of government is interpreted and adjudicated by any branch of that government. I should mention that nowhere in the *Constitution* is it mentioned that that august body we call the Supreme Court is to be the arbiter and arbitrator of our rights. And because of that, the *10th Amendment* actually forbids it. It says:

The powers not delegated to the United States by the Constitution, nor prohibited by it to the States, are reserved to the States respectively, or to the people.

I'm not saying it's not a good idea to have the Court intercede for us and hope for the best. I'm just saying it's not "constitutional."

What the Founders had intended was for *us* to guard our rights ourselves. That's why they're written in everyday language rather than the legalese we've come to expect from lawyers, lawmakers, bureaucrats, and the courts. Think of it this way: Had the Founders thought our rights should be determined by a branch of the government, by men who were appointed or confirmed to their judicial seats by the very people who would deprive us of our rights, then the Founders would have taken their case to an English court in 1776, heard the inevitable decision, and today we could still be subjects of the Crown.

So, was there anything in the decision I *did* like? Yes. I was stunned to discover that the majority decision ruling was based on the *Natural* right of self-defense.

Why is this important? Because I rarely hear anyone, in any branch of government, talk about our Natural or God-given rights. Even the mainstream media rarely uses either of these

terms. But Natural or God-given rights are *exactly* what the Founders had in mind when they wrote the *Declaration of Independence*, the *Constitution*, and the *Bill of Rights*. But on June 26th, though the Natural right to self-defense is mentioned nowhere in the *Constitution*, at least five of the justices suddenly acknowledged its existence. *That's good.*

I've tried, again and again, to point out to people that the primary reason the *Bill of Rights* was included in the *Constitution* was to remind the citizenry and the government that we have rights under *any* government. But they never intended it to be an exhaustive or comprehensive list of our rights nor was it intended to be the *source* of our rights as many people, including lawyers and politicians, have come to believe. Hence the term we commonly use: *constitutional rights.*

But we don't have constitutional rights, folks. The English, Canadians, and even the Russians have constitutional rights. We have Natural or God-given rights. The Founders had intended us to be the first (and, so far, the only) country where the citizens have rights that are *not* gifts from politicians, bureaucrats, the courts, or even the Founders themselves.

John C. Eastman, Associate Dean of Chapman University's School of Law and director of the Claremont Institute's Center for Constitutional Jurisprudence, commenting on the decision said, "...the Second Amendment, like its sister amendments, does not confer a right but rather recognizes a natural right inherent in our humanity." This kind of sentiment is rarely reported by the press, nor is it taught in our schools. Frankly, I don't think either the people who inform us nor the people who educate us are any longer aware of it.

Worse, I don't think many so-called legal experts are aware of it. Consider this: Justice Stephen Breyer's dissenting opinion was based on the fact that self-defense is not explicitly mentioned as a reason for the *2nd Amendment*. Apparently, neither he nor the three justices who joined him understand where our rights come from. Presumably, they feel what rights we have are a gift from him and the rest of the government. *That's dangerous.*

If the American people will just sit up and listen to what the decision was based on, and realize where our rights really come from, maybe we can stop the erosion of our freedoms, and perhaps we can even get back the ones we've lost.

Finally, there's the question: "What would Washington, Adams, Jefferson, or any of the other Founders have done if confronted by the loss of rights we're experiencing today. Well, there's a little ditty making the rounds on the Internet that says the ultimate defense of our liberties is in three boxes:

• the ballot box
• the jury box
• the ammo box.

When the first two failed them, the Founders had to reluctantly turn to the third. I hope we never have to resort to it again. But it is *one* of the reasons for the *2nd Amendment*.

— **John Silveira**

Nov/Dec 2008
Issue #114
$5.95 US
$7.50 CAN

Backwoods
Home magazine

practical ideas for self-reliant living

Whole grain bread

Energy crisis solutions

Crabapples

Storage pantry meals

Homestead guns

Fire wick fire starter

A shared treasure chest

Community supported agriculture

www.backwoodshome.com

My view

A momentous event that puts the Presidential race in perspective

My son, Jake, turned 17 years of age between issues. What a momentous occasion! Coincidentally, either McCain or Obama is about to be elected America's next President. What a minor event!

How can I say this? Elevating my son's 17th birthday above the election of America's President? Have I lost all perspective?

Hardly! Having your oldest son turn 17 just before the Presidential election *gives* you perspective. It contrasts honesty with, to put it euphemistically, truth bending. It highlights the vital personal decisions a young man must make to succeed at this critical stage of his life against the meaningless doubletalk of politicians who seek to win election no matter how many facts they must hammer and twist to fit the moment.

Do I sound too cynical about the political process?

My son, even while besieged by the hormonal flood that accompanies the teenage years, sincerely seeks truth to make informed decisions, while politicians, all too aware of the dark side of truth, namely, that it can be molded by clever men to appear to be what it is not, seek election to lead the rest of us.

Which event is most important? Which is the harbinger of good for the nation? I'll put my money on Jake and the thousands of other teenagers in his position. They'll create the future we'll rely on. We'll have to suffer through whoever wins the election.

If each of us reaches into our own memories, we will find events in our lives, peopled by heroes and villains and all sorts of characters in between, who made a significant difference in how we have lived. The heroes are the ones who stand out for me. They include high school teachers like Sister Helena, who taught me confidence in myself, my father, who taught me how to work hard, my older brother, Hugh, who taught me the importance of family, and my friend of 44 years, John Silveira, who taught me the meaning of friendship. I could go on and on, but no politician or political event comes to mind.

In my opinion, politics is a big circus populated by clowns. The only significant role they have ever played in my life is to hinder my progress or frustrate my belief in the innate goodness of mankind. They are the bogeymen of my memories, always meddling in the affairs of hard working people, passing senseless laws, and stifling the individual efforts of people instead of letting them combine to push the nation forward.

I see the Presidential election as a temporary spectacle like the Superbowl. Everybody is talking about it, but in the end

Jake installs a batten Dutch door he and his brothers made for the 2-story clubhouse they built.

it's relatively meaningless, at least when compared to youngsters like Jake gearing up to solve the world's problems.

It is a sad commentary on our times, I think, that so many people disagree with me on this matter. They think electing either Obama or McCain is one of the most critical decisions of their lifetime. They think it will dictate the future of America. It is a "group" mentality that has been fostered over many years by the colossus that makes up America's large political and bureaucratic establishment.

Well, I've got news for you. If you think getting a certain politician elected is going to favorably affect your life, you're in for a disappointment. Only you paying attention to the details of your own life will favorably affect your future. It doesn't matter worth a damn who becomes President.

Incidentally, the *Large Hadron Collider* in Europe is also revving up as I write this. The LHC is about as big an event as launching *Sputnik*, or putting a man on the moon, or coming up with Einstein's *Special Theory of Relativity*. It will likely unlock the fundamental secrets of science and open the door to the TOE — the *Theory of Everything*. It represents the *Holy Grail* of science.

But you may not read much about the LHC in this Presidential year. It was one of those incredible scientific achievements that should have taken place in the United States. But 15 years ago the U.S. Congress, after spending $2 billion on it, killed the funding because of politicians' complaints the money could be better used elsewhere. It was an incredibly shortsighted decision, and now that Europe has built the LHC to the applause of scientists and engineers around the world, it is expected to cause a scientific brain drain from the United States to Europe. But I doubt you will hear much talk of either the LHC or the loss of American scientists to Europe from politicians.

But even though the LHC is obviously more important than America's Presidential race, I'm still leaning towards Jake's coming of age as the main event. Δ **— Dave Duffy**

Whole grain breads
baked at home
part 2

By Richard Blunt

Since ancient times home-baked bread has invoked deeply-felt emotions in people around the world. The breads common to the early Egyptians and Greeks were simple crushed grains mixed with water and baked under a pile of ashes on a bake stone or griddle. They were usually dry, gritty, and rather hard. Not exactly the well-risen, light, and spongy breads so common today. Even these basic breads, however, were considered a treat while still hot.

When they arrived, the Romans were quick to make refinements to the whole process. Improvement in the quality of bread depended on improvements in the way grains were milled. The Romans at first ignored this fundamental fact and continued to enjoy their favorite grain food—*puls*, a simple, thick porridge or gruel made from roasted emmer wheat or barley, crushed with a mortar and pestle, and mixed with water, salt, and fat. It was sort of a forerunner of polenta.

The Romans introduce the Pompeian rotary mill

Eventually, they gave up the crude simplicity of the mortar and pestle in favor of the more efficient Pompeian rotary mill. These mills consisted of two large stones, made of lava, and nestled one inside the other. Turned by animal power, the upper stone moved around crushing grain that was fed through a hopper into a small space separating the two stones. The milled grain fell onto a ledge below the stones where it could be ground further and sifted into various grades of flour. A few wealthy homes had scaled down versions of this mill, usually powered by slaves.

The rotary mill made it possible for Romans to be the first civilization to centralize bread baking, making it possible for most citizens in the cities to buy their daily bread at a central bakery. The concept of having someone else do the baking was apparently very popular. These public bakeries were barely able to keep up with demand. Bakeries often ran as 24-hour-a-day operations with slaves working in shifts. This was the ancient forerunner of today's fast-paced bread industry.

As popular as the central bakeries were, home-baked bread still had the same unique appeal to the ancient Romans as it does to us today, and some wealthy people in Roman cities, along with almost all the ordinary people in the surrounding countryside, ground their own grains and baked their favorite breads at home.

As the Roman Legions conquered other countries and imposed their rule on them, those countries were obligated to export their products to Rome. From Britain came millet, flax, and emmer wheat—one of the most ancient of all wheats. From the Mediterranean came a variety of cultivated wheats like einkorn and durum. By all accounts these high quality wheats, when milled through a Pompeian rotary mill and baked in stone ovens, produced breads close to the familiar loaves we enjoy today.

Avoiding chronic hunger during the Middle Ages

Later, during the Middle Ages, wars, diseases, and natural disasters created serious food shortages in Europe. Only the wealthy, supported by powerful feudal lords, had the ability to avoid chronic hunger. And, using their power and influence, these folks passed laws that made it illegal for ordinary people to grind their own grain. These laws mandated that all grain be brought to a central mill for processing. The mills, of course, were owned by the feudal lords and rented to the millers who paid a toll, usually in the form of grain, to the lord for the privilege. The grain was then secured in massive strongholds inside thick-walled castles. Complying with this oppressive system, called a soke system, was often the only way to avoid starvation. Also, most peasant homes did not have an oven, and folks had to prepare their dough at

307

home and bring it to a communal bakery to be baked. Here, also, there was a fee to be paid.

Bread during this period of history was truly the staff of life. Unlike today, it was not an accompaniment to a meal, but more often it *was* the meal, especially in peasant homes.

Historically, during prosperous times, bread sales seem to decline as people eat more "elegant" foods. But during times of hardship bread assumes a role of magnified importance in our lives.

A feeling of security

World War II was a time of severe food rationing for all the countries engaged. In Britain, the government introduced the "National Loaf" as part of their food-rationing program. Even though commercial white bread was the bread of choice, this supply of whole grain bread gave the British people a feeling of security. That is, despite the war, despite the rationing, they still had bread to eat. But, when the wartime rationing program ended in 1954, folks returned to their favorite loaf, Mother's Pride, the British version of Wonder Bread.

White bread

For a variety of reasons, since about the fifth century the belief that white bread is superior to whole grain bread has existed in almost all societies where bread is eaten. This despite the fact the refined flour is deficient in vitamins, minerals, and the dietary fiber we need. Dense, dark breads made from low-gluten grains like rye and barley were considered food for poor people, while white bread made with refined wheat flour was, and still is to some extent, considered food for the upper class.

The long-standing prejudice against dark, whole grain breads started to change in the 1960s as the public's sense of health consciousness began to change. Since then medical research has uncovered convincing evidence that dramatically increasing the amount of whole grain foods in our diet is a vital step to maintaining optimum health. Today, we seem to be taking this advice seriously and making sweeping changes in our eating habits. We are eating more whole grain cereals at breakfast and more fresh and frozen fruits and vegetables at other meals.

However, unless we are willing to eat breakfast several times a day, eating enough whole grain to maintain optimum health can get tricky. The most convenient and satisfying way to

meet our goal for increasing the amount of whole grains in our diet is to have high quality whole grain breads available as a regular complement to other meals.

But shopping for these breads at a local retail bakery or supermarket can prove to be frustrating, as well as expensive. As you read ingredient labels on many of the so-called whole grain and multigrain breads, you realize they are really colored copies of the soft, white, pillow breads that occupy most of the space in the bread aisle.

This article is intended to help you make your own real whole grain bread with all its nutritious health benefits.

Encouraging your family to make the switch

Over the years I have written several articles in *BHM* featuring various types of bread, and the test loaves I prepared at home for my family were always popular.

So when I got the idea to write an article on whole grain breads, I was confident that this enthusiasm would continue. But for reasons that have only recently become clear, during the past several weeks many of the early whole grain breads I baked received a somewhat ho-hum response from my wife and three kids.

After watching several loaves age and go stale in the bread cabinet, I felt something must be wrong with my recipe formulas.

One day at the dinner table I shared my observations with the group. My daughter, Sarah, came right to point: "Dad, all of these breads taste good but we are not accustomed to the texture. These breads are denser than the bread that we normally eat. If they were a little lighter I would find them easier to eat."

Click! the light bulb finally came on and I realized what the missing piece to this puzzle was. My family, me included, had been eating commercial breads most of our lives. The taste, mouth-feel, and visual structure of most commercial breads was fixed, and was not going to be changed by a sudden leap into whole grains. Modifications in my recipes were necessary.

The Taggert Bread Co. (the bakery that introduced Wonder Bread) started selling sliced white bread in this country in 1930. It was an instant success that continues to this day. I think it is safe to say that most people in America have been raised eating the soft, marshmallow-like commercial breads that are so prevalent in most food stores.

My family, I realized, needed time to adjust to whole grain bread.

To encourage my family to embrace my whole grain bread program, I began incorporating incremental amounts of traditional white flour into my recipes. Adding 40 to 50 percent white flour to a bread recipe gives the finished loaf a somewhat lighter crumb (crumb is baker-speak for describing the inner consistency of bread), without compromising the integrity of the loaf.

To test this theory, I made eight loaves of whole grain oatmeal bread over a three-week period. The first was made with about 15 percent white bread flour. In each subsequent loaf I increased the amount of bread flour until I got to 50 percent. From 40 percent on, none of these breads went to waste.

When the last loaf was finished, it was eaten completely by the next day. The vote for the last was unanimous. My son, Michael, spoke for the rest of the test committee. "When are you going to make that bread again, Dad?"

In the coming months I will reverse this process, taking out the white flour, and see if we can develop an appreciation for bread made with 100 percent whole grain.

So, all the recipes I offer here contain *some* white flour. In three of the recipes, instead of commercial bread or all-purpose flour, I ground enough hard red winter wheat to use in the recipe, and sifted it through a small fine-mesh sifter that I purchased at Wal-Mart. After grinding and sifting one pound of wheat berries I get about 12 ounces of almost white flour. This flour, which still contains fine bits of wheat germ and bran, performs as well as commercial white flour, while still containing most of the nutritional value of whole grain flour.

The loaves made with the recipes that follow were eaten with an enthusiasm that I thought might not be possible. They are proof that it is possible to grind a variety of whole grains in your own kitchen, and fashion the resulting flour into an endless variety of nutritious breads that will be eaten and enjoyed.

Grains

The quality and price of whole grains has remained stable, even now, with prices going up. Health food stores and upscale markets like Whole Foods carry a limited selection of whole grains and sell them out of bulk-purchase bins. In my area the only wheat that is consistently available is hard red winter wheat. But none of the stores could or would tell me how long the wheat had been sitting in the bin or if it was properly rotated. So I opted to buy my grains from more reliable sources, all of which sell quality grain from their websites.

The four sources I use most often are:
• Bob's Red Mill
1-800-349-2173
(www.bobsredmill.com)
• Sun Organic Farms
1-888-269-9888
(www.sunorganic.com)
•King Arthur Flour
1-800-827-6836

(www.kingarthurflour.com)
• Home Grown Harvest
1-866-900-3321
(www.homegrownharvest.com)

If you are not ready to buy a grain mill right away, high-quality flours milled by King Arthur Flour, Arrowhead Mills, Hodgson Mill, and Bob's Red Mill are available in most supermarkets and health food stores. Whether you opt for whole grains or milled flours, it is important that you store them in airtight containers in a cool, dry place. I store all of my flours and grains in a small refrigerator in my basement. Without careful storage, even the highest quality grains will become stale and possibly rancid, and milled flour—commercial

or home-processed—is even more prone to spoilage.

My grain mill sits on my kitchen counter next to my mixer and other baking equipment. When I bake, I mill only enough flour to complete my recipe. If I have any left I pack it in a clean, plastic food storage container with a tight-fitting lid, and put it in the refrigerator or freezer.

Baking bread

Before you start working with these recipes, I suggest you read the "Elements of Baking" section of my first article of this series in this anthology. The article is titled, *Whole grain breads baked at home.* (**BHM has sold out of this issue, but the article is available free at our web-**site, **www.backwoodshome.com —** **Editor**) The 13 principles of baking I outlined there apply to these recipes as well.

If you have trouble developing a sourdough starter, or prefer not to make one from scratch, don't worry. King Arthur Flour sells a dried starter that is a great product. It comes in a one-ounce jar with complete instructions and is ready for use after adding flour and water. If you feel like you're "cheating" doing it this way, you're *not*. You're joining a very exclusive club that boasts many high-end professional bakeries as members. If you're a lover of rye bread, an active sourdough culture is not a frivolous luxury—it is a *must*. I will expand on

Grain mill, sifter, and whole grains

Soaker and pre-ferment ready for mixing

ent rates, especially when using whole grain flour. Because of these different rates, to prepare the recipes that follow we will use three slightly different **pre-ferments**: *biga, pâte fermenté,* and *poolish.* The only difference between the first two pre-ferments is that biga contains salt, pâte fermenté doesn't. Poolish is biga but with more water in it.

A **soaker** is actually a type of pre-ferment that does not contain yeast. Coarsely ground flours, other grains, and seeds are soaked overnight in water or milk. The purpose is to activate the enzymes in the grains and release some of the sugars trapped in the starch. Salt is added to the soaker as a means of controlling this enzyme activity which if left unchecked will result in bread that is gummy and gelatinous.

Finally, we have the **sourdough culture**, which is a pre-ferment that has many uses. My personal favorite is to use it to develop flavor and texture in rye breads. The versatility of

this when we get to my rye bread recipe.

Simply adding water or water-containing liquid, such as milk, to flour triggers chemical and biological activity in the flour. Two proteins, gliadin and glutenin, that are naturally present in wheat and a few other grains, combine to create the protein gluten. Gluten provides both elasticity (ability to stretch and spring back) and extensibility (ability to stretch without tearing) to bread dough.

The water also activates enzymes which immediately start converting the starch—and to a lesser extent the proteins in the flour—into a variety of complex sugars. Activating, maintaining, and controlling this activity is essential to success when working with whole grain flour.

Pre-ferment dough, **soakers**, and **sourdough culture** are the primary tools I employ in the recipes that follow. These three elements, which when mixed separately and allowed to mature in the proper environment, control enzyme activity and contribute to the development of a strong gluten structure in each recipe.

So, why is it necessary to separate them? The answer is simple. Enzyme conversion, gluten development, and leavening action move along at differ-

Mill, sifted flour, soaker

Sourdough seed starters from left: wheat, white, rye.

sourdough culture allows it to enhance flavor, improve keeping-qualities, and develop texture in almost any bread recipe. It is compatible with commercial yeast when used in the same recipe, or it can be used independently, without commercial yeast, as both a flavor enhancer and a leavening agent.

One final note before we move on to the recipes. All of these recipes incorporate a developing process called "delayed fermentation." This is simply mixing a measured amount of flour with a small amount of yeast and placing it in the refrigerator to ferment overnight. This initial cold fermentation develops the dough through a complex symphony of chemical and biological actions. When the pre-fermented dough is added to the rest of the ingredients the next day, it transfers this perfect chemical and physical balance to the entire batch and the finished loaf will have more flavor, a uniform crumb, and will last longer.

Readers of my previous article might remember that I said it is best to use only enough yeast to leaven the bread. That's because conventional bread recipes, such as those in the previous article, incorporate a full complement of yeast along with the other ingredients, which are then mixed, kneaded, and set aside to ferment. Then, *voila*, you're on the road to successfully making a loaf of bread.

But the recipes in this article are different. There will be additional yeast added to the final dough. This will be to ensure that the bread leavens before putting it in the oven.

I also recommend that, for these recipes, you resist the temptation to work the raw dough in a mixer as you might when making bread with white flour. When making whole grain bread, it is important for the baker to develop an ability to know what the dough should feel and look like when it is time to move from one step in the recipe to another. The best way to develop this ability is to hand-work the dough as much as possible.

The initial mixing is best done with a sturdy wooden or stainless steel spoon. When the dough can no longer be mixed with the spoon, wet your hands and finish the mixing and kneading, wetting your hands as needed to prevent the dough sticking to them. As the flour absorbs the water and the gluten network begins to form, the dough will become smooth, soft, and supple. From start to finish this whole initial mixing is done in less than five minutes.

Once you become familiar with the look and feel of properly mixed whole grain bread dough, mixing and kneading can be done in a sturdy stand-mixer or food processor.

Good luck with these recipes. As you gain experience, feel free to increase or decrease the amount of whole grain flour to suite your individual taste.

As in my first article, all the recipes that follow are for a single loaf, each weighing less than 40 ounces.

Pizza bianka

My family loves pizza, especially my food review committee which consists of my children, Sarah, Jason, and Michael. When we visit one of the many upscale pizza restaurants in our area the most difficult decision at our table is what kind of pizza to order. My wife, Tricia, and I are both open to the selection. The committee members, however, are completely at odds over what constitutes an acceptable pizza. One wants a thin crust, the others want a thick crust. Sarah does not like red sauce on her pizza and will always request a white pizza. Jason loves hamburger, sausage, and pepperoni. Michael is a vegetarian.

One day, this past June, my wife and I decided it was too hot to cook and that it might be fun to go to a new high-end pizza restaurant that just opened in our town.

As is our habit, we sat at our table for at least 30 minutes, sipping beverages and trying to decide on pizzas that would make everyone happy. Jason and Michael came to a compromise and ordered a "medium" with half pepperoni and half spinach and onion. Tricia and Sarah decided to order dinner salads instead of pizza. I was about to do the same until I spotted a familiar item—pizza bianka. A few years had passed since I last tasted this very basic, yet delicious and satisfying pizza. The version of this pizza that came to mind as I read the menu was a focaccia-like bread with no cheese or sauce. The topping consisted simply of a few sprinkles of coarse salt, extra virgin olive oil, and fresh rosemary.

Our waiter confirmed that the restaurant made *this* version as well as several others that had a variety of cheeses, fresh vegetables, and herb toppings. When made properly, this is a light, chewy bread with a crisp exterior and a bubbly crumb. I ordered a small pizza bianka and had it cut into squares so that everyone could have a piece.

As soon as my pizza came to the table, I made a mental note for the future to use my new grain mill and my supply of hard red winter wheat to develop a whole wheat version.

The preparation procedure I employ to make this dough is similar to other recipes in this section, but with a couple of important differences.

Most bread created in Italy contains a high percentage of water in the dough. For example, standard pizza in this country would be made with about 6 ounces of water for every 10 ounces of flour. Pizza bianka dough contains 9 ounces of water for every 10 ounces of flour. This high water content is why the crust is so light. The dough, after mixing, resembles a very sticky pancake batter. This batter consistency totally defies traditional kneading. This is a blessing because you can let your electric mixer do all the work, and you don't need a workhorse mixer to get the job done. If you can make pancakes with your mixer, you can make this pizza dough.

Finally, in this recipe we will be using a different type of pre-fermented dough called poolish. This poolish has equal amounts of water and flour along with a small amount of yeast.

Also, this recipe is the *basic* version of pizza bianka. I suggest you make this version before you consider sauces, cheeses, and other toppings.

For preparation of the final dough use an electric mixer. Since this dough is very soft and somewhat fluid, a workhorse type mixer is not necessary. Even your grandmother's old Sunbeam will handle this dough without a problem. Hand mixing with a wooden spoon is not out of the question, but it is a workout.

Last, I want you to remember that all of the ounce measurements in these recipes are weight, *not* volume. So, use a scale.

Ingredients for the soaker:

9 ounces whole wheat flour
1 tsp. kosher salt
8¼ oz. bottled spring water

Procedure for soaker:

1. Combine all the ingredients in a small stainless steel, glass, or plastic bowl and stir with a wooden spoon until all ingredients are completely incorporated.

2. Cover the bowl with plastic wrap and set aside to rest overnight.

Ingredients for poolish:

9 ounces unbleached bread or all-purpose flour
8 oz. bottled spring water at room temperature
¼ tsp. instant yeast

Procedure for poolish:

1. Combine all ingredients in a medium stainless steel or other sturdy non-reactive bowl. Stir vigorously with a wooden spoon or wire whisk for two or three minutes. Set the dough aside to rest for 10 minutes. Then stir it vigorously with a wooden spoon or wire whisk for another two minutes.

2. Transfer the dough to a small bowl. Cover the bowl with plastic wrap and set the bowl in the refrigerator to ferment overnight.

3. Remove the poolish from the refrigerator at least one hour before starting the final dough and let it come to room temperature.

Pizza bianka

Sliced whole wheat

Final dough ingredients:

1 oz. whole wheat flour
1¼ tsp. instant yeast
1 tsp. kosher salt
all of the soaker
all of the poolish
2 Tbsp. plus 1 tsp. extra virgin olive oil
1½ tsp. brown sugar
nonstick cooking spray

Topping ingredients:

1 tsp. kosher salt
2 Tbsp. extra-virgin olive oil
¼ cup grated Pecorino Romano cheese
2 Tbsp. fresh rosemary leaves, chopped

Procedure for final dough and topping:

1. Combine the flour, instant yeast, and salt in a small bowl and stir with a spoon until well-blended. Set aside.

2. Combine the soaker, poolish, two tablespoons of oil, and brown sugar in the bowl of your electric mixer. Attach the dough hook or paddle.

3. Sprinkle the yeast mixture from step 1 over the dough. Mix the dough at low speed until no patches of dry flour remain. Depending on the mixer this will take two to four minutes. Occasionally, stop the mixer and scrape the sides and bottom of the bowl with a rubber spatula. Turn off the mixer and let the dough rest for 15 minutes.

4. Increase the speed of the mixer to high and mix/knead the dough until smooth and it pulls away from the sides of the bowl.

5. Generously coat a large straight-sided stainless steel, glass, or plastic bowl with non-stick cooking spray. Transfer the dough to this bowl and sprinkle an additional one teaspoon of olive oil over the dough. Tightly cover the bowl with plastic wrap and set it aside at room temperature to proof until the dough is nearly triple in bulk. Depending on the ambient temperature of the room this will take from 1½ to 2 hours.

5. One hour before baking set your oven to 450° F if have a baking stone; set it to 500° F if you don't.

6. When you are ready to bake, liberally coat a 17x13-inch rimmed baking sheet with non-stick cooking spray. With a rubber spatula turn the fully proofed dough onto the baking sheet. Lightly coat your fingers with cooking spray and gently press the dough out to the edges of the pan. Take care not to break or tear the dough. It will not fit snug into the corners. If the dough becomes too elastic and resists spreading, let it rest

Whole wheat sandwich bread

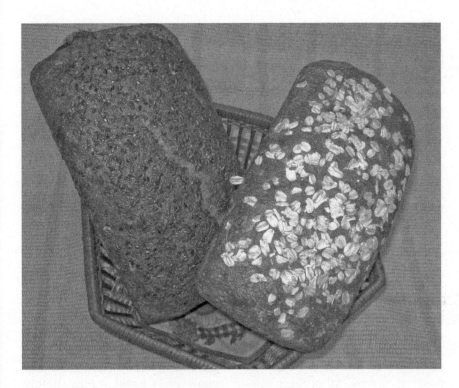

Rye and oatmeal breads

for about 10 minutes before continuing.

7. Use a dinner fork to randomly poke the dough 30 to 40 times.

8. Now, apply the topping ingredients. Sprinkle the surface of the dough with kosher salt and place the pan in the oven to bake for 20 to 30 minutes. Halfway through the baking, evenly sprinkle the Romano cheese and chopped rosemary over the crust.

9. Remove the baked pizza from the oven, cut into squares, and serve.

Whole wheat bread

This is a basic wheat bread that contains a little over 60 percent white flour. As an alternative, you can grind 30 ounces of wheat berries, separate 13½ ounces for use in the whole wheat component of the recipe, then sift the remainder through a fine sifter. There will enough sifted whole wheat flour to substitute for the all-purpose flour, and use for dusting the counter when kneading the final dough.

This sifted flour still retains some of the bran and germ from the wheat

berry, giving the baker a two-fold benefit. First, it removes most of the coarse outer layer of bran which,

when left in, weakens the delicate gluten structure of the dough. Second, it raises the nutritional value of the bread by adding more wheat germ. If you think that you will be making this bread often, simply cut off roughly a 6 oz. piece from the finished dough in this recipe. Degas it (i.e., squeeze out the carbon dioxide), wrap tightly in plastic wrap, and place it in the refrigerator. It will remain usable for up to three days. If you don't plan to use it by then, put it in the freezer for up to a week.

Old dough (pâte pre-fermenté) ingredients :

4 ounces bread flour
½ tsp. kosher salt
¼ tsp. instant yeast
2½ oz. bottled spring water, room temperature, or about 74° F

Procedure for old dough pre-ferment:

1. Combine the flour, yeast, and salt and stir until well-mixed. Add the

Traditional rye bread with flax seeds.

water and stir with a spoon until all of the flour is hydrated.

2. Lightly dust the counter with flour, transfer the dough to the counter, and knead for about a minute or until the dough forms a smooth ball.

3. Place the dough in a small bowl coated with Pam or other quick release spray, cover it with plastic wrap, and place it in the refrigerator overnight.

Final dough ingredients:

13½ oz. whole wheat flour
4½ oz. unbleached all-purpose flour
    or sifted whole wheat flour
1 tsp. instant yeast
1 tsp. kosher salt
all of the pre-ferment
11½ oz. bottled spring water
1 Tbsp. vegetable oil
1 Tbsp. honey

Final dough procedure:

1. One hour before you plan to start preparing the final dough, remove the pre-ferment from the refrigerator to warm up.

2. Combine the flours, instant yeast, and salt. Stir with a spoon until well-blended. Using a bench scraper or knife, cut the pre-ferment into six or eight small pieces and add them to the flour mixture. Add the water, vegetable oil, and honey. Stir this mixture with a sturdy spoon until all of the flour is hydrated and the dough forms a shaggy ball.

3. Lightly coat the counter with flour and transfer the dough to this work surface.

4. Knead the dough, adding more flour as needed for about five minutes or until it forms a smooth ball that is a little tacky but not sticky.

6. Cover the dough with a clean kitchen towel and let rest for 15 minutes. This is the autolyse period explained in my previous article about whole grain breads. Resume kneading for two more minutes.

7. Remove a small piece of dough, hold it up to the light, and gently

stretch it, using the thumbs and fore-fingers of both hands. If it stretches enough so that light will shine though this translucent membrane, the gluten is sufficiently formed. If the dough tears instead of stretching, return it to the counter and continue kneading for another two minutes and test again. This is called a "windowpane test." It is the best way to determine if the gluten network in the dough is sufficiently formed.

8. Coat a straight-sided stainless steel or glass bowl with quick-release spray. Place the dough in this bowl, cover tightly with plastic, and let the dough ferment until it is 1½ times its original size.

For all of my breads I use a two quart plastic or glass-measuring bowl. After putting the dough in the bowl, I take note of how many cups the dough represents. All of these sandwich breads initially represent about 3 cups. When they ferment to the point where they reach 4½ cups, they're ready for the final proofing. This will take about 45 minutes to one hour.

9. While the dough is fermenting, coat a 9x5-inch bread pan with quick release spray and set it aside. When the dough is fully proofed, gently remove it from the bowl. Be careful not to squeeze or punch the dough. The object here is to retain as much gas in the fermented dough as possible. Fold the dough in half, gently stretching it to fit the length of the pan. Place the dough in the pan, seam side down, and cover the pan with plastic wrap. Let the dough proof until it is 1½ times the size it was when you put it in this pan.

10. While the dough is proofing, preheat the oven to 450° F.

11. When fully proofed, place the dough in the preheated oven and *immediately reduce* the heat to 350° F. Bake the loaf for 20 to 25 minutes. Turn the loaf 180 degrees and continue baking until the internal tempera-

ture of the bread is 195° F to 200° F as explained in my previous article.

12. Remove the loaf from the pan as soon as you take it from the oven, and let it cool at room temperature for at least two hours.

Whole wheat and oat sandwich bread

I love oatmeal and this is why I added it to this bread. Oatmeal is a great source of soluble fiber and adds a great deal of character to this loaf. Since we are using an uncooked cereal grain and a higher percentage of whole grain flour in this recipe, I have added a soaker, which will convert more of the flour starch into complex sugars. These sugars will add a natural sweetness to the finished bread and provide additional food for the yeast. All of this translates to a lighter whole grain bread with a slightly moist texture and a rich nutty taste. You will notice that the pre-ferment is biga. That is, it contains no salt.

Soaker ingredients:

6 oz. whole wheat flour
2 oz. old-fashioned rolled oats
¾ tsp. kosher salt
7 oz. rice milk, milk, soy milk, or
    bottled spring water

Procedure for the soaker:

1. Combine all ingredients of the soaker and stir with a wooden spoon until the flour is completely hydrated.

2. Place this mixture in a plastic or stainless steel bowl, cover tightly with plastic wrap, and set aside overnight at room temperature.

Pre-ferment ingredients:

8 oz. sifted whole wheat flour
¼ tsp. instant yeast
5 oz. bottled spring water

Procedure for pre-ferment:

1. Combine the flour, yeast, and water. Stir the mix until the flour is completely hydrated.

2. Knead the dough, inside the bowl, for two minutes. Let the dough rest for 10 minutes, then knead for an additional two minutes. Place the dough into a small plastic or stainless steel bowl and place it in the refrigerator overnight.

Final dough ingredients:

all of the soaker
all of the pre-ferment
1 oz. rye flour
¾ tsp. kosher salt
2¼ tsp. instant yeast
2 Tbsp. honey
1 Tbsp. canola oil
1 oz. sifted whole wheat flour (for adjustments)

Procedure for final dough:

1. One hour before you plan to assemble the final dough, remove the pre-ferment from the refrigerator and let warm to room temperature.

2. Combine the rye flour, salt, and instant yeast in a bowl large enough to hold all of the dough. Make a dough sandwich by placing the soaker in the bowl followed by the pre-ferment. Coat one side of this sandwich by pressing it into the flour mixture. Turn the dough over and coat the other side. Remove the coated dough sandwich to the counter and, using a dough scraper or knife, cut the sandwich into 12 pieces. Return the cut dough to the bowl and coat with the flour mixture to prevent the pieces from sticking together.

3. Combine the honey and oil and add it to the dough.

4. Now comes the fun part. Wet your hands and grab the dough with both hands and squeeze it between your fingers. It will be a little sticky and some of it will stick to your hands. Continue mixing until all ingredients are well incorporated. If you own a sturdy stand mixer, like those made by KitchenAid, you can perform this step by mixing the dough with the dough hook. I prefer hand-mixing because it much easier for me to determine what adjustments will be necessary right away. You will also find this to be a benefit as you gain experience working with this type of dough.

5. When the dough is evenly mixed, transfer it to a well-floured counter for kneading. Knead the dough, adding additional flour, as needed, until it forms a smooth, supple ball that is tacky without feeling sticky. This will take five or six minutes. Cover the dough with a towel and let it rest for 10 minutes. Resume kneading for an additional three or four minutes or until a small piece of dough passes the windowpane test.

6. Place the dough in a suitable size bowl, cover the bowl with plastic wrap, and let the dough ferment until it is 1½ times its original size.

7. Remove the fully-fermented dough from the bowl, place it on the counter, gently fold it into a loaf, and place it in a 9x5-inch bread pan. Cover the pan with plastic wrap and let the dough proof until it is again 1½ times its original size.

8. While the dough is proofing, preheat the oven to 450° F.

9. Bake and cool this bread using the same method as the whole wheat bread.

10. Take the bread from the oven, remove it from the pan, and cool it on a wire rack, at room temperature, for at least two hours.

Traditional rye bread with flax seeds

My mother grew up in a small town in southwestern Pennsylvania. My grandmother moved to this country after the First World War from Germany. With her came many Old World bread recipes. My mother loved her mother's rye bread recipes and continued to bake them long after she left home and got married.

It wasn't until I was nine years old that I learned that rye bread was sold in stores. Unfortunately, most of the store-bought rye breads were, and still are, a total disappointment for me. They simply lack the flavor complexity and texture of the rye breads I grew up with.

Two years after my mother died, I was still trying to catalog the hundreds of recipes she had stuffed into shoeboxes and notebooks. One day I found a formula for an all-rye flour sourdough culture. The recipe card was simply labeled "For Leinsamenbrot," which translates to "flaxseed bread." But the recipe was only for the sourdough starter, not the bread itself. I was never able to find her recipe for the bread, but I still have vivid memories of what the bread looked, smelled, and tasted like.

The bread that follows is not an exact replica of my mother's bread but it is close. I make my starter from a white flour sourdough seed culture and a combination of rye and sifted whole wheat flour instead of the full rye culture that my mother used. I have also incorporated a soaker because of all the benefits this addition adds to the final loaf.

Important note: You can use any sourdough seed culture you have available: white, rye, or whole wheat. However, it is important your culture has been fed and allowed to mature at least two days before you use it in this recipe.

Ingredients for soaker:

5 oz. medium rye flour
3 oz. whole wheat flour
½ oz. whole flax seed
1 tsp. kosher salt
7½ oz. bottled spring water

Procedure for soaker:

Prepare the soaker using the same procedure as

Grain Mills

Milling at home has been gaining popularity for several years. If you are serious about having the freshest flour whenever you decide to bake, owning one of the many available electric or hand-operated grain mills is a must.

I used one of the most popular electric mills on the market to grind the grain used in all of the recipes that you find here. Since I was planning to bake a lot of bread, I needed a machine that was easy to clean and could produce a lot of flour quickly. This mill fit my needs perfectly.

Currently there are several excellent electric and hand-operated mills on the market. Before buying one of these mills, it is important to carefully consider what your baking needs will be.

If you're looking for a mill to function during a period of long-term disaster, your best bet is to look for an efficient hand-cranked model. If you only bake bread once or twice a week, only making one or two loaves at a session, a smaller hand-cranked mill will probably suit your needs.

All bread mills are not created equal. Some of the high-speed electric mills spit out clouds of flour dust, are loud, noisy, hard to clean, and very expensive. There are slow and medium-speed electric mills that are much less messy to use and have very specific and accurate grinding settings. I have seen one of these mills being used in a local bakery that bakes breads for customers who can afford the price of these custom loaves. However, mills of this type start at about $500 and go up from there.

In my previous article I indicated that inexpensive hand mills, like the Corona grain mill I use for cracking malted barley when making beer, were a good bet for grinding grains for bread. I was wrong! Malted barley is not nearly as hard as wheat.

Grinding eight ounces of hard red winter wheat is a workout that any serious body builder would appreciate. So choose your grain mill accordingly.

The oldest style is the stone mill. In centuries past, these mills used real stone to do the grinding. Modern stone mills are made of hard materials that look and feel like natural stone but are more durable and have a longer life. The Egyptians, Greeks, and Romans used mills of this type, and the operating principle hasn't changed in the last 3000 years. They have two circular stones, one of which turns and grinds against a non-movable stone. Grooves are cut into the movable stone and radiate out from its center. As the grain is ground, these grooves in the rotating stone pull the grain through the channels to the outer edges of the stones. The ground flour, depending on the design of the mill, is deposited in a bowl or a hopper attached to the mill. These mills are designed to last a lifetime. They are usually the most adjustable, and will produce everything from cracked wheat to very fine flour. They are, however, bulky, heavy, and the stones will become clogged and incapable of grinding if they are used to grind oil-bearing seeds or nuts.

A second type of mill is based on a principal similar to a stone mill. It's the burr mill. Like the stone grinder, these mills have grinding wheels, but they are made of steel with small teeth that shear the grain and turn it into flour. Burr grinders will grind oil-bearing seeds, dried beans, and grains like corn, wheat, and barley. They are also capable of producing flour that is nearly as fine as that produced by a quality stone mill.

The third type is the impact mill. These mills use rows of blades on circular wheels. One wheel is movable and intermeshes with a stationary wheel. Grain is deposited into a closed chamber and falls into the center of the fixed wheel. The high speed motion of the moving wheel pulverizes the grain as it rotates in very close tolerance to the stationary wheel. Impact mills are usually light and compact. They can be put away in a cupboard or a closet when not in use. They grind quickly and will also grind any grain into very fine flour. On the downside they can be fairly noisy. When running with no grain in the hopper, my *Wonder Mill* sounds like an idling jet engine waiting for take off at the airport. This loud whine is only noticeable for short periods before adding grain to the hopper, then again after the mill is through grinding.

When I decided to buy a home grain mill, my first choice was what I consider the best of all the hand-cranked mills: the *Country Living Grain Mill*. It is well-built and efficient. It outperforms any of the other mills I have tried. However, as a result of what seemed to be a sudden wave of panic-motivated disaster buying, I was not able to get a delivery commitment prior to the writing of this article. At $395 apiece you might get the impression that not many folks are willing to spend that much money for a grain mill. But the lack of availability seems to contradict this notion.

Without a good grain mill, I knew that I would not be able to write this article, so I started searching for an alternative. I found the *Wonder Mill* on sale, and although I was skeptical of how it would compare to the *Country Living Grain Mill,* I ordered one anyway. To date, I have processed nearly 25 pounds of grain, beans, and rice through this mill and it continues to produce high quality flour without any problems. There is an electric model as well as a hand-cranked model.

you did in the two preceding recipes, and set aside, overnight, at room temperature.

Ingredients for sourdough starter:

1 oz. sourdough seed culture
5 oz. whole wheat flour, sifted
2 oz. medium rye flour
6 oz. bottled spring water

Procedure for sourdough starter:

1. Remove one ounce of your mature sourdough seed culture from the refrigerator and let it sit at room temperature for 30 minutes before you use it.

2. Combine the sourdough seed culture with the other three ingredients in a suitable size bowl and mix until the flour is completely hydrated.

3. Transfer the starter to a clean plastic, stainless steel, or glass bowl. Cover the bowl tightly with plastic wrap and set it aside, at room temperature for five to six hours or until it has doubled in size.

Ingredients for final dough:

2 oz. medium rye flour
2 oz. whole wheat flour, sifted
½ tsp. anise seeds
1½ tsp. instant yeast
1¼ tsp. kosher salt
all of the sourdough starter
all of the soaker
1 Tbsp. vegetable oil
1½ Tbsp. dark molasses
1 oz. whole wheat flour for adjustments and kneading
nonstick cooking spray

Procedure for final dough:

1. Combine the flours, anise seeds, yeast, and salt in a bowl large enough to hold the entire dough, and stir until incorporated.

2. Combine the sourdough starter and the soaker using the same procedure outlined in the oat sandwich bread.

3. Again, using the same procedure outlined in the oat bread recipe, combine the soaker/starter sandwich with the flour mixture along with the oil and molasses.

4. Hand mix until all ingredients are well blended.

5. Transfer the dough onto a well-floured counter and knead for five or six minutes, adding flour as needed until the dough forms a smooth ball that is tacky without being sticky.

6. Cover the dough with a clean kitchen towel and let it rest for 15 minutes. Resume kneading until a small piece of dough passes the windowpane test.

7. Place the dough in a suitable size bowl coated with quick release spray. Cover the bowl with plastic wrap and let the dough ferment until it is 1½ its original size. This should take between 45 minutes and an hour.

8. While the dough is fermenting, coat a 9x5-inch baking pan with quick release spray and set it aside.

9. When the dough is fully fermented, gently remove it from the bowl, fashion it into a loaf, and place it into the loaf pan. Cover the pan loosely with plastic wrap and let the dough proof until it is 1½ times its original size.

10. While the loaf is proofing, preheat the oven to 425° F.

11. If you want to garnish the loaf before baking, brush it with a mixture of one egg white mixed with one teaspoon of water and sprinkle the loaf with whole flax seeds.

12. Place the fully-proofed loaf in the oven and immediately reduce the heat to 375° F. Bake the loaf 25 to 30 minutes, rotate the loaf 180 degrees and continue baking until it reaches an internal temperature of 195° to 200° F. This will take about 15 to 20 minutes.

13. Remove the fully-baked loaf from the oven and cool as outlined in the previous recipe. Δ

Backwoods Home Cooking

- *Breads*
- *Casseroles*
- *Cookies*
- *Desserts*
- *Jams & jellies*
- *Main dishes*
- *Pasta*
- *Salads*
- *Seafood*
- *Soups*
- *Vegetables*

Our energy crisis
Part 2 of 3: nuclear energy is sensible and safe

By John Silveira

When an atomic bomb was detonated over Nagasaki, Japan, August 9, 1945, the amount of energy released by the explosion amounted to roughly 21,000 tons of TNT. The blast destroyed much of the city and killed as many as 80,000 thousand people.

That bomb and the one dropped three days earlier on Hiroshima were the two most fearsome weapons ever used in warfare. They introduced the world to what some commentators deemed the "nuclear age," an age filled with both terror and promise.

While some feared this new weapon would destroy civilization—and even send the human species into extinction—others looked at what fueled that explosion and saw promise.

The Nagasaki bomb, nicknamed "Fat Man" because of its shape, contained some 13½ pounds of plutonium, shaped in a sphere about the size of a softball, of which only about 2¼ pounds underwent fission. The rest was simply blown away before it could come into play.

So, how does plutonium cause an explosion?

When many of the heavy, unstable elements undergo fission, i.e., when their atomic nuclei are split, the results are new, lighter atomic nuclei, some neutrons, and the release of a *huge amount of energy*. The source of that energy is the conversion of part of the mass of the original atom into pure energy—either radiation or kinetic energy. (To see how an atomic bomb works see my article, *Nuclear Terrorism*, in *BHM's Issue 74, March/April 2002*, also contained in *BHM's 13th Year Anthology*. The article is also on the *BHM* website.)

But, of that 2¼ pounds that underwent fission, how much of it was actually converted into energy? Only about *one gram*. That's approximately .035 ounces of the plutonium nuclei—or the weight of a one dollar

The atomic bomb dropped on Nagasaki was 10 2/3 feet long, 5 feet in diameter, and weighed 10,800 pounds. But for all its size and all the destructive power unleashed, the amount of mass that was converted into energy amounted to only about one gram of the bomb's weight—about the weight of a one dollar bill.

bill—that, when converted to energy, created that terrible explosion.

Search for an alternative

And it is exactly *this* that makes the conversion of matter into energy, either by fission or, as you'll see, by fusion, such an attractive alternative as we search for a better way to fuel our civilization.

Energy is the basic commodity on which modern civilization runs. Whether it's cars and trucks, planes, factories, or TV and cell phones, without economical and easily obtainable energy, civilization will grind to a halt. It is the lifeblood of our modern world.

When World War II ended, many of the world's scientific and technical minds turned to the energy locked up in the atomic nucleus as a source of power for something other than a destructive explosion.

The military looked at the applications of atomic power to power ships.

Under the direction of Admiral Hyman Rickover, the U.S. Navy soon produced the nuclear-powered submarine Nautilus, and since then have produced more than 200 nuclear submarines, 23 nuclear aircraft carriers, and a variety of nuclear missile cruisers.

But there was also the hope that we could electrify the nation, and perhaps the world, with the power locked up in the atom.

Today it may be more than just a hope, it may be an imperative. With the skyrocketing price of petroleum, the United States is witnessing the biggest transfer of wealth from one set of countries to another in history. The damage it is doing to the American economy is inestimable.

Unlike countries such as Japan that created its wealth by building one of the mightiest technological and industrial bases in history and selling their products at fair-market prices, the OPEC countries are accumulating their prodigious wealth merely

The rising cost of OPEC oil has created the largest transfer of wealth between nations in history. Nuclear energy will help reduce this.

because they are sitting on top of some of the greatest accretions of natural resources ever discovered. (Never mind that the U.S. is also sitting on another massive deposit of useable fossil fuel, namely coal, but we have failed to exploit it properly. See *Backwoods Home Magazine* Issue 113, Sept./Oct 2008.)

Practical energy solutions, such as the pursuit of viable nuclear power, are going to be needed to extricate the United States from the grip of OPEC and its expensive energy.

Nuclear fission

Six years after Hiroshima and Nagasaki, the first nuclear reactor built to generate electricity was the Arco reactor built near Arco, Idaho, in 1951. But the first one to generate electricity to be fed into an electric power grid was the Obninsk Nuclear Power Plant, built in 1954, in the former Soviet Union.

Following that, in 1956 the first commercial reactor, Calder Hall, came on line in Sellafield, England. A year later, the first commercial reactor to come on line in the United States was the Shippingport Reactor in Pennsylvania, about 25 miles from Pittsburgh. The Shippingport reactor was another Rickover project he developed at the request of the Atomic Energy Commission.It looked like we were on our way to developing into a nuclear power-fueled nation.

It's fair to say that, almost from the beginning, nuclear fission, as a source of energy, was essentially solved. Today there are at least 439 nuclear power plants around the world, located in 31 countries, including 104 operational commercial nuclear power plants in the United States.

Talk about a small world! As I was finishing this article on nuclear energy, I met, by chance, Capt. John D. Richardson, U.S. Navy (Retired). Capt. Richardson spent 32 years in the Navy, 7 under Admiral Hyman G. Rickover, the father of America's nuclear fleet, and another five in the maintenance and repair of nuclear ships. He was kind enough to talk with me about many aspects of nuclear power.

Breeder reactors: the fuel that creates more fuel—and atomic bombs

When talking about nuclear reactions, a **fissile** material is an isotope of an element that is capable of being split and releasing energy, such as uranium-235 (^{235}U). A **fertile** material is an element that is not fissile but which by absorption of neutrons can be converted to a fissile element. An example is the isotope of uranium called ^{238}U which can absorb a neutron and be converted to plutonium-239 (^{239}Pu). ^{239}Pu can then be used to create even more energy. The problem, however, is that ^{239}Pu is also used to make nuclear weapons.

The "doubling time" in a breeder reactor is the amount of time it takes for the breeder to create as much fuel as it consumes—while all the while it's generating power. Today's reactors strive to have doubling times of 10 years. For example, a 10-year supply of ^{235}U would produce another 10-year supply of ^{239}Pu for use in either this reactor or another one.

One of the better fertile-to-fissile reactions is the use of thorium-232 (^{232}Th) in a breeder reactor because thorium is so much more plentiful than uranium. (In nature, it's about as common as lead.) Through neutron capture, the thorium is converted to ^{233}U, another fissile isotope of uranium.

Because some of the world's largest known reserves of thorium are located on the Indian subcontinent, India, already an atomic power, is likely to become a leader in building thorium-based breeder reactors.

Other large reserves are located in Australia, Norway, and the United States.

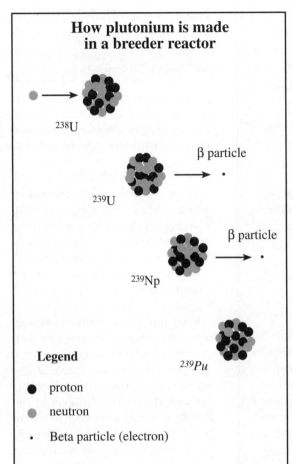

How plutonium is made in a breeder reactor

^{238}U

β particle

^{239}U

β particle

^{239}Np

^{239}Pu

Legend

● proton

● neutron

· Beta particle (electron)

From top to bottom, here is how the most common isotope of uranium, nonfissile ^{238}U, is converted to fissile plutonium in a breeder reactor: The uranium nucleus absorbs a neutron creating an unstable isotope of uranium, ^{239}U. This isotope, with a half-life of 23½ minutes, decays into an isotope of the element neptunian, Np_{239}, by emitting a beta particle (electron). But Np_{239} is also unstable, with a half-life of about 56½ hours, and it emits yet another beta particle and becomes a fissile isotope of plutonium, ^{239}Pu, which has a half-life of 24,400 years. The ^{239}Pu can be used to fuel other reactors—or to make nuclear weapons.

About 6½% of the world's power, including some 15% of the world's electricity, now comes from nuclear power with the U.S., France, and Japan accounting for more than half of it.

In 1960, the Atomic Energy Commission estimated there would be as many as 1,000 nuclear power plants in the United States by the year 2000. But that never happened.

Nuclear falls out of favor

In the 1970s and through the 1980s, events occurred that caused nuclear power to fall into disfavor in the United States. Not only did the growth slow, but more than 120 orders for commercial reactors were cancelled. The last reactor to come on line in the United States was the the Watts Bar 1 reactor in Tennessee, which became operational in 1996.

The two crucial events that began to turn the American public against nuclear power were the partial meltdown of one of the reactors at *Three Mile Island* in Pennsylvania, in 1979, and the meltdown and reactor fire at *Chernobyl*, in Ukraine, in 1986.

The first, *Three Mile Island*, was a "contained" accident whereas the accident at *Chernobyl* resulted in a fire and a meltdown which soon killed at least 56 people, affected several million others, may have caused as many as 9,000 extra cancers, and temporarily contaminated, to a greater or lesser degree, an area spread over tens of thousands of square miles. Today, in Ukraine, there is a 19-mile radius zone, sometimes referred to as the Zone of Alienation, surrounding the site of the reactor, from which most people are excluded.

However, according to the World Nuclear Association, as of June 2008 *Three Mile Island* and *Chernobyl* are still the only two major accidents in 12,700 cumulative reactor-years for commercial reactors in 32 countries.

To the press *Three Mile Island* and *Chernobyl* were black eyes for nuclear power. The two events, along with scare tactics used by environmental groups, brought a nuclear dark age to the United States. But, in reality, Three Mile Island was an unparalleled success story — *the safety features worked as intended*. That is the reason the damage was minimized.

On the other hand, the problems at Chernobyl were that the reactors there were built with no provision for containment and they were built without "passive safety" features. (See sidebar on *Nuclear accidents and passively safe reactors*.) Reactors in the West, and particularly in this country, have always been built with *containment* as a priority, and now *passive safety* is a priority.

China has ordered 100 nuclear power plants

Though nuclear power is almost in a deep freeze in the United States, the 104 nuclear power plants currently operating account for almost 20 percent of our electricity. But in the European Union, about 30% of the electricity comes from nuclear sources. In France, nearly 80% of their electricity comes from nuclear power plants.

Today France, Germany, and Japan, three countries poor in other energy resources, are quietly building more reactors. Meanwhile, the People's Republic of China, which has 11 nuclear power reactors, has recently ordered 100 more nuclear power plants from Westinghouse. Theirs is one of the most ambitious nuclear programs on the planet. They intend, by 2030, to have roughly 2½ times the nuclear power capacity of the United States. It has been pointed out by proponents of nuclear energy that one of the reasons China is able to embark on a program to bring nuclear

Nuclear accidents and passively safe reactors

Nuclear safety seems to be the biggest concern people have when they hear the words "nuclear power." And the press is quick to trot out images of *Three Mile Island* and *Chernobyl* when nuclear safety issues are raised. But today's nuclear reactors, at least in western countries, are now safer than ever.

At the *Chernobyl* reactor in Ukraine, the "accident" was created by a lethal combination of bad reactor design and operator error. Reactor safety at *Chernobyl*, like most early reactors, involved "active" safety procedures, meaning that electrical or mechanical actions had to be initiated by the operators or computers monitoring the reactor to slow or stop fission at the reactor's core. Worse yet, the Soviets built the reactors at *Chernobyl* without regard for containment if the worst-case scenario occurred. *Chernobyl* was a disaster waiting to happen.

But the way modern reactors are built, there are two primary safety features that will slow or stop fission at the reactor's core when the reactor's core gets out of hand and *neither requires any kind of human or computer intervention*. They occur naturally. They are what are known as "negative temperature coefficient" and "negative void coefficient."

To understand how this works, you first have to understand how fission works. We think of fission happening because a high-speed neutron hits a uranium nucleus and splits it the way a cue ball splits a rack of balls on a pool table. The faster the cue ball, the more violently the rack of balls splits. But that is *not* what happens in nuclear fission. The fact it, if the neutron is moving too fast, it just passes through the nucleus. To get fission, the neutron has to be moving slow enough for the nucleus to capture it. To slow the neutrons down, moderators such as water are used. Then, only after the nucleus captures a slow neutron, the nucleus becomes unstable and splits, releasing vast amounts of energy.

Back to the terms: Negative temperature coefficient means that in water cooled reactors, once the temperature rises beyond an optimal level, the water that is cooling the reactor expands and there is less water to slow down the neutrons. The efficiency of the nuclear reactions decrease on their own and the reactor, itself, automatically and inevitably slows down.

Negative void coefficient means that if steam forms in the cooling water there is a further decrease in moderating effect so even fewer neutrons are able to cause fission and, again, the reaction slows down automatically.

This combination of negative temperature coefficient and negative void coefficient are called "passive safety" and they are built into virtually all western reactors. If fission in the reactor starts running away, these features will turn it down automatically without the intervention of the operators or the computers, and even if the operators and computers don't yet realize there's a problem.

Had the reactor at Chernobyl had this feature, the disaster, as it happened, could not have occurred.

energy to their country is that many of the upper-echelon members of the Chinese political elite are engineers by training, not lawyers.

In the meantime, while the development of nuclear power goes on in the rest of the world, the United States has not brought a nuclear power plant on line in more than a dozen years.

Nuclear advantages

There are obvious advantages to going nuclear, including becoming less energy dependent on foreign sources. Notice, I did not say "achieve total energy independence." That's not going to happen. It doesn't even make sense to try to make it happen.

What this nation needs are enough alternative sources of energy to keep the cost of foreign energy down to a fair price. If petroleum is sold at free market prices instead of cartel prices, we can afford it. Petroleum at the wellhead would now cost less than $30 a barrel—and OPEC would still be making a profit—if we'd had a sensible energy policy, including more nuclear power plants, for the last four decades.

Among its uses, nuclear power has natural applications in the production of other fuels. Half the excessive pollutants from Coal-To-Liquid (CTL) fuels are the result of burning other fossil fuels to provide energy for processing the coal. The use of nuclear power to produce these and other fuels will dramatically reduce these pollutants. And the production of alternative motor fuels from coal is one way to drive down the price of imported oil. (See the article in this anthology.)

Nuclear power can also provide the electricity to produce hydrogen from the electrolysis of water, which may become a fuel for powering automobiles and trucks. It is also a way of producing the electricity for electric cars and hybrids.

Another attractive feature of nuclear reactors is that some can be used to create more fuel than they "burn." These are called breeder reactors. These reactors allow us to make more nuclear fuel from otherwise "unusable" heavy elements. (See sidebar.)

Nuclear power is safe

Because of *Three Mile Island* and *Chernobyl*, nuclear safety is one of the first thoughts that comes to mind when nuclear power is mentioned. But one thing the public is largely unaware of is that a *Chernobyl* disaster *cannot* occur in the United States, simply because we have *no* reactors of that design, nor would we ever allow one to be built.

Another thing that *cannot* happen in a nuclear reactor is a nuclear explosion. Atomic bombs are hard to make and the conditions for one just don't exist in a reactor.

Safety features for modern nuclear reactors account for about a quarter of the capital costs for the building of the reactor. Reactor safety is always paramount when building a plant and it is estimated that the likelihood of reactor damage, such as leaks or a meltdown, in modern reactors is less than one in 1,000,000 years of reactor operation.

New nuclear power plants are now designed to survive natural catastrophes including earthquakes, tornados,

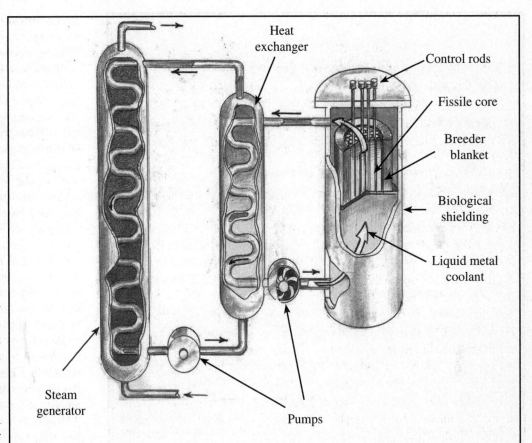

This is how a breeder reactor works. In this case, it's a "liquid metal" cooled reactor. In the reactor's core "fissile" material, i.e., material that can undergo fission, will generate both heat and neutrons. The heat will be carried by the liquid metal, pass through a heat exchanger, and be passed on to the steam generator where steam will be created. The steam is used to turn a turbine which will generate electricity. In the meantime, the neutrons will interact with the "fertile" material, i.e., an element such as ^{238}U, that is in the breeder blanket to form yet another fissile material such as ^{239}Pu. This way, the reactor is creating fuel while it's consuming fuel.

and hurricanes as well as man-made disasters including terrorist threats.

Today's nuclear reactors are so robust that it is expected they would survive the impact of a fully-fueled Boeing 767-400 slamming into the containment building at over 300 mph. (Why 300 mph? That's probably the highest speed at which terrorists, even if they are experienced pilots, can control the plane for precise impact with a target the size of the containment building.)

New safety features built into modern reactors, in particular the construction of what are called "passively safe" reactors, are going to make new reactors even safer. A passively

safe reactor is one that is designed to *shut itself down* when the reactor begins to malfunction. (See sidebar.)

According to *PBS Online*, no deaths have been attributed to U.S. nuclear power in its entire history. On the other hand, factoring in deaths from mining, transportation accidents, respiratory complications, and other factors, more than 30,000 deaths have been attributed to coal since 1930.

Nuclear waste problem political, not technical

The other bogeyman in nuclear power is nuclear waste. It's a problem. But it's a *political* problem, not

E = mc²

The above equation is so simple, yet it describes a concept so powerful it could either save or destroy civilization.

Most often associated with Albert Einstein, it didn't originate with him. Among others, the English physicist, J.J. Thomson, derived it from the equations of one of history's most underrated scientists, James Clerk Maxwell. The French physicist, Poincaré, also derived it, as did several others, all before Einstein independently derived it himself.

Elegantly simple, the equation sprung into the public's awareness in August 1945 with the dropping of the atomic bomb on Hiroshima. It is now the most famous equation in history.

But when did humans first convert mass into energy? Most people with a sense of history, including many scientists, would probably say just before World War II when scientists were working with atomic piles or in 1945 with the detonation of the first atomic bomb. But they would be *way* off. The first person to create energy from mass, in accordance with the above equation, was the first caveman to build a fire.

How can this be?

By rearranging the components of the $e = mc^2$ equation, you can calculate how much mass is *lost* when you extract energy from *anything*.

$$m = E/c^2$$

What this means is that every time you build a fire in your stove or fireplace, every time you turn on your gas oven, every time you drive your car or truck, you are converting mass, however miniscule, into energy.

How much? You could calculate it from the equations (as I did). On the other hand, you could weigh it. But to do that you'd need a very accurate scale, one capable of determining the tiniest differences in measurements. Say you had such a scale and you *precisely* weighed 20 pounds of logs you were about to burn, along with the ambient oxygen that would feed the flames. After that, if you were to gather up all the ashes and recover all the CO_2 along with any other by-products of combustion once the flames went out, and precisely weighed them again, you would find a miniscule difference, about .00000053 ounces. That is less than the weight of the ink comprising the period that is at the end of this sentence.

Where did the mass go? It was converted into energy that was radiated away as both light and heat, in accordance with the equation. And anything that absorbed that energy, including the warmth, is now ever so slightly heavier—until it gives that energy up.

Now, compare this to the conversion of hydrogen into helium. During nuclear fusion, 0.7% of the mass of the hydrogen is transformed straight into energy. This means that if you convert 20 pounds of hydrogen to helium, you'll also have converted about 2¼ ounces of mass into energy, more than 60 times the energy released by the Nagasaki bomb.. This is enough energy to light up a city for months, using a fusion reactor, or to level it with a hydrogen bomb. It's the reason scientists doggedly search for a way to build an economical fusion reactor.

a technological one. There are viable solutions today for its disposable, and future solutions just get better.

First, it's worth noting that the first commercial nuclear plant, the Shippingport plant mentioned earlier, was decommissioned in 1982. The reactor was removed for burial in Washington State, and the Pennsylvania site where it once stood was cleaned up and released for unrestricted use. Cleanup is not just possible, but it's been done.

Second, we already have the technology to make more efficient reactors that will burn their own waste, creating even more energy. This is particularly true for breeder reactors that use thorium-232 in their breeder blankets. The extra neutrons that are produced will convert the thorium to uranium 233, another fissile isotope of uranium that can be used to fuel the reactor, thereby decreasing the amount of waste the reactor produces.

Third, there are various strategies for disposing of reactor waste. Among some that already work well is embedding the waste in molten glass, pouring it into stainless steel containers, sealing them, then storing the containers away. The waste can be stored this way for thousands of years or until future technologies can dispose of them in other fashions.

Promising future strategies are to irradiate the radioactive components in reactors to form other isotopes which are either stable or have extremely short half-lives so they decay to stable isotopes in a short time. (At the same time, the irradiating plant would be creating electric power. It's a double bonus.)

But one of the best alternatives, and one we're likely to see used in the future, is to bury the wastes at subduction zones in deep ocean trenches. Subduction zones are places along the earth's crust where old rock sinks into the mantle where it is recycled and it will not reappear for millions of years. In that time, their radioactivity will have been both diluted and reduced.

Fusion power

Nuclear fusion is another source of atomic energy scientists are pursuing. Fusion is what powers many stars including our sun. Scientists now hope it will be the solution to civilization's quest for a practical source of affordable energy.

We have already released fusion power with the hydrogen bomb, the most powerful weapon mankind can now manufacture. We have even created fusion in the laboratory and, if we can ever perfect it so it's economical and sustainable, we will have virtually unlimited energy with which to power our world.

But therein is the rub: Can we ever get fusion out of the lab and into the economy? It is the power locked up in as little as one gram of mass that makes the reward for achieving it so attractive. But there are scientists who think man-made fusion power will never be any more than a laboratory curiosity. And they may have good reason to think so.

While fission is the splitting of the nuclei of very heavy elements to release energy, fusion involves the fusing of the nuclei of very light elements to release energy.

It was very easy to make fusion weapons, which were immediately more efficient than the fission weapons they've now largely replaced. The very first hydrogen bombs released about 500 times the energy of the first atomic bombs. But using fusion to produce energy for the generation of electricity has proved to be much more difficult than the the fission-based nuclear reactors that are now in place all over the world.

In the simplest fusion picture, we see the nuclei of atoms of hydrogen somehow combining to form helium. Things are not that simple. The most promising way to fuse atomic nuclei to form helium, thus releasing vast amounts of energy, is to use two different isotopes of hydrogen, namely, deuterium (which is a hydrogen atom whose nucleus is made up of one pro-

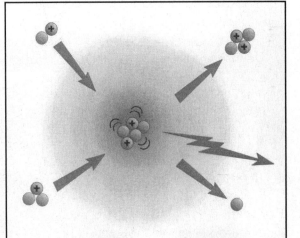

The grandest hope for almost unlimited energy is if we can build a practical fusion reactor. At its simplest, a deuterium nucleus, consisting of a single proton and a single neutron, will be fused with a nucleus of tritium, which is a single proton with two neutrons. The result will be a helium atom, another neutron, and a burst of energy.

ton and one neutron) and tritium (which is a hydrogen atom whose nucleus is made up of one proton and two neutrons).

The difficulties with fusing atoms is that they must be brought close enough together to allow their nuclei to fuse. However, the like positive charges of their nuclei means the nuclei are going to repel each other when they get close together. Herein is the problem scientists have had; power must be supplied to overcome these repulsive forces, because only after that's accomplished is it possible for fusion to take place. But the usable power that results from the fusion must be greater than the power required to create and sustain the fusion or it's of no use to us. And no one has done that yet.

Fusion naturally takes place in the sun because the sun's gravitational field holds the hot plasma in place, allowing it to occur. Here on earth we must use other strategies and the best one we've come up with relies on the fact that the hot plasma can be influenced by a magnetic field. The

---

Obtaining fuel for fusion

To fuel a deuterium-tritium plant, we must first create the tritium.

Deuterium exists in nature. About one hydrogen atom in 6500 has deuterium as its nucleus. Tritium, though it is constantly being formed in the upper atmosphere from cosmic rays, is rare because it has a half-life of just 28 years. It's estimated there are actually only about five pounds of naturally formed tritium, at any moment, on the surface of this planet. Fortunately, however, it can be manufactured by bombarding the metal lithium with neutrons in reactors. The result is one atom of tritium and one of helium. Lithium is plentiful in the earth's crust and in seawater. Deuterium can be extracted from water.

The deuterium contained in about a half-gallon of water and the lithium contained in about a half-pound rock would be enough to power an average home for a year.

If that isn't impressive, think of it this way: a pound of fusion fuel will produce the same energy as 10,000,000 pounds of a typical fossil fuel.

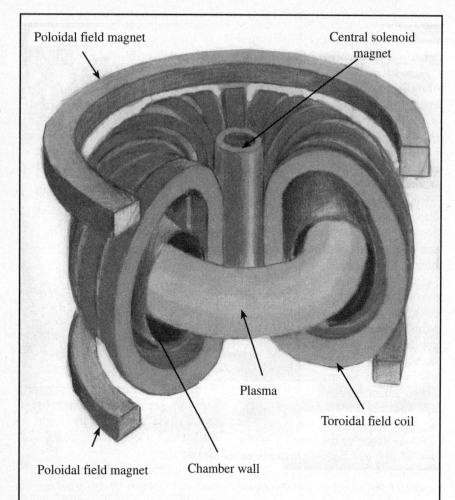

Poloidal field magnet

Central solenoid magnet

Plasma

Toroidal field coil

Poloidal field magnet   Chamber wall

The Tokamak reactor was conceived in 1951 by Soviet physicists Igor Yevgenyevich Tamm and Andrei Sakharov. The reactor uses a scheme of high-powered magnets to confine a plasma of deuterium and tritium that has been heated to a temperature of 100 million degrees C. When confined at such a high temperature, it is possible for fusion to take place. The problem, to date, is that no one has ever extracted more energy from any fusion reactor, including a Tokamak, than they have had to put into to make it run. Unless scientists can find a way to do that, fusion reactors will never become practical.

Russians surprised scientists in the West when they created the Tokamak reactor, a torus (donut shape) that confines the hot plasma, using powerful magnets, allowing the deuterium and tritium to remain in close enough proximity for fusion to happen and, at the same time, keep the plasma away from the chamber's walls. The name Tokamak is a Russian acronym standing for "toroidal chamber with magnetic coils." The Tokamak design is now the standard by which most scientists are trying to make a practical fusion reactor.

In the meantime, there are other strategies by which scientists are trying to create fusion. One involves compressing pellets containing deuterium and tritium with powerful lasers. A test reactor that will be as large as a football stadium when it's completed, is now under construction at the Lawrence Livermore National Laboratory, located in the San Francisco Bay Area. The hope is that by using 192 lasers, focused on the fuel pellets, they can heat and implode them to fuse the deuterium-tritium mixture inside.

These and other strategies tried so far almost all create fusion, but none so far has produced more energy than it consumes.

Back in 1970 it was predicted we'd have the first commercial fusion reactors on line and producing electricity by the year 2000. But 2000 came and went with no fusion reactors on line. Today, the forecast is grimmer.

A third type of nuclear power

Another type of nuclear power is similar to fission: It's nuclear decay. In part, the interior of the earth is molten because of the heat generated by the gradual decay of radioactive elements beneath its crust. There's more power there than you may think. Nuclear decay may be the ultimate source of energy that moves the continents and causes them to drift. It may also be the reason volcanoes continue to exist today. Were it not for this decay, the earth might have cooled off sufficiently since its formation that there would be no more continental drift and all volcanoes might now be extinct.

Commercially, batteries that operate on the principle of nuclear decay have been used to power everything from pacemakers to space probes. However, nuclear decay is not something we expect to tap on a grand scale and, though it is at least part of the source of geothermal power that has been harnessed by man, it is not currently an important source of power in this country, so it won't be discussed in this series of articles.

Researchers are hoping *maybe* we'll have one by 2050. In the meantime, there are others who think we may be a century or more away. But, as I said, there are yet others who believe we may never see a commercial fusion reactor at all.

So the race goes on because, compared to *any other* sources of energy, the advantages of fusion power are:

- The fuel would be virtually limitless.
- It's essentially clean because it will emit little or no pollutants including the so-called greenhouse gases.
- A meltdown isn't possible because the second the plasma is compromised, the reaction instantly stops. So, in its "worst-case scenario" a fusion reactor is not only safer than a fission reactor, but it is safer than any conventional fossil fuel power station.

There is a small problem of one of the radioactive isotopes of hydrogen—tritium—getting released into the environment. But the half-life of tritium is relatively short and the dilution factor is so great that by the time it reached the fences where the reactor is housed it would be diluted to acceptable quantities.

The future of nuclear

The *Nuclear Power 2010 Program*, initiated in 2002, was initiated to examine the needs and prospects for resuming the construction of nuclear power plants in the United States. Because of that and other programs, today, after a long moratorium, there are now more than 20 new nuclear plants planned in the United States. Construction on Watts Bar 2 reactor, in Tennessee, which was suspended in 1995 when it was 80 percent completed, was resumed in late 2007. It is scheduled to be completed in 2013.

None of the other 20 or so will come on line until 2013 to 2015. They're late in coming, but the use of nuclear power will make us less dependent on fossil fuels and, despite the cries of the naysayers, they'll make a cleaner world for us and our children.

Energy shortages, rising fuel prices, and pollution concerns including heavy metals and the so-called greenhouse gases that are by-products of the burning of fossil fuels are going to force us take a hard new look at the nuclear power that is possible today.

Next issue I'll conclude this three-part series by examining the alternative energies such as wind, solar, hydro, etc. They are the energies the individual person can adopt in his or her personal lifestyle to relieve the energy crisis on a local level. Many readers of *BHM* are already using these energy alternatives. ∆

A Backwoods Home Anthology
The Eighth Year

- ❊ Considering life in rural Arkansas
- ❊ Where I live: Nine-patch, baby, and log cabin quilts
- ❊ Here's the best way to split gnarly firewood
- ❊ Here's an easier (and cheaper) way to make wooden beams
- ❊ Rid your garden of snails and slugs — organically
- ❊ Try these 13 metal cleaning tips to keep your house shining
- ❊ I remember the day the lynx attacked
- ❊ Raise your own feed crops for your livestock
- ❊ Lay vinyl flooring the foolproof way
- ❊ These double-steep half stairs save space
- ❊ Think of it this way...Science and truth — are they related?

- ❊ Commonsense preparedness just makes sense
- ❊ Grandma will love this personal "Helping Hands" wall hanging
- ❊ Try these pasta desserts for unusual holiday fare
- ❊ Winterize your animals without going broke
- ❊ Enjoy snap beans — fresh from the garden
- ❊ Set 100 steel fence posts a day with a home-made driver
- ❊ Plant your Irish potatoes this fall or winter
- ❊ From apple crisp to French tarts, tasty apple treats are just right for fall
- ❊ Here are four sure catfish baits
- ❊ Save time and energy with the fenced chicken coop/garden
- ❊ Rough day? You need to sip some yeller wine

The fire wick fire starter

By Len McDougall

When my hunting buddy Dar met me for lunch at our rendezvous point, he said he doubted we could make a small cook-fire on the wet, snow-covered ground. After a hot meal of canned pork-and-beans and instant coffee, our innards were rewarmed, and he was very interested in the tinder I'd pulled from my daypack.

In a wilderness environment, no ability is more likely to save your life than fire-making, regardless of latitude or season. Air temperatures below 98.6° F steal body heat, especially with the added cooling effects of wind and rain; smoke repels insects, and can be seen from a long distance; flames are a fearsome thing to most animals; and the ability to cook wild flesh (never eat raw fish) insures that any parasites are dead. In one respect or another, fire is vital to human survival, and when not being able to make one might equal dying, every trick in the proverbial book is fair.

The fire starter my friend had been impressed by employed the simplest technology to create a cheap, water-proof, easily-lighted tinder that has been part of every survival kit I've owned for the past two decades. In my youth I'd employed the classic woodsman's trick of using a candle to ignite damp tinder materials, but while the technique worked as well for me as it had for Kit Carson, it became evident that an entire candle was overkill. All that was really needed to get even wet tinder flaming was a candle wick saturated with enough paraffin to make it burn hotly for the minute or two needed to create a self-sustaining fire.

The most basic type of "fire wick" consists of nothing more than thick cotton laundry or packaging string that has been saturated with molten paraffin, allowed to cool and harden, then cut to the desired lengths. The string used must be cotton, never nylon or any other type of synthetic, because these not only don't burn well, but emit noxious fumes while burning. Cotton string is usually found in the housewares aisle, priced at about two dollars for one hundred yards.

In the simplest process, a ten-foot length of cotton string is lowered carefully into an old saucepan containing a pound of paraffin (canning wax) that has been heated to a liquid by a camp stove or hotplate. Paraffin is sold in supermarkets for about one dollar per pound. Or you can melt down the stubs from used candles, which works just as well for making fire wicks, but imparts to them whatever scents or dyes were in the candle wax.

Always take sensible precautions when melting paraffin; do the job in a well-ventilated place where there is little risk of fire and plenty of fresh air. Wear heavy gloves (not latex or rubber) when handling molten wax, and never allow the paraffin to get hot enough to smoke, because this is a warning that it is about to catch fire. If the melting pot does burst into flames, don't panic; the flaming wax is still safely contained. Simply cover the pot with a loose-fitting lid, which

Shown here burning atop hardpack snow, fire wicks might be the best fire-starting tinder available—but you have to make them yourself.

will smother the fire, and turn off the heat. Even with the heat off, the wax will remain liquid for a half hour or so.

The next step is to pluck one end of the string from the melting pot using pliers (wear your gloves, too)—always do this in a place where you won't mind a few wax drippings. Pull the string outward in a straight line, allowing it to drag over the rim of the pot, until the entire length has been extracted. Hang the wax-soaked string over a convenient nail or rail until it cools and hardens—usually about 15 minutes. The cooled strings will be stiff enough to lay across a cutting board and cut into sections using a sharp knife, or with sharp scissors. I package the completed fire wicks into "tinder bottles" adapted from pill bottles, 35mm film canisters, or just zip-lock bags, and scatter the hundreds I generally make at a time throughout my gear. My backpack and survival knife sheaths carry fire wicks, but you'll also find them in my kayak, my vehicle's glove box, and next to my wood-fired smoker grill. I even carry them in the toolbox,

where they've come in handy for re-lighting gas furnaces and other pilot lights.

In most instances, a single-strand fire wick is all that's needed, but sometimes I prefer a thicker, longer-burning tinder. To accomplish this, I use a twist-lock doubling technique that has been used to make rope from plant fibers since primitive humans discovered that skill. Just twist the string in a single direction until tension causes it to coil around itself when pull from either end is relaxed. Hold the twisted string taut while folding it in half to bring the two ends together. Slowly ease tension on the doubled string, allowing it to wrap evenly around itself like a small rope. This doubled (or quadrupled if you repeat the twisting process again) cord can then be dipped into molten paraffin, cooled, and sectioned to make thicker fire wicks that burn twice as long.

A good alternative to cotton string is wool felt weatherstripping, or old felt pac-boot liners cut into sections. Fire wicks made from felt produce longer-burning fire because they

Demonstrating how well fire wicks work, this one continues to flame hotly while melting a hole into hardpack snow.

absorb more paraffin, and ignite nearly as well as those made from cotton string. Again, use only felt made from pure wool, because some is comprised of synthetic fibers that not only don't burn well, but emit soot and toxic gases.

To use a fire wick, you'll need an initial source of combustion. A butane or liquid-fuel lighter is recommended survival gear at all times, but I've had little trouble igniting a well-frayed fire wick using only sparks from the Strike Force flint-and-steel in my knife sheath. The trick is to fray one end of the fire wick into a small airy mass that flames at the touch of a lighted match. Lay the lighted fire wick onto a small platform of sticks to keep it from being hampered by evaporating ground moisture, add more fire wicks as needed, and slowly build a tepee of pencil-thick dead twigs around its perimeter. Add larger sticks as the fledgling fire grows, until you've achieved a crackling blaze.

Considering the value this simple yet very effective fire starter has had for me through many years of survival classes in pouring rains and heavy snowstorms, when not having fire is simply not an option, I'm surprised that no company is manufacturing fire wicks. Until someone does, I'll keep making and using my own because the fire wick has earned a place as a must-have item in my own never-fail fire making kit. Δ

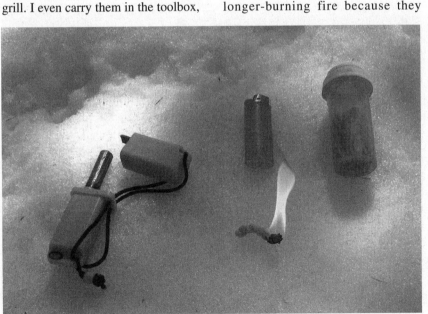

The Strike Force flint-and-steel, a butane lighter, and fire wicks kept together in a container; throw in a little fire-making know-how, and this pocket-size kit virtually guarantees fire in any weather.

Never too busy to make bread

By Ilene Duffy

Summer vacation came to an abrupt end. Sons are back in school. My "soccer mom" folding chair is in the trunk of the car. The daytimer is getting filled with dates and times of cross country meets and soccer games. The living room of our house is undergoing a renovation. Step-daughter, Annie, and the two darling grandkids have recently moved in to live with us while her Marine Corp hubby heads off to Iraq. I'm *busy*, but never bored.

So when I thought about what this issue's cooking column should be about, I thought of baking bread. I might be a busy mom, but it doesn't really take that much time to throw ingredients into my bread machine, let it run through the dough cycle, then take that nice elastic dough out and shape it into rolls or a long loaf for some fresh bread for my family. And I know I'm not the only mom with a busy schedule, so I thought I'd share some cookbooks and recipes for some easy, nutritious breads.

It's easy to get inspired to bake more when we have such talented writers like Claire Wolfe, who in this anthology, gave us good reasons *why* we might want to bake more bread. Also in this anthology, our friend, Richard Blunt, goes into depth about the use of whole grains in home-baked breads. Hence, the idea came to us for this issue's cover. Why not bake a bunch of breads, set them in a nice display, take a picture, and *voila*, the makings of the cover for this issue as well as a nice snack for the staff. So the other night, husband Dave and I loaded up my car with bowls, measuring cups, the bread machine, and most of the ingredients needed to make several loaves of bread right in our office kitchen. It smelled *really* good in our office for a couple of days while I took turns between bread making and editorial duties. Our office crew wasn't too happy with me though, when I wouldn't let them eat the breads until after we got a good picture to use for the cover. Sometimes you just have to be patient.

I baked a total of seven loaves of bread over the course of two days here in the office. Just some of those breads are pictured on the cover of this issue, but I'll share as many recipes as this space allows.

One of the things that amazed me while mixing up these loaves was how few ingredients were needed to make quite a variety of breads. Some of the breads I made were sweet, some were savory, others full of nuts and oatmeal, some with eggs and milk. But all these breads had one thing in common. I only spent between 5 and 10 minutes of preparation before each loaf was ready to start the dough cycle in my bread machine.

And I have a confession to make. I can't leave well enough alone. Every recipe I decided to try was changed to accommodate the ingredients I brought from home or already had here at the office. Sometimes I changed the recipe just because I felt like it. I've learned from past bread making mistakes that if I decide to add more dry ingredients than the original recipe calls for, I also add a

Pretty as a picture. This is one batch of bread that became a braided loaf as well as a dozen dinner rolls.

bit more liquid. You'll notice in the recipes below when I say "plus 2 Tbsp. milk," you can bet that this was a change I made in the recipe to allow for more dry ingredients that I had added.

I'd be lost without some of my favorite cookbooks. The three I used were: *The Olive and the Caper* by Susanna Hoffman, Workman Publishing (available through our bookstore and online at www.backwoodshome.com), *Whole Grain Breads by Machine or Hand* by Beatrice Ojakangas, Wiley Publishing, Inc., and a Better Homes and Gardens publication titled *Bread Machine Bounty*.

This first recipe is taken from the *Whole Grain Breads by Machine or Hand* book. I've changed it significantly from the original recipe which uses poppy and sesame seeds as well. Also, I decided to grind the flax seeds since you get more nutrition from the ground seeds, as compared to leaving them whole.

Surprisingly, it doesn't take very many ingredients to make a variety of breads. From left: Italian seasoning, yeast, salt, sugar, flax seeds, poppy seeds, butter, milk, cinnamon, sunflower seeds, eggs, olive oil, bread flour, whole wheat flour, brown sugar, oat bran, and yogurt. Not pictured are bananas.

Oatmeal seed bread

1$^1/_3$ cups water, plus 2 Tbsp.
2 Tbsp. olive oil
¾ tsp. salt
2 Tbsp. sugar
2 tsp. flax seeds, ground
¼ cup raw sunflower seeds
2 Tbsp. dry cereal mix
2 pgks. instant plain oatmeal
1 cup whole wheat flour
2$^1/_3$ cups bread flour
2 tsp. active dry yeast or bread
   machine yeast

Put water and olive oil in a ceramic bowl or measuring cup and warm in microwave until just warmed through. Pour into bread machine.

In a separate bowl, mix all dry ingredients except yeast. Dump dry mixture on top of liquid in bread machine. Form a well in center of flour mixture and place the yeast into the well. Start the dough cycle in bread machine.

When the dough cycle is done, prepare a cookie sheet with a bit of olive oil spread in the center as well as a sprinkling of flour. Take dough out of bread machine. Knead gently on floured board and shape into a circle. Place on cookie sheet, cover with a damp cloth, and let rise in a warm place for about an hour. Bake at 350° F for about 25 minutes until golden.

The next recipe is about the easiest and quickest recipe I've ever found. It's based on a bread recipe from *The Olive and the Caper* which is a really nice Greek cookbook I've recently discovered. Maybe before next issue

Here's the wheat and seed bread dough just out of the bread machine.

I'll have time to let my family be guinea pigs for some of the recipes in this book and I'll let you know how they turn out.

Country bread

¼ cup olive oil
1 cup warm water, plus 2 Tbsp.
2 cups bread flour
1 cup whole wheat flour
1 Tbsp. sugar
2 Tbsp. dry cereal mix
½ tsp. salt
2 tsp. active dry yeast or bread
   machine yeast

Put the olive oil and water in a ceramic bowl, then warm in microwave until just warmed through. Add liquid to the bread machine pan. In a separate bowl, mix together all dry ingredients except yeast. Add dry ingredients to the bread machine pan. Make a well in the center of the flour. Place yeast in the well. Set machine to the dough cycle.

When done, prepare one long loaf pan or 2 regular bread loaf pans with oil and flour. Gently knead the dough to release the gas. Form dough to fit pan(s). Cover with a damp cloth and let rise in a warm place about 1 hour.

Wheat and seed bread is hearty, but not heavy. Sliced thin, this makes a nice grilled cheese sandwich. Yum.

Bake at 350° F for about 25 minutes until golden.

Everybody winds up with a few overripe bananas at some point. This recipe is even faster to throw together than an unleavened sweet bread.

Banana cinnamon bread

²/₃ cup milk plus 2 Tbsp.
½ cup mashed ripe banana (1 small banana)
1 egg
2 Tbsp. butter
2 cups bread flour
1 cup whole wheat flour
2 Tbsp. dry cereal mix
3 Tbsp. sugar
½ tsp. salt
1 tsp. ground cinnamon
2 tsp. active dry yeast or bread machine yeast

In a ceramic bowl mix together the milk, mashed banana, egg, and butter. Warm in microwave until butter is very soft. Mix gently, then add to bread machine pan. In a separate bowl, mix all dry ingredients except the yeast. Make a well in center of flour mixture. Add yeast to the well. Set machine to the dough cycle.

When done, prepare one long loaf pan with oil and flour. Gently knead the dough to release the gas. Form dough to fit pan. Cover with a damp cloth and let rise in a warm place about 1 hour. Bake at 350° F for about 25 minutes until golden.

Sometimes you just have to try something new. With the following recipe, I decided to halve the dough and braid one of the halves to fit into a regular loaf pan. I divided the other half into 12 equal portions, rolled them into balls, and placed in a greased and floured muffin pan to make rolls. See the picture on page 62 to see the end result from this batch of bread. So pretty!

Egg bread with raisins

1 cup milk plus 2 Tbsp.
1 egg
1 Tbsp. butter
2 cups bread flour
1 cup whole wheat flour
2 Tbsp. dry cereal mix
¼ cup sugar
½ tsp. salt
½ cup raisins
2 tsp. active dry yeast or bread machine yeast

In a ceramic bowl mix together the milk, egg, and butter. Warm in microwave until butter is very soft. Mix gently, then add to bread machine pan. In a separate bowl, mix all dry ingredients and the raisins, but not the yeast. Make a well in center of flour mixture. Add yeast to the well. Set machine to the dough cycle.

When done, prepare one regular-sized loaf pan and 1 muffin pan with oil and flour. Gently knead the dough

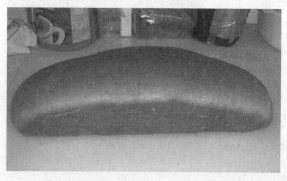

This loaf is the finished banana bread, baked in my long loaf pan

All banana bread ingredients are in the bread machine pan ready to start the dough cycle.

to release the gas. Divide the dough into 2 equal portions. Take one of the halves and divide into thirds. Form each of the thirds into a strip of dough about 12 inches long and braid. Gently squeeze ends together so the braid won't come apart as it's rising. Place the braid into a loaf pan. Divide the remaining half into 12 portions, roll by hand into balls, and place in muffin pan. Cover loaf and rolls with a damp cloth and let rise in a warm place about 1 hour. Loaf needs to bake about 25 minutes at 350° F, but the rolls only need to bake for 15-20 minutes until golden.

And before I forget, for all of you internet users, we're about to launch a new part of our website called www.backwoodscooking.com. With this new website, we'll be sharing recipes, menus of the week, and articles about cooking. People who wish to will have the ability to post their own recipes to be included and shared on the site. We'll keep things organized and indexed to make it easy to navigate. Cool, huh?

Nothing like starting another project when I'm already busier than the average soccer mom. But at least I'm not too busy to make bread. Δ

Great home-cooked meals from your
Storage Pantry

By Jackie Clay

For some reason, cooking from a long-term storage pantry makes many people cringe. Maybe they are envisioning endless meals of boiled beans and plain piles of white rice. You know, "survival" food.

We eat out of our pantry, three meals a day, seven days a week, at least to some extent. And we aren't forcing down unpalatable food, just to "rotate" our foods, either. I'm no gourmet cook, but visitors tend to sniff the air when coming into our house. "Mmmm...what's that?" We

answer, somewhat smugly, I'll admit, and laughingly set another plate or two at the table.

Eating out of a pantry is not just something you do during an emergency. It is a tasty, very economical way of meal planning. But don't you have to spend hours cooking meals from the pantry? Hardly. A lot of days, I don't have fifteen minutes to cook a meal and the storage pantry is a real lifesaver. (We live an hour and a half from a fast food restaurant, so we can't just run to Mickie D's for a take out when we're busy.)

So, to better acquaint you with just what can be done with storage foods,

I've picked out a few of our favorites. They are very flexible; if you have fresh or home-canned veggies, you can substitute those for reconstituted dehydrated vegetables. Or if you have fresh meat, you can substitute it for home-canned. You get the picture.

Casseroles

Casseroles of all types are among the most versatile ways to use our pantry foods. They stick to your ribs, are fast and easy to put together, and make good use of a wide variety of foods from our pantry shelves. Here are a few of our favorites.

Cheesie vegetable casserole

In a two quart casserole dish, layer the following, in this order:

3 large potatoes, peeled and sliced, or 1½ cups dehydrated potatoes, reconstituted in 1 cup of boiling water until nearly tender, or 1 pint sliced, home canned potatoes without liquid

1 pint sweet corn or 1 cup dehydrated corn reconstituted the day before in 2 cups boiling water and set overnight in fridge

1 pint carrots or 1 cup dehydrated carrots, reconstituted the day before in 2 cups boiling water and set overnight in fridge

½ cup cheddar cheese powder

½ cup dehydrated milk

dehydrated onions

grated cheese

Mix ½ cup of cheddar cheese powder and ½ cup of dehydrated milk with enough warm water to cover

With a good storage pantry you can eat well all of the time.

335

A well-stocked pantry and kitchen cheers up any hard times!

vegetables slightly. Sprinkle top with dehydrated sliced onions. Bake at 350° F until almost done, then sprinkle top with grated cheese and finish baking until cheese is melted and bubbly.

This casserole is flexible; you can vary the vegetables as you want or need to, or you can add any leftover pieces of boneless meat or poultry. We use it often and never get tired of it. It's especially good with home baked whole wheat rolls.

Chicken noodle bake

3 cups dry wide noodles or homemade noodles
2 Tbsp. margarine
1 onion, sliced or 1 Tbsp. dehydrated
1 pint boneless chicken breast
1 tsp. black pepper
2 cups milk (dry or fresh)
2 Tbsp. flour
half pint mushrooms or a quarter
  cup dehydrated and rehydrated in
  boiling water
1 cup coarse bread crumbs
1 tsp. salt
1 tsp. ground sage
3 Tbsp. margarine

In a large saucepan, simmer noodles in water until tender.

Meanwhile in a medium saucepan, over medium heat, melt the margarine. Then saute onion and mushrooms in it until slightly browned. Add flour while stirring. Add 2 cups of milk and stir over heat until beginning to thicken. Quickly add salt, pepper, and sage and stir in well. Add more milk, if needed to make a medium sauce, a bit on the thin side. Stir in drained noodles and stir gently. Then add sliced, boneless, skinless chicken and stir once again, gently.

Slide mixture into a casserole dish and pat down evenly. Sprinkle with coarse bread crumbs and drizzle with melted margarine. (You can add a layer of half mushrooms, stuffed with minced chicken, mixed with creamed cheese and a pinch of dehydrated onion for special occasions! Then add bread crumbs and melted margarine.) Bake at 350° F until done.

Again, this recipe is versatile; you can add vegetables, double the recipe for larger gatherings, or "fancy" it up with the chicken-creamed cheese stuffed mushrooms (our favorite is wild morels), stuffed jalapeños, or even carrot curls.

Chili cheese bake

1 quart of home-canned chili with
  beans (To make a quart of chili
  for this recipe I use 1 cup dry
  pinto or red kidney beans soaked
  overnight and simmered the next
  day to tender, ½ pound fried,
  crumbled hamburger with 1
  chopped onion (or dehydrated
  equivalent), one pint of tomato
  sauce or chopped tomatoes, ½
  tsp. cumin, 1 tsp. salt, 1 Tbsp.
  mild chili powder and 1 Tbsp.
  brown sugar)
2 cups cooked rice
6 homemade corn tortillas
1 cup shredded cheddar cheese

In casserole dish, layer the rice first, then the chili.

Cut tortillas into quarters and quickly deep fry until crisp and puffy. Drain. Layer on top of chili and sprinkle with shredded cheese. Bake at 350° F until done. Serve with more tortilla chips and salsa.

Stews

Stews are filling, comforting, and pretty darned good, to boot. And, like casseroles, you can add or take away to suit your taste or use just what you have today. All this good food makes you forget that it's from your emergency pantry, doesn't it?

Brunswick stew

¼ cup bacon TVPs (textured soy
  protein)
1½ pints canned boneless chicken
  with liquid
1 qt. tomatoes
1 cup potatoes (cubed) or dehydrated equivalent
1 tsp. dehydrated onion powder
½ pint sliced celery
1 tsp. sugar
2 tsp. salt
half a lemon, sliced thin (or dehydrated equivalent)
1 tsp. black pepper
½ tsp. ground cloves
2 cups butter beans or sweet corn
  (or dehydrated equivalent)

With dehydrated margarine and eggs, a recipe is always doable, even when chickens aren't laying and you don't have butter.

Add all the ingredients in a large pot. Simmer gently until flavors blend well and serve.

This is a great leftover use-er-upper. I toss in leftover holiday turkey we're a bit tired of instead of chicken. Throw in that leftover half pint of carrots, those tomatoes that are getting a bit over the hill (chopped), or whatever. The combination of poultry and tomatoes works well.

Venison stew

1 pint cubed, canned venison
¼ cup dehydrated onions or 2 large onions, quartered
1 qt. canned cut carrots or 3 large carrots, cut into chunks
1 pint sweet corn
1 tsp. dehydrated minced garlic or 1 large clove garlic, minced
1 qt. canned new potatoes or 4 medium potatoes, cubed
1 qt. tomato sauce
1 pint rutabagas, diced
1 tsp. salt
1 tsp. celery salt
2 tsp. black pepper

Combine all ingredients in a large, heavy stew pot, and heat with lid on slowly for half an hour (longer if fresh vegetables are used). When all ingredients are very tender, take off lid and slowly simmer until thick enough, but not scorched. Serve hot with thick slices of homemade bread or top with dumplings (recipe on page 50) instead of cooking down further, place top on and cook for an additional 20 minutes until dumplings are fluffy and done.

Chicken chowder

2 Tbsp. butter
1 pint cubed, canned white boneless chicken meat
1 pint diced raw carrots or 1½ cups dehydrated
$\frac{1}{8}$ tsp. pepper
3 Tbsp. flour
1 Tbsp. dehydrated onion or ¼ cup chopped fresh
1 pint cubed canned potatoes or 1½ cups cubed raw potatoes
1 tsp. salt
2½ cups milk

Melt butter in heavy 3-quart saucepan. Add any raw vegetables with enough water to simmer until tender. Drain. Add cooked vegetables, chicken, seasonings together in saucepan. Add ½ cup milk and flour in a jar. Shake until blended well. Add this and remaining 2 cups of milk to the vegetable/chicken mixture. Cook over medium heat, stirring constantly until mixture thickens. We like this served with hot flour tortillas and homemade butter.

Meat pies

Although the very thought of eating store-bought "pot pies" gives me the willies, some of our favorite meals are flaky crusted, steaming pies of meat and vegetables. Tender crusted, they are quick to make and oh so good. They also make good use of rehydrated vegetables and leftover dabs of this and that. (I'll bet I can put together a "to die for" meat pie as fast as anyone can open four cardboard frozen imposters.)

I usually bake my meat pies in a medium cast iron frying pan, as we like lots of yummy filling. While you can use a bottom crust, I prefer a top crust only. It's quicker, and it's plenty of pastry.

Crust:

The crust for any of my meat pies is a basic fruit pie crust. I usually make a "double" batch of dough, as the crust for a meat pie is usually thicker and when I use a medium-sized cast iron frying pan, it is larger in diameter than a 9" pie tin.

Basic double pie crust

4 cups flour
1¾ cups shortening
enough ice water to make dough workable
1½ tsp. salt

Mix flour and salt, then cut in shortening until the size of peas; don't overwork. Add half a cup of ice water and mix. Add just enough more ice water to allow the dough to form a ball and be worked with; you don't want it sticky. Again, don't overwork or it will get tough. Form in a ball and chill if the day is warm. Roll out onto a floured surface to about a ¼ inch

We recycle old tins for use as dry storage containers.

thick. Using a plate or other properly sized disc, cut the top crust of your meat pie. I usually cut steam slots in the top in the shape of two stems of wheat. It's pretty and lets steam out so the pie doesn't "grow bubbles." (Your crust should be just the size to fit snugly on top of frying pan. I often cut them half an inch oversized and flute the edge, just for appearance, but you don't have to.)

The ingredients of the pie are mixed and put in the pan, then the top is placed carefully on. A hint: I carefully roll the crust up on my rolling pin and unroll it gently into place so it doesn't break up on me.

Turkey pot pie

2 Tbsp. butter
2 Tbsp. flour
2 cups milk
1 pint diced boneless turkey
1 cup canned carrots, sliced
1 Tbsp. dehydrated onion or 1 raw
    onion, chopped
¼ cup dehydrated peas
1 tsp. dehydrated green peppers
1 pint cubed canned potatoes or 2
    large raw potatoes, cubed
crust (from recipe above)

In medium-sized cast iron frying pan, melt butter gently, stirring in flour to make roux. Add milk until your white sauce is medium thick; add more milk if necessary. Add the rest of ingredients and stir gently. Top with crust. Bake at 350° F until crust is bubbly and light brown. It's great and quick to do, too.

Beef cowboy pie

2 Tbsp. butter
2 Tbsp. flour
1 pint tomato sauce
1 pint diced canned stewing beef
2 Tbsp. dehydrated onion or 2
    medium raw onions, chopped
1 pint cubed canned potatoes
1 tsp. pepper
1 Tbsp. dehydrated beef stock soup
    base
1 tsp. chili powder
1 tsp. celery seed
crust from recipe above

Melt butter in heavy medium cast iron frying pan. Add flour, mixing well, then tomato sauce. If necessary, add just enough water to make a medium sauce. Add rest of ingredients, stirring gently. Top with crust and bake at 350° F until perfect.

Shepherd's pie

Shepherd's pie is a no-pastry meat pie and is one of our favorite quickies. The topping is browned mashed potatoes instead of a pastry. Give it a try. Folks will never believe it came from your storage food.

1 Tbsp. butter
1 qt. beef or venison meat slices
3 cups hot mashed potatoes (use
    dehydrated, reconstituted)
2 cups gravy (use meat juice,
water, flour, and soup base)

Generously butter bottom of medium cast iron frying pan. Spread mashed potatoes over bottom and up sides, about half inch thick. Layer sliced meat on top (I often add mushroom slices, too), topping it with the gravy. Top with a few spoonfuls of mashed potatoes over it, drizzling a little melted butter over them. Cover and bake at 350° F for about half an hour. You can add any vegetables to the meat before covering with gravy or top with cheese, powdered or grated, for ten minutes before taking out of the oven. This is an old-time standby.

Three very handy "goodies" from the storage pantry are dumplings, biscuits, and cornbread. All are great with stews and mixed dishes. Use them often and see how contented your "stuffed" family leaves the table!

Dumplings

1 cup flour
½ tsp. salt
2 tsp. baking powder
1 egg
⅓ cup melted butter
3 Tbsp. milk

Mix all dry ingredients and butter. Add egg and milk. Stir until just moistened. Drop by tablespoons into boiling gravy. Cover and simmer for 15-20 minutes. Do not remove cover until this time or they will fall flat! Serve at once when done. These dumplings will be tender and fluffy, just like Grandma's.

Cornbread

```
1 cup hot milk—dry, reconstituted
1 cup cornmeal
1 cup flour
1/3 cup honey
2 Tbsp. vegetable oil
1 egg
1 tsp. salt
3 tsp. baking powder
```

I use dry milk, reconstituted with boiling water, to mix with, first the cornmeal, then the rest of the ingredients. In this way, the cornbread is tender, and not as crumbly as it often is. I tried it and really like the difference. Mix the batter well and pour into a 9"x9" greased pan or a medium cast iron frying pan. Bake at 400° F about 20 minutes, until just done. I also often add a half pint of drained canned sweet corn and 1 tsp. mild chili powder for a Mexican style cornbread. Ole!

Biscuits

```
2 cups flour
½ cup shortening
1 tsp. salt
3 tsp. baking powder
1 cup milk or buttermilk
```

Mix flour and shortening until pieces are the size of a pea. Add salt and baking powder. Then mix in milk. If you use buttermilk, also add 1 tsp. baking soda. The dough should be moist, but dry enough to hold together for a brief kneading on a floured board. Pat down or roll out to about 1 inch thick and cut. I use a greased canning jar ring. Pat them a bit to fluff them up and place on a lightly greased cookie sheet. The biscuits should touch each other; this way they'll be tender and fluffy, not crunchy on the edges! Bake at 400° F until just golden on the edges. Serve hot with gravy or your favorite jam.

Along with these quick breads, you'll want to serve plenty of yeast rolls and breads of all types. There are so many possibilities, especially when you use an assortment of whole grains. We think of them as "special" breads—not "survival" foods! And with my breads and rolls, I constantly change my recipes a bit, adding a little of this or that, as the mood hits. For instance, I may toss in a handful of hulled sunflower seeds, rolled oats, poppy seeds, ground dehydrated pumpkin (very good in whole wheat bread), or chopped nuts. I don't add enough to drastically alter a recipe, only spice it up a bit.

Prairie whole wheat bread

```
3 cups lukewarm liquid (potato
   water, milk, or water)
2½ Tbsp. dry yeast
1 cup warm water
2 beaten eggs
2 Tbsp. butter
1 cup cornmeal
2 tsp. salt
¼ cup honey
13 cups whole wheat flour
```

Heat liquid till very hot and remove from heat. Dissolve yeast in 1 cup warm water. When heated liquid is lukewarm, add 2 beaten eggs and softened butter. Add softened yeast. Add cornmeal and salt. Beat well. Then add honey, followed by flour, one cup at a time, mixing well between cups, until the dough is able to be turned out on a floured board to knead. Add extra flour, if necessary to make an elastic, yet moist dough. Knead well and place in a greased bowl, turning once to grease top. Cover with damp towel and let rise in warm place till doubled. Punch down and divide into 3 loaves and place in greased bread pans or cookie sheets for free-shaped loaves (braid 'em, for a fancy look). Again let rise and bake at 350° F, until tops are nicely browned. Take out of oven and grease tops with butter or margarine.

For an extra nice dinner, even in hard times, take the extra few minutes to make a pan of butter horns (crescent rolls) for the family. The ingredients aren't extraordinary, but the results are.

Butter horns

```
2 tsp. dry yeast
1 cup warm water
1 Tbsp. sugar
3 eggs, beaten
½ cup sugar
½ tsp. salt
½ cup shortening
5 cups white flour
```

Mix yeast, warm water, 1 Tbsp. sugar, and eggs in a mixing bowl and let stand 15 minutes. Then add ½ cup sugar, salt, shortening, and flour. Mix, then knead well. Place in greased, covered bowl and let stand in fridge overnight. Divide in 2 parts and roll out in 12 inch circles, cut into 16 wedges. Roll up, starting with the wide end. Let rise 3-4 hours. Bake at 400° F for 15 minutes. Brush with butter and serve piping hot.

Sometimes the thing we miss most in "survival" situations or just plain hard times is desserts! Maybe it's like when we were kids and were sad or sick, and Mom or Grandma fixed us something extra nice for dessert. Here are a few ideas that work well from the storage pantry.

Desserts
Oatmeal sunny cookies

```
1½ cups sifted flour
½ tsp. salt
1 tsp. baking powder
1 tsp. soda
2 cups brown sugar
1 cup shortening
2 eggs, beaten
1 tsp. vanilla
3 cups rolled oats
¾ cup sunflower seeds
powdered sugar
```

Sift flour, salt, baking powder, and soda. Cream sugar and shortening. Add beaten eggs and vanilla and beat well. Add dry ingredients and oats. Chill dough. Form into balls the size of a walnut. Roll in powdered sugar until heavily coated. Place 2 inches apart on greased cookie sheets. Put pecan in center of each, if desired. Press balls down. Bake at 375° F until just starting to brown.

Raised donuts

1 cup milk
½ cup sugar
1 tsp. salt
½ cup shortening
2 eggs, well beaten
1 Tbsp. dry yeast
3²/3 cups flour

Scald milk. Add sugar, salt, and shortening. Let cool to lukewarm, then add eggs. Mix well. Then add yeast and let dissolve. Add flour and mix well. Let rise about 1 hour.

Punch dough and let rise again. Roll out dough on floured board and cut. If you don't have a donut cutter, cut in strips or use a wide mouth canning ring and another small cutter to cut out hole. Deep fry, then glaze or roll in granulated sugar.

Mock pecan pie

¼ cup butter or margarine
½ cup sugar
1 cup dark corn syrup
¼ tsp. salt
3 eggs, well beaten
½ cup coconut
½ cup quick rolled oats
9" unbaked pie crust

Cream butter, add sugar and corn syrup, mix till fluffy. Add salt, beat well. Add eggs, one at a time, beating well. Stir in coconut and oatmeal. Pour into unbaked pie crust. Bake at 350° F. until knife inserted in center comes out clean. Cool before serving.

Fruit cobbler

2 Tbsp. margarine
2 cups sugar
3 cups flour
½ tsp. salt
3 tsp. baking powder
milk
drained, canned fruit

Soften margarine and mix with sugar, then add flour, salt, baking powder, and enough milk to make a cake batter. Pour a quart of drained home-canned fruit, such as blueberries, peaches, or pie cherries (If these have been canned without sugar or with a very light syrup, add ½ cup sugar to drained fruit.) into a baking dish. Top with batter. You can add nuts or raisins on top if you wish. Bake at 350° F 45-60 minutes or until crust is golden brown. Serve warm with sweetened cream or whipped cream. You'll forget these are hard times.

By now, you get the idea; just because the world (or your corner of it) is in turmoil, doesn't mean you have to suffer and eat boiled beans three meals a day. If you have your storage pantry, with at least a year—preferably two years' worth—of food available, you can eat well. Probably better than you are now! Rotating these foods by using them in your daily cooking assures that they remain fresh and nutritious.

You do not want to simply buy the touted "year's worth" of survival food and stash it under the bed and forget about it. By using these foods, you'll develop a knack for finding recipes your family loves. And by adding dozens and dozens of home-canned and dehydrated foods, as well as those from your garden, orchard, and homestead, you can eat very well. Δ

A Backwoods Home Anthology
The Ninth Year

❋ Build your own solar hot tub
❋ Make "split pulley" bookends
❋ Save big $$$ by installing your own septic system
❋ Compost the quickie way
❋ Forget the dog, the chicken is man's best friend
❋ Remembering the good life
❋ Perk up the cash flow by selling farm produce
❋ Build a fish pond, just for fun

❋ Try growing the popular potato
❋ Kerosene lamps — a brilliant idea
❋ Try this gravel road waterbreak
❋ Cash in on those windfalls
❋ Whole-grain sourdough recipes
❋ Build a simple through-the-wall woodbox
❋ Victory gardens
❋ Long term food storage
❋ Use common herbs to treat the common cold

The community treasure chest

By Sandy Coates

Do you have odds and ends sitting around that you no longer need? Are you a "green" thinker, hating to throw items away that are still useful? Do you enjoy trading and swapping and just treasure hunting in general? Is your mantra "one man's junk is another man's treasure?" Do you enjoy being thrifty and love to recycle; taking cast-offs and finding a new use for them? Do you know other like-minded souls that live in your neighborhood or that you see on a regular basis? If you can answer yes to any of these questions then why not start a community treasure chest?

The rural community I call home consists mainly of ranch families, small home businesses, young couples, and retirees. Most families are on fixed budgets or they have been raised to abhor wastefulness, even before "green was the thing."

With that thought in mind, my neighbors and I found ourselves always passing around a large bag of "hand-me-downs." This bag shuffled from house to house as we claimed new treasures and added a few of our own. The bag was awkward and cumbersome and, as large trash bags tend to do, it seemed to disintegrate at the most inopportune times, more likely than not involving rain and mud! So, on a trip to town I picked up an 18-gallon rubber tote with a snap lid and a loose-leaf notebook. On the first few pages of the notebook I compiled some simple guidelines and rules and then I attached this to the tub with a heavy cord. *Voila!* Our community treasure chest was born.

If this seems like a fun endeavor to you, here is how to get your own community treasure chest started.

You will need to find 5-10 like-minded friends, neighbors, co-workers, community, club, or church members. It helps if you are in contact with each other on a daily or at least weekly basis. Purchase a medium sized rubber tote with handles and a lid. An 18-gallon tote is large enough for a nice selection of items but small enough that it is easy to carry and to load in the trunk of a car. I suggest you attach a wire bound notebook that includes a list of all members and their phone numbers as well as the treasure chest rules. With these minor details out of the way, you are ready to begin.

The object of the chest is for members to pass on or trade clothing and/or other items in good condition that they no longer have a use for with hopes that those items may find a home elsewhere. At the same time this gives each member the opportunity to acquire new treasures at no

One man's junk might be another man's treasure.
Here are some items that showed up in our community treasure chest.

member on the list. The chest continues down the list moving from household to household until it has gone full circle and comes back to the first member. The first member then gets to pick from the treasures and removes any of their original items that have been left in the chest after making a complete cycle. The first member again adds items looking for new homes. It continues to be passed on with each member removing their items that have made the full circle, helping themselves to new items and then again adding more unwanted items. It is that simple! It is a good idea to have a person assigned as a chest monitor. Each member is required to let the monitor know when they have passed it on and to whom. The monitor helps keep the chest moving smoothly and promptly. We lost our chest when it mysteriously disappeared and none of the members knew where it was. When it did not surface for several months, we bought another tub and started again. Suddenly, more than a year later, the first chest reappeared at a central drop off point used by several members. No one ever confessed to having it, but I believe it had gotten shoved in an inconspicuous corner of a member's home and when it was finally found, they were too embarrassed to admit it!

Here are our guidelines and rules that you might find useful.

Rules:

1. You are welcome to take as many items from the chest as you find useful. Please share the contents with family and friends. They are free.

2. Try to contribute at least one item per cycle. This can be a household item, clothing, or shoes. These must be clean and in good condition. You are welcome to contribute as much as the chest will easily hold.

3. Please keep the chest moving. Pass it on to the next person promptly, preferably within 3 days. Make sure

cost to them; thus extending the life of these items by continuing to recycle them within the community and keeping them out of the trash. It also gives members the opportunity to advertise items that are too large or too perishable to be placed in the chest. Items that have found new homes via our community treasure chest have been cookbooks, paperbacks, educational items, toys, clothing (from baby to adult), shoes, purses, socks, mittens, hats, jewelry, fabric, kitchen gadgets and dishes, toiletries—including hair products, perfumes, makeup, lotions and soaps, craft and hobby items, gifts, trinkets, garden items and seeds, packaged food, holiday decorations, linens, gift items, computer and office supplies, videos, tools, and hardware.

The treasure chest works something like this. The first member on the list deposits their cast off treasures into the tub and passes it on to the next person. The next member may then take any or all items from the tub that they find useful. Then they add their own cast offs to the menagerie of treasures and pass it on to the next to call the monitor when you have passed it on.

4. When the chest has made a full cycle and returned to you, please remove any of your previously donated items and pass them on to charity. This will allow us to always have room for new items.

5. No soiled, tattered, or bulky clothing or rags, no heavy items such as large quantities of books, appliances, cleansers, or paint. Please advertise these in the ad section of the notebook.

6. Food must be sealed and within the package's expiration dates. Other food items can be advertised in the notebook.

7. Please keep the chest neat and tidy, refold items after looking at them.

8. The attached notebook contains member's names, phone numbers, and chest rules with the remainder of the notebook devoted to classified ads. Use it as much as you want. Please mark out any old ads that are no longer applicable. Remember to include your name and contact number or email with your ad. Please make sure the notebook remains with the chest.

Guidelines:

1. Ten members seem to be about the right amount to allow a nice array of items without the chest taking too long to make a cycle. We try to have a cycle completed at least once a month.

2. The chest works best if members live close to one another or have a common connection through a job or organization. In our rural community, our member order coincides with our location on the county road. This allows us to easily pass from one house to the next without anyone having to make an extended drive. If you have a secure central drop off point this also works well. We have a corner in our small country post office/ fire hall/ meeting hall, where we are allowed to leave it for the next person.

3. It is nice if you can change the member order about every 6 months. Let's face it, some people just have better treasures than others and it is only fair that the same person doesn't always get first dibs. We usually just reverse the order.

4. The notebook attached to the chest has become the traveling classifieds and is used to advertise items that can't be put in the chest. Members advertise items to give away, sell, or trade. They can also request items they are looking for or add services they have to offer. I once requested baby food jars for a gift project and when the chest showed up the next time, there amongst the treasures was a bag of jars with my name on it! Through our traveling classifieds, members have found homes for livestock and pets, bought and sold refrigerators, furniture, boats, cars, and hay. They have traded services and acquired jobs, canning jars, yard and garden tools, coats, boots, paints, plant cuttings, seeds, composted manure, and even unloaded their excess zucchinis!

Now more than 3 years strong, our community treasure chest has been a continued source of entertainment and resourcefulness. Through our chest we have helped each other save money, save resources, and save the environment. We have secretly helped families in need who have been too proud to take public handouts but in the privacy of their own home have found within the chest a little something to get them through. Best of all, we have become better acquainted with our friends and neighbors. It seems the treasure chest has overflowed into other aspects of our lives. Like the worldly goods passed on in the chest, we too have something to offer, something to pass on to be admired and cherished. The greatest treasures our chest holds are the friendships and sense of community it has helped to create. Δ

Ayoob on Firearms

An economical battery of guns for the backwoods home

By Massad Ayoob

Everything's getting more expensive. Food. Gasoline. Guns and ammunition. Not everyone who appreciates the rural lifestyle was "born with a gun in their hand" the way some of us feel as if we've been. Many are urban-dwellers who've figured out for themselves that living closer to nature is a better way, and nothing from their previous metropolitan lifestyle has prepared them for their sudden realization that firearms are important, routinely-used tools for those who live "in the country."

Reading is good, but training is better. My advice to the people new to guns would be to take a firearms safety course before buying their first firearm. It'll give them a better idea of what they want, what they need, and what will suit them in terms of the size, the power, and the mechanics of the many, many firearms they have the option of buying. Your local office of the state Fish and Wildlife Department will be able to steer you toward hunter safety and firearms safety courses. As adult education goes, these courses are extremely affordable. If self-defense is your primary concern, your local gun shop or police department can direct you to armed citizen training programs. Most of these are geared toward folks about to apply for concealed carry permits, but the advice encompassed in their curricula are essential even for those only concerned with defending the home against violent intrusion.

Building a battery

A "battery" of firearms is a selection of guns that will cover multiple needs. The collector has "a collection," but the person who uses guns as tools has a working "battery," like a carpenter having multiple saws for different cutting purposes, and different screwdrivers for dealing with different sizes of screws.

At an absolute minimum, I would suggest four guns for the backwoods home. These would be a .22, a shotgun, a defensive-type handgun, and a high-powered rifle.

Just for the sake of argument, let's assume some frugality at work. I know trapshooters whose custom shotguns cost more than my SUV did new off the showroom floor, and gun collectors who might buy a single rare firearm that's worth more than my home and the real estate it sits on. Common sense economy is one of the values this publication celebrates, after all.

The .22

The .22 Long Rifle cartridge is the most popular in the United States. It has mild blast and mild recoil. Above all, it is cheap. With careful shopping, at this writing you can buy 500 cartridges for $12 to $15. Because it is a low-pressure cartridge, the manufacturers don't have to wrap a lot of super-strong metallurgy around it, and .22s tend to be cheaper than more powerful guns of similar quality.

Let me say it here and now: because it is so mild and inexpensive to shoot, the .22's single biggest advantage for the new shooter is that it lets them

Massad Ayoob

shoot enough to grow accustomed to shooting, and to become good at it!

As to shooting needs on a rural property, the .22 Long Rifle is a small game cartridge. It's suitable for rabbits, squirrels, raccoons, groundhogs, and the like. It's good for crows. It's a good choice for feral cats. It can certainly kill feral dogs, or foxes and coyotes, but frankly it's a little on the light side for animals that size. Remember, even if the animal must die so your livestock may live, you owe it a quick and humane death.

The .22 is a traditional gun for slaughtering livestock. In that situation, however, the animal must be penned under control, and the person performing the slaughter must take their time to put the bullet exactly through the skull in the right spot to reach the brain for an instant, painless death. That won't be possible when shooting a wild animal. When a steer goes wild and tries to trample you, or Ol' Yeller turns rabid and is coming at you, trust me: you'll want something a lot more powerful than a .22.

In most cases, the .22 is a rifle. Whether it has traditional "iron sights" or a telescopic sight, the two-hand grasp and the brace of the butt against your shoulder maximizes accuracy. If you get really good with

*Steve Sager is a Master competitive shooter who has learned
to appreciate the inexpensive Mossberg Plinker .22 rifle as a "best buy."
Here, he checks out a used specimen at Daddy's Gun Shop in Mayo, Florida.*

it, a target grade handgun will get the job done at a typical "house to barn distance" of, say, 25 to 50 yards.

The .22 is available in many formats. There is the single-shot, the traditional "young hunter's starter gun" of yesteryear. Today, the scaled down Chipmunk or Henry bolt action single shot is the right size for grade-school age kids, and a great choice for getting the young 'uns off to a good start in firearms safety. There are Western style lever actions, and pump-action .22s like the ones we geezers can remember from the live-fire shooting arcades on the boardwalks of our youth. The bolt-action repeating rifle makes a lot of sense for the user who won't be able to keep the working gun as clean and pristine as they'd like. In the humid, rust-inducing atmosphere of the slaughterhouse, the "killing gun" I'm most likely to see is a bolt-action .22. Its mechanism operates like a turnbolt lock, and allows main physical force to operate it should it stick due to rust or crud in its neglected mechanism.

The semiautomatic .22 rifle would be my personal choice. If the fisher cat is about to devour your prize pet Persian, or the rabid skunk is about to lunge at your beloved family dog, one shot may not be enough. You'll want a follow-up shot, and maybe another and another and another. The semiautomatic will fire as fast as you can hold on target and you don't have to think about anything but holding your aim and pressing the trigger. You will, however, have to keep it cleaned and lubricated.

Cost-effective choices: Mossberg now imports a little semiautomatic .22 rifle from Brazil that they market as The Plinkster. It's great for "plinking" tin cans off the back fence, as its name implies, but Master competitive shooter Steve Sager tells me his will put five shots in one hole at 25 paces…and never seems to jam. The price? Steve just bought his for $107 plus tax, brand new, from a big box store. The Ruger 10/22 and the Marlin Model 60 will cost somewhat more, but are longer-established, time-proven choices as splendidly reliable and surprisingly accurate semiautomatic .22 "utility rifles." In an accurate .22 pistol, I've seen the polymer-framed Ruger 22/45 and the Smith & Wesson Model 22A both selling new for $250, and the Browning Buckmark is another cost-effective choice. The shooter more comfortable with the simple mechanism of a revolver can get a Taurus .22 for an MSRP (manufacturers' suggested retail price) of $389 new.

The shotgun

Designed primarily to put a large spray of multiple pellets called "shot" in the air with each pull of the trigger, the shotgun is the logical choice for flying birds and is a top choice of small game hunters for shooting running rabbits and squirrels for the same reason. Loaded with the small pellets of birdshot for the feathered

*This Mossberg Plinkster with vari-X scope, only slightly used
and in excellent condition, is a bargain at under $140.*

stuff and the small furred stuff, and with buckshot for close-range deer, bad dogs, and worse humans, the shotgun can also fire a single slug. Slug loads are fine for deer out to plus/minus 100 yards (assuming good rifle-type sights and a steady hand on the trigger), and many Alaskan guides think a short, fast-handling shotgun loaded with slugs is just the ticket for huge, angry wounded bears in the thickets. Because its "shells" can carry so many different types of projectiles, the shotgun is the most versatile of backwoods home utility firearms.

The giant 10-gauge shotgun is a long-range duck and turkey hunter's weapon, and the tiny .410 shotgun is strictly for close range on small targets. Your all-around shotgun should be somewhere between 12- and 20-gauge. The less powerful 20 tends to have lighter recoil but, at close range, will probably do all you need done. The 12 is more versatile because it can carry more of its leaden payload, but you pay the price in notoriously hard recoil, or "kick."

Shotguns can be had in economy bolt-action formats, but they tend to be cheaply made and I never saw one that didn't kick mercilessly for a gun of its size with the shells it was chambered for. The single-shot break-open design has been a staple of American farms since the 19th century because it's relatively cheap to manufacture, but it's light for its power, kicks like hell, and doesn't offer a follow-up shot if the first one hasn't solved the problem. The double barrel is better, but a magazine-type shotgun such as the slide-action or the semiautomatic tends to be more practical for workaday rural needs. The semiautomatic is faster to shoot, nothing to do but pull the trigger, and in a gas-operated model will kick less since much of the recoil is absorbed in operating its cycling mechanism. However, as with .22 rifles, the "auto" demands more maintenance than it often gets. The

Some bargains pass the point of diminishing returns. Author is checking out an old Stevens single-shot 12 gauge shotgun. With fore-end missing, barrel will come off frame when action is "broken" to load or reload... but, that said, it will still shoot, and price is only 30 bucks.

rugged, manually operated slide-action, or "pump gun," may be the better choice, and will certainly be cheaper.

Cost effective choices: In either 12- or 20-gauge, the Mossberg 500 and the Remington 870 Express models are quality pump shotguns commonly available at affordable prices. I'd give the Mossberg the point for ergonomics (ambidextrous safety right under the thumb, easy loading without pushing shells past a spring-loaded magazine gate), and the Remington the point for smoothness of action and trigger pull. The Mossberg will start at around $350 MSRP, and the Remington, at $359.

The high powered rifle

Jackie Clay, probably our most popular featured writer at *Backwoods Home Magazine*, considers venison a staple of her larder and shoots her annual supply with a lever-action Winchester Model 94 .30-30, the classic "deer rifle." Marlin makes the comparable Model 336, currently in production and in the low $500 range MSRP. Both are suitable for deer and black bear-size game.

If you're located where the meat-bearing critters are bigger (northern moose, western mule deer), or farther (plains antelope, let's say), you want a higher velocity, more accurate rifle, and you'll definitely want a telescopic sight. We're talking a bolt action in the .270, .308, .30-06 etc. caliber range. Bolt action is the overwhelming choice here: its more rigid receiver, or frame, enhances precision. As with other firearm types, the bolt action high power rifle gives the shooter manual leverage that helps when the mechanism is gunked up by mud, bad weather, or owner neglect.

If you're in big, bad bear country, you might want to ratchet the power level up a notch. A .338 Winchester Magnum or 7mm Remington Magnum is more in line here. If I needed to ruin a really big bruin, I'd pony up $1,122 suggested retail for the semiautomatic BAR (Browning Automatic Rifle) in caliber .338 Winchester Magnum and consider every penny well spent. The bear attacks I've studied have happened very, very fast, and the big guys have soaked up a lot of firepower and kept fanging and clawing. Follow-up rounds of the hefty .338 persuasion as fast as you can pull the trigger would make huge sense here.

The "high power rifle" title also encompasses smaller bullets going faster: rounds like the ubiquitous .223 Remington or the super-fast .22/250. Great for long-range shots on the woodchucks that are tearing up your crops and are WAY out there, but not quite generating the smack and penetration you need for deer size game.

If you're not planning on hunting and don't have problems with either very large, mean animals or very distant ones, the high powered rifle—the "deer rifle," if you will—is probably the one gun in the battery you can most easily do without.

Cost effective choice: You're looking at MSRP in the $600-700 range for a plain-Jane bolt action Remington Model 700, Ruger Model 77, etc.; the Savage bolt action is often found new at "best buy" prices. I'm comfortable with any of them. A lower price is featured on Remington's fairly new, economy-grade Model 770. I've heard good things about this rifle, but haven't had a chance to check one out yet myself.

The defensive handgun

Folks move to the boonies to get away from the sort of lifestyle that makes you feel more comfortable carrying a gun 24/7. Hate to be the one to break it to you, but wherever you are, the need to defend yourself from man or beast tends to arise suddenly, without time to run to the gun cabinet.

A .22 pistol is handy for pot meat from ptarmigan to tree rat ("squirrels," for the city folk), and while it can certainly kill a large, aggressive creature, it won't necessarily stop it in its tracks. A .44 Magnum double action revolver would be my choice if I had big brown bears in my backyard. Most of us south of Alaska don't have to deal with that, though, and a more moderately powerful sidearm that you can wear whenever you're dressed makes a lot of sense. If being visibly armed is not part of your vision of ambient rural living, I understand; however, compact .38 Special or .357 Magnum revolvers are available in a discreet pocket size, and can be with you constantly.

Each of us lives in a different place with different situations that will guide our choices in everything from clothing to vehicles to, yes, firearms. I can only say that on the rural property where I have lived for the last four years, I have a battery that encompasses everything from varmint rifles to elephant guns, yet every time I've had to kill something on this particular turf (multiple poisonous snakes, and one really angry hog) I did it with the .357 or .45 pistol that was on my hip because nothing more suitable was within immediate reach in time.

Cost effective choice: For a small .38 Special or .357 Magnum revolver with a short barrel that lives in your pants pocket, a Ruger, Taurus, or Smith & Wesson will do nicely. The MSRP can range from low $400 to around a grand. In a holster-size semiautomatic pistol in a caliber with authority (9mm, .40, .45, or .357 SIG) you're looking at Glock, Ruger, SIG, Smith & Wesson and Taurus in a roughly $400-700 range bought new.

Purchasing used

The mechanic who purchases a pre-owned automobile is unlikely to get burned on the deal. He or she knows what to look for. The person who doesn't know much about cars except how to drive them won't get burned on a used car either…if he takes an

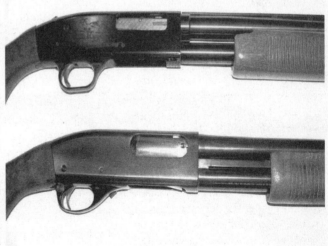

Mossberg 500 (top) and Remington 870 (below) are both good quality, affordable slide action shotguns available in various gauges.

auto mechanic he can trust with him to review the vehicle in question before he plunks down his cash.

Just as a spanking new automobile becomes a used car the moment the first buyer wheels it out of the dealer's lot, a brand-new firearm becomes a second-hand gun as soon as it fires its first shot outside the factory testing range. In either case, unless the machine in question is a rare collector's item, that first transfer of ownership drops cash value precipitously.

This means that careful shopping can get you a helluva deal on a gun someone else has broken in for you. It's all about the condition of the individual specimen. I know some purist collectors who act as if a single freckle of rust on the otherwise perfect blue finish of the gun they want is as much a deal-breaker as if they were collecting Picasso paintings and a cat had urinated on the canvas.

With a working gun, external blemishes are going to happen anyway. The stock and even some of the metal is going to get dinged and dented in the natural course of use. Some of the finish is going to get worn anyway.

Thus, a rough finish is perfectly acceptable for a backwoods working gun, so long as the arm is mechanically in perfect working order.

Case in point: In 1995, I found myself at Jack First's outstanding gun shop in Rapid City, South Dakota. Looking up at me from the used gun case was a very well-worn Smith & Wesson Combat Masterpiece Model 15 .38 Special, carrying the even-then unbelievably low price tag of $130. On a whim, I asked to see it.

It was the classic example of what the late, great gun expert Jeff Cooper characterized as a gun that had been "carried much and shot seldom." More of its famously beautiful S&W blued finish had worn off than still remained. The frame was literally pitted, as if it had been worn in an outside holster through the snows and rains of many years of extreme Dakota weather. Someone had probably scoured off the rust with steel wool. Yet the lockup was as tight as a brand new revolver, and the bore—the inside of the barrel—was absolutely pristine.

I reached for my checkbook, and made the arrangements to ship the gun to a licensed dealer for me, in the state where I lived. When I finally got it to the range, I discovered it would put every round of Federal Match grade 148 grain .38 Special ammunition into about an inch at 25 yards. I often used it thereafter to teach classes with, to reinforce the point that shooting is more about the shooter than the gun. This year, that ugly old beast won for me the Stock Service Revolver Champion plaque at the Tri-State Regional Championship (Arkansas, Mississippi, Tennessee) of the International Defensive Pistol Association. We shot that match in a driving rainstorm and, you know, I didn't worry about rusting the gun for a moment. That's as good an example as I can think of for the sort of value you can get in carefully shopping for used firearms.

I'm writing this on a quiet, rainy Saturday afternoon in North Florida. Some friends and I were heading south to Hernando this morning for an IDPA match, but turned back when we met a solid wall of thunderstorms halfway there. We returned home in leisurely fashion, doing a "gun shop tour" on the way. With this article in mind, I paid more attention than usual to the prices on good, used stuff.

At Southern Sportsman in Chiefland, I found a Marlin Model 336 with a generic 3-to-9-power variable telescopic sight. The caliber was .30-30 Winchester, adequate for anything one would be likely to hunt in this part of the country. The scope was the kind we associate with more powerful, longer range hunting rifles, but its magnification is always a one-last-check safety net for making certain that what we're aiming at in the forest at twilight really is a deer, and really does have antlers. This carbine had led a hard life, with a gray patina and some pitting where its blue finish used to be, and lots of dents and dings in the buttstock and fore-end.

In days of old…When author's dad "moved to the country" in 1945, his household gun battery included a .22 rifle (Stevens Model 87) for his young daughter (top), a Winchester '94 deer rifle (center), and the 12-gauge Winchester '97 pump shotgun (bottom).

An example of an effective four-gun battery today. From top: .22 rifle (Ruger 77/22). .30-06 "Deer rifle" (Ruger 77). All-around 20 gauge shotgun (Mossberg 500). Defensive pistol (9mm Glock 19).

However, I could find no rust in the bore, and the action still worked smoothly. The price? Thanks to its ugly duckling appearance, a mere $199.95 and certainly a solid value.

Moving north to Mayo, Daddy's Gun Shop had one of those Brazilian-made Mossberg Plinksters, in virtually new condition, apparently traded in on something fancier. Its owner had installed a 3-9X variable power Tasco telescopic sight, decent optics for ordinary work. This was a full size (one-inch diameter) scope for a deer rifle, not one of those narrow little scopes designed for .22s and BB guns that you can barely find an image in. For sure, neither a .22 nor a BB gun is a toy, but the scopes made for them damn sure are. This new-condition .22 rifle and its good scope were tagged together at $138.

Further up the road, on the southern outskirts of Live Oak, Lundy's Gun Shop had an old Stevens Model 77 12-gauge pump shotgun, tagged at $167. It was an economy gun the day it left the factory, but a sturdy one: the military used a bunch of them for jungle warfare during the Vietnam conflict. It had the same patina and dented wood that spoke of years in the corner of the barn or the back of the pickup truck, but it was in perfect working order.

For $505, plus sales tax and five bucks to each dealer for the NICS computer clearance to purchase a firearm from a licensed dealer, that would have put a .22 rifle, a .30-30 deer rifle, and a shotgun into the backwoods home gun rack, with telescopic sights on the rifles to boot. At manufacturers' suggested retail pricing (MSRP), the Marlin .30-30 alone (without the scope) would have been more than that.

Quality handguns tend to run a bit higher than utilitarian "farm guns." We finished our gun shop tour at Pro Arms in Live Oak, where a gentleman had just purchased a traded-in S&W Model 15 .38 Special Combat Masterpiece like the one I discussed above, but his was in virtually new condition. It appeared to have been fired very little, and was fitted with Uncle Mike's Boot Grips, which allow the gun to conceal in an inside the waistband holster as well as a snub-nosed Detective Special, despite its accuracy-assisting four-inch barrel. The price was $325 before tax. S&W no longer produces the blue steel Model 15 version of the Combat Masterpiece, but its stainless steel Model 67 version has an MSRP of $774 at this writing. Whether for concealed carry or home defense, I could be happy with that.

Counting the revolver, the day's shopping would have yielded a before-tax cost of $830 for enough guns to cover my basic firearms needs if I lived in a cabin in the area where we were shopping. Hell, the lightweight Smith & Wesson Model 340 Military & Police .357 Magnum snub-nose revolver that's in my pocket as I type this would go that at suggested retail, by itself.

Bottom line

Don't go for an A+ in one class at the expense of a grade of Incomplete on the rest of the curriculum. One screwdriver won't do it all for you, nor will one saw, and neither will one firearm. A good, functional, representative example of each type puts a lot more versatility in your toolbox than the most expensive specimen of just one type. That's how it is with tools... and, in a rural home, the working gun IS a tool. No more, no less.

Choose your tools carefully. Learn to use them well. And, above all, demand of yourself and others that they be used responsibly and safely. Δ

City girl & Country life

Community supported agriculture:
Where town meets country

By Claire Wolfe

We've all heard the old expression, "East is east and west is west and ne'er the twain shall meet." (Or "Yeast is yeast and nest is nest and ne'er the mane shall tweet"—but that's another shaggy-dog story.)

Sometimes it seems that the same is true of city and country. There's such a gulf of lifestyle and attitude between plain, simple, country us and the zoom-zoom urban fast-laners, with their glittering materialism, their sense of entitlement, and their bizarre desire to pave absolutely everything (including, paradoxically, their walking paths for getting "back to nature"), that the cultural Grand Canyon often appears unbridgeable.

But despite the old proverb, east and west have, these days, done a pretty good job of meeting: "Sushi meet American pop culture. Kia meet the Big Mac. Acupuncture meet modern western medicine."

So is it also possible for city to meet country on friendly, symbiotic terms? Wow, that's a tougher issue.

Often in this cozy little corner of *Backwoods Home Magazine*, I muse about the differences between the city/suburban life I grew up with and the hermit country life I lead now. Not just the differences for me, but differences—and struggles—that affect a lot of us who trade freeways for open spaces. It can be a hard, if gratifying, transition to go from being a city person to a country mouse. We often have long-term "issues."

I, for instance, can barely make weeds grow on what ought to be a very fertile patch of land. That's ridiculous for somebody known as an advocate of self-reliance. But give me a break! I grew up where concrete and blacktop were the only crops and where I spent half my life imagining that carrots came from the carrot factory.

But individual struggles and dislocations are only part of the big gulf. Sometimes it seems as if City is making downright war on Country.

With the exception of a few states (bless you Wyoming!) the United States' population is increasingly urban. En masse—en *political* masse—city-zens tend either to disregard country people or actively agitate against rural interests.

They treat rural areas primarily as their personal vacation paradise, their nature preserve, their weekend getaway, the quaint little place they might like to move to someday when they retire. They don't care how we feel about their attitudes or their plans for us. They don't care whether we might starve or be driven into urban-ghetto-like trailer parks if they legislate our livelihoods away. They want us kept "picturesque" and "unspoiled." Therefore, we end up as their ecological and sentimental playgrounds, to be preserved—even if preservation destroys us.

After all, our interests don't matter. We're just a bunch of gap-toothed, gun-totin' Billy-Bobs who need either to die off or to be jerked forcibly into the twenty-first century. Right? Yeah. (Well, at least the gun-totin' part is true.)

Ever since "one man, one vote" (that noble-sounding, who-could-possibly-be-against-it fraud!) shifted representation away from rural counties, we in the country have never had a chance.

Of course, we may feel contempt for city-zens, too. A lot of us sneer right back at them. We shudder at their fetid air, their traffic jams, their government-loving politics, their materialistic emptiness, and the cities' bizarre combination of yuppies and unlettered masses.

But mutual contempt doesn't make us equal. Country contempt of the city is just people standing on the outside, spitting at their fence. City contempt of country is—alas—wielded by the monumental powers of legislature and bureaucracy.

For instance, The People (all hail!) of Washington state recently made it illegal to do almost anything except picnic and hike within 200 feet of the normal high watermark of nearly any body of water. Doing anything else requires the dreaded Government Permit. But the Department of Ecology exempted one body of water. Guess which one. Yep, you've already got it figured out, haven't you? If not, check your Rand McNally and draw the logical conclusion.

That's right, they exempted the overwhelmingly largest body of water in the state, Puget Sound, because that's where *they* live. But, by golly, country streams will remain pristine, even if it costs rural Washingtonians their farms, fishing industry, and logging companies.

Some of the city-zens most responsible for such moves against country life are young activists who, of course, have never done more than ride through our parts of the world on their $2,500 mountain bikes. But they don't have to be here and experience how their policies disrupt our way of life because, of course, they already *know* what's best for us.

Seems like those folks would be our least likely allies in anything. But we—that is, you who can grow things—have an opportunity to do an "east meets west" with some people we might never have touched before.

Some of those haughty activists will be among the people who might help us bridge the big gulf. So will a few soccer moms, health buffs, and retirees looking for natural cures for what ails them.

I just learned about this recently. But talented growers may have known about it for a long time. Maybe a few of you reading this are already participating.

But for those who don't know, or those who'd like a refresher… I'm talking about Community Supported Agriculture.

Community Supported Agriculture (CSA) is a voluntary, 100 percent non-government program in which "shareholders" or "subscribers" who want wholesome, locally-produced foods purchase seasonal shares in certified organic or uncertified but "biodynamic" farms.

The farmers retain complete ownership in their land and operations. They remain beholden to nobody—no subsidies, no grants, no begging for loans. They still make all the decisions about what to plant or raise (though some operations go out of their way to open communications about crops with their subscribers). But since subscriptions are taken (usually) in the fall, winter, and early spring, the farmers start the growing season knowing just how much to plant and they have the money up front to buy seeds, tools, and equipment.

So clearly the farmer benefits.

Most of the people subscribing to CSAs are urban or suburban. (The farms routinely deliver fresh-picked crops to central points in cities as much as 50 or 60 miles away.) They're interested in healthy foods grown in harmony with the earth. They're more educated than most, and they're often able to pay quite a premium for getting what they want.

Each week during the season (which may range from 10 weeks to 20, and in a few cases run year-round), the subscriber gets a box full of whatever the farm provides— which may be wildly varied.

Take a look at one of the websites that function as central clearing houses for CSAs, *www.localharvest.org*. You'll see that a few farms boast of growing up to 100 vegetables and herbs. Fifty or more is common. (As journalist and food guru Michael Pollan said in his book "In Defense of Food," some of these vegetables will send you scurrying for your cookbook, trying to figure out what to do with kohlrabi or a rutabaga.)

Some CSA farms also "do" flowers, eggs, chicken, beef, pork, lamb, honey, grains, and more. Generally in those cases subscribers pay for and receive only certain services.

The buyer faces a few drawbacks. Aside from usually not having a choice of what he gets each week, she (Don't you just love these politically correct pronouns? I think I'll just switch from he to she and she to he for the rest of the article and hope the numbers come out even so the Feminarmy

won't come jackbooting all over me)… anyway, aside from not usually being able to choose whether to get kale or carrots, the buyer also faces financial risk.

Once a person pays his subscription of $250 or $450 or $600 or whatever the seasonal fee is, there are no guarantees of *anything*. A flood rolls through and wipes the entire crop out? Sorry, you've lost your investment. A new 12-legged fluorescent-green beetle species arrives from the planet Megatron and devastates all the farmer's summer squash? No squash for you this year.

But, overall, it all works out to mutual benefit. Farmers get capital and at least a bit of predictability in this capricious world dominated by a permanently PMSing Mother Nature. Buyers get fresher, healthier food, wholesomely grown. Each bears a little risk for the other.

That's a simplified version. There are variations. Some CSAs are created and driven by the subscribers. (Essentially a group gets together and "hires" a farmer to grow what they want.) There are often half shares or "small shares" available and occasionally even requirements that subscribers put in labor on the farm. A few CSA farms offer sliding-scale fees to encourage low-income families to feed themselves better. Some are affiliated with food banks or church groups.

In other words, variations abound to suit different needs.

(Let's hope the government never gets wind of all that freely chosen variety. If bureaucrats get their hands on the CSA concept, next year we'll have one-size-fits-all agriculture and five years after that, all the farmers will either be on welfare or have barricaded themselves inside the barns (aka "bunkers") on their depleted spreads (read "compounds"), screaming incoherent pleas for justice. But for the moment, things are good.)

But things could be better.

A few minutes ago I mentioned Michael Pollan and his manifesto "In Defense of Food." I highly recommend that book. It's a pleasant combination of good writing, good sense, and good humor. Among other things, Pollan examines the current environment of "nutritionism" (the place where the extremely faulty science of nutrition becomes more like a religion—"Fats evil! Carbs good!"—or simply becomes so wrapped up in erroneous methodologies that its billions of dollars in research turn out to have political value, but do nothing to help humans eat well).

Pollan shows that nutritional research is usually flawed because it attempts to isolate one factor (a type of fat, for instance, or a single vitamin or trace mineral) in a system that is unknowably complex. In truth, our food and the way our bodies use it is probably much more than the sum of its parts. As Pollan notes, the goodness of our food may depend not just on scientifically isolatable "nutrients" but upon complex interactions, and even upon *how* we eat, as well as what we eat, and how much we eat. In any case, science is far, far, far from being able to define what makes good eating.

Yet scientists continue to conclude and governments continue to decree things like this: "If we just add vitamin B1 to that bucket of library paste and call it 'Wonder Bread' all will be well." (Yes, Wonder Bread and other bad food is still on my mind from last column, but I promise not to get repetitious on you.)

Researchers have known for nearly 100 years that every time a population newly adopts the so-called Western diet, they suddenly develop an explosion of so-called Western diseases: hypertension, diabetes, heart disease, and a certain family of cancers known to be diet-related.

But because of the way the Western "nutritional-industrial complex" operates, few eaters consider going back to known-healthier fundamentals. No, instead we're introduced to 17,000 new or re-manufactured food-like products proclaiming "now with oat bran!" or "low-fat!" or "contains folic acid!" Or whatever the latest nutritionalist wisdom of the day dictates.

But an increasing number of smart people are saying NO to all that. They're saying that they want healthy, whole foods that are the product of farm, not factory.

Unfortunately, people who see through the food fraud and seek to adopt more wholesome (and whole-food) diets may have a hard time making substantial enough change.

Say you're a city person who vows to give up (as Pollan recommends) "things your great-grandmother wouldn't recognize as food" or anything with unfamiliar ingredients, unpronounceable ingredients, high-fructose corn syrup, or more than five ingredients.

So you head for the produce department.

Well, that rosy apple looks good—but since it's been bred for commercial advantages (uniform time of harvest, durability during shipment, etc.), it has far fewer nutrients than the apple great-granny munched.

And over there in the meat case...?

You know darned well how those animals have been raised. They've endured conditions that make Guantanamo Bay look like a vacation paradise. If that alone doesn't touch your heart, they've been fed and injected with substances they were never meant to have in their bodies—and now those chemicals are about to go into yours.

Caught in the triple vise of nutrition science, government, and industrial food marketing, all those growingly conscious city people have probably felt powerless. Heck, even their much-vaunted Whole Foods (motto: "If you have to ask the price, you can't afford it") has let them down by being revealed as a purveyor of beef from some unsanitary bovine hellhole.

So there they are, waving money and calling out for fresh, healthy food, grown in healthy, humane ways. Grown within 100 miles of home, if possible, for both freshness and community spirit. And here we are. Well, here you are, you people who can grow things.

What an opportunity!

Community Supported Agriculture first came to the U.S. in 1984 as an import from Switzerland. It started slowly at first. But it was a good, simple idea whose time has finally come. Along with farmers' markets (which are also growing at a rapid pace), it's a perfect way to bring money into the country, good food into the city, and goodwill and better understanding on both sides.

No longer are country farmers mere Billy-Bobs to those city cousins. Nor are we useful only for catering to passing tourists. Heck, we're not even quaint any more. No. Now, we have the opportunity to be on the ecological, nutritional, and humane forefront—and making a living at it, to boot.

Maybe our city cousins will even come to understand that the rural world isn't something to be preserved for their amusement or to make them feel environmentally righteous. Maybe they'll gradually get that a healthy, diverse country economy is essential to healthy, diverse life in the city.

Could be. In any case, it's a win-win for all.

It's also (I always seem to keep coming back to this), another blow against Authority. Do we really need or want government and scientists telling us what we should eat? Even if they were right in their proclamations (and so far time has proven them repeatedly, often disastrously wrong), our lives are ours, not theirs. Do we really want Archer Daniels Midland, Pillsbury, Sara Lee, or anybody else defining "food" for us—let alone engineering it, manufacturing, re-manufacturing, and marketing it to us?

Do we, especially, want anyone narrowing down our food choices while in fact pretending to offer us more and more and more? (Despite those 17,000 new or re-engineered food-like products brought to market every year, the underlying *actual* foods in those products become ever more limited. As Pollan points out, $2/3$ of the calories in the typical American diet now come from just *four* plants—corn, soy, wheat, and rice—and only from the highly processed seeds of those plants.)

Maybe it's time to rediscover kohlrabi and rutabagas, not to mention emmer and quinoa. And CSAs give a great chance for growers and subscribers alike to do just that—along with discovering common cause and solidarity.

Wow, it almost makes me want to go out and plant kiwi fruit or jicama. But—sigh—in my case I fear that would only lead to the slow, tortured death of an innocent plant.

Me, I'll be scraping together my pennies to buy a half-share and spending my winter evenings surfing the web sites of nearby CSAs. Δ

Making bouillon cubes

By Selina Rifkin

The word "bouillon" comes from French cuisine and simply means "broth." Sometimes the term broth is used for liquid flavored with only the meat, while the term "stock" includes bones. But this is not a hard and fast rule. Bouillon cubes were commercialized in 1908 as a cheaper version of meat extract, which was a highly concentrated meat stock. Bouillon cubes are a great short cut when making soups and gravies. A couple little cubes in the pot add flavor and makes the whole process easier. Bouillon cubes also take up much less space than canned or frozen broth and last a long time. Of course, unless you are buying organic, store-bought bouillon cubes also contain MSG, hydrogenated oils, and plenty of salt.

Making your own bouillon cubes is easy and means you will have a much healthier product. In addition, you can make use of parts of the chicken, lamb, pork, or beef from your table that might otherwise be thrown out. But the real health benefits are not just from what gets left out. Making your own bouillon means that it will contain gelatin.

Gelatin? You mean Jell-O? Like in grandma's aspic salads? *Yuck!* Well, yes, it is the same stuff, but there are very good reasons why you want it in your soup or gravy. In fact, more often than not, if you are already making soup stock from scratch, it's already there. Have you put soup in the refrigerator, or out in the cold so it would be easier to scrape off the fat? The jelly-like consistency of the broth when it's chilled means that it has gelatin in it.

Gelatin is highly beneficial to the digestion, making the process easier on the body. Gelatin is what's called a hydrophilic colloid, meaning that it attracts liquid. When you eat foods with hydrophilic colloids, they attract digestive juices to the food. This both speeds up the process of digestion and makes it more efficient. When food is well digested, we get more nutrients out of what we eat. Usually, hydrophilic colloids are found in raw foods, while cooked foods are often hydrophobic, meaning they repel liquids. Hydrophobic foods slow the digestive process. Gelatin is unusual in that it is hydrophilic after cooking. This means it is one of the only cooked foods that support digestion in this way.

There are vegetable sources of gelatin, but to make bouillon cubes we will be using only animal sources. Gelatin comes from the connective tissue attached to bones including cartilage, tendons, and ossein (the protein matrix of bones). It can also be found in skin and hooves or horns. Because it is mostly protein—although not a complete one—it can be used to replace some protein in the diet.

Making bouillon is simply a matter of making broth from bones and then boiling it down. Bones may be pre-cooked or raw. For example, when we have baked chicken for dinner, the bones get salvaged. Raw bones will produce a more pale broth, although this will darken as it boils down.

If you are doing your own butchering, obtaining bones is no problem. I recently ordered part of a free-range cow and bagged bunches of bones for boiling later. If you are going to freeze the bones for a while, it's a good idea to pre-sort them. Try to include at least one joint bone with each bunch. The cartilage will provide a substantial amount of gelatin.

Another source is the bones from whatever cut of meat you are having for dinner. Keep them in a bag in the freezer until you have enough to make broth. When saving chicken carcasses, be sure to keep the neck, gizzard and heart, but don't use the liver for soup.

There are two schools of thought about making soup stock. If I am going to make soup right away or freeze part of it for later use I include vegetables like onions, carrots, and celery. But this stock will go bad more quickly if unused. If I am making bouillon cubes, I use only the bones.

Ideally, you need a deep stockpot and enough bones to fill it halfway. This allows the liquid to circulate freely around the bones. I have successfully done smaller batches, but this works better for broth you will use right away rather than what you will make into cubes. Start by placing the bones in the pot and filling the pot with enough clean water to cover your bones. Your pot should be about half full of bones. Add ¼ cup of apple cider vinegar to help leach minerals out of the bones, and let this set for 15 minutes or so. Then add enough water to finish filling the pot and bring to a boil.

At this point, foam will rise to the top of the pot and this must be skimmed off or the broth will taste less than ideal and will be quite murky. Your stock will need to simmer for 12 to 24 hours to dissolve all

On the left, one batch of bouillon fills a pint jar that lasts me for two or three months.
The batch on the right in the picture was a triple; three large stockpot's worth.

of the cartilage off the bones. You will need to periodically add water so that the bones stay covered and the liquid keeps circulating. Once the cartilage is all dissolved, remove the bones and any meat and leave nothing but the broth.

It is a good idea at this time to transfer your broth to a smaller pot. Just leave enough room for boiling and leave the lid off for evaporation. Now we boil and boil until the liquid reduces by about three quarters. Keep an eye on the pot and periodically put a lid on. This will wash gelatin off the sides of the pot. Be sure to remove the lid again, so evaporation can continue. When the liquid is reduced this much, I like to transfer to a smaller pot. As it further reduces, it will start to look sticky, and it will be! When the whole top of the pot is one big bubble it is very close to done.

Because of the gelatin, bouillon is astoundingly sticky. There is a reason they make glue out of this stuff. If it cooks down too far, you will have to add some water and start over because it just won't come out of the pot. When the big bubble stage is reached, I prepare an oiled piece of aluminum foil with edges turned up

to catch my bouillon. Put the lid back on one last time to melt the film on the top of the gelatin. Two minutes is plenty, then pour immediately into your foil. It should be just a bit slow when it comes out of the pot—the consistency of syrup. Once in the foil, allow it to harden.

When cool, it should be stiff enough to cut, and the texture should be like stiff rubber. If not, put it back in the pot and heat gently until it loses more water. It takes a bit of practice to judge this and cook-down times vary depending on the amount of broth.

Cut into cubes about ¼ inch square, and wrap with small pieces of waxed paper. You may be able to store them at room temperature, but try it first by putting one in a jar and leaving it out, while the rest go in the freezer. I spend time in both Maine and Connecticut. In Connecticut, I must keep my cubes in the freezer or they mold. In Maine, they last over a year at room temp. One batch fills a pint jar and lasts me for two or three months. The batch in the picture was a triple—three large stockpots worth.

To reconstitute them, they need to have heat. Unlike store bouillon, these will not just dissolve in a bit of

hot tap water. They will have to boil for a few minutes until dissolved. Generally use one cube to one cup of water. But do taste, and remember there is no salt added! I use these any time a recipe calls for broth, and for gravies and sauces, and they are fine to use in canning. I also throw one in the pot when cooking rice, and my stepdaughter is very fond of bouillon cube broth with some rice noodles when she gets sick, since it settles her stomach. I find this to be an efficient, tasty, and space-saving technique that benefits both my health and my cupboard!

Selina may be contacted for questions at gelfling2364@sbcglobal.net. Δ

CASH IN ON AUTUMN'S BOUNTY OF CRABAPPLES

By Linda Gabris

When I was a kid, my grandparents had a small orchard of the best producing crabapple trees in the whole countryside. Not only did the bountiful trees produce enough fruit for me to sell throughout the season at my roadside fruit stand to passing tourists, but also plenty of crabapples left over for grandpa to load into his wine barrel and for grandmother to do up into countless delicious treats over the cold winter months when fresh fruit in our remote neck of the woods was hard to come by.

Crabapples, like apples, belong to the *Malus* genus of trees, which is a member of the rosaceae (rose) family. The only difference between a "regular" apple and a crabapple is the size.

Fruit that is two inches in diameter or smaller is technically considered a crabapple and anything larger is classified as an apple—meant to be eaten out of hand.

They are native to temperate zones of the Northern Hemisphere (Europe, Asia, and North America), and are one of the most widely cultivated fruit trees in the world. There are many varieties including Oregon Crabapple, Southern Crabs, Spring Snow, Siberian, Dolgo, Japanese, Pacific, Sir Lancelot, Prairie, Asian, European Wild, Sweet, and Orchard Crabs... just to name a few.

In my book, every yard should be graced by at least one crabapple tree, but, according to grandpa, two or more is always better! A reliable nursery can recommend a tree that's perfectly suited for almost any grow-

ing conditions and climates but be sure to follow the planting instructions that come with your tree for best results.

The hardiest crabapple tree in my little grove is one that I "rescued" a number of years ago from a grown-in homestead not far from where I live. When I dug up the tree—which was an offshoot of a mature tree—it was about 3 feet tall. I transplanted it in my yard where it quickly took root and has been a great producer ever since, perhaps because it was climatized for my zone or maybe just because I pampered it with mulch and water until I was sure it was holding its own. In any event, that's one way to go if you know where there's an abandoned tree that needs a new home!

Autumn crabapples—a beautiful tree, a bountiful fruit

In olden days, North American homesteaders planted crabapple trees in order to cash in on the wonderful bounty of tart autumn fruit that is perfect for making into jellies, wine, cider, preserves, and relishes. Since crabapples are hardier than regular apple trees, they were—and still are—a better suited, more dependable tree for colder climates and some enthusiasts vouch that crabs are less prone to typical apple tree diseases such as black rot and apple scab than are their bigger kin.

When my husband was a boy growing up in Hungary, he claims that the number one reason folks in his homeland grew tons of crabapples was to "fatten up" their autumn pig. In the Old World, it is said that the best tasting pork—especially an animal whose fat is intended for pastries and baking—is that from a pig that has feasted heartily on crabapples toward his demise. I don't know about pigs, but I do know that horses love crabapples because I used to feed the ones that fell on the ground to grandpa's

team and they would devour them fast as I could gather.

Since crabapple trees are very decorative they have gained popularity in more recent years as an ornamental, landscaping tree for residential as well as commercial grounds. Not only are they breathtaking in spring when they burst into full flower—a showy display of fragrant, snowy white to delicate pinks and deep reddish blooms depending on species—but they also dish up wonderful green foliage throughout the summer.

Come autumn, crabapple trees flaunt their bountiful display of fruits that are traditionally pinkish to deep reds when ripe, although newer hybrids like "Golden Hornet" have luscious yellow fruits. Crabs are popular with birds, making them an ideal tree for bird watchers and nature lovers to plant outside their windows. Fruits that are not harvested in fall will sometimes cling to the bare branches long into winter or until eaten off by woodland foragers.

Squirrels and chipmunks, deer and other wildlife, including black bears,

are very fond of juicy, bite-sized crabapples. If you want to deter bears from fattening up for their winter den on your autumn bounty and discourage them from visiting your yard, get the fruits off early before they beat you to the harvest!

Apples require cross-pollination between individual trees by insects, typically honey bees which swarm to the flowers for nectar and pollen. Since most species of trees are self-sterile (with the exception of a few newer strains) pollinating insects are of vital importance for healthy, producing trees.

Grandpa always quipped that one crabapple tree could not stand alone, vouching that if you want lots of fruit, you need at least one other tree nearby to spur fertility. Many growers of fruit trees will agree that planting more than one tree produces better results. Crabapple trees are great way to attract bees to the flower and vegetable gardens, too—vital in helping flowers to bloom and garden goods to ripen.

Crabapples, like their larger kin, are loaded with vitamins and minerals and they dish up fiber needed for good health and well-being. Adding them to one's diet helps to keep the digestive system running smoothly. However, as any crabapple-loving kid knows, if the fruits are consumed "green" or eaten in great quantities, upset stomach and "trots" or diarrhea are bound to happen!

Being a well-respected herbalist in the countryside where I grew up, grandmother was often called upon to cure various everyday ailments and common complaints, and crabapples were one of her favorite medicinal cures.

It is written in her old doctoring journals that crabapple tea is useful treatment for flushing impurities from the kidneys. It can also be called upon for treating constipation, relieving sore throats, breaking up head colds and congestion, calming nerves,

*There are many delicious old world recipes to help you
put up a bushel of tart little "crabs."*

inducing sleep, and clearing sinus pain.

For a general good health tonic, steep 1 cup of dried crabapple slices in a teapot of boiling water until the tea is fragrant and all the goodness has been extracted from the fruit. Sweeten with honey and serve hot in the wintertime to cure the chilblains or in tall glasses over ice in the summertime to cool the body down.

As a medicinal cure, steep 4 or 5 slices of dried crabapple in ½ cup boiling water and drink as required. For cold and flu treatment, add a slice of lemon or some fresh grated ginger root. For sore throat, add a couple whole cloves to the cup.

If you want to put your bounty of backyard crabapples to good use, try the Old World recipes below. You might find that you'll have to plant another tree or two just to keep up with demand!

Good news is, crabapples can be bought by the bushel at autumn farmers' markets and fruit stands. I have even seen them being offered "free for the taking" by those who have more bounty than they can use and want to remove them from their yards before the bears come to visit! So even folks who don't have their own trees can cash in on the joys of putting these wonderfully tart, delightfully delicious fruits up for winter use.

Drying crabapples

Dried crabapples make fragrant tea and since the dried fruit is not intended for everyday snacking as are traditional apple rings, you don't have to fuss and muss with peeling and coring. I do it the same way as I learned from grandmother and that is to simply string and hang.

Wash crabs and slice into thin rings—the thinner they are, the faster they will dry. Using a needle and uncolored thread or fishing line, string them up into long chains. Grandma hung hers on the wall behind the old McClary woodstove that sat in the corner of her kitchen. I hang mine from the ceiling of my sunroom and within a few days they are tan and leathery and the house is filled with the mouthwatering aroma of dried apples. Or if you have a food dehydrator, crabapples can be dried in the same manner as apple rings, following directions in your manual.

Once moisture is gone, unstring the dried crabs into a cotton or burlap bag and store them on the pantry shelf or in a cool dry place. They are now ready for making into tea or for nibbling on.

Crabapple tea can be brewed to any strength, the more rings the more potent the tea will be. It is delicious, especially when sweetened with honey. Even children can indulge in this nutritious, caffeine-free drink that makes great thermos fill for cold weather outings or is excellent served over ice in the summertime.

Of course, just like when I was a kid, I still like eating the steeped

Best ever crabapple jelly

Clove-spiked crabapples are one of my favorite preserves on the pantry shelf. They make appetizing decorations for roast meat platters, especially pork.

Clove-spiked crabapples make a delightful dessert drizzled with cream that you can pick up and "eat by the tail."

apples out of the pot after all the tea has been poured. And I still can't resist passing the pantry without stopping to snack on a dried crabapple ring—even if the pits have to be spit out when all the joy has been chewed out of the little gem.

Root cellaring crabapples

Like grandpa and grandma, every fall I pick a bushel of crabapples especially for root cellaring. It's easy as filling up a mesh or net bag and hanging the bag from a hook in the rafters in the root cellar where air can circulate evenly around the crabs.

The less crabs per bag, the better they will save as they can bruise under their own weight. They require the same temperature as apples so if you've had good luck wintering big apples, you should be able to enjoy fresh crabapples at least up until Christmastime or even longer, depending on variety.

A firm-bodied crabapple saves better in this method that those that are softer upon ripening. Only fill the net with prime pick as the moisture from one rotten or bruised crab can spur mold and cause rot amongst the others.

They can be used for nibbling on fresh out of hand, which I always enjoy, or chopped into the porridge bowl, or stewed and strained into sauce.

Clove-spiked crabapples

This Old World preserve always makes a big hit at my table and it's surprising how fast they disappear— even when intended as decoration! The stems are left on so that they can be picked up and eaten as grandpa would say, "by the tail." They are studded with cloves and preserved in sugar syrup.

Spiced crabapples make delightfully elegant decoration for meat platters, especially pork roasts, game birds and meats, including venison, and are wonderful for adding an enlivening touch of color to the turkey, goose, or duck platter as well as being great garnish for cold meat platters and pickle trays.

Grandma's favorite way to serve them was to remove the cloves and set about 5 of the crabs in a little dessert bowl, pour over some of the syrup in which they were canned, and then drizzle with fresh cream. The apples are picked up with the fingers by the stem or "tail," eaten, and then the core containing the pits put back down on the saucer. After all the apples have been eaten, the juice and cream are spooned up as the grand finale. Delicious.

I use spiked crabapples to add color and flair to the punch bowl. They are very attractive floating in fruit punches, mulled wine, or in the wassail bowl and add a wonderful "apple-y" flavor and aroma. And if you take a few from the jar, sprinkle them with sugar, and let them sit on waxed paper until dry, they can be used as decorations for cakes or other special desserts.

Below is grandma's old recipe for making clove-spiked crabapples. There are many different recipes for making preserved whole crabapples with some recipes calling for vinegar-based solutions which makes more of a "pickle" than a "sweet fruit." I prefer the sweeter version which I grew up with.

Use the best crabapples the tree has to offer. Those with soft spots or mars can be set aside and used for wine, cider, jelly, or relish recipes. Wash the crabs and leave on the stems. Stick 2 or 3 whole cloves into each apple, pushing them in as far as they will go—the more cloves you use, the spicier they will be. For variation, orange rind can be added to the jar or a piece of cinnamon stick.

Wash Mason or other approved canning jars in hot soapy water, scald well, and then boil for 10 minutes. Hold hot in the water until ready to fill. For safety's sake, use the modern-day canning jars that have the two-piece lids and use new lids for each canning session. Prepare lids according to manufacturer's directions which usually call for the lids to be heated in boiling water in order to soften the rubber seal.

Ensure that you have as many jars and new lids for them as you do apples. For each quart of crabapples you will need about 1½ cups of medium sugar syrup. To make the syrup, use 1 cup of sugar per 2 cups of water.

Measure sugar and water into large heavy-bottomed kettle, bring to a boil over medium heat, and stir until sugar is dissolved.

Carefully drop crabapples into the boiling syrup. It will lose its boil so bring it back to the boiling point and cook for 1 minute. Remove from heat.

Remove jars from boiling water and fill with the hot crabapples. Cover with boiling sugar syrup up to the neck, ensuring that apples are thoroughly covered. Wipe rim of jar to remove traces of spilled syrup. This will ensure a proper, secure seal. Center on the lid, screw on the cap.

At this point, like grandma, I let the jars completely cool and then label them and store on my pantry shelf but if you are a modern-day canner who uses a pressure canner for your home canning projects, follow the directions in your canner's manual for processing further.

These will save indefinitely but it is best to estimate how many jars you will need to do from one season to the next rather than canning more than you can use within the year.

Old World apple wine

This is a dependable and easy olden day recipe that produces a light fruity wine that is perfect for serving as an aperitif or dessert wine.

As a general rule of thumb, you will need about 6 pounds of sugar per 12 quarts of crabapples which will produce about 6 gallons of wine, depending on juice content of apples. The recipe can be halved or doubled as desired, but yeast content will remain the same.

Slice apples—peels, pits and all—into a large tub. Grandpa had a wooden barrel especially for the purpose. You can use a food grade plastic tub or primary fermentor bought specially for the purpose of wine making.

Add enough water to cover apples. Cover the tub with a cloth and let stand for two days, stirring several times a day with a wooden stick.

Dissolve needed amount of sugar in enough boiling water to cover and stir into the tub. Cover and let stand overnight.

Sprinkle one package of baker's yeast on a piece of crispy stale toast. Or if you are a modern-day winemaker, you can use real wine yeast according to directions on the packet. Float the toast across the surface of the juice.

Cover again and let stand for one week, stirring once a day.

Strain the apples through several layers of cheesecloth, twisting and

Homemade crabapple wine is a great way to toast your autumn bounty of crabs.

Crabapple tea steeped from dried crabapple rings

pressing until all juice is extracted. Apples can now be discarded. Put them on your compost heap for a big boost of energy.

Put juice into clean fermenting jar—one which can be fitted with an air lock. Grandpa had a homemade air lock—a complicated contraption made out of a piece of rubber hose. I would advice that you buy an air lock as they are fairly inexpensive and well worth the investment. Adjust lock and leave jar until fermentation has stopped. You will know it is done working when the action has ceased—no more bubbling.

Using a siphon or clean rubber hose, siphon the wine from the fermentor into sterilized wine bottles and then cork. Label and store the bottled wine in wine cellar or cool place, on their sides, for at least six months before sampling. The longer you can resist temptation, the better the vintage will be.

Best ever apple jelly

Grandma made her apple jelly without the use of store-bought pectin, one reason being it was hard to come by in the rural woods where I grew up. Another reason being, according to grandma, "fancy stuff like that is just too dear to bother with…"

Of course, today I use pectin as it not only cuts down on the jelly making process but also takes the guesswork out of having to do grandma's old test of "dropping a drop of jelly onto a cold plate to see if it is set…" Grandma was good at guessing, I am not. So here is my super-easy updated recipe below and I am sure that grandma would approve of this mouthwatering ruby jelly that turns out perfect every time.

Wash jelly jars or Mason sealers in hot water and scald. Put in kettle of boiling water and boil 10 minutes to sterilize. Hold hot until ready to fill. Prepare new lids as directed by manufacturer. Or in the case of jelly, the jar can be sealed with hot paraffin wax as grandmother always did.

Remove blossom and stem ends off 4 quarts of washed ripe, tart crabapples, the redder the variety, the brighter the jelly will be.

Cover with 6 cups of water, bring to a boil and simmer 15 minutes. Using a potato masher, mash the apples and cook another 5 minutes.

Line a large sieve or colander with a double layer of cheesecloth and set over a large kettle.

Pour the cooked apples into the sieve and allow juice to drain through but do not force it. If you force it, the jelly will be cloudy.

Measure juice and work in batches rather than doubling up on recipe. Put 7 cups of crabapple juice and 2 tablespoons lemon juice into a heavy-bottomed saucepan.

Measure 9 cups of sugar into a bowl, set aside.

Bring crabapple juice and 1 box of pectin (any brand will do) to a boil over high heat. Add the sugar and stir until dissolved.

Bring back to a full rolling boil and let boil 1 minute.

Remove from heat. Skim. Ladle into sterilized jelly jars and seal. This yields about 10 cups of jelly.

Crabapple chutney

This tasty chutney goes nicely with roast meats, poached fish, or to add excitement to burgers or hot dogs. It can be used in place of traditional chutneys as a side dish to curries.

---

2 pounds crabapples
1 cup raisins or currants
2 cups thinly sliced celery
2 cups minced red pepper
2 minced jalapeños
2 minced onions
1½ cups apple cider vinegar
3 cups brown sugar
1 tsp. ground cloves
1 tsp. ground cumin
1 tsp. each whole coriander and
 whole black mustard seeds

Remove stems and blossom ends from washed crabapples. Quarter and cut out the centers. Grind in grinder or processor, or chop fine. Add celery, peppers, and onions. Let stand five minutes.

Heat cider vinegar and sugar in heavy-bottomed saucepan to boiling then add apple mixture and spices. Bring to a boil, reduce heat, and simmer over low heat for 1 hour, stirring occasionally. Mixture should be thick as relish when done. Ladle into sterilized hot jars and seal. Or let cool and freeze in zip-lock freezer bags. Δ